DISCARDED
MILLSTEIN LIBRARY

Alice Munro

*An Annotated Bibliography
of Works and Criticism*

Compiled by
Carol Mazur

Edited by
Cathy Moulder

The Scarecrow Press, Inc.
Lanham, Maryland • Toronto • Plymouth, UK
2007

SCARECROW PRESS, INC.

Published in the United States of America
by Scarecrow Press, Inc.
A wholly owned subsidiary of
The Rowman & Littlefield Publishing Group, Inc.
4501 Forbes Boulevard, Suite 200, Lanham, Maryland 20706
www.scarecrowpress.com

Estover Road
Plymouth PL6 7PY
United Kingdom

Copyright © 2007 by Carol Mazur and Cathy Moulder

All rights reserved. No part of this publication may be reproduced, stored in a retrieval system, or transmitted in any form or by any means, electronic, mechanical, photocopying, recording, or otherwise, without the prior permission of the publisher.

British Library Cataloguing in Publication Information Available

Library of Congress Cataloging-in-Publication Data

Mazur, Carol.
 Alice Munro : an annotated bibliography of works and criticism / compiled by Carol Mazur ; edited by Cathy Moulder.
     p. cm.
 Includes indexes.
 ISBN-13: 978-0-8108-5924-1 (alk. paper)
 ISBN-10: 0-8108-5924-6 (alk. paper)
 1. Munro, Alice—Bibliography. 2. Munro, Alice—Criticism and interpretation—Bibliography. I. Moulder, Cathy, 1949– II. Title.

Z8605.55.M39 2007
[PR9199.3.M8]
016.813'54—dc22

2007001000

∞™ The paper used in this publication meets the minimum requirements of American National Standard for Information Sciences—Permanence of Paper for Printed Library Materials, ANSI/NISO Z39.48-1992.
Manufactured in the United States of America.

Contents

Acknowlegements	v
Introduction	vii

Part I: Primary Works

Books	3
Stories	22
Poems	76
Memoirs	77
Nonfiction	78
Television and Radio	89
Films and Videocassettes	95
Sound Recordings	98
Interviews	106

Part II: Secondary Works

Theses and Dissertations	133
Book Reviews	165
Books about Alice Munro	205
Audiovisual	219
Articles and Chapters in Books about Alice Munro	220
Bibliographies	318
Reference Works	320
Awards	326

Appendix	
Stories in the Collected Works	337
Chapters in the Novel	338
Unverified Radio Broadcasts	338
Archives	339
Collections	339

Author and Title Index	340
Introduction to the Subject Index	360
Subject Index	362
About the Authors	457

Acknowledgements

This bibliography was inspired by the late David Cook, who was a friend and colleague of ours at Mills Memorial Library, McMaster University. Mr. Cook was personally acquainted with Alice Munro, and a faithful devotee of her writing. He would often speak about her work with awestruck admiration, summing up an attempt to capture the essence of one of her complex stories by saying, "She gets it right." For many years he spent his personal time reading these stories and recording them, and to a lesser extent, the articles written about Munro and her writing. In 1976, he was the first to complete an extended bibliography on Alice Munro, which was published in the *Journal of Canadian Fiction*.[1] Since that time, Mr. Cook's bibliography has been cited again and again in the scholarly criticism. It is in his honour that we have expanded his original bibliography and have carried it forward to the present.

We would like to also acknowledge the fine work of Robert Thacker, professor in the Department of English at St. Lawrence University, who produced the first annotated bibliography on Alice Munro in 1984.[2] Mr. Thacker has provided us with the encouragement and advice which only a dedicated Munro scholar and bibliographer can give. We are also indebted to another Munro scholar, Tim Struthers, associate professor in the School of English and Theatre Studies at the University of Guelph, for his time and most helpful advice related to publication and content. Elizabeth Thompson in her capacity as a professional indexer gave much-needed practical direction in the formation of the subject index. Finally, Lorraine York, professor of English at McMaster University, kindly offered her comments on our publication proposal and the subject index.

Many other individuals contributed to the making of this work. We would especially like to thank Apollonia Steele, special collections librarian at the University of Calgary Library, who supplied us with many of the anthology entries in the primary works section. She also gave generously of her time at the University of Calgary Library and provided access to book reviews in the clipping files located in the Munro Fonds. We would like to also acknowledge the help of Shirley Onn at the same institution.

Our very deep gratitude goes to our friends and colleagues at McMaster University, especially to Helen Creedon, Laurie Crompton, Greta Culley, Tafila Gordon-Smith, and Donna Millard of the Interlending and Document Supply department in Mills Memorial Library. They were all indispensable in locating and obtaining a large number of the theses and articles which would have been otherwise difficult to obtain. These dedicated, cheerful, and efficient staff members were very much a part of our working team and have our fullest appreciation for obtaining material from Canadian, American, British, and other European libraries. The interest and support of many other staff members at Mills Memorial Library has sustained us through the many years of our work.

Other librarians and archivists across the country and abroad have provided assistance in verifying references and supplying information on specific items in their libraries. We would like thank Ted Uranowski at the Toronto Reference Library, Luba Frastacky at the University of Toronto, David McKnight at McGill University, Lynne Macdonald at the Vancouver Public Library, Kimberley Hintz at the University of British Columbia, Raymond Karen at the National Library of Canada, and Tove Dahl Johansen at the National Library in Oslo, Norway.

The CBC Radio Archives in Toronto were especially generous in allowing us access to their database and to the taped interviews of Alice Munro in their collection. For their assistance, our deepest thanks go to Gail Donald, Keith Hart, and Ken Puley. Elsewhere at the CBC, we would like to thank Liliane Hunkeler, Ann Jansen, Roy Harris, and James Roy.

We are grateful to John Munro, who allowed us access to a box of primary and secondary articles from the estate of David Cook at the beginning of the project, and to Virginia Barber, Munro's agent, who supplied us with a list of Munro's permissions for reproduction in recent anthologies.

Our family and friends have shared this long journey with us and made our steps lighter with their unflagging and very much appreciated support.

And finally, our deepest appreciation goes to Alice Munro herself, who has created the body of very fine work that is the 'raison d'être' of this bibliography.

Notes

1. D. E. Cook, "Alice Munro: A Checklist (to December 31, 1974)," *Journal of Canadian Fiction* 16 (1976): 131-136.

2. Robert Thacker, "Alice Munro: An Annotated Bibliography," *The Annotated Bibliography of Canada's Major Authors*, ed. Robert Lecker and Jack David, Vol. 5 (Downsview, ON: ECW Press, 1984) 354-414.

Introduction

Alice Munro's style and technique have been often compared with those of writers such as Anton Chekhov and James Joyce. In 1996, A. S. Byatt wrote, "She is the equal of Chekhov and de Maupassant and the Flaubert of the *Trois Contes*, as innovatory and as illuminating as they are."[1] Mona Simpson called her "the living writer most likely to be read in a hundred years."[2] Over a period of half a century, Alice Munro has established herself as one of Canada's major authors and as one of the world's finest short story writers. She has attained this status for a combination of qualities found in her writing—qualities that have been discussed in the hundreds of books, theses, and articles found listed in this bibliography. Her style and narrative technique combine in the creation of complex and often disturbing stories of everyday people—characters who on the surface are as ordinary and real as our neighbours, yet whose lives below the veneer of everyday life have a dimension of strangeness and mystery that throws everyday reality into question and reshapes it into another less definable yet more truthful reality. This "double vision" informs much of Munro's writing.

Her vision, her narrative techniques of disarrangement, multiplicity, fragmentation, and resistance to closure have caused Munro to be classified as a post-modernist writer. Much like the art of Edward Hopper, whom Munro herself admires, her writing, with its close attention to surface detail accompanied by a sense of the fantastic or surreal, is also categorized with the label of "magic realism." Other labels of realism associated with Munro's style are those of "super-realism" and documentary or "photographic realism." Munro's fiction vividly describes ordinary people and settings with which readers identify. As Hugh Garner said in his foreword to her first collection, *Dance of the Happy Shades*, "These are not characters on a printed page but are parts of you, your present and your past."[3] The regional setting is another aspect that characterizes Munro's fiction and has invited comparisons with certain writers of the American South, among them James Agee, Eudora Welty, and Flannery O'Connor, all of whom Munro has acknowledged as literary influences.

As a female writer writing from the female perspective, Munro delves into the psychological and social lives of girls and women as few other contemporary writers have. Her novel, *Lives of Girls and Women,* and many of her stories include feminine themes: women's roles, female socialization, the female body, sexuality, feminism, self-identity, personal development, mother-daughter relationships, and relationships between men and women. Other themes that recur throughout Munro's writing are those of love, death, time, human connection, the gothic and the grotesque, the wilderness and the garrison mentality.

Narrative structure and technique have been just as intensely examined as Munro's themes. Narrative time, point-of-view, and narrative voice figure prominently in the focus of critical works. Adult narrators looking back at the past and multiple narrators with multiple points of view move between past and present, here and there, memory and reality, truth and fiction. These complex movements of the narrative sometimes baffle, but inevitably bring the protagonist and the reader to a higher level of understanding, so that in the end they are able to glimpse a truth that lies behind the surface reality.

Use of narrative devices such as symbols, metaphors, and imagery, which Munro states is not a conscious or deliberate act on her part but something which naturally occurs in the writing process, have been highlighted in a number of critical works. On the other hand, Munro in interviews has consistently and deliberately used the house as a metaphor for the story to illustrate her aesthetic for both reading and writing fiction.

The use of paradox is again, not so much a conscious technique, as a reflection of the way Munro sees the world, her double vision of reality which has been the leit-motif throughout the years of criticism. Paradox is often paired with photography and Munro's photographic vision, where the grotesque is beautiful and the beautiful grotesque, where the object is something to be both feared and revered, and where the ordinary becomes strange and something unknown.

Language has been studied in a number of different contexts: its inherent inadequacy to express feeling and the reality of experience; its association with women particularly in its relation to the female body and female sexuality; and the controlling power of male discourse.

While Munro and her writing receive the critical attention of serious scholars and she is considered to be a "writer's writer," she is one of the few authors who has achieved not only scholarly but also great popular appreciation. Her collection *Hateship, Friendship, Courtship, Loveship, Marriage* rose to the top of the *Maclean's* "Best-Sellers" list in less than two months following its release.[4] Her first collection, *Dance of the Happy Shades*, received the Governor General's Award in 1969. Since then, she has garnered not only two more Governor General's awards and numerous other Canadian honours, but she has also been recognized abroad with The Canada-Australia Literary Prize, The Commonwealth Writers' Prize, The Lannan Literary Award (U.S.), The Rea Award (U.S.), The National Book Critics Circle Award (U.S.) and the W. H. Smith Award (U.K.).

Munro's first collections of stories, *Dance of the Happy Shades* and *Something I've Been Meaning to Tell You*, were published in Canada, the United States, and the United Kingdom, and were positively reviewed in all these countries. However, it wasn't until Virginia Barber, her sole agent, introduced her stories to the *New Yorker* in 1977 that Munro started receiving regular exposure to the North American audience. Subsequently her reputation as a writer grew not only in her native Canada and in the United States, but throughout the world. Her new collections, always eagerly anticipated and reviewed, receive generous space and praise in major world newspapers such as the *New York Times* and the *London Times*, not to mention most of the larger Canadian and American newspapers. Translations of the story collections and the novel have been published in seventeen foreign languages in a number of European countries, Asia, the Middle East, and South America.

Introduction

Scope of This Bibliography

While absolute comprehensiveness is an unattainable goal for any bibliographer when considering the numerous unindexed sources, the inaccessibility of a broad range of foreign language materials, and the relentless stream of new publications, the goal of this bibliography has been to attain as comprehensive a coverage as possible. The years covered are from April 1950, when Munro published her first story "The Dimensions of a Shadow" in *Folio*, to December 2005 when the story "Wenlock Edge" was published in the *New Yorker*.

A small number of items which could not be verified have been excluded from this work. They include such things as radio broadcasts of early stories, articles from small circulation journals and newspapers, and some foreign theses. Also excluded were photographs of Munro published in journals and magazines. Under the books of criticism about Munro, the reviews of those books are selective. Generally the reviews of Munro's books published in the smaller local newspapers were not included.

Primary Works

Primary works include all of Munro's published writings and interviews. Beginning the Primary Works section are the published collections of Munro's stories and her novel, *Lives of Girls and Women*. Each book entry includes the Canadian, American, and British editions, the reprints, and the foreign translations. Several Munro story collections compiled by others appear at the end of this listing.

The next section covers Munro's individual stories. Under each story will be found a citation to its original publication in a periodical or collection and subsequent appearances in anthologies and textbooks. Every effort was made to identify the anthology sources, but it was a challenge since these books are not usually indexed. A large number of stories in anthologies were supplied by Apollonia Steele at the University of Calgary. Others were found through online library catalogues which sometimes analyse the contents of books and through specialized short story indexes, bibliographies, and electronic databases.

Following the listing of Munro's fictional work is a section of her nonfiction writings including essays and memoirs, her commentaries on stories, and letters to editors.

Non-print formats are next. A good number of Munro's stories have been recorded in the form of braille, sound cassettes, video recordings, television plays, and films. Except for editions in braille, which are listed with the book translations, these audiovisual formats are listed following Munro's published works.

The last part of the Primary section is devoted to interviews found in published and unpublished sources including taped radio interviews that are stored in the Radio Archives of the Canadian Broadcasting Corporation in Toronto. These interviews reflect the same thoughtful and precise articulation in Munro's speech as in her writing, and they provide insight into Munro's aesthetic vision, her writing, and her life. A small number of unpublished interviews, while less accessible, have nevertheless been included for the sake of comprehensiveness. It should also be noted that while Munro has been routinely interviewed upon release of each new collection, these interviews have usually been edited by the interviewer and incorporated into a newspaper article. These therefore are listed in the Secondary Sources section.

Secondary Works

The Secondary materials fall into the categories of theses, book reviews, books of criticism or biography, critical articles and book chapters, bibliographies, reference works, and awards. The Secondary Sources section begins with a listing of 134 theses and dissertations. All of these have Munro's writing either as their main subject or included in a comparative study with the writing of other authors. In several cases, theses have been published in book form and so appear in both the theses and book sections. The majority of theses listed were written in Canada and have been examined firsthand. However, those completed outside of Canada, particularly in the United Kingdom and the European countries, were not as readily accessible. In these cases, copies of the title pages, tables of contents, and abstracts provided essential information for the annotations and indexing.

Book reviews were found in periodicals, newspapers, and in specialized sources such as *The New York Times Book Review*, or the *T.L.S.: The Times Literary Supplement*. The numerous reviews published in the smaller local newspapers were less accessible because these papers generally are not indexed. The clippings files in the Munro archives at the University of Calgary Library and in the Macmillan archives at McMaster University's Mills Memorial Library contained reviews of Munro's early works published in the smaller Canadian and American newspapers. Acquired from outside sources, these clippings unfortunately did not always include a page number. This fact and the problem of accessibility to such local newspapers made the inclusion of such sources questionable, but for the sake of completeness they were inserted as a separate section following the body of reviews under an individual title. All the reviews vary in length and quality, from detailed scholarly analyses of several pages to brief descriptive synopses. Furthermore, a small number of entries are not reviews in the strict sense of the word, but are rather notices or announcements of "best books" or "editor's choice." These were included to show the consistent acclaim with which Munro's successive books have been received.

Following the book reviews, twenty-four books are listed. These include biographies, works of criticism, published theses, published conferences, and special issues of periodicals devoted to Munro criticism.

In the next section, comprised of articles and chapters of books, there is a great variation in the scope and quality of the articles written about Munro, ranging from brief newspaper articles of public interest to detailed scholarly examinations of a single aspect of a story. While no distinction was made with respect to level of audience, nor was selection done on the basis of quality, those sources, which mentioned Munro only briefly, that is in a few sentences, have not been included.

The bibliographies and reference works listed next include published sources and selective internet sources.

All awards identified through the newspapers or through reference sources are listed. In some cases, such as the Booker Prize, nomination or short-listing for an award was considered significant enough for inclusion even though it was not awarded.

Arrangement of Entries

Primary Works

The books by Munro are listed alphabetically by title. Under each title, there are groupings of editions, reprints, and translations all given in order of publication date. In the stories section, individual story titles are listed alphabetically. Under each title, reprints of the story are given in chronological order by date of publication, so the first entry for a story will be its first appearance in print. Nonfiction writing by Munro is arranged alphabetically by title. Television/radio adaptations, films/videocassettes, and sound recordings all appear in an alphabetical arrangement by title of the story or collection, and under each title they are arranged chronologically by date of production. The interviews are given in chronological order because this arrangement best shows the course of Munro's life and career and the evolution of her fictional aesthetics over time. For users who approach this work with the name of the interviewer rather than date, the Author and Title Index will provide them with quick access to the interview citation.

Secondary Works

The sections for books and theses are arranged alphabetically by author or by editor. The same applies to the section for articles and chapters in books. In cases where no author is present the article is listed by title in the alphabetical sequence of authors. In the book review section, the book titles are given in alphabetical order, with the reviews listed for each in alphabetical order by reviewer's name or by title. The sections listing bibliographies and reference works are arranged in an alphabetical sequence by author's name or title. Names of awards are shown alphabetically, while entries under individual awards are chronological. In cases where there are two or more of these entries with the same date, sub-arrangement is by author and title.

Sources Consulted

The checklists of David Cook and Tim Struthers as well as Robert Thacker's annotated bibliography were consulted first. Then, in the course of the research, hundreds of other bibliographies found in reference works, theses, books, and articles were examined for possible additions.

The compiler used electronic databases and the Internet extensively, taking advantage of the online catalogues of libraries throughout the world to conduct searches in all the major national library catalogues including those of the National Library of Canada, the Library of Congress, and the British Library. To be comprehensive with respect to Canadian library holdings, searches were also done of individual university library catalogues and those of the major public libraries.

However, these technological tools, as invaluable as they were, did not provide complete coverage of Munro's career, which spans over half a century. This was especially true for publications issued before the 1970s and prior to the computerization of the major scholarly indexes. Older indexes only available in printed form filled the gap where electronic coverage was not available.

The major paper and electronic sources consulted were the following: *Amicus* (the union catalogue of Canadian library holdings, including the National Library of Canada), *American Book Publishing Record, Annual Bibliography of English Language and Literature, ArticleFirst, Biography and Genealogy Master Index, Book Review Digest, Book Review Index, CBCA (Canadian Business and Current Affairs), Canadian News Index, Canadian Newspaper Index, Canadian Periodical Index, Canadian Research Index, CPI Q* (electronic version of Canadian Periodical Index), *Canadiana, Dissertation Abstracts International, Ebsco Host: Master File Premier* and *Canadian MAS Elite, Humanities Index, Index Translationum, InfoTrac: Web-Expanded Academic ASAP, InfoTrac: General Reference Center Gold, Literature Online, Ingenta, MLA International Bibliography, Readers' Guide to Periodical Literature, Short Story Index* and *WorldCat*.

Methodology

The research began in the summer of 2000, when the compiler conducted a systematic search in the sources listed above for works by Alice Munro and for criticism of her works. Most of the sources were searched by author, subject, and keyword. At this stage, patterns of possible organization emerged and a draft outline was prepared for the Primary Works and the Secondary Works.

The most painstaking and time-consuming aspect of the compilation was the firsthand verification and examination of each item. The majority of the items in this bibliography have been seen after numerous library visits and interlibrary loan transactions between the McMaster University library and other libraries in Canada, the United States, and Europe. The resources of the libraries at McMaster University, the University of Toronto, the University of Calgary, and the Toronto and Hamilton public libraries proved to be the most helpful in the direct verification of items.

The bibliography progressed into a later stage, and throughout the six-year span of its compilation, additional searches were required to keep the content up to date with Munro's new writings and the recent criticism. *Runaway* is the latest collection listed, and "The View from Castle Rock" and "Wenlock Edge" are the most recent stories listed.

The compiler and editor collaborated throughout the project, communicating not only in person but to a great extent electronically. Files of completed and updated material, revisions, and corrections were sent back and forth electronically on a regular basis.

Style of Entry

The MLA style of entry was chosen because of its preferred use in literary scholarship. When considered necessary for clarification, fuller information is given, as in the case of periodical page numbering or periodical issue and date information.

Abbreviations Used

To conserve space in the annotations, the following abbreviations have been used for the collected works:

Beggar	*The Beggar Maid: Stories of Flo and Rose*
Dance	*Dance of the Happy Shades*
Friend	*Friend of My Youth*
Hateship	*Hateship, Friendship, Courtship, Loveship, Marriage*
Lives	*Lives of Girls and Women*
Love	*The Love of a Good Woman*
Moons	*The Moons of Jupiter*
Open	*Open Secrets*
Progress	*The Progress of Love: Stories*
Runaway	*Runaway*
Something	*Something I've Been Meaning to Tell You*
Who	*Who Do You Think You Are?*

Other abbreviations used:

Dir.	Directed by
Ed.	Edited by
Introd.	Introduced by
Prod.	Produced by
Rpt.	Reprinted
Sel.	Selected by
Trans.	Translated by

Notes

1. A. S. Byatt, "Alice Munro: One of the Great Ones," *Globe & Mail* 2 November 1996, weekend ed.: D18.

2. Mona Simpson, "A Quiet Genius," *Atlantic Monthly* December 2001: 126.

3. Hugh Garner, "Foreword," *Dance of the Happy Shades: Stories* by Alice Munro. (Toronto: Ryerson, 1968) viii.

4. "Best-Sellers," *Maclean's* 5 November 2001: 70.

Part I
Primary Works
(Works by Alice Munro)

Books

P1. The Beggar Maid: Stories of Flo and Rose

First published 1978 in Canada under the title *Who Do You Think You Are?* (See entries under that title for the Canadian edition.)

Editions

1st American ed. New York: Alfred A. Knopf, distributed by Random House, 1979, c1978. 210 pp. ISBN 0394506820.
London: Allen Lane, 1980, c1979. 210 pp. ISBN 0713913177.

Reprints

London: Penguin Books; New York: Viking Penguin, 1980, c1979. 210 pp. ISBN 0140054006.
A King Penguin. Harmondsworth, Eng.: Penguin Books, 1980, 1981, 1984. 210 pp. ISBN 0140060111.
Bantam Windstone ed. Toronto; New York: Bantam, 1982, c1978. 242 pp. ISBN 0553202928.
1st Vintage Contemporaries ed. New York: Vintage Books, 1991, c1978. 210 pp. ISBN 0679732713.
London: Vintage, 2004. 224 pp. ISBN 0099458357.

Translations

Braille

Stockport, Eng.: National Library for the Blind, n.d. 3 vols.
London: Royal National Institute for the Blind, 1981. 3 vols.

Danish

Hvem tror du egentlig, du er?: Fortaellinger om Flo og Rose. Trans. Arne Herløv Petersen. København: Hekla, 1984, c1978. 263, [1] pp. ISBN 8774741004.

Finnish

Kerjäläistyttö: Tarinoita Flosta ja Rosesta. Trans. Kristiina Rikman. Helsinki: Tammi, 1985. 258, [1] pp. ISBN 9513057623.

German

Das Bettlermädchen: Geschichten von Flo und Rose. Trans. Hildegard Petry. Stuttgart: Klett-Cotta, 1981, c1978. 289 pp. ISBN 312905571.
Das Bettlermädchen: Geschichten von Flo und Rose. Trans. Hildegard Petry. Ungekürzte Ausg. Ullstein-Buch 39066. Frankfurt am Main; Berlin; Wien: Ullstein, 1983. 288 pp. ISBN 3548390668.
Das Bettlermädchen: Geschichten von Flo und Rose. Trans. Hildegard Petry. 1 Aufl. München: Klett-Cotta im Deutcher Taschenbuch, 1989, c1981. 244 pp. ISBN 3423110368.
Das Bettlermädchen: Geschichten von Flo und Rose. Trans. Hildegard Petry. Berlin: Berliner Taschenbuch, 2003. 327 pp. ISBN 3442761492.

Norwegian

Tiggerpiken: Fortellinger om Flo og Rose. Trans. Berit Hoff. Oslo: Gyldendal Norsk Forlag, 1982, c1978. 290, [1] pp. ISBN 8205131988.

Swedish

Tiggarflickan. Trans. Karin Benecke. Stockholm: Norstedt, 1984, c1978. 252, [1] pp. ISBN 9118310923.

P2. Dance of the Happy Shades: Stories

American and British editions have the title *Dance of the Happy Shades and Other Stories*.

Editions

Foreword by Hugh Garner. Toronto: Ryerson Press, 1968. xi, 224 pp. ISBN 0770002390. Also issued with the imprint of McGraw-Hill Ryerson.
1st edition in the United States. New York: McGraw-Hill, 1973, c1968. 224 pp. ISBN 0070440484.
London: Allen Lane, 1974. 224 pp. ISBN 0713907703.

Reprints

A King Penguin. Harmondsworth, Eng.; Markham, ON: Penguin Books, 1983, c1968. 224 pp. ISBN 0140066810.

London; New York: Penguin Books, 1983, c1968. ISBN 014012408X.

2nd Canadian Paperback ed. Toronto: McGraw-Hill Ryerson, 1988, c1968. 224 pp. ISBN 0075497174.

Large Print ed. [Teeswater, ON]: Reference Press, 1995. 326 pp. ISBN 0919981526.

Foreword by Hugh Garner. Toronto: Penguin Books, 1997, c1968. xi, 227 pp. ISBN 0140270043.

1st Vintage Contemporaries ed. New York: Vintage Contemporaries, 1998, c1968. 224 pp. ISBN 067978151X.

London: Vintage, 2000, c1974. 224 pp. ISBN 0099273772.

Introduction by Annie Proulx. Toronto: Penguin Canada. 2005. xvi, 199 pp. ISBN 0143051431.

Translations

Braille

Stockport, Eng.: National Library for the Blind, n.d. 4 vols.
Longueuil, PQ: Institut Nazareth et Louis-Braille, 1979? 6 vols.
Toronto: CNIB [Canadian National Institute for the Blind], 1982. 6 vols.

French

La danse des ombres: Nouvelles. Trans. Colette Tonge. Collection littérature d'Amérique. Montréal: Québec/Amérique, 1979. 273 pp. ISBN 2890370135.

Italian

La danza delle ombre felici. Trans. Gina Maneri. Postfazione di Oriana Palusci. Milano: La Tartaruga, 1994. 248 pp. ISBN 8877381671.

Norwegian

Forunderlig er Kjærligheten: Noveller. Trans. Unni Eri. [Oslo]: J.W. Cappelens, 1988. 295, [1] pp. ISBN 8202111463.

P3. Friend of My Youth: Stories

Editions

A Douglas Gibson Book. Toronto: McClelland and Stewart, 1990. 273 pp. ISBN 077106697X.

A Borzoi Book. New York: Alfred A. Knopf, distributed by Random House, 1990. 273 pp. ISBN 0394584422.
London: Chatto & Windus, 1990. 273 pp. ISBN 0701136634.

Reprints

London: Vintage, 1991. 273 pp. ISBN 0099820609.
1st Vintage Contemporaries ed. New York: Vintage Books, 1991, c1990. 274 pp. ISBN 0679729577.
Toronto: Penguin Books, 1991, c1990. 273, [1] pp. ISBN 014014319X.
Toronto: Penguin Books Canada, 1995. 273, [1] pp. ISBN 0140241620.
Foreword by Elizabeth Thompson. Fitzhenry & Whiteside Canadian Literary Classics. Large Print Library. Markham, ON: Fitzhenry & Whiteside, 1997. xiv, 361 pp. ISBN 1550413163.
Introduction by Annie Proulx. Toronto: Penguin Canada, 2005. xvi, 199 pp. ISBN 0143051431.

Translations

Braille

Toronto: CNIB [Canadian National Institute for the Blind], 1993. 8 vols. of computer braille.

Danish

Min ungdoms veninde. Trans. Lisbeth Møller-Madsen. [København]: Gyldendal, 1993, c1990. 178, [1] pp. ISBN 8701778609.

Dutch

Vriendin van mijn jeugd: Verhalen. Trans. Dorien Veldhuizen. Baarn: Anthos, 1991. 268 pp. ISBN 9060746813.

French

Amie de ma jeunesse: Nouvelles. Trans. Marie-Odile Fortier-Masek. Les grandes traductions. Paris: Albin Michel, 1992. 284 pp. ISBN 2226056734.
Amie de ma jeunesse. Trans. Marie-Odile Fortier-Masek. Rivages poche 198. Bibliothèque étrangère. Paris: Payot & Rivages, 1996. 359, [1] pp. ISBN 2743601116.

German

Glaubst du, es war Liebe?: Erzählungen. Trans. Karen Nölle-Fischer. Stuttgart: Klett-Cotta, 1991. 308 pp. ISBN 3608957545.
Glaubst du, es war Liebe?: Erzählungen. Trans. Karen Nölle-Fischer. Berlin: Berliner Taschenbuch, 2005. 379 pp. ISBN 3833300035.

Italian

Stringimi forte, non lasciarmi andare. Trans. Gina Maneri and Anna Rusconi. Milano: La Tartaruga, [1998]. 330 pp. ISBN 8877382813.

Spanish

Amistad de juventud. Trans. Esperanza Pérez. 1st. ed. Meridianos 70. Barcelona: Versal, 1991. 277 pp. ISBN 8478760725.

Swedish

Äpplen eller apelsiner: Noveller. Trans. Karin Benecke. Stockholm: Norstedts, 1993. 321, [1] pp. ISBN 9119112521.

P4. Hateship, Friendship, Courtship, Loveship, Marriage: Stories

Editions

A Douglas Gibson Book. Toronto: McClelland and Stewart, 2001. vii, 322 pp. ISBN 0771065256.
A Borzoi Book. New York: Alfred A. Knopf, 2001. vii, 323 pp. ISBN 0375413006.
London: Chatto & Windus, 2001. 323 pp. ISBN 0701172924.

Reprints

Toronto: Penguin Canada, 2002. 327 pp. ISBN 0143012312.
London: Vintage, 2002. 256 pp. ISBN 0099422743.
Large print ed. Thorndike Press Large Print Women's Fiction Series. Waterville, ME: Thorndike Press, 2002. 519 pp. ISBN 0786242310.
1st Vintage Contemporaries ed. New York: Vintage Contemporaries, 2002. 323 pp. ISBN 0375727434.

Translations

Chinese

Gan qing you xi. Trans. Zhang Rang. Chu ban. Da shi ming zuo fang 81. Taibei Shi: Shi bao wen hua chu ban qi ye gu fen you xian gong si, 2003. 341 pp. ISBN 9571339644.

Dutch

Liefde slaapt nooit: Verhalen. Trans. Kathleen Rutten. Breda, Neth.: Uitgeverij De Geus, 2003. 351 pp. ISBN 9044502441.

Finnish

Viha, ystävyys, rakkaus: Kertomuksia. Trans. Kristiina Rikman. Keltainen kirjasto 344. Helsinki: Tammi, 2002. 398 pp. ISBN 9513124037.

French

Un peu, beaucoup . . . pas du tout. Trans. Geneviève Doze. Collection de littérature étrangère. Paris: Payot & Rivages, 2004. 340 pp. ISBN 2743613238.

German

Himmel und Hölle: Neun Erzählungen. Trans. Heidi Zerning. Frankfurt am Main: S. Fischer, 2004. 380 pp. ISBN 3100488199.

Hebrew

Sin'ah, yedidut, hizur, ahavah, ni suim: sipurim. 'Adi Gintsburg. Moshav Ben-Shemen: Modan, 2005. 286 pp.

Italian

Nemico, amico, amante . . . . Trans. Susanna Basso. Torino: Einaudi, 2003. 315 pp. ISBN 8806165917.
Nemico, amico, amante . . . . Trans. Susanna Basso. Torino: Einaudi, 2005. 315 pp. ISBN 8806174681.

Norwegian

Uvennskap, vennskap, forelskelse, forlovelse, ekteskap. Trans. Kia Halling. [Oslo]: Gyldendal, 2004. 319 pp. ISBN 8205303452.
Uvennskap, vennskap, forelskelse, forlovelse, ekteskap. Trans. Kia Halling. Gyldendal Pocket. [Oslo]: Gyldendal, 2005. 319 pp. ISBN 8205335451.

Portuguese

Ódio, amizade, namoro, amor, casamento. Trans. Cássio de Arantes Leite. São Paulo: Globo, 2004. 359 pp. ISBN 8525038547.

Spanish

Odio, amistad, noviazgo, amor, matrimonio. Trans. Marcelo Cohen. Barcelona: RBA, 2003. 257 pp. ISBN 8479019654.

Swedish

Kärlek, vänskap, hat: Noveller. Trans. Rose-Marie Nielsen. [Stockholm]: Wahlström and Widstrand, 2003. 306, [1] pp. ISBN 9146200983.

P5. Lives of Girls and Women: A Novel

Editions

Toronto: McGraw-Hill Ryerson, 1971. 254 pp. ISBN 0070929327.
New York: McGraw-Hill, [1972], c1971. 250 pp. ISBN 0070440433.
London: Allen Lane, 1973, c1971. 250 pp. ISBN 0713906537.

Reprints

Large print ed. Boston: G. K. Hall, 1973, c1971. 483 pp. ISBN 0816161429.
A Signet Book. New York: New American Library, 1974, c1971. 211 pp.
A Signet Book. Scarborough, ON: New American Library of Canada, 1974, c1971. 211 pp.
London: Women's Press, 1978, c1971. 211 pp. ISBN 0704338211.
A King Penguin. Harmondsworth, Eng.: Penguin, 1982, 1984, c1971. 250 pp. ISBN 0140059962.
New York: New American Library, 1983, c1971. 339 pp. ISBN 0452259754.
Plume Fiction. New York: New American Library, 1983, c1971. 211 pp. ISBN 0452261848.
A Plume Book. New York; Scarborough, ON: New American Library, 1983. 211 pp. ISBN 0452254337; 0452254345.
Markham, ON: Penguin Books Canada, 1990. 211 pp. ISBN 0140121617.
London: Bloomsbury, 1994, c1973. 281 pp. ISBN 0747517436.
Toronto: Penguin, 1995, c1971. 211 pp. ISBN 0140251618.
Toronto: Penguin Books, 1996, c1971. 278 pp. ISBN 0140241671.
Toronto: Penguin Canada, 1997, c1971. 278 pp. ISBN 0140256113.
Winnipeg: Manitoba Education and Training, 1998. [Large print reproduced from Markham, ON: Penguin Books Canada, 1990. ISBN 0140121617.]
1st Vintage Contemporaries ed. New York: Vintage Contemporaries, 2001, c1971. 277 pp. ISBN 0375707492.
Introd. Jane Smiley. Toronto: Penguin Canada, 2005. xiii, 237 pp. ISBN 014305144X.

Translations

Braille

Toronto: CNIB [Canadian National Institute for the Blind], 1980. 6 vols.

Danish

Pigeliv & kvindeliv. Trans. Lisbeth Møller-Madsen. København: Hekla, 1986, c1971. 271, [1] pp. ISBN 8774741349.

German

Kleine Aussichten: Ein Roman von Mädchen und Frauen. Trans. Hildegard Petry. Stuttgart: Klett-Cotta, 1983. 321 pp. ISBN 3608950133.
Kleine Aussichten: Ein Roman von Mädchen und Frauen. Trans. Hildegard Petry. Ungekürzte Ausg. München: Klett-Cotta im Deutschen Taschenbuch-Verlag, 1988. 269 pp. ISBN 3423109165.
Kleine Aussichten: Ein Roman von Mädchen und Frauen. Trans. Hildegard Petry. Frankfurt am Main; Olten; Wien: Büchergilde Gutenberg, 1988. 321 pp. ISBN 3763234233.
Kleine Aussichten: Ein Roman von Mädchen und Frauen. Trans. Hildegard Petry. Berlin: Berliner Taschenbuch, 2005. 362 pp. ISBN 3833300248.

Hebrew

Haye na''arot ve-nashim. Trans. Sarah Ripin. Tel Aviv: Zmora-Bitan, 1991. 229 pp.

Korean

Op 'eret'a tchaksarang - kurigo sulp'un yonin. Trans. Pak Mi-gyong. Soul [Seoul]: Sihan Kihoek, 1995. 304 pp. ISBN 8985820079.

P6. The Love of a Good Woman: Stories

Editions

A Douglas Gibson Book. Toronto: McClelland and Stewart, 1998. 339, [1] pp. ISBN 0771066856.
A Borzoi Book. New York: Alfred A. Knopf, distributed by Random House, 1998. 339, [1] pp. ISBN 0375403957.
London: Chatto & Windus, 1998. 339 pp. ISBN 0701168307.

Reprints

1st Vintage Contemporaries ed. New York: Vintage Contemporaries, 1999, c1998. 339 pp. ISBN 0375703632; 0375403957.
Toronto: Penguin Books Canada, 1999, c1998. 395 pp. ISBN 0140281940.
London: Vintage, 2000, c1998. 339 pp. ISBN 0099287862.

Translations

Braille

Bredbury, Eng.: National Library for the Blind, 2000. 7 vols.

Danish

En god kvindes kærlighed: Noveller. Trans. Lisbeth Møller-Madsen. [Kobenhavn]: Centrum, 2002. 356, [1] pp. ISBN 8758311858.

Dutch

De liefde van een goede vrouw: Verhalen. Trans. Pleuke Boyce. Breda, Neth.: Uitgeverij De Geus, 2000. 365 pp. ISBN 9052267529.

Finnish

Hyvän naisen rakkaus: Kertomuksia. Trans. Kristiina Rikman. Keltainen kirjasto 329. Helsinki: Tammi, 2000. 392 pp. ISBN 9513116131.

French

L'amour d'une honnête femme: Nouvelles. Trans. Geneviève Doze. Paris: Rivages, 2001. 348, [1] pp. ISBN 2743607459.
L'amour d'une honnête femme: Nouvelles. Trans. Geneviève Doze. Rivages poche. Bibiothèque étrangère. Paris: Payot & Rivages, 2003. 396 pp. ISBN 2743610891.

German

Die Liebe einer Frau: Drei Erzählungen und ein kurzer Roman. [Selections]. Trans. Heidi Zerning. Frankfurt am Main: S. Fischer, 2000. 223, [1] pp. ISBN 3100488113.
Contains stories "Die Liebe einer Frau" (The Love of a Good Woman), "Jakarta," "Cortes Island," and "Einzig der Schnitter" (Save the Reaper).
Der Traum meiner Mutter: Erzählungen. [Selections]. Trans. Heidi Zerning. Afterword Judith Hermann. Frankfurt am Main: S. Fischer, 2002. 221 pp. ISBN 3100488172.
Contains stories "Der Traum meiner Mutter" (My Mother's Dream), "Die Kinder bleiben Hier" (The Children Stay), "Stinkreich" (Rich as Stink), and "Vor dem Wandel" (Before the Change).

Die Liebe einer Frau: Drei Erzählungen und ein kurzer Roman. [Selections]. Trans. Heidi Zerning. Frankfurt am Main: Fischer Taschenbuch, 2004. 223 pp. ISBN 3596157080.

Der Traum meiner Mutter: Erzälungen. [Selections]. Trans. Heidi Zerning. Frankfurt: Fischer Taschenbuch, 2005. 224 pp. ISBN 3596161630.

Italian

Il sogno di mia madre. Trans. Susanna Basso. Torino: Einaudi, 2001. 362 pp. ISBN 8806153420.

Il sogno di mia madre. Trans. Susanna Basso. Einaudi tascabili 1232. Torino: Einaudi, 2004. 362 pp. ISBN 8806169092.

Norwegian

En god kvinnes kjærlighet. Trans. Kia Halling. [Oslo]: Gyldendal, 2000. 299 pp. ISBN 8205267332.

Spanish

El amor de una mujer generosa: Relatos. Trans. Javier Alfaya Bula, José Hamad, and Javier Alfaya McShane. La creación literaria. Madrid: Siglo XXI de España, [2002]. 336 pp. ISBN 8432310859.

P7. The Moons of Jupiter: Stories

Editions

Toronto: Macmillan of Canada, 1982. 233 pp. ISBN 0771597258.

A Borzoi Book. New York: Alfred A. Knopf, distributed by Random House, 1983, c1982. 233 pp. ISBN 0394529529.

London: A. Lane, 1983, c1982. 233 pp. ISBN 0713915498.

Reprints

A Penguin Book. Harmondsworth, Eng.; Markham, ON: Penguin Books, 1983, c1982. 233 pp. ISBN 0140068414.

A King Penguin. Harmondsworth, Eng.: Penguin Books, 1984, c1982. 233 pp. ISBN 0140065474.

Introduction by Alice Munro. Markham, ON.: Penguin Books Canada, 1986, c1982. xvi, 233 pp. ISBN 0140092390.

1st Vintage Contemporaries ed. New York: Vintage Books, 1991, c1983. 233 pp. ISBN 0679732705.

Introduction by Alice Munro. Toronto: Penguin Books Canada, 1995. xvi, 233 pp. ISBN 0140244034.

London: Vintage, 2004, c1996. 240 pp. ISBN 0099458365.

Translations

Braille

Toronto: CNIB [Canadian National Institute for the Blind], 1983. 6 vols.

Dutch

De manen van Jupiter. Trans. Ton Heuvelmans, m.m.v. J. Polderman. Tricht, Neth.: Goossens, 1988. 236 pp. ISBN 9065510710.

French

Les lunes de Jupiter. Trans. Colette Tonge. Les grandes traductions. Paris: Albin Michel, 1989. 283, [1] pp. ISBN 2226036180.
Les lunes de Jupiter: Nouvelles. Trans. Colette Tonge. Rivages poche 147. Bibliothèque étrangère. Paris: Payot & Rivages, 1995, c1989. 380 pp. ISBN 2869308825.

German

Die Jupitermonde: Erzählungen. Trans. Manfred Ohl and Hans Sartorius. Stuttgart: Klett-Cotta, 1986, c1982. 276 pp. ISBN 3608953221.
Die Jupitermonde: Erzählungen. Trans. Manfred Ohl and Hans Sartorius. 2. Aufl. Stuttgart: Klett-Cotta, 1987. 280 pp. ISBN 3608953221.
Die Jupitermonde: Erzählungen. Trans. Manfred Ohl and Hans Sartorius. Berlin: Berliner Taschenbuch, 2002. 345 pp. ISBN 3442760496.

Japanese

Mokusei no tsuki. Trans. Yokoyama Kazuko. Tokyo: Chuo Koronsha, 1997. 366 pp. ISBN 4120026558.

Spanish

Las lunas de Júpiter. Trans. Esperanza Pérez Moreno. Meridianos 55. Barcelona: Versal, 1990. 301, [1] pp. ISBN 8478760385.

Swedish

Jupiters månar: Noveller. Trans. Karin Benecke. Stockholm: Norstedt, 1985. 296, [1] pp. ISBN 9118511821.

P8. Open Secrets: Stories

Editions

A Douglas Gibson Book. Toronto: McClelland and Stewart, 1994. 293, [1] pp. ISBN 0771066996.
A Borzoi Book. New York: Alfred A. Knopf, distributed by Random House, 1994. 293, [1] pp. ISBN 0679435751.
London: Chatto & Windus, 1994. 293 pp. ISBN 0701161450.

Reprints

London: Vintage, 1995. 293, [1] pp. ISBN 009945971X.
1st Vintage Contemporaries ed. New York: Vintage Contemporaries, 1995, c1994. 293 pp. ISBN 0679755624.
Toronto: Penguin Books Canada, 1995, c1994. 344 pp. ISBN 0140247300.
Large print ed. Rothley, Leicester, Eng.: W. F. Howes, 2003, c1994. 377 pp. ISBN 184197594X.

Translations

Albanian

Virgjëresha shqiptare: Novela. [Selections]. Trans. Betim Muço. Tiranë: Shtëpia Botuese "Mësonjëtorja," 1999-2002? 131 pp.
   Contains stories "Virgjëresha shqiptare" (The Albanian Virgin), "Një Jetë e vërtetë" (A Real Life), and "E Fry mëzuar" (Carried Away).

Danish

Offentlige hemmeligheder: Noveller. Trans. Lisbeth Møller-Madsen. [København]: Samleren, 1996, c1994. 313, [1] pp. ISBN 8756812531.

Finnish

Julkisia salaisuuksia: Kertomuksia. Trans. Kristiina Rikman. Keltainen kirjasto 287. Helsinki: Tammi, 1994. 328 pp. ISBN 9513106020.

French

Secrets de Polichinelle. Trans. Céline Schwaller-Balaÿ. Paris: Rivages, 1995. 315, [1] pp. ISBN 286930966X.
Secrets de Polichinelle. Trans. Céline Schwaller-Balaÿ. Rivages poche 328. Bibliothèque étrangère. Paris: Payot & Rivages, 2001. 336 pp. ISBN 2743607505.

German

Offene Geheimnisse: Erzählungen. Trans. Karen Nölle-Fischer. Stuttgart: Klett-Cotta, 1996. 334 pp. ISBN 3608933719.
Offene Geheimnisse: Erzählungen. Trans. Karen Nölle-Fischer. Berlin: Berliner Taschenbuch-Verlag, 2004. 376 pp. ISBN 3833300043.

Italian

Segreti svelati. Trans. Marina Premoli. Milano: La Tartaruga, [2000]. 337 pp. ISBN 887738316X.

Norwegian

Den albanske jomfru: Og andre fortellinger. Trans. Ebba Haslund. Oslo: Gyldendal Norsk Forlag, 1996. 261 pp. ISBN 8205238332.

Spanish

Secretos a voces. Trans. Flora Casas. Versión castellana. Colección literatura. Madrid: Debate, 1996. 284 pp. ISBN 8474449766.
Secretos a voces. Trans. Julio Paredes Castro. La Otra Orilla. Cuentos. Bogotá: Norma, 2000. 122 pp. ISBN 9580435804.

P9. The Progress of Love: Stories

Editions

A Douglas Gibson Book. Toronto: McClelland and Stewart, 1986. 309 pp. ISBN 077106666X.
A Borzoi Book. New York: Alfred A. Knopf, distributed by Random House, 1986. 309 pp. ISBN 0394552725.
London: Chatto & Windus, 1987, c1986. 309 pp. ISBN 0701131616.

Reprints

Markham, ON: Penguin Books Canada, 1987, c1986. 421 pp. ISBN 0140098798.
A King Penguin. New York: Penguin Books, 1987. 309 pp. ISBN 0140098798; 0140105530.
London: Flamingo; Fontana, 1988, c1987. 309 pp. ISBN 0006542697.
Toronto: Penguin Books Canada, 1995. 411 pp. ISBN 0140241612.
London: Vintage, 1996, c1986. 309 pp. ISBN 0099741318.
1st Vintage Contemporaries ed. Vintage Contemporaries. New York: Vintage Books, 2000. 309 pp. ISBN 0375724702.
Large print. Rothley, Leicester, Eng.: W. F. Howes, 2003. 455 pp. ISBN 1841976679.

Translations

Braille

Bredbury, Eng.: National Library for the Blind, 1996. 6 vols.

Danish

Forunderlig er kærligheden. Trans. Lisbeth Møller-Madsen. [København]: Hekla, 1991, c1986. 245 pp. ISBN 8774741748.

Dutch

Liefdes vorderingen. Trans. Pleuke Boyce and Jeanne Polderman. Tricht, Neth.: Goossens, 1990. 300 pp. ISBN 9065510761.

Finnish

Valkoinen tunkio: Kertomuksia. Trans. Kristiina Rikman. Helsinki: Tammi, 1987. 327 pp. ISBN 9513068331.

French

Miles City, Montana. Trans. Florence Petry and Jean-Pierre Ricard. Paris: Deuxtemps Tierce, 1991. 404 pp. ISBN 2903144702.

German

Der Mond über der Eisbahn: Liebesgeschichten. Trans. Helga Huisgen. Stuttgart: Klett-Cotta, 1989. 391 pp. ISBN 3608955593.
Der Mond über der Eisbahn: Liebesgeschichten. Trans. Helga Huisgen. Berlin: Berliner Taschenbuch-Verlag, 2001. 442 pp. ISBN 344276016X.

Italian

Il percorso dell'amore. Trans. Chiara Spallino Rocca. Milano: Serra e Riva, 1989. 357 pp. ISBN 8877980168.

Spanish

El progreso del amor. Trans. Flora Casas. Versión castellana. Colección literatura 77. Madrid: Debate, 1990. 327 pp. ISBN 8474444586.
El progreso del amor. Trans. Flora Casas. 1a ed. en bolsillo. Debate bolsillo. Madrid: Debate, 1996. 326 pp. ISBN 8474449952.

Swedish

Kärlekens vägar: Noveller. Trans. Karin Benecke. Stockholm: Norstedts, 1991, c1986. 331, [1] pp. ISBN 9118915728.

P10. Queenie: A Story

Originally published in *London Review of Books* July 1998.

Editions

London: Profile Books, in association with *London Review of Books*, 1999, c1998. 64 pp. ISBN 1861971192.

P11. Runaway: Stories

Editions

A Douglas Gibson Book. Toronto: McClelland and Stewart, 2004. 335 pp. ISBN 077106506X.
New York: Alfred A. Knopf, 2004. 335 pp. ISBN 140004281X.
London: Chatto & Windus, 2005. 335 pp. ISBN 0701177500.

Reprints

Toronto: Penguin Canada, 2005. 335 pp. ISBN 0143050710.
1st Vintage Contemporaries ed. New York: Vintage Contemporaries, 2005. 335 pp. ISBN 1400077915.
New York: Random House Large Print, 2005. 576 pp. ISBN 0375435301.

Translations

Dutch

Stilte. Trans. Pleuke Boyce. Breda, Neth.: De Geus, 2005. 382 pp. ISBN 9044506056.

Finnish

Karkulainen: Kertomuksia. Trans. Kristiina Rikman. Keltainen kirjasto 364. Helsinki: Tammi, 2005. 386 pp. ISBN 9513132250.

German

Tricks: Acht Erzählungen. Trans. Heidi Zerning. Frankfurt am Main: S. Fischer, 2006. 384 pp. ISBN 3100488261.

Italian

In fuga. Trans. Susanna Basso. Torino: Einaudi, 2004. 316 pp. ISBN 8806171836.

Spanish

Escapada. Trans. Carmen Aguilar. Barcelona: RBA, 2005. 286 pp. ISBN 8478714049.

P12. Selected Stories

Editions

A Douglas Gibson Book. Toronto: McClelland and Stewart, 1996. 545 pp. ISBN 0771066708.
A Borzoi Book. New York: Alfred A. Knopf, distributed by Random House, 1996. 545 pp. ISBN 0679446273.
[Selections]. London: Chatto & Windus, 1996. 412 pp. ISBN 0701165219.

Reprints

[Selections]. London: Vintage, 1997. 412 pp. ISBN 0099732416.
Introduction by Alice Munro. 1st Vintage Contemporaries ed. New York: Vintage Contemporaries, 1997. xxi, 664 pp. ISBN 067976674X.
Introduction by Alice Munro. Toronto: Penguin Books Canada, 1998. xvii, 686 pp. ISBN 0140267751.

Translations

Braille

Stockport, Eng.: National Library for the Blind, n.d. 12 vols.
Trans. Associated Services for the Blind. [Washington, DC]: Library of Congress, NLS [National Library Service], 1997. 6 vols. (Also available from Web-braille as a grade 2 braille digital file.)
Bredbury, Eng.: National Library for the Blind, 1999- . Diskettes, double sided, high density, 3.5 in. (Remote access through VisuTEXT. Braille formatted file.)

French

La danse des ombres heureuses. [Selections]. Trans. Geneviève Doze. Collection de littérature étrangère. Paris: Payot & Rivages, 2002. 165, [1] pp. ISBN 2743609605. Contains stories "Le cow-boy des frères Walker," "La danse des ombres heureuses," "La carte postale," "Images," "Quelque chose que j'avais l'intention de te dire," "La vallée de l'Ottawa," and "Material."

P13. Something I've Been Meaning to Tell You . . . : Thirteen Stories

Editions

Toronto; Montreal; New York: McGraw-Hill Ryerson, 1974. 246 pp. ISBN 0070777608.
New York; St. Louis; San Francisco: McGraw-Hill, 1974. 246 pp. ISBN 0070777608.

Reprints

New York: New American Library, 1975. 197 pp. ISBN 0451143434.
A Signet Book. Scarborough, ON: New American Library of Canada, 1975, c1974. 197 pp. ISBN 0451088654; 0451126297; 0451112466.
A Plume Book. New York: New American Library, 1984, c1974. 246 pp. ISBN 0452255155; 0452260213.
A King Penguin. Harmondsworth, Eng.; Markham, ON: Penguin Books, 1985, c1974. 235 pp. ISBN 0140072896; 0140147543.
Markham, ON: Penguin Books, 1990. 246 pp. ISBN 0140128395.
Toronto: Penguin Books Canada, 1996, c1974. 246 pp. ISBN 0140241604.
1st Vintage Contemporaries ed. New York: Vintage Contemporaries, 2004, c1974. 246 pp. ISBN 0375707484.

Translations

Braille

Toronto: CNIB [Canadian National Institute for the Blind], 1980. 5 vols.
Stockport, Eng.: National Library for the Blind, n.d. 5 vols.

Hindi

Main tumse kuchh kahna chahti hoon. Trans. Anand. Ottawa: VK Canada; copublished by Viplava Karyalaya, Lucknow, India, 1993. 231 pp.

P14. Who Do You Think You Are?: Stories

Published in the United States and Britain under the title *The Beggar Maid: Stories of Flo and Rose*. (See entries under that title for American and British editions.)

Editions

Toronto: Macmillan of Canada, 1978. 206 pp. ISBN 0770517129.

Reprints

A Signet Book. Scarborough, ON: Macmillan-NAL, 1979, c1978. 210 pp. ISBN 0772300275.
A Signet Book. Toronto: New American Library of Canada, 1979. 210 pp. ISBN 0772300984.
Macmillan Paperback 43. Toronto: Macmillan of Canada, 1989. 206 pp. ISBN 0771592981.
Toronto: Penguin Books Canada, 1991, c1978. 277 pp. ISBN 0140149775.
Toronto; London: Penguin Books, 1996, c1978. 256 pp. ISBN 0140241582.

Translations

Braille

Toronto: CNIB [Canadian National Institute for the Blind], 2001. 4 vols. (431 pp.) of computer braille.

Dutch

Wie denk je dat je bent? Trans. P. de Vos and J. Polderman. Tricht, Neth.: Goossens, 1987. 221 pp. ISBN 9065510710.

French

Pour qui te prends-tu?: Roman. Trans. Colette Tonge. Collection littérature d'Amérique. Montréal: Québec/Amérique, 1981. 297 pp. ISBN 2890370593.
Un demi-pamplemousse: Nouvelles. Trans. Michèle Causse. Éd. hors commerce. Rivages poche. Bibliothèque étrangère. Paris: Payot & Rivages, 2002. [89] pp. ISBN 2743608935. Contains stories "De sacrées raclées" (Royal Beatings) and "Un demi-pamplemousse" (Half a Grapefruit).

Italian

Chi ti credi di essere. Trans. Anna Rusconi. Roma: Edizioni e/o, 1995. 214 pp. ISBN 887641259X.

Other Story Selections

P15. *No Love Lost*. Sel. and afterword Jane Urquhart. New Canadian Library. Toronto: McClelland and Stewart, 2003. 421 pp. ISBN 0771034814.
Contains stories "The Albanian Virgin," "Bardon Bus," "The Bear Came Over the Mountain," "Carried Away," "The Children Stay," "Hateship, Friendship, Courtship, Loveship, Marriage," "The Love of a Good Woman," "Meneseteung," "Mischief," "Simon's Luck."

P16. *Vintage Munro*. New York: Vintage, 2004. 196 pp. ISBN 1400033950.
Contains stories "The Moons of Jupiter," "The Progress of Love," "Differently," "Carried Away," "Hateship, Friendship, Courtship, Loveship, Marriage."

Translations

Czech

P17. *U dávno ti chci n co íct: a jiné povídky*. Trans. Alena Jindrová-Špilarová. Afterword Josef Jarab. Sv tová próza 6. Praha [Prague]: Paseka, 2002. 302 pp. ISBN 8071855324.

Norwegian

P18. *Noveller*. Trans. Ragnhild Eikli. Sel. and foreword Gordon Hølmebakk. [Oslo]: Den norske Bokklubben, 1993. 553 pp. ISBN 8252516998.

Stories

Accident

P19.   "Accident." *Toronto Life* November 1977: 60-61, 87-88, 90-95, 149-150, 153-156, 159-160, 162-165, 167, 169-173.

P20.   "Accident." *The Moons of Jupiter: Stories.* Toronto: Macmillan of Canada, 1982. 77-109.

The Albanian Virgin

P21.   "The Albanian Virgin." *New Yorker* 27 June & 4 July 1994: 118-121, 123-127, 129-134, 136-138.

P22.   "The Albanian Virgin." (Revised) *Open Secrets: Stories.* Toronto: McClelland and Stewart, 1994. 81-128.
Originally entitled "Lottar."

P23.   "The Albanian Virgin." *Selected Stories.* Toronto: McClelland and Stewart, 1996. 465-497.

P24.   "The Albanian Virgin." *The Oxford Book of Stories by Canadian Women in English.* Ed. Rosemary Sullivan. Don Mills, ON: Oxford University Press, 1999. 180-212.

P25.   "The Albanian Virgin." *No Love Lost.* Sel. and afterword Jane Urquhart. New Canadian Library. Toronto: McClelland and Stewart, 2003. 312-358.

Translations

Albanian

P26.   "Virgjëresha shqiptare." *Virgjëresha shqiptare: Novela*. Trans. Betim Muço. Tiranë: Shtëpia Botuese "Mësonjëtorja," 1999-2002? 5-51.

At the Other Place

P27.   "At the Other Place." *Canadian Forum* 35 (September 1955): 131-133. [as Alice Laidlaw]

Baptizing

Chapter from the novel *Lives of Girls and Women*.

P28.   "Baptizing (excerpt)." *Touching Fire: Erotic Writings by Women*. Ed. Louise Thornton, Jan Sturtevant, and Amber Coverdale Sumrall. New York: Carroll & Graf, 1989. 15-16.

P29.   "Baptizing." *The HarperCollins World Reader: The Modern World*. [Ed.] Mary Ann Caws and Christopher Prendergast. New York: HarperCollins College, 1994. 2526-2531.

Bardon Bus

P30.   "Bardon Bus." *The Moons of Jupiter: Stories*. Toronto: Macmillan of Canada, 1982. 110-128.

P31.   "Bardon Bus." *The World of the Short Story: A Twentieth Century Collection*. Sel. and ed. Clifton Fadiman. Boston: Houghton Mifflin, 1986. 685-701.

P32.   "Bardon Bus." *Likely Stories: A Postmodern Sampler*. Ed. George Bowering and Linda Hutcheon. Toronto: Coach House, 1992. 179-201.

P33.   "Bardon Bus." *No Love Lost*. Sel. and afterword Jane Urquhart. New Canadian Library. Toronto: McClelland and Stewart, 2003. 1-22.

A Basket of Strawberries

P34.   "A Basket of Strawberries." *Mayfair* November 1953: 32-33, 78-80, 82. [as Alice Laidlaw]

P35.   "A Basket of Strawberries." *First Fiction: An Anthology of the First Published Stories by Famous Writers*. Ed. Kathy Kiernan and Michael M. Moore. Introd. Jane Smiley. Boston: Little, Brown, 1994. 270-279.

The Bear Came Over the Mountain

P36.   "The Bear Came Over the Mountain." *New Yorker* 27 December 1999 & 3 January 2000: 110-121, 124-127.

P37.   "The Bear Came Over the Mountain." *Best Canadian Stories, 00.* [Ottawa]: Oberon, 2000. 9-41.

P38.   "The Bear Came Over the Mountain." *Hateship, Friendship, Courtship, Loveship, Marriage: Stories.* Toronto: McClelland and Stewart, 2001. 274-322.

P39.   "The Bear Came Over the Mountain." *No Love Lost.* Sel. and afterword Jane Urquhart. New Canadian Library. Toronto: McClelland and Stewart, 2003. 263-311.

Before the Change

P40.   "Before the Change." *New Yorker* 24 & 31 August 1998: 132-136, 138-143.

P41.   "Before the Change." (Revised) *The Love of a Good Woman: Stories.* Toronto: McClelland and Stewart, 1998. 254-292.

P42.   "Before the Change." *Valentine's Day: Women Against Men: Stories of Revenge.* London: Duck Editions, 2000. 166-199.

Translations

Czech

P43.   "Nez prijde zmena." *Uz dávno ti chci neco ríct: A jiné povídky.* Trans. Alena Jindrová-Špilarová. Afterword Josef Jarab. Svetová próza 6. Praha [Prague]: Paseka, 2002. 258-295.

German

P44.   "Vor dem Wandel." *Der Traum meiner Mutter: Erzählungen.* Trans. Heidi Zerning. Afterword Judith Hermann. Frankfurt am Main: S. Fischer, 2002. 215-221.

The Beggar Maid

P45.   "The Beggar Maid." *New Yorker* 27 June 1977: 34-40, 43-46, 51.

P46.   "The Beggar Maid." *Best Canadian Stories, 78.* Ed. John Metcalf and Clark Blaise. [Ottawa]: Oberon, 1978. 9-42.

P47. "The Beggar Maid." (Revised) *Who Do You Think You Are?: Stories*. Toronto: Macmillan of Canada, 1978. 65-97.

P48. "The Beggar Maid." *Best Canadian Short Stories*. Ed. John Stevens. Toronto: McClelland-Bantam, 1981. 96-121.

P49. "The Beggar Maid." *The Norton Anthology of Contemporary Fiction*. Ed. R. V. Cassill and Joyce Carol Oates. New York: Norton, 1988. 316-343.

P50. "The Beggar Maid." *The Houghton Mifflin Anthology of Short Fiction*. Patricia Hampl. Boston: Houghton Mifflin, 1989. 942-963.

P51. "The Beggar Maid." *Major Writers of Short Fiction: Stories and Commentaries*. [Ed.] Ann Charters. Boston: Bedford Books of St. Martin's Press, 1993. 989-1015.

P52. "The Beggar Maid." *Selected Stories*. Toronto: McClelland and Stewart, 1996. 124-151.

Translations

Norwegian

P53. "Tiggerpiken." *Noveller*. By Alice Munro. Trans. Ragnhild Eikli. Sel. and foreword Gordon Hølmebakk. [Oslo]: Den norske Bokklubben, 1993. 188-224.

A Better Place Than Home

P54. "A Better Place Than Home." *The Newcomers: Inhabiting a New Land*. Ed. Charles E. Israel. Toronto: McClelland and Stewart, 1979. 113-124.

Boys and Girls

P55. "Boys and Girls." *Montrealer* 38.12 (December 1964): 25-34.

P56. "Boys and Girls." *Dance of the Happy Shades: Stories*. Toronto: Ryerson Press, 1968. 111-127.

P57. "Boys and Girls." *Sixteen by Twelve: Short Stories by Canadian Writers*. Ed. and introd. John Metcalf. Toronto: Ryerson, 1970. 112-124.

P58. "Boys and Girls." *Four Hemispheres: An Anthology of English Short Stories From Around the World*. Ed. W. H. New. Toronto: Copp Clark, 1971. 89-101.

P59. "Boys and Girls." *Diary of a Mad Tourist*. [Comp.] Ernest H. Winter. Don Mills, ON: Nelson, 1975. 27-43.

P60. "Boys and Girls." *Women in Canadian Literature*. Ed. M. G. Hesse. Ottawa: Borealis, 1976. 11-21.

P61. "Boys and Girls." *New Worlds: A Canadian Collection of Stories With Notes*. Ed. John Metcalf. Toronto: McGraw Hill Ryerson, 1980. 120-132. Questions about the stories, pp. 162-164.

P62. "Boys and Girls." *The Norton Introduction to Literature*. [Ed.] Carl E. Bain, Jerome Beaty, and J. Paul Hunter. New York: Norton. Shorter 3rd ed. 1982. 293-304. 6th ed. 1995. 465-475. Shorter 6th ed. 1995. 338-348.

P63. "Boys and Girls." *A 20th Century Anthology: Essays, Stories, and Poems*. Ed. W. E. Messenger and W. H. New. Scarborough, ON: Prentice-Hall Canada, 1984. 351-360.

P64. "Boys and Girls." *The Norton Introduction to Fiction*. [Comp.] Jerome Beaty. 3rd ed. New York: Norton, 1985. 339-350.

P65. "Boys and Girls." *Classic Short Fiction*. Charles H. Bohner. Englewood Cliffs, NJ: Prentice-Hall, 1986. 796-805.

P66. "Boys and Girls." *Literature for Composition: Essays, Fiction, Poetry, and Drama*. Sylvan Barnet, Morton Berman, and William Burto. 2nd ed. Glenview, IL: Scott, Foresman, 1988. 519-529.

P67. "Boys and Girls." *The New Canadian Anthology: Poetry and Short Fiction in English*. Ed. Robert Lecker and Jack David. Scarborough, ON: Nelson Canada, 1988. 360-372.

P68. "Boys and Girls." *An Introduction to Literature: Fiction, Poetry, Drama*. Ed. Sylvan Barnet, Morton Berman, and William Burto. 9th ed. Glenview, IL: Scott, Foresman, 1989. 320-332.

P69. "Boys and Girls." *Contemporary Canadian Short Stories: Atwood, Findley, MacLeod, Munro, Richler, Valgardson, Wiebe*. Introd. Klaus Peter Müller. Stuttgart: Reclam, 1990. 95-119.

P70. "Boys and Girls." *The Blair Reader*. Ed. Laurie G. Kirszner and Stephen R. Mandell. Englewood Cliffs, NJ: Prentice Hall, 1992. 454-466.

P71. "Boys and Girls." *Major Writers of Short Fiction: Stories and Commentaries*. [Ed.] Ann Charters. Boston: Bedford Books of St. Martin's Press, 1993. 1015-1026.

P72. "Boys and Girls." *An Anthology of College Readings*. Prepared by the School of English Studies, Seneca College of Applied Arts and Technology. Scarborough, ON: Prentice-Hall Canada, 1994. 293-303.

P73.   "Boys and Girls (excerpt)." *Explorations in World Literature.* Carole M. Shaffer-Koros and Jessie M. Reppy. New York: St. Martin's Press, 1994. 169-172.

P74.   "Boys and Girls." *The Norton Introduction to Literature.* [Ed.] Carl E. Bain, Jerome Beaty, and J. Paul Hunter. New York: Norton. 6th ed. 1995. 465-475. Shorter 6th ed. 1995. 338-348.

P75.   "Boys and Girls." *Discovering Literature: Stories, Poems, Plays.* Hans P. Guth and Gabriele L. Rico. 2nd ed. Upper Saddle River, NJ: Prentice Hall, 1996. 81-92.

P76.   "Boys and Girls." *Elements of Literature. Fourth Course. Pupil Text.* Robert E. Probst, et al. Austin, TX: Holt, Rinehart and Winston, 1997. 53-64.

P77.   "Boys and Girls." *The Norton Introduction to Literature.* [Ed.] Jerome Beaty and J. Paul Hunter. New York: Norton. 7th ed. 1998. 422-432. Shorter 7th ed. 1998. 365-375.

P78.   "Boys and Girls." *Short Fiction: Classic and Contemporary.* Ed. Charles Bohner and Dean Dougherty. 4th ed. Upper Saddle River, NJ: Prentice Hall, 1999. 764-773.

P79.   "Boys and Girls." *The Wascana Anthology of Short Fiction.* Ed. Ken Mitchell, Thomas Chase, and Michael Trussler. Regina: Canadian Plains Research Center, 1999. 326-336.

P80.   "Boys and Girls." *An Introduction to Literature: Fiction, Poetry, Drama.* Sylvan Barnet, et al. 12th ed. New York: Longman, 2000. 252-262.

P81.   "Boys and Girls." *Literature: Reading, Reacting, Writing.* Laurie G. Kirszner and Stephen R. Mandell. Compact 4th ed. Forth Worth, TX: Harcourt College Publishers, 2000. 424-435.

P82.   "Boys and Girls." *Literature for Composition: Essays, Fiction, Poetry, and Drama.* Ed. Sylvan Barnet, et al. 5th ed. New York: Longman, 2000. 714-723.

P83.   "Boys and Girls." *Exploring Literature: Writing and Thinking about Fiction, Poetry, Drama and the Essay.* New York: Longman, 2001. 843-853.

P84.   "Boys and Girls." *Short Fiction: Classic and Contemporary.* Charles Bohner and Lyman Grant. 5th ed. Upper Saddle River, NJ: Prentice Hall, 2002. 810-819.

Translations

German

P85.   "Jungen und Mädchen." *Die weite Reise: Kanadische Erzählungen und Kurzgeschichten.* Trans. Karl Heinrich. Ed. Ernst Bartsch. Berlin: Verlag Volk und Welt, 1974. 284-303.

Carried Away

P86. "Carried Away." *New Yorker* 21 October 1991: 34-46, 48-51, 54-58, 60-61.

P87. "Carried Away." *The Best American Short Stories, 1992.* Sel. Robert Stone with Katrina Kenison. Introd. Robert Stone. Boston: Houghton Mifflin, 1992. 179-217.

P88. "Carried Away." *Best English Short Stories IV.* Ed. Giles Gordon and David Hughes. New York: Norton, 1992. 199-241.

P89. "Carried Away." *Open Secrets: Stories.* Toronto: McClelland and Stewart, 1994. 3-51.

P90. *Carried Away.* s.l.: s.n., 1994. 51pp. Excerpt from *Open Secrets: Stories.* A limited edition, numbered and signed by the author.

P91. "Carried Away." *Selected Stories.* Toronto: McClelland and Stewart, 1996. 431-464.

P92. "Carried Away." *No Love Lost.* Sel. and afterword Jane Urquhart. New Canadian Library. Toronto: McClelland and Stewart, 2003. 23-69.

Translations

Albanian

P93. "E Fry mëzuar." *Virgjëresha shqiptare: Novela.* Trans. Betim Muço. Tiranë: Shtëpia Botuese "Mësonjëtorja," 1999-2002? 83-129.

Czech

P94. "Závrat'." *Uz dávno ti chci neco ríct: A jiné povídky.* Trans. Alena Jindrová-Špilarová. Afterword Josef Jarab. Svetová próza 6. Praha [Prague]: Paseka, 2002. 181-226.

Norwegian

P95. "Rykket bort." *Noveller.* By Alice Munro. Trans. Ragnhild Eikli. Sel. and foreword by Gordon Hølmebakk. [Oslo]: Den norske Bokklubben, 1993. 509-552.

Chaddeleys and Flemings: 1. Connection
See also "Connection."

P96. "Chaddeleys and Flemings. 1: Connection." (Revised) *The Moons of Jupiter: Stories.* Toronto: Macmillan of Canada, 1982. 1-18.

P97. "Chaddeleys and Flemings. 1: Connection." *Canadian Short Fiction: From Myth to Modern.* Ed. W. H. New. Scarborough, ON: Prentice-Hall Canada, 1986. 323-334.

P98. "Chaddeleys and Flemings. Connection." *A Corner in Each Life: Contemporary Canadian Stories, Reflections in Fiction*. Ed. Sean Armstrong and Carole Corbeil. Scarborough, ON: Nelson Canada, 1994. 130-146.

P99. "Chaddeleys and Flemings. I: Connection." *Selected Stories*. Toronto: McClelland and Stewart, 1996. 171-184.

P100. "Chaddeleys and Flemings. 1: Connection." *Canadian Short Fiction*. Ed. W. H. New. 2nd ed. Scarborough, ON: Prentice-Hall Canada, 1997. 287-300.

Translations

Norwegian

P101. "Familiene Chaddeley og Fleming: forbindelser." *Noveller*. By Alice Munro. Trans. Ragnhild Eikli. Sel. and foreword Gordon Hølmebakk. [Oslo]: Den norske Bokklubben, 1993. 225-243.

Chaddeleys and Flemings: 2. The Stone in the Field
See also "The Stone in the Field."

P102. "Chaddeleys and Flemings. 2: The Stone in the Field." (Revised) *The Moons of Jupiter: Stories*. Toronto: Macmillan, 1982. 19-35.

P103. "Chaddeleys and Flemings. 2: The Stone in the Field." *Canadian Short Fiction: From Myth to Modern*. Ed. W. H. New. Scarborough, ON: Prentice-Hall Canada, 1986. 334-345.

P104. "[Chaddeleys and Flemings: 2.] The Stone in the Field." *Elements of Literature*. [Ed.] Robert Scholes, et al. Canadian ed. Toronto: Oxford University Press, 1987. 319-332.

P105. "[Chaddeleys and Flemings: 2.] The Stone in the Field." *Contest Essays by Canadian Students*. Ed. Robert Hookey and Joan Pilz. Toronto: Holt, Rinehart and Winston of Canada, 1991. 218-231.

P106. "Chaddeleys and Flemings. II: The Stone in the Field." *Selected Stories*. Toronto: McClelland and Stewart, 1996. 185-198.

P107. "Chaddeleys and Flemings. 2: The Stone in the Field." *Canadian Short Fiction*. Ed. W. H. New. 2nd ed. Scarborough, ON: Prentice-Hall Canada, 1997. 300-311.

Translations

Norwegian

P108. "Familiene Chaddeley og Fleming: steinen i åkeren." *Noveller*. By Alice Munro. Trans. Ragnhild Eikli. Sel. and foreword Gordon Hølmebakk. [Oslo]: Den norske Bokklubben, 1993. 244-261.

Chance

P109. "Chance." *New Yorker* 14-21 June 2004: 130-142.

P110. "Chance." *Runaway: Stories*. Toronto: McClelland and Stewart, 2004. 48-86.

Characters

P111. "Characters." *Ploughshares* 4.3 (1978): 72-82.

The Children Stay

P112. "The Children Stay." *New Yorker* 22 & 29 December 1997: 90-96, 98-100, 102-103.

P113. "The Children Stay." *Prize Stories, 1998: The O. Henry Awards*. Ed. and introd. Larry Dark. New York: Anchor Books/Doubleday, 1998. 53-78.

P114. "The Children Stay." (Revised) *The Love of a Good Woman: Stories*. Toronto: McClelland and Stewart, 1998. 181-214.

P115. "The Children Stay." *An Introduction to Literature: Fiction, Poetry, Drama*. Sylvan Barnet, et al. 12th ed. New York: Longman, 2000. 262-278.

P116. "The Children Stay." *Literature for Composition: Essays, Fiction, Poetry, and Drama*. Ed. Sylvan Barnet, et al. 5th ed. New York: Longman, 2000. 735-750.

P117. "The Children Stay." *Fault Lines: Stories of Divorce*. Collected and ed. Caitlin Shetterly. New York: Berkley Books, 2001. 74-104.

P118. "The Children Stay." *Modern Stories in English*. Ed. W. H. New and H. J. Rosengarten. 4th ed. Toronto: Addison Wesley, 2001. 328-352.

P119. "The Children Stay." *No Love Lost*. Sel. and afterword Jane Urquhart. New Canadian Library. Toronto: McClelland and Stewart, 2003. 384-415.

P120. "The Children Stay." *Women Write: A Mosaic of Women's Voices in Fiction, Poetry, Memoir, and Essay*. Ed. and introd. Susan Cahill. New York: New American Library, 2004. 199-218.

Translations

Czech

P121. "Deti zùstanou tady." *Uz dávno ti chci neco ríct: A jiné povídky*. Trans. Alena Jindrová-Špilarová. Afterword Josef Jarab. Svetová próza 6. Praha [Prague]: Paseka, 2002. 227-257.

German

P122. "Die Kinder bleiben Hier." *Der Traum meiner Mutter: Erzählungen*. Trans. Heidi Zerning. Afterword Judith Hermann. Frankfurt am Main: S. Fischer, 2002. 71-113.

Circle of Prayer

P123. "Circle of Prayer." *Paris Review* 28 [no. 100] (Summer/Fall 1986): 31-51.

P124. "Circle of Prayer." (Revised) *The Progress of Love: Stories*. Toronto: McClelland and Stewart, 1986. 254-274.

P125. "Circle of Prayer." *The Best American Short Stories, 1987: Selected from U.S. and Canadian magazines*. Sel. Ann Beattie with Shannon Ravenel. Boston: Houghton Mifflin, 1987. 118-137.

Comfort

P126. "Comfort." *New Yorker* 8 October 2001: 66-77.

P127. "Comfort." *Hateship, Friendship, Courtship, Loveship, Marriage: Stories*. Toronto: McClelland and Stewart, 2001. 118-153.

Connection
See also "Chaddeleys and Flemings. 1: Connection."

P128. "Connection." *Chatelaine* November 1978: 66-67, 97-98, 101, 104, 106, 108, 111-112. Revised version pub. as "Chaddeleys and Flemings: 1. Connection" in *The Moons of Jupiter: Stories*.

Cortes Island

P129. "Cortes Island." *New Yorker* 12 October 1998: 72-80.

P130. "Cortes Island." (Revised) *The Love of a Good Woman: Stories*. Toronto: McClelland and Stewart, 1998. 117-145.

Translations

German

P131. "Cortes Island." *Die Liebe einer Frau: Drei Erzählungen und ein kurzer Roman*. Trans. Heidi Zerning. Frankfurt am Main: S. Fischer, 2000. 147-182.

Dance of the Happy Shades

P132. "Dance of the Happy Shades." *Montrealer* 35.2 (February 1961): 22-26.

P133. "Dance of the Happy Shades." *Dance of the Happy Shades: Stories*. Toronto: Ryerson Press, 1968. 211-224.

P134. "Dance of the Happy Shades." *Canadian Short Stories (Second Series)*. Sel. Robert Weaver. Toronto: Oxford University Press, 1968. 285-300.

P135. "Dance of the Happy Shades." *The Narrative Voice: Stories and Reflections by Canadian Authors*. Ed. and introd. John Metcalf. Toronto: McGraw-Hill Ryerson, 1972. 171-180.

P136. "Dance of the Happy Shades." *The Canadian Century: English-Canadian Writing Since Confederation*. Ed. and introd. A. J. M. Smith. Toronto: Gage, 1973. 491-501. Volume 2 of *The Book of Canadian Prose*.

P137. "Dance of the Happy Shades." *The Canadian Experience: A Brief Survey of English-Canadian Prose*. Ed. A. J. M. Smith. Toronto: Gage, 1974. 287-297.

P138. "Dance of the Happy Shades." *Here and Now: Best Canadian Stories*. Ed. Clark Blaise and John Metcalf. [Ottawa]: Oberon, 1977. 85-95.

P139. "Dance of the Happy Shades." *Toronto Short Stories*. Ed. Morris Wolfe and Douglas Daymond. Toronto: Doubleday Canada, 1977. 260-272.

P140. "Dance of the Happy Shades." *Introduction to the Short Story*. Robert W. Boynton and Maynard Mack. 4th ed. Portsmouth, NH: Boynton/Cook, 1992. 34-43.

P141. "Dance of the Happy Shades." *Selected Stories*. Toronto: McClelland and Stewart, 1996. 16-25.

Translations

Czech

P142. "Tanec šťastných stínů." *Uz dávno ti chci neco ríct: A jiné povídky*. Trans. Alena Jindrová-Špilarová. Afterword Josef Jarab. Svetová próza 6. Praha [Prague]: Paseka, 2002. 25-37.

French

P143. "La danse des ombres heureuses." *La danse des ombres heureuses*. Trans. Geneviève Doze. Collection de littérature étrangère. Paris: Payot & Rivages, 2002. 31-46.

The Dangerous One

P144. "The Dangerous One." *Chatelaine* July 1957: 48-51.

Day of the Butterfly
See also "Good-By, Myra."

P145. "Day of the Butterfly." *Dance of the Happy Shades: Stories*. Toronto: Ryerson Press, 1968. 100-110. Revised version of "Good-By, Myra," originally published in *Chatelaine*.

P146. "Day of the Butterfly." *Kaleidoscope: Canadian Stories*. Sel. John Metcalf. Toronto: Van Nostrand Reinhold, 1972. 92-102.

P147. "Day of the Butterfly." *The Ontario Experience*. Ed. John Stevens. Themes in Canadian Literature. Toronto: Macmillan, 1976: 102-112.

P148. "Day of the Butterfly." *Inquiry into Literature 4*. Bryant Fillion and Jim Henderson. Don Mills, ON: Collier Macmillan Canada, 1982. 54-63.

P149. "Day of the Butterfly." *World Literature: An Anthology of Great Short Stories, Drama, and Poetry*. Donna Rosenberg. Lincolnwood, IL: National Textbook, 1992. 707-716.

P150. "Day of the Butterfly." *Junior Great Books, Series 7*. Chicago: Great Books Foundation, 1992. 162-173.

Differently

P151. "Differently." *New Yorker* 2 January 1989: 23-36.

P152.   "Differently." *Friend of My Youth: Stories*. Toronto: McClelland and Stewart, 1990. 216-243.

P153.   "Differently." *The Best American Short Stories, 1990*. Sel. Richard Ford with Shannon Ravenel. Boston: Houghton Mifflin, 1990. 190-214.

P154.   "Differently." *Selected Stories*. Toronto: McClelland and Stewart, 1996. 410-430.

The Dimensions of a Shadow

P155.   "The Dimensions of a Shadow." *Folio* [University of Western Ontario] 4.2 (April 1950): [4-10]. [as Alice Laidlaw]

Dulse

P156.   "Dulse." *New Yorker* 21 July 1980: 30-39.

P157.   "Dulse." (Revised) *The Moons of Jupiter: Stories*. Toronto: Macmillan of Canada, 1982. 36-59.

P158.   "Dulse." *The Penguin Book of Modern Canadian Short Stories*. Ed. Wayne Grady. Harmondsworth, Eng.: Penguin, 1982. 462-481.

P159.   "Dulse." *Selected Stories*. Toronto: McClelland and Stewart, 1996. 199-217.

P160.   "Dulse." *The Harbrace Anthology of Short Fiction*. Ed. Jon C. Stott, Raymond E. Jones, and Rick Bowers. 2nd ed. Toronto: Harcourt Brace, 1998. 1051-1066.

Translations

Norwegian

P161.   "En gave." *Noveller*. By Alice Munro. Trans. Ragnhild Eikli. Sel. and foreword Gordon Hølmebakk. [Oslo]: Den norske Bokklubben, 1993. 262-286.

The Edge of Town

P162.   "The Edge of Town." *Queen's Quarterly* 62.3 (Autumn 1955): 368-380. [as Alice Munroe (sic)]

Emily

See also "Simon's Luck."

P163.   "Emily." *Viva* August 1978: 99-105.
Revised version pub. as "Simon's Luck" in *Who Do You Think You Are?: Stories*.

Epilogue: The Photographer see The Photographer

Eskimo

P164.   "Eskimo." *GQ - Gentlemen's Quarterly* (December 1985): 262-266, 301-302, 304.

P165.   "Eskimo." *The Progress of Love: Stories*. Toronto: McClelland and Stewart, 1986. 189-207.

Translations

Norwegian

P166.   "Eskimo." *Noveller*. By Alice Munro. Trans. Ragnhild Eikli. Sel. and foreword Gordon Hølmebakk. [Oslo]: Den norske Bokklubben, 1993. 352-371.

Serbo-Croatian (Cyrillic)

P167.   "Eskim." *Lišaj: Dve novele*. Trans. Velimir Kostov. Pancevo: Zajednica Knjizevnika Pancevo, 1992.

Executioners

P168.   "Executioners." *Something I've Been Meaning to Tell You . . . : Thirteen Stories*. Toronto: McGraw-Hill Ryerson, 1974. 138-155.

Family Furnishings

P169.   "Family Furnishings." *New Yorker* 23 July 2001: 64-70, 72-77.

P170.   "Family Furnishings." *Hateship, Friendship, Courtship, Loveship, Marriage: Stories*. Toronto: McClelland and Stewart, 2001. 84-117.

P171.   "Family Furnishings." *The Best American Short Stories, 2002: Selected from U.S. and Canadian Magazines*. Sel. Sue Miller and Katrina Kenison. Boston: Houghton Mifflin, 2002. 276-303.

P172.   "Family Furnishings." *Best Canadian Stories, 02*. Ed. Douglas Glover. [Ottawa]: Oberon, 2002. 40-69.

Fathers

P173.   "Fathers." *New Yorker* 5 August 2002: 64-71.

P174. "Fathers." *The O. Henry Prize Stories, 2003*. Ed. and introd. Laura Furman. New York: Anchor Books, 2003. 256-271.

The Ferguson Girls Must Never Marry

P175. "The Ferguson Girls Must Never Marry." *Grand Street* 1.3 (Spring 1982): 27-64.

Fits

P176. "Fits." *Grand Street* 5.2 (Winter 1986): 36-61.

P177. "Fits." (Revised) *The Progress of Love: Stories*. Toronto: McClelland and Stewart, 1986. 106-131.

P178. "Fits." *Canadian Mystery Stories*. Ed. Alberto Manguel. Toronto: Oxford University Press, 1991. 108-130.

P179. "Fits." *Selected Stories*. Toronto: McClelland and Stewart, 1996. 353-373.

P180. "Fits." *Short Fiction: An Anthology*. Ed. Rosemary Sullivan and Mark Levene. Don Mills, ON: Oxford University Press, 2003. 463-481.

Five Points

P181. "Five Points." *New Yorker* 14 March 1988: 34-43.

P182. "Five Points." *Friend of My Youth: Stories*. Toronto: McClelland and Stewart, 1990. 27-49.

Translations

Norwegian

P183. "Five Points." *Noveller*. By Alice Munro. Trans. Ragnhild Eikli. Sel. and foreword Gordon Hølmebakk. [Oslo]: Den norske Bokklubben, 1993. 396-417.

Floating Bridge

P184. "Floating Bridge." *New Yorker* 31 July 2000: 64-72.

P185. "Floating Bridge." *Best Canadian Stories, 01*. Ed. Douglas Glover. [Ottawa]: Oberon, 2001. 15-43.

P186. "Floating Bridge." *Prize Stories, 2001: The O. Henry Awards*. Ed. and introd. Larry Dark. New York: Anchor Books, 2001. 85-105.

P187.   "Floating Bridge." *Hateship, Friendship, Courtship, Loveship, Marriage: Stories.* Toronto: McClelland and Stewart, 2001. 53-83.

P188.   "Floating Bridge." *More Stories We Tell: The Best Contemporary Short Stories by North American Women.* Ed. Wendy Martin. New York: Pantheon Books, 2004. 239-264.

Forgiveness in Families

P189.   "Forgiveness in Families." *McCall's* April 1974: 92-93, 138, 140, 142, 144, 146.

P190.   "Forgiveness in Families." *Something I've Been Meaning to Tell You . . . : Thirteen Stories.* Toronto: McGraw-Hill Ryerson, 1974. 93-105.

P191.   "Forgiveness in Families." *The West Coast Experience.* Ed. Jack Hodgins. Toronto: Macmillan of Canada, 1976. 32-44.

P192.   "Forgiveness in Families." *Heartland: An Anthology of Canadian Stories.* Ed. Katheryn Maclean Broughton. [Scarborough, ON]: Nelson, 1983. 107-108, 110-117.

P193.   "Forgiveness in Families." *West of Fiction.* Ed. Leah Flater, Aritha van Herk, and Rudy Wiebe. Edmonton: NeWest Press, 1983. 220-230.

P194.   "Forgiveness in Families." *Traditions in Literature.* James E. Miller, Helen McDonnell, and Russell J. Hogan. 7th ed. Glenview, IL: Scott, Foresman, 1985. 39-45.

P195.   "Forgiveness in Families." *Vancouver Short Stories.* Ed. Carole Gerson. Vancouver: University of British Columbia Press, 1985. 94-103.

P196.   "Forgiveness in Families." *Slices of Life: Writing from North America.* [Ed.] Thalia Rubio. Englewood Cliffs, NJ: Regents/Prentice-Hall, 1993. 135-144.

P197.   "Forgiveness in Families." *Go Tell It on the Mountain: And Related Readings.* Literature Connections. Evanston, IL: McDougal Littell, 1998. 349-363.

The Found Boat

P198.   "The Found Boat." *Something I've Been Meaning to Tell You . . . : Thirteen Stories.* Toronto: McGraw-Hill Ryerson, 1974. 125-137.

P199.   "The Found Boat." *The Role of Woman in Canadian Literature.* Ed. Elizabeth McCullough. Toronto: Macmillan, 1975. 70-81.

P200.   "The Found Boat." *Introduction to Fiction.* Ed. Jack David and Robert Lecker. Toronto: Holt, Rinehart and Winston, 1982. 366-370.

P201. "The Found Boat." *To Read Fiction*. Donald Hall. New York: Holt, Rinehart and Winston, 1987. 541-548.

P202. "The Found Boat." *Literature: Experience and Meaning*. Martha McGowan. San Diego: Harcourt Brace Jovanovich, 1989. 76-84.

P203. "The Found Boat." *Longman Anthology of World Literature by Women, 1875-1975*. Marian Arkin and Barbara Shollar. New York: Longman, 1989. 832-839.

P204. "The Found Boat." *Literature: An Introduction to Reading and Writing*. Edgar V. Roberts and Henry E. Jacobs. 3rd ed. Englewood Cliffs, NJ: Prentice-Hall, 1992. 286-293.

P205. "The Found Boat." *The McGraw-Hill Introduction to Literature*. Gilbert H. Muller and John A. Williams. 2nd ed. New York: McGraw-Hill, 1995. 44-51.

P206. "The Found Boat." *A Pocketful of Prose: Vintage Short Fiction*. Vol. 2. Ed. David Madden. Fort Worth, TX: Harcourt Brace Jovanovich College Publishers, 1996. 142-150.

P207. "The Found Boat." *The Stories: Contemporary Short Fiction Written in English*. Ed. Bruce Meyer. Scarborough, ON: Prentice Hall Canada, 1997. 434-443.

P208. "The Found Boat." *Literature: An Introduction to Reading and Writing*. Edgar V. Roberts and Henry E. Jacobs. Compact ed. Upper Saddle River, NJ: Prentice-Hall, 1998. 299-306.

Friend of My Youth

P209. "Friend of My Youth." *New Yorker* 22 January 1990: 36-48.

P210. "Friend of My Youth." *Friend of My Youth: Stories*. Toronto: McClelland and Stewart, 1990. 3-26.

P211. "Friend of My Youth." *The Best American Short Stories, 1991*. Sel. Alice Adams and Katrina Kenison. Introd. Alice Adams. Boston: Houghton Mifflin, 1991. 314-334.

P212. "Friend of My Youth." *Best Short Stories, 1991*. Ed. Giles Gordon and David Hughes. London: Heinemann, 1991. 194-216.

P213. "Friend of My Youth." *Best English Short Stories III*. Ed. Giles Gordon and David Hughes. New York: Norton, 1991. 194-216.

P214. "Friend of My Youth." *The Short Story in English*. Ed. Neil Besner and David Staines. Toronto: Oxford University Press, 1991. 658-674.

P215. "Friend of My Youth." *Short Fiction: An Introductory Anthology*. Ed. David Rampton and Gerald Lynch. Toronto: Harcourt Brace Jovanovich, 1992. 1045-1061.

P216. "Friend of My Youth." *Selected Stories*. Toronto: McClelland and Stewart, 1996. 374-391.

P217. "Friend of My Youth." *Short Fiction: Classic and Contemporary*. Ed. Charles Bohner and Dean Dougherty. 4th ed. Upper Saddle River, NJ: Prentice Hall, 1999. 750-763.

Translations

Norwegian

P218. "En ungdomsvenninne." *Noveller*. By Alice Munro. Trans. Ragnhild Eikli. Sel. and foreword Gordon Hølmebakk. [Oslo]: Den norske Bokklubben, 1993. 372-395.

Good-By, Myra

See also "Day of the Butterfly."

P219. "Good-By, Myra." *Chatelaine* July 1956: 16-17, 55-58. Revised version pub. as "Day of the Butterfly" in *Dance of the Happy Shades: Stories*.

Goodness and Mercy

P220. "Goodness and Mercy." *New Yorker* 20 March 1989: 38-48.

P221. "Goodness and Mercy." *Friend of My Youth: Stories*. Toronto: McClelland and Stewart, 1990. 156-179.

P222. "Goodness and Mercy." *Best English Short Stories II*. Ed. Giles Gordon and David Hughes. New York: Norton, 1990. 224-246.

Half a Grapefruit

P223. "Half a Grapefruit." *Redbook* May 1978. 132-133, 176, 178, 180, 182-183.

P224. "Half a Grapefruit." (Revised) *Who Do You Think You Are?: Stories*. Toronto: Macmillan of Canada, 1978. 38-54.

P225. "Half a Grapefruit." *Children Playing before a Statue of Hercules*. Ed. and introd. David Sedaris. New York: Simon & Schuster Paperbacks, 2005. 101-120.

Translations

French

P226. "Un demi-pamplemousse." *Un demi-pamplemousse: Nouvelles*. Trans. Michèle

Causse. Éd. hors commerce. Rivages poche. Bibliothèque étrangère. Paris: Payot & Rivages, 2002. 55-89.

Hard-Luck Stories

P227. "Hard-Luck Stories." *The Moons of Jupiter: Stories*. Toronto: Macmillan of Canada, 1982. 181-197.

P228. "Hard-Luck Stories." *In the Stacks: Short Stories About Libraries and Librarians*. Ed. and intro. Michael Cart. Woodstock, NY: Overlook Press, 2002. 230-245.

Hateship, Friendship, Courtship, Loveship, Marriage

P229. "Hateship, Friendship, Courtship, Loveship, Marriage." *Hateship, Friendship, Courtship, Loveship, Marriage: Stories*. Toronto: McClelland and Stewart, 2001. 1-52.

P230. "Hateship, Friendship, Courtship, Loveship, Marriage." *No Love Lost*. Sel. and afterword Jane Urquhart. New Canadian Library. Toronto: McClelland and Stewart, 2003. 211-262.

Hired Girl

P231. "Hired Girl." *New Yorker* 11 April 1994: 82-88.

P232. "Hired Girl." *Best Canadian Stories, 95*. Ed. David Helwig. [Ottawa]: Oberon, 1995. 51-70.

P233. "Hired Girl." *Best Short Stories, 1995*. Ed. Giles Gordon and David Hughes. London: Heinemann, 1995. 205-223.

Hold Me Fast, Don't Let Me Pass

P234. "Hold Me Fast, Don't Let Me Pass." *Atlantic Monthly* December 1988: 58-66, 68-70.

P235. "Hold Me Fast, Don't Let Me Pass." *Best Canadian Stories, 89*. Ed. David Helwig and Maggie Helwig. [Ottawa]: Oberon, 1989. 153-187.

P236. "Hold Me Fast, Don't Let Me Pass." *Friend of My Youth: Stories*. Toronto: McClelland and Stewart, 1990. 74-105.

P237. "Hold Me Fast, Don't Let Me Pass." *The Literary Traveler: An Anthology of Contemporary Short Fiction*. Ed. and introd. Larry Dark. New York: Penguin Books, 1996. 245-274.

Translations

Norwegian

P238.   "Hold meg, slipp meg ei forbi." *Noveller*. By Alice Munro. Trans. Ragnhild Eikli. Sel. and foreword Gordon Hølmebakk. [Oslo]: Den norske Bokklubben, 1993. 442-472.

Home

P239.   "Home." *New Canadian Stories: 74*. Ed. David Helwig and Joan Harcourt. [Ottawa]: Oberon, 1974. 133-153.

P240.   "Home." (Revised) *New Statesman* 17 December 2001: 84-93.

The Honeyman's Granddaughter
See also "Privilege."

P241.   "The Honeyman's Granddaughter." *Ms*. October 1978: 56-57, 75-76, 79. Revision of the story "Privilege," originally published in *Tamarack Review*.

How Could I Do That?

P242.   "How Could I Do That?" *Chatelaine* March 1956: 16-17, 65-70. [as Alice Laidlaw Munro]

Translations

Swedish

P243.   "Hur Kunde Jag?" *Vecko-revyn* July 1956: 10, 26, 29, 33.

How I Met My Husband

P244.   "How I Met My Husband." *McCall's* February 1974: 84-85, 123-127.

P245.   "How I Met My Husband." (Revised) *Something I've Been Meaning to Tell You . . . : Thirteen Stories*. Toronto: McGraw-Hill Ryerson, 1974. 45-66.

P246.   "How I Met My Husband." *Modern Canadian Stories*. Ed. John Stevens. New York: Bantam Books, 1975. 1-20.

P247.   "How I Met My Husband." [dramatized version] *The Play's the Thing: Four Original Television Dramas*. Ed. Tony Gifford. Toronto: Macmillan of Canada, 1976. 15-34.

42 Primary Works

P248. "How I Met My Husband." *Personal Fictions: Stories by Munro, Wiebe, Thomas, and Blaise*. Sel. Michael Ondaatje. Toronto: Oxford University Press, 1977. 21-37.

P249. "How I Met My Husband." *The Borzoi Book of Short Fiction*. David H. Richter. New York: Knopf, 1983. 1139-1152.

P250. "How I Met My Husband." *Timely and Timeless: Contemporary Prose*. Comp. and ed. Priscilla Galloway. Toronto: Clarke, Irwin, 1983. 12-30.

P251. "How I Met My Husband." *Fictions*. [Comp.] Joseph F. Trimmer and C. Wade Jennings. San Diego: Harcourt Brace Jovanovich, 1985. 887-899. 2nd ed. 1989. 889-901.

P252. "How I Met My Husband." *Modern Canadian Short Stories: Second Series*. Ed. with notes by Keiichi Hirano and Suzanne Firth. Kenkyusha Pocket English Series. Tokyo: Kenkyusha, [1988]: 18-47.

P253. "How I Met My Husband." *The Bedford Introduction to Literature: Reading, Thinking, Writing*. [Ed.] Michael Meyer. 2nd ed. Boston: Bedford Books of St. Martin's Press, 1990. 133-145. 5th ed. Boston: Bedford/St. Martin's, 1999. 442-453.

P254. "How I Met My Husband." *The Story and Its Writer: An Introduction to Short Fiction*. Ed. Ann Charters. Shorter 2nd ed. Boston: Bedford Books of St. Martin's Press, 1990. 594-607.

P255. "How I Met My Husband." *Kitchen Talk: Contemporary Women's Prose and Poetry*. Ed. Edna Alford and Claire Harris. Red Deer, AB: Red Deer College Press, 1992. 199-212.

P256. "How I Met My Husband (excerpt)." *Seeing and Believing: A Drama Anthology Organized by Themes*. Comp. and ed. David Perlman and Masha Buell. Toronto: Irwin, 1992. 264-265.

P257. "How I Met My Husband." *Literature: An Introduction to Fiction, Poetry and Drama*. X. J. Kennedy and Dana Gioia. New York: Longman. 2nd Compact ed. 2000. 453-466. 8th ed. 2002. 680-692.

P258. "How I Met My Husband." *Literature for Composition: Essays, Fiction, Poetry, and Drama*. Ed. Sylvan Barnet, et al. 5th ed. New York: Longman, 2000. 723-734.

P259. "How I Met My Husband." *The Longman Anthology of Short Fiction: Stories and Authors in Context*. [Comp.] Dana Gioia and R. S. Gwynn. New York: Longman, 2001. 1303-1315.

P260. "How I Met My Husband." *The Hudson Book of Fiction: 30 Stories Worth Reading*. Boston: McGraw-Hall, 2002. 246-260.

P261. "How I Met My Husband." *Literature: The Human Experience*. Richard Abcarian and Marvin Klotz. 8th ed. Boston: Bedford/St. Martin's, 2002. 1039-1051.

P262. "How I Met My Husband." *Literature: Reading and Writing with Critical Strategies*. Steven Lynn. New York: Pearson/Longman, 2004. 500-511.

Translations

Norwegian

P263. "Da jeg møtte min mann." *Noveller*. By Alice Munro. Trans. Ragnhild Eikli. Sel. and foreword Gordon Hølmebakk. [Oslo]: Den norske Bokklubben, 1993. 121-140.

The Idyllic Summer

P264. "The Idyllic Summer." *Canadian Forum* 34 (August 1954): 106-107, 109-110. [as Alice Laidlaw Munro]

Images

P265. "Images." *Dance of the Happy Shades: Stories*. Toronto: Ryerson Press, 1968. 30-43.

P266. "Images." *The Narrative Voice: Stories and Reflections by Canadian Authors*. Ed. and introd. John Metcalf. Toronto: McGraw-Hill Ryerson, 1972. 161-171.

P267. "Images." *Double Vision: An Anthology of Twentieth-Century Stories in English*. Sel. Rudy Wiebe. Toronto: Macmillan, 1976. 229-241.

P268. "Images." *Personal Fictions: Stories by Munro, Wiebe, Thomas, and Blaise*. Sel. Michael Ondaatje. Toronto: Oxford University Press, 1977. 9-20.

P269. "Images." *The Possibilities of Story. Volume 1*. Ed. J. R. (Tim) Struthers. Toronto: McGraw-Hill Ryerson, 1992. 178-188.

P270. "Images." *Selected Stories*. Toronto: McClelland and Stewart, 1996. 40-49.

Translations

Czech

P271. "Predstavy." *Uz dávno ti chci neco ríct: A jiné povídky*. Trans. Alena Jindrová-Špilarová. Afterword Josef Jarab. Svetová próza 6. Praha [Prague]: Paseka, 2002. 58-71.

French

P272. "Images." *La danse des ombres heureuses.* Trans. Geneviève Doze. Collection de littérature étrangère. Paris: Payot & Rivages, 2002. 71-88.

The Jack Randa Hotel

P273. "The Jack Randa Hotel." *New Yorker* 19 July 1993: 62-70.

P274. "The Jack Randa Hotel." *Open Secrets: Stories.* Toronto: McClelland and Stewart, 1994. 161-189.

P275. "The Jack Randa Hotel." *The New Oxford Book of Canadian Short Stories in English.* Sel. Margaret Atwood and Robert Weaver. Introd. Margaret Atwood. Toronto: Oxford University Press, 1995. 131-148.

P276. "The Jack Randa Hotel." *Nothing But You: Love Stories from The New Yorker.* Ed. Roger Angell. New York: Random House, 1997. 87-109.

P277. "The Jack Randa Hotel." *The Writer's Path: An Introduction to Fiction.* Ed. Constance Rooke and Leon Rooke. Toronto: ITP Nelson, 1998. 570-589.

Jakarta

P278. "Jakarta." *Saturday Night* February 1998: 44-60.

P279. "Jakarta." *The Love of a Good Woman: Stories.* Toronto: McClelland and Stewart, 1998. 79-116.

Translations

German

P280. "Jakarta." *Die Liebe einer Frau: Drei Erzählungen und ein kurzer Roman.* Trans. Heidi Zerning. Frankfurt am Main: S. Fischer, 2000. 101-145.

Jesse and Meribeth

See also "Secrets between Friends." Originally published in *Mademoiselle* under that title.

P281. "Jesse and Meribeth." (Revised) *The Progress of Love: Stories.* Toronto: McClelland and Stewart, 1986. 162-188.

Translations

Norwegian

P282.   "Jesse og Meribeth." *Noveller*. By Alice Munro. Trans. Ragnhild Eikli. Sel. and foreword Gordon Hølmebakk. [Oslo]: Den norske Bokklubben, 1993. 324-351.

Labor Day Dinner

P283.   "Labor Day Dinner." *New Yorker* 28 September 1981: 47-56, 59-60, 65-66, 70, 75-76.

P284.   "Labor Day Dinner." *The Moons of Jupiter: Stories*. Toronto: Macmillan of Canada, 1982. 134-159.

P285.   "Labor Day Dinner." *You've Got to Read This: Contemporary American Writers Introduce Stories That Held Them in Awe*. Ed. Ron Hansen and Jim Shepard. Introd. David Leavitt. New York: HarperPerennial, 1994. 381-399.

P286.   "Labor Day Dinner." *Selected Stories*. Toronto: McClelland and Stewart, 1996. 231-251.

Lichen

P287.   "Lichen." *New Yorker* 15 July 1985: 26-36.

P288.   "Lichen." *The Progress of Love: Stories*. Toronto: McClelland and Stewart, 1986. 32-55.

P289.   "Lichen." *Celebrating Canadian Women: Prose and Poetry by and about Women*. Ed. Greta Hofmann Nemiroff. [Markham, ON]: Fitzhenry & Whiteside, 1989. 303-320.

Translations

Serbo-Croatian (Cyrillic)

P290.   "Lišaj." Trans. Velimir Kostov. *Gradina* 27.3/4/5 (1992): 128-144.

P291.   "Lišaj." *Lišaj: Dve novele*. Trans. Velimir Kostov. Pancevo: Zajednica Knjizevnika Pancevo, 1992.

Lives of Girls and Women
Chapter from the novel *Lives of Girls and Women*.

P292.   "Lives of Girls and Women." *The Lexington Introduction to Literature*. [Comp.]

Gary Waller, Kathleen McCormick, and Lois Josephs Fowler. Lexington, MA: D.C. Heath, 1987. 296-318.

P293. "Lives of Girls and Women." *The Art of Short Fiction: An International Anthology*. Ed. Gary Geddes. Toronto: HarperCollins, 1993. 513-535.

P294. "Lives of Girls and Women." *Jo's Girls: Tomboy Tales of High Adventure, True Grit, and Real Life*. Ed. Christian McEwen. Boston: Beacon Press, 1997. 131-158.

The Love of a Good Woman

P295. "The Love of a Good Woman: A Murder, A Mystery, A Romance." *New Yorker* 23 & 30 December 1996: 102-105, 107-108, 110-114, 116-122, 124-132, 134-138, 140-141.

P296. "The Love of a Good Woman." *Best Canadian Stories, 97*. Ed. Douglas Glover. [Ottawa]: Oberon, 1997. 122-189.

P297. "The Love of a Good Woman." *Prize Stories, 1997: The O. Henry Awards*. Ed. and introd. Larry Dark. New York: Anchor Books/Doubleday, 1997. 85-149.

P298. "The Love of a Good Woman." *The Love of a Good Woman: Stories*. Toronto: McClelland and Stewart, 1998. 3-78.

P299. "The Love of a Good Woman." *The Norton Introduction to the Short Novel*. [Comp.] Jerome Beaty. 3rd ed. New York: Norton, c1999. 721-756.

P300. "The Love of a Good Woman." *No Love Lost*. Sel. and afterword Jane Urquhart. New Canadian Library. Toronto: McClelland and Stewart, 2003. 112-184.

Translations

German

P301. "Die Liebe einer Frau." *Die Liebe einer Frau: Drei Erzählungen und ein kurzer Roman*. Trans. Heidi Zerning. Frankfurt am Main: S. Fischer, 2000. 9-99.

Lying under the Apple Tree (Fictionalized Memoir)

P302. "Lying under the Apple Tree." *New Yorker* 17 & 24 June 2002: 88-90, 92, 105-108, 110-114.

Marrakesh

P303. "Marrakesh." *Something I've Been Meaning to Tell You . . . : Thirteen Stories*. Toronto: McGraw-Hill Ryerson, 1974. 156-174.

Material

P304. "Material." *Tamarack Review* 61 (November 1973): 7-25.

P305. "Material." *Something I've Been Meaning to Tell You . . . : Thirteen Stories.* Toronto: McGraw-Hill Ryerson, 1974. 24-44.

P306. "Material." *Double Vision: An Anthology of Twentieth-Century Stories in English.* Sel. Rudy Wiebe. Toronto: Macmillan of Canada, 1976. 242-259.

P307. "Material." *Personal Fictions: Stories by Munro, Wiebe, Thomas, and Blaise.* Sel. Michael Ondaatje. Toronto: Oxford University Press, 1977. 55-71.

P308. "Material." *The Best Modern Canadian Short Stories.* Ed. Ivon Owen and Morris Wolfe. Edmonton: Hurtig, 1978. 24-38.

P309. "Material." *Canadian Short Stories (Third Series).* Ed. Robert Weaver. Toronto: Oxford University Press, 1978. 241-263.

P310. "Material." *Canadian Literature in the 70's.* Ed. Paul Denham and Mary Jane Edwards. Toronto: Holt, Rinehart and Winston, 1980. 19-35.

P311. "Material." *Selected Stories.* Toronto: McClelland and Stewart, 1996. 81-95.

Translations

Czech

P312. "Látka." *Uz dávno ti chci neco ríct: A jiné povídky.* Trans. Alena Jindrová-Špilarová. Afterword Josef Jarab. Svetová próza 6. Praha [Prague]: Paseka, 2002. 115-136.

French

P313. "Material." *La danse des ombres heureuses.* Trans. Geneviève Doze. Collection de littérature étrangère. Paris: Payot & Rivages, 2002. 141-166.

Norwegian

P314. "Råmateriale." *Noveller.* By Alice Munro. Trans. Ragnhild Eikli. Sel. and foreword Gordon Hølmebakk. [Oslo]: Den norske Bokklubben, 1993. 101-120.

Memorial

P315. "Memorial." *Something I've Been Meaning to Tell You . . . : Thirteen Stories.* Toronto: McGraw-Hill, 1974. 207-226.

Translations

Norwegian

P316. "Minnestunden." *Noveller*. By Alice Munro. Trans. Ragnhild Eikli. Sel. and foreword Gordon Hølmebakk. [Oslo]: Den norske Bokklubben, 1993. 157-175.

Meneseteung

P317. "Meneseteung." *New Yorker* 11 January 1988: 28-38.

P318. "Meneseteung." *The Best American Short Stories, 1989*. Sel. Margaret Atwood with Shannon Ravenel. Boston: Houghton Mifflin, 1989. 247-268.

P319. "Meneseteung." (Revised) *Friend of My Youth: Stories*. Toronto: McClelland and Stewart, 1990. 50-73.

P320. "Meneseteung." *The Best American Short Stories of the Eighties*. Sel. and introd. Shannon Ravenel. Boston: Houghton Mifflin, 1990. 351-372.

P321. "Meneseteung." *Canadian Short Stories (Fifth Series)*. Sel. Robert Weaver. Toronto: Oxford University Press, 1991. 154-177.

P322. "Meneseteung." *Literature: An Introduction to Reading and Writing*. Edgar V. Roberts and Henry E. Jacobs. 3rd ed. Englewood Cliffs, NJ: Prentice-Hall, 1992. 221-234.

P323. "Meneseteung." *Canadian Classics: An Anthology of Short Stories*. Critical commentary John Metcalf. Bibliographical and textual research J. R. (Tim) Struthers. Toronto: McGraw-Hill Ryerson, 1993. 124-142.

P324. "Meneseteung." *Myths and Voices: Contemporary Canadian Fiction*. Ed. David Lampe. Fredonia, NY: White Pine Press, 1993. 386-411.

P325. "Meneseteung." *Literature*. James H. Pickering and Jeffrey D. Hoeper. 4th ed. New York: MacMillan, 1994. 502-515.

P326. "Meneseteung." *The Oxford Book of Modern Women's Stories*. Ed. Patricia Craig. Oxford: Oxford University Press, 1994. 485-502.

P327. "Meneseteung." *Selected Stories*. Toronto: McClelland and Stewart, 1996. 392-409.

P328. "Meneseteung." *The Best American Short Stories of the Century*. Ed. John Updike. Coed. Katrina Kenison. Boston: Houghton Mifflin, 1999. 633-651.

P329.   "Meneseteung." *The Scribner Anthology of Contemporary Short Fiction: Fifty North American Stories Since 1970*. Ed. Lex Williford and Michael Martone. Introd. Rosellen Brown. Scribner Paperback Fiction. New York: Simon & Schuster, 1999. 470-487.

P330.   "Meneseteung." *No Love Lost*. Sel. and afterword Jane Urquhart. New Canadian Library. Toronto: McClelland and Stewart, 2003. 359-383.

Translations

Norwegian

P331.   "Meneseteung." *Noveller*. By Alice Munro. Trans. Ragnhild Eikli. Sel. and foreword Gordon Hølmebakk. [Oslo]: Den norske Bokklubben, 1993. 418-441.

Miles City, Montana

P332.   "Miles City, Montana." *New Yorker* 14 January 1985: 30-40.

P333.   "Miles City, Montana." *Canadian Short Stories (Fourth Series)*. Sel. Robert Weaver. Toronto: Oxford University Press, 1985. 160-182.

P334.   "Miles City, Montana." *Best Canadian Stories, 86*. Ed. David Helwig and Sandra Martin. [Ottawa]: Oberon, 1986. 7-32.

P335.   "Miles City, Montana." (Revised) *The Progress of Love: Stories*. Toronto: McClelland and Stewart, 1986. 84-105.

P336.   "Miles City, Montana." *New American Short Stories: The Writers Select Their Own Favorites*. Ed. Gloria Norris. New York: New American Library, 1987. 141-165.

P337.   "Miles City, Montana." *The Secret Self 2: Short Stories by Women*. Sel. and introd. Hermione Lee. London: Dent, 1987. 351-370.

P338.   "Miles City, Montana." *The Faber Book of Contemporary Canadian Short Stories*. Ed. Michael Ondaatje. London: Faber and Faber, 1990. 656-675.

P339.   "Miles City, Montana." *From Ink Lake: Canadian Stories*. Ed. Michael Ondaatje. Toronto: Lester and Orpen Dennys, 1990. 656-675.

P340.   "Miles City, Montana." *Reading Our World: The Guelph Anthology*. Ed. Constance Rooke, Renée Hulan, and Linda Warley. Needham Heights, MA: Ginn, 1990. 163-174.

P341.   "Miles City, Montana." *Selected Stories*. Toronto: McClelland and Stewart, 1996. 308-324.

P342. "Miles City, Montana." *The Penguin Anthology of Stories by Canadian Women.* Ed. Denise Chong. Toronto: Viking-Penguin Books, 1997. 41-65.

P343. "Miles City, Montana." *The Bedford Introduction to Literature: Reading, Thinking, Writing.* [Ed.] Michael Meyer. Boston: Bedford/St. Martin's. 5th ed. 1999. 458-472. 6th ed. 2002. 458-472.

P344. "Miles City, Montana." *The Compact Bedford Introduction to Literature: Reading, Thinking, Writing.* [Ed.] Michael Meyer. Boston: Bedford/St. Martin's, 2000. 375-388.

P345. "Miles City, Montana." *The Broadview Anthology of Short Fiction.* Ed. Julia Gaunce and Suzette Mayr. Peterborough, ON: Broadview, 2004. 182-196.

Translations

Czech

P346. "Miles City." *Uz dávno ti chci neco ríct: A jiné povídky.* Trans. Alena Jindrová-Špilarová. Afterword Josef Jarab. Svetová próza 6. Praha [Prague]: Paseka, 2002. 156-180.

Serbo-Croatian (Cyrillic)

P347. "Majls Siti, Montana." Trans. Branka Robertson. *Sveske: Èasopis za knjizevnost, umetnost i kulturu* 7.23 (1995): 154-166.

Spanish

P348. "Miles City, Montana." *10 Relatos de viajes.* Traduccíon de Flora Casas cedida por Editorial Debate. 1 ed. Colección Diez relatos. Barcelona: Plaza & Janés, 1995. 165-196.

Mischief

P349. "Mischief." *Viva* April 1978: 99-109.

P350. "Mischief." (Revised) *Who Do You Think You Are?: Stories.* Toronto: Macmillan of Canada, 1978. 98-132.

P351. "Mischief." *No Love Lost.* Sel. and afterword Jane Urquhart. New Canadian Library. Toronto: McClelland and Stewart, 2003. 70-111.

Monsieur les Deux Chapeaux

P352. "Monsieur les Deux Chapeaux." *Grand Street* 4.3 (Spring 1985): 7-33.

P353.	"Monsieur les Deux Chapeaux." *The New Press Anthology, Number 2: Best Stories*. Ed. John Metcalf and Leon Rooke. New Press Canadian Classics. Toronto: General Pub., 1985. 76-105.

P354.	"Monsieur les Deux Chapeaux." *The Best American Short Stories, 1986: Selected from U.S. and Canadian Magazines*. Sel. Raymond Carver with Shannon Ravenel. Introd. Raymond Carver. Boston: Houghton Mifflin, 1986. 180-206.

P355.	"Monsieur les Deux Chapeaux." *The Progress of Love: Stories*. Toronto: McClelland and Stewart, 1986. 56-83.

The Moon in the Orange Street Skating Rink

P356.	"The Moon in the Orange Street Skating Rink." *New Yorker* 31 March 1986: 26-36, 38-41, 44.

P357.	"The Moon in the Orange Street Skating Rink." (Revised) *The Progress of Love: Stories*. Toronto: McClelland and Stewart, 1986. 132-161.

P358.	"The Moon in the Orange Street Skating Rink." *Best Short Stories, 1987*. Ed. Giles Gordon and David Hughes. London: Heinemann, 1987. 227-255.

The Moons of Jupiter

P359.	"The Moons of Jupiter." *New Yorker* 22 May 1978: 32-39.

P360.	"The Moons of Jupiter." (Revised) *The Moons of Jupiter: Stories*. Toronto: Macmillan of Canada, 1982. 217-233.

P361.	"The Moons of Jupiter." *An Anthology of Canadian Literature in English. Vol. 2*. Ed. Donna Bennett and Russell Brown. Toronto: Oxford University Press, 1983. 314-326.

P362.	"The Decision." [Excerpt adapted from "The Moons of Jupiter"] *American Health* October 1993: 108.

P363.	"The Moons of Jupiter." *Victory: An English Textbook*. Signe Pihl Clausen, Haege Hestnes, and Sigmund Ro. Oslo: Gyldendal Norsk Forlag, 1993. 228-235.

P364.	"The Moons of Jupiter." *Literature: An Introduction to Critical Reading*. Lee A. Jacobus. Upper Saddle River, NJ: Prentice Hall, 1996. 434-444.

P365.	"The Moons of Jupiter." *Selected Stories*. Toronto: McClelland and Stewart, 1996. 252-265.

P366.	"The Moons of Jupiter." *The Nelson Introduction to Literature*. Ed. Jack

Finnbogason and Al Valleau. Scarborough, ON: Nelson Thomson Learning, 2000. 446-457.

Translations

Czech

P367. "Jupiterovy mesíce." *Uz dávno ti chci neco ríct: A jiné povídky.* Trans. Alena Jindrová-Špilarová. Afterword Josef Jarab. Svetová próza 6. Praha [Prague]: Paseka, 2002. 137-155.

Norwegian

P368. "Jupiters måner." *Noveller*. By Alice Munro. Trans. Ragnhild Eikli. Sel. and foreword Gordon Hølmebakk. [Oslo]: Den norske Bokklubben, 1993. 306-323.

Mrs. Cross and Mrs. Kidd

P369. "Mrs Cross and Mrs Kidd." *Tamarack Review* 83 & 84 (Winter 1982): 5-24.

P370. "Mrs. Cross and Mrs. Kidd." *The Moons of Jupiter: Stories.* Toronto: Macmillan of Canada, 1982. 160-180.

P371. "Mrs. Cross and Mrs. Kidd." *Harbrace Anthology of Short Fiction.* Ed. Jon C. Stott, Raymond E. Jones, and Rick Bowers. Toronto: Harcourt Brace Canada, 1994. 1692-1707.

My Mother's Dream

P372. "My Mother's Dream." *The Love of a Good Woman: Stories.* Toronto: McClelland and Stewart, 1998. 293-340.

Translations

German

P373. "Der Traum meiner Mutter." *Der Traum meiner Mutter: Erzählungen.* Trans. Heidi Zerning. Afterword Judith Hermann. Frankfurt am Main: S. Fischer, 2002. 9-70.

Nettles

P374. "Nettles." *New Yorker* 21 & 28 February 2000: 254-256, 258-259, 262-264, 266-269.

P375. "Nettles." *Hateship, Friendship, Courtship, Loveship, Marriage: Stories.* Toronto: McClelland and Stewart, 2001. 154-185.

The Office

P376. "The Office." *Montrealer* 36.9 (September 1962): 18-23.

P377. "The Office." (Revised) *Dance of the Happy Shades: Stories*. Toronto: Ryerson Press, 1968. 59-74.

P378. "The Office." *Great Canadian Short Stories*. Sel. and introd. Alec Lucas. New York: Dell, 1971. 263-275.

P379. "The Office." *Women and Fiction: Short Stories by and about Women*. Ed. Susan Cahill. New York: New American Library, 1975. 301-313.

P380. "The Office." *Transitions II: Short Fiction. A Source Book of Canadian Literature*. Ed. Edward Peck. Vancouver: Commcept, 1978. 141-152.

P381. "The Office." *Literature and Composition I. Engl. 100 - Fiction File*. Don Stanley. Richmond, BC: Open Learning Agency, 1988. 109-120.

P382. "The Office." *Worlds of Fiction*. Ed. Roberta Rubenstein and Charles R. Larson. New York: Macmillan; Toronto: Maxwell Macmillan Canada, 1993. 915-923.

P383. "The Office." *Literature*. [Comp.] James H. Pickering and Jeffrey D. Hoeper. 4th ed. New York: Macmillan, 1994. 494-501.

Translations

Slovenian

P384. "Pisarna." Trans. Marcello Potocco. *Literatura* 15 no. 141 (March 2003): 143-159.

Oh, What Avails

P385. "Oh, What Avails." *New Yorker* 16 November 1987: 42-52, 55-56, 58-59, 62, 64-65, 67.

P386. "Oh, What Avails." *The Second Macmillan Anthology*. Ed. John Metcalf and Leon Rooke. Toronto: Macmillan of Canada, 1989. 63-90.

P387. "Oh, What Avails." *Friend of My Youth: Stories*. Toronto: McClelland and Stewart, 1990. 180-215.

P388. "Oh, What Avails (excerpt)." *Vancouver Sun* 25 August 1990: D1, D8.

Translations

Norwegian

P389.   "Alt det som var deg gitt." *Noveller*. By Alice Munro. Trans. Ragnhild Eikli. Sel. and foreword Gordon Hølmebakk. [Oslo]: Den norske Bokklubben, 1993. 473-508.

Open Secrets

P390.   "Open Secrets." *New Yorker* 8 February 1993: 90-101.

P391.   "Open Secrets." (Revised) *Open Secrets: Stories*. Toronto: McClelland and Stewart, 1994. 129-160.

Oranges and Apples

P392.   "Oranges and Apples." *New Yorker* 24 October 1988: 36-48, 52, 54.

P393.   "Oranges and Apples." *The Second Macmillan Anthology*. Ed. John Metcalf and Leon Rooke. Toronto: Macmillan of Canada, 1989. 91-123.

P394.   "Oranges and Apples." *Friend of My Youth: Stories*. Toronto: McClelland and Stewart, 1990. 106-136.

The Ottawa Valley

P395.   "The Ottawa Valley." *Something I've Been Meaning to Tell You . . . : Thirteen Stories*. Toronto: McGraw-Hill Ryerson, 1974. 227-246.

P396.   "The Ottawa Valley." *Selected Stories*. Toronto: McClelland and Stewart, 1996. 67-80.

Translations

Czech

P397.   "Ottawské údolí." *Uz dávno ti chci neco ríct: A jiné povídky*. Trans. Alena Jindrová-Špilarová. Afterword Josef Jarab. Svetová próza 6. Praha [Prague]: Paseka, 2002. 95-114.

French

P398.   "La vallée de l'Ottawa." *La danse des ombres heureuses*. Trans. Geneviève Doze. Collection de littérature étrangère. Paris: Payot & Rivages, 2002. 117-140.

An Ounce of Cure

P399. "An Ounce of Cure." *Montrealer* 35.5 (May 1961): 26-30.

P400. "An Ounce of Cure." *Dance of the Happy Shades: Stories.* Toronto: Ryerson Press, 1968. 75-88.

P401. "An Ounce of Cure." *Sixteen by Twelve: Short Stories by Canadian Writers.* Ed. and introd. John Metcalf. Toronto: Ryerson, 1970. 102-112.

P402. "An Ounce of Cure." *McCall's* October 1973: 92-93, 130, 132-134.

P403. "An Ounce of Cure." *Singing Under Ice.* Ed. M. Grace Mersereau. Toronto: Macmillan, 1974. 147-160.

P404. "An Ounce of Cure." *Sunlight and Shadows.* James A. MacNeill and Glen A. Sorestad. Don Mills, ON: Nelson, 1974. 51-62.

P405. "An Ounce of Cure." *Canadian Humour and Satire.* Ed. Theresa Ford. Themes in Canadian Literature. Toronto: Macmillan of Canada, 1976. 99-111.

P406. "An Ounce of Cure." *Canadian Stories of Action and Adventure.* Ed. John Stevens and Roger J. Smith. Toronto: Macmillan, 1978. 51-64.

P407. "An Ounce of Cure." *A Land, A People: Short Stories by Canadian Writers.* Ed. Michael Nowlan. St. John's, NF: Breakwater Books, 1986. 119-128.

P408. "An Ounce of Cure." *The Story Begins When the Story Ends: Canadian and World Short Fiction.* Ed. Gayle Rosen, Marilyn Chapman, and Lesley Elliott. Scarborough, ON: Prentice-Hall Canada, 1991. 31-40.

P409. "An Ounce of Cure." *Ounce of Cure, Alcohol in the Canadian Short Story.* Ed. Mark Anthony Jarman. Victoria, BC: Beach Holme, 1992. 23-33.

P410. "An Ounce of Cure." *The Bedford Introduction to Literature: Reading, Thinking, and Writing.* [Ed.] Michael Meyer. 4th ed. Boston: Bedford Books of St. Martin's Press, 1996. 474-481.

P411. "An Ounce of Cure." *The Compact Bedford Introduction to Literature: Reading, Thinking, Writing.* [Ed.] Michael Meyer. Boston: Bedford/St. Martin's, 2000. 361-371.

Passion

P412. "Passion." *New Yorker* 22 March 2004: 76-89.

56   Primary Works

P413.   "Passion." *Runaway: Stories*. Toronto: McClelland and Stewart, 2004. 159-196.

The Peace of Utrecht

P414.   "The Peace of Utrecht." *Tamarack Review* 15 (Spring 1960): 5-21.

P415.   "The Peace of Utrecht." *The First Five Years: A Selection from the Tamarack Review*. Ed. Robert Weaver. Introd. Robert Fulford. Toronto: Oxford University Press, 1962. 149-164.

P416.   "The Peace of Utrecht." (Revised) *Dance of the Happy Shades: Stories*. Toronto: Ryerson Press, 1968. 190-210.

P417.   "The Peace of Utrecht." *Canadian Short Stories (Second Series)*. Sel. Robert Weaver. Toronto: Oxford University Press, 1968. 259-284.

P418.   "The Peace of Utrecht." *Stories From Ontario*. Sel. Germaine Warkentin. Toronto: Macmillan of Canada, 1974. 241-259.

P419.   "The Peace of Utrecht." *Personal Fictions: Stories by Munro, Wiebe, Thomas, and Blaise*. Sel. Michael Ondaatje. Toronto: Oxford University Press, 1977. 38-54.

P420.   "The Peace of Utrecht." *Stories by Canadian Women*. Ed. Rosemary Sullivan. Toronto: Oxford University Press, 1984. 267-283.

P421.   "The Peace of Utrecht." *The Oxford Book of Canadian Short Stories in English*. Sel. Margaret Atwood and Robert Weaver. Toronto: Oxford University Press, 1986. 191-206.

P422.   "The Peace of Utrecht." *Contemporary Women's Short Stories: An Anthology*. Sel. and introd. Susan Hill. London: Michael Joseph, 1995. 248-268.

P423.   "The Peace of Utrecht." *The Moral of the Story: An Anthology of Ethics through Literature*. Ed. Peter Singer and Renata Singer. Oxford: Blackwell, 2005. 102-109.

Translations

Norwegian

P424.   "Freden i Utrecht." *Noveller*. By Alice Munro. Trans. Ragnhild Eikli. Sel. and foreword Gordon Hølmebakk. [Oslo]: Den norske Bokklubben, 1993. 53-72.

The Photographer
Chapter from the novel *Lives of Girls and Women*.

P425.   "The Photographer." *The Artist in Canadian Literature*. Ed. Lionel Wilson. Toronto: Macmillan of Canada, 1976. 96-104.

P426. "The Photographer." *The Arnold Anthology of Post-Colonial Literatures in English*. Ed. John Thieme. London: Arnold, 1996. 392-399.

Pictures of the Ice

P427. "Pictures of the Ice." *Atlantic Monthly* January 1990: 64-68, 70, 72-73.

P428. "Pictures of the Ice." *Friend of My Youth: Stories*. Toronto: McClelland and Stewart, 1990. 137-155.

P429. "Pictures of the Ice." *Reading Narrative Fiction*. Seymour Chatman with material contrib. by Brian Attebery. New York: Macmillan, 1993. 518-529.

P430. "Pictures of the Ice." *God: Stories*. Ed. C. Michael Curtis. Boston: Houghton Mifflin, 1998. 151-166.

Post and Beam

P431. "Post and Beam." *New Yorker* 11 December 2000: 96-106, 108-109.

P432. "Post and Beam." *The Best American Short Stories, 2001: Selected from U.S. and Canadian Magazines*. [Ed.] Barbara Kingsolver and Katrina Kenison. Introd. Barbara Kingsolver. Boston: Houghton Mifflin, 2001. 176-200.

P433. "Post and Beam." *Hateship, Friendship, Courtship, Loveship, Marriage: Stories*. Toronto: McClelland and Stewart, 2001. 186-216.

Postcard

P434. "Postcard." *Tamarack Review* 47 (Spring 1968): 23-31, 33-39.

P435. "Postcard." *Dance of the Happy Shades: Stories*. Toronto: Ryerson Press, 1968. 128-146.

P436. "Postcard." *Selected Stories*. Toronto: McClelland and Stewart, 1996. 26-39.

Translations

Czech

P437. "Pohlednice." *Uz dávno ti chci neco ríct: A jiné povídky*. Trans. Alena Jindrová-Špilarová. Afterword Josef Jarab. Svetová próza 6. Praha [Prague]: Paseka, 2002. 38-57.

French

P438. "La carte postale." *La danse des ombres heureuses.* Trans. Geneviève Doze. Collection de littérature étrangère. Paris: Payot & Rivages, 2002. 47-70.

Norwegian

P439. "Prospektkort." *Noveller*. By Alice Munro. Trans. Ragnhild Eikli. Sel. and foreword Gordon Hølmebakk. [Oslo]: Den norske Bokklubben, 1993. 34-52.

Powers

P440. "Powers." *Runaway: Stories.* Toronto: McClelland and Stewart, 2004. 270-335.

Princess Ida

Chapter from the novel *Lives of Girls and Women.*

P441. "Princess Ida." *Close Company: Stories of Mothers and Daughters.* Ed. Christine Park and Caroline Heaton. London: Virago, 1987. 209-235.

Translations

Norwegian

P442. "Prinsesse Ida." *Noveller*. By Alice Munro. Trans. Ragnhild Eikli. Sel. and foreword Gordon Hølmebakk. [Oslo]: Den norske Bokklubben, 1993. 73-100.

Privilege

See also "The Honeyman's Granddaughter."

P443. "Privilege." *Tamarack Review* no. 70 (1977): 14-28. Revised versions pub. as "The Honeyman's Granddaughter" in *Ms.*; and as "Privilege" in *Who Do You Think You Are?: Stories.*

P444. "Privilege." (Revised) *Who Do You Think You Are?: Stories.* Toronto: Macmillan, 1978. 23-37.

The Progress of Love

P445. "The Progress of Love." *New Yorker* 7 October 1985: 35-46, 49-50, 53-54, 57-58.

P446. "The Progress of Love." (Revised) *The Progress of Love: Stories.* Toronto: McClelland and Stewart, 1986. 3-31.

P447. "The Progress of Love." *Among Sisters: Short Stories by Women Writers.* Ed. Susan Cahill. A Mentor Book. New York: New American Library, 1989. 175-201.

P448. "The Progress of Love." *Selected Stories.* Toronto: McClelland and Stewart, 1996. 266-288.

P449. "The Progress of Love." *A New Anthology of Canadian Literature in English.* Ed. Donna Bennett and Russell Brown. Don Mills, ON: Oxford University Press, 2002. 660-679.

Providence

P450. "Providence." *Redbook* August 1977: 98-99, 158-163.

P451. "Providence." (Revised) *Who Do You Think You Are?: Stories.* Toronto: Macmillan of Canada, 1978. 133-151.

Prue

P452. "Prue." *New Yorker* 30 March 1981: 34-35.

P453. "Prue." *The Moons of Jupiter: Stories.* Toronto: Macmillan of Canada, 1982. 129-133.

P454. "Prue." *Best Canadian Stories, 82.* Ed. John Metcalf and Leon Rooke. [Ottawa]: Oberon Press, 1982. 74-79.

P455. "Prue." *The Treasury of English Short Stories.* Sel. and introd. Nancy Sullivan. Garden City, NY: Doubleday, 1985. 588-592.

P456. "Prue." *The Norton Anthology of Short Fiction.* Ed. R. V. Cassill. New York: Norton. 3rd ed. 1986. 1101-1104. 4th ed. 1990. 1212-1216.

P457. "Prue." *The Possibilities of Story.* Ed. J. R. (Tim) Struthers. Vol. 2. Toronto: McGraw-Hill Ryerson, 1992. 119-124.

P458. "Prue." *The McGraw-Hill Book of Fiction.* Robert DiYanni and Kraft Rompf. New York: McGraw-Hill, 1995. 787-790.

P459. "Prue." *The Bedford Introduction to Literature: Reading, Thinking, Writing.* [Ed.] Michael Meyer. Boston: Bedford/St. Martin's. 5th ed. 1999. 454-458. 6th ed. 2002. 454-458.

P460. "Prue." *The Compact Bedford Introduction to Literature: Reading, Thinking, Writing.* [Ed.] Michael Meyer. Boston: Bedford/St. Martin's, 2000. 372-374.

P461. "Prue." *The Norton Anthology of Short Fiction.* R. V. Cassill and Richard Bausch. 6th ed. New York: Norton, 2000. 1236-1239.

Translations

Dutch

P462. "Prue." Trans. Charles Forceville. *De Tweede Ronde* 6.4 (Winter 1985/86): 161-165.

Queenie: A Story

P463. "Queenie: A Story." *London Review of Books* 30 July 1998: 11-16.

P464. "Queenie." *Hateship, Friendship, Courtship, Loveship, Marriage: Stories.* Toronto: McClelland and Stewart, 2001. 242-273.

A Queer Streak

P465. "A Queer Streak. Part One: Anonymous Letters." *Granta* 17 (Autumn 1985): 187-212.

P466. "A Queer Streak. Part Two: Possession." *Granta* 18 (Spring 1986): 201-219.

P467. "A Queer Streak." (Revised) *The Progress of Love: Stories.* Toronto: McClelland and Stewart, 1986. 208-253.

A Real Life

P468. "A Real Life." *New Yorker* 10 February 1992: 30-40.

P469. "A Real Life." *The Best American Short Stories, 1993.* Sel. Louise Erdrich and Katrina Kenison. Boston: Houghton Mifflin, 1993. 25-48.

P470. "A Real Life." *Best Short Stories 1993.* Ed. Giles Gordon and David Hughes. London: Heinemann, 1993. 195-221.

P471. "A Real Life." *Best English Short Stories V.* Ed. Giles Gordon and David Hughes. New York: Norton, 1994. 195-221.

P472. "A Real Life." *Open Secrets: Stories.* Toronto: McClelland and Stewart, 1994. 52-80. Originally entitled "A Form of Marriage."

P473. "A Real Life." *Identity and Self-Respect.* The Great Books Foundation 50th anniversary series. Chicago: Great Books Foundation, 1997. 85-113.

Translations

Albanian

P474. "Një Jetë e vërtetë." *Virgjëresha shqiptare: Novela*. Trans. Betim Muço. Tiranë: Shtëpia Botuese "Mësonjëtorja," 1999-2002? 53-81.

Red Dress - 1946

P475. "Red Dress - 1946." *Montrealer* 39.5 (May 1965): 28-34.

P476. "Red Dress - 1946." *Dance of the Happy Shades: Stories*. Toronto: Ryerson Press, 1968. 147-160.

P477. "The Red Dress." *McCall's* March 1973: 66-67, 138-141, 146.

P478. "Red Dress - 1946." *In the Looking Glass: Twenty-One Modern Short Stories by Women*. Ed. Nancy Dean and Myra Stark. New York: Putnam's, 1977. 199-211.

P479. "Red Dress - 1946." *Childhood and Youth in Canadian Literature*. Ed. M. G. Hesse. Themes in Canadian Literature. Toronto: Macmillan, 1979. 74-86.

P480. "Red Dress - 1946." *Rites of Passage*. Don Gutteridge. Casebooks in Canadian Literature. Toronto: McClelland and Stewart, 1979. 8-19.

P481. "The Red Dress." *Seasons of Life: Stories of the Human Cycle*. [Comp.] Eva Taube. Toronto: McClelland and Stewart, 1989, c1985. 74-84.

P482. "Red Dress - 1946." *McDougal, Littell Literature and Language. Orange Level*. Jane N. Beatty. Evanston, IL: McDougal, Littell, 1992. 557-566.

Rich As Stink

P483. "Rich As Stink." *The Love of a Good Woman: Stories*. Toronto: McClelland and Stewart, 1998. 215-253.

Translations

German

P484. "Stinkreich." *Der Traum meiner Mutter: Erzählungen*. Trans. Heidi Zerning. Afterword Judith Hermann. Frankfurt am Main: S. Fischer, 2002. 115-164.

P485. *Stinkreich*. Trans. Heidi Zerning. Frankfurt am Main: Fischer-Taschenbuch-Verl., 2003. 111 pp.

Royal Beatings

P486. "Royal Beatings." *New Yorker* 14 March 1977: 36-44.

P487. "Royal Beatings." (Revised) *Who Do You Think You Are?: Stories*. Toronto: Macmillan of Canada, 1978. 1-22.

P488. "Royal Beatings." *Images of Women in Literature*. Comp. Mary Anne Ferguson. 3rd ed. Boston: Houghton Mifflin, 1981. 137-155.

P489. "Royal Beatings." *The Norton Anthology of Short Fiction*. Ed. R. V. Cassill. New York: Norton. 2nd ed. 1981. 1041-1059. 3rd ed. 1986. 1082-1100. 4th ed. 1990. 1193-1212. Shorter 5th ed. 1995. 646-664.

P490. "Royal Beatings." *Making It New: Contemporary Canadian Stories*. Ed. John Metcalf. Toronto: Methuen, 1982. 181-204.

P491. "Royal Beatings." *The Heath Introduction to Fiction*. John J. Clayton. 3rd ed. Lexington, MA: Heath, 1988. 792-810.

P492. "Royal Beatings." *We Are the Stories We Tell: The Best Short Stories by North American Women Since 1945*. Ed. Wendy Martin. New York: Pantheon, 1990. 164-187.

P493. "Royal Beatings." *The Short Story in English*. Ed. Neil Besner and David Staines. Toronto: Oxford University Press, 1991. 640-658.

P494. "Royal Beatings." *Canadian Classics: An Anthology of Short Stories*. Critical commentary John Metcalf. Bibliographical and textual research J. R. (Tim) Struthers. Toronto: McGraw-Hill Ryerson, 1993. 101-123.

P495. "Royal Beatings." *Family Matters: Readings on Family Lives and the Law*. Ed. Martha Minow. New York: New Press, 1993. 5-19.

P496. "Royal Beatings." *Stories: An Anthology and an Introduction*. Eric S. Rabkin. New York: HarperCollins College, 1995. 994-1009.

P497. "Royal Beatings." *Selected Stories*. Toronto: McClelland and Stewart, 1996. 96-114.

P498. "Royal Beatings." *The Writer's Path: An Introduction to Fiction*. Ed. Constance Rooke and Leon Rooke. Toronto: ITP Nelson, 1998. 550-569.

P499. "Royal Beatings." *Literature and the Writing Process*. Ed. Elizabeth McMahan, Susan X. Day, and Robert Funk. 5th ed. Upper Saddle River, NJ: Prentice Hall, c1999. 406-420.

P500. "Royal Beatings." *The Norton Anthology of Short Fiction*. [Ed.] R. V. Cassill and Richard Bausch. New York: Norton. 6th ed. 2000. 1220-1236. Shorter 6th ed. 2000. 642-658

Translations

French

P501. "De sacrées raclées." *Un demi-pamplemousse: Nouvelles*. Trans. Michèle Causse. Éd. hors commerce. Rivages poche. Bibliothèque étrangère. Paris: Payot & Rivages, 2002. 7-53.

Runaway

P502. "Runaway." *New Yorker* 11 August 2003: 62-75.

P503. "Runaway." *Runaway: Stories*. Toronto: McClelland and Stewart, 2004. 3-47.

P504. "Runaway." *The Best American Short Stories, 2004: Selected from U.S. and Canadian Magazines*. Sel. Lorrie Moore and Katrina Kenison. Boston: Houghton Mifflin, 2004. 304-335.

Save the Reaper

P505. "Save the Reaper." *New Yorker* 22 & 29 June 1998: 120-128, 130-132, 134-135.

P506. "Save the Reaper." (Revised) *The Love of a Good Woman: Stories*. Toronto: McClelland and Stewart, 1998. 146-180.

P507. "Save the Reaper." *The Best American Short Stories, 1999: Selected from U.S. and Canadian Magazines*. Sel. Amy Tan with Katrina Kenison. Boston: Houghton Mifflin, 1999. 273-293.

P508. "Save the Reaper." Introd. Lorrie Moore. *Prize Stories, 1999: The O. Henry Awards*. Ed. and introd. Larry Dark. 1st Anchor Books original ed. New York: Anchor Books, 1999. 59-90.

Translations

German

P509. "Einzig der Schnitter." *Die Liebe einer Frau: Drei Erzählungen und ein kurzer Roman*. Trans. Heidi Zerning. Frankfurt am Main: S. Fischer, 2000. 183-[224].

Secrets between Friends
See also "Jesse and Meribeth."

P510. "Secrets between Friends." *Mademoiselle* November 1985: 116, 118, 120, 122, 124, 126, 128, 130, 228, 230. Revised version pub. as "Jesse and Meribeth" in *The Progress of Love: Stories*.

The Shining Houses

P511. "The Shining Houses." *Dance of the Happy Shades: Stories*. Toronto: Ryerson Press, 1968. 19-29.

P512. "The Shining Houses." *Canadian Anthology*. Ed. Carl F. Klinck and Reginald E. Watters. 3rd ed. rev. and enl. Toronto: Gage, 1974. 520-526.

P513. "The Shining Houses." *The Anthology Anthology: A Selection from 30 Years of CBC Radio's "Anthology."* Ed. Robert Weaver. Toronto: Macmillan of Canada, 1984. 1-9.

P514. "The Shining Houses." *Vancouver, Soul of a City*. Ed. Gary Geddes. Vancouver: Douglas & McIntyre, 1986. 57-64.

Silence

P515. "Silence." *New Yorker* 14-21 June 2004: 157-158, 160, 163-164, 166, 168-172, 175-176, 178-180, 183.

P516. "Silence." *Runaway: Stories*. Toronto: McClelland and Stewart, 2004. 126-158.

P517. "Silence." *The Best American Short Stories, 2005: Selected from U.S. and Canadian Magazines*. Sel. Michael Chabon and Katrina Kenison. Boston: Houghton Mifflin, 2005. 149-173.

Simon's Luck
See also "Emily."

P518. "Simon's Luck." *Who Do You Think You Are?: Stories*. Toronto: Macmillan of Canada, 1978. 152-173. Revised version of "Emily," originally published in *Viva*.

P519. "Simon's Luck." *Love and Loss: Stories of the Heart*. Ed. Georgina Hammick. London: Virago, 1992. 105-126.

P520. "Simon's Luck." *Selected Stories*. Toronto: McClelland and Stewart, 1996. 152-170.

P521. "Simon's Luck." *No Love Lost*. Sel. and afterword Jane Urquhart. New Canadian Library. Toronto: McClelland and Stewart, 2003. 185-210.

Translations

Spanish

P522. "La suerte de Simon." *Libro del amor y de la péridada: Historias del corazón*. Ed. Georgina Hammick. Trans. Enrique Ibáñez. Femenino Lumen, 35. Barcelona: Editorial Lumen, 1997. 130-152.

Something I've Been Meaning to Tell You

P523. "Something I've Been Meaning to Tell You." *Something I've Been Meaning to Tell You... : Thirteen Stories*. Toronto: McGraw-Hill Ryerson, 1974. 1-23.

P524. "Something I've Been Meaning to Tell You." *Canadian Literature in the 70's*. Ed. Paul Denham and Mary Jane Edwards. Toronto: Holt, Rinehart and Winston, 1980. 19-37.

P525. "Something I've Been Meaning to Tell You." *An Anthology of Canadian Literature in English*. Ed. Donna Bennett and Russell Brown. Vol. 2. Toronto: Oxford University Press, 1983. 301-314.

P526. "Something I've Been Meaning to Tell You." *Elements of Fiction*. [Ed.] Robert Scholes and Rosemary Sullivan. Shorter Canadian ed. Toronto: Oxford University Press, 1986. 570-586.

P527. "Something I've Been Meaning to Tell You." *Selected Stories*. Toronto: McClelland and Stewart, 1996. 50-66.

Translations

Chinese

P528. "Yu tui ni shuo." *Yu tui ni shuo... : Jia na da duan pian xiao shuo jing xuan*. Li-chu Chian and Yu-tsan Yang. Chia-na-ta wen hsueh ts'ung shu chih 4. Beijing: Chong-kuo wen lien ch'u pien she, 1991. 47-69.

Czech

P529. "Uz dávno ti chci neco ríct." *Uz dávno ti chci neco ríct: A jiné povídky*. Trans. Alena Jindrová-Špilarová. Afterword Josef Jarab. Svetová próza 6. Praha [Prague]: Paseka, 2002. 72-94.

French

P530. "Quelque chose que j'avais l'intention de te dire." *La danse des ombres heureuses*. Trans. Geneviève Doze. Collection de littérature étrangère. Paris: Payot & Rivages, 2002. 89-116.

Soon

P531. "Soon." *New Yorker* 14-21 June 2004: 142-149, 151-157.

P532. "Soon." *Runaway: Stories*. Toronto: McClelland and Stewart, 2004. 87-125.

Spaceships Have Landed

P533. "Spaceships Have Landed." *Paris Review* 36 [no. 131] (Summer 1994): 265-294.

P534. "Spaceships Have Landed." (Revised) *Open Secrets: Stories*. Toronto: McClelland and Stewart, 1994. 226-260.

P535. "Spaceships Have Landed." *The Paris Review Book of Heartbreak, Madness, Sex, Love . . . , and Everything Else in the World Since 1953*. Editors of The Paris Review. Introd. George Plimpton. New York: Picador, 2003. 261-282.

The Spanish Lady

P536. "The Spanish Lady." *Something I've Been Meaning to Tell You . . . : Thirteen Stories*. Toronto: McGraw-Hill Ryerson, 1974. 175-191.

P537. "The Spanish Lady." *Dumped: An Anthology*. Ed. B. Delores Max. New York: Grove Press, 2003. 5-19.

Translations

Norwegian

P538. "Den spanske damen." *Noveller*. By Alice Munro. Trans. Ragnhild Eikli. Sel. and foreword Gordon Hølmebakk. [Oslo]: Den norske Bokklubben, 1993. 141-156.

Spelling

P539. "Spelling." *Weekend Magazine* (*Globe & Mail*, Toronto) 17 June 1978: 24-27.

P540. "Spelling." (Revised and expanded) *Who Do You Think You Are?: Stories*. Toronto: Macmillan of Canada, 1978. 174-188.

P541. "Spelling." (Abridged) *The Best American Short Stories, 1979*. Sel. Joyce Carol Oates with Shannon Ravenel. Boston: Houghton Mifflin, 1979. 150-156.

P542. "Spelling." *Story: Fictions Past and Present*. [Comp.] Boyd Litzinger and Joyce Carol Oates. Lexington, MA: D.C. Heath, 1985. 972-981.

P543. "Spelling." *Night Light: Stories of Aging*. Ed. Constance Rooke. Toronto: Oxford University Press, 1986. 83-96.

P544. "Spelling." *Literature and Aging: An Anthology*. Ed. Martin Kohn, Carol Donley, and Delese Wear. Kent, OH: Kent State University Press, 1992. 281-292.

The Stone in the Field

See also "Chaddeleys and Flemings. 2: The Stone in the Field."

P545. "The Stone in the Field." *Saturday Night* April 1979: 40-45. Revised version pub. as "Chaddeleys and Flemings: 2. The Stone in the Field" in *The Moons of Jupiter: Stories*.

P546. "The Stone in the Field." *Best Canadian Stories, 80*. Ed. Clark Blaise and John Metcalf. [Ottawa]: Oberon, 1980. 115-131.

P547. "The Stone in the Field (excerpt)." *Inquiry into Literature 2*. [Ed.] Bryant Fillion and Jim Henderson. Don Mills, ON: Collier Macmillan Canada, 1980. 182-183.

Translations

Croatian

P548. "Kamen u polju." *Antologija kanadske pripovijetke*. Preveli i priredili Branko Gorjup i Ljiljanka Lovrincevic. Opca knjiznica 12/20. Zagreb: Nakladni zavod Matice Hrvatske, 1991. 148-162.

German

P549. "Der Stein im Feld." *Du* 9 (1985): 4, 6, 8, 11, 13.

Story for Sunday

P550. "Story for Sunday." *Folio* [University of Western Ontario] 5.1 (December 1950): 4-8. [as Alice Laidlaw]

Sunday Afternoon

P551. "Sunday Afternoon." *Canadian Forum* 37 (September 1957): 127-130.

P552. "Sunday Afternoon." *A Book of Canadian Stories*. Ed. Desmond Pacey. Rev. ed. Toronto: Ryerson, 1962. 327-336.

P553. "Sunday Afternoon." *Dance of the Happy Shades: Stories*. Toronto: Ryerson Press, 1968. 161-171.

P554. "Sunday Afternoon." *Selections from Major Canadian Writers*. [Ed.] Desmond Pacey. Toronto: McGraw-Hill Ryerson, 1974. 244-249.

P555. "Sunday Afternoon (excerpt)." *Toronto Star* 4 September 1983: D5.

Tell Me Yes or No

P556. "Tell Me Yes or No." *Chatelaine* March 1974: 34-35, 54, 56-60, 62.

P557. "Tell Me Yes or No." *Something I've Been Meaning to Tell You . . . : Thirteen Stories*. Toronto: McGraw-Hill Ryerson, 1974. 106-124.

Thanks for the Ride

P558. "Thanks for the Ride." *Tamarack Review* 2 (Winter 1957): 25-37.

P559. "Thanks for the Ride." *Dance of the Happy Shades: Stories*. Toronto: Ryerson Press, 1968. 44-58.

P560. "Thanks for the Ride." *The Story-Makers: A Selection of Modern Short Stories*. Ed. Rudy Wiebe. Toronto: Macmillan of Canada, 1970. 47-60.

P561. "Thanks for the Ride." *Modern Stories in English*. Ed. W. H. New and H. J. Rosengarten. Toronto: Copp Clark Pitman, 1975. 273-284. 2nd ed. 1986. 282-292. 3rd ed. 1991. 277-288.

P562. "Thanks for the Ride." *Fiction 100: An Anthology of Short Stories*. [Comp.] James H. Pickering. 3rd ed. New York: Macmillan, 1982. 783-789.

P563. "Thanks for the Ride." *The Penguin Book of Modern Canadian Short Stories*. Ed. Wayne Grady. Harmondsworth, Eng.: Penguin, 1982. 70-82.

P564. "Thanks for the Ride." *The Story-Makers: A Selection of Modern Short Stories*. Ed. Rudy Wiebe. Toronto: Gage, 1984. 47-60.

P565. "Thanks for the Ride." *The Story-Makers: A Selection of Modern Short Stories*. Ed. and introd. Rudy Wiebe. 2nd ed. Agincourt, ON: Gage Educational, 1987. 80-95.

The Time of Death

P566. "The Time of Death." *Canadian Forum* 36 (June 1956): 63-66. [as Alice Laidlaw]

P567. "The Time of Death." *Canadian Short Stories*. Sel. and introd. Robert Weaver. Toronto: Oxford University Press, 1960. 398-410.

P568. "The Time of Death." (Revised) *Dance of the Happy Shades: Stories*. Toronto: Ryerson Press, 1968. 89-99.

P569. "The Time of Death." *Modern Canadian Stories*. Ed. Giose Rimanelli and Roberto Ruberto. Toronto: Ryerson, 1969. 314-323.

P570. "The Time of Death." *Contemporary Voices: The Short Story in Canada*. Sel. Donald Stephens. Scarborough, ON: Prentice-Hall, 1972. 128-134.

P571. "The Time of Death." *The Secret Self: Short Stories by Women*. Sel. and introd. Hermione Lee. London: Dent, 1985. 235-243.

P572. "The Time of Death." *Trio: A Book of Stories, Plays and Poems*. [Comp.] Harold P. Simonson. 6th ed. New York: Harper & Row, 1987. 138-146.

Trespasses

P573. "Trespasses." *Runaway: Stories*. Toronto: McClelland and Stewart, 2004. 197-235.

Tricks

P574. "Tricks." *Runaway: Stories*. Toronto: McClelland and Stewart, 2004. 236-269.

A Trip to the Coast

P575. "The Trip to the Coast." *Ten For Wednesday Night: A Collection of Short Stories Presented for Broadcast by CBC Wednesday Night*. Ed. Robert Weaver. Toronto: McClelland and Stewart, 1961. 74-92.

P576. "A Trip to the Coast." (Revised) *Dance of the Happy Shades: Stories*. Toronto: Ryerson, 1968. 172-189.

P577. "A Trip to the Coast." *The Evolution of Canadian Literature in English, 1945-1970*. Ed. Paul Denham. Toronto: Holt, Rinehart and Winston, 1973. 200-211.

The Turkey Season

P578. "The Turkey Season." *New Yorker* 29 December 1980: 36-44.

P579. "The Turkey Season." (Revised) *The Moons of Jupiter: Stories*. Toronto: Macmillan of Canada, 1982. 60-76.

P580. "The Turkey Season." *Worlds Unrealized. Volume II: Short Stories of Adolescence by Canadian Writers*. St. John's, NF: Breakwater, 1991. 228-241.

P581. "The Turkey Season." *I Know Some Things*. Ed. Lorrie Moore. Boston: Faber and Faber, 1992. 184-197.

P582. "The Turkey Season." *Meanwhile, in Another Part of the Forest: Gay Stories from Alice Munro to Yukio Mishima*. Ed. Alberto Manguel and Craig Stephenson. 1st Canadian ed. Toronto: Knopf Canada, 1994. 192-207. Also published in London, Eng. by Flamingo under the title *In Another Part of the Forest: The Flamingo Anthology of Gay Literature*.

P583. "The Turkey Season." *Into the Widening World: International Coming-of-Age Stories*. Ed. John Loughery. New York: Persea Books, 1995. 75-87.

P584. "The Turkey Season." *Selected Stories*. Toronto: McClelland and Stewart, 1996. 218-230.

Vandals

P585. "Vandals." *New Yorker* 4 October 1993: 179-182, 184-190.

P586. "Vandals." *Open Secrets: Stories*. Toronto: McClelland and Stewart, 1994. 261-294.

P587. "Vandals." *Selected Stories*. Toronto: McClelland and Stewart, 1996. 523-545.

The View from Castle Rock

P588. "The View from Castle Rock." *New Yorker* 29 August 2005: 64-77.

Visitors

P589. "Visitors." *Atlantic Monthly* April 1982: 90-98.

P590. "Visitors." *The Moons of Jupiter: Stories*. Toronto: Macmillan of Canada, 1982. 198-216.

P591. "Visitors." *American Stories II: Fiction from the Atlantic Monthly.* Ed. C. Michael Curtis. San Francisco: Chronicle Books, 1991. 145-160.

Translations

Norwegian

P592. "Besøk." Trans. Gordon Hølmebakk. *Canada forteller: Kanadiske noveller.* Sel. and introd. Gordon Hølmebakk. [Stabekk]: Den norske Bokklubben, 1985. 331-347.

P593. "Gjester." *Noveller.* By Alice Munro. Trans. Ragnhild Eikli. Sel. and foreword Gordon Hølmebakk. [Oslo]: Den norske Bokklubben, 1993. 287-305.

Walker Brothers Cowboy

P594. "Walker Brothers Cowboy." *Dance of the Happy Shades: Stories.* Toronto: Ryerson Press, 1968. 1-18.

P595. "Walker Brothers Cowboy." *Canadian Writing Today.* Ed. Mordecai Richler. Harmondsworth, Eng.: Penguin, 1970. 105-120.

P596. "Walker Brothers Cowboy." *The Oxford Anthology of Canadian Literature.* Ed. Robert Weaver and William Toye. Toronto: Oxford University Press, 1973. 347-361. 2nd ed. 1981. 325-339.

P597. "Walker Brothers Cowboy." *Stories from Ontario.* Sel. Germaine Warkentin. Toronto: Macmillan of Canada, 1974. 156-171.

P598. "Walker Brothers Cowboy." *The Depression in Canadian Literature.* Alice K. Hale and Sheila A. Brooks. Themes in Canadian Literature. Toronto: Macmillan of Canada, 1976. 92-109.

P599. "Walker Brothers Cowboy." *Literary Review* [Madison, NJ] 28.3 (Spring 1985): 425-437.

P600. "Walker Brothers Cowboy." *The Graywolf Annual Two: Short Stories by Women.* Ed. Scott Walker. Saint Paul, MN: Graywolf, 1986. 33-48.

P601. "Walker Brothers Cowboy." *Writers in Aspic.* Ed. John Metcalf. Montreal: Véhicule, 1988. 171-185.

P602. "Walker Brothers Cowboy." *The Story and Its Writer: An Introduction to Short Fiction.* [Ed.] Ann Charters. 4th ed. Boston: Bedford Books of St. Martin's Press. 1995. 987-998. Compact 4th ed. 1995. 546-557.

P603. "Walker Brothers Cowboy." *Selected Stories*. Toronto: McClelland and Stewart, 1996. 3-15.

P604. "Walker Brothers Cowboy." *Literature and Its Writers: An Introduction to Fiction, Poetry and Drama*. Ann Charters and Samuel Charters. Boston: Bedford Books, 1997. 484-495.

P605. "Walker Brothers Cowboy." *The Norton Anthology of World Literature. Vol. F: The Twentieth Century*. Gen. ed. Sarah Lawall and Maynard Mack. 2nd ed. New York: Norton, 2002. 3010-3020.

Translations

Czech

P606. "Kovboj Bratří Walker." *Uz dávno ti chci neco říct: A jiné povídky*. Trans. Alena Jindrová-Špilarová. Afterword Josef Jarab. Svetová próza 6. Praha [Prague]: Paseka, 2002. 7-24.

French

P607. "Le cow-boy des frères Walker." *La danse des ombres heureuses*. Trans. Geneviève Doze. Collection de littérature étrangère. Paris: Payot & Rivages, 2002. 9-30.

Norwegian

P608. "Walkerbrødrenes cowboy." *Noveller*. By Alice Munro. Trans. Ragnhild Eikli. Sel. and foreword Gordon Hølmebakk. [Oslo]: Den norske Bokklubben, 1993. 17-33.

Walking on Water

P609. "Walking on Water." *Something I've Been Meaning to Tell You . . . : Thirteen Stories*. Toronto: McGraw-Hill Ryerson, 1974. 67-92.

Wenlock Edge

P610. "Wenlock Edge." *New Yorker* 5 December 2005: 80-91.

What Is Remembered

P611. "What Is Remembered." *New Yorker* 19 & 26 February 2001: 196-207.

P612. "What Is Remembered." *Hateship, Friendship, Courtship, Loveship, Marriage: Stories*. Toronto: McClelland and Stewart, 2001. 217-241.

P613. "What Is Remembered." *The Vancouver Stories: West Coast Fiction from Canada's Best Writers*. Introd. Douglas Coupland. Vancouver: Raincoast Books, 2005. 59-90.

White Dump

P614. "White Dump." *New Yorker* 28 July 1986: 25-39, 42-43.

P615. "White Dump." (Revised) *The Progress of Love: Stories*. Toronto: McClelland and Stewart, 1986. 275-309.

P616. "White Dump." *Selected Stories*. Toronto: McClelland and Stewart, 1996. 325-352.

Who Do You Think You Are?

P617. "Who Do You Think You Are?" *Who Do You Think You Are?: Stories*. Toronto: Macmillan of Canada, 1978. 189-206.

P618. "Who Do You Think You Are?" *The Penguin Book of Canadian Short Stories*. Ed. Wayne Grady. Harmondsworth, Eng.: Penguin, 1980. 299-316.

P619. "Who Do You Think You Are?" *Making It New: Contemporary Canadian Stories*. Ed. John Metcalf. Toronto: Methuen, 1982. 205-222.

P620. "Who Do You Think You Are?" *Introduction to Literature: British, American, Canadian*. Ed. Robert Lecker, Jack David, and Peter O'Brien. New York: Harper & Row, 1987. 966-986.

P621. "Who Do You Think You Are?" *Short Fiction: An Introductory Anthology*. Ed. David Rampton and Gerald Lynch. Toronto: Harcourt Brace Jovanovich, 1992. 1030-1045.

Translations

German

P622. "Was glaubst du, wer du bist?" *Kanada Erzählt: 17 Erzählungen*. Ed. Stefana Sabin. Frankfurt am Main: Fischer Taschenbuch, 1992. 199-222.

The Widower

P623. "The Widower." *Folio* [University of Western Ontario] 5.2 (April 1951): [7-11]. [as Alice Laidlaw]

Wigtime

P624. "Wigtime." *New Yorker* 4 September 1989: 34-46, 48, 50.

P625. "Wigtime." *The Best American Short Stories, 1990*. Sel. Richard Ford with Shannon Ravenel. Boston: Houghton Mifflin, 1990. 215-241.

P626. "Wigtime." *Friend of My Youth: Stories*. Toronto: McClelland and Stewart, 1990. 244-273.

P627. "Wigtime." *Woman's Hour Book of Short Stories: Volume II*. Sel and introd. Pat McLoughlin. London: BBC Books, 1992. 199-227.

Wild Swans

P628. "Wild Swans." *Toronto Life* April 1978: 52-53, 124-125.

P629. "Wild Swans." *Who Do You Think You Are?: Stories*. Toronto: Macmillan of Canada, 1978. 55-64.

P630. "Wild Swans." *The Norton Anthology of Literature by Women: The Tradition in English*. [Comp.] Sandra M. Gilbert and Susan Gubar. New York: Norton, 1985. 2184-2193. 2nd ed. 1996. 2072-2079.

P631. "Wild Swans." *The Norton Anthology of Contemporary Fiction*. Ed. R. V. Cassill and Joyce Carol Oates. New York: Norton, 1988. 316-343. 2nd ed. 1998. 403-411.

P632. "Wild Swans." *Fiction*. [Comp.] R. S. Gwynn. A HarperCollins Pocket Anthology. New York: HarperCollins College Publishers, 1993. 253-261.

P633. "Wild Swans." *Selected Stories*. Toronto: McClelland and Stewart, 1996. 115-123.

P634. "Wild Swans." *The Vintage Contemporaries Reader*. New York: Vintage Books, 1998. 224-235.

Translations

Norwegian

P635. "Ville svaner." *Noveller*. By Alice Munro. Trans. Ragnhild Eikli. Sel. and foreword Gordon Hølmebakk. [Oslo]: Den norske Bokklubben, 1993. 176-187.

A Wilderness Station

P636. "A Wilderness Station." *New Yorker* 27 April 1992: 35-46, 48-51.

P637.   "A Wilderness Station." *Best Canadian Stories, 93*. Ed. David Helwig and Maggie Helwig. [Ottawa]: Oberon, 1993. 18-53.

P638.   "A Wilderness Station." *Open Secrets: Stories*. Toronto: McClelland and Stewart, 1994. 190-225.

P639.   "A Wilderness Station." *Points of View: An Anthology of Short Stories*. Ed. James Moffett and Kenneth R. McElheny. Rev. ed. New York: Mentor, 1995. 96-125.

P640.   "A Wilderness Station." *The Penguin Book of International Women's Stories*. Sel. and introd. Kate Figes. New York: Penguin Books, 1996. 88-116.

P641.   "A Wilderness Station." *Selected Stories*. Toronto: McClelland and Stewart, 1996. 498-522.

P642.   "A Wilderness Station." *Other People's Mail: An Anthology of Letter Stories*. Ed. Gail Pool. Columbia: University of Missouri Press, 2000. 10-36.

Translations

Norwegian

P643.   "En utpost i ødemarken." Trans. Ebba Haslund. *Den må du lese!: 24 favorittfortellinger*. [Oslo]: Gyldendal, 2002. 179-207.

Winter Wind

P644.   "Winter Wind." *Something I've Been Meaning to Tell You . . . : Thirteen Stories*. Toronto: McGraw-Hill Ryerson, 1974. 192-206.

P645.   "Winter Wind." *Family Portraits*. Ian Underhill. Casebooks in Canadian Literature. Toronto: McClelland and Stewart, 1978. 57-67.

P646.   "Winter Wind." *Literature in Canada*. Ed. Douglas Daymond and Leslie Monkman. Vol. 2. Toronto: Gage Educational, 1978. 477-487.

Wood

P647.   "Wood." *New Yorker* 24 November 1980: 46-54.

P648.   "Wood." *The Best American Short Stories, 1981*. Ed. Hortense Calisher with Shannon Ravenel. Introd. Hortense Calisher. Boston: Houghton Mifflin, 1981. 241-254.

P649.   "Wood." *Best Canadian Stories, 81*. Ed. John Metcalf and Leon Rooke. [Ottawa]: Oberon, 1981. 93-110.

Poems

P650. "Poem (Untitled)." *Canadian Forum* 46 (February 1967): 243. [as Anne Chamney, pseud.]

Memoirs

P651.   "Working for a Living." *Grand Street* 1.1 (Autumn 1981): 9-37.

P652.   "Working for a Living." *A Grand Street Reader*. Ed. B. Sonnenberg. New York: Summit Books, 1986. 17-45.

Nonfiction

(Alphabetical by Title)

P653.   "About This Book." *Alice Munro. Selected Stories: A Tribute*. [Toronto]: McClelland & Stewart, n.d. 1-7.
    Also pub. as "Introduction to the Vintage Edition" in *Selected Stories*. New York: Vintage, 1997. xiii-xxi.
    Rpt. as "Introduction" in *Selected Stories*. Toronto: Penguin Books Canada, 1998. ix-xvii.
Munro initially began writing short stories because it was the form most suited to her life as a wife and mother. She says that her strong affinity to the Huron County landscape and way of life is the reason she writes about this area. Inspired in adolescence by Emily Brontë's *Wuthering Heights*, Munro began a romantic novel which she later abandoned. A scene she viewed from the window of the library in Wingham affected her and began to make her think about writing in a different way. She talks about creating stories built around scenes like these, and about stories begun from anecdotes and personal experience, using as examples many of her stories including "Open Secrets," "The Albanian Virgin," "Images," "Royal Beatings," "Friend of My Youth," and "The Turkey Season." Munro goes on to elaborate on her writing and revision process, saying that she knows the ending before she begins writing a story and that it may or may not change as the story evolves. Her fictional aesthetic is captured in her description of the unconventional way she reads a story which, in metaphorical terms, is like exploring the rooms of a house.

P654.   Afterword. *Emily of New Moon*. By L. M. Montgomery. Toronto: McClelland & Stewart, 1989. 357-361.
    Rpt. as "Lucy's Lives: Emily of New Moon" in *Brick* 36 (Summer 1989): 46-48.
As a child of nine or ten, Munro says that *Emily of New Moon* struck her as being "good but different," the latter being the key word on which Munro focuses. The elements which Munro talks about as being different and affecting her as a young reader are the suffering and punishment that Emily undergoes at the hands of tyrannical and cruel adults, the latent sexual tension in the novel, and the development of a girl-child into a writer. Montgomery's original intention in writing *Emily of New Moon* for young readers is not clear. But Munro summarizes the positive tone of the book by saying that the protagonist finds she is alone

and makes a choice about her life without knowing it and without feeling "the shadow of a compromise." However, what Munro most admires about Montgomery's writing is the suggestion of a "life spreading out behind the story," something she incorporated at the time as a young reader, and later as a writer.

P655.   Afterword. *The Equations of Love; With an Afterword by Alice Munro*. By Ethel Wilson. Toronto: McClelland & Stewart, 1990. 259-262.

Munro has reread Ethel Wilson's book after a lapse of thirty-five years and writes about her present impression of the two stories in the book, one of which ("Tuesday and Wednesday") she had always claimed to be her very favourite story. Now Munro says she cares more about Lilly in "Lilly's Story" than any of the characters in "Tuesday and Wednesday." But "this is another kind of fiction," she adds of the latter, and proceeds to comment on the coming together of the characters at the end. Munro admires Wilson's skill in evoking a sense of place and comments on a Chinese character in "Lilly's Story." However, she admits that she finds Wilson's tone now "too composed, too self-assured," while on the other hand some of the sentences still "deliver whole worlds."

P656.   "Alice Munro Writes." Letter. *National Post* 29 June 2000: A15.

Responding to John Metcalf's article published in *National Post* on 17 June 2000, Munro writes that Robert Weaver did not in fact function as her agent in either Canada or the United States, but as someone who gave her friendly advice and encouragement. She is also critical of JoAnn McCaig's essay referenced in Metcalf's article and claims that it is not factual.

P657.   "An Appreciation." *Room of One's Own* 9.2 (1984): 32-33.

Munro praises Marian Engel's bravery in writing serious fiction about women's lives at a time when it was not fashionable to do so. Although not mentioning specific works, Munro's comments relate to her first reading of Engel's *No Clouds of Glory*. She says that Engel's writing gave her pleasure both as a reader and writer. She appreciated her skill in capturing the spirit of women when, for instance, they are talking amongst themselves. Munro says that this excited her and gave her a glimpse of what was possible when writing about women.

P658.   "Author Denies Statement." Letter. *London Free Press* 4 March 1975: 6.

This very brief statement by Munro is a denial that her childhood was "hideously painful" as reported in a recent article.

P659.   "Author's Commentary [on 'An Ounce of Cure' and 'Boys and Girls']." *Sixteen by Twelve: Short Stories by Canadian Writers*. Ed. John Metcalf. Toronto: Ryerson, 1970. 125-126.
   Rpt. in *How Stories Mean*. Ed. John Metcalf and J. R. (Tim) Struthers. Erin, ON: Porcupine's Quill, 1993. 185-187.

"An Ounce of Cure" originated from an anecdote. Munro comments on the protagonist, who changes from a participant to an observer in the same way as a writer does. "Boys and Girls" is about gender roles, responsibility, and freedom. Because females are denied action and full responsibility, they have more freedom than males. Males are not free to show their feelings. Munro does not feel satisfied that she has covered all she wanted to convey in the story.

P660. "The Authors on Their Writing." *Personal Fictions: Stories by Munro, Wiebe, Thomas, and Blaise*. Sel. Michael Ondaatje. Toronto: Oxford University Press, 1977. 224-225.

The text is excerpted from an interview with Graeme Gibson published in *Eleven Canadian Novelists* and from Munro's essay "The Colonel's Hash Resettled." Munro says that she learned to disguise early in life, because her view of the world was different from that of other people in her conservative rural community. The writers of the American south excited her because the type of country they wrote about was gothic like her own. Her motivation to write has something to do with the fight against death. Munro says she is excited about the surface of life. She sees it as an act of treachery to remove an object from its obscurity and set it down in print. Talking about writing makes her uncomfortable, and Munro expresses her doubts about writing, fearing that it might be "a questionable trick, an evasion . . . an unavoidable lie."

P661. "Bob Weaver Has Lots of Friends - Timid Beverages." *Performing Arts in Canada* 10.3 (Fall 1973): 13.

Munro reveals a humorous anecdote about her first meeting with Weaver. She acknowledges his generosity and the support he has given her as a writer.

P662. "The Case of Wei Jingsheng." Alice Munro, et al. Letter. *New York Review of Books* 43.3 (15 February 1996): 41-42.

This open letter, signed by Munro along with twenty-six other writers belonging to PEN around the world, was sent to the political leaders of ten countries. It expresses their concern for the imprisoned Chinese writer, Wei Jingsheng, and other prisoners of conscience in China, and requests their release.

P663. "Changing Places." *Writing Home: A PEN Canada Anthology*. Ed. Constance Rooke. Toronto: McClelland & Stewart, 1997. 190-206.

In this essay written for the anthology, Munro talks about her Scottish ancestors and the emigration of one of them, James Laidlaw, from Scotland to Canada. She gives details of her ancestors' history in Canada, including information about her great-grandfather, Thomas Laidlaw. She includes some of his correspondence.

P664. "The Colonel's Hash Resettled." *The Narrative Voice: Short Stories and Reflections by Canadian Authors*. Ed. and introd. John Metcalf. Toronto: McGraw-Hill Ryerson, 1972. 181-183.
Rpt. in *How Stories Mean*. Ed. John Metcalf and J. R. (Tim) Struthers. Erin, ON: Porcupine's Quill, 1993. 188-191.
Rpt. (excerpts) in *Personal Fictions: Stories by Munro, Wiebe, Thomas, and Blaise*. Sel. Michael Ondaatje. Toronto: Oxford University Press, 1977. 224-225.

Munro begins with a consideration of objects as physical realities and their use as symbols in writing. She ties this in to the writing of "Images," in which her memory plays a part and provides many of its details. The house in the ground described in the story is real. But Munro feels that removing an innocent object like this from its "natural obscurity" and extracting it as a "bloodless symbol" is like a betrayal to the object. The characters in the story are also similar to people in her area. She says that real memories are difficult to

Nonfiction

separate from fictional memories. These are as true to her as dreams are true. In discussing the origin of the story "Dance of the Happy Shades," Munro says that it came from the outside, an anecdote told to her by a family member, but she needed to see it in her own terms. Fictional "remembered" things made up the detail in the story.

P665. "Contributors' Notes ['Carried Away']." *The Best American Short Stories, 1992: Selected from U.S. and Canadian Magazines.* Sel. Robert Stone with Katrina Kenison. Introd. Robert Stone. Boston: Houghton Mifflin, 1992. 370-371.

"All the time I felt a parallel story going on," Munro says on the writing of the story. The story began as a realistic account of a small-town industry during the period of the first World War. But a parallel story developed. She explains how even drastic events such as the accident, which may or may not have occurred, do and don't matter.

P666. "Contributors' Notes ['The Children Stay']." *Prize Stories, 1998: The O. Henry Awards.* Ed. and introd. Larry Dark. New York: Anchor Books/Doubleday, 1998. 412.

Munro says that the story is about making choices which are sometimes not about the things we think they are. The woman in the story saves herself, but "on what pretext and at what cost?"

P667. "Contributors' Notes ['Circle of Prayer']." *The Best American Short Stories, 1987: Selected from U.S. and Canadian Magazines.* Sel. Ann Beattie with Shannon Ravenel. Boston: Houghton Mifflin, 1987. 314.

The story originated from a combination of ideas, images, and personal knowledge: a conversation heard between women about the circle of prayer and how it worked, a strong image of young girls dropping their jewellery, and knowledge of the feelings between mothers and daughters. But, Munro adds, "most of it came out of thin air."

P668. "Contributors' Notes ['Differently']." *The Best American Short Stories, 1990: Selected from U.S. and Canadian Magazines.* Sel. Richard Ford with Shannon Ravenel. Boston: Houghton Mifflin, 1990. 352.

Munro views the story from the perspective of place (Victoria, B.C.) and the time period of 1968 to 1974 in the lives of people who are in their thirties. She describes the atmosphere of the time as being like "a late outbreak of adolescence."

P669. "Contributors' Notes ['Family Furnishings']." *The Best American Short Stories, 2002: Selected from U.S. and Canadian Magazines.* Sel. Sue Miller and Katrina Kenison. Boston: Houghton Mifflin, 2002. 355.

The "kernel incident" was based on a true story which Munro had "somewhat rearranged." The story includes personal and autobiographical elements.

P670. "Contributors' Notes ['Floating Bridge']." *Prize Stories, 2001: The O. Henry Awards.* Ed. and introd. Larry Dark. New York: Anchor Books, 2001. 396.

The train of thought in developing the story began with the characters, and was followed with what Munro calls "two gifts": the joke which includes the family in the trailer, and the road which is based on a real road. The road led to the drive, the boy, and all that followed.

P671. "Contributors' Notes ['Friend of My Youth']." *The Best American Short Stories, 1991: Selected from U.S. and Canadian Magazines.* Sel. Alice Adams and Katrina Kenison. Introd. Alice Adams. Boston: Houghton Mifflin, 1991. 406.

A friend told Munro about a Cameronian family he had known, including details about the drama in the family and the half-painted house. Munro says she was not conscious of when she wrote herself and her mother into the story and began writing through the perspectives of each.

P672. "Contributors' Notes ['The Love of a Good Woman']." *Prize Stories, 1997: The O. Henry Awards.* Ed. Larry Dark. New York: Anchor Books/Doubleday, 1997. 442-443.

The idea for the story originated from a real incident of sex, murder, and marital cooperation in disposing of a body in a boat off the coast of British Columbia. Munro transposed the setting to Huron County and added details and characters, but concluded the story with the enigmatic boat by the river.

P673. "Contributors' Notes ['Meneseteung']." *The Best American Short Stories, 1989: Selected from U.S. and Canadian Magazines.* Sel. Margaret Atwood with Shannon Ravenel. Boston: Houghton Mifflin, 1989. 322-323.

The protagonist and her situation began with Munro's interest in local poetesses who lived in the small towns of 19th-century southwestern Ontario. Living on the edge of Victorian civilization, they were looked upon with "an uneasy mingling of mockery and respect." Munro says she imagined one of these women and gave her some talent, but did not want her to be particularly odd. She wanted her to have some choices.

P674. "Contributors' Notes ['Post and Beam']." *The Best American Short Stories, 2001: Selected from U.S. and Canadian Magazines.* [Sel.] Barbara Kingsolver and Katrina Kenison. Introd. Barbara Kingsolver. Boston: Houghton Mifflin, 2001. 350-351.

The story came to be written because Munro says that she knew of a similar situation and was interested in the common human experience of making a secret bargain. She considers the reasons why the young wife in the story made the bargain.

P675. "Contributors' Notes ['A Real Life']." *The Best American Short Stories, 1993: Selected from U.S. and Canadian Magazines.* Sel. Louise Erdrich and Katrina Kenison. Boston: Houghton Mifflin, 1993. 370.

The story's protagonist is described by Munro as a sexless woman-heroine of a romance that has a happy ending. Munro had learned about the tradition of the Albanian virgin in the early years of the 20th century. Relating this concept to modern times, she says that sex makes women unfit for lives of independence.

P676. "Contributors' Notes ['Runaway']." *The Best American Short Stories, 2004: Selected from U.S. and Canadian Magazines.* Sel. Lorrie Moore and Katrina Kenison. Boston: Houghton Mifflin, 2004. 440.

The dour landscape of the Dundalk Plain, not far from Munro's home in Clinton, lead to the image of the horse barn, the "uneasy couple," and other details of the story.

Nonfiction

P677. "Contributors' Notes ['Save the Reaper']." *The Best American Short Stories, 1999: Selected from U.S. and Canadian Magazines.* Sel. Amy Tan with Katrina Kenison. Boston: Houghton Mifflin, 1999. 387-388.

Munro says that the story is an expression of changes she has felt and observed in the rural life of Ontario and in the lives of people of her own generation who are in their sixties. "It is about things you feel and don't quite know why or things you pay attention to without being able to say why they are important."

P678. "Contributors' Notes ['Save the Reaper']." *Prize Stories, 1999: The O. Henry Awards.* Ed. and introd. Larry Dark. 1st Anchor Books original ed. New York: Anchor Books, 1999. 404.

The story grew from the real experience of a woman who had visited a similar house she had known from childhood and her discovery of a sinister scene within it.

P679. "Contributors' Notes ['Silence']." *The Best American Short Stories, 2005: Selected from U.S. and Canadian Magazines.* Sel. Michael Chabon and Katrina Kenison. Boston: Houghton Mifflin, 2005. 389.

The story is the last of a trilogy of stories. It is about a woman and "her coming to be alone" after being with, and then without, a child. Munro says she does not feel it to be a particularly sad story or one that is all about loss. "There is some gain."

P680. "Contributors' Notes ['Wigtime']." *The Best American Short Stories, 1990: Selected from U.S. and Canadian Magazines.* Sel. Richard Ford with Shannon Ravenel. Boston: Houghton Mifflin, 1990. 352.

Beginning with an anecdote about a woman going to a trailer park in disguise to spy on her husband, Munro explains how she thought about the woman and what she would do if she had caught her husband in adultery. The story and characters evolved from this and include some personal details.

P681. "Distressing Impression." Letter. *Globe and Mail* 22 December 1982: 6.
   Rpt. in *Wingham Advance-Times* 29 December 1982: 4.

In an article, "Writing's Something I Did Like the Ironing" published in the *Globe and Mail* on December 11, 1982, the author referred to Munro's father as a failed fox and turkey farmer. The impression given of her father distresses Munro, who says that he was not a failure, but a man who worked hard, suffered bad luck, and was brave and uncomplaining.

P682. "Everything Here Is Touchable and Mysterious." *Weekend Magazine* [*Globe and Mail*, Toronto] 11 May 1974: 33.

Munro recalls her youthful memories of the Maitland River in Huron County. She gives a detailed description of the river and its physical surroundings, including the low fields and pasture along the river, called "The Flats." She recounts the flooding of the area in the spring and the way the local people, including the children, would react to this. The numerous species of fish, plants, and flowers are detailed. As a child, Munro says, she would imagine deep holes in one section of the river and expresses the mythic quality it held for her. "This ordinary place is sufficient, everything here touchable and mysterious," she writes.

P683. Foreword. *The Anthology Anthology: A Selection from 30 Years of CBC Radio's "Anthology."* Ed. Robert Weaver. Toronto: Macmillan, 1984. ix-x.

Munro credits Robert Weaver for giving her, and other unknown Canadian writers, unflagging faith and encouragement from the very beginning. Weaver promoted Canadian writing in the Canadian market when it was not popular to do so. He had purchased one of Munro's stories in 1951 for the radio program *Canadian Short Stories*.

P684. "Going to the Lake." *Ontario: A Bicentennial Tribute*. Toronto: Key Porter Books, 1983. 51-52.

Munro recalls her childhood memories of Sunday family outings to Lake Huron.

P685. "Golden Apples." *Georgia Review* 53.1 (Spring 1999): 22-24.
 Rpt. in *Eudora Welty: Writers' Reflections upon First Reading Welty*. Ed. Pearl Amelia McHaney. Athens, GA: Hiss Street Press, 1999. 73-76.

Golden Apples was the first and favourite book of Welty's that Munro had read. In her appraisal, Munro includes a passage from the book and says that there is more than skill involved, more than the right details and dialogue. She says that what the writer is writing about must be imagined so deeply and devoutly that readers feel a connection to it in their personal lives.

P686. "Good Woman in Ireland." *Prize Writing: The 10th Anniversary Collection*. Ed. Gary Stephen Ross. Toronto: Giller Prize Foundation in association with Coach House Books, 2003. 57-64.
 Rpt. in *Brick* 72 (Winter 2003): 26-30.

During a stay in Ireland, Munro revised "The Love of a Good Woman." But after her return to Canada she was dissatisfied with it, threw it out, and went back to the original version, which she then revised. Munro realized that being in Ireland, where the influence of Irish writers was so immediate, had caused her to change the tone of the story and it was all wrong.

P687. Introduction. *The Moons of Jupiter: Stories*. Markham, ON: Penguin Books, 1986. xiii-xvi; Toronto: Penguin Books Canada, 1995. xiii-xvi.

In her introduction, Munro gives insight into the creative process of transforming autobiographical material into fiction. Some stories such as "The Moons of Jupiter" begin with facts, but a different story forms and comes together. Thus, personal stories are carried away from the real. Conversely, anecdotal stories become familiar. In some detail, Munro relates the origin and writing of "The Turkey Season."

P688. "A Leaven of Alice." Letter. *Today* [*Toronto Star* and other Canadian newspapers] 27 February 1982: 2.

Munro responds to an article by Wayne Grady published in *Today Magazine* on 5 December 1981, which caused a hostile reaction in Wingham. Grady's article included a quotation from an interview in which Munro describes Lowertown as a "kind of ghetto." Elsewhere in the article Grady labels the town as "stultifyingly provincial." Munro denies that she passed any such judgement on the town. Rather, she "always found Wingham lively and interesting."

Munro further states that she is not writing autobiography and the towns appearing in her books are not Wingham, but a composite of real and imagined places.

P689.　Letter. *Books in Canada* 16.6 (August-September 1987): 38-39.
Munro supports Raymond Knister's daughter in her efforts to stop rumours about the cause of her father's death.

P690.　"No Snub Was Intended." Letter. *Vancouver Sun* 19 December 1981: A5.
Munro, who was reported in the *Vancouver Sun*, 13 November 1981, to have snubbed Mavis Gallant at a short-story conference in Edmonton, denies that she had ever snubbed Gallant and says that the idea of doing so appalls her. In fact she had spoken to Gallant and told her how much she admired her work.

P691.　"The Novels of William Maxwell." *Brick* 34 (Fall 1988): 28-31.
　　Rpt. in *Brick* 65/66 (Fall 2000): 23-29.
　　Rpt. revised and expanded in "Maxwell." *A William Maxwell Portrait: Memories and Appreciation*. Ed. Charles Baxter, Michael Collier, and Edward Hirsch. New York: W. W. Norton, 2004. 34-47.
Munro prefaces her commentary on several of Maxwell's books, notably *Time Will Darken It* and *So Long, See You Tomorrow*, with some general remarks, saying that when she had first read Maxwell's work in the early 1960s she did not appreciate the quality of his writing as much as she did later on. She praises his simplicity and naturalness of style and goes as far as to say that at one point she wished she could rewrite her own work so that it could be informed with his spirit. In the expanded essay published in *A William Maxwell Portrait*, Munro gives a more detailed commentary on the two books and also briefly discusses *They Came Like Swallows* and *The Folded Leaf*.

P692.　"On John Metcalf: Taking Writing Seriously." *Malahat Reveiw* 70 (March 1985): 6-7.
In this section of the article, Munro writes about her literary friendship and early correspondence with Metcalf and his qualities as a literary mentor.

P693.　"On Stuewe and Censorship." Letter. *Books in Canada* 7.10 (December 1978): 39-40.
Munro reacts to the article written by Paul Stuewe on the banning of Laurence's *Diviners* in schools in Huron county. She wonders whether he was aware that the small group of book-banners did not represent the whole community, that the "children" being protected were grade 13 students, and that the book was not required reading. Munro believes that children have a natural resistance to values being "over-sold" to them, and that it is healthy for them to encounter different opinions.

P694.　"On Writing 'The Office.'" *Transitions II: Short Fiction. A Source Book of Canadian Literature*. Ed. Edward Peck. Vancouver: Commcept, 1978. 259, 261-262.
　　Rpt. in *How Stories Mean*. Ed. John Metcalf and J. R. (Tim) Struthers. Erin, ON: Porcupine's Quill, 1993. 192-194.
"The Office" is based on a personal experience in Vancouver in 1960 and 1961, which was "a little bit rearranged and pointed up to make a story." Munro writes, "It is the most straightforward autobiographical story I have ever written." Looking back at the story now, she would

write it differently and make it more open and less pointed and contrived. She proceeds to describe the intrusions of the landlord and summarizes that, in the end, the experiment of renting an office space for writing a novel did not solve her writer's block and was not a success.

P695.   "An Open Letter." *Jubilee* [Gorrie, ON] [1] (1974): 4-7.

The fictional town of Jubilee in Munro's writing is based on Wingham, Ontario. Munro describes her impressions of the town in her youth and writes about the emotional power of local detail in writing.

P696.   "Remember Roger Mortimer: Dickens' *Child's History of England* Remembered." *Montrealer* 36.2 (February 1962): 34-37.

Charles Dickens' *A Child's History of England* is the first real book Munro had ever read. The copy had belonged to her father. Munro recalls different sections and stories in the book, and comments on the historical figure of Roger Mortimer.

P697.   "Sin of Omission." Letter. *Books in Canada* 16.3 (April 1987): 40.

No stories by John Metcalf appeared in the recently published *Oxford Book of Canadian Short Stories in English*. Munro protests this omission.

P698.   "The Sweet Second Summer of Kitty Malone." *Uncommon Ground: A Celebration of Matt Cohen*. Ed. Graeme Gibson, et al. Toronto: Knopf Canada, 2002. 91-94.

Munro has read *The Sweet Second Summer of Kitty Malone* several times, not from beginning to end, but from part to part, beginning with a part that interests her and moving back and forth between other parts to discover the interconnections in the story. After presenting a succinct interpretation of Cohen's story about the Malone family, Munro concludes that she wants to reread a story such as this because it presents a "good feeling . . . of an ongoing discovery, that rambles out beyond the story." She goes on to praise Cohen's commitment to his characters and story, his style, literary integrity, and the way he fuses "sharp seeing and feeling."

P699.   "Through the Jade Curtain." *Chinada: Memoirs of the Gang of Seven*. Gary Geddes, et al. Dunvegan, ON: Quadrant, 1982. 51-55.

A group of Canadian writers, including Munro, was invited to China by the Chinese Writers' Association. In this piece, which is based on an interview by Geoff Hancock on February 20, 1982, Munro gives her impressions of the Chinese countryside, the farming practices, the people, physical sites, and the lives of women. She is disappointed with the state control of writers and with the Chinese writers' belief that it is their duty to write in the service of the state.

P700.   "A Walk on the Wild Side: One of Canada's Best-Loved Authors (Alice Munro) Wants to Turn Old Tracks into New Trails." *Canadian Living* October 1989: 38-39, 41-42. Rpt. in *Hooray for Canada: Special Canadians Talk about What Canada Means to Them*. Toronto: Canadian Living, 1989. 51-54.
          Rpt. in *Far and Wide: Essays from Canada*. Ed. Sean Armstrong. Toronto: Nelson Canada, 1995. 102-105.

In this article, Munro argues her case for the preservation of old railway lands and their conversion into walking trails. She begins by describing the area where she grew up and how the land and people have changed since she left. On coming back to Ontario, Munro says that much of the land is now privately owned and there is no access to natural areas. She advocates that access to land is a right and necessity, and says that the natural landscape of rural Ontario should be preserved.

P701. "What Do You Want to Know For?" *Writing Away: The PEN Canada Travel Anthology*. Ed. Constance Rooke. Toronto: McClelland and Stewart, 1994. 203-220.

Munro writes of two parallel journeys: one, a car trip with her husband over the physical landscape of Grey and Bruce Counties in Ontario; the other, a personal journey within herself. Both journeys revolve around a mystery: in the first case, the mystery inside two crypts found in an old cemetery in Sullivan Township; and in the second case, the mystery of a lump, as yet undiagnosed, within her body.

P702. "What Is Real?" *Making It New: Contemporary Canadian Stories*. Ed. John Metcalf. Toronto: Methuen, 1982. 223-226.
Rpt. in *Canadian Forum* 62 (September 1982): 5, 36.
Rpt. in *The Art of Short Fiction: An International Anthology*. Ed. Gary Geddes. Toronto: HarperCollins, 1993. 824-827.
Rpt. (excerpt) in *Canadian Classics: An Anthology of Short Stories*. Critical commentary John Metcalf. Bibliographical and textual research J. R. (Tim) Struthers. Toronto: McGraw-Hill Ryerson, 1993. 143-145.
Rpt. in *How Stories Mean*. Ed. John Metcalf and J. R. (Tim) Struthers. Erin, ON: Porcupine's Quill, 1993. 331-334.
Rpt. in *The Norton Anthology of Short Fiction*. R.V. Cassill. Shorter 5th ed. New York: Norton, 1995. 939-942.
Rpt. (excerpt) in *Contemporary Novelists*. Ed. Susan Windisch Brown. 6th ed. New York: St. James Press, 1996. 743.
Rpt. in *Contemporary Literary Criticism: Excerpts from Criticism of the Works of Today's Novelists, Poets, Playwrights, Short Story Writers, Scriptwriters, and Other Creative Writers*. Ed. Brigham Narins and Deborah A. Stanley. Vol. 95. Detroit: Gale, 1997. 289-291.
Rpt. in *The Writer's Path: An Introduction to Fiction*. Ed. Constance Rooke and Leon Rooke. Toronto: ITP Nelson, 1998. 970-973.
Rpt. in *Literature for Composition: Essays, Fiction, Poetry, and Drama*. Ed. Sylvan Barnet, et al. 5th ed. New York: Longman, 2000. 750-752.
Rpt. in *The New Millennium Reader*. [Comp.] Stuart Hirschberg and Terry Hirschberg. 2nd ed. Upper Saddle River, NJ: Prentice Hall, 2000. 687-690.
Rpt. in *The Norton Anthology of Short Fiction*. R. V. Cassill and Richard Bausch. New York: Norton. 6th ed. 2000. 1706-1709. Shorter 6th ed. 1002-1005.
Rpt. (excerpt) as "How I Write Short Stories [Author's Perspective]" in *The Longman Anthology of Short Fiction: Stories and Authors in Context*. [Comp.] Dana Gioia and R. S. Gwynn. New York: Longman, 2001. 1315-1316.
Rpt. in *The Broadview Anthology of Expository Prose*. Ed. Tammy Roberts, et al. Peterborough, ON: Broadview Press, 2002. 318-321.

Munro explains her aesthetics of reading and writing fiction. She describes in metaphorical terms the way she reads a short story, saying that it is like entering a house which encloses interconnecting spaces and rooms through which she slowly wanders. Of her writing, Munro says that she wants to make a certain kind of structure, and knows the feeling she wants to get from being inside the structure. How a story feels plays into much of the revision. Things from the real world, such as people and events, jump-start the creative process.

P703. "What Should Cynthia Do with the Rest of Her Life?" *Chatelaine* June 1987: 84.
In a short paragraph, Munro answers the question of what type of advice she would give a recent university graduate. She advises graduates to take time to decide how they want to live, adding that a career should not be the measure of who they are.

P704. "Writer Denies Her Books Were Based on Wingham." Letter. *Wingham Advance-Times* 13 January 1982: 4.
Munro denies two points made in an editorial by Barry Wenger on December 16, 1981. She says that she was never interviewed by the journalist Wayne Grady nor had she ever spoken to him about Wingham. Secondly, she points out that the assumption by both Grady and Wenger that her fictional towns were based on Wingham is false. "Far from being bitter," Munro says, "I have always had a certain affection for Wingham." (See entries under Grady and Wenger in the Secondary Works-Articles section.)

P705. "Writers Compiled Handbook." Letter. *London Free Press* 24 January 1979: A6.
In her letter, Munro addresses several erroneous details reported on the censorship issue in Huron County. She says that writers did not call the book-banners names and that it was the Writer's Union of Canada, not the publishing industry, which produced the censorship handbook.

P706. "Writing the O. Henry Prize Stories 2003: The Authors on Their Work ['Fathers']." *The O. Henry Prize Stories, 2003*. Ed. and introd. Laura Furman. New York: Anchor Books, 2003. 339.
Munro addresses the concepts of good fathers and bad fathers, and the boundaries of power between parents and children. She eschews calling the story autobiographical, but says that it is personal, in the sense that it contains remembered feelings.

Television and Radio

"The Albanian Virgin"

P707.   "The Albanian Virgin." *Between the Covers*. CBC Radio. 11-15 March 1996. (5 part series, 75 min.)

"Baptizing"
Chapter from the novel *Lives of Girls and Women*.

P708.   "Baptizing." Narr. Deborah Turnbull. Adapt. Patricia Watson. Prod. David Peddie. Dir. Allan King. *Performance*. CBC TV. 19 January 1975. (22 min.)
Also on film.

"Bardon Bus"

P709.   "Bardon Bus (excerpt)." Narr. Alice Munro. *Morningside*. CBC Radio. 20 October 1982. (2 min.)

A Better Place Than Home
See "1847: The Irish. [The Newcomers Series]."

"Boys and Girls"

P710.   "Boys and Girls." *Sons and Daughters*. Coproduced by Atlantis Films. CBC TV. 5 January 1984. (23 min.)
Rebroadcast 3 June 1984. Also on film.

"Carried Away"

P711.   "Carried Away." Narr. Kate Lynch. *Between the Covers*. CBC Radio. 6-10 February 1995. (5 part series, 75 min.)
Rebroadcast *Between the Covers*. 4-8 March 1996.

"Cortes Island"

P712.   "Cortes Island." Narr. Susan Hogan. *Between the Covers*. CBC Radio One. 14-18 September 1998. (5 part series)
Rebroadcast *Between the Covers*. 17-21 July 2000.

"Forgiveness in Families"

P713.   "Forgiveness in Families." Narr. Aileen Seaton. *Anthology*. CBC Radio. 10 March 1973. (26 min.)

"The Found Boat"

P714.   "The Found Boat." Narr. Aileen Seaton. *Anthology*. CBC Radio. 6 April 1974. (25 min.)
Rebroadcast (excerpt) *Sunday Supplement*. CBC Radio. 18 August 1974. (13 min., 30 sec.)

"Friend of My Youth"

P715.   "Friend of My Youth (excerpt)." Narr. Alice Munro. *Writers and Company*. CBC Radio One. September? 1990.
Rebroadcast 15 October 2000.

Hateship, Friendship, Courtship, Loveship, Marriage: Stories

P716.   "Hateship, Friendship, Courtship, Loveship, Marriage." Narr. Dixie Seatle. *Between the Covers*. CBC Radio One. 29 October-7 November 2001. (8 part series)

"How I Met My Husband"

P717.   "How I Met My Husband." Narr. Nonnie Griffin. Prod. George Jonas. Dir. Herbert Roland. Perf. Lynne Griffin, George R. Robertson, Jackie Burroughs, and others. *The Play's the Thing*. CBC TV. 17 January 1974. (21 min.)
Printed in *The Play's the Thing: Four Original Television Dramas*. Ed. Tony Gifford. Toronto: Macmillan of Canada, 1976. 15-34.

"Images"

P718. "Images." Narr. Aileen Seaton. *CBC Tuesday Night*. CBC Radio. 17 September 1968. (25 min.)

The Irish: 1847
See "1847: The Irish. [The Newcomers Series]."

Lives of Girls and Women: A Novel

P719. *Lives of Girls and Women* (excerpts and summarized contents). Narr. Alice Munro. *CBC Monday Evening*. CBC-FM Radio. 18 February 1974.

P720. *Lives of Girls and Women*. Adapt. Laura Common. *Judy*. CBC Radio. 29 September-25 November 1975. (30 part series, 10 min. each part)

P721. *Lives of Girls and Women* (selections). Narr. Alice Munro. *Gzowski on FM*. CBC-FM Radio. 19 February 1976.

P722. *Lives of Girls and Women*. Narr. Judith Mahbey. Adapt. Ruth Fraser. Prod. Lawrie Seligman. *Booktime*. CBC Radio. 8-12, 15-19, 22-26 June 1981. (15 part series, 15 min. each part)

P723. *Lives of Girls and Women* (stereodrama). Adapt. Martin Hunter. Prod. and dir. James Roy. Perf. Sheila McCarthy, Nonnie Griffin, Janet Amos, and others. *Arts National*. CBC-FM Radio. 22 June 1992. (2 hrs.)
Review:
Adilman, Sid. "Lively Munro Tales Worth a Second Listen." *Toronto Star* 26 April 1993: C7.

P724. "Lives of Girls and Women." Script Charles K. Pitts and Kelly Rebar. Dir. Ronald Wilson. Perf. Tanya Allen, Wendy Crewson and others. Prod. Paragon Entertainment Corp., Toronto. CBC TV. 11 February 1996. (90 min.)
Also on film.
Reviews:
"Munro's 'Lives' Drip 1940s Mood: Newcomer Tanya Allen Stars as Del Jordan, a Small-Town Teen-ager with an Overpowering Mother." *Globe and Mail* 27 January 1996: C9.
Turbide, Diane. "Sense and Sensuality: A Young Woman Gets Sidetracked by Desire." *Maclean's* 12 February 1996: 93.

"Miles City, Montana"

P725. "Miles City, Montana." Adapt. by Alberto Manguel. Perf. Jennifer Dale, Tom Butler, Gina Samptoria, Lisa Yamanaka, Marlow Vella, Gina Bertoia, Philip Williams. *Morningside*. CBC Radio. 9 September 1988.

"The Moons of Jupiter"

P726.   "The Moons of Jupiter (excerpt)." Read by Alice Munro at the International Festival of Authors at Harbourfront. *Arts National*. CBC-FM Radio. 25 November 1981. (21 min.)

P727.   "The Moons of Jupiter (excerpt)." Narr. Alice Munro. *Morningside*. CBC Radio. 22 October 1982. (2 min.)

"Mrs. Cross and Mrs. Kidd"

P728.   "Mrs. Cross and Mrs. Kidd (excerpt)." Narr. Alice Munro. *Morningside*. CBC Radio. 21 October 1982. (2 min.)

"My Mother's Dream"

P729.   "My Mother's Dream (excerpt)." Narr. Alice Munro at The International Festival of Authors, Fall 1998. *The Arts Today*. CBC Radio One. 14 February 1999. Rebroadcast *The Arts Today*. 19 February, 10 March 1999.

The Newcomers Series
See "1847: The Irish. [The Newcomers Series]."

"Oranges and Apples"

P730.   "Oranges and Apples (excerpt)." Narr. Alice Munro. *Writers and Company*. CBC Radio One. September? 1990.
Rebroadcast 15 October 2000.

"The Ottawa Valley"

P731.   "The Ottawa Valley." Adapt. Anna Reiser. Prod. Maxine Samuels. Dir. Daniele J. Suissa. *Performance*. CBC TV. 23 November 1975. (21 min.)

P732.   "The Ottawa Valley (excerpt)." Narr. Alice Munro. *Don Harron's Morningside*. CBC Radio. 5 January 1978. (7 min.)

"An Ounce of Cure"

P733.   "An Ounce of Cure." Adapt. John Frizzell. Prod. Janice Platt, Michael MacMillan, Seaton McLean. Dir. Don McBrearty. *Sons and Daughters*. CBC TV. 27 January 1985. (20 min., 30 sec.)
Rebroadcast 13 October 1985. Also on film.

"The Peace of Utrecht"

P734. "The Peace of Utrecht." Adapt. James W. Nichol. Prod. David Peddie. Dir. René Bonnière. *To See Ourselves*. Canadian Short Stories. CBC TV. 17 November 1972. (21 min., 30 sec.)
Rebroadcast 5 September 1974. Also on film.

"Postcard"

P735. "Postcard." Adapt. René Bonnière and David Peddie. Ex. prod. David Peddie. Prod. and dir. René Bonnière. *Theatre Canada*. CBC TV. 1 October 1970. (22 min.)
Rebroadcast *Double Exposure*. CBC TV. 2 April 1971. *To See Ourselves*. CBC TV. 18 April 1973. Also on film.

P736. "Postcard." Narr. Kristina Nicholl. *Between the Covers*. CBC Radio One. 8-9 November 2001. (20 min.)

"Providence"

P737. "Providence." Narr. Lynn Henderson. Prod. Susan Lumsden. *Anthology*. CBC Radio. 9 April 1977. (27 min., 50 sec.)

"Rich as Stink"

P738. "Rich as Stink." Narr. Nicky Guadagni. *Between the Covers*. CBC Radio One. 21-25 September 1998.
Rebroadcast 5-9 February 2001. (5 part series)

"The Shining Houses"

P739. "The Shining Houses." Narr. Joy Coghill. *CBC Wednesday Night*. CBC Radio. 6 June 1962. (30 min.)

"The Stone in the Field"

P740. "The Stone in the Field (excerpt)." Narr. Alice Munro. *Morningside*. CBC Radio. 19 October 1982. (2 min.)

"Thanks For the Ride"

P741. "Thanks For the Ride." Adapt. Nika Rylski. Prod. David Peddie. Dir. Grahame Woods. *To See Ourselves*. Canadian Short Stories. CBC TV. 28 October 1971. (21 min., 30 sec.) Rebroadcast *To See Ourselves.* 6 September 1973. Also on film.

P742. "Thanks For the Ride." Adapt. Judy Curnew. Prod. and dir. Bill Lane. *Monday Night Playhouse; Summerfest*. CBC Radio Two. 14 August 2000.

"A Trip to the Coast"

P743. "The Trip to the Coast." Adapt. James W. Nichol. Prod. David Peddie. Dir. Paul Lynch. Perf. David Hughes, Cynthia Dale, and Nan Stewart. *To See Ourselves*. CBC TV. 5 December 1973. (20 min., 30 sec.)
Also on film.

"The Turkey Season"

P744. "The Turkey Season." Narr. Corinne Langston. *Anthology*. CBC Radio. 16 October 1982. (20 min.)

"Wild Swans"

P745. "Wild Swans." Narr. Tedde Moore. *Anthology*. CBC Radio. 7 April 1984. (24 min., 15 sec.)

P746. "Wild Swans." Narr. Nicky Guadagni. Prod. Ann Jansen. *Sunday Showcase*. CBC Radio One. 6 April 1997. (22 min., 47 sec.)
Rebroadcast *Monday Night Playhouse*. CBC Radio Two. 7 April, 1997.

"The Yellow Afternoon"

P747. "The Yellow Afternoon." Narr. Dorothy Davies. *Anthology*. CBC Radio. 22 February 1955. (25 min.)
Broadcast but never published.

"1847: The Irish. [The Newcomers Series]"

P748. *The Newcomers* [series]. *1847: The Irish*. Prod. Richard Nielsen and Pat Ferns. Dir. Eric Till. CBC TV. 8 January 1978.
Retelecast 16 March 1980. Later published as "A Better Place Than Home."
Review:
Kirby, Blaik. "The Irish Newcomers—No TV Formula Here." *Globe and Mail* 6 January 1978: 12.

Films and Videocassettes

"Baptizing"

P749.   *Baptizing*. National Film Board of Canada. Toronto: Canadian Broadcasting Corporation, 1975. Film, 16 mm. (50 min.)

"Boys and Girls"

P750.   *Boys and Girls*. Canadian Literature Series. Prod. Janice Platt, Seaton McLean, and Michael MacMillan. Dir. Don McBrearty. Script, Joe Wiesenfeld. Perf. Megan Follows, David Fox, Clare Coulter. Produced by Atlantis Films in association with the Canadian Broadcasting Corporation, 1982. Dist. Magic Lantern Films, Oakville, ON; Beacon Films, Norwood, MA. Film, 16 mm. Videocassette, VHS, ½ in. (24 min.)
   Also issued in French under the title *Garcons et filles*.
Academy Award 9 April 1984: Best Achievement in Live Action Short Film.

"Connection"

P751.   *Connection*. Canadian Short Story Video Series. Prod. Cindy Hamon-Hill and William Weintraub. Dir. and ed. Wolf Koenig. Script Kelly Rebar. Perf. Kate Trotter, Patricia Hamilton, Tom Butler, and others. Produced by the National Film Board of Canada and Atlantis Films with the participation of Telefilm Canada and the Global Television Network, 1986. Dist. Magic Lantern Communications, Oakville, ON; Beacon Films, Norwood, MA. Film, 16 mm. Videocassette, VHS, ½ in. (24 min.)
   Also issued in French under the title *Contact*.

"Differently"

P752.   [*Alice Munro*]. TVOntario, Authors at Harbourfront series (Nippising). Produced for TVOntario, Toronto, by Tier One Communications, 1990. Videocassette. (30 min.)

"Forgiveness in Families"

P753.   *Alice Munro: Forgiveness in Families.* (Dramatized excerpts and interview with Alice Munro) Canadian Literature (Authors). Produced by TVOntario for the Council of Ministers of Education, Canada, 1984. Dist. Image Media Services, Richmond, BC.; Access Network, Calgary, AB. Videocassette, VHS, ½ in. (Munro segment 15 min.)
Videocassette also includes Michel Tremblay, Janis Rapoport, and Al Purdy.

Lives of Girls and Women: A Novel

P754.   *Lives of Girls and Women.* Prod. Richard Borchiver. Dir. Ronald Wilson. Script Charles Kristian Pitts and Kelly Rebar. Perf. Tanya Allen, Wendy Crewson. Produced by Paragon Entertainment in association with Canadian Broadcasting Corporation and Telefilm Canada, 1995. Dist. McNabb & Connolly Films, Port Credit, ON. Videocassette, VHS, ½ in. (90 min.)

P755.   *Lives of Girls and Women.* [Selections] Introduction to Literature. Prod. Fraser Steele. Ed. Bill Grier. Host/writers Catherine Ross and Allan Gedalof. Perf. Tanya Allen, Wendy Crewson. Selections read by Leanna Brodie. TVOntario, Toronto, 1993. Dist. International Tele-Film, Mississauga, ON; Films for the Humanities & Sciences, Princeton, NJ, 1996. Videocassette, VHS, ½ in. (28 min.)

The Newcomers
See "1847: The Irish [The Newcomers Series]."

"An Ounce of Cure"

P756.   *An Ounce of Cure.* Canadian Literature Series. Prod. Michael MacMillan, Seaton McLean, and Janice Platt. Dir. Don McBrearty. Script John Frizzell. Perf. Cathy Burns, Martha Cronyn, Greg Spottiswood. Produced by Atlantis Films in association with the Canadian Broadcasting Corporation, 1983? Dist. Magic Lantern Communications, Oakville, ON; Beacon Films, Norwood, MA. Film, 16 mm. Videocassette, VHS. ½ in. (26 min.)
Also issued in French on film under the title *Coeur Chagrin*, and on videocassette under the title *Un Rayon des remedes*.

"Thanks for the Ride"

P757.   *Thanks for the Ride.* Prod. John Kramer and John Spotton. Dir. and script John Kent Harrison. Perf. Carl Marotte, Lesleh Donaldson, Peter Krantz, and Melissa Bell. Produced by the National Film Board of Canada, 1983. Film, 16 mm. Videocassette, VHS, ½ in. (29 min.)
Review:
Shoebridge, Tom. *Cinema Canada* 102 (December 1983): 29.

"A Wilderness Station"

P758. "A Wilderness Station." *Edge of Madness*. Prod. Bill Gray. Dir. Anne Wheeler. Script Charles K. Pitts. Perf. Caroline Dhavernas, Paul Johansson, Corey Sevier, and Brendan Fehr. Produced by Cinegroupe, Credo Entertainment and Gregorian Films. Dist. Lions Gate Home Entertainment, 2002. (99 min.)
Also issued in 2003 with Spanish subtitles by Studio Home Entertainment, Los Angeles, CA on videocassette, VHS, ½ in. and videodisc, 4 3/4 in.

"1847: The Irish [The Newcomers Series]"

P759. *1847: The Irish [The Newcomers Series]*. Story and screenplay by Alice Munro. Prod. Pat Ferns and Richard Nielsen. Dir. Eric Till. Produced by Nielsen-Ferns International for Imperial Oil, 1977. Film, 16 mm. Videocassette, VHS, ½ in. (59 min.)

Other Videocassettes and Films

P760. Alice Munro at Bentley College / English Dept., Bentley College. 1 videotape.
Copy located in the University of Calgary Library, Special Collections.

P761. *Voices on the Water*. [1986 Harbourfront International Festival of Authors]. Prod., dir. Andrew Johnson. Script Andrew Johnson. Narr. Shelagh Rogers. Produced by Toronto Open City Productions Ltd. 1987. Dis. McNabb and Connolly Films. Videocassette, VHS, ½ in. (58 min.)
Footage of writers, including Alice Munro, with readings, interviews and seminars.

Sound Recordings

"The Albanian Virgin"

P762. "The Albanian Virgin." (excerpts); "Vandals." (excerpts). Read by Alice Munro. Introd. Verlyn Klinkenborg. Recorded 15 March 1994, in Longfellow Hall, Harvard University. Sponsored by the Woodberry Poetry Room, Harvard College Library. Morris Gray Reading series. 1 audiotape, 2 track (50 min.)

The Beggar Maid: Stories of Flo and Rose

P763. *The Beggar Maid: Stories of Flo and Rose.* Read by George Backman. Recorded and distributed by AFB. [Washington, DC]: Library of Congress, NLS [National Library Service], 1980. LP 6 s. 10 in. 8 rpm.

P764. *The Beggar Maid: Stories of Flo and Rose.* Read by Jeanne Hopson. Special library ed. Newport Beach, CA: Books on Tape, 1983. 9 audiocassettes, 2 track (9 hrs.)

Dance of the Happy Shades: Stories

P765. *Dance of the Happy Shades.* Read by Pat Barlow. Vancouver: Library Development Commission, 1978. 6 audiocassettes, 2 track (7 hrs., 35 min.)

P766. *Dance of the Happy Shades, and Other Stories.* [Peterborough, ON: Ontario Audio Library Service, 1982]. 1 audiotape, 4 track, master.

P767. *Dance of the Happy Shades and Other Stories.* Princeton, NJ: Recording for the Blind and Dyslexic, 1999. 2 audiocassettes, 4 track.

Translations

French

P768.　*La danse des ombres*. Read by René Chouteau. Longueuil, PQ: Institut Nazareth et Louis-Braille, 1980. 6 audiocassettes, 2 track.

"Forgiveness in Families"

P769.　"Forgiveness in Families." *Canadian Short Stories*, pgm. 11-12. [Montreal?]: Radio Canada International, [197?]. LP. 33 1/3 rpm. mono.; 12 in. (52 min.) Transcript.
LP also includes "Words for the Winter" by Clarke [i.e., Clark] Blaise.

P770.　"Forgiveness in Families." Read by Barbara Barrie. *Selected Shorts: A Celebration of the Short Story*. Vol. 6, cassette b. Recorded live at Symphony Space. New York: Symphony Space, 1992. 1 audiocassette (29 min., 13 sec.)
Cassette also includes "The Jewbird" by Bernard Malamud and "Palais de justice" by Mark Helprin.

Friend of My Youth: Stories

P771.　*Friend of My Youth: Stories*. (Selections). Read by Alice Munro. New York: Random House AudioPublishing, 1990. 2 audiocassettes (2 hrs., 41 min.)
Unabridged readings of selected stories from *Friend of My Youth*.

P772.　*Friend of My Youth: Stories*. Read by Mitzi Friedlander. Recorded and distributed by American Printing House for the Blind. [Washington, DC]: Library of Congress, NLS [National Library Service], 1991. 2 audiocassettes, 4 track.
Reissued by CNIB, Toronto, 1991 in 7 audiocassettes, 2 track (10 hrs., 30 min.); 2 audiocassettes, 4 track.

P773.　*Friend of My Youth: Stories*. Read by Elizabeth Caton. Vancouver, BC: Crane Memorial Library, 1991. 7 audiocassettes, 2 track.

P774.　*Friend of My Youth: Stories*. Read by Beth Fowler. Chivers Sound Library. Hampton, NH: Chivers North America, 2000. 8 audiocassettes, 2 track (ca. 9 hrs., 35 min.)

Hateship, Friendship, Courtship, Loveship, Marriage: Stories

P775.　*Hateship, Friendship, Courtship, Loveship, Marriage*. Read by Kymberly Dakin. Chivers Sound Library. Hampton, NH: Chivers North America, 2002. 8 compact discs, 4 3/4 in.; 6 audiocassettes (ca. 7 hrs., 30 min.)

P776.　*Hateship, Friendship, Courtship, Loveship, Marriage*. Read by Kymberly Dakin. Auburn, CA: Audio Partners, 2002. 8 compact discs, 4 3/4 in.; 6 audiocassettes (10 hrs.)

P777. *Hateship, Friendship, Courtship, Loveship, Marriage*. Read by Gina Clayton. Toronto: CNIB [Canadian National Institute for the Blind], 2002. 6 computer laser optical discs, 12 cm.; 2 audiocassettes, 4 track (10 hrs., 38 min.)

P778. *Hateship, Friendship, Courtship, Loveship, Marriage*. Read by Martha Harmon Pardee. Recorded and distributed by American Printing House for the Blind. [Washington, DC]: Library of Congress, NLS [National Library Service for the Blind and Physically Handicapped], 2002. 2 audiocassettes, 4 track.

P779. *Hateship, Friendship, Courtship, Loveship, Marriage*. AudioPlus Book. Princeton, NJ: Recording for the Blind and Dyslexic, 2002. 1 compact disc; 4 audiocassettes.

P780. *Hateship, Friendship, Courtship, Loveship, Marriage*. Read by Liza Ross. Rothley, Leicester, Eng.: W. F. Howes, 2002? 8 audiocassettes (10 hrs., 45 min.)

P781. *Hateship, Friendship, Courtship, Loveship, Marriage*. Read by Gina Clayton. Toronto: CNIB [Canadian National Institute for the Blind], 2003. 1 computer laser optical disc.

Translations

German

P782. *Himmel und Hölle* [Selections]. Read by Judith Hermann. [Zurich]: Kein & Aber Records; Frankfurt am Main: Vertrieb Buchhandel, 2005. 2 compact discs. (2 hrs., 9 min.) Contains stories "Was in Erinnerung bleibt" (What is Remembered), "Trost" (Comfort).

"The Jack Randa Hotel"

P783. "The Jack Randa Hotel." Read by Liza Ross. *Woman's Hour Short Stories. Vol. 5.* BBC Radio Collection. London: BBC, 1999. On cassette 1 of 2 audiocassettes.

Lives of Girls and Women: A Novel

P784. *Lives of Girls and Women*. Read by Susan Stevens. Washington, DC: Library of Congress, NLS [National Library Service] /BPH (New York: American Foundation for the Blind), n.d.
Reissued by CNIB, Toronto, 1975 in 7 audiocassettes, 2 track (10 hrs., 30 min.); 1980 in 2 audiocassettes, 4 track (9 hrs., 15 min.)

P785. *Lives of Girls and Women: A Novel*. [Peterborough, ON: Ontario Audio Library Service, 1982]. 1 audiotape, 4 track, master.

P786. *Lives of Girls and Women*. Read by Jeanne Hopson. Newport Beach, CA: Books on Tape, 1983. 7 audiocassettes, 2 track (10 hrs., 30 min.)

P787. *Lives of Girls and Women.* (Abridged). Read by Judy Mahbey. Ed. Ruth Fraser. Toronto: Key Porter Audio, copublished with Canadian Broadcasting Corporation, [1989?]. 2 audiocassettes (3 hrs., 6 min.)

P788. *Lives of Girls and Women.* Read by Laura Giannarelli. [Washington, DC]: Library of Congress, NLS [National Library Service], 1997. 2 audiocassettes, 4 track.

P789. *Lives of Girls and Women.* (Abridged). Read by Judy Mahbey. Prod. Lawrie Seligman. Between the Covers Classics Collection. Fredericton, NB: Goose Lane Editions, 1998, c1981. 3 audiocassettes (3 hrs., 10 min.)

P790. *Lives of Girls and Women.* Read by Ida Reichardt Osler. Winnipeg: Manitoba Education and Training, 1998. 11 audiocassettes, 2 track (10 hrs., 30 min.)

P791. *Lives of Girls and Women.* Read by Chris Grove. Vancouver: Crane Resource Centre, 1998. 7 audiocassettes, 2 track.

P792. *Lives of Girls and Women.* Read by Paula Parker. Chivers Sound Library. Hampton, NH: Chivers North America, 1999. 8 audiocassettes (12 hrs.)

P793. *Lives of Girls and Women.* (Abridged). Read by Judy Mahbey. Fredericton, NB: BTC Audiobooks, 2005. 3 compact discs (ca. 3 hrs.)

The Love of a Good Woman: Stories

P794. *The Love of a Good Woman: Stories.* Read by Paula Parker. Chivers Sound Library, CLS 205. Hampton, NH: Chivers North America, 1999. 8 audiocassettes (9 hrs., 53 min.)

P795. *The Love of a Good Woman: Stories.* Read by Mitzi Friedlander. Recorded and distributed by APH. [Washington, DC]: Library of Congress, National Library Service for the Blind and Physically Handicapped, 1999. 3 audiocassettes, 4 track.

P796. *The Love of a Good Woman: Stories.* Read by Sondra Bolton. Toronto: CNIB [Canadian National Institute for the Blind], 1999. 8 audiocassettes, 2 track; 2 audiocassettes, 4 track (11 hrs., 1 min.)

P797. *The Love of a Good Woman: Stories.* Read by Tory Ross. Vancouver: Crane Resource Centre, 1999. 8 audiocassettes, 2 track.

P798. *The Love of a Good Woman: Stories.* Princeton, NJ: Recording for the Blind and Dyslexic, 1999. 3 audiocassettes, 4 track.

P799. *The Love of a Good Woman: Stories.* Read by Sondra Bolton. Toronto: CNIB [Canadian National Institute for the Blind], 2002. 1 computer laser optical disc (16 hrs., 36 min.)

The Moons of Jupiter: Stories

P800.   *The Moons of Jupiter*. Read by Catherine Mead. Vancouver: Crane Library, 1982. 6 audiocassettes, 2 track.

P801.   *The Moons of Jupiter*. Read by Aileen Seaton. Toronto: CNIB [Canadian National Institute for the Blind], 1983. 7 audiocassettes, 2 track (10 hrs., 30 min.); 2 audiocassettes, 4 track (9 hrs., 40 min.)

P802.   *The Moons of Jupiter: Stories*. Read by Rita Knox. Recorded and distributed by AFB. [Washington, DC]: Library of Congress, NLS [National Library Service], 1983. 2 audiocassettes, 4 track.

P803.   *The Moons of Jupiter*. Read by Susan Mellor. Vancouver: Crane Resource Centre, 2002. 6 tape reels, 4 track, master; 6 audiocassettes, 2 track.

P804.   *The Moons of Jupiter*. Read by Aileen Seaton. Toronto: CNIB [Canadian National Institute for the Blind], 2004. 1 computer laser optical disc (9 hrs., 17 min.)

Translations

Swedish

P805.   *Jupiters Månar*. Produced for Minnesota Library for the Blind and Physically Handicapped, Braille and Sight Saving School. Recording agency Synskadades Riksförbund (De Blindas Förening), Sweden. 8 audiocassettes, 2 track.

Open Secrets: Stories

P806.   *Open Secrets: Stories*. (Selections). Read by Jackie Burroughs. Prod. Peter Sellers. Burlington, ON: Durkin Hayes, 1995. 4 audiocassettes (6 hrs.)
Contains stories "Carried Away," "A Real Life," "Open Secrets," "The Jack Randa Hotel," "Vandals."

P807.   *Open Secrets: Stories*. Read by Sandra Scott. Toronto: CNIB [Canadian National Institute for the Blind], 1995. 2 audiocassettes, 4 track.

P808.   *Open Secrets: Stories*. [Princeton, NJ]: Recording for the Blind and Dyslexic, 1995. 3 audiocassettes, 4 track.

P809.   *Open Secrets: Stories*. Read by Catherine Byers. Recorded and distributed by AFB. [Washington, DC]: Library of Congress, NLS [National Library Service], 1995. 2 audiocassettes, 4 track.

P810.   *Open Secrets: Stories*. Read by Pat Barlow. Vancouver: British Columbia Library Services Branch, Audiobook Program, 1996. 8 audiocassettes, 2 track (10 hrs., 5 min.)

P811. *Open Secrets: Stories*. Read by Joan Vieira and Catherine Mead. Vancouver: Crane Resource Centre, 2001. 9 audiocassettes, 2 track.

P812. *Open Secrets: Stories*. Read by Liza Ross. Rothley, Leicester, Eng.: W. F. Howes, 2003. 8 audiocassettes (11 hrs.)

P813. *Open Secrets*. Read by Sandra Scott. Toronto: CNIB [Canadian National Institute for the Blind], 2004. 1 computer laser optical disc. (8 hrs., 57 min.)

"An Ounce of Cure"

P814. "An Ounce of Cure." Read by Mary Louise Wilson. Recorded 16 April 1986 at Symphony Space, NYC. *Selected Shorts*. New York: n.p., 1986. 1 audiocassette.

The Progress of Love: Stories

P815. *The Progress of Love*. Read by Mauralea Austin. Toronto: CNIB [Canadian National Institute for the Blind], 1986. 9 audiocassettes, 2 track (13 hrs., 30 min.); 3 audiocassettes, 4 track (12 hrs., 35 min.)

P816. *The Progress of Love*. Read by Catherine Mead. Vancouver: Crane Library, 1986. 8 audiocassettes, 2 track.

P817. *The Progress of Love*. Read by Flo Gibson. Recorded by NLS, distributed by MTX. [Washington, DC]: Library of Congress, NLS [National Library Service], 1987. 2 audiocassettes, 4 track.

P818. *The Progress of Love*. (Selections). Read by Alice Munro. Audio Encore Recording. Toronto: McClelland and Stewart, 1990. 2 audiocassettes (ca. 3 hrs.)
Contains stories "The Progress of Love," "Miles City, Montana," "Circle of Prayer" (all unabridged).

P819. *The Progress of Love*. Read by Mauralea Austin. Toronto: CNIB [Canadian National Institute for the Blind], 2004. 1 computer laser optical disc. (12 hrs., 13 min.)

"The Progress of Love"

P820. *Alice Munro Reads "The Progress of Love."* AAPL 7051. Columbia, MO: American Audio Prose Library, 1987. 1 audiocassette (1 hr., 10 min.).
Cassette 2 of a 2-cassette recording: [Cassette 1] Alice Munro interview with Kay Bonetti.

"Providence"

P821. "Providence." *Canadian Short Stories*, pgm. 5-6. [Montreal?]: Radio Canada International, 197?. 1 LP, 33 1/3 rpm. (56 min.) Transcription.
LP also includes "God Has Manifested Himself Unto Us as Canadian Tire" by Hugh Hood.

Runaway: Stories

P822.   *Runaway*. Read by Kymberly Dakin. Auburn, CA: Audio Partners, 2004. 6 audiocassettes; 9 compact discs. (11 hrs., 3 min.)

P823.   *Runaway*. Read by Kymberly Dakin. Hampton, NH: BBC Audiobooks America, 2004. 7 audiocassettes. (11 hrs., 3 min.)

P824.   *Runaway*. Princeton, NJ: Recording for the Blind and Dyslexic, 2005. 1 compact disc.

Selected Stories

P825.   *Selected Stories*. Princeton, NJ: Recording for the Blind and Dyslexic, 1998. 7 audiocassettes, 4 track.

P826.   *Selected Stories*. Read by Mary Kane. Recorded and distributed by Potomac Talking Book Services, Bethesda, MD. [Washington, DC]: Library of Congress, NLS [National Library Service], 1999. 5 audiocassettes, 4 track.

Something I've Been Meaning to Tell You . . . : Thirteen Stories

P827.   *Something I've Been Meaning to Tell You*. Read by Catherine Crowell. Vancouver, Charles Crane Memorial Library, University of British Columbia, 1975. 5 audiocassettes (7 hrs., 30 min.)

P828.   *Something I've Been Meaning to Tell You*. Read by Aileen Seaton. Toronto: Canadian National Institute for the Blind, 1977. 6 audiocassettes, 2 track (9 hrs.); 2 audiocassettes, 4 track (8 hrs., 30 min.)

P829.   *Something I've Been Meaning to Tell You*. [Peterborough, ON: Ontario Audio Library Service, 1982]. 1 audiotape, 4 track, master.

P830.   *Something I've Been Meaning to Tell You*. Read by Jeanne Hopson. Special library ed. Newport Beach, CA: Books on Tape, 1984. 6 audiocassettes (8 hrs., 35 min.)

P831.   *Something I've Been Meaning to Tell You*. Read by Shirley Gent. [Toronto]: CNIB, [Canadian National Institute for the Blind], 1991. 6 audiocassettes, 2 track; 2 audiocassettes, 4 track (8 hrs., 35 min.)

P832.   *Something I've Been Meaning to Tell You*. Read by Shirley Gent. Toronto: CNIB [Canadian National Institute for the Blind], 2003. 1 computer laser optical disc. (8 hrs., 34 min.)

"Walker Brothers Cowboy"

P833.   "Walker Brothers Cowboy." Read by Buffy Davis. *Woman's Hour Short Stories. Vol. 4.* BBC Radio Collection. London: BBC, 1998. On cassette 1 of 2 audiocassettes.

Who Do You Think You Are?: Stories

P834.   *Who Do You Think You Are?* Read by Stephanie Taylor. Toronto: Canadian National Institute for the Blind, 197? and 1980. 5 audiocassettes, 2 track; 2 audiocassettes, 4 track (7 hrs., 30 min.)

P835.   *Who Do You Think You Are?* Read by Carol Andrews. Vancouver: Crane Resource Centre, 1998. 6 audiocassettes, 2 track.

P836.   *Who Do You Think You Are?* Read by Stephanie Taylor. Toronto: CNIB [Canadian National Institute for the Blind], 2003. 1 computer laser optical disc. (7 hrs., 30 min.)

P837.   *Who Do You Think You Are?* Vancouver: Crane Resource Centre, 2004. 1 compact disc, in MP3 audio format.

Translations

French

P838.   *Pour qui te prends-tu?* Read by René Chouteau. Trans. Colette Tonge. [Longueuil, PQ: Institut Nazareth et Louis-Braille, 1981]. 6 audiocassettes, 2 track.

Interviews

(In Chronological Order)

P839. Stainsby, Mari. "Alice Munro Talks with Mari Stainsby." *British Columbia Library Quarterly* 35.1 (July 1971): 27-31.

Munro tells Stainsby about her writing process, specifically how ideas form into stories. She talks about writing as a career and about the balancing of writing and raising children. In listing the writers of the American South she has read, Munro mentions Eudora Welty as being her favourite.

P840. Anderson, Allan. "Aspects of the Canadian Novel." Interview with Alice Munro and other Canadian authors. *Anthology*. Ed. Robert Weaver. Prod. Doug MacDonald. CBC Radio. 4 November-16 December 1972. (7 part series)
Pt. 1 (4 November 1972). Alice Munro, Robertson Davies, and Margaret Atwood. (4 min.); Pt. 6 (9 December 1972). Alice Munro. (2 min.); Pt. 7 (16 December 1972). Alice Munro, Robertson Davies, and Margaret Atwood. (1 min.)

Pt. 1—Davies, Atwood, and Munro answer the questions: What motivates the writer? How do you view your work and that of others? Why are you an artist? Pt. 6—Munro explains her writing process and says that she works by trial and error. She does not find writing the short story any more difficult than the novel. The merits of short stories are compared to those of the novel. Pt. 7—Writers, because of their low income, need help from the Canada Council to survive, says Munro. Then she and Sylvia Fraser discuss different aspects of writing, specifically technical composition and editing.

P841. Metcalf, John. "A Conversation with Alice Munro." *Journal of Canadian Fiction* 1.4 (Fall 1972): 54-62.

Metcalf's conversation with Munro brings out details about Munro's childhood and the start of her writing. Munro speaks also on a variety of topics: her method of writing, the importance of "emotional exactness" in her choice of words, regionalism, her opinions on other writers including short story writers, her choices in reading, magic realism in art, and autobiography in her work. Munro also responds to Metcalf's question about the order in which she wrote the stories in *Dance*. In the rest of the interview, she gives her thoughts on feminism, on the problems of women writers, and on women writing about men, and men writing about women. She discusses *Lives* as a novel, telling how it was written and explaining the structure. This is followed by her comments on the differences between writing a novel and short stories.

P842.   Gibson, Graeme. Interview with Alice Munro. *Anthology*. CBC Radio. 10 March 1973. (29 min.)

The interview begins with a general discussion about writing. What Munro likes about her writing is the humour, and what she dislikes is wordiness, slow approach, and failures. Surface details are very important. Munro says that she cannot get into people without describing all the things around them. The discussion moves to the novel *Lives*, and Munro explains how it was written, revised, and rearranged. She says that the only way she can work is on a single tension string, that is, on a segment or story. Using *Lives* as a point of reference, Munro then talks about the male-female relationship and the ambiguity of women's feelings toward men. She says that women are tougher than men. They are afraid of criticizing men for fear of crushing them and destroying their confidence. This fear, and the fundamental condescension of women toward men, however, is contrasted with their need for men in their lives. Preadolescent boys, on the other hand, hate girls, and this carries into adolescence and is based on a hatred and fear of sex. Munro also talks about autobiography in some of the stories in *Dance*, and mentions that "The Peace of Utrecht" is the most autobiographical.

P843.   Gibson, Graeme. "Alice Munro." *Eleven Canadian Novelists*. Toronto: Anansi, 1973. 241-264.
    Rpt. (excerpts) in *Personal Fictions: Stories by Munro, Wiebe, Thomas, and Blaise*. Sel. Michael Ondaatje. Toronto: Oxford University Press, 1977. 224-225.
    Rpt. (with 3 short omissions) in *Short Story Criticism: Excerpts from Criticism of the Works of Short Fiction Writers*. Ed. Sheila Fitzgerald. Vol. 3. Detroit: Gale Research, 1989. 322-328.
    Rpt. (excerpt) as "An Interview with Munro on Writing" in *The Bedford Introduction to Literature: Reading, Thinking, Writing*. [Ed.] Michael Meyer. Boston: Bedford/St. Martin's. 5th ed. 1999. 472-473. 6th ed. 2002. 472-473.

In this expanded version of the radio interview listed above, Munro talks also on other subjects. She expands on her vision and how she is very excited about the surface of life. She finds it very important to get the exact tone or texture of things. Her motivation to write might have something to do with the fight against death and getting control over experience. Munro describes her early life and the beginning of her writing career, noting the fact that she disguised her writing. She speaks also about being a Canadian writer, about the gothic nature of the Southwestern Ontario region, about having no sense of social role as a writer, the conflict between her writing and her expected role as a wife and mother, and her writing process. She says that a writer needs to have inner confidence and to be selfish. As a writer, Munro says she needs to use personal material. She describes her writing technique as traditional, although she admires the new techniques and superrealism in art, mentioning the work of Edward Hopper.

P844.   Frum, Barbara. "Great Dames: Interviews with Barbara Frum." *Maclean's* April 1973: 32, 38.

Munro tells Frum that when she was young, then later as a housewife, she kept her writing secret. She talks of traditional gender roles which prevent women from saying what they really think and feel. In the past, she tried to please people and deferred to men in arguments, but not anymore. Munro continues to discuss women's relationships with men and talks about the emotional energy women expend in trying to have long-term relationships. As she ages, Munro is afraid of no longer being sexually attractive. She confesses that looks matter more in middle age.

P845.   Gardiner, Jill Marjorie. "Text of an Interview with Alice Munro by Jill Gardiner, June 1 1973" in "The Early Short Stories of Alice Munro." M.A. thesis, University of New Brunswick, 1973. 169-182.

The interview begins with an informal discussion about Munro's uncollected stories. Munro comments that the setting of Huron County in Southwestern Ontario shapes the experiences she writes about. She describes the region as similar to that of the American South and as gothic in nature. She admits that in her early stories setting was more important than the characters. Atmosphere and the use of details are also discussed. Munro then comments on stylistic changes she made between the versions of the same story, "Good-by Myra" and "Day of the Butterfly." Writing, Munro believes, does not clarify the mysteries and difficult things in life; it only recognizes them. Following this, Munro draws the distinction between the autobiographical and the personal, and says that she considers her work to be personal or coming from the inside. Writing sometimes creates incidents that are more real than personal ones, she says, illustrating this with "Walker Brothers Cowboy" and "Images." In her remarks on "Thanks for the Ride," Munro gives the origin of the story and talks about Lois and other similar female characters who cannot get out of their communities. Munro expresses her feelings about the character of Miss Marsalles in "Dance of the Happy Shades."

P846.   Komisar, Elizabeth. Interview with Alice Munro. *CBC Monday Evening*. CBC-FM Radio. 18 February 1974. (47 min.)

Munro reads excerpts from each chapter in *Lives*, gives a brief summary of the chapter, and answers questions from Komisar. "The Flats Road" began chiefly with place, Munro says. The details evoke the feeling of place and time. In "Heirs of the Living Body," death is viewed by Del as something obscene. Komisar comments on the sense of distance in Del's reaction to her traumatic experience of death. Munro says that she is never conscious of how she is doing things and speculates that the distance may be due to the fact that the writing was autobiographical. Munro summarizes "Age of Faith" by saying that Ada Jordan is an agnostic, Del is trying to have faith, and she questions at the end of the chapter whether prayer will have any effect in saving the dog Major. "Changes and Ceremonies" began as a story about an operetta which Munro later introduced into *Lives*. It takes place in a stage of Del's life when boys have a hatred against girls. In writing the chapter "Lives of Girls and Women," Munro says that she was aware that Ada Jordan was an early feminist who was against prudery and felt suppressed not by men but by the situation of a whole society. Unlike Ada, Del wants the best of both worlds—sexual experience and personal freedom. Del's escape in "Baptizing" represents an escape from the whole community. In reference to "Epilogue: The Photographer," Munro talks about Del's wish to write about the town, the perfect gothic novel.

P847.   Boyle, Harry. Interview with Alice Munro. *Sunday Supplement*. CBC Radio. 18 August 1974. (19 min.)

Munro and Boyle discuss Huron County, where they both grew up, noting the aspects of the macabre, or "Canadian Gothic," in the life of rural Southwestern Ontario. Munro talks about *Something* and the stories "Material," "The Spanish Lady," and "The Ottawa Valley." Among the themes and ideas she presents are the relationships between men and women, the necessity of truth in writing, the use of real people, and the genesis of her stories. In addition, there is a reading by Aileen Seaton from "The Found Boat."

P848.   Martineau, Barbara. Unpublished interview. 16 February 1975, London, ON.
   Typescript copy located in the University of Calgary Library, Special Collections, Alice Munro Papers [series 37.20.20].

Munro begins by comparing the short story genre to that of the novel and says that she didn't set out to write a novel when she began *Lives*. She observes that her early stories had more conclusive endings than the later ones, and also talks about the autobiographical content in her stories. Munro continues on a number of other topics: not consciously writing as a Canadian, being influenced by certain American writers, writing about her writing in "Home," her excitement in seeing "the other side," her need for isolation and introspection, her reaction to publication and feedback from readers, and her thoughts on publicity and book promotions. In speaking of reader recognition, Munro notes that the reality experienced in popular reading is not similarly found in Canadian literature and history as taught in schools, and she questions whether education is effective in opening the self. Turning to personal subjects, Munro talks about the influence of her mother on herself as a mother, her views on feminism, her emotional dependence on men, sexual relationships and aging, women and childbirth, physical appearance, and playing the roles of mother and writer. She says that women are less boxed in by their identities than men. She looks at the conflict between the traditional roles of women and women as writers, and at the depiction of women in writing by men.

P849.   Murch, Kem. "Taped Interview with Alice Munro." *London Ontario Women's Centre Review* February 1975: [8-19].
   Rpt. revised as "Name: Alice Munro; Occupation: Writer." *Chatelaine* August 1975: 42-43, 69-72.

At the beginning of the interview, Munro refers to *Lives* in her discussion about the relationships between men and women. Munro says that women are forced to view their bodies through the eyes of men. In her portrayal of male characters, Munro says that rather than portraying them as real characters, she shows them as they appear through the eyes of the female characters. Briefly speaking about her relationship with her daughters and her mother, Munro says that "The Ottawa Valley" contains some of her feelings toward her mother. She speaks of her ability to recall visual detail as something "like having an ear for music."

P850.   Gane, Margaret Drury. "Do You Use Real People in Your Fiction?" *Saturday Night* November 1975: 41.

In answering the question posed by Gane, Munro says "Mostly I use composites." She admits that she sometimes uses real people and real incidents, but changes the characters and settings. She only uses real things out of faith and necessity.

P851.   Watson, Patrick. "Interview with Alice Munro." *Gzowski on FM*. CBC-FM Radio. 19 February 1976. (35 min.)
Rebroadcast *Gzowski on FM*. CBC-FM Radio. 1 March 1977.

Munro talks about how her writing is linked with memory. She tells what feelings and associations come to mind when she hears the words "resignation," "brutality," and "intimacy." Munro and Watson read selections from *Lives*, which Munro characterizes as being autobiographical in feel but not in incident. In speaking of the public life of writers, Munro says that writers are continually being asked to give pronouncements on things. She credits Robert Weaver as being enormously helpful to her throughout her career.

P852.   Harron, Don. Interview with Alice Munro. *Don Harron's Morningside*. CBC Radio. 5 January 1978. (24 min., 20 sec.)

The interview begins with Munro telling Harron about her early career and the role Robert Weaver played in getting her started. In answering a question about style, Munro says that she is not sure what it is, but that she aims for an effect. Her ideal is to make something so clear that words don't come between the story and the reader. She says that she leaves in only what is essential. The aim in her writing is to make a reality more real than reality. The story "Boys and Girls" elicits the comment that girls have greater freedom of speech than boys because they have no power. In terms of her preferences in writing, Munro says she will continue writing short stories, but that she has also written a novel and two scripts for television ("How I Met My Husband" and *1847: The Irish* for the Newcomers Series). The latter includes the type of tough-minded women she wanted to portray in *Lives*. The interview continues with Munro's thoughts on other topics: the way men write about women, growing up in a culture where you were pressed to achieve but had to pretend that you were not trying, and the roles of men and women in rural and urban settings.

P853.   Harron, Don. Interview with Alice Munro. *Don Harron's Morningside*. CBC Radio. 13 November 1978. (20 min.)
Rebroadcast *Morningside in the Summer*. 3 July 1979.

The interview opens with a question from Harron about the harsh settings found in *Who*. Munro explains that this came from material in her life which she had never used before. She then says that she writes short stories rather than novels because they are more in keeping with her vision of life as progressing in "little jumps" rather than in an orderly way. Munro describes Rose's reaction to "something unthinkable" in "Wild Swans" as one not of passivity but of curiosity. In writing the book, Munro says that she wanted to show the division between social classes in Canada. She feels that women writers should get away from a simplified view when writing about women who leave their husbands in order to find themselves.

P854.   Campbell, Terry. Interview with Alice Munro. *Stereo Morning*. CBC-FM Radio. 15 November 1978. (7 min., 35 sec.)
Rebroadcast *Stereo Morning*. 5 April 1979.

Much of the interview is taken up with a discussion of *Who*. Munro first talks about the writing of the book, saying that the first story she wrote was "Privilege" because she wanted to portray the first school she attended, including its brutal environment. She also wanted to write about the delicate feeling of a girl's crush on an older girl. Munro calls "The Beggar

Maid" a pivotal story. She says that at first the character Rose was not clear to her, and that she skipped about with stories like "Mischief" and was slow to see what she was doing. The character of Rose had a strong hold on her, coming as she did from the same small town environment and sharing the same personal feelings about what it was to be an artist. Despite her use of real places, Munro says that the book is not entirely autobiographical. Moving on to the genre of the short story, Munro remarks that in the beginning she wrote stories for practical reasons, but now writes them because the episodic nature of stories is how she sees things. While it is not in her nature to be solitary, Munro needs privacy to preserve herself and lives in a small town for that reason. In response to the banning of her books in Huron County, Munro muses that local writers are not liked in small towns until much later.

P855.   Davidson, Joyce. Interview with Alice Munro. *Authors*. CBC TV. 8 January 1979. (30 min.)

Munro tells Davidson that *Who* is "less autobiographical in incident as in feeling." She says that the characters were created from many real experiences and that the school in "Privilege" is completely true to fact. Munro describes herself in childhood as being easily hurt and eager to please. She says that her mother, who was unconventional and ambitious, is not the model for the mother in *Lives* or *Who*, but that she may be in some stories. Munro feels that older readers will identify with life in the Depression found in the book. The conversation turns to fathers, Munro's own father and Rose's father depicted in "Royal Beatings." She sees men of this era as not uncaring but uninvolved in the upbringing of daughters. Extremes of behaviour occurred, as in the beating scene, but she doesn't condemn men like these. Rose uses men who are uncaring people like herself. On the subject of Munro's marriages, she says that no marriage is entirely successful or unsuccessful, and that getting married gave her the chance to write. Shame, stoicism, and the Protestant ethic are deeply ingrained in her. Writing helps her to explore difficult subjects and to tell the truth. Munro admits to being very curious about people and what happens to them. She says that privacy is necessary for her to write.

P856.   Brown, Harry. Interview with Alice Munro. *Take 30*. CBC Radio. 19 January 1979. (6 min., 35 sec.)

According to Munro, the removal of *Lives* from high school reading lists in Huron County was caused by pressure groups with Christian fundamentalist beliefs. She talks generally about the reasons for banning books and advocates that people can fight against censorship by organizing groups against it. Teachers use books that they are excited about in their teaching. They stimulate students' imaginations through books. Munro says that in her case reading broadened the world and gave an extra dimension to her life. In answer to the question of whether *Who* is autobiographical, she states that the heroine and other characters are not based on real people, but that the school is real.

P857.   Twigg, Alan. "Writer Alice Munro: 'If a Woman Comes on Shouting She Won't Be Forgiven.'" *Vancouver Free Press* 15-21 June 1979: 15, 18.
Same interview, somewhat expanded, pub. as "What Is: Alice Munro." in *For Openers: Conversations with 24 Canadian Writers*. Alan Twigg. Madiera [sic] Park, BC: Harbour, 1981. 13-20.

Rpt. in *Strong Voices: Conversations with Fifty Canadian Authors*. Alan Twigg. Madeira Park, BC: Harbour, 1988. 215-219.

In Huron County, Christian fundamentalism and a total lack of appreciation of literature were responsible for the deletion of *Lives* from the high school reading list, according to Munro. She says that literature should not be used to teach morals. Going on to talk about her writing, Munro says that the writer writes to get "on top of experience" and to try to get control over it. She talks on a number of topics: writing with a design in mind, the short story as her preferred form, the magazine market, the triggering experience for stories, the need to get at the emotional core, and the use of personal material in her writing. While always wanting to write, Munro explains that what prompted her to write in the beginning were her feelings of isolation and the sense of power writing offered her. She describes her early life in Wingham, where her family lived outside the social structure. She admits that love and emotions have an effect in writing. Commenting on Rose in *Who*, Munro says that by the end of the book she gets a knowledge of herself. In her opinion, male writers are freer than females because if a woman writer, no matter what her achievements or abilities, behaves badly or outrageously, men will disapprove of her because she lacks feminine qualities. Aging for Munro brings freedom, happiness, and clearer perspective.

P858. Robertson, Tony. Interview with Alice Munro and Marion Engel. *Audience*. CBC-FM Radio. 15 September 1979. (4 min., 17 sec.; 12 min., 5 sec.)

In responding to the label of regional writer, Munro says that at an early age the world caught hold of her and made her want to write, not only about all the surface details but everything that was "deep down." She discusses a break in her writing after *Something*, the change in her personal life, and her return to Huron County. In *Who*, there is a maturity of vision. Munro says that male writers, like Cheever, do not portray women with truth or realistically, but as they think they ought to be. Responding to a question on gender differences, Munro says that women sometimes see more clearly than men and that they are freer to be themselves, whereas men are forced into professional or work roles. Aging and the burden of years brings greater uncertainty of who you are, and in the end you can fail but there is still a glimpse of something that is positive. Happiness, she says, is possible even if you are alone. Men do not write about old age and death, but women do because they are personally involved with these things.

P859. Gerson, Carole. "Who Do You Think You Are?: Review-Interview with Alice Munro." *Room of One's Own* 4.4 (1979): 2-7.

Rpt. (excerpt) in *Short Story Criticism: Excerpts from Criticism of the Works of Short Fiction Writers*. Ed. Sheila Fitzgerald. Vol. 3. Detroit: Gale Research, 1989. 333-335.

Within the context of the interview, Gerson includes her own commentary on *Who*. At the beginning of the interview, Munro tells Gerson about the last-minute changes to the Canadian and American editions of the book. She explains the distinction in form between *Lives* and *Who*, saying that she views *Lives* as an episodic novel and *Who* as linked stories. She also details the differences in treatment of minor characters and points out the gaps in *Who*. Munro goes on to talk about Rose and her situation as a middle-aged woman who decides to keep herself whole instead of being involved in erotic love. Some of the early stories of Rose, notably "Privilege," are autobiographical. The inclusion of retrospectives in stories, such as "Half a Grapefruit," makes it possible to show the changes to places and characters which are brought about by time. Munro describes Flo as a character who is very strong, complex, and direct.

P860.   Kroll, Jeri. "Interview with Alice Munro." *LiNQ: Literature in North Queensland* 8.1 (1980): 47-55.

Following a preliminary section of background information on Munro's career and writing, the interview begins with Munro telling Kroll that the purpose of her writing and revision is to get at the truth of something important. She says that the short story form is more natural to her because it reflects the way she looks at life, that is, in segments. Commenting on some of her works, Munro says that in *Something* the characters have epiphanies, but need the grace to act. She says that *Lives* was written to show the development of a young girl and an artist. "The Ottawa Valley" is a story containing her view of the artist's function, why she writes, the material, and the result. Writing, Munro says, always falls short because the final truth cannot be reached. She discusses the teaching of writing and advises new writers to write what is important to them and to discover writers with whom they can identify. In her case, they were writers from the American South. Finally, Munro talks about writing about places, from a distance.

P861.   Rasporich, Beverly J. [Selected comments from personal interviews conducted in February 1981, June 1982, and from private correspondence with Alice Munro]. *Dance of the Sexes: Art and Gender in the Fiction of Alice Munro*. Edmonton: University of Alberta Press, 1990. 14-31.

Munro answers questions on a variety of subjects. Beginning with personal topics, she says that the grandmother in "Winter Wind" is based on her own grandmother. She then talks about her first husband's reaction to her success, her life as a housewife and writer, her relationship with men, aging, and the capacity for happiness. Female writers, Munro says, experience a conflict in roles between being females and being writers. But she attributes the restraint in *Dance* to her immaturity as a writer rather than to fear of showing female passion. The origin of "Bardon Bus" is given. Speaking about characters in her work, Munro says that they are either aspects of herself or composites of other people. "The Stone in the Field" is based on factual material, whereas Ada Jordan in *Lives* is one of the few characters she has created. The topic of women and power leads Munro to talk about *Lives* and Del's intellectual power. The characters of Rose and Flo in *Who* are also discussed. Narrative jumps in her work, says Munro, reflect the intersections and lack of continuity in real life. She also talks of her attraction to the landscape and about the aging of women.

P862.   Struthers, J. R. (Tim). Interview with Alice Munro. London, ON. 27 April 1981.
Published as "The Real Material: An Interview with Alice Munro." *Probable Fictions: Alice Munro's Narrative Acts*. Ed. Louis K. MacKendrick. Downsview, ON: ECW Press, 1983. 5-36.
Rpt. [excerpts] in Struthers, J. R. (Tim). "Alice Munro: Influences and Attitudes." *London Magazine* [London, ON] September 1983: 14, 36-39.

The interview begins with the subject of fictionalizing in writing and in photography, particularly in the photography of Diane Arbus and Walker Evans. Munro says that she greatly admires James Agee's technique in *A Death in the Family*. She then talks about her early reading and writing, revision, and writing stories for *The New Yorker*. In naming her favourite stories and short story writers, Munro says that she was particularly affected by Eudora Welty's *The Golden Apples*. On the topic of writing, Munro feels that changing techniques in writing give the writer fresh perception. She says she cannot write novels because they lack the tension of short stories. She elaborates on her writing and rewriting of *Lives*, and her treatment of the chapters as stories. Responding to a question about other authors she has read and how she responded to them as a reader, Munro says that *Emily of New Moon* by L. M. Montgomery made the greatest impression in her childhood. Turning to her books *Dance*, *Something*, *Who* and *Lives*, Munro tells Struthers the order in which the stories were written and how the stories were selected, ordered, and juxtaposed in each book. Commenting on many of the stories, Munro tells which are significant and what she likes and dislikes about them. She talks about revision, specifically the revisions made to *Who*. Her attitudes to rural Ontario and the use of local places in her fiction are also discussed.

P863.   Wright, Jim. Interview with Alice Munro. *Arts National*. Host Karen Wells. CBC-FM Radio. 25 November 1981. (21 min.; 12 min.)

The program begins with a 21 minute segment of Munro reading from "The Moons of Jupiter" at the International Festival of Authors in Toronto. Munro then says she would prefer not to give public readings, but that they are necessary to help publishers to promote books and it is exciting for readers to meet living writers. Speaking about the short story genre, Munro says that she started writing short stories because they were all she had time for as a mother. Although she began writing *Lives* as a novel, she rearranged it into discrete segments that were more like short stories. This is how she sees things in life. When Wright asks her "What makes a good short story?" Munro responds by saying that she never thinks about questions like this and that every story is a different problem, starting with an anecdote or picture. While Munro has taught writing, she says she would prefer to be an editor, helping students to see their own stories. Writers by nature need to be good observers and listeners. She says she likes dialogue and can hear in her head her characters speaking.

P864.   Hancock, Geoff. "Canadian Writers in China." *Anthology*. Host Harry Mannis. CBC Radio. 20 February 1982. (Munro segments total 7 min.)
   Printed [excerpts] as "Through the Jade Curtain." in *Chinada: Memoirs of the Gang of Seven*. Garry Geddes, et al. Dunvegan, ON: Quadrant, 1982. 51-55.

Munro was one of the Canadian writers invited as guests to China by the Chinese Writers' Association. She speaks about her impressions of the physical and rural landscapes of China, contrasting the rural landscape with that of Ontario. Commenting on the disturbing amount of self-censorship among writers in China, Munro says that it must be very disheartening to write in a climate where writers cannot express their own viewpoint. She expresses her awe for the courage of the Chinese writer, Ding Ling, whose book, *Miss Sophie's Diary and Other Stories*, got her into trouble with the authorities.

P865.   Hancock, Geoff. "An Interview with Alice Munro." [Interview conducted September 15, 1982] *Canadian Fiction Magazine* 43 (1982): 74-114.
   Rpt. in *Canadian Writers at Work: Interviews with Geoff Hancock*. Toronto: Oxford University Press, 1987. 187-224.
   Rpt. (excerpts) in *The Writer's Path: An Introduction to Short Fiction*. Ed. Constance

Rooke and Leon Rooke. Scarborough, ON: ITP Nelson, 1998. 964-969.

Munro begins with many comments related to her writing: her excitement in writing and reading stories, never being satisfied with her work, revision, the triggering moment in the writing process, atmosphere in the early stories, the influence of the southern writers, surprise endings, and angle of vision. In speaking of her aesthetic vision, Munro says there has to be a "feeling" and the writer has to be "in" the story. She cites Eudora Welty's "The Worn Path" as a perfect story. There is an abdication of the writer in the process of writing, so that only the story remains. Elsewhere in the interview, Munro says that there is a necessary detachment of the writer from the physical world, whether it is beautiful or ugly. Munro's view of life is reflected in her writing. She says that she sees people's lives as snapshots, where gaps in time show changes in characters and their situations. Pivotal moments occur. In explaining her vision of the world, Munro says that she is very interested in the surface of things, and that objects have always had an importance for her and that they have a meaning beyond themselves. Munro describes the writing process as seeing the picture and fitting in the pieces. She explains how she starts a story from an idea or scene and discovers the story as she goes along. Using "Bardon Bus" as an example, Munro describes how she produces a "climate." She does not consciously use symbols or metaphors. Her narrative technique varies with the materials and the feeling she wants to convey in the story. *Who* is mentioned in different contexts: revisions, titles, and autobiography. Munro believes that reading is important in learning to write. She names the authors she reads. The complicated relationship of Munro with her home territory in Huron County comes out in her comments on its rural and gothic nature, its Scots-Irish culture and Protestant ethic. She feels that her poor background was an advantage to her writing. Major characters, Munro says, develop themselves, but she has to know them first. Minor characters such as those in "Images" are necessary. She comments on Ada Jordan in *Lives* and the characters in "Dulse." Finally, gender and class issues are brought up.

P866. French, William. "The Untold Story of Canadians' Writing Abroad." [Interview with Alice Munro and other writers] *Anthology*. Host Harry Mannis. CBC Radio. 25 September 1982. (Munro segments total 10 min.)

French asks a number of Canadian writers and critics questions about the international acceptance of Canada's best writers. Munro's comments total some 10 minutes. She mentions a request from a person in Inner Mongolia to translate "The Turkey Season" and speculates that it might have been chosen because it is a story about workers. In Norway, *The Beggar Maid* was very well received and promoted across the country. While she cannot attest to the quality of the translation, Munro says that the book jacket was tastefully done. She comments that writers cannot live off their income in one country alone, and that translations serve to increase their income.

P867. French, William. Interview with Alice Munro. *Anthology*. CBC Radio. 16 October 1982. (14 min., 5 sec.)

Munro tells French that "The Turkey Season" started with a photograph. Why the story was chosen to be translated in Inner Mongolia she doesn't understand, but what interests her is what the Chinese think about the story which is so foreign to their culture. Munro says that she wanted to portray the sexual byplay and conversations that make a workplace bearable, even enjoyable. The intelligent narrator, coming from a conservative environment, is proving herself by learning a manual skill. Munro then comments on the difference in the importance placed on education for males and females. In *Moons*, Munro says she is not writing about women, but about people. They are women who are not necessarily being exploited by men, but women who want to make connections. Reviewers tend to stereotype female characters who are alone or divorced as lonely, unlike male characters. Munro expresses her feelings about publicity and fame. She describes her method of reading stories, saying that she starts somewhere in the middle. On the other hand, when writing stories, she starts at the beginning. For her, the plot is secondary, and her aim is to recreate intense moments of experience.

P868.   Kelman, Suanne. Interview with Alice Munro. *Sunday Morning*. CBC Radio. 17 October 1982. (13 min., 30 sec.)

For Munro, home is a private place where she does not allow interviews. She describes her writing routine and process, saying that much of her time involves sitting and thinking, and that social intrusions destroy the possibility of work for the day. Munro says that she needs reality as a basis for her fiction, but that her plots are not based on real things. The question of the feminist perspective in her work is raised by Kelman, followed by the reading of a brief passage from "Lives of Girls and Women." Munro explains the passage, saying that it is concerned with women's preoccupation with their personal appearance and that it was based on a magazine article she had read and been horrified by as an adolescent. For her, reading a story is like visiting a house. Inhabiting a story gives her a "feeling of delight." Munro goes on to say that she worries about negative reviews after a book comes out and that she feels nervous and exposed at public readings. During the interview, short excerpts are played of Clare Coulter reading from *Lives* and *Moons*.

P869.   Gzowski, Peter. Interview with Alice Munro. Part 1. *Morningside*. CBC Radio. 18 October 1982. (17 min., 30 sec.)
Rebroadcast *The Best of Morningside*. 18 July 1983.
Printed (edited) as "Conversations with Writers I: Alice Munro" in *The Morningside Years*. Peter Gzowski. Toronto: McClelland and Stewart, c1997. 2-6.

In this first of five consecutive interviews about *Moons*, Munro tells Gzowski that the book is a collection of individual stories, separately written. She then describes the way she reads stories and finds herself in a certain environment, in a texture of a created world. This interests her more than what is happening. "The Chaddeleys and Flemings" are the two sides of the narrator's family. In "The Stone in the Field," Munro comments on Poppy Cullender as an outsider who typifies certain characters in small towns of the period. By carving out their identities as outsiders or freaks, they can enjoy the freedom of playing the part. In answer to Gzowski's question of whether she writes from any sense of "outsiderness," Munro tells him that she writes only from a remembrance of this feeling as a child. Like most writers, she says, she had a sense of being different, of being an observer, but not of being a recorder. She had an overwhelming sense of place. Reading excited her, and made her want to write and be part of the magic by writing stories.

P870.   Gzowski, Peter. Interview with Alice Munro. Part 2. *Morningside*. CBC Radio. 19 October 1982. (8 min., 40 sec.)
Rebroadcast *The Best of Morningside*. 19 July 1983.
Printed (edited) as "Conversations with Writers I: Alice Munro" in *The Morningside*

Years. Peter Gzowski. Toronto: McClelland and Stewart, c1997. 6-9.

After reading a short excerpt from "The Stone in the Field," Munro says that the narrator's father's family lives on a farm where their life is isolated and comprised of rituals. While to outsiders, the family might seem to be withdrawn and even total failures, their life is not grim to them. Rather, there is a pattern to their lives that gives them satisfaction. Munro says she remembers people like this, and she knows people who get satisfaction in hard work. The story started with a picture of the women. Munro says she wanted to get into the quality of their lives and find out why they made choices not to do certain things, such as to get hydro. She mentions the Scottish-Irish Protestant attitude.

P871.   Gzowski, Peter. Interview with Alice Munro. Part 3. *Morningside*. CBC Radio. 20 October 1982. (7 min., 48 sec.)
Rebroadcast *The Best of Morningside*. 20 July 1983.
Printed (edited) as "Conversations with Writers I: Alice Munro" in *The Morningside Years*. Peter Gzowski. Toronto: McClelland and Stewart, c1997. 9-11.

Munro reads an excerpt from "Bardon Bus." She summarizes the themes of erotic obsession and unconsummated love. Using the story as her frame of reference, Munro then describes how she wants to get a feeling out of a story. In "Bardon Bus," she explains the atmosphere of desperation, hysteria, and eroticism after the end of a love affair. The puritanical exterior of someone's life, she says, can hide inner obsessions. The character is living a modern woman's life of free choice in which she has an intense response to an experience, but at the same time she is living in a society where things are taken more lightly.

P872.   Gzowski, Peter. Interview with Alice Munro. Part 4. *Morningside*. CBC Radio. 21 October 1982. (11 min.)
Rebroadcast *The Best of Morningside*. 21 July 1983.
Printed (edited) as "Conversations with Writers I: Alice Munro" in *The Morningside Years*. Peter Gzowski. Toronto: McClelland and Stewart, c1997. 11-14.

Munro begins with a short reading from "Mrs. Cross and Mrs. Kidd." She says that the story is about love. Contrary to their expectations, people in nursing homes continue to live social lives and form attachments. Munro doesn't find it difficult to imagine herself getting old, looking back to the person she was in childhood. "We stay pretty much the way we are," she says. Old people are quick to pick up on other people's attitudes toward them. Their sense of irony or humour is not gone. Their jokes contain black humour and humour about the grotesque that relates to their situations. Munro says that, in the course of visiting her mother-in-law in a nursing home, she formed friendships with people there, and some of the details of the home were included in stories in *Moons*.

P873.   Gzowski, Peter. Interview with Alice Munro. Part 5. *Morningside*. CBC Radio. 22 October 1982. (14 min., 22 sec.)
Rebroadcast *The Best of Morningside*. 22 July 1983.
Printed (edited) as "Conversations with Writers I: Alice Munro" in *The Morningside Years*. Peter Gzowski. Toronto: McClelland and Stewart, c1997. 14-18.

Munro reads a short excerpt from "The Moons of Jupiter," then comments on the passage, saying that the daughter is disturbed by her dying father's irrational hope of living. When Gzowski asks "Are you afraid of dying?" Munro answers yes, but that she is not preoccupied with death as she was when she was young. The meaning of life, too, is not a burning question for older people, as it is for the young. Turning back to the story, Munro explains that it is about the narrator's feelings toward death and also her feelings toward her daughters and her father. "Could you have written this story at twenty-two?" Gzowski asks. Munro answers no, just as twenty years from now she will be thinking about things differently. Once a story is written, she says, you push it away from you. Speaking on the effects of aging on her writing, Munro says that things come harder and there is a thinning out of energy and motivation. She worries about the story and about getting at what she wants to say.

P874. Scobie, Stephen. "A Visit with Alice Munro." *Monday Magazine* [Victoria, BC] 19-25 November 1982: 12-13.

Scobie interviews Munro while she is on a promotional tour in Victoria, BC for *Moons*. Munro admits to having conflicting feelings about promotional tours, but knows they are necessary for her survival as a writer and for the publisher. She says that she can write on tours and almost anywhere, except in a study. She mentions that another Christopher Pratt painting on the cover of *Moons* would have better reflected her writing. She then comments on several stories in the collection: "Bardon Bus," "Accident," and "The Turkey Season." For the last story, Munro tells how it originated and mentions her interest in describing work processes. She lists her story preferences in the book. Several other topics are covered: the differences between the genders in friendships and conversations, Canadian writers she admires, and the reason why she cannot write novels.

P875. Watson, Patrick. "A Portrait of Morley Callaghan." *Anthology*. CBC Radio. 19 February 1983. (Munro segment 3 min., 35 sec.)

"Patrick Watson talks to Morley Callaghan, his friends, family, and critics." Munro comments on Morley Callaghan's writing, saying that his stories made a great impression on her. She describes them as powerful, simple, and truly felt. They have a sense of place, Toronto in the late 1930s and early 1940s, that is mysterious. There is a feel of a whole story beyond the story. Munro ends by relating a chance encounter with Callaghan in a subway in Toronto.

P876. Sand, Cy-Thea. "Alice Munro Talks about Her Work, Her Life." *Kinesis* [Australia] (December 1982-January 1983): 20-21.

Munro responds to Sand's question about class by saying that she doesn't have a strong sense of class in Canada, but admits that she comes from a poor background. She describes how she felt about this later in life. The anti-artistic, anti-intellectual strain in the middle class is mentioned. Munro then shares her thoughts on feminism, the balance in her life between work as a writer and a housewife, and having confidence as a writer. The discussion turns to social attitudes toward the roles of women. Munro describes the gender roles in her parents' and grandparents' time, when both genders did equally valued work on farms. She says that she has never been hindered by men or felt discrimination as a female writer in Canada. "Dulse" is mentioned in her remarks on lesbian relationships.

P877. "30th Anniversary Special." *Anthology*. Prod. Eithne Black. Host Bronwyn Drainie. CBC Radio. 20 October 1984. (Munro segment 12 min.)

This 12 minute segment contains reminiscences of Robert Weaver, Morley Callaghan, and Alice Munro on the 30th anniversary of the CBC program *Anthology* originated by Robert

Weaver. Munro relates her first meeting with Robert Weaver at her home in Vancouver. She talks also about her early years as a writer, beginning with her secret writing in school. She says that early on she was impressed with certain writers like Chekhov and the writers of the American South, whose writing she could personally identify with. This showed her the possibility of using her own material in a similar way. The fact that she wrote in isolation from the literary world saved her from discouragement, since she was unaware of how difficult it was for a Canadian, a woman, and a short story writer to be published during the 1950s. Munro mentions Sandra Birdsell as a current writer who interests her.

P878.   *Alice Munro: Forgiveness in Families.* (Dramatized excerpts and interview with Alice Munro). Canadian Literature (Authors). Prod. TVOntario for the Council of Ministers of Education, Canada, 1984. Dist. Image Media Services, Richmond, BC.; Access Network, Calgary, AB. Videocassette, VHS, ½ in. (15 min.)
Videocassette also includes Canadian authors Michel Tremblay, Janis Rapoport, and Al Purdy.

In a 15 minute segment, including dramatized excerpts of the story, Munro talks about her beginnings as a writer, the writing process, and her preference for the short story genre. She also discusses "Forgiveness in Families."

P879.   Horwood, Harold. "Interview with Alice Munro." *The Art of Alice Munro: Saying the Unsayable, Papers from the Waterloo Conference.* Ed. Judith Miller. Waterloo, ON: University of Waterloo Press, 1984. 123-135.
Rpt. in *Major Writers of Short Fiction: Stories and Commentaries.* [Ed.] Ann Charters. Boston: Bedford Books of St. Martin's Press, 1993. 1026-1034.

Munro talks about her writing in youth and how reading books inspired her to write. She names *Wuthering Heights* and *Emily of New Moon* as influences. In the context of gender roles and fiction writing, Munro says that writing fiction is a questionable profession, especially for women. She describes her early writing and publication in Canadian magazines. When *Dance* was published, sales were low because Ryerson did not promote the book well. Also, at that time, there was no market for work by women writers or for short stories. The important role of editors, especially Douglas Gibson at Macmillan, is mentioned. Munro says her writing process is unanalytical in the sense that she does not plan things like symbolism. "Getting" the story is important. A "writing room" is the only place in which Munro cannot write. Although she considers herself a feminist in the political sense, Munro keeps political causes separate from her writing. She comments on the removal of *Lives* from the school reading lists in Huron County and her personal affinity to Ontario and the landscape of her home area.

P880.   Slopen, Beverly [Beverley]. "PW Interviews Alice Munro." *Publishers Weekly* 230.8 (22 August 1986): 76-77.
Rpt. as "Alice Munro." in *Writing for Your Life.* Ed. Sybil Steinberg. Wainscott, NY: Pushcart, dist. W. W. Norton, 1992. 370-374.

This edited version of an interview with Munro is interspersed with quotations. Munro talks about the difference between writing stories and novels, and says that stories give intense but not connected moments of life. Munro talks about her life, career, and her thoughts on privacy and interviews. In explaining the writing process, she says that what happens isn't important, but that "getting into" a story is.

P881.   Gzowski, Peter. Interview with Alice Munro. Part 1. *Morningside*. Hour Two. CBC Radio. 22 September 1986. (19 min.)

This is the first in a 5 part consecutive series of interviews on *The Progress of Love*. In answer to Gzowski's question "How does a story come about?" Munro says that she starts with a central idea or nucleus of a story, then "lets her mind drift" so it is loose enough to know what to do with it. Her ideas for stories originate from different places—relationships, people, anecdotes. The better stories start with a very strong picture, colour, smell, or dialogue. Munro says that the time-shifts and doubling back in time in her writing come from a process similar to telling stories to oneself. A trip through small-town America brought Munro and her husband to a tent revival meeting in Kentucky. Munro describes her awareness at this meeting of herself as an observer. She says that she does not like the idea of herself as a cold observer. At the beginning of a writing career, she says, there is a pressure of reality, getting out all the things you have observed. But later, you become conscious of your voyeurism and have a kind of guilt. Watching and expressing don't mean as much as they once did.

P882.   Gzowski, Peter. Interview with Alice Munro. Part 2. *Morningside*. Hour Two. CBC Radio. 23 September 1986. (17 min.)
Rebroadcast 2 June 1987.

The interview relates mainly to the theme of "Lichen." Munro first explains the choice of the title of the collection and the significance of the story title to the story. Symbolism, such as the lichen in the story, is something Munro does not purposely write into a story. Munro stresses the importance of knowing and understanding the characters she writes about, and of being nonjudgmental. When Gzowski asks how she can write from the perspective of a man so well, Munro answers that feelings are not necessarily gendered. She describes the situation of the middle-aged man, David, who is foolishly in love with a younger woman. The situation of his middle-aged former wife is compared to his. These two characters, Munro explains, illustrate the different options men and women still have as they grow into middle age and try to cope with their problems. Munro reads a brief excerpt from the story.

P883.   Gzowski, Peter. Interview with Alice Munro. Part 3. *Morningside*. Hour Two. CBC Radio. 24 September 1986.

Munro talks about pivotal moments in life when fate hangs in the balance, and if it tips one way, one's life changes irrevocably. (Based on an abstract)

P884.   Gzowski, Peter. Interview with Alice Munro. Part 4. *Morningside*. Hour Two. CBC Radio. 25 September 1986. (13 min.)

The focus of the interview is the story "The Moon in the Orange Street Skating Rink." After preliminary remarks about the title and story, Munro reads an excerpt from it. Callie, the female character, is the centre of the story. What interests Munro about this character is her impenetrability and the mystery associated with her story. The story is focussed through a male character, Sam, who attempts to understand the mystery. The writer does not have to know the mystery, Munro says, but only has to see it through Sam's eyes. She tells Gzowski that she knows people like Callie who are fabulists and stick to their stories whether they are true or not.

P885.   Gzowski, Peter. Interview with Alice Munro. Part 5. *Morningside*. Hour Two. CBC Radio. 26 September 1986. (16 min.)

Love is the theme of *Progress*, and Munro talks about the nature of love in modern times. She says that the situations of love have changed and, since religion is gone, people give their lives meaning through relationships with people. "Is love a legitimate hope for ourselves?" Gzowski asks. Sometimes it will work, Munro answers, but love is not capable of fulfilling as much as we expect it to. Munro then sets up the story "A Queer Streak" and reads a short excerpt from it. She comments on the female character who marries for romantic love, but is disappointed in the marriage and chooses to be a "saint" to restore her self-respect. Munro says that she is sympathetic to the critical moment of revelation. People of Violet's generation are from a different civilization and try to fit events into a scheme of beliefs. For Munro, characters are real but not simple; there is more to them than she knows. "Do you like them?" Gzowski asks. She says she does, even David in "Lichen."

P886.   Connolly, Kevin, Douglas Freake, and Jason Sherman. "Interview: Alice Munro." *What* 6 (September-October 1986): 8-10.

Munro says that in her early stories detail and texture were important, but that later she became more interested in people and story. The story must be a combination of both idea and scene. Writing sympathetically about real life is important, even if it is not pretty. She mentions "The Peace of Utrecht" as being a pivotal story in her writing, saying that it gave her some idea of what writing could do. Munro then considers the morality of using this type of personal and autobiographical material. She says that faith in the importance of art is lost in middle age, but that reading and writing make her life bearable. Referring to "The Progress of Love," Munro considers social change and changes in values. She has become more of a social writer in her approach to Huron County and middle-aged women. Expressing her distrust of writing, Munro says that she now shies away from tricks in technique used in stories such as "Home" and "Thanks for the Ride." She explains the change in her writing as a tightening up of the structure to get at the story. Munro goes on to talk about the writing of "White Dump," the characters, and the differences in the portrayal of characters in short stories and novels. She proceeds on a number of subjects: first- and third-person narrators, her identity as a writer, book promotions, the need of writers for reassurance, the relationship between memory and reality, people's lives as drama, types of women in her writing, and female-male and female-female relationships.

P887.   Sandor, Suzanne. "Q & A: Alice Munro—An Intimate Appeal." *Maclean's* 17 November 1986: 12j, 12l.

Munro is interviewed after winning the Marian Engel Award. She tells Sandor that the award means a lot to her since she knew Engel personally. The award, solely for female writers, redresses the inequality between males and females in the allocation of grant money to writers. Munro mentions her own application for a Canada Council grant being turned down. In answer to why readers feel a personal connection with her, Munro says that in youth she felt like an outsider and as a writer she sees things differently, and that through her writing she has drawn together women who have similar sensibilities of feeling alone. She finds it unsettling when, occasionally, a story she has written happens in reality. Munro believes that the one purpose of writing is "to organize experience, organize reality to make sense of it" and "to express another dimension in it that is felt to be there." For her, reading and writing are vital and give meaning to life.

P888.   Margaret Laurence: Tribute. *State of the Arts*. CBC-FM Radio. 11 January 1987. (6 min., 30 sec.)

In this tribute to Laurence, Munro recalls her first meeting with her in Vancouver. She says that Laurence's writing had a bearing on hers, but that she was not influenced by it. Munro considers Laurence to be a good writer who has directness and compassion, and is straightforward in her view and style. Munro reads an excerpt from *A Bird in the House*.

P889.   Bonetti, Kay. "Interview with Alice Munro." Columbia, MO: American Audio Prose Library, 1987. 1 audiocassette. (71 min.)
Cassette 1 of a set; Cassette 2, Alice Munro reads *The Progress of Love*. (70 min.)
Printed in Cencig, Elisabeth. "Gestaltete Erinnerung: Alice Munros Ich-Erzählungen im Kontext der kanadischen Gegenwartsliteratur." Ph.D. dissertation, Universität Graz, 1992. 356-386.

Munro first describes her fascination with surface details and her heightened sense of the physical world. She then talks of the illusive nature of autobiography and the maturing of her artistic vision, progressing from autobiographical material as in "Miles City, Montana" to writing about others. Moving on to other topics, she touches on the politics of feminism and feminist critics, the importance of the feel of place, the relationship between art and life, Southwestern Ontario, and her position as a writer in a small town. The town of Hanratty in *Who* is based on Wingham, Ontario. Munro then talks about her relationship with her mother and father. Gender issues discussed include the female position in "Boys and Girls" and the relative freedoms of female writers compared with males. She says that the lack of time as a mother and housewife forced her into the short story form. She describes the writing and revisions to *Lives* and *Who*. Using "Miles City, Montana" and "The Progress of Love" as examples, Munro explains how stories are shaped from anecdotes or images. Style, she says, is deeply part of the story. The story should shine through the prose and surface details. The narrative should be true to the narrator's voice. Munro identifies with the writers of the American South. She talks briefly about her critical reception in Canada and the United States, the pressure in Canada to be a "great" Canadian writer, and her ear for dialogue.
Review:
Rasporich, Beverly. "Munro Tapes." *Canadian Literature* 138-139 (Fall-Winter 1993): 147-148.

P890.   Ross, Catherine. "An Interview with Alice Munro." [Interview conducted 12 October 1988] *Canadian Children's Literature* 53 (1989): 14-24.

In the interview, Munro talks about her childhood reading and the connection between reading and writing. She says that, in the beginning, she made up imitative stories, but eventually found an authentic voice and a personal vision. Works and authors described as having influenced her are Charles Dickens's *A Child's History of England*, L. M. Montgomery's *Emily of New Moon*, Emily Brontë's *Wuthering Heights*, and the poetry of Alfred

Lord Tennyson. One book that Munro says she disliked when she was young was Mabel Hale's *Beautiful Girlhood*, which told girls how they should behave.

P891.　Gzowski, Peter. Interview with Alice Munro. Part 1. *Morningside*. Hour Two. CBC Radio. 25 April 1990.
　　　Rebroadcast 23 August 1990.

The interview takes place after the publication of *Friend of My Youth*. Munro tells Gzowski about her contact with readers when a book first comes out, and the connections of readers to material in her books. She says that collecting material from the real world is an ongoing subconscious activity. Afterwards, in the process of writing, she changes reality to such an extent that it is difficult to remember what is real and what is fiction. The story "Friend of My Youth" came from an anecdote about the Cameronians. Munro explains how the story started and changed when she began seeing it through her mother, and her relationship with her mother. She goes on to give her views about how her own perception and that of others constantly changes, in the way they see the lives of others. Even people close to her are getting more mysterious. The mother's life in the story is a mystery to her daughter, just as her own mother is a mystery to herself. A version of her mother is all she can do in her fiction, Munro says, but fiction is inadequate. Social trends and values across time also influence the way we think about things at a particular time in our lives. For Munro, the writing process is a private investigation and not a final pronouncement. Her aim in writing is to get to the truth.

P892.　Gzowski, Peter. Interview with Alice Munro. Part 2. *Morningside*. Hour Two. CBC Radio. 26 April 1990.
　　　Rebroadcast 24 August 1990.

Good stories should be separate experiences for the reader, Munro says. Explaining her writing process, she says that she writes the first draft quickly as she sees it, telling the story to herself. She hears the dialogue of the characters in her head. Dialogue, she says, has to carry the story. For Munro, writing a story is like conducting an investigation in which the craft of writing almost gets in the way. She has always lived an "intense imaginative life" and finds it difficult when she isn't writing. Turning to *Friend*, the observation is made that the stories are about women who are either married or divorced. Munro comments on the situations of marriage in "Oranges and Apples" and "Wigtime." This leads Gzowski to ask about happiness in middle age, and where happiness comes from. Munro answers that it is not altogether from circumstance, but from a "harmonious relationship between yourself and something beyond yourself." She derives a central happiness from writing, and now in middleage she has more time to enjoy life. Sex contributes to happiness, she says in response to another question, but it can also disrupt it. Munro says she would like to write a book of nonfiction and a novel, but admits that she can't write novels. She does not see herself as "a star," but only as an ordinary person.

P893.　Wachtel, Eleanor. Interview with Alice Munro. *Writers and Company*. CBC Radio. September? 1990.
　　　Rebroadcast CBC Radio One. 15 October 2000.
　　　Printed as:
　　　"An Interview with Alice Munro." *Brick* 40 (1991): 48-53.

Rpt. (edited) in *The Brick Reader*. Ed. Linda Spalding and Michael Ondaatje. Toronto: Coach House, 1991. 288-294.

Rpt. (edited) in *Writers and Company*. Eleanor Wachtel in collaboration with Richard Handler and Sandra Rabinovitch. Toronto: Knopf, 1993. 101-112.

Rpt. (edited excerpts) in *The Writer's Path: An Introduction to Short Fiction*. Ed. Constance Rooke and Leon Rooke. Scarborough, ON: ITP Nelson, 1998. 974-977.

Munro portrays the environment where she grew up as one where physical work was the norm, and reading and writing were considered degenerate. This made her keep her reading and writing hidden. Her own feeling of being "phoney" after returning to her rural hometown causes her to muse on the Canadian characteristic of reprimanding people who construct themselves into someone other than themselves. She talks about a summer job she had when she was 16, working as a servant in a house in the Rosedale area of Toronto, and says that this was used in the story "Sunday Afternoon." Munro talks about her mother's illness and her relationship with her, admitting a feeling of guilt when she left home and a regret for her mother as a person. She says that her mother's story was woven around the story in "Friend of My Youth." Talking about her aesthetics and technique, Munro says that she writes stories to figure something out, rather than for plot. She likes open-endedness, where moments of insight lead to something else and the story continues in the mind of the reader. Absences, loss, and complexity are also mentioned. Munro explains that she uses memory as a technique, and that she cannot get at what she is doing unless she uses memory. The resulting complexity leads to moments of insight. Finally, Munro expresses her thoughts on happiness in fiction and in life in general, and on love and sex.

P894. Bigsby, Christopher. "In Conversation with Alice Munro." [Interview conducted October 1990] *Writers in Conversation with Christopher Bigsby*. Sel. and introd. Christopher Bigsby. Vol. 2. East Anglia, Norwich: Pub. for the Arthur Miller Centre for American Studies by EAS Publishing, 2001. 119-128.

In the 1950s, Munro wasn't aware of the problems of being a regional, female, short story writer. In her early writing, she imitated European writers, but was later influenced by the writers of the American south such as Eudora Welty. Munro says that reading stories should take as long as writing them. As a female writer, she tries not to feel pressured by groups like the feminists. Even in her youth Munro says she felt threatened by conformity. She points out differences in communication between men and women, and between women, saying that the latter results in bonds and friendships. On topics of writing, Munro talks about the necessary detachment of the writer, recapturing the sensibility of childhood in her past self, writing about a past that was not gentler or simpler, and her inability to write novels. What excites her is what makes a story—the layers, intertwinings, blanks, jumps, and the unexpected. She says that time changes you as a person and the way you perceive things, and she feels that her writing is more complex. She loves the "dream-like quality" of people reentering your life after the passing of time. The changes in people's lives give a different perspective of the past and she likes to use this in her fiction. The endings of her stories are crucial because they cause a fundamental shift by which the story that came before is made clear.

P895. McCulloch, Jeanne and Mona Simpson. "Alice Munro: The Art of Fiction CXXXVII." *Paris Review* 36 [No. 131] (Summer 1994): 226-264.

Munro begins by talking about revision, the need to detach oneself from a story once it is written, and the role of editors, specifically at *The New Yorker*. She then describes her life in Vancouver as a young wife and mother and in the context of her early writing career, making the admission later on that she feels guilty about not being wholly absorbed with her children. *Lives* was first intended as a novel but was rewritten as a series of stories. At several points, Munro brings up the autobiographical dimensions of her writing, especially the central position of her mother in it, in stories such as "Princess Ida" and "Friend of My Youth." She later describes her feelings toward her mother, and also toward her grandmother and great-aunt, who filled an important role in her life. Speaking about *Who*, Munro says the character Flo is a composite person who embodies the culture of her youth. Several stories are mentioned as originating from anecdotes passed on to her by her husbands. Munro describes her writing process and admits that getting a grasp on what she wants to write about is difficult. Although she had a lot of confidence in her writing, there was also a dread that it was misplaced. Munro says her writing has changed, in that it is less personal, includes historical stories that require facts and involves alternate realities. What makes her want to continue is her excitement and faith in writing. Other topics covered in the interview are Munro's sympathy with the writing of women of the American South, her meeting with her second husband Gerald Fremlin, her affinity to the Huron County landscape, the reaction in Wingham to some of her comments, and her close relationship with her father.

P896.   Smith, Stephen. "Layers of Life: No More 'Single Paths' for Alice Munro." *Quill & Quire* August 1994: 1, 24.

The topic of the title choice for *Open Secrets* prompts Munro to say that "a lot of fiction writing is about open secrets." She disavows any planning in what she writes about, saying that the historical stories in the collection were only stories she was interested in writing at the time. Munro then describes how she wrote "Carried Away" and developed two parallel stories to bring out the possibility of a parallel life. She says that in writing, she wants the story to have many layers so that the reader can think not so much about the plot but "something else about life." Social history is important in that it provides a framework of time and place into which something complex and mysterious can be set. Munro believes that aging brings a more multilayered perspective to life and has affected her approach to writing. She writes now to find out "something else" in the story, following not a single path but multiple paths. In speaking of revision, Munro says that she spends a good deal of time on the crucial paragraph, which should not be obtrusive. She does not like the thought of being a "literary institution."

P897.   Gzowski, Peter. Interview with Alice Munro. Part 1. *Morningside*. Hour One. CBC Radio. 30 September 1994.
        Rebroadcast 11 July 1995.

In this interview, centred around *Open Secrets*, Munro tells Gzowski that she has done riskier things in this collection. She wants the reader to see alternate possibilities in what might have happened in characters' lives, as for example in the story "Carried Away." She explains the different threads in the story and where they originated. In "The Albanian Virgin," the main character has a position similar to that of a virgin with honorary male status in Albania. The couple at the end of the story are based on real people. Munro says that the story did not come in a planned way, and she explains how the two plot lines were brought together at the end. She describes the writing process in general as finding out about a story that is happening and changing it to make it better; to do justice to something. Munro says that short stories are the only thing she is interested in doing, but admits that length can be a problem for some magazines. *The New Yorker*, while it did not accept some of her early stories, is the only magazine that didn't refuse her stories on the basis of length. It did, however, refuse "Spaceships Have Landed" which was later published by the *Paris Review* with the first part edited out.

P898. Gzowski, Peter. Interview with Alice Munro. Part 2. *Morningside*. CBC Radio. 3 October 1994.
Rebroadcast 26 December 1994.

The cover illustration of *Open Secrets* was done by Munro's daughter Jenny, and the author says that it reflects the feeling of the collection. After speaking briefly about her role as a juror for the Giller Prize, Munro talks about the importance of books for readers, whether the books are good or not so good. As an interviewee, Munro doesn't like talking about her personal life or about writing in general, but doesn't mind talking about stories. She mentions an extensive interview she did for her friend Mona Simpson for the *Paris Review*. "Writing Away," says Munro, is a nonfiction piece that is based on a personal experience and a real trip she and her husband had taken. For the rest of the interview, Munro talks on a number of subjects: the fact that she is not a public writer, the effect of aging on her writing, her compelling need to write, the teaching of writing, and her reacquaintance with Gerald Fremlin, who later became her second husband. Munro also comments on two of the stories in *Open Secrets*, saying that "A Wilderness Station" contains some family history, and that in "The Jack Randa Hotel" the plot is far-fetched and coincidental.

P899. Gittings, Chris. "The Scottish Ancestor: A Conversation with Alice Munro." *Scotlands* 1994: 83-96.

Munro tells Gittings that her interest in her Scottish ancestors did not come until later in life. She feels that Canadian Presbyterianism is a much stricter form than that practiced in Scotland, and relates this to the Cameronianism in "Friend of My Youth." It was important for her to trace her family history and her Scottish ancestors, including the author James Hogg and his mother, the storyteller Margaret Hogg. She says that "The Wilderness Station" was based on letters of early Scottish ancestors who had come to Canada. For the remainder of the interview, Munro discusses the two stories, "Friend of My Youth" and "Hold Me Fast, Don't Let Me Pass." In the first story, Munro talks about the cocooning of stories, the mother's story as narrated and viewed by the daughter. The daughter's view of the story, and her view of her mother, change over time. Neither story received much of a response in Scotland, Munro admits. "Hold Me Fast, Don't Let Me Pass" was faulted for a lack of understanding of the Border country. Munro counters this by saying the landscape was portrayed as it was seen through the eyes of a Canadian woman, and that the setting was of secondary significance in the story, as it was in "Bardon Bus." She goes on to talk about the Scottish ballad "Tam Lin" in the story, and the importance of getting back to one's roots for connection and personal identity.

P900. Wainwright, J. A. Excerpts from an interview with Alice Munro on the subject of Margaret Laurence. *A Very Large Soul: Selected Letters from Margaret Laurence to*

Canadian Writers. Ed., pref. and introd. J. A. Wainwright. Dunvegan, ON: Cormorant Books, 1995. 142-145.

Munro says she felt an instant rapport with Laurence because they were both writers who were also housewives and mothers. Munro relates both her own and Laurence's reaction to the censorship of Laurence's books. She speculates that Laurence became a public person because of her need to be involved in social, political, and cultural issues.

P901.   Boyce, Pleuke and Ron Smith. "A National Treasure: An Interview with Alice Munro." [Interview conducted 30 January 1995] *Meanjin* 54.2 (1995): 222-232.

Munro tells Boyce and Smith there are no intended social or political messages in her writing, although some readers may find them. Expressing her fondness for Eudora Welty and her book, *The Golden Apples*, Munro says that Welty writes truthfully and accurately, but may sometimes be politically incorrect. In describing the change in her writing since her first book, Munro says that her stories are more open-ended. When readers comment that her stories are grim and depressing, Munro says this bothers her and she does not agree. She says that she started *Open Secrets* as a type of novel, and describes the stories in the book as an extension of the short story form. In it, she wanted to record how women adapt when they are trying to protect men. The book is also concerned with time and how we relate to time and space, for example the house in "Carried Away." Other points brought up include the origin and writing of "The Albanian Virgin," the writing of novels versus short stories, sex and sexuality, and writing from a male point of view. Her impressions after living in Australia are that it is very similar to Canada but is more openly male-dominated, more open to literary controversy, and more independent.

P902.   Gzowski, Peter. Interview with Alice Munro. *Morningside*. CBC Radio. 9 October 1996. Rebroadcast in part on *This Morning*. CBC Radio One. 28 January 2002.

When asked about the choice of stories included in *Selected Stories*, Munro says that they are her favourite stories, but that "The Albanian Virgin" is one "she really likes." She explains that Albania is a country of the mind, and that the story originated from a rumour she had heard about a librarian from Clinton. This brings to mind the subject of libraries and Munro briefly recalls her work as a clerk in the Vancouver Public Library. The conversation moves to Munro's close working relationship with her literary agent, Virginia Barber. Munro says that Barber is the first person to read her stories and offer suggestions. Earlier in her career, she sometimes asked her husband for his opinion and Munro tells an anecdote related to this. Her most detailed advice comes from the editors at *The New Yorker* and she may or may not accept their advice. She recalls that her first story accepted by the magazine was "Royal Beatings." The editors wanted all the crude language changed, but Munro says she stood firm and the story was published as written. In speaking of her fictional aesthetics, Munro says that structure interests her immensely, and that a good narrative structure is like a light that shines from different angles. Everything in a story hangs on a crucial paragraph. The idea starts like a picture that has to stay clear. Munro believes in getting the dialogue right and brings up the case of the "klutsy" dialogue in "The Hired Girl" before it was changed.

P903.   Wachtel, Eleanor. Interview with Alice Munro. *Writers and Company: The Arts Today*. CBC Radio One. 14 February 1999.
Rebroadcast *Writers and Company: The Arts Today*. 19 February and 10 March 1999.

Munro begins by acknowledging Robert Weaver as the most important person in her writing life, because he gave her encouragement, access to publication, and contact with other writers. Munro says that she began writing not as an escape but because it was something wonderful that she had discovered. But she needed to keep it secret because of the attitude toward ambition in her community. At the beginning of her career, Munro was oblivious to the fact that it was a bad time to be a Canadian female short-story writer. Robert Weaver was her main encouragement and accepted many of her stories. Once she began earning an income as a writer, Munro says that it gave validity to her work and she no longer felt the need to keep her writing secret. She then describes how "Cortes Island" originated from the image of a curtain. Wachtel notes the frustrated mothers and women in *Love*. Munro answers that the stories are from a time in her life when she had difficult demands as a writer, wife, and mother. She says that she always looks back in her writing, and writes about an earlier period of her life. Aging does not make writing any easier, Munro admits, but getting older brings a more balanced view of things. When she was young, she did not think about being famous but about writing "the beautiful thing." She has since discovered the enormous gap between what you want to do and what you do. Munro says she is always trying to do something better, and to give greater justice to an idea. The interview includes a recorded excerpt of Munro reading from "My Mother's Dream" at the International Festival of Authors, Fall 1978.

P904.   Quinn, Alice. "Go Ask Alice." [Interview with Alice Munro] *New Yorker. On-Line Only.* 12 February 2001. Accessed 3 May 2006. <http:// www.newyorker.com/online/content/articles/010219on_online_munro>

Munro tells Quinn, her editor at *The New Yorker,* about the time element and the split way of thinking when you are a writer and a mother and housewife. She says she reads a story not to find out what happened but to get inside the feel of it. Munro talks about her writing schedule, daydreaming to gather thoughts for stories, and beginning a story. People, she says, become more real as she rewrites. Stories are built around key scenes, as in "Miles City, Montana." Munro goes on to discuss the personal element of stories, as well as childhood and writing about childhood. The fact that she is detached from her stories once they are written makes Munro feel like a fraud when talking about them. In the rest of the interview, Munro tells Quinn about the importance of *The New Yorker* to her career. Selling stories to *The New Yorker* gave validity to her work as a short story writer and came at the right time of her career. Unlike the view in Canada that she was a "slightly outmoded writer," the readership of *The New Yorker* was more discerning and the magazine allowed her to write about whatever she wanted, no matter how out-of-fashion or quaint it was.

P905.   Gzowski, Peter. "'You're the Same Person at 19 That You Are at 60.'" *Globe and Mail* 29 September 2001: F4-F5.

The interview takes place after the publication of *Hateship.* In answer to Gzowski's question of where the details of her stories originate, Munro says they often come from what she hears from other people, giving as an example the joke in "Floating Bridge." She relates the objection of the editors at *The New Yorker* to the crude language she used in some of her earlier stories. The discussion then centres around jokes, dirty jokes, and jokes as a form of literary composition. The subject of sexuality in "Nettles" and "What is Remembered" is raised. Munro responds to questions on aging and death, then comments on "The Bear

Came Over the Mountain," saying that it deals with old age and loss of memory. She briefly touches on the title of the collection, autobiography in writing, and writers as characters in stories.

P906. Feinberg, Cara. "Bringing Life to Life." *Atlantic Online. Atlantic Unbound*. 14 December 2001. Accessed 3 May 2006. <http://www.theatlantic.com/doc/prem/200112u/int2001-12-14.htm> (Available only to subscribers)

Throughout the interview, Munro comments on stories in her latest collection, *Hateship*. Munro says she writes what interests her and doesn't follow conventional rules for short story writing. She also talks about her use of time in stories, and expresses particular interest in how time relates to memory and how the past appears to people as they age and change. Men and women tell the stories of their lives differently, in what they include and what they leave out. She says that most of her stories are written from the perspective of the current stage of her life and usually look back to the past. The period of the 1960s is one that especially interests her. In talking about using real people in fiction, Munro says that the people in her home town of Wingham are upset because they think that her fictional characters are real people. Other topics touched on are feminism, regionalism, literary influences, her method of reading stories, her choice of the short story genre, writing about childhood events, and writing as a discovery process. As a child, Munro said she learned to disguise, like most children. However, today there is a trend for adults to try to protect children from trauma, illness, and death, but children see through this because they have a natural wisdom.

P907. "A Conversation with Alice Munro." *Reading Group Center*. Vintage Books-Random House. Accessed 18 March 2004. <http://www.randomhouse.com/vintage/read/secrets/munro.html>

Munro responses briefly to a range of questions asked: her thoughts on the short story form; the genesis of stories; writing habits; literary influences; reaction to being compared with Chekhov; the need for complete knowledge of characters; the effect of rural Ontario on her writing; the relationship between memory, truth, and experience; and favourite stories she has written. Munro also gives words of advice to young writers.

P908. Treisman, Deborah. "Telling Stories." *The New Yorker-Online Only. Audio Q&A*. 6 July 2004. Accessed 14 September 2006. <http://www.newyorker.com/online/covers/articles/040614onco_covers_gallery> (7 min.)

The interview centres around three stories recently published in *The New Yorker*: "Chance," "Soon," and "Silence." Speaking to her editor at the magazine, Munro tells Treisman that the stories had been in her mind for a long time. They are all about the same woman. "Soon" and "Silence" were envisioned as part of one long story or novella, but that wasn't what they turned out to be. Saying that she is not a novelist, or ever meant to be one, Munro views life "as pieces that don't fit together very well." People's lives interest her very much, in that they do not follow a straight trajectory but have startling and interesting things happening in them. In "Chance," Munro says she is trying to show the problem of being oneself. "Soon" has autobiographical elements related to the attitude toward bookish intelligence in small towns and to the competent women characters, such as Irene. Penelope is looking for a regular life and freedom away from her parents.

P909.   Wachtel, Eleanor. Interview with Alice Munro. *Writers and Company*. CBC Radio One. 7 November 2004. (55 min.)
Printed [edited by Lisa Godfrey] as "Alice Munro: A Life in Writing; A Conversation with Eleanor Wachtel." *Queens Quarterly* 112.2 (Summer 2005): 266-280.

Using the concept of "runaway" as a point of reference, Munro talks about infidelity in middle-aged women of her generation, and how they see love and passion as a way of escaping the predictability of their lives. Munro considers infidelity as a popular subject for writers because of the drama inherent in it. In the spoken interview, she looks at how male writers of the past wrote about unfaithful women, specifically D. H. Lawrence in "The Fox" and Leo Tolstoy in *War and Peace*. Munro says she tries to write truthfully about female sexuality. Discussing "Passion," she talks about women's attraction to brooding, troubled men. Munro says her stories are getting darker because the ideas are coming from things that are close to her life as she ages. What some people see as tragic, such as the loss of the daughter in "Silence," could be something quite natural in life, the result of "things people do." The discussion moves on to the regional and personal dimensions of Munro's writing. Munro, who dislikes being called a regional writer, describes the changes in small town Ontario and notes a more tolerant attitude toward the lower social classes. She contrasts this with the past and the violent atmosphere in the school she attended. The circumstance of being a middle-class child living close to a disadvantaged class gave her a greater understanding of life and a confidence in her abilities as a writer. Munro goes on to talk about her guilt in leaving home when her mother was ill, her close relationship with her father, his support of her writing, and the novel he completed before his death. The interview ends with Munro's thoughts about the past and writing about the past, her present life, and plans for the future.

P910.   Todd, Paula. "Literarily Speaking with Alice Munro." *Person 2 Person*. Studio 2. TVO, Toronto. 5 April 2006. (60 min., including film clips)

Early in life, Munro composed stories in her head while walking home from school. At the age of fourteen, she decided that she wanted to be a writer. Her mother's illness forced her to do housework, which she didn't mind. Munro describes her first meeting with Jim Munro at university and her conventional ideas about marriage and having children at that time. In the early fifties, she was considered to be "queer" for writing the stories as she did. As a young mother, Munro used her daughter's nap time to think about stories. She talks candidly about the death of her infant daughter, Catherine, and says that "My Mother's Dream" came from that period. For some years, Munro experienced writer's block, attributing it to a crisis in confidence in her ability to write and to a physical anxiety disorder. When her first book *Dance* won the Governor General's Award, Munro thought "it was a kind of fluke." Even now she is delighted but surprised when she wins an award. When a book is published, it is a thing of the past, written by someone else. It is only the next story that is important. The "silly period" around the time of her divorce affected her attitude and behaviour and influenced the way she related to her daughters. Now, Munro says that aging brings her greater freedom. Giving a personal interview is easier because the humiliation of exposure is no longer there. When asked about writing, Munro answers that it is about "tackling the experience of being alive as best you can" and as "the best thing you can do with your life."

Part II
Secondary Works
(Works about Alice Munro)

Theses and Dissertations

S1.   Aherne, Catherine Lynne. "The Poetics of the Short Story Cycle: Alice Munro's *Lives of Girls and Women* and *Who Do You Think You Are?*" M.A. thesis, Acadia University, 1992.

Begins with a general examination of the poetics of the short story cycle within the context of English world literature. The thesis compares and contrasts Munro's own statements regarding the two works with the interpretations of the critics. It then examines each work in detail, showing, by means of a series of signals found in the texts, that each follows the short story cycle form and that this form can be used to read the text in new ways.

S2.   Arbing, Susan. "Webs and Hierarchies: Individuation in Munro and Hemingway." M.A. thesis, McMaster University, 1993.

The search for self and the formation of masculine and feminine identities are examined in Hemingway's *The Nick Adams Stories* and Munro's *Lives*. The role of the family, and in particular Del's relationship with her mother, is seen as an important influence in Del's early development. Socialization and an environment where gender roles and expectations are clearly demarcated further affects the formation of Del's female identity.

S3.   Armstrong, Carol A. "'The Fascinating Pain, the Humiliating Necessity': Delicate Moments of Exposure in Alice Munro's Fiction." M.A. thesis, McMaster University, 1987.

The theme of human relationships and the pain inflicted between people as a necessary part of these relationships are examined in selected stories from *Who*, *Moons*, and *Progress*. Painful experiences of loss, humiliation, and disillusionment often have the effect of delivering the characters to an altered state of self-acceptance or self-knowledge. Munro's view of life and her use of time shifts are also discussed.

S4.   Assad, Mavis. "Female Sexuality in the Fiction of Alice Munro." M.A. thesis, Concordia University, 1992.

Assad examines, from a feminist theoretical perspective, the central role of sexuality in the identity formation of Munro's female characters. Sexuality is seen as a rite of passage and connected to self-representation, female desire, and the assumption of gender roles. Further discussion revolves around Munro's narrative strategy and her use of figurative language when writing of the female body and sexuality.

S5.   Babineau, Nicole. "The Narrative Use of Atmospheric Evocation in the Fiction of Alice Munro: An Image of Superrealism." M.A. thesis, Université de Montréal, 1976 (accepted 1977).

A study of the superrealist perspective in *Dance*, *Lives*, and *Something*. Influenced by American writers like Eudora Welty and James Agee, Munro evokes feelings and texture through description, language, and her approach to characters and objects, especially in the first two books. In *Something*, however, Munro's style, treatment of time, and point of view have changed and the frames around characters and their emotional expression have tightened. The thesis ends with a discussion of Munro's style, poeticism, and use of words. An appendix looks into the elements of humour in the three books.

S6.   Ballon, Heather M. "The Bildungsroman in Recent Canadian Fiction." M.A. thesis, McGill University, 1977.

A comparative study dealing with the influence of love, death, and time on the self-development of the protagonists in the three Canadian novels: *Anne of Green Gables* by L. M. Montgomery, *The Mountain and the Valley* by Ernest Buckler, and *Lives* by Munro. Del Jordan's path to self-discovery and independence is traced through an analysis of her relationship with her mother and other members of her family, her encounters with death, and later her sexual relationships with Jerry Story and Garnet French.

S7.   Batstone, Kathleen [Loren]. "Feminist Themes in Alice Munro's *Lives of Girls and Women*." Honours B.A. thesis, Acadia University, 1993.

The repression of female sexuality, confining female roles, and the feminist struggles against both are the themes which are examined in *Lives*, particularly in the chapter "Princess Ida." Using as a frame of reference three prominent feminist literary works (*The Feminine Mystique* by Betty Friedan, *The Female Eunuch* by Germaine Greer, and *Sexual Politics* by Kate Millett), Batstone illustrates how the novel reflects the pro-feminist atmosphere of the time in which it was written. (Based on abstract)

S8.   Batstone, Kathleen Loren. "Unlocking Pandora's Box: Female Desire in Three Works by Canadian Female Writers." M.A. thesis, Acadia University, 1994.

Three novels (*Songs My Mother Taught Me* by Audrey Thomas, *Lady Oracle* by Margaret Atwood, and *Lives* by Munro) are discussed in this thesis. By examining the articles published in *Chatelaine* during the 1970s, Batstone shows the social climate of Canada as one in which women are caught in the middle of conflicting social forces—one of liberation as personified in the Women's Liberation Movement and, at the same time, one of continuing restriction, notably in the area of female sexuality and desire. These restrictions are considered in the context of the socialization process of young girls and women's sexuality.

S9.   Bellamy, Connie. "The New Heroines: The Contemporary Female Bildungsroman in English Canadian Literature." Ph.D. dissertation, McGill University, 1986.

Contends that the female *Bildungsroman* exemplified by Margaret Laurence's *A Jest of God*, Margaret Atwood's *Lady Oracle*, and Munro's *Lives* goes beyond the male protagonist version of the *Bildungsroman* and explores not only the self-development of the protagonist but also her development as a woman. It is shown how work, love, family, and traditional expectations conflict with the female's development as an individual.

S10. Belyea, Andy. "Redefining the Real: Gothic Realism in Alice Munro's *Friend of My Youth*." M.A. thesis, Queen's University, 1998.

Friend is studied in the context of the Southern Ontario gothic. The thesis is an examination of typical gothic conventions and gothic themes such as dread, repression, madness, and death. It also looks at the various gothic narrative devices used in different stories: dreams, diaries, and letters. The surface of everyday life is seen to have gothic undercurrents, and characters have difficulty distinguishing between what they see and what they feel; between what is real and what is imagined.

S11. Bezanson, Bridget. "'Her Infinite Variety': The Function of Role-Playing in the Early Fiction of Alice Munro." Honours B.A. thesis, Acadia University, 1995.

A thesis on the development of an alternative female identity in *Lives* and *Who*. It begins with Munro's first book, *Dance*, to illustrate the conditioning of young girls to traditional female roles. In *Lives*, the adolescent female protagonist experiments with both conventional and alternative roles. The protagonist in *Who*, from her adolescence to adulthood, uses role-playing as a method of creating alternative identity. The conclusion reached is that an alternative female identity based on a plurality of selves or roles allows Munro's female characters to experience the freedoms associated with the male identity. (Based on abstract)

S12. Bowen, Deborah. "Mimesis, Magic, Manipulation: A Study of the Photograph in Contemporary British and Canadian Novels." Ph.D. dissertation, University of Ottawa, 1990.

An examination of the works of a number of British and Canadian writers, including Munro. Through a study of their use of photography and photographic imagery, a comparison is made between the writers in each culture regarding their approach to the real and the fictive, and the relationship between them. There is a brief treatment of magic realism in four of Munro's stories: "Something I've Been Meaning to Tell You," "The Turkey Season," "Epilogue: The Photographer," and "Simon's Luck."

S13. Boynton, Danelle Gail. "Theme and Image in Alice Munro's Fiction." M.A. thesis, McMaster University, 1980.

Shows how main themes such as death, human relationships, illusion, and quest for identity are dramatized in significant images in *Dance*, *Lives*, *Something*, and *Who*. Images are shown to be essential components of themes in the many stories discussed.

S14. Brown, Daniel J. "Unintelligible Marks: Antidetection in Alice Munro's Recent Uncollected Short Fiction." M.A. thesis, University of Guelph, 1994.

Elaborates on the differences between classic detective fiction and the antidetection found in Munro's fiction. Rather than solving a mystery in the rational way of detective fiction, antidetection reveals a multiplicity of truths in the mysteries of human experience and, as a result, provides no sense of resolution. These mysteries and the multiplicity of possible truths are examined in "Open Secrets" and "A Wilderness Station."

S15. Campbell, Leslie Marion. "Scottish Influence and the Construction of Canadian Identity in Works by Sara Jeannette Duncan, Alice Munro, and Margaret Laurence." M.A. thesis, Dalhousie University, 2000.

In Chapter 2, pages 50-74, Campbell discusses how Munro subverts and revises the Scots nation-builder and female pioneer myths in "A Wilderness Station," "Meneseteung," "Friend of My Youth," *Lives,* and "The Stone in the Field." The transfer of religious Puritanism to the New World resulted in the continuation of rigid ethical codes which repressed and disempowered women. Munro's female characters resist and reject these constrictions and struggle to find ways to adjust and empower themselves. Robert Laidlaw's *The McGregors* and its relevance to Scots pioneer mythology is also discussed.

S16. Carver Taylor, Mary Anne. "The Quest for Connection: A Comparative Analysis of the Fiction of Flannery O'Connor and Alice Munro." M.A. thesis, Dalhousie University, 1993.

Demonstrates how the ordinary regional settings and characters portrayed by O'Connor and Munro have universal recognition. While O'Connor's settings are small communities in the American South and Munro's are small towns in Southwestern Ontario, both writers use the environment of the community, home, and family to show the interdependence of these factors on the self-discovery and identity of their characters. Female characters and their authority are also discussed.

S17. Caskey, Sarah A. "Open Secrets: Ambiguity and Irresolution in the Australian, New Zealand, and Canadian Short Story." Ph.D. dissertation, University of Western Ontario, 2000.

In Chapter 6, pages 139-197, Caskey looks at Munro's open, ambiguous, and complex narrative structures and analyses her use of ambiguity and indeterminacy in "Real Life," "Open Secrets," "The Chaddeleys and Flemings," and "Meneseteung." Then, with Munro's aesthetic and life visions as a reference point, Caskey demonstrates Munro's use of disarrangement as a device in uncovering the multiple layers of reality, especially in "A Wilderness Station" and "The Love of a Good Woman."

S18. Cencig, Elisabeth. "Gestaltete Erinnerung: Alice Munros Ich-Erzählungen im Kontext der kanadischen Gegenwartsliteratur." Ph.D. dissertation, Universität Graz, 1992.

A study of Munro's portrayal of memory and time structure in her first-person narrative stories in *Dance, Lives, Something, Who, Moons,* and *The Progress of Love.* The thesis examines both vertical and horizontal time structures and their relationship with each other. The treatment of first-person narrative is shown to evolve in complexity over Munro's writing career. The structure of both *Lives* and *Who* is discussed. Comparison is made between James Joyce's *A Portrait of the Artist as a Young Man* and Munro's *Lives.* The considerable revisions made to the role and viewpoint of the principal character in *Who* are detailed. Memories, specifically childhood memories, are viewed in relation to fictional topography. Memories and daughter-mother and daughter-father relationships are discussed. The appendix is of note: "An Interview with Alice Munro, conducted by Kay Bonetti for the American Prose Library in June 1987."

S19. Daziron, Héliane Catherine. "Angles of Vision on Alice Munro's Short Fiction." Ph.D. dissertation, York University, 1985.

A semiotic approach to the analysis of nine stories that exemplify Munro's angles of vision. The five angles of vision are classified as rhetorical, archetypal, syntactical, stylistic, and structural. The narrative techniques of contradiction or opposition associated with each angle of vision are illustrated by particular stories: oxymoron by "Dance of the Happy Shades," contradiction by "Thanks for the Ride," inclusion by "Flats Road," exclusion by "Day of the Butterfly," irony and inversion by "Memorial," embedding by "Half a Grapefruit," separation and distance by "Dulse," mystification by "Walking on Water," and contrapuntal technique by "Mrs. Cross and Mrs. Kidd."

S20. Dickman, Amy G. "From Development to Deconstruction: The Contemporary Female *Künstlerroman*." Ph.D. dissertation, University of South Florida, 2003.

In the developmental model of the contemporary female *Künstlerroman*, women writers manage to avoid the dissolution of self that occurs in the traditional male model of the *Künstlerroman*. The process of self-affirmation contained in Carolyn Heilbrun's *Writing a Woman's Life* involves the female resistance to the conventional marriage plot in favour of a quest plot to find a subject-position that will enable her to speak in her own voice. Del's process of development as an artist reflects the steps in Heilbrun's process and the developmental model of the female *Künstlerroman*. Also discussed is *Push* by Sapphire.

S21. DiLeo, Michael. "Stream of Conscience: A Collection of Short Stories." M.F.A. thesis, Warren Wilson College, Asheville, NC, 1996.

Discusses or mentions embedding in "Wigtime," "Meneseteung," and "Five Points" on pages 4-5, 17-28, 36, 39, and 45-47. (Note from the author)

S22. Drysdale, Andrea. "Fragmentation and the Canadian Short Story: The Work of Alice Munro." M.A. research essay, Carleton University, 1992.

Shows how structural and thematic fragmentation are central to Munro's work. Munro's vision sees life not as orderly, but as a mixture of order and disorder. This reflects a fundamental stance of Canadians in a multicultural society and Canadian literature where otherness is asserted and the received order is subverted. However, Munro's stories show hope in the fact that her characters accept this flux in their lives.

S23. Dufault, Roseanna Lewis. "Metaphors of Childhood: Personal and Political Identity in Three Québécois Novels." Ph.D. dissertation, University of Colorado, 1986.

Includes a chapter comparing the treatment of childhood in Gabrielle Roy's *Rue Deschambault* and Munro's *Lives* as an illustration of the difference between the French and English cultures in Canada. Childhood is studied as a theme in Québécois literature, and also as a metaphor for Quebec's struggle for political autonomy and national identity. The section also includes a comparison with Fredelle Bruser Maynard's *Raisins and Almonds*.

S24. Duncan, Isla. "'The Complicated Reflections; The Accidental Clarity': An Analysis of the Narrative Viewpoints in the Short Fiction of Alice Munro." M.Phil., University of Strathclyde, 1991 (degree 1992).

Narrative viewpoints are analysed through the progression of Munro's writing, beginning with the first person in *Dance* (retrospective) and *Something* (confessional) and ending with the more unusual and complex perspectives such as the third person viewpoint with a shifting perspective and the double-distancing perspective found in the stories of *Progress* and *Friend*. Other viewpoints studied include the rare, for Munro, viewpoint of the first person male, the third person detached omniscient narrative in *Beggar*, and the omniscient and first person narratives in *Moons*. The first person female viewpoint is illustrated in the "filial guilt" stories: "The Peace of Utrecht," "The Ottawa Valley," and "Friend of My Youth."

S25.   Duteau, Claire L. "The Dramatis Personae of Alice Munro." M.A. thesis, University of Alberta, 1973.

Begins by proposing that readers view Munro's female characters as variant faces of Munro herself. The rest of the thesis focuses on three roles portrayed by the female characters in *Dance* and *Lives*. The role of the girl maturing into a woman is demonstrated in the girl's relationship with her parents and other adults, her attitudes toward feminine skills, and her impressions about her body and sex. The role of the believer focuses on Del Jordan's private religious quest and the areligious nature of the towns found in the stories of *Dance*. The role of the writer is personified in Del and her interest in words and reading, and in her development as a realistic writer.

S26.   Dyment, Betty J. "Escaping Girlhood: Gender and Growth in Four Works by Margaret Laurence and Alice Munro." M.A. thesis, Carleton University, 1988.

A study of the heroines in Margaret Laurence's *Bird in the House* and *Diviners*, and Munro's *Lives* and *Who*. The four books are viewed as female versions of the *Bildungsroman* where female, spiritual, and creative development are restricted by patriarchal society. The thesis expands on the heroine's personality, family, town environment, role models, and rites of passage. Style and narrative structures are also examined.

S27.   Etter, Kathryn. "Genre of Return: The Short Story Volume." Ph.D. dissertation, University of Iowa, 1985.

Separate chapters explore Eudora Welty's *The Golden Apples*, Renata Adler's *Speedboat*, and Munro's *The Beggar Maid*. Etter analyses the structure of *Beggar* and brings attention to the unity of the work as a whole, but also points out the distinctness of each story. In Chapter 2, specific focus is directed to language, power, and authority in the work and to the fragmentation of time.

S28.   Evans, Jennifer. "The Gothic Elements of the Early Fiction of Alice Munro." Honours B.A. thesis, Mount Allison University, 1982.

Shows how Munro's photographic style and technique best illustrate the gothic realism found in *Dance* and *Lives*. The impact of the gothic world, both real and fictional, on the characters is outlined. Munro's style is compared to writers of the American South and to French-Canadian writers. Chapter 2 of the thesis gives a comparative analysis of themes and techniques in six stories from *Dance*: "Images," "Walker Brothers Cowboy," "Thanks for the Ride," "The Time of Death," "A Trip to the Coast," and "The Peace of Utrecht." Chapter 3 looks at the gothic elements in *Lives*. Del Jordan's world is presented as restricted, impoverished, gothic, and rural in nature. The thesis brings attention to gothic elements of this world that impinge on Del's growth as a female and artist.

S29.   Fisher, Don. "The Ordinary and the Epiphanic/Death and Eros: Religious and Spiritual Questing in the Fiction of Alice Munro." Ph.D. dissertation, University of Alberta, 2004.

Explores Munro's implicit spiritual/religious vision and her treatment of "the ordinary life" which is central to this vision. The concept of the "affirmation of ordinary life" is taken from the work of Charles Taylor. The spiritual elements associated with Eros, death, and the epiphanic are first discussed. The second chapter looks at Munro and Christianity, and at the ultimate mystery of death in "The Time of Death," "Age of Faith," and "Boys and Girls." The third and fourth chapters examine respectively the failure and the success of questing for spiritual fulfillment in the realm of Eros or sexuality/the body as illustrated by selected stories from *Dance*, *Lives*, *Something*, *Who*, *Moons*, *Progress*, and *Friend*. Chapter five discusses the experience of the religious/spiritual through epiphany or epiphanic moments, treating "Walker Brothers Cowboy" as a microcosm of the epiphanic in Munro's work. Epiphanic moments are also exemplified in stories such as "Miles City, Montana" and "Labor Day Dinner." The final chapter uses "Jakarta," "Post and Beam," "Comfort," and "Floating Bridge" to show how Munro's implicit spiritual/religious vision has increased in the later stages of her career.

S30.   Forkash, Diana Grace. "The Female Voice of Realism in the Fiction of Alice Munro." M.A. thesis, University of Wisconsin-Eau Claire, 1992.

A study of the female voice in selected stories: "Boys and Girls," "Postcard," "Memorial," "Tell Me Yes or No," "Bardon Bus," and "Dulse." Using the same stories, Forkash considers the feminist view of the female body as an active subject and applies the concept of desiring female body to the voice in each story and shows how it relates to female characters' power and identity, especially in relation to men.

S31.   Foy, Nathalie. "'Our Unfixed Vision': The Undermining of Vision in Contemporary Canadian Fiction." Ph.D. dissertation, University of Toronto, 2004.

Examines thematic and narratological responses to the problems of vision in selected fiction by Alistair MacLeod, Jane Urquhart, Thomas King, and Alice Munro. In *Who*, Munro troubles vision narratologically. Chapter three of the dissertation, entitled "Vision and Aurality in Alice Munro's *Who Do You Think You Are?*," expands on the friction and gaps between the aural and the visual. The auditory effect of a shifting narrative voice that is hard to place is unsettling for the reader. Munro counters Cartesian perspectivalism through a narrative perspective that is profoundly embodied in Rose. Rose is the focalizer, or the one who "sees." She also is the one who controls the "telling" of the story. In "Royal Beatings," the comic structure is seen as the key to understanding the interplay of the visual and the aural. The visual/aural friction is also discussed for the Canadian and American versions of the title.

S32.   Gardiner, Jill Marjorie. "The Early Short Stories of Alice Munro." M.A. thesis, University of New Brunswick, 1973.

Early uncollected stories and stories from *Dance of the Happy Shades* written up to 1960 are studied in chronological order to trace the reciprocal development of Munro's personal vision and her technical skill as a artist. The uncollected stories examined are "The Dimensions of a Shadow," "Story for Sunday," "The Idyllic Summer," "At the Other Place," and "The Edge of Town." In the beginning, Munro's writing shows a central concern with character, a sombre vision, and a spare evocative style. By the writing of "The Peace of Utrecht," Munro's vision and skill have reached their peak. The regional aspects of Munro's writing are also considered. Gardiner's personal interview with Munro is found in the appendix.

S33.   Garrett, Charlotte K. "The Laurel Tree: An Archetypal Perspective of the Sacrifice of Soul in *Who Do You Think You Are?* and *Kamouraska*." M.A. thesis, University of Alberta, 1993.

Presents an archetypal approach to the subject of sacrifice in the two books based on the depth psychology of Carl Gustav Jung. The thesis first examines the nature of sacrifice and the idea that sacrifice is necessary to escape patriarchal domination. It then turns to the violent relationship between Rose and her father, linking Rose to the classical archetype of Iphigeneia. The study moves on to the mother-daughter relationship and postulates that Rose's weak identity is the result of parental loss. Also considered is the connection between ritual, violence, and sacrifice.

S34.   Gholamain, Mitra. "The Attachment and Personality Dynamics of Reader Response." Ph.D. dissertation, Ontario Institute for Studies in Education, University of Toronto, 1998.

The attachment theory, used in psychology, is applied to Munro's "Bardon Bus" to study reader response to the story. Reader literary response is measured in terms of personal impression and memories evoked. The connection is shown between object representations, literary experience, and fictional identification. The dissertation also examines personality style and reader response using Carson McCullers' "Sojourner."

S35.   Gittings, Christopher E. "'Sounds in the Empty Spaces of History': Re-Placing Canadian and Scottish Literatures." Ph.D. dissertation, University of Edinburgh, 1993.

Chapter 3, pages 71-105, of this dissertation is entitled "Transforming Memory: Family History and Cultural Translation in Alice Munro." The stories "Friend of My Youth," "Hold Me Fast, Don't Let Me Pass," and "A Wilderness Station" have been chosen to illustrate a cross-cultural view of Canadian and Scottish narratives. The Scot and the Canadian descendant of white European settler culture is found in the paradoxical role of both "agent and victim of British imperialism—the colonizer and the colonized." (Based on abstract)

S36.   Grieve, Meghan. "Writing Women's Lives: The Fictional Aesthetic of Alice Munro." M.A. thesis, Lakehead University, 1997.

Explores Munro's fictional aesthetic through a study of the female artist figure in *Lives*, "The Office," "The Ottawa Valley," "Dulse," "Lichen," and "Meneseteung." A study of the female artist at different stages of life (youth, middle age, and old age) is used to shed light on Munro's own development as a writer and to distill from this analysis the basic elements of Munro's aesthetic of fiction. These basic elements are found in the importance in her work of texture and surface detail, the aesthetic tension between fiction and reality, the difficulties associated with being a female writer, and the use of personal experience in her fiction.

S37.   Hagen, Anne Marie. "Portrayals of Space and Identity in the Fiction of Elizabeth Bowen and Alice Munro." Cand. Philol. thesis, University of Oslo, 2003.

The mutually influencing relationship between space and identity is examined in Elizabeth

Bowen's *The Last September* and *A World of Love*, and Munro's "The Peace of Utrecht" and "The Love of a Good Woman." In the four works, individual characters try to establish their identities through their surroundings, or space. The division of space is a question of gender and textual space as characters form their personal identities. In Munro's stories, the central loci or spaces in which the characters are examined are the enclosed, private spaces of the house, and the public space of the small town, represented by Jubilee in the first story and Walley in the second. The narrative structure of both works is discussed in relation to the theme. The thesis ends by questioning whether a whole self and a whole reality exist, and in continuation.

S38. Hammerstad, Gerd. "A Make-Believe World?: The Problem of Reality in Alice Munro's *Lives of Girls and Women*." Cand. Philol. thesis, University of Oslo, 1989.

Follows Del Jordan's progression from youth to maturity with a focus on how she acquires a greater understanding of reality and hence an ordering of the chaotic world around her. The thesis begins with Del's struggle to gain a realistic picture of herself and her role in society. Ada Jordan is considered from Del's point of view. Del's confrontation with the reality of death, her search for faith through religion, and her initiation into sex all serve to bring her closer to the "real world." Consideration then is given to the problem of reality and perception, and the difficulty of interpreting perceptions. Ambiguity and contradictions in the descriptions of persons are examined. The final chapter of *Lives* ends with a holistic view of reality, where Del discovers that reality can only be understood in terms of the past, present, and future.

S39. Hartmann, Eva Maria. "'Deep Caves Paved with Kitchen Linoleum': Aspects of Alice Munro's Art." Dr. Phil. dissertation, Universität Wien, 2001.

A broad study of Munro's work beginning with her early life and her development as a short story writer in Canada. A chapter is devoted to the critical reception of her work. The rest of the dissertation examines her works mainly in chronological order, beginning with *Dance* and ending with *Love*. The two story cycles, *Lives* and *Who*, are studied from the perspective of "a portrait of the artist as a young woman." (Based on the Table of Contents)

S40. Hayes, Elizabeth J. "Legend and Experience in the Stories of Alice Munro." M.A. thesis, Cleveland State University, 2001.

This is a study of the dialectical relationship in Munro's writing between reality and legends. It is shown how this relationship mirrors the workings of the minds of characters as they encounter experience and contemplate memories. Epiphanies result at the point at which legends are made from real experience or when legends break down, or separate from experience. The progression of Munro's writing is examined in terms of stylistic changes, particularly the change from "sense" to "sensibility," where introspection is centred on tricks of memory and language. The reality-legend dialectic, associative connections, epiphany, and sensibility are considered in comparative studies of *Lives* and *Beggar*, and "Images" and "The Love of a Good Woman." The power of unspoken reality or the absence of language is considered in "Baptizing." Fathers and father-type characters are viewed as legendary figures in *Lives* and "Images."

S41. Heble, Ajay. "'The Tumble of Reason': Paradigmatic Reservoirs of Meaning in the Fiction of Alice Munro." Ph.D. dissertation, University of Toronto, 1990.
Pub. revised and updated as *The Tumble of Reason: Alice Munro's Discourse of Absence*. Toronto: University of Toronto Press, 1994.

Paradigmatic discourse is one which presents possibilities taken from potential or absent levels of meaning. This thesis looks at latent meaning, subtext, implication, irony, and symbol and the techniques Munro uses to produce them. Heble moves chronologically through the works from *Dance* to *Progress* and studies the ways in which paradigmatic discourse operates in each work. In *Dance*, he considers the process of memory turning into legend; in *Lives*, the opposition of reality and fiction; in *Something*, power and suspicion and gaps in communication; in *Who*, disruptive patterns, gaps in time, and discourse of absence; in *Moons*, the poetics of surprise manifested through the collapse or absence of connections; in *Progress*, patterns of complicity and deception to promote and undo reality at the same time.

S42. Hesse, Nicole Christine. "Piecing Together the 'Who': The Construction and Perception of Character in *Who Do You Think You Are?*" M.A. thesis, Queen's University, 1993.

Examines Munro's technique of creating character identity, particularly in the protagonist Rose. Hesse works from the theory that fragmentation, alienation, role-playing, and uncertainty of identity found in the characters in the book reflect the framework of the society during the time in which *Who* was written. By means of narrative gaps and discontinuous time, the character of Rose is shown to undergo inexplicable transformations, and the reader is challenged to piece together her character from the fragments of the often conflicting information provided.

S43. Holton, Danica Lynn. "Class and Stratification in the Works of Alice Munro and Margaret Laurence." M.A. thesis, Dalhousie University, 1999.

Begins with an analysis of class structure in Canadian society and the myths of classlessness that are found in Canadian literary criticism. Chapter 2 examines the fiction of Munro with attention to the class-related experiences of female characters, particularly those of impoverished women, to illustrate how class-based ideologies and their values prohibit women's upward mobility. *Lives* and stories in many other works are discussed.

S44. Hornosty, Janina Camille. "Hunter, Adult Adolescent, and Wounded Warlock: Images of Men in English-Canadian Women's Fiction (1960-93)." Ph.D. dissertation, McMaster University, 1994.

A section of this thesis studies masculinity and male types in the two stories "Bardon Bus" and "Who Do You Think You Are?" The male-female sexual relationship is explored in the first story, where the male is seen as an adult adolescent type and the woman as a consumable object. Also discussed in relation to the story are female adolescent attitudes and behaviour, women's experience of extramarital affairs, and the vulnerability of women. In the second story, the man is seen as "warlock." Ralph is a spiritual twin to Rose, a healer and a counterpart to her identity. Male types are briefly considered in "Lichen" and "Labor Day Dinner."

S45. Huang, Shu. "The Myth of Amor and Psyche and Female Autobiographical Writing." M.A. thesis, University of Manitoba, 1991.

Texts covered include *The Early Diary of Anaïs Nin*, Mary McCarthy's *Memories of a Catholic Girlhood*, and Munro's *Lives*. Chapter 4 of the thesis discusses the myth of Amor and Psyche as a paradigmatic story of female development and applies it to the *Bildungsroman*, *Lives*. In *Lives*, the growth of the female self mirrors Psyche's development. Different relationships in Del's world are explored: husband and wife, aunt and uncle, mother and daughter; and finally Del's sexual relationships. In the end, Del sees writing as a way of controlling the helplessness of sensuality and femaleness.

S46. Hulan, Renée. "Shaping a Space of One's Own: Time and Form in *Lives of Girls and Women*, *Kamouraska*, and *The Linnet Muir Stories*." M.A. thesis, University of Guelph, 1990.

A study of time, both as an element of the narrative and as a narrative technique. Del's narrative moves in two directions, forward from her early years to her artistic awakening but also backward since the narrative is an account of her memories. Time is also studied as an integral part of the narrative form. Del is examined as a first person narrator and as a female artist who lives and writes her/self as subject. The narration is one of associative remembering, one of a remembered past in nonchronological order. The narrative past is overlaid with the voices of future selves.

S47. Hunter, Shaun M. "The Apprenticeship of Alice Munro: Seeing through the World of Flannery O'Connor." Honors [B.A.] thesis, Smith College, Northampton, MA, 1984.

Demonstrates the similarities between O'Connor's and Munro's early writing to show the former's seminal influence on Munro's artistic development. The points of similarity shown in *Dance* and "The Ferguson Girls Must Never Marry" include regionalism and a sense of place, surface details of ordinary life, Gothic elements, and eccentric and mysterious characters. Classified as imitative stories are "The Time of Death" and "A Trip to the Coast." "The Peace of Utrecht" is discussed as Munro's first personal story, followed by *Lives* with a double narrator. The major difference between the two writers comes in the fact that Munro does not write from the Christian viewpoint as O'Connor does.

S48. Hunter, Shaun M. "Growing Up United: The United Church in the Fiction of Laurence, Atwood, Engel and Munro." M.A. research essay, Carleton University, 1985.

Discusses the United Church as a continuation of a repressive Methodist and Presbyterian morality, and as the embodiment of middle-class society, which sees the function of the church in a social rather than a spiritual sense. Through their fictional characters, the four authors explore the experience of standing outside the church, separating church from religion, and seeking spiritual sustenance in areas outside the church. Chapter 4, pages 65-82, entitled "Alice Munro: Seeing Beyond Surfaces of 'Sociable Noise,'" discusses Munro's work, including *Lives*.

S49. Irvine, Lorna. "Hostility and Reconciliation: The Mother in English Canadian Fiction." Ph.D. dissertation, American University, 1977.

The love-hate tension in mother-daughter relationships, the pervasive influence of the maternal past, and traumas of separation are studied in the fiction of Margaret Atwood, Marian

Engel, Sylvia Fraser, Margaret Laurence, and Alice Munro. The autobiographical aspect of "The Peace of Utrecht" is considered. In "The Ottawa Valley," the daughter's attempts to exorcize grotesque memories of her mother fail. The mother personifies the humiliation and shame of the female body. A tension in the love-hate relationship between mother and daughter is seen sometimes to split the mother into two people. In *Lives*, Del both repudiates and acknowledges her mother. "The Peace of Utrecht" and "Red Dress-1946" show a daughter's feelings of failure to measure up to her mother's expectations that she will take over her role.

S50.   Iyer, Lalitha. "Adolescence: A Social Construct as Portrayed in *Pratham Pratishruti*, *Who Do You Think You Are* and *Lives of Girls and Women*." M. Phil. thesis, S.N.D.T. Women's University, Bombay, 1994.

A close study of the three adolescent protagonists in these books illustrates the differences between East and West in the socialization of girls and the social situation of the female adolescent in the respective cultures. Chapter 3, pages 45-75, takes the view of adolescence as a social construct of Western society. Stories in *Who* and *Lives* illustrate the conflict of adolescent females in the areas of sex, sex roles, and identity.

S51.   Johnson, Brian R. "Schools of Scandal: Gossip in Theory and Canadian Fiction." M.A. thesis, University of Manitoba, 1996.

Looks at the depiction of gossip in Robertson Davies' *Fifth Business*, Margaret Atwood's *The Handmaid's Tale*, and Munro's *Who*. Using Michel Foucault's theories of power/knowledge and self-constitution, Johnson examines the relationship between Flo and Rose and the function of gossip as a means of self-aggrandizement. Moral and functional aspects are considered in the evolution of Rose's development and her eventual rejection of gossip. The thesis considers both the story-telling and parodic aspects of gossip.

S52.   Johnson, Katherine M. "Responsible Deceits: Love, Infidelity, and Metafiction in Alice Munro." M.A. thesis, University of Denver, 1999.

Reveals connections between love as experienced by Munro's characters and how they tell their stories. Among the works discussed are: *Lives*, *Who*, "An Ounce of Cure," "Material," "Accident," "Dulse," and "Visitors." Betrayals and infidelities in love are linked with betrayals in narration and the narrator's use of metafiction. The characters' stories reveal the ambivalent way they view their lives and love. The thesis examines how they use varying narrative strategies, both in their storytelling and within their lives. Their stories are ambiguous, mysterious, and open-ended. Love is shown to hinder powers of observation and control. Its connection to faith is explored.

S53.   Kerr, Alison Patricia. "Towards a Therapeutics of Reading Literature: The Influence of Aesthetic Distance and Attachment." Ph.D. dissertation, University of Toronto, 2005.

Explores the connections between aesthetic distance, adult attachment type, and reader response. The thesis begins with an overview of reader response theory and how reading literature may produce changes in readers' identity, psyche, or way of thinking. The study involved two sample texts and the questionnaires given to 100 graduate students enrolled in English and Psychology. Underdistanced, overdistanced, and original versions of "Winter

Wind" by Alice Munro and "An Occurrence at Owl Creek Bridge" by Ambrose Bierce were used. The results indicated a strong relationship between adult attachment type and literary response. Securely attached participants had stronger emotional reactions to the stories than those who were insecurely attached. Less connection was found between aesthetic distance and reader emotional response. However, readers of the overdistanced version identified less with the main character.

S54.   Kim, Helen M. "Living the Fantasy: The Politics of Pleasure in Mass Culture." Ph.D. dissertation, University of Michigan, 1994.
The discussion on pages 124-133 shows how culture, as constituted in masculine terms, and mass-mediated femininity are rejected by Del Jordan in *Lives*, and how self-invention enables her to reinvent Jubilee through memory and art.

S55.   Lallier, Lily Marie. "L'univers féminin dans l'oeuvre romanesque d'Alice Munro." M.A. thesis, Université de Sherbrooke, 1993.
Explores the feminine world in *Dance*, *Lives*, *Who*, *Moons*, *Progress*, and *Friend* through an examination of feminine characters, cultural feminine models, the concept of love, ethical values, and the changing nature of the feminine world. The thesis first outlines the social milieu of women in *Dance* and *Lives*. It then continues with a discussion of the feminine ideal in the middle ages and the 1940s, the social status of women, and their literary representation. Three aspects of the concept of love are examined: the dream, the fulfilment, and the death of love. Values, broadly classified as ethical conscience and knowledge of the body, include a discussion of sexual puritanism, the law of causality, beauty of the body, and female sexuality. The changing feminine world is seen in terms of feminine discourse and new ways of thinking and expressing the feminine.

S56.   Lamont, Linda. "Absurdity and Horror in the Fiction of Clark Blaise and Alice Munro." M.A. thesis, University of Calgary, 1979.
Conformance to and divergence from Gothic romance are studied in *A North American Education*, *Tribal Justice*, and *Lunar Attractions* by Blaise, and in *Dance*, *Lives*, *Something*, and *Who* by Munro. Selections from these works are shown to be horror stories in the sense that they portray the disruption of ordinary daily life by the absurd and grotesque. The thesis looks at the isolation of the protagonist. It further examines how horror derives from the realization that fantasy and reality are indistinguishable. Writing is seen as an imaginative ordering response to a chaotic reality.

S57.   Langley, Sandra Wynne. "The Ideology of Form: Political Interpretation and Alice Munro's *Lives of Girls and Women*." M.A. thesis, Concordia University, 1988.
A socialist-feminist interpretation of *Lives*, seeing the novel as a process within the historical conditions of its production and reception. Langley gives a critique of the humanist criticism of Munro, then goes on to discuss the novel as a realist narrative. She outlines the narrative conventions and strategies used by Munro in light of her aesthetics. After an examination of different chapters in the work, it is shown that Del's survival is found in her accommodation to dominant authority and her simultaneous dissent from it.

S58.	Leitch, Linda. "Alice Munro's Fiction: Explorations in Open Forms." M.A. thesis, University of Guelph, 1980.

An examination of the structure of the open form in *Lives* and *Who*. The thesis begins with the emergence of the form in Munro's writing, looking at the unifying techniques of setting, character, and narrative structure, as well as the linking devices used in *Dance* and *Lives*. Munro's third book, *Something*, while without the same unity, marks an important development in the form with the introduction of time shifts and the moving away from a reliance on structural devices to create unity. Prior to final publication, earlier versions of the stories found in *Who* are shown to have undergone extensive alterations in both their texts and in their story arrangement in Munro's attempt to unify them.

S59.	Lewochko, Mary. "Circular Patterns of Change in the Feminine Quest for Self-Identity in the Novels of Margaret Atwood and Alice Munro." M.A. thesis, Concordia University, 1989.

A study of Atwood's *The Edible Woman*, *Lady Oracle*, *Dancing Girls*, *Surfacing*, and *The Handmaid's Tale*, and Munro's *Lives* and *Who*. Del's quest for self-identity in *Lives* is outlined in her rebellion against the social norms for women and her subsequent rejection of marriage and traditional female roles. Rose, the protagonist in *Who*, attempts to find her identity through a career by moving away from the roles of wife and mother. For both protagonists, the price of their deviation and freedom is loneliness, isolation, alienation, and rejection by men. However, they find consolation in the fact that they have reached a higher understanding of reality and of themselves.

S60.	Liu, Xiujie. "Narrative Structures in Alice Munro's Short Stories." M.A. thesis, Harbin Institute of Technology, 1999.

Uses theories of narratology and narrative structure to examine five types of narrative structures in Munro's stories. "The Jack Randa Hotel" is classified as a "narrative circle," while "The Progress of Love" is considered as an abstract structure. Features of stories are then examined in light of narrative time. These are exemplified by the use of contrast (repetitive narrative) structure in "The Progress of Love" and retrospective structure in "A Wilderness Station." The fifth type, applied to "The Office," is the open structure, characterized by alternation of scenes and ellipses in scenes.

S61.	Lowery, Adrien Jeanette. "The Unconvincing Truth: The Dialogical Politics of Identity Creation in the Novels of Atwood, Munro, and Gilchrist." Ph.D dissertation, University of Southern California, 2001.

Examines the path of Del Jordan's transcendental quest for identity in *Lives*. The role of the family is considered as a formative factor in Del's development. Underlined are the father's, but more especially, the mother's role in reinforcing social role expectations. Del's mother, Ada, is shown to be an atypical mother in that she outwardly conforms but at the same time holds private nonconformist views. The thesis goes on to explore the body image, the conflict of the female artist, and the use of language as a means of self-definition. Includes also a study of Margaret Atwood's *Surfacing*, *Lady Oracle*, and *Cat's Eye*, and Ellen Gilchrist's *In the Land of Dreamy Dreams*, *Net of Jewels*, and *Rhoda: A Life in Stories*.

S62. MacPherson, Cheryl S. "Speaking Silences: Narrative, Social and Metafictional Reverberations in Selected Stories by Alice Munro." M.A. thesis, University of Guelph, 1992.

A study of the significance of silence found in selected stories of *Moons*, *Progress*, and *Friend*. More specifically, it looks at silences in the experience of the characters and the narrative strategies used to present these silences. The thesis also deals with issues of classism, racism, and gender relations which relate to these silences. In the first-person stories, such as "Bardon Bus," silence suggests an interpenetration of fantasy or imagining in the narrator's perception of reality. In third-person stories, such as "Fits," silences suggest concerns with mysteries which remain unsolved. These concerns with the imagined and real, mystery and truth, imply a metafictional interest in writing and the writing process.

S63. Martin, Betty Ann. "Liberating Female Identity and Narrative from the Confines of Masculine Discourse in Alice Munro's *Lives of Girls and Women*." M.A. thesis, McMaster University, 1995.

An examination of the discovery of feminine identity and language, and the development of the female artist in the context of a patriarchal society dominated by masculine culture, discourse, and literary tradition. Del is shown to struggle for self-definition by rejecting the conventional definition of femininity which confines, imprisons, and suffocates women. Her conflicting desires of subjectivity and social acceptance result in duplicity and play-acting. In her narrative, she is both subject and witness. Sexuality is shown to mark Del's initiation into the world of feminine language. Del's narrative voice is influenced by the different forms of masculine and feminine narratives she encounters in life, especially that of her mother. The epilogue conveys Del's struggle, as a female artist, with the conflict between reality and fiction.

S64. Martin, Margaret Kathleen. "Alice Munro's Re/visionary Later Stories." M.A. thesis, University of Saskatchewan, 1995.

Uses three feminist critical approaches in the study of "Chaddeleys and Flemings," "Hold Me Fast, Don't Let Me Pass," and "The Jack Randa Hotel." First, seen from the view of feminist revisionary mythopoesis, where dissent from narrative patterns implies dissent from the social norms, the stories discussed are seen to delegitimate cultural myths embedded in the traditional story patterns of realist and romance fiction and thus challenge the power hierarchies. Viewed secondly from the materialist-feminist theory, the analysis focuses on dialectics, process, and change, specifically the physical and social changes experienced by middle-aged women. Thirdly, feminist theories of aging are used in the study of the middle-aged women in the stories. (Based on abstract)

S65. Matsell, Ruth. "Alice Munro and the Problematic Nature of Self-Definition." M.A. thesis, Memphis State University, 1992.

Perceptual and actual frames of reference are used to study self-definition in *Progress*, *Friend*, and *Moons*. In the story "Lichen," frames are shown to offer a sense of power and control and to make individual human connection possible, while in "Miles City, Montana," the characters are seen as victims of self-awareness. With reference to "Oranges and Apples," "Friend of My Youth," and "Meneseteung," fragments of personal identity appear in the universal frame of Canadian identity or historical reality. The frames in *Moons*, specifically in the stories "Connection," "Accident," and "Labor Day Dinner," centre around the theme of self-knowledge and the "shock of recognition."

S66.   Matthews, Carol Anne. "'Innumerable Repetitions, Innumerable Variations': The Vision and Craft of Alice Munro." M.A. thesis, Dalhousie University, 1983.

A study of Munro's double or dual-world vision through an analysis of the structure, language, and description found in her first four books. Selected stories in *Dance* present "the other world" as a world to fear. An attempt to reconcile "the other world" with the real world is made by the protagonist in *Lives*. In *Something*, duality is created by the tension between order and chaos. The tension between past and present, fantasy and reality, ugliness and beauty, and the roles of wife and lover create in the protagonist of *Who* a "multi-world" vision. The dual-world vision resumes in *Moons*.

S67.   McCaig, JoAnn Elizabeth. "Beggar Maid: Alice Munro's Archives and the Cultural Space of Authorship." Ph.D dissertation, University of Calgary, 1997.

The literary archives of Alice Munro, located in the University of Calgary Library, were used in the research for this study. Looking at the factors of nationality (Canadian), gender (female), and social class, McCaig shows the development of Munro's career in Canada and the United States. The thesis examines the role Robert Weaver played in Munro's early career in Canada and Virginia Barber's critical role in establishing Munro as an author of authority. Munro's relationship with her publishers is explored through the complicated publishing history of *Who*. Readers' response to Munro's writing is found in the letters at the archives.

S68.   McGill, Robert J. "Travelling through Fiction: Alice Munro's Topographies." M.Phil. thesis, University of Oxford, 2001.
    Pub. revised as "Somewhere I've Been Meaning To Tell You: Alice Munro's Fiction of Distance." *Journal of Commonwealth Literature* 37.1 (April 2002): 9-29.
    Pub. revised as "Where Do You Think You Are? Alice Munro's Open Houses." *Mosaic* 35.4 (December 2002): 103-119.

See annotations under these entries in the Articles and Chapters in Books section.

S69.   McLatchie, Ian B. "*Spit Delaney's Island* and *Lives of Girls and Women*: The Experiments in Cyclical Form." M.A. thesis, University of Toronto, 1981.

After an initial discussion of the short story cycle and the short story as literary form, McLatchie proceeds to show how the meaning of the fragmentary form of *Lives* emerges in the final pages. First he considers the form of each chapter as a short story, then as a part of the whole. The chapter structure, and the methods used to produce it, are shown to progress from the discrete, self-enclosed chapter, "The Flats Road," to the novella-type story found in "Baptizing," which is the most removed from the short story form. It is in the final chapter, "Epilogue: The Photographer," that the narrative elements are brought together. Unity is also present in the consistent narrative tone, something which is not present in Jack Hodgin's *Spit Delaney's Island*.

S70.   Mokros, Anne. "Subversion and Empowerment: Mother-Daughter Story Telling in Selected Texts of Margaret Laurence and Alice Munro, and in Authorial Experience." M.A. research essay, Carleton University, 1992 (degree 1993).

Uses two theories, the materialist theory of dialectical relations of reproduction and the feminist theory of language and the feminine, as reference points. In "The Peace of Utrecht," "Princess Ida," "The Progress of Love," and "Royal Beatings" storytelling of mothers to daughters is related to the material conditions of women's lives and to the language they use. The stories told are a source of empowerment for women, in that they subvert the patriarchal discourse and provide strong role models and examples for young daughters.

S71. Moschapidakis, Helen Kafatou. "Discovery through Fiction: Rethinking the Paradox of Sacrifice and Desire." Psy.D. dissertation, Massachusetts School of Professional Psychology, 2001.

A discussion of "The Love of a Good Woman" appears on pages 41-58. The study focuses on the tensions between the care of others and self-interest, between duty and pleasure, and between collectivism and individualism. It outlines the nature of duty and caring for others, and the resultant joy and therapeutic growth of the caregiver, which in turn enables her to accept pleasure and desire into her life.

S72. Moss, Laura F. "'An Infinity of Alternate Realities': Reconfiguring Realism in Postcolonial Theory and Fiction." Ph.D. dissertation, Queen's University, 1998.

Chapter 4, pages 89-116, entitled "Quilting 'Many-Dimensionality' into Canadian Realism," looks at Margaret Atwood's *Alias Grace* and Munro's "Wilderness Station" with a focus on the authors' use of literary realism to destabilize notions of authenticity, historical reality, and cultural reliability. The analysis points out the overwhelming sense of contradiction and ambiguity in Munro's story by reviewing the multiple versions of Simon's death, the ambivalent characterization of Annie, and the lack of closure.

S73. Nadkarny, Prema. "The Small Town in the Fiction of Alice Munro." M. Phil. thesis, S.N.D.T. Women's University, Bombay, 1993.

An exploration of the natural, physical, historical, and social aspects of the small town in Munro's fiction. The thesis begins with a look at the influence of the natural landscape and environment on the growth of the small town and its way of life. Aspects of regionalism illustrated in the landscape, the mythic quality of rivers, animal and bird motifs, elements of nature, and animals are studied in relation to *Lives* and selected stories from other works. The small town in Munro's fiction, particularly Jubilee in *Lives*, is perceived in its rootedness and limitedness where the inhabitants are surrounded by tradition, myth, and story, and at the same time are imprisoned within their ordinary lives. The thesis goes on to explore the variety of relationships of the people in small towns, the meaning of lineage, and the relationships between towns and the outside world.

S74. Næss, Gunn Reinertsen. "'Real Life': Alice Munro's Girls and Women." Cand. Philol. thesis, University of Oslo, 1984.

Examines technique, prevalent themes, and style in stories which depict childhood and adolescence in *Dance*, *Lives*, *Something*, *Who*, and *Moons*. The thesis shows how Munro's use of time perspectives creates irony in the narrator's retrospective telling of a story and how this irony produces humour. Aspects of the theme of mother-daughter relationships are considered, namely daughters' emotions of ambivalence and feelings of confusion toward their mothers, and the problems of communication between them. In a separate chapter,

Næss looks at the female artists, both girls and women, who either aspire to become artists or are artists. In one of the final chapters, Munro herself is the subject of study and is considered as a woman writer who gives shape to the female experience with her "female approach."

S75. Obexer, Regina. "Three Portraits of the Artist as a Young Woman: Womanhood, Art, and Other (Im)possibilities in *Violet Clay*, *Lives of Girls and Women* and *A Bird in the House*." Mag. Phil. thesis (Leopold-Franzens), Universität Innsbruck, 1996.

Elaborates on the patterns of artistic and female development in the three works. The thesis considers the autobiographical impulses of artists writing about artists and covers the growth of the woman and artist through an examination of different formative factors, notably the mother-daughter relationship, storytelling, power, and love. (Based on the Table of Contents)

S76. Osachoff, Margaret Gail. "Pastoralism and Technology in Recent Canadian Fiction." Ph.D. dissertation, University of Alberta, 1978.

The section discussing Munro's fiction is found on pages 263-307. Osachoff posits that in Munro's work there is no sense of new technology, nor can her small town scenes be considered pastoral. Neither technology nor nature are seen as good or bad, or as superior to each other. The treatment of each subject is studied in *Lives* and in selected stories from *Dance* and *Something*. Technology in the form of cars and modern household conveniences is examined in "Thanks for the Ride" and "Sunday Afternoon" respectively. Pastoralism is considered in "Memorial," "Walking on Water," and "Marakesh."

S77. Østby, Inger-Mette. "What Constitutes the Artistic Mind?: A Study of L. M. Montgomery's *Emily of New Moon* and Alice Munro's *Lives of Girls and Women*." Cand. Philol. thesis, University of Oslo, 1991.

An inquiry into what makes the artist different from the ordinary person. The constitution of an artistic mind, like that of Del Jordan, is determined to be influenced by a number of factors both in the artist's environment and in her personality. The first characteristic of the artistic mind is found in her/his realistic approach to art and life. This is examined both in Munro herself and in Del, who has a clear and detailed vision of life, and searches for realism in her art. Three personal qualities in Del (the capacity for observation, her sensitivity to the feelings of others, and a temperament which is characterized by the need for independence) are all shown to be other qualities of the artist. Finally the artist is considered in light of artistic ambition and the need to write. *Lives* is proposed as an autobiographical novel, based on Munro's own childhood.

S78. Packer, Miriam. "Beyond the Garrison: Approaching the Wilderness in Margaret Laurence, Alice Munro, and Margaret Atwood." Ph.D. dissertation, Université de Montréal, 1977 (degree 1978).

A comparative study of the theme of defense, and of tone and style in Margaret Laurence's *The Stone Angel*, *A Jest of God*, *The Fire-Dwellers*, and *The Diviners*, Margaret Atwood's *The Edible Woman*, *Surfacing*, and *Lady Oracle*, and Munro's *Dance*, *Lives*, and *Something*. Women are studied as victims, both of class structure and of the conditions of their lives. Many are threatened by deep feelings and by painful pasts. These are conceptualized as real and metaphorical wildernesses, from which they seek to escape by means of a destructive psychological defense, called an "imprisoning garrison." Female characters in many of Munro's stories are studied—those imprisoned in the garrison mentality such as abandoned maiden figures, and those who have survived the wilderness and learned to accept pain and even to have cause for faith and hope.

S79. Paletta, Anna. "From Subordinate to Subversive: Feminist Fiction as an Instrument in Expanding and Changing the Social Meaning of Gender." M.A. thesis, University of Victoria, 1985, c1990.

Views contemporary feminist fiction, as exemplified by Margaret Atwood's *The Handmaid's Tale*, Alice Walker's *The Color Purple*, and Munro's *Lives*, as counter-hegemonic cultural production. In this fiction, the subordination of women is presented in terms of their victimization in marriage and in the organization of the household. Women are also considered as victims of sexual violence. In *Lives,* Del and Addie are shown to resist subordination and to provide for the reader an alternative and liberating image of women.

S80. Passek, Lynn. "Techniques of Closure in the Short Stories of Alice Munro." M.A. thesis, San Francisco State University, 1992.

Direct and indirect forms of closure and the methods used to achieve these are examined in stories from *Dance, Lives, Something, Beggar,* and *Moons*. Direct closure is found in stories which end with the most resolution. It is propelled by major grotesque characters or situations. Grotesque characters and Munro's compassionate treatment of them are shown to reflect her vision of the world. "Images," "Royal Beatings," and "Dance of the Happy Shades" are some of the stories discussed. Indirect closure is found in stories which have indeterminate endings and which change direction after a pivotal point occurs, such as in "Memorial" and "Mrs. Cross and Mrs. Kidd."

S81. Penner, Maxine Dawn. "Narrative Preoccupations: The Interconnectedness of Technique and Subject in the Fiction of Alice Munro." M.A. thesis, University of Saskatchewan, c1985, 1986.

Studies the relationship between the retrospective technique and the major theme of the developing artist in *Dance, Lives, Something, Who,* and *Moons*. The thesis first looks at Munro's first-person approach to the retrospective narrator, followed by the third-person approach where the narration is from the point of view of the protagonist. It is shown how these approaches are appropriate in the case of artist figures and their retrospective accounts of their development through a detailing of their past and their relationships, especially mother-daughter, as females and artists. The retrospective technique continues in *Moons*, but changes somewhat with the insertion of more recent adult experiences into the narrative, especially those relating to father-daughter relationships. (Based on abstract)

S82. Perkin-McFarland, Anne Louise. "Connection and Dislocation: Themes in Recent Short Stories by Canadian Women Writers." M.A. thesis, University of New Brunswick, 1992.

Munro's portrayal of human relationships is shown through this study of connection and dislocation/alienation. Her treatment is contrasted with stories by Miriam Waddington, Margaret Atwood, and Janette Turner Hospital. Family heritage and a sense of belonging are discussed for stories such as "Chaddeleys and Flemings." The thesis goes on to examine relationships within the family, especially the mother-daughter relationship in stories such as "Friend of My Youth," the grandmother-mother-daughter relationship in "The Progress of Love," and the father-daughter relationship in "The Moons of Jupiter." Women's search for connection through relationships with men is exemplified by stories such as "Material" and "Bardon Bus."

S83.   Potter, John. "Ordinary Children, Extraordinary Journeys: The Role of Imagination in the Early Life and Selected Fiction of Alice Munro." M.ED. thesis, University of Western Ontario, 1998.

Munro's fiction and her early life, including a study of her early reading and writing, are used to illustrate the role of imagination in childhood and its application to the education of children in the classroom. The thesis looks at six of Munro's stories and discusses each in terms of patterns and connections involving a specific type of imagination. Romantic imagination is associated with examples of childhood fantasizing, the heroic imagination with questing in childhood, and the mythic imagination with storytelling in childhood. "Walker Brothers Cowboy," "Boys and Girls," "Heirs of the Living Body," "Changes and Ceremonies," "Winter Wind," and "The Ottawa Valley" are the stories used as illustrations.

S84.   Powell, Barbara Pezalla. "Narrative Voices of Alice Munro." Ph.D. dissertation, York University, 1980 (degree 1981).

An examination of typical stylistic and structural features of "How I Met My Husband," "Forgiveness in Families," "Postcard," "The Time of Death," "Something I've Been Meaning to Tell You," "Thanks for the Ride," and "Material." The thesis sets out to show how Munro can make an unsophisticated narrator speak within a literary short story. Based on the literary theory of story and voice, the framework used in the discussion of each text is narrative structure, rhetorical structure, and voice. Also applied to the description is a linguistic framework, including linguistic theory and linguistic structure.

S85.   Prendergast, Kathleen. "'The Facts Are Not to be Reconciled': Alice Munro's Use of the Grotesque as a Narrative Strategy in Six Short Stories." M.A. thesis, University of Saskatchewan, 2001.

In the stories discussed, the grotesque is used as a strategy in furthering the development of the protagonist. It serves as a catalyst or turning point which transforms the life of characters by revealing truths about themselves or changing the way they view themselves, their lives, or their world. The grotesque, associated with the motif of bodily degradation and insanity and termed 'bodily grotesque,' is examined in "Heirs of the Living Body" and "The Ottawa Valley." Embodied in the motif of comic violence is the 'comic grotesque,' as found in "Thanks for the Ride" and "Carried Away." Revelatory grotesque is illustrated by the stories "Visitors" and "Five Points." (Based on abstract)

S86.   Rankin, Linda Marie. "Sexual Roles in the Fiction of Alice Munro." M.A. thesis, University of New Brunswick, 1977 (degree 1978).

Examines sexual roles as portrayed in *Dance*, *Something*, *Lives*, and the uncollected story "The Beggar Maid." First, interviews of Munro are used to illustrate her personal views on the subject. The thesis goes on to describe Munro's methods of characterization, then the characteristics common to her female and male characters. Sexual roles are discussed as they relate to females in different age groups, from preteen adolescents through to middle-aged women, married or single, and finally the elderly. Detailed attention is paid to the gender roles of male and female characters in *Lives*, and contrasts are made between conforming and non-conforming characters.

S87.   Reid, Susan E. Bryan. "Two Portrait of the Artist Novels: Writing the Creative Ordering of Experience." M.A. research paper, Carleton University, 1978.

Compares Gabrielle Roy's universal approach to human experience in *La Route d'Altamont* to Munro's individualistic and superrealistic one in *Lives*. By means of retrospection, characters are shown to come to terms with their experience and to take control over it, as the narrator attempts to do in "The Ottawa Valley." The creative reworking of experience produces a new reality for characters like Del Jordan in *Lives*. As a narrator with two levels of consciousness, one in the past and the other in the present, Del is able to retrospectively order all the contradictory and incongruous experiences of her past to create a new clarity.

S88.   Reid, Verna M. "Perceptions of the Small Town in Canadian Fiction." M.A. thesis, University of Calgary, 1972.

A thematic study of fictional towns in the work of eight authors, including Munro. *Lives* is used as a touchstone in the discussion. The fictional small town is characterized as a place from which one is forced to escape and to which one is compelled to return. The fiction portrays towns as being seen through characters' memory—"towns of the mind," products of the imagination and environment. Ada Jordan's and Del's relationship with Jubilee are discussed in terms of the small town as a colonial outpost, as a garrison-prison, as a female domain, and as a symbol of home.

S89.   Reimer, Elizabeth Anne. "Reconceiving the Feminist Biographical Subject: A Study In Metabiography." Ph.D dissertation, University of Toronto, 2003.

The chapter on pages 58-91,"'Rescuing One Thing from the Rubbish': Salvaging Feminist Biography in Alice Munro's 'Meneseteung,'" analyses the story as a revisionist feminist biography and as a mock-metabiography. A narrator, as a metabiographer, has the function of both "fictionalizing" and "representing" history. The illusion of historical fact challenges the reader to distinguish between fact and fiction. The narrator in the story is set up as an objective reporter, but later proceeds to deconstruct Almeda for the sake of biographical truth. The use of dialogism and dialogue are discussed.

S90.   Roark, Margaret S. "A Spacious Story: Moral Agency and Empathy in Alice Munro's 'My Mother's Dream.'" M.A. thesis, University of North Carolina at Wilmington, 2001.

Examines the story from the perspective of an ethical narrative, with concepts from feminist ethics. The thesis shows how two aspects of moral life, agency and empathy, function in the assumption of responsibility. Ethicality is first studied in the substance of the story where dream narrative, fragility of self, meaning and connection, and responsibility and love are demonstrated and discussed. The second consideration of how ethicality functions in the story is that of the narrative strategies used, or how the story is told by the daughter-narrator who is shown to have inherited her mother's tools of agency and empathy.

S91. Robson, H. P. Nora. "Wawanash County: Parallels Between the World of Alice Munro and the White American South." M.A. thesis, McGill University, 1978.

A sense of place, history, family tradition, quest, and the grotesque are used as points of comparison between Munro's fiction and that of Eudora Welty, Flannery O'Connor, and Carson McCullers. The Wawanash County and river are shown to have mythic and folkloric counterparts in the regions and rivers of the Southern writers. Similarities are also found in areas of family heritage and family bonds. The image of the father is examined in "Images" and "Walker Brothers Cowboy." Different family dynamics evident in *Lives* and other stories are discussed. Finally, the thesis looks at the three themes of alienation, isolation, and rejection found in *Lives* and in selected stories of *Dance*.

S92. Rogalus, Paul William. "Alice Munro and the Craft of Short Fiction." Ph.D. dissertation, Purdue University, 1992.

Shows how Munro's narrative technique is intimately bound up with theme or meaning and how both have changed over Munro's writing career. In *Dance*, the stories dwell on private individual problems. The characters often experience moments of insight or epiphanies. Larger social issues are dealt with in *Something*. Stories in *Beggar* and in *Moons* show life as being less coherent and more mysterious. Fragmentary techniques are used to convey the chaotic nature of characters' lives. By *Progress* and *Friend*, characters are shown to impose patterns of meaning on their lives and the stories have a more coherent technical framework and connectedness of form.

S93. Rønnestad, Trude. "Treachery Is the Other Side of Dailiness: Om representasjon, identitet og skam i Alice Munro's *The Beggar Maid*." Hovedoppgave, Universitet i Oslo, 2005.

Begins with a consideration of *Beggar* in terms of modern short story theory and whether the work is a collection of separate or continuous stories. Then, narratology is examined in "Royal Beatings" with reference to voice, narrative perspective, and distancing. A thematic approach to the same story looks at the protagonist's environment of poverty and isolation in West Hanratty, the dynamics between Rose and her parents, and Rose's tendency to fantasize and role-play as evidenced in "the royal beating." Mirroring the format of the story analysis, Beggar is then treated as a short story cycle with attention paid to the recurring themes of social class, alienation, identity, role-playing, love, shame, speech and silence, and home place.

S94. Rose, Anita R. "The Female Hero in the Short Fiction of Eudora Welty and Alice Munro." M.A. thesis, Western Carolina University, 1991.

The hero's quest of female characters is compared in Welty's "Livvie," "A Curtain of Green," and "Lily Daw and the Three Ladies," and in Munro's "The Office," "Dulse," and "Meneseteung." Munro's postmodern sensibility is contrasted with Welty's mythic sensibility and use of mythology. The protagonists in all the stories derive their heroic status from their struggle to stay true to themselves in the face of contradictory expectations. The stories illustrate the marginality of women and their conflict between individual freedom and "biological destiny."

S95. Roy, Michel. "Traduction de l'anglais au français des deux premiers chapitres du roman *Lives of Girls and Women* d'Alice Munro." M.A. thesis, Université de Sherbrooke, 1990.

Presents a French translation of "The Flats Road" and "Heirs of the Living Body." A preliminary section of critical analysis outlines the near-magical powers associated with Uncle Benny and the fantastic world in which he lives. Uncle Craig's writing of history is seen in the wider context of "the body of literature." The character of Mary Agnes is also discussed. An "Annexe Technique" gives a review and examination of translation problems.

S96. Rubens, Pamela. "Internship at *Stories* Magazine and Critical Essay on Alice Munro." M.F.A. thesis, Emerson College, 1988.

Examines the themes and the female point of view in *Progress*. The thesis compares and contrasts these with stories from *Dance* and *Moons*. (Based on abstract)

S97. Rubio, Jennie. "'In an Alphabet I Did Not Know': Reading Space in Montgomery, Laurence and Munro." M.A. thesis, McMaster University, 1992.

A study of cultural and noncultural space in Montgomery's *Emily of New Moon*, Laurence's *The Diviners*, and Munro's *Lives*. In "The Flats Road," noncultural space is found in the undefined natural world and in the fantastic world of the imagination. Del, in her preadolescence, finds connections to the natural and imaginary worlds. As she grows older, she finds that cultural space is a terrifying world where connections are replaced by social expectations and she struggles as a female to fit into this cultural script. The place of nonconformity or eccentricity is demonstrated in "Changes and Ceremonies." Del's explorations in spaces outside the cultural scripts lead her to the creation of her own script through writing and language.

S98. Saint-Louis, Louise. "Traduction de deux nouvelles d'Alice Munro: suivie d'un commentaire." M.A. thesis, Université Laval, 1986.

This translation into French of "The Spanish Lady" and "How I Met My Husband" is followed by a commentary on modern literary translation. Peter Newmark's and Jean-Paul Vinay's theories of translation are applied to sentences in the two stories to illustrate the difference between literal and free translation. The comments also include the difficulties associated with the translation of metaphors.

S99. Samuels, Selina. "Fertile Soil: Short Stories by Women from Australia, Canada and the Caribbean, 1968-1995." Ph.D. dissertation, Queen Mary and Westfield College, 1997.

Posits that the links between the structure of the short story, feminist theory, and regional theory create a model of the short story as counter-narrative. Chapter 3, pages 97-134, looks at Margaret Atwood's "Significant Moments in the Life of My Mother" and Munro's "The Ottawa Valley," "The Peace of Utrecht," and "Friend of My Youth." Areas examined are the interrelationships and continuity across female generations, female literary inheritance, cross-generational storytelling, and narrator/daughter and mother relationships. The regional aspects are brought out in discussions of small-town Ontario, the mythologized motherland, and the Canadian wilderness as a positive space for female creativity. Chapter 5, pages 171-206, examines Jamaica Kincaid's *At the Bottom of the River* and Munro's *Lives* and *Beggar* as short-story cycles. The structure and the strategies, and the themes of female relationships and storytelling are examined.

S100. Selby, Pamela. "The Artistic Vision of Alice Munro." M.A. thesis, Eastern Washington University, 1988.

Examines *Lives*, *Beggar*, and selected stories in light of the role of art in both Munro's and her characters' vision of life. The absurdity, banality, and lack of any divine guidance in the lives of the characters lead them on a quest for meaning and answers. For the protagonists in the two books, the answers are not found in faith or fantasy, but in artistic expression. The personas of Del and Rose are used by Munro to express her own vision of reality. This vision is examined in association with her technique of magic realism. The art and artifice of fiction writing is examined in the story "Material."

S101. Sexton, Melanie. "The Woman's Voice: The Post-Realist Fiction of Margaret Atwood, Mavis Gallant and Alice Munro." Ph.D. dissertation, University of Ottawa, 1993.

Discusses language, dialogism, and self-construction as they relate to women and their voice. Language, narrative control, and power are elements which dominate the stories in *Something*. In *Lives*, a study is made of the diverse discourses which impinge upon, or are integral to, Del's search for her own voice: tabloids, oral stories of the female body, of childhood, discourses of religion, and discourses of sex. The construction of the self is illustrated by Rose in *Who*. The book is examined in its adherence to and departure from the *Bildungsroman*. The significance of role-playing, public performance, and disguise is discussed as part of Rose's difficult journey to self-definition.

S102. Shojania, Moti Gharib. "Descartes' Doubting Daughters: The Care of the Self in the Fiction of Atwood, Laurence, and Munro." Ph.D. dissertation, University of Manitoba, 1995.

Examines each writer's approach to the Cartesian mind/body problem and Michel Foucault's notion of the "care of the self." In Chapter 3, pages 138-228, entitled "Constructed with Terrible Care: Self-Fashioning in Munro's Fiction," Munro's approach and techniques are discussed. The chapter begins with a survey of the discursive practices found in *Lives* and a consideration of their role in subject formation. The analysis turns to the care of the self as a body to be made beautiful and to the construction of the self as illustrated in Del's aunts, including Nile. The construction of persona through mimesis is detailed in Rose, the protagonist of *Who*. Deception, a technique of self-care in *Something*, is described as being in conflict with the need of characters to tell the truth. Other mind/body problems appearing in the same collection include the inability of characters to articulate what they need to say or the suffering caused by complicity and duplicity.

S103. Sinklier, Laurie Jill. "Rose by Any Other Word: A Textual Study of the Stories in Alice Munro's *The Beggar Maid: Stories of Flo and Rose*." M.A. thesis, Texas Tech University, 1999.

Details the extensive revisions Munro made to the original versions of the stories in order to produce one clear and consistent character as the protagonist of the book. A comparison of the original and final versions revealed name changes in seven of the stories where the main character's name was not Rose. Munro also made a major alteration in the narrative perspective, changing from a first-person narrative to a third-person. Substantial revisions and added details were found to add clarity and vividness to the narrative. Changes in the form of anecdotes and physical description aided in the characterization of Rose.

S104.   Smythe, Karen E. "Works of Mourning: The Elegiac Fiction of Mavis Gallant and Alice Munro." Ph.D. dissertation, University of Toronto, 1990.
Pub. revised as *Figuring Grief: Gallant, Munro and the Poetics of Elegy*. Montreal: McGill-Queen's University Press, 1992.

Proposes that the use of realism invokes an "anti-entropic" documentation of life as a way to stop the process of natural decay. Smythe examines Munro's technique of photographic realism in her stories of death, loss, grief, and mourning. She looks at both the reader's and character's experience of epiphany, much like that of "photographic shock," and the way this provides consolation. The dissertation examines stories containing deaths in families, anticipatory grief, storytelling and mourning, love and loss, sexuality and human mortality. The chapters on Munro are: "Munro and Modern Elegy," pages 267-314; "Munrovian Melancholy", pages 315-354.

S105.   Snyder, Rebecca Lynn. "'Living a Life Out Here': Place, Gender, and Marriage in Three Stories from Munro's *Open Secrets*." M.A. thesis, California State University, Fresno, 1997.

Investigates how the imagery and mystique associated with place or landscape are transformed by the presence of women in traditionally male stories or roles, particularly when marriage is involved. Three types of landscape enter into the discussion: the landscape of the wilderness or natural world as found in "A Real Life"; the landscape of the frontier or unexplored unsettled area exemplified in "A Wilderness Station"; and the landscape of the community, illustrated by Carstairs in "Carried Away." Within this context of place, an examination is made of the association of women to the wilderness, real or metaphorical, and to the nontraditional and traditional roles women play outside and within marriage.

S106.   Somerville, J. Christine. "Stories and Storytelling in Alice Munro's Fiction." M.A. thesis, University of British Columbia, 1985.

Elaborates on the function of stories and storytelling as a counterpoint to experience for Munro's characters. Memory makes recollected stories resemble recollected experience. Stories in *Dance*, specifically "Images," "Boys and Girls," and "The Peace of Utrecht," show how stories affect the perception, personality, and memories of children. In *Lives* and *Who*, storytelling is central to both protagonists as developing artists. In *Something*, the embedding of stories within the narrative imitates the workings of memory. In this work, Munro also experiments with different points of view. Stories about family, connection, and time in *Moons* reveal the differences between male and female ways of thinking. "The Moons of Jupiter," "Dulse," and "Mrs. Cross and Mrs. Kidd" are examined in more detail.

S107.   Stead, Katrina M. "From Cowlike Contentment, Good Lord Deliver Us: Narrative Strategies in 20th-Century English-Canadian Fiction Written by Women." Ph.D. dissertation, Reading University, 1994.

Chapter 8, pages 316-350, entitled "The Twinkling of an 'I': Alice Munro and Helen Weinzwieg," is concerned with stories in *Friend* and Munro's narrative strategy of approaching their themes through an investigation of the shifting subject of self. The theme of mother-daughter relationships in the collection and the title story is expanded on. In the title story, there is a question of truth in the description of the mother in the narrative text. The metaphor of the house is examined in "Wigtime," in addition to the constructed image of self.

"Pictures of the Ice" also presents a case of a constructed self-image, but one which is physical and another which is imaginary. Almeda in "Meneseteung" appears as a series of selves hidden beneath the outer woman.

S108.   Steele, Clare. "Adolescent Heroines: The Mother-Daughter Relationship in Laurence, Munro and Thomas." M.A. thesis, Université de Montréal, 1991.

A comparative study of mother-daughter conflict in Margaret Laurence's *A Bird in the House*, Audrey Thomas's *Songs My Mother Taught Me*, and Munro's *Lives*. Comparisons are made between the young literary heroines, between the personal backgrounds of the three authors and their novels, and between the fictional mothers. Chapter 3, pages 34-49, is entitled "Del Jordan: Lives of Girls and Women." Beginning with a look at the personality and independence of Ada Jordan, the thesis then proceeds to outline the differing views of the mother and daughter on death, religion, and sex. For Del, sex is a rite of passage which brings her to maturity and frees her from her mother. In the end, Del develops Ada's strengths while rejecting her weaknesses.

S109.   Stone, Claire L. "Understatement, Ellipsis and the Non-Ending in Selected Stories by Anton Chekhov and Alice Munro." M.A. thesis, University of North Carolina at Chapel Hill, 1994.

Begins by pointing out thematic and stylistic similarities between the two authors in their use of understatement, and the subsequent undercurrents of suggestion in their depiction of everyday life. Munro's technique of using small incidental developments and understatement brings prominence to the emotional lives of her characters. Understatement is discussed in "Walker Brothers Cowboy," "The Turkey Season," "The Peace of Utrecht," and "The Moons of Jupiter." Ellipsis, used more extensively by Munro than Chekhov, is illustrated in "The Time of Death," where temporal ellipsis is used, and in "Material," "Miles City, Montana," and "The Moons of Jupiter," where ellipsis is found in narrative disarrangement. Nonendings are examined in "The Peace of Utrecht," "The Moons of Jupiter," "The Spanish Lady," and "Hold Me Fast, Don't Let Me Pass."

S110.   Straif, Barbara. "A Room of Her Own: The Woman Artist and Space in Alice Munro's *Lives of Girls and Women* and *Who Do You Think You Are?*" Mag. Phil. thesis (Leopold-Franzens), Universität Innsbruck, 2001.

Follows the paths of the protagonists from their childhood and restrictive home environments to their emancipation and pursuit of artistic ambitions in a space of their own. The rural-urban nature of Jubilee and its surroundings and the social environment are compared with those of Hanratty. Female stereotypes in the lives of the protagonists receive scrutiny, especially the mothers of the protagonists and their influence on their daughters. The development of Del and Rose is studied in its progression from their early interest in boys and relationships with girls, through to their search for faith, and finally their experiences with sexuality and love. Both come to the realization that their ambitions cannot be fulfilled at home but in a private space elsewhere. The thesis concludes by examining the influences that shaped Del's life as an artist and how she used writing as a space.

S111.   Struthers, J. R. (Tim). "Intersecting Orbits: A Study of Selected Story Cycles by Hugh Hood, Jack Hodgins, Clark Blaise, and Alice Munro, in Their Literary Contexts."

Ph.D. dissertation, University of Western Ontario, 1981 (accepted 1982).
A study of Hugh Hood's *Around the Mountain*, Jack Hodgins' *Spit Delaney's Island*, Clark Blaise's *A North American Education*, and Munro's *Who*. The unifying features in Munro's short story cycle, *Who*, are explored in Chapter 5, pages 319-323, "Wide Open Windows: Who Do You Think You Are?" Generally these features include narrative method, a consistent vision of reality, artistic distortion, recurring storytelling, dreams and memoirs, patterns, rituals, and ceremonies in life, and the use of imagery and similes. These features are then specifically applied to the book, showing how, chapter by chapter, unity is achieved in the structure, theme, characterization, and images.

S112. Sturgess, Charlotte Jane. "A Politics of Location: Subjectivity and Origins in the Work of Mavis Gallant, Alice Munro and Margaret Atwood." Ph.D. dissertation, Queen Mary and Westfield College, 1993.

Links the concepts of feminine identity and place/locality (real or metaphorical) in Canadian women's writing. Chapter 2 looks at stories in *Friend* and *Something* which are concerned with women's relationships with men and the dominant place of men in their desires and fantasies. It also examines female sexuality and "erotic landscapes of the mind." The chapter goes on to explore, in *Beggar*, the relationship between female selfhood and roleplaying by Flo and Rose. In Chapter 9, family secrets and the search for identity through the community are discussed as central themes in the story "The Progress of Love." Turning to *Lives*, the focus is on Madeleine and her place in Flats Road, which is neither inside nor outside the town. The chapter ends with a study of female sexuality as a landscape and language. Spaces of identity are discussed in "The Progress of Love" and "Wild Swans."

S113. Suppan, Christiane. "Alice Munros *Lives of Girls and Women* und *The Progress of Love* als Kurzgeschichtenzyklen. (Unter Berücksichtigung von *Dubliners* und *Winesburg, Ohio*)." Diplomarbeit zur Erlangung des Magistergrades, Universität Graz, 1991.

Examines the structure of the two works as short-story cycles. The thesis shows how levels of integration (unification) and segmentation (separation) with respect to setting, characters, plot, time, themes, motifs, and narrative situation are used to create unity in a series of linked stories. After looking at the unifying elements in *Lives*, the thesis compares the novel to Sherwood Anderson's *Winesburg* and comes to the conclusion that the former is closer to the novel form than the latter. On the other hand, *Progress*, in which the unity relies on a central thematic complex, is considered to be closer to a collection than James Joyce's *Dubliners*. The thesis contains a summary in English.

S114. Sutherland, Katherine Gail. "Bloodletters: Configurations of Female Sexuality in Canadian Women's Writing." Ph.D. dissertation, York University, 1993.

Chapter 3, pages 302-313, entitled "The Gypsies Have Departed," focuses on "Meneseteung." In the discussion on female sexuality, Sutherland links menstruation to the female voice. The feminine body is discussed. Space, represented by the house, is viewed as synonymous with the protagonist. Sexuality and voice are seen to be inherent to identity. Identity is seen as fluid and as hiding beneath the surface more than it reveals. Female sexual blood, incest, and witchcraft are symbolically linked in a history of female sexuality. In this context, the concept of the protagonist as a witch is explored.

S115. Switocz, Barbara M. "The Language of Power: Authentic Selfhood in Alice Munro's Protagonist." M.A. research essay, Carleton University, 1987.

Features the protagonists' struggle against male domination in Munro's fiction. Switocz looks at the role of language in men's control over women. The feeling of injustice of young female protagonists and their brief painful experiences in their father's sphere cause them to reject both male and female spheres, and to seek an alternative sphere through imagination and silence or a refusal to speak the male language. The adult female protagonist seeks beyond the existing systems to fulfil her desires and obtain a balance of power in her relationships with men, thus achieving authentic selfhood and finding a language of her own. (Based on abstract)

S116. Tanaszi, Margaret. "Emancipation of Consciousness in Alice Munro's *Lives of Girls and Women*." M.A. thesis, Queen's University, 1972.

Within the context of feminist literary criticism, the thesis illustrates how Del's journey to maturity and independence has the effect also of freeing her mind. Thematic and structural tensions are discussed for the chapters, along with the stylistic devices used to support them. Del's early family and community environment, her response to her mother's attitudes and beliefs, and the gradual formation of her own values and aspirations through her experiences with religion, sex, and love are outlined. The analysis finally covers the theme and structure of the introspective last chapter. A concluding section evaluates the place of *Lives* in literature by and about women.

S117. Tanaszi, Margaret. "Feminine Consciousness in Contemporary Canadian Fiction, with Special Reference to Margaret Atwood, Margaret Laurence and Alice Munro." Ph.D. dissertation, Leeds University, 1977.

The section on Munro, pages 289-414, discusses "feminine sensibility" in terms of sensitivity to tone and texture in *Dance*, *Something*, and *Lives*. *Dance* is characterized by an inexpressible reality that can be felt. This comes about through the surface details of features, feelings, and situations which cumulate to produce a distilled quality of reality. It is shown how tension and emotions produce an emotional tone in many of the stories in which there is conveyed a vague distress of being female. The stories in *Something* continue with feminine problems—eccentricities, contrasts, abstractions, and situations of instability which are mirrored in the tone and texture. In a detailed coverage of *Lives*, Tanaszi reveals Munro's craftsmanship at its best.

S118. Teahen, Kelley. "Hopechests and Cashmere, or How to Be a Woman: Rebelling against the Small Town in the Fiction of Margaret Laurence and Alice Munro." M.A. thesis, Dalhousie University, 1984.

Compares the influence of the small town on the identity of the female protagonist in Margaret Laurence's *The Stone Angel*, *A Jest of God,* and *The Diviners*, and Munro's *Lives*, *Who*, and "Chaddeleys and Flemings." The values of the small town in Munro are associated with a rigid Protestant mentality and work ethic. These values are seen to influence the expected role of women and women's ideals of femininity. As Del and Rose mature, they rebel against the repression of individuality and leave the town in pursuit of their own identity. They eventually discover, however, that their identity lies in their heritage and links to the past.

S119. Thacker, Robert W. "A Fine and Lucky Benevolence: The Development of Alice Munro's Narrative Technique." M.A. thesis, University of Waterloo, 1976.

An examination of the development of Munro's dual-voiced retrospective narrative technique in the early uncollected stories and in *Dance*. In Munro's early stories, the denouement is shown to be dependent upon setting, plot, and inarticulate characters. Munro's first use of the retrospective technique appears in "How Could I Do That?" and "Good-by Myra." The merging of the two distinct modes (mute character and weight of setting, and articulate character explaining past experience) appears in "Thanks for the Ride" and three other stories. Six more stories in *Dance*, such as "The Peace of Utrecht," illustrate Munro's experimentation in the use of the variable dual perspective which involves the subjective awareness of an adult narrator. The last five stories in *Dance* show a coalescence of the aspects of all previous stories and the maturity of Munro as an artist.

S120. Thorburn, Jan Ellen. "An Examination of the Presentation of the Small Town in Works by Alice Munro and David Adams Richards." Honours B.A. essay, Mount Allison University, 1990.

A study of Richards' *Blood Ties* and *Road to the Stilt House*, and Munro's *Lives* and *Who*. The towns of Jubilee and Hanratty are shown to cage or entrap the characters in Munro's works, particularly Del and Rose, who desire to escape from the stifling moral and social values of their environments. The towns, and the protagonists' lives in them, are examined in light of three interrelated themes—ethics and religion, education and experience, and external influences. The study shows how Del and Rose finally escape, but learn to come to terms with their small-town heritage.

S121. Trant, Jennifer. "Perfect and Familiar: Alice Munro's Narrative Voices." M.A. thesis, University of Guelph, 1988.

Examines the narrative strategy used in *Moons*, *Progress*, and "Home" as it relates to voice and the theme of connection. In "Home," Trant discusses the limiting influence of one narrative voice and single point of view. She goes on to examine first-person and third-person narratives in *Moons* and the relationship of each of these to the theme of connection. The third-person multiple-voiced stories create an element of distance between the narrator(s) and character(s). In this type of narrative, the overlapping and the merging or blurring of the voices allow the characters to make connections to truths. In *Progress*, the scope of narrative voices widens to include males. Relationships between the male and female narrative voices are explored in many of the stories.

S122. Trudel, Danielle. "Vers une nouvelle théorie de la littérature régionale (appliquée à une oeuvre de Munro, Roy, Brodeur et Vanderhaeghe)." M.A. thesis, Université de Sherbrooke, 1985 (degree 1986).

Chapter 1, pages 12-27, uses *Lives* as an example of regional literature and analyses the functional relationship between Jubilee and its surroundings. It looks at the relationships between Jubilee and Flats Road, and Del's life in both. Uncle Craig and his sisters are seen to form the nucleus essential to the whole region. The functional relationship between Jubilee and the outside world is represented by the contrasts between Ben Jordan and Garnet French, who represent the world of the region, and Uncle Bill, his wife Nile, Ada Jordan, Jerry

Story, and Del, who are linked with the industrial, civilized, technological, or educated outside world. Eccentrics, like Uncle Benny, are seen living outside the centre of the region.

S123. Turner, Gordon Philip. "The Protagonists' Initiatory Experiences in the Canadian Bildungsroman: 1908-1971." Ph.D. dissertation, University of British Columbia, 1979.

On pages 191-211, a study of the quest motif in *Lives* follows Del's search for self from her early years and the influence of her family, to the time of her sexual awakening. The emphasis is on Del's particular attitudes toward life during the different stages of her journey.

S124. Varley, Jill. "'Not Real But True': Evolution in Form and Theme in Alice Munro's *Lives of Girls and Women, The Progress of Love* and *Open Secrets*." M.A. thesis, Concordia University, 1997.

Through an examination of the interrelationship of narrative techniques and dominant themes, this thesis shows how Munro's narrative approach and multifaceted vision of life and reality have changed over time. In *Lives*, the theme of female quest and self-development is supported by a chronological presentation of events, with a view of life and characters as composites. In *Progress*, where the protagonists are older, the stories explore the mysterious aspects of reality through the subjective interpretation of the characters. There is a significant change in the narrative techniques used. One of three types of narration is used, depending on the theme of the story. The thematic concentration in *Open* is on the connections between characters and their destinies. This is reflected in the choice of narrative techniques and in the interconnections between the stories and segments of text.

S125. Velden, Maria Cecilia. "Surfaces and Depths: The Fiction of Alice Munro." M.A. thesis, University of Western Ontario, 1979.

A study of *Dance, Lives, Something,* and *Who* shows the development of style and realism of texture in Munro's work. Each book is examined in terms of its themes and how surfaces and depths are used in relation to the major themes. The stories in *Dance*, centred around elements of regionalism and childhood, are not consistent in their use of surfaces and depths. *Lives*, which is linked together by a consistent narrator and consistent themes, is heavy with surface details of everyday life, but beneath this surface are mysteries. In the book *Something*, where stories involve the lack of communication or the inadequacy of language, the surface is language which characters must penetrate to understand the truth. In *Who*, the surfaces are the pretensions and affectations used by the characters to disguise their frailties and vulnerability.

S126. Visser, Carla. "Canadian Short Fiction: A Comparative Study." Ph.D. dissertation, University of Toronto, 1990.

Chapter 5, entitled "Alice Munro's 'Documentary Realism,'" looks at Munro's use of documentary details to produce an extratextual reality for the reader. The extratextual reality consists of the illusion of the continuity between fiction and reality, and the unmediated recognition by the reader of the fictional world. Elements which create this fictional reality include references to topography and landscape, narrator's language and voice, and details of everyday reality. An analysis is made of the narrator-character-reader relationship and the communicative strategies used in the choice of narrators, first or third person, and their roles in the stories.

S127.   Wang, Yuanfei. "Feminine Fantasies and Reality in the Fiction of Eileen Chang and Alice Munro." M.A. thesis, University of British Columbia, 2004.

A comparative study looking mainly at *Romance* by Eileen Chang and *Who* by Alice Munro. In *Who*, Rose struggles between her attraction to social prestige offered by marriage and her inner need for love. While love takes precedence, self-identity is a more essential concern. Rose's escape from Hanratty and the acting out of her sexual fantasies involve both moral chaos and ritual performance. In a similar "immoral" situation, Frances in "Accident" is helped to escape and eventually marry because of an accident and death, but her female selfhood remains unchanged. Disarrangement between real life and art affects both Del in "Changes and Ceremonies" (*Lives*) and Rose in "Wild Swans" (*Who*). But through imagination and daydreaming, they can indulge freely in their sexual fantasies.

S128.   Ward, Sandra Lee. "To 'Rearrange' These Facts: Space and Time in Alice Munro's Short Fiction." M.A. thesis, Bishop's University, 1986.

In *Dance*, time and space is expressed in the sense of impermanence and transience in several stories, including "Walker Brothers Cowboy." The stories in *Something* dwell on the past and the memories of old or middle-aged characters who are submerged in the past. A sense of disorientation found in some of the stories is analogous to the displacement of time and space. The protagonist in *Who* "rearranges" the facts of her life to impose order on its chaos. The isolation of the characters in *Moons* is emphasized by their disjunction in time and space, and they seek to find connection to themselves and others.

S129.   Weaver, Rosalie Mary. "Innovation within the Modern Short Story through the Interaction of Gender, Nationality and Genre: Margaret Atwood's *Wilderness Tips* and Alice Munro's *Open Secrets*." Ph.D. dissertation, University of Manitoba, 1996, c1997.

Chapter 3 begins by looking at Munro's preference for the short-story genre, and how her present vision and the epic scope of her writing was shaped by her gender and nationality. The rest of the chapter examines Munro's style and innovative narrative techniques in the following areas: the representation of women's experience in "A Real Life"; the inadequacy of language to represent women's experience in "The Albanian Virgin"; the concept of subjectivity in "The Wilderness Station"; the story structure in "Carried Away"; and the narrative of community in "Open Secrets."

S130.   Wehmeyer, Paula J. "Universality and the Self-Discovery Narrative: Three Works by Contemporary Writers." M.A. thesis, South Dakota State University, 1997.

An examination of Margaret Atwood's *Cat's Eye*, Lorrie Moore's *Who Will Run the Frog Hospital?* and Munro's *Lives*. The thesis illustrates how the three works go beyond the typical female self-discovery narrative to become a narrative of universal human experience. This is shown in the character's quest to find her own identity outside that which is dictated by society. In Chapter 2, pages 20-41, entitled "Childhood Wonders and Adult Realities in Alice Munro's *Lives*," Del is described as a girl who romanticizes her childhood. Later she discovers the dichotomy between real life and the imaginary, and she finds that social values and expectations of gender roles are in conflict with her own. She feels a nostalgia for the past, and later, apprehension about adulthood.

S131. Wilson, Patricia A. "Women of Jubilee: A Commentary on Female Roles in the Work of Alice Munro." M.A. thesis, University of Guelph, 1975.

Wilson examines stories in *Dance, Lives,* and *Something* in terms of the female roles played by characters living in rural southwestern Ontario during the 1930s and 1940s. Female roles are examined within the framework of three life stages. The roles of young girls in all three books are shown to be not only learned but imposed and in conflict with the girl's true self. The role of the mother, or mother figure, is also dictated by the rural and social environment of the time. She is seen in different stories as caregiver, teacher (to her daughter), and lady. In the first two books, the portrayal of older women epitomizes the defeated landscape of the Depression, and shows the humiliation and embarrassment of old age. *Something* contains examples of older women who risk being different.

S132. Wise, Kristyn. "Conversations with My Mother: The Daughter-Mother Relationship and the Contemporary Women Writer." D. Phil. dissertation, University of Sussex, 1988.

Chapter 3, entitled "'The Living Body' and Literary Production: Munro's *Lives of Girls and Women*," considers the mother-daughter relationship in terms of the literary parentage of the woman writer. Del Jordan finds a number of literary models within her own family: Uncle Craig, Aunts Elspeth and Grace, and Ada Jordan. While none of these provide a satisfactory model, Del does inherit something from each of them, especially her mother. Links are made between the woman's body, bodily awareness, female creativity, and language. "The Ottawa Valley" is presented in the thesis as another example of a female writer's ambivalent relationship with her mother and her inability to describe or to have a total knowledge of her.

S133. Yan, Qigang. "A Comparative Study of Contemporary Canadian and Chinese Women Writers." Ph.D. dissertation, University of Alberta (Edmonton), 1997.

In a section entitled "Search for Identity in Canadian Women's Writing: Achievements and Ambivalence," the process of Del's and Rose's search for identity is examined in *Lives* and *Who*. Del achieves selfhood partly by realizing the differences between herself and others, and through experience, especially her sexual experience with Garnet French. Rose also goes through "the humiliations of love" and comes closer to an understanding (although still incomplete) of herself.

S134. York, Lorraine Mary. "'The Other Side of Dailiness': Photography in Recent Canadian Fiction." Ph.D. dissertation, McMaster University, 1985.
   Pub. revised as *'The Other Side of Dailiness': Photography in the Works of Alice Munro, Timothy Findley, Michael Ondaatje and Margaret Laurence*. Toronto: ECW Press, 1988.

The chapter on pages 26-99, entitled "'The Delicate Moment of Exposure': Alice Munro and Photography," examines the photographic qualities of Munro's vision and narrative technique in *Dance*, *Something*, *Who*, and *Lives*, especially "The Epilogue." Her writing reflects the paradoxical nature of photography, where the boundaries between the perceived and real are blurred. York points out the juxtaposition of the grotesque and the beautiful, control and helplessness, motion and stillness. Munro's use of photographs and photography as a technique in the treatment of past and present is examined. Her narrative form is seen as a series of snapshots. Munro's appreciation of Edward Hopper, James Agee, Walker Evans, and Diane Arbus is also noted.

Book Reviews

The Beggar Maid: Stories of Flo and Rose

S135. Balakian, Nona. "Books of the Times." *New York Times* 13 December 1979, late ed.: C21.

S136. Balakian, Nona. *Books of the Times* 3.1 (January 1980): 18-20.

S137. Beatty, Jack. *New Republic* 13 October 1979: 40.

S138. *Booklist* 76 (1 September 1979): 26.

S139. *British Book News* March 1982: 133.

S140. Cadogan, Mary. *Books and Bookmen* June 1980: 43-44.

S141. Cameron, Marsaili. "Who Do You Think You Are?" *Gay News* 191 [1980]: 22.

S142. Edwards, Thomas R. "It's Love!" *New York Review of Books* 6 March 1980: 43-44.

S143. Epps, Garrett. "Real Short Stories and Static Prose." *Washington Post* 21 December 1979: C10.

S144. Esmonde de Usabel, Frances M. *Library Journal* 104 (1 October 1979): 2120.

S145. Hollinghurst, Alan. "Elapsing Lives." *New Statesman* 25 April 1980: 630-631.

S146. *Kirkus Reviews* 47 (1 August 1979): 882.

S147. Lothian, Andrew. *Blackwood's Magazine* 328 (August 1980): 159.

S148. Morgan, Ted. "Writers Who Happen to Be Women." *Saturday Review* 6 (13 October 1979): 76-78.

S149. Oates, Joyce Carol. "The Canadian Inheritance: Engel, Munro, Moore." *Ontario Review* 11 (Fall-Winter 1979-1980): 87-90.

S150. Oates, Joyce Carol. "Rich Texture." *Mademoiselle* October 1979: 72, 74.

S151. O'Faolain, Julia. "Small-Town Snobbery in Canada." *New York Times Book Review* 16 September 1979: 12.
Rpt. in *Short Story Criticism: Excerpts from Criticism of the Works of Short Fiction Writers*. Ed. Sheila Fitzgerald. Vol. 3. Detroit: Gale Research, 1989. 333.

S152. *Publishers Weekly* 216.3 (16 July 1979): 57-58.

S153. Rabinowitz, Dorothy. "The Flash Floodings That Love Breeds." *Wall Street Journal* 7 November 1979, eastern ed.: 26.

S154. Reed, Nancy Gail. "We Can Find Ourselves, Like Rose." *Christian Science Monitor* 2 January 1980: 17.

S155. Stone, William B. *Studies in Short Fiction* 17 (1980): 353-354.

S156. Tamarkin, Civia. "Complex Insights, Simple Truths." *Chicago Tribune* 11 November 1979: G10.

S157. Tucker, Eva. "Ancient Mariner Mannerisms." *Hampstead and Highgate Express* 17 October 1980: 60.

S158. Wilner, Paul. "Virtue Wins." *Village Voice* 15 October 1979: 42.

Reviews from the following sources are located in the Alice Munro archives at the University of Calgary Library, Special Collections Division:

Des Moines Register 24 February 1980.
Glasgow Herald 10 May 1980.
Lone Star Book Review February 1980: 9, 29.
Los Angeles Times 10 October 1979?
Minnesota Daily 19 November 1979: 14.
Pacific Sun 11 April 1980.
Paperback and Hardback Book Buyer April 1980.
Philadelphia Inquirer 13 January 1979?
Pittsburgh Press 18 November 1979?
San Jose Mercury News 18 November 1979?
Sojourner January 1980.

Dance of the Happy Shades: Stories

S159. Blumberg, Myrna. "Short Stories." *Times* [London] 13 June 1974: 14.

S160. Blythe, Ronald. "Keeping a Foothold." *Listener* 13 June 1974: 777.

S161. *Booklist* 70 (1 November 1973): 274.

S162. Brockway, James. "A Measure of Life." *Books and Bookmen* August 1974: 92.

S163. Callaghan, Barry. "Digging into the Pits and Caves, Cellars and Tombs Where We Kill." *Telegram* [Toronto] 19 October 1968: 5.

S164. *Choice* December 1973: 1551.

S165. Dafoe, Christopher. "Books and Bookmen." *Vancouver Sun* 2 May 1969: Leisure section 29a.

S166. "La face secrète du quotidien." *Québec/Amérique* 2.3 (n.d.): 4-5.

S167. Fischman, Sheila. "To Maturity along a Rural Route." *Globe Magazine* [*Globe and Mail*, Toronto] 19 October 1968: 24.

S168. Gould, Jan. "Memory, Experiences of 'Normal Life' Feed Her Fiction." *Victoria Daily Times* 9 August 1969: 9.

S169. Grosskurth, Phyllis. "Our Dull Short Stories Can Come Alive." *Toronto Daily Star* 2 November 1968: 27.

S170. Harvor, Beth. "The Special World of the WW's." *Saturday Night* August 1969: 33.

S171. Helwig, David. *Queen's Quarterly* 77.1 (Spring 1970): 127-128.

S172. Kirkwood, Hilda. *Canadian Forum* 48 (February 1969): 260.

S173. Levin, Martin. *New York Times Book Review* 23 September 1973: 48.

S174. *Library Journal* 98 (15 October 1973): 3021-3022.

S175. "Lost Choices." *TLS: The Times Literary Supplement* 10 May 1974: 493.

S176. Morgan, William. "Small Town." *Winnipeg Free Press* 21 December 1968, Leisure Magazine: 12.

S177. Oates, Joyce Carol. "Rich Texture." *Mademoiselle* October 1979: 72, 74.

S178.   Peter, John. *Malahat Review* 11 (July 1969): 126.

S179.   Portman, Jamie. "Ordinary People, Ordinary Situations, Ordinary Lives." *Herald Magazine* [*Calgary Herald*, late city ed.] 21 March 1969: 6.

S180.   Prince, Peter. "Paragons." *New Statesman* 3 May 1974: 633.

S181.   Pritchett, V. S. *New Yorker* 5 November 1973: 186.

S182.   [Radio Review]. *Speaking of Books*. CBC-FM Radio, Vancouver. 15 June 1969. Panel discussion of *Dance of the Happy Shades* by Alice Munro and *The Street* by Mordecai Richler. Panel: Dr. Warren Tallman, Bill Duthie, and Don Stainsby.

S183.   Rasporich, Beverly. *Canadian Book Review Annual* 1988: 3205.

S184.   Simpson, Leo. [Radio Review]. *Anthology*. CBC Radio, Toronto. 19 October 1968. Review of *Dance of the Happy Shades* by Alice Munro and *Miracle at Indian River* by Alden Nowlan.

S185.   Stuewe, Paul. "Sparkling Fictional Realities Kindle the Imagination." *Toronto Star* 24 September 1988: M6.

S186.   Tench, Helen. "Turning-Points in Young Lives Subjects of Fine Short Stories." *Ottawa Citizen* 4 January 1969: 25.

S187.   Thomas, Audrey. "'She's Only a Girl,' He Said." *Canadian Literature* 39 (Winter 1969): 91-92.

S188.   Thompson, Kent. *Fiddlehead* 82 (November/December 1969): 71-72.

S189.   Thompson, Kent. [Radio review]. *Music and the Arts*. CBZ Radio. Fredericton, NB. May 1969.

S190.   Ward-Harris, E. D. "These Stories Have the Maugham Touch." *Victoria Daily Colonist* 10 November 1968: 14.

S191.   Weiss, Charlotte. *English Quarterly* 9.3 (Fall 1976): 72.

Reviews from the following sources are located in the Alice Munro archives at the University of Calgary Library, Special Collections Division:

Anniston Star [Anniston, AL] 14 October 1973.
Birmingham Post 4 May 1974.
Daily Colonist [Victoria] 10 November 1968: 14.
Daily Telegraph [UK] 2 May 1974.
Daily Times Advocate 11 November 1973: 13.

Des Moines Sunday Register 16 September 1973.
Edmonton Journal 20 December 1968.
Erie Daily Times 1 December 1973.
Fredericton Daily Gleaner 26 October 1968.
King Features Syndicate [New York] 2 September 1973.
Kingsport Times-News 27 January 1974.
Legal Advertiser and Gazette-Times [Ferndale, MI] 13 September 1973.
Nashville Tennessean 7 October 1973.
News American [Baltimore, MD] 11 November 1973: 8E.
News and Observer [Raleigh, NC] 9 June 1974.
Philadelphia Inquirer 27 January 1974.
Pittsburgh Press 27 September 1973.
Plain Dealer 7 October 1973.
Regina Leader Post 26 October 1968.
St. Catharines Standard 7 December 1968.
Saskatoon Star-Phoenix 21 November 1968.
Seattle Post-Intelligencer 12 August 1973.
Seattle Times 14 October 1973.
Sunday Bulletin [Philadelphia] 7 October 1973.
Unitarian Universalist World 1 April 1974.
Victoria Daily Times 2 November 1968.

Friend of My Youth: Stories

S192.   Bailey, Paul. "The Top Ten." *Listener* 18 October 1990: 27.

S193.   Boston, Anne. "Hidden Reasons." *New Statesman and Society* 19 October 1990: 32-33.

S194.   Brookner, Anita. "The Different Ages of Women." *Spectator* 265 (20 October 1990): 37-38.

S195.   Buitenhuis, Peter. "The Wilds of the Past." *Books in Canada* May 1990: 19-22.

S196.   Caldwell, Gail. "Short Stories Endowed with Solid Grace." *Boston Globe* 18 March 1990, city ed.: B44.

S197.   Carrington, Ildikó de Papp. "Rubble or Remedy?" *Essays on Canadian Writing* 44 (Fall 1991): 162-169.

S198.   Coles, Joanna. "Postcards from the Nightmare." *Guardian* [London and Manchester] 15 November 1990: 24.

S199.   Congram, John. *Presbyterian Record* 114 (November 1990): 37.

S200. Craig, Patricia. "Pungent Connections." *TLS: The Times Literary Supplement* 19 October 1990: 1130.

S201. "Critics' Choice: Our Aisle-Sitters Give the Morning-After Verdict on the Year's Best Books." *Publishers Weekly* 238.1 (4 January 1991): 34.

S202. Crosbie, Lynn. "Remembered Friends." *Paragraph Magazine* 12.3 (1990): 25-26.

S203. Eckstein, Barbara J. *World Literature Today* 64.4 (Autumn 1990): 639.

S204. "Editors' Choice." *New York Times Book Review* 2 December 1990: 3.

S205. Farmer, Lesley S. J. *Wilson Library Bulletin* 65.3 (November 1990): Booktalker 7.

S206. Flam, Jack. "Life in Soft and Sharp Focus." *Wall Street Journal* 7 May 1990, eastern ed.: A12.

S207. Freeman, Judith. "Chekhov on Lake Huron." *Los Angeles Times Book Review* 1 April 1990, home ed.: 4.

S208. French, William. "Just Folks." *Globe and Mail* 21 April 1990: C17.

S209. Godley, Elizabeth. "Nary a Wasted Word from Masterful Munro." *Vancouver Sun* 14 April 1990: C4.

S210. Hooper, Brad. *Booklist* 86 (1 February 1990): 1049.

S211. Jones, Malcolm. "The Glory of the Story." *Newsweek* 2 April 1990: 56-57.

S212. Kakutani, Michiko. "Alice Munro's Stories of Changes of the Heart." *New York Times* 9 March 1990, late ed.: C36.

S213. Kemp, Peter. "The Past Is Ourselves." *Sunday Times* [London] 14 October 1990: 8: 8.5.

S214. *Kirkus Reviews* 58 (15 January 1990): 74.

S215. Lucas, Alec. "Subtle Probing." *Matrix* 32 (Fall 1990): 70-71.

S216. Marchand, Philip. "Telling Stories." *Saturday Magazine* [*Toronto Star*] 21 April 1990: M12-M13.

S217. Martin, Sandra. *Saturday Night* 105.4 (May 1990): 75.

S218. Matthews, Mike. *Malahat Review* 93 (December 1990): 119-121.

S219. McLennan McCue, Sharon A. *CM: A Reviewing Journal of Canadian Materials for Young People* 18.4 (July 1990): 189-190.

S220. Motei, Angela Cozea. "Munro Writes a 'Common Story.'" *Calgary Herald* 5 May 1990: D14.

S221. Mukherjee, Bharati. "Hometown Horrors." *New York Times Book Review* 18 March 1990: 1, 31.
Rpt. (excerpts) as "A Writer of Extraordinary Richness." in *Globe and Mail* 23 March 1990: A7.

S222. *New York Magazine* 26 March 1990: 30.

S223. Oates, Joyce Carol. "Women of a Certain Age." *Book World* [*Washington Post*] 18 March 1990: 1-2.

S224. Osmond, Rosalie. "Shy Romances with Rubble and Strife." *Independent* [London] 20 October 1990: Weekend Books 26.

S225. Prokop, Mary. *Library Journal* 115 (15 March 1990): 115.

S226. *Publishers Weekly* 237.3 (19 January 1990): 94.

S227. Redekop, Magdalene. "Enchanted Space." *Canadian Literature* 129 (Summer 1991): 208-210.

S228. Salter, Mary Jo. "In Praise of Accidents." *New Republic* 14 May 1990: 50-53.
Rpt. in *Contemporary Literary Criticism*. Ed. Brigham Narins and Deborah A. Stanley. Vol. 95. Detroit: Gale, 1997. 308-311.

S229. Scott, Jay. "Alice Munro Makes the Mundane Magical." *Chatelaine* July 1990: 10.

S230. Shields, Carol. "In Ontario." *London Review of Books* 7 February 1991: 22-23.
Rpt. in *Contemporary Literary Criticism*. Ed. Brigham Narins and Deborah A. Stanley. Vol. 95. Detroit: Gale, 1997. 312-314.

S231. Slavitt, David R. "Not-So-Simple Gifts: The Elegant Craftsmanship of Alice Munro, the Awkward Short Fiction of John Hersey." *Chicago Tribune* 25 March 1990, Tribune Books: 8.

S232. Thomas, Audrey. "Alice Munro, the Laureate of 'Bad Girls.'" *Gazette* [Montreal] 5 May 1990: I2.

S233. Thomas, Joan. "Where Only Women Walk." *Winnipeg Free Press* 5 May 1990: 24.

S234. Thorpe, Michael. "Letters in Canada 1990: Fiction." *University of Toronto Quarterly* 61.1 (Fall 1991): 35-36.

S235. Timson, Judith. "Merciful Light." *Maclean's* 7 May 1990: 66-67.

S236. Tomalin, Claire. "The Times of Their Lives." *Independent Sunday Review* [London] 4 November 1990: 34.

S237. Towers, Robert. "Short Satisfactions." *New York Review of Books* 17 May 1990: 38-89. [Munro on page 38]

S238. Walbert, Kate. "Munro Doctrine." *Nation* 14 May 1990: 678-680.

S239. Walters, Colin. "Stories of People Coping with Change." *Washington Times* 2 April 1990, final ed.: E6.

S240. Warren, Rosalind A. "Of Cats and Women." *Women's Review of Books* 7 (May 1990): 8-9.

S241. Wayne, Joyce. "Wallace and Munro: Day-to-Day Life Empowers Each Word." *Quill & Quire* June 1990: 29.

Friend of My Youth: Stories. French Translation

S242. Brisac, Geneviève. "Les petits riens de la vie." *Monde* 5 octobre 1996: 3.

S243. Picard, Geneviève. "Amie de ma jeunesse." *Voir Arts et Spectacles* 26 mars 1992: 24.

Hateship, Friendship, Loveship, Courtship, Marriage: Stories

S244. Adams, Lorraine. "Cheating Hearts." *Book World* [*Washington Post*] 16 December 2001: 5.

S245. Allardice, Lisa. "Small-Town Blues." *New Statesman* 19 November 2001: 51.

S246. Allen, Bruce. "Wide-Ranging Ingenuities from Pen of 'Canada's Chekhov.'" *Washington Times* 2 December 2001, final ed.: B8.

S247. Aulin, Virginia. *Room of One's Own* 24.2 (January 2002): 201.

S248. Bailey, Paul. "Word Perfect." *Independent* [London] 17 November 2001, Features: 11. Accessed 24 April 2006. <http://www.independent.co.uk>

Book Reviews

S249. Balée, Susan. "America the Innocent." *Hudson Review* 55.2 (2002): 308-309.

S250. Beattie, Ann. "Alice Munro's Amazingly Ordinary World." *Globe and Mail* 29 September 2001: D2-D3.

S251. Bemrose, John. "Alice's Looking Glass." *Maclean's* 8 October 2001: 66, 68.

S252. "Best Books of 2001." *Library Journal* 127 (January 2002): 50.

S253. "The Best Books of 2001." *Quill & Quire* February 2002: 30.

S254. Brookner, Anita. "Much Matter within a Small Compass." *Spectator* 287 (3 November 2001): 52-53.

S255. Caldwell, Gail. "Places in the Heart." *Boston Globe* 4 November 2001, 3rd ed.: C3.

S256. Ciabattari, Jane. "Mysteries and Revelations." *Los Angeles Times Book Review* 4 November 2001, home ed.: 1.

S257. Clark, Alex. "What's the Story? Is Brevity the Soul of It?" *Guardian* [London and Manchester] 10 November 2001: Saturday 10.

S258. Davis, Amanda. "Alice's Wonderland." *Esquire* November 1998: 31.

S259. Deignan, Tom. "Life in a Sentence." *Commonweal* 129.4 (22 February 2002): 26-27.

S260. Drainie, Bronwyn. "Relationship Roulette." *Quill & Quire* August 2001: 22.

S261. D'Souza, Irene. *Herizons* 16.1 (Summer 2002): 42.

S262. "Editors' Choice." *New York Times Book Review* 2 December 2001: 12.

S263. Enright, Anne. "New Ways to Leave." *National Post* 29 September 2001: RB7.

S264. Fertile, Candace. "The Mistress of Style." *Vancouver Sun* 29 September 2001: D15.

S265. Franklin, Ruth. "Assent and Lamentation." *New Republic* 25 February 2002: 33-37.

S266. Freeman, John. *Wall Street Journal* 9 November 2001, eastern ed.: W8.

S267. Giles, Jeff. "The Heart of Her Matter: Munro's Lonely Terrain." *Newsweek* 12 November 2001: 66.

S268. Greenstein, Michael. "Munrogue's Progress." *Books in Canada* 31.2 (April 2002): 6.

S269.   Howells, Coral Ann. "Double Vision." *Canadian Literature* 178 (Autumn 2003): 160-161.

S270.   Kakutani, Michiko. "Home Is Where the Heart Is, an Independent One." *New York Times* 20 November 2001, late ed.: E8.

S271.   Knapp, Mona. *World Literature Today* 76.2 (Spring 2002): 152.

S272.   Lewis, Trevor. "Pick of the Week." *Sunday Times* [London] 28 July 2002: 46.

S273.   Lockerbie, Catherine. "The Loving Literature of Alice Munro." *Ottawa Citizen* 30 September 2001: C11, C15.

S274.   Marchand, Philip. "The Way Things Are." *Toronto Star* 30 September 2001: D12-D13.

S275.   Markovits, Benjamin. "Suspicion of Sentiment." *London Review of Books* 13 December 2001: 26-27.

S276.   McClay, Jill Kedersha. *Resource Links* 8 (October 2002): 57.

S277.   McGahern, John. "Heroines of Their Lives." *TLS: Times Literary Supplement* 9 November 2001: 23-24.

S278.   Moore, Lorrie. "Artship." *New York Review of Books* 17 January 2002: 41-42.

S279.   Morrissy, Mary. "Short, Sharp Subtle Surprises." *Irish Times* 1 December 2001: 70.

S280.   Myerson, Jonathan. "No Need to Bring Your Own Food and Wine." *Independent on Sunday* [London] 25 November 2001, Features: 17.

S281.   Neufeld, K. Gordon. "Wondrous Tales from Munrovia." *Calgary Herald* 29 September 2001: ES8.

S282.   "Out of the Ordinary." *Economist* (U.S. ed.) 361 (24-30 November 2001): 80.

S283.   Patterson, Troy. "Small Worlds." *Entertainment Weekly* 7 December 2001: 95.

S284.   Pritchard, William H. "Road Map Not Included." *New York Times Book Review* 25 November 2001, late ed.: 9.

S285.   Rasporich, Beverly. *Canadian Book Review Annual* 2001: 3145.

S286.   Ravitch, Michael. "Fiction in Review." (Review article) *Yale Review* 90.4 (October 2002): 160-170.

S287. Schiedel, Bonnie. "Go Ask Alice." *Chatelaine* November 2001: 26.

S288. Seaman, Donna. *Booklist* 98.2 (15 September 2001): 164.

S289. Simonds, Merilyn. "Munro's Wit Is Undiminished." *Gazette* [Montreal] 29 September 2001: I1, I2.

S290. Simpson, Mona. "A Quiet Genius." *Atlantic Monthly* December 2001: 126, 128-132, 134-136.

S291. Tong, Murray. "Munro Creates a Masterpiece with Stories Set in the Depths of the Soul." *Magazine* [*Hamilton Spectator*] 29 September 2001: 19.

S292. Truax, Alice. "Alice Munro Constructs Another Masterly Short-Story Collection." *Vogue* November 2001: 405-406.

S293. Williams, Lynna. "Imperfect Worlds That Seem Just Right." *Chicago Tribune* 11 November 2001, Chicagoland, Books: 1.

S294. Zaleski, Jeff. *Publishers Weekly* 248.41 (8 October 2001): 41.

Hateship, Friendship, Courtship, Loveship, Marriage: Stories. Audio

S295. Edwards, Harriet. *Library Journal* 127.13 (August 2002): 170, 172.

Lives of Girls and Women: A Novel

S296. Barrett, Mary Ellin. "Cosmo Reads the New Books." *Cosmopolitan* March 1973: 26.

S297. Beer, Patricia. "Beside the Wawanash." *TLS: The Times Literary Supplement* 17 March 1978: 302.

S298. Blythe, Ronald. "Blob." *Listener* 29 November 1973: 752.

S299. *Booklist* 69 (1 March 1973): 620.

S300. "Briefly Noted." *New Yorker* 6 January 1973: 75.

S301. *British Book News* October 1984: 581.

S302. Coldwell, Joan. "A Small World Re-Created." *Victoria Times* 6 November 1971: 17.

S303. Currie, Sheldon. *Antigonish Review* 15 (Autumn 1973): 99-100.

Secondary Works

S304. Dafoe, Christopher. "The Causerie." *Vancouver Sun* 26 November 1971: Leisure 39A.

S305. Dobbs, Kildare. "This First Novel Is Solid, Beautiful." *Toronto Daily Star* 30 October 1971: 71.

S306. Ferrari, Margaret. "Lives of Girls and Women." *America* 24 February 1973: 168.

S307. Foote, Audrey C. "Nostalgia for Jubilee." *Washington Post* 4 January 1973: C12.

S308. Gersoni-Stavn, Diane. *Library Journal* 98 (1 January 1973): 86.

S309. Grosskurth, Phyllis. "A Delight. Goodbye to Inhibitions." *Globe Magazine* [*Globe and Mail*] 30 October 1971: 17.

S310. Hill, William B. *Best Sellers* 1 January 1973: 452.

S311. Howard, Irene. "An Elegant Book about Women." *Monday Morning* 6.6 (February 1972): 22-23.

S312. Jackson, Heather. *Canadian Forum* 51 (January-February 1972): 76-77.

S313. Johnson, Marigold. "Mud and Blood." *New Statesman* 26 October 1973: 618-619.

S314. *Kirkus Reviews* 40 (1 November 1972): 1266-1267.

S315. Klein, Norma. "A Quartet of Novels." *Ms* August 1973: 30-31.

S316. "Lives of Girls and Women." *Publishers Weekly* 202.5 (31 July 1972): 68.

S317. McAlpine, Mary. "An Expansive Vision, a Fulfilled Promise." *Saturday Night* January 1972: 36-37.

S318. McMullen, Lorraine. *Canadian Fiction Magazine* 11 (Autumn 1973): 93, 95, 97-98.

S319. Metcalf, John. "Growing Up." *Montreal Star* 20 November 1971: B6.

S320. Overduin, Hendrik. "Glimpsing the Female Psyche." *Windsor Star* 27 November 1971, final ed.: 50.

S321. Peltier, Mary Damon. *Second Wave* 2.4 (July 1973): 46.

S322. Peterson, Kevin. "A Penetrating Look at the World of Women." *Herald Magazine* [*Calgary Herald*] 4 February 1972, late city ed.: 6.

S323. Polk, James. "Deep Caves and Kitchen Linoleum." *Canadian Literature* 54 (Autumn 1972): 102-104.

S324. Poteet, Lewis J. "Review of *Lives of Girls and Women*." *Le Chien d'Or/The Golden Dog* 2 (August 1973): n.p.

S325. Rix, Beverley. "Sensitive Novel Chronicles a Romantic Girl's Maturing." *Ottawa Citizen* 15 January 1972: 29.

S326. Rudzik, O. H. T. "Letters in Canada 1971: Fiction." *University of Toronto Quarterly* 41.4 (Summer 1972): 314.

S327. Rule, Jane. "The Credible Woman." *Books in Canada* 1.4 (November 1971): 4-5.

S328. Smith, Stephen. "Forty Great Works of Canadian Fiction: A Q&Q Panel Selects the Century's Literary 'Best.'" *Quill & Quire* 65.7 (July 1999): 21-23.

S329. Sonnenfeld, Jean E. *Presbyterian Record* 98.2 (February 1974): 29.

S330. Symons, Julian. "Scenes from Provincial Life." *Sunday Times* [London] 14 October 1973: 14.

S331. Thomas, Clara. "Woman Invincible." *Journal of Canadian Fiction* 1.4 (Fall 1972): 95-96.

S332. Tomalin, Claire. "Harvest and Holocaust." *Observer* 21 October 1973: 40.

S333. Wolff, Geoffrey. "Call It Fiction." *Time* (Canadian ed.) 15 January 1973: 64, 66. (American ed.) 15 January 1973: 79.

S334. Wordsworth, Christopher. "Maple Leaf in Bud." *Manchester Guardian Weekly* 3 November 1973: 24.

Reviews from the following sources are located in the Alice Munro archives at the University of Calgary Library, Special Collections Division:

Argus Roundup [Rock Island, IL] 3 February 1973: 6.
Daily Gleaner 31 December 1971.
Daily Pilot [Costa Mesa, CA] 2 February 1979.
Daily Telegraph [UK] 25 October 1973.
Daytona Beach Sunday News-Journal 24 December 1972: 10E.
Edmonton Journal 21 January 1972.
Fort Wayne Journal-Gazette 31 December 1972: 5E.
Fort Worth Star-Telegram 31 December 1972: 7G.
Gazette [University of Western Ontario] 17 March 1972.
Glasgow Herald 20 October 1973?
Herald American and Call-Enterprise 1 February 1973: 68.
Idahonian [Moscow, ID] 4 May 1973.
Milwaukee Journal 28 January 1973: Pt. 5:4.

Minneapolis Star 4 October 1972.
Moncton Transcript 18 October 1975.
News [Athens, GA] 10 June 1973.
News-Sun [Waukegan, IL] 22 March 1973.
Oklahoma Journal 3 December 1972.
Philadelphia Inquirer 18 February 1973.
Plain Dealer [Cleveland, OH] 14 January 1973: 7H.
Red Deer Advocate [Red Deer College?] 28 January 1972.
Spare Rib Magazine January 1974.
Star [Anniston, AL] 26 November 1972.
Sun-Telegram [San Bernardino, CA] 19 November 1972: E13.
Sunday Bulletin [Philadelphia, PA] 4 March 1973.
Sunday Telegraph [UK] 4 November 1973.
Tallahassee Democrat 19 November 1972: 12E.
Telegram [San Bernardino, CA].
Times-Advocate [Escondido, CA] 15 April 1973.
Unitarian Universalist World 1 February 1974.
Yorkshire Post 1 November 1973?

Radio Transcripts

S335.   Bulpitt, Mildred. KMCR-FM Phoenix, AZ. 17 February 1973.

Lives of Girls and Women: A Novel. Audio Version

S336.   "December Audio Titles." *Quill & Quire* December 1998: 34.

The Love of a Good Woman: Stories

S337.   Aulin, Virginia. *Room of One's Own* 21.4 (Winter 1998/99): 85-86.

S338.   Baillieul, J.G. "On the Brink of a Changing World." *Contemporary Verse Two* 21.4 (Spring 1999): 61-64.

S339.   Balée, Susan. "Victorian Voyages and Other Mind Trips." *Hudson Review* 52 (Spring 1999): 171-172.

S340.   Bemrose, John. "Telling Tales in Canada: The Season's Best Ranges from Punches to Pachyderms." *Maclean's* 7 December 1998: 69.

S341.   Besner, Neil. "Letters in Canada 1998: Fiction." *University of Toronto Quarterly* 69.1 (Winter 1999-2000): 25-42. [Munro on page 27]

S342.   Byatt, A. S. "Munro: The Stuff of Life." *Globe and Mail* 26 September 1998, weekend ed.: D16.

Book Reviews 179

S343. Caldwell, Gail. "The Edge of Sadness." *Boston Globe* 22 November 1998, city ed.: D1.

S344. Carey, Barbara. "Tapping Our Shadowy Compulsions." *Toronto Star* 19 September 1998: K18.

S345. Croft, Barbara. "Indirect Objects." *Women's Review of Books* 16.4 (January 1999): 15-16.

S346. Curb, Randall. "When Is a Story More Than a Story?: A Fiction Chronicle." *Southern Review* 35.3 (Summer 1999): 617-620.

S347. Davis, Amanda. "Alice's Wonderland." *Esquire* November 1998: 43.

S348. D'Souza, Irene. *Herizons* 13.4 (March 2000): 32.

S349. "Editors' Choice." *New York Times Book Review* 6 December 1998: 8.

S350. Frank, Michael. "Fiction in Review (review article)." *Yale Review* 87.2 (April 1999): 157-174. [Munro on pages 166-174]

S351. Gardam, Jane. "A Passion for the Particular." *Spectator* 282 (13 March 1999): 36-37.

S352. Garebian, Keith. "Love in Full Summer Leaf." *Books in Canada* 28.1 (February 1999): 8-9.

S353. Garebian, Keith. *Quill & Quire* September 1998: 55-56.

S354. Gorra, Michael. "Crossing the Threshold." *New York Times Book Review* 1 November 1998, late ed.: 6-7.

S355. Govier, Katherine. "Queen of the Gothic." *Time* (Canadian ed.) 16 November 1998: 86.

S356. Harvey, Caroline. "What Darkness Within." *Vancouver Sun* 10 October 1998: J5, J6.

S357. Hughes-Hallett, Lucy. "Life Goes On." *Sunday Times* [London] 13 December 1998, sec. 8: 13.

S358. Jensen, Liz. "Recipes for Repression in the Well-Ordered Household." *Independent* [London] 9 January 1999, Features: 14.

S359. Johnston, Ingrid. *Resource Links* 7.1 (October 2001): 58.

S360. Kephart, Beth. "Life, Woman, Truth by Alice Munro." *Baltimore Sun* 1 November 1998: 14F.

S361. *Kirkus Reviews* 66 (1 September 1998): 1224.

S362. Knapp, Mona. *World Literature Today* 73.3 (Summer 1999): 526.

S363. Lee, Hermione. "Dark and Handsome." *Observer* 8 November 1998: Observer Review 14.
Rpt. as "Dark and Disturbing" in *Manchester Guardian Weekly* 29 November 1998: Books 33.

S364. "Less Is More." *Economist* 12-18 December 1998, Economist Review of Books and Multimedia: Insert 14-15.

S365. Love, Barbara. *Library Journal* 123 (15 September 1998): 115.

S366. Lowry, Elizabeth. "Getting Over Love." *TLS: The Times Literary Supplement* 4 December 1998: 22.

S367. Macdonald, Jenny. *Woman: Canadian Women's Quarterly Newsmagazine* Winter 1999: 51.

S368. Mallick, Heather. "Short but Not So Sweet." *Calgary Sun* 8 November 1998, final ed.: SC7.

S369. Martin, Sandra. "Munro Is Tops on Amazon Book List." *Globe and Mail* 24 August 2004: R1.

S370. McGoogan, Ken. "She Provides No Easy Answers." *Calgary Herald* 19 September 1998: J7.

S371. Miller, Judith Maclean. "Rooms within Rooms within Alcoves." *Canadian Notes & Queries* 54 (Winter 1998): 25-28.

S372. Persky, Stan. "Writers Clear Trails through the Fourth Dimension." *Vancouver Sun* 9 January 1999: A23.

S373. Posesorski, Sherie. "Realism Is Implacable in Munro Stories." *Gazette* [Montreal] 24 October 1998: J3.

S374. *Publishers Weekly* 245.36 (7 September 1998): 81.

S375. Putnam, Conan. "Listening In: Alice Munro's Short Fiction Lets Readers Eavesdrop on Her Characters' Lives." *Chicago Tribune* 1 November 1998, Chicagoland, Books: 6.

S376. "PW's Best Books." *Publishers Weekly* 245.44 (2 November 1998): 41.

S377. Renwick, Meredith. "The Best Books of 1998." *Quill & Quire* February 1999: 42.

S378. Robertson, Sarah. *Canadian Book Review Annual* 1998: 3132.

S379. Schiefer, Nancy. "More Masterly Munro: Latest Short Stories Can Only Strengthen Public's Love of a Good Writer." *London Free Press* 3 October 1998, final ed.: C14.

S380. Schuck, Paula. "Munro Lives Up to Her Wonderful Reputation." *Kitchener-Waterloo Record* 14 November 1998, final ed.: H9.

S381. Seaman, Donna. *Booklist* 95 (1 September 1998): 6.

S382. Sheppard, R. Z. "Quiet Virtues." *Time* (American ed.) 30 November 1998: 119.

S383. Stipe, Stormy. *Biblio* 4.3 (March 1999): 61.

S384. Tessier, Vanna. "Womanly Virtues: A Masterful New Book from Alice Munro." *Edmonton Sun* 1 November 1998, final ed.: SE16.

S385. Tillinghast, Richard. "Bookmarks." *Wall Street Journal* 30 October 1998, eastern ed.: W4.

S386. Todd, Tamsin. "The Detail Kills." *New Statesman* 12 February 1999: 54-55.

S387. Turbide, Diane. "'That Life Beating.'" *Maclean's* 12 October 1998: 78.

S388. Urquhart, Jane. "The Art of Alice Munro." *Ottawa Citizen* 20 September 1998. Rpt. as "The Superb Art of Alice Munro." *Hamilton Spectator* 3 October 1998, final ed.: W7.

S389. Van Herk, Aritha. "Between the Stirrup and the Ground." *Canadian Forum* 77 (October 1998): 49-52.

S390. *Virginia Quarterly Review* 75.2 (Spring 1999): 58.

S391. Walters, Colin. "Not-So-Still Life in the Northwest." *Washington Times* 8 November 1998, final ed.: B6.

The Moons of Jupiter: Stories

S392. Adachi, Ken. "Munro: Ironic, Observant and Always Subtle." *Toronto Star* 16 October 1982: G14.

S393. Balpataky, Elaine. *CM: Canadian Materials for Schools and Libraries* 11.2 (March 1983): 59-60.

S394. Becker, Robin. "Fear-of-Success Stories?" *Women's Review of Books* 1.7 (April 1984): 5-6.

S395. Beddoes, Julie. "Books by Winners." *Flare* November 1982: 74.

S396. "Best Books of 1983." *New York Times Book Review* 4 December 1983: 74.

S397. Black, Barbara. "Munro Delivers Yet Another Superb Collection." *Gazette* [Montreal] 16 October 1982, final ed.: A9.

S398. Blake, Patricia. "Heart-Catching." *Time* (Canadian ed.) 28 February 1983: 75-76. (American ed.) 28 February 1983: 71, 73.

S399. Blodgett, E. D. "Winging It." *Canadian Literature* 97 (Summer 1983): 98-101.

S400. *Booklist* 79 (15 February 1983): 763.

S401. Brookner, Anita. "Good Girls and Bad Girls." *London Review of Books* 2-15 June 1983: 20.

S402. Broyard, Anatole. "Books of the Times." *New York Times* 16 February 1983, late ed.: C27.

S403. Buitenhuis, Peter. "Life's Texture in Short Form." *Vancouver Sun* 29 October 1982: Leisure & TV Week, L27.

S404. Buitenhuis, Peter. *Reader* 1.6 (December 1982): 29-30.

S405. Carter, Alixe. *Writer's Lifeline* December 1982: 25.

S406. Collins, Anne. "The Fantasy of Perfect Mastery." *Maclean's* 18 October 1982: 74-75.

S407. Crerar, Tom. "A Sentence to Life." *Brick* 18 (Spring 1983): 10.

S408. Crittenden, Yvonne. *Sunday Sun* [*Toronto Sun*] 23 January 1983: S17.

S409. De Wiel, Alexa. "Mothers, Moons and Mafiosi." *Broadside* [Toronto] May 1983: 11, 13.

S410. DeMott, Benjamin. "Domestic Stories." *New York Times Book Review* 20 March 1983: 1, 26.

S411. Dooley, D .J. *Canadian Churchman* December 1982: 16-17.

S412. Edwards, Caterina. "Munro's Latest Short Stories Lack Power of Earlier Works." *Edmonton Journal* 6 November 1982: A11.

S413. Faustmann, John. "Two Alices." *Western Living* June 1983: 63-64.

S414. Flower, Dean. "Fiction Chronicle." *Hudson Review* 36 (Summer 1983): 359-377. [Munro on pages 366-368]

S415. Franks, Lucinda. "Fiction Chronicle." *Ontario Review* 19 (Fall-Winter 1983/1984): 91-98. [Munro on pages 91-95]

S416. Freeman, Suzanne. "A Gift for Telling Moments: Two Story Collections." *Ms* April 1983: 34-35.

S417. French, William. "The Moons of Jupiter." *Globe and Mail* 16 October 1982: E15.

S418. Gervais, Marty. "An Ability to Strike the Right Chords." *Windsor Star* 16 October 1982: C9.

S419. Grady, Wayne. "A House of Her Own." *Books in Canada* 11.8 (October 1982): 12, 14.

S420. Hill, Douglas. "Letters in Canada 1982: Fiction." *University of Toronto Quarterly* 52 (Summer 1983): 324.

S421. Hollinghurst, Alan. "The Secrets of Failing Lives." *TLS: The Times Literary Supplement* 6 May 1983: 457.

S422. Hulbert, Ann. "The Country and the City." *New Republic* 7 March 1983: 37-38.

S423. Kareda, Urjo. "Double Vision." *Saturday Night* November 1982: 63-64.

S424. Kaveney, Roz. *Books and Bookmen* August 1983: 35.

S425. Kemp, Peter. "Making Connections." *Observer* 1 May 1983: 28.

S426. *Kirkus Reviews* 50 (1 December 1982): 1308.

S427. LaBarge, Dorothy. "Alice Munro Turns to Women in Love." *Calgary Herald* 6 November 1982: J4.

S428. Lehman, David. "When Short Is Beautiful." *Newsweek* 25 April 1983: 85-86. [Munro on page 85]

S429. McMullen, Lorraine. "Magic Realism in Fiction." *Fiddlehead* 138 (January 1984): 77-80.

S430. Mellors, John. "Canada Swans." *Listener* 9 June 1983: 26.

S431. Morley, Patricia. "Munro Explores Familiar Terrain." *Citizen* [Ottawa] 16 October 1982: 40.

S432. Mort, Mary-Ellen. *Library Journal* 108 (15 February 1983): 413.

S433. Mukherjee, Bharati. "Alice Munro's Visionary Lyricism Dazzles." *Quill & Quire* September 1982: 57.

S434. O'Faolain, Nuala. "Alice Munro: Soaring Clear." *Sunday Tribune* [Dublin, Ire.] 26 August 1984: 14.

S435. Osborne, Linda Barrett. "Love's Many Contradictions." *Book World* [*Washington Post*] 17 April 1983: 8.

S436. Palmer, Jill. *Scrivener* [McGill University] 4.2 (Summer 1983): 30-31.

S437. Philip, Neil. *British Book News* August 1983: 518.

S438. *Publishers Weekly* 222.24 (17 December 1982): 63.

S439. Quigly, Isabel. "When Auntie Came to Dinner . . ." *Financial Times* [London] 14 May 1983: sec. I:12.

S440. Redmon, Anne. "Women in the Wilderness." *Sunday Times* [London] 5 June 1983: 42.

S441. Rexford, Alex. "Moons of Jupiter a Superb Display of Munro's Talent for the Short Story." *the newspaper* [Toronto] 3 November 1982: 6.

S442. Sand, Cy-Thea. "Munro's Latest Preoccupied with Romantic Love." *Kinesis* [Australia] November 1982: 21, 29.

S443. Scanlan, Larry. "Believing Alice Munro." *Whig-Standard Magazine* [Kingston, ON] 4 December 1982: 21.

S444. Schiefer, Nancy A. "Munro Turns Poetic Precision, Uncommon Observation into Art." *London Free Press* 16 October 1982: F7.

S445. Seidenbaum, Art. "Canadian Stories and Warmly Told." *Los Angeles Times* 23 February 1983, part V: 6.

S446. Shapiro, Anna. *Saturday Review* 9.8 (May-June 1983): 56.

S447. Simpson, Leo. "Story by Story, a Stronger Collection than Joyce's *Dubliners*." *Spectator* [Hamilton] 20 November 1982: C3.

S448. Solecki, Sam. "Lives of Girls and Women." *Canadian Forum* 62 (October 1982): 24-25.

S449. Solomon, Charles. "Paperbacks." *Los Angeles Times Book Review* 9 June 1991, home ed. 3: 14.

S450. Stone, William B. *Studies in Short Fiction* 21 (1984): 160.

S451. Tamarkin, Civia. "Munro's Honest Stories Reveal the Complexity of 'Simple' Lives." *Chicago Tribune Book World* 8 May 1983, sec. 7: 3.

S452. Taylor, David. "Connections." *London Magazine* new series 23.4 (July 1983): 94-95.

S453. Timson, Judith. "News and Reviews." *Chatelaine* November 1982: 10.

S454. Twigg, Alan. "The Flawless Alice Munro." *Vancouver Province. The Magazine* 7 November 1982: 5.

S455. *Virginia Quarterly Review* 59.4 (Autumn 1983): 128.

S456. *West Coast Review of Books* 9.4 (July/August 1983): 26.

S457. Williamson, David. "Alice Munro at Her Best." *Winnipeg Free Press* 30 October 1982: 46.

S458. Withers, Jim. "Alice Munro: Close to Home." *Edmonton Sunday Sun* 14 November 1982: S16.

S459. Wordsworth, Christopher. "Dissolved in the Sludge." *Guardian* [London and Manchester] 6 May 1983: 24.

Reviews from the following sources are located in the Alice Munro archives at the University of Calgary Library, Special Collections Division:

Baltimore Sun 13 March 1983.
Berkeley Gazette 24 April 1983: 11.
Boston Globe 21 February 1983: 28.
Cambridge Times [Cambridge, ON] 3 November 1982.
Chicago Sun Times 13 March 1983.
Chronicle and Echo [Northampton, Eng.] 30 August 1984.
Daily Telegraph [London? Dublin?] 28 April 1983.
Desert Sun [Palm Springs, CA] 4 March 1983: A20.
Glasgow Herald 2 July 1983.
Grand Rapids Press 13 March 1983: 4F.
Herald Examiner [Los Angeles] 1 May 1983: F5-F6.
Miami Herald 27 February 1983.
Monterey Peninsula Herald 26 June 1983.

Newspaper [University of Toronto] 3 November 1982.
North Bay Nugget 27 November 1982.
Philadelphia Inquirer 20 February 1983: 6.
Sunday Telegraph [London] 10 July 1983.
World-Herald [Omaha?] 25 February 1983.

Radio Transcripts

S460.   Russ, Margaret. WEBR. Buffalo. 28 March 1983.

Reviews from the following sources are located in the Macmillan archives in Mills Memorial Library, McMaster University:

Cambridge Times [Cambridge, ON] 3 November 1982.
Chronicle Journal [Thunder Bay, ON] 15 November 1982.
Medicine Hat News 15 April 1983.
North Bay Nugget 27 November 1982.
Times Colonist [Victoria, BC] 30 October 1982.

Moons of Jupiter: Stories. French Translation

S461.   Rerolle, Raphaelle. "Infimes moments intimes." *Monde* 18 mars 1995: 5.

Open Secrets: Stories

S462.   Allen, Bruce. "Neighbors and Neighborhoods." *Chicago Tribune* 30 October 1994, Chicagoland, Tribune Books: 5.

S463.   Andrews, Audrey. "Secrets Revealed Can Be Horrifying." *Calgary Herald* 1 October 1994: C8.

S464.   *Antioch Review* 54.1 (Winter 1996): 116.

S465.   "Best Books of 1994. [L.J. Editors' Choices]." *Library Journal* 120 (January 1995): 50.

S466.   Brookner, Anita. "The Sense of Unending." *Spectator* 273 (29 October 1994): 35-36.

S467.   Bush, Catherine. "Where the Wild and the Everyday Collide." *Financial Post* 1 October 1994: S7.

S468.   Butala, Sharon. "A Walk on the Wild Side with Alice Munro." *Globe and Mail* 17 September 1994, metro ed.: C30.

S469.   Caldwell, Gail. "Munro's Stories Are a World All Their Own." *Boston Globe* 18 September 1994, city ed.: A14.

Book Reviews 187

S470. Clapp, Susannah. "The Present Imperfect Tense." *Independent. Sunday Review.* [London] 23 October 1994: 32.

S471. Dubus, Andre. *America* 173.1 (1-8 July 1995): 27-28.

S472. "Editors' Choice." *New York Times Book Review* 4 December 1994: 32.

S473. Fisher, Ann H. *Library Journal* 119 (August 1994): 137.

S474. Gamerman, Amy. "Glowing Stories of Charred Hearts." *Wall Street Journal* 9 September 1994, eastern ed.: A12.

S475. Gironnay, Sophie. "Alice Munro, l'ensorceleuse." *Devoir* 22 octobre 1994: D4.

S476. Gorjup, Branko. *World Literature Today* 69.2 (Spring 1995): 363.

S477. Harris, Gale. *Belles Lettres* 10.2 (Spring 1995): 10-11.

S478. Heeger, Susan. "Pluck, Luck and Destiny." *Los Angeles Times Book Review* 30 October 1994, home ed.: 2.

S479. Hefferman, Teresa. "Letters in Canada 1994: Fiction." *University of Toronto Quarterly* 65.1 (Winter 1995/6): 15.

S480. Helwig, David. "Alice in Wonderland." *Gazette* [Montreal] 24 September 1994: I1, I3.

S481. Higgins, Krystyna. "Looking for a Summer Reading Challenge? Try Open Secrets." *Catholic New Times* 9 July 1995: 7.

S482. Holstrom, David. "Compassion, Surprise Shape Work of Two Veteran Storytellers." *Christian Science Monitor* 11 October 1994: 14.

S483. Hughes-Hallett, Lucy. "The World in a Nutshell." *Sunday Times* [London] 9 October 1994, sec. 7: 7.12.

S484. Hulbert, Ann. "Writer without Borders." *New York Review of Books* 22 December 1994: 59-60.
Rpt. in *Contemporary Literary Criticism*. Ed. Brigham Narins and Deborah A. Stanley. Vol. 95. Detroit: Gale, 1997. 320-323.

S485. Humphreys, Josephine. "Mysteries Near at Hand." *New York Times Book Review* 11 September 1994: 1, 36-37.
Rpt. in *Contemporary Literary Criticism*. Ed. Brigham Narins and Deborah A. Stanley. Vol. 95. Detroit: Gale, 1997. 319-320.

S486.   Jones, Malcolm. "Ordinary People." *Newsweek* 26 September 1994: 63.

S487.   Kakutani, Michiko. "Love, Found and Lost, Amid Sharp Turns of Fate." *New York Times* 6 September 1994, late ed.: C17.

S488.   Kenyon, Linda. "Reality off Kilter: Alice Munro Approaches Life from the Most Unusual Angles." *Kitchener-Waterloo Record* 22 October 1994, final ed.: F10.

S489.   *Kirkus Reviews* 62 (1 July 1994): 875-876.

S490.   Lesser, Wendy. "The Munro Doctrine." *New Republic* 31 October 1994: 51-53.

S491.   London, Joan. "Never Ending Story." *Meanjin* 54.2 (1995): 233-240. Rpt. in *Contemporary Literary Criticism*. Ed. Brigham Narins and Deborah A. Stanley. Vol. 95. Detroit: Gale, 1997. 323-325.

S492.   Marchand, Philip. "More Stories from a Virtuoso." *Toronto Star* 24 September 1994: J20.

S493.   McGraw, Erin. "Exclusionary Principles." *Georgia Review* 49.4 (Winter 1995): 957-959.

S494.   McKenzie, Sandra. "Complex Human Knots Remain Tied." *Vancouver Sun* 8 October 1994: D16.

S495.   Meek, Jim. "Munro Master of Short Story." *Chronicle-Herald* [Halifax] 28 October 1994, provincial ed.: C2.

S496.   O'Faolain, Julia. "In the Territory of Dreams." *TLS: The Times Literary Supplement* 14 October 1994: 24.

S497.   *Publishers Weekly* 241.31 (1 August 1994): 72.

S498.   "PW's Best Books '94." *Publishers Weekly* 241.45 (7 November 1994): 40.

S499.   Quinn, Anthony. "Secrets Hugged to the Chest." *Independent* [London] 12 November 1994, Weekend Books Page: 26.

S500.   Rifkind, Donna. "Canada's Master Storyteller." *Book World* [*Washington Post*] 18 September 1994: 2.

S501.   Robertson, Sarah. *Canadian Book Review Annual* 1994: 3122.

S502.   Rosborough, Linda. "Munro Stories Delight: Secrets Exposed with Grace." *Winnipeg Free Press* 16 October 1994: D5.

S503. Ross, Val. "A Writer Called Alice." *Globe and Mail* 1 October 1994: C1, C21.

S504. Ruta, Suzanne. *Entertainment Weekly* 14 October 1994: 57.

S505. Segedin, Benjamin. *Booklist* 91 (1 September 1994): 24.

S506. Sheppard, R.Z. "Women on the Edge." *Time* (Canadian ed.) 7 November 1994: 70. (American ed.) 3 October 1994: 80.

S507. Solotaroff, Ted. "Life Stories." *Nation* 28 November 1994: 665-668.

S508. Struthers, J. R. (Tim). "How Real, How Magical." *Books in Canada* 23.7 (October 1994): 32-33.

S509. Summers, Merna. *Canadian Forum* 73 (January-February 1995): 38-39.

S510. Turbide, Diane. "The Incomparable Storyteller." *Maclean's* 17 October 1994: 46-49.

S511. Ware, Tracy. *Studies in Short Fiction* 33.1 (Winter 1996): 123-124.

S512. Woodcock, George. "The Secrets of Her Success." *Quill & Quire* August 1994: 25.

Open Secrets: Stories. Audio Version

S513. Arnold, Sue. "In a Northern Light." *Guardian* 20 March 2004, final ed.: 32.

S514. Granatstein, J. L. "Commuter Bestsellers." *Quill & Quire* April 1997: 22-23.

S515. *Kliatt* 30.1 (January 1996): 48.

S516. *Publishers Weekly* 242.23 (5 June 1995): 34.

Open Secrets: Stories. French Translation

S517. Brisac, Geneviève. "La vie selon les femmes de Carstairs." *Monde* 20 octobre 1995: 5.

S518. Chaput, Sylvie. *Nuit blanche* 63 (printemps 1996): 41-42.

S519. Crom, Nathalie. "Littérature canadienne." *Croix* 1 octobre 1995: 17.

S520. Devarrieux, Claire. "La doctrine Munro." *Libération* 28 septembre 1995: VII.

S521. Mercier, Christophe. "Et aussi . . ." *Point* 20 janvier 1996: 76.

The Progress of Love: Stories

S522.   Adachi, Ken. "Alice Munro: At the Very Top of Her Form." *Toronto Star* 21 September 1986: G11.

S523.   "Alice (Laidlaw) Munro: *The Progress of Love*. Governor General's Literary Award: Fiction." *Contemporary Literary Criticism. Yearbook 1987*. Ed. Sharon K. Hall. Vol 50. Detroit: Gale Research, 1988. 207-221.
Reprints of reviews from various sources.

S524.   Andrews, Audrey. "Munro Plumbs Emotional Depths." *Calgary Herald* 19 October 1986: C11.

S525.   Austin, Allan. *World Literature Written in English* 27.1 (Spring 1987): 58-59.

S526.   Austin-Smith, Brenda. "A Way of Seeing." *Prairie Fire* 9.2 (Summer 1988): 73-75.

S527.   Beddoes, Julie. "Country Manners." *Brick* 29 (Winter 1987): 24-26.
Rpt. (in part) in *Contemporary Literary Criticism. Yearbook 1987*. Ed. Sharon K. Hall. Vol 50. Detroit: Gale Research, 1988. 213-215.

S528.   "The Best Books of 1986. [L.J. Editors' Choices]." *Library Journal* 112 (January 1987): 57.

S529.   Blodgett, E. D. "Perfect and Familiar." *Canadian Forum* 66 (October 1986): 32-33.

S530.   *Booklist* 83 (15 September 1986): 102.

S531.   Bradbury, Patricia. "The Realism of Munro and the Romance of Turner Hospital." *Quill & Quire* August 1986: 42.
Rpt. in *Contemporary Literary Criticism. Yearbook 1987*. Ed. Sharon K. Hall. Vol 50. Detroit: Gale Research, 1988. 208.

S532.   Byatt, A. S. "Vanishing Time." *Listener* 29 January 1987: 22-23.
Rpt. in *Contemporary Literary Criticism. Yearbook 1987*. Ed. Sharon K. Hall. Vol 50. Detroit: Gale Research, 1988. 215-216.

S533.   Caplan, Brina. "Objects of Desire." *Nation* 8 November 1986: 497.

S534.   Craig, Patricia. "Minor Upheavals." *Sunday Times* [London] 25 January 1987: 59.

S535.   Daurio, Beverley. *Cross-Canada Writers' Quarterly* 9.1 (1987): 18-19.

S536.   Duchêne, Anne. "Respect for the Facts." *TLS: The Times Literary Supplement* 30 January 1987: 109.

Book Reviews 191

Rpt. (in part) in *Contemporary Literary Criticism. Yearbook 1987*. Ed. Sharon K. Hall. Vol 50. Detroit: Gale Research, 1988. 216.

S537. Durrant, Digby. *London Magazine* new series 27.1&2 (April-May 1987): 158-159.

S538. "Editors' Choice: The Best Books of 1986." *New York Times Book Review* 7 December 1986: 37.

S539. French, William. "Less Is Much More in the Short Story." *Globe and Mail* 20 September 1986: F19.

S540. Gorra, Michael. "Fiction Chronicle." *Hudson Review* 40.1 (Spring 1987): 140-142.
Rpt. (with minor revisions) in *Contemporary Literary Criticism. Yearbook 1987*. Ed. Sharon K. Hall. Vol 50. Detroit: Gale Research, 1988. 217-218.

S541. Gorse, Oliver. *Idler* 12 (March-April 1987): 59-60.

S542. Graham, Barbara J. *CM: A Reviewing Journal of Canadian Materials for Young People* 15.1 (January 1987): 19.

S543. Gray, Paul. "Amplitudes." *Time* (Canadian ed.) 22 September 1986: 82-83. (American ed.) 22 September 1986: 95.

S544. Haviland, Beverly. "Missed Connections." *Partisan Review* 56 (Winter 1989): 154-157.

S545. Henderson, Heather. "Gently Unsettling Songs of Experience." *Maclean's* 22 September 1986: 57.

S546. Howard, Philip. "Life for Us All from Canada." *Times* [London] 22 January 1987: 13.

S547. Jones, D. A. N. "What Women Think about Men." *London Review of Books* 5 February 1987: 23.
Rpt. in *Short Story Criticism: Excerpts from Criticism of the Works of Short Fiction Writers*. Ed. Sheila Fitzgerald. Vol. 3. Detroit: Gale Research, 1989. 348-350.
Rpt. (excerpts) in *Contemporary Literary Criticism. Yearbook 1987*. Ed. Sharon K. Hall. Vol 50. Detroit: Gale Research, 1988. 216-217.

S548. Kakutani, Michiko. "Books of the Times." *New York Times* 3 September 1986, late ed.: C22.
Rpt. in *Contemporary Literary Criticism. Yearbook 1987*. Ed. Sharon K. Hall. Vol 50. Detroit: Gale Research, 1988. 208-209.

S549. *Kirkus Reviews* 54 (1 August 1986): 1148-1149.

S550. LaHood, Marvin J. *World Literature Today* 61.2 (Spring 1987): 295.

S551. Levene, Mark. "Letters in Canada 1986: Fiction." *University of Toronto Quarterly* 57.1 (Fall 1987): 7-9.
Rpt. in *Contemporary Literary Criticism. Yearbook 1987*. Ed. Sharon K. Hall. Vol 50. Detroit: Gale Research, 1988. 218.

S552. Levine, Norman. "A Way with Words." *Books in Canada* 15.7 (October 1986): 14, 16.

S553. Macfarlane, David. "Writer in Residence." *Saturday Night* 101 (December 1986): 51-52, 54, 56.

S554. Mallinson, Jean. "Alice Munro's *The Progress of Love*." *West Coast Review* 21.3 (Winter 1987): 52-58.
Rpt. in *Contemporary Literary Criticism. Yearbook 1987*. Ed. Sharon K. Hall. Vol 50. Detroit: Gale Research, 1988. 219-221.

S555. Millar, Mary. *Queen's Quarterly* 94.4 (Winter 1987): 1015-1017.

S556. Milne, Kirsty. "Wife on Warpath." *Financial Times* [London] 7 February 1987, Weekend: xiv.

S557. Oates, Joyce Carol. "Characters Dangerously Like Us." *New York Times Book Review* 14 September 1986: 7, 9. Correction 28 September 1986: 39.
Rpt. (in part) in *Contemporary Literary Criticism. Yearbook 1987*. Ed. Sharon K. Hall. Vol 50. Detroit: Gale Research, 1988. 210-212.
Rpt. (in part) in *Short Story Criticism: Excerpts from Criticism of the Works of Short Fiction Writers*. Ed. Sheila Fitzgerald. Vol. 3. Detroit: Gale Research, 1989. 346-348.

S558. *Publishers Weekly* 230.1 (4 July 1986): 60.

S559. "PW's Choice: The Year's Best Books." *Publishers Weekly* 231.1 (9 January 1987): 51.

S560. Radin, Victoria. "On the Map." *New Statesman* 27 February 1987: 31.

S561. Robinson, Helen. *Canadian Churchman* December 1986: 20.

S562. Rooke, Constance. *Malahat Review* 78 (March 1987): 152.

S563. Rouse, L. J. *Canadian Book Review Annual* 1986: 3136.

S564. Schwartz, Lynne Sharon. "Alice Munro's Fictions for Our Fickle Times." *Book World* [*Washington Post*] 14 September 1986: 3-4.
Rpt. in *Contemporary Literary Criticism. Yearbook 1987*. Ed. Sharon K. Hall. Vol 50. Detroit: Gale Research, 1988. 209-210.

Book Reviews

S565. Seidenbaum, Art. *Los Angeles Times Book Review* 31 August 1986, home ed.: 8.

S566. Shaumian, Mariam. *Canadian Woman Studies* 10.4 (Winter 1989): 107-108.

S567. Slopen, Beverley. "Alice Munro's U.S. Audience Grows." *Toronto Star* 3 August 1986: G11.

S568. Soete, Mary. *Library Journal* 111 (15 September 1986): 101.

S569. Stewart, Robert. "Exploring Alice Munro's Country." *Gazette* [Montreal] 20 September 1986, final ed.: B7.

S570. Thacker, Robert. "Munro's Progress." *Canadian Literature* 115 (Winter 1987): 239-242.

S571. Tomalin, Claire. "Generation to Generation." *Observer* 25 January 1987: 26. Rpt. as "Time and Distance: *The Progress of Love* by Alice Munro" in *Several Strangers: Writing from Three Decades*. London: Viking, 1999. 136-138.

S572. Tyler, Anne. "Canadian Club." *New Republic* 15 & 22 September 1986: 54-55. Rpt. in *Contemporary Literary Criticism. Yearbook 1987*. Ed. Sharon K. Hall. Vol 50. Detroit: Gale Research, 1988. 212-213.

S573. West, Kathleene. *Prairie Schooner* 61.2 (Summer 1987): 113-114.

S574. Williamson, David. "Munro Excels at Short Story." *Winnipeg Free Press* 20 September 1986: 54.

The Progress of Love: Stories. French Translation

S575. Laniel, Carole-Andrée. "Des univers qui peuvent surprendre . . ." *Presse* 8 mars 1992: C5.

The Progress of Love. Audio Version

S576. "Audio Reviews: Author Readings. Alice Munro Reading." *Publishers Weekly* 232.19 (6 November 1987): 41.

S577. Peters, Joanne K. *CM: A Reviewing Journal of Canadian Materials for Young People* 18.5 (September 1990): 223.

S578. Rasporich, Beverly. "Munro Tapes. Alice Munro Reading *The Progress of Love* (Selections)." *Canadian Literature* 138/139 (Fall/Winter 1993): 147.

Queenie: A Story

S579.   Gardam, Jane. "A Passion for the Particular." *Spectator* 282 (13 March 1999): 36-37.

Runaway: Stories

S580.   Aitken, Lee. *People* 15 November 2004: 47.

S581.   Allen, Bruce. "Complicated Sorrowful Lives." *Sewanee Review* 113.2 (Spring 2005): xxxvi-xxxviii.

S582.   Alvarez, A. "Life Studies." *New York Review of Books* 10 February 2005: 23-24.

S583.   Bailey, Paul. "The Power and the Story." *Independent* [London] 28 January 2005: 29.

S584.   Bautz, Mark. "Compelling Narratives Packed into Precise Prose." *Washington Times* 25 September 1994, final ed.: B8.

S585.   Bender, Elaine. *Library Journal* 129.15 (15 September 2004): 53.

S586.   Boddy, Kasia. "When You Look at the Moon." *Daily Telegraph* 29 January 2005, Books: 9.

S587.   Brown, Rosellen. "Rural and Restless." *New Leader* 87.6 (November-December 2004): 31-33.

S588.   Curtis, Gary. "High-Brow Chicklit." *Hamilton Spectator* 2 October 2004: Go15.

S589.   Cusk, Rachel. "Private Lives." *New Statesman* 134 (24 January 2005): 50.

S590.   Dhuibhne, Éilis Ní. "A Cause for Celebration." *Irish Times* 29 January 2005: 13.

S591.   D'Souza, Irene. *Herizons* 18.4 (Spring 2005): 33.

S592.   Duguid, Lindsay. "The Rhythm of Life." *Sunday Times* [London] 30 January 2005, Culture: 53.

S593.   Erskine, Bruce. "Mastery of Munro." *Chronicle Herald* [Halifax] 26 September 2004, provincial ed.: NS11-NS12.

S594.   Fish, Maria. "Munro's 'Runaway' Hits Home." *USA Today* 18 November 2004: 4D.

S595.   Frank, Michael. "Illuminating Lives in Flight." *Los Angeles Times* 14 November 2004, home ed., Part R: 6.

S596.   Franzen, Jonathan. "Alice's Wonderland." *New York Times Book Review* 14 November 2004, final ed.: 1, 14-15.

S597.   Freeman, John. "Three Masters Invite Us into the Worlds of Their Short Stories." *Chicago Tribune* 28 November 2004, final ed., Books: 3.

S598.   Gatti, Tom. "You Can Run, But You Can't Hide." *Times* [London] 5 February 2005, Weekend Review: 13.

S599.   Goldberg, Carole. "Eight Tales of the Twists Women's Lives Take." *Hartford Courant* 19 December 2004: G3.

S600.   Hawthorne, Mary. "Disconnected Realities." *London Review of Books* 17 February 2005: 17-18.

S601.   Herford, Oliver. "The Impulse of Avoidance." *TLS: The Times Literary Supplement* 18 February 2005: 21.

S602.   Hooper, Brad. *Booklist* 101.2 (15 September 2004): 180.

S603.   Kakutani, Michiko. "Realizing That Certainty Is Inevitably Uncertain." *New York Times* 7 December 2004: E1, E8.

S604.   *Kirkus Reviews* 72.18 (15 September 2004): 887.

S605.   Kritenbrink, Angie. *Identity Theory* 7 November 2004. Accessed 19 January 2006. <http://www.identitytheory.com>

S606.   Lacayo, Richard. "Small Is Beautiful." *Time* (American ed.) 6 December 2004: 109.

S607.   Lalonde, Jeremy. "Beyond the Familiar." *Books in Canada* 33.7 (October 2004): 9-10.

S608.   Marchand, Philip. "Time Passing." *Toronto Star* 26 September 2004: D12-D13.

S609.   Matthews, Mike. *Malahat Review* 150 (March 2005): 96-98.

S610.   McDowell, Lesley. "How Sylvia Was Saved by an Absconding Goat." *Independent on Sunday* [London] 13 March 2005: 29.

S611.   McGovern, Clare. *Iris: A Journal about Women* 50 (Spring-Summer 2005): 66.

S612.   Messud, Claire. "Our Chekhov, Our Flaubert." *Globe and Mail* 25 September 2004: D6.

S613.   Miller, Karl. "Not Bad for a Housewife." *Scottish Review of Books* 1.2 (2005): 18-19.

Secondary Works

S614. Miner, Valerie. "Survival of the Adaptable." *Ms* 14.4 (Winter 2004/2005): 90-91.

S615. Moore, Lorrie. "Leave Them and Love Them." *Atlantic Monthly* December 2004: 125-128.

S616. Passaro, Vince. "Between Freedom and Love: Masterful Stories from the Incomparable Alice Munro." *O, The Oprah Magazine* 5.11 (November 2004): 200.

S617. "Peripheral Visions." *Economist* (American ed.) 18 December 2004: 134.

S618. *Publishers Weekly* 251.41 (11 October 2004): 53.

S619. Reese, Jennifer. *Entertainment Weekly* 12 November 2004: 131.

S620. Reid, Robert. "Master of Her Craft." *Record* [Kitchener-Waterloo] 25 September 2004, final ed.: E6.

S621. Ridge, Mary Blanche. "Ripples in the Backwaters." *Tablet* [London] 12 February 2005.

S622. Roberts, Michele. "The Kindest of Pathologists." *Financial Times* [London] 19 February 2005, Weekend Magazine, Books: 32.

S623. Robertson, Sarah. *Canadian Book Review Annual* 2004: 3143.

S624. Schiefer, Nancy. "Munro's Short Tales Unmatched." *London Free Press* 25 September 2004, final ed.: D8.

S625. See, Carolyn. "The Munro Doctrine." *Washington Post* 19 November 2004, final ed.: C03.

S626. Shilling, Jane. "Life as a Game of Chance." *Sunday Telegraph* 6 February 2005: 17.

S627. Showalter, Elaine. "A Mother's Love." *Literary Review* [London] February 2005: 49.

S628. Skinner, David. "Intricate Stories Told with Craft and Feeling." *Washington Times* 19 December 2004: B08.

S629. Skurnick, Lizzie. *New York* 1 November 2004: 79.

S630. Smee, Sebastian. "The Dangerous Edge of Things." *Spectator* 297 (22 January 2005): 32.

S631. Stern, Bezalel. "Running in Circles." *Jerusalem Post* 4 March 2005, Books: 27.

S632. Thoreen, David. "From Munro, Lives of Canadian Desperation." *Boston Globe* 14 November 2004: E7.

S633. Timson, Judith. "Do Not Write Gently." *Maclean's* 4 October 2004: 48.

S634. Todaro, Lenora. "Ladies in Waiting." *Artforum International* 11.4 (December 2004/January 2005), Supplement: 47.

S635. Upchurch, Michael. "Challenging Journeys through Women's Eyes." *Seattle Times* 31 October 2004: K10.

S636. Urquhart, Jane. "Master of Missed Clues." *National Post* 25 September 2004: RB7.

Runaway. Audio Version

S637. Saricks, Joyce. *Booklist* 101.13 (1 March 2005): 1216.

Selected Stories

S638. "25 Up: Our Favorite Books of the Year." *VLS* [Village Voice Literary Supplement] Winter 1996: 10.

S639. Ackerman, Marianne. "In Short, The Best." *Gazette* [Montreal] 2 November 1996, early ed.: J1, J3.

S640. Archer, Bert. "Mavis and Alice." *Quill & Quire* October 1996: 33.

S641. Banville, John. "Revelations." *New York Review of Books* 20 February 1997: 19-20, 22.

S642. Bell, Millicent. "Fiction Chronicle." *Partisan Review* 64.3 (Summer 1997): 424-427.

S643. "Best Books of 1996. [L.J. Editors' Choices]." *Library Journal* 122 (January 1997): 50.

S644. "Best of the Century: Fiction." *Maclean's* 1 January 2000: 241.

S645. Boyt, Susie. "Household Hints from Jilted Lovers." *Independent* [London] 23 November 1996, Books: 8.

S646. Brookner, Anita. "Daughter's Eye View." *Spectator* 277 (9 November 1996): 47.

S647. Byatt, A. S. "Alice Munro: One of the Great Ones." *Globe and Mail* 2 November 1996, weekend ed.: D18, D14.

S648. Caldwell, Gail. "The Munro Doctrine." *Boston Globe* 3 November 1996, city ed.: D15. Rpt. as "Monarchs of the World: A Celebration" in *Vancouver Sun* 4 January 1997: H6.

S649. Duffy, Dennis. "Something She's Been Meaning to Tell Us." *Books in Canada* 25.9 (December 1996): 8-10. Response to reader's comments: "Not Exactly a Beast." Letter to the editor. *Books in Canada* 26.4 (May 1997): 40.

S650. "Editors' Choice." *New York Times Book Review* 8 December 1996: 11.

S651. Fertile, Candace. "Alice Munro: Stories Confirm Reputation." *Calgary Herald* 9 November 1996: E6.

S652. Ford, Richard. "International Books of the Year." *TLS: The Times Literary Supplement* 29 November 1996: 13.

S653. Fraser, Marian Botsford. "Munro's Short Story Collection Rivals the World's Best." *Financial Post* 23 November 1996: 33.

S654. Heble, Ajay. "Letters in Canada 1996: Fiction." *University of Toronto Quarterly* 67.1 (Winter 1997/1998): 13-15.

S655. Hoffert, Barbara. *Library Journal* 121 (1 October 1996): 130.

S656. Hughes-Hallett, Lucy. "Tales to Take Your Breath Away." *Sunday Times* [London] 3 November 1996, sec. 7: 7.13.

S657. Jacobs, Rita D. *World Literature Today* 71.3 (Summer 1997): 589.

S658. Jones, Malcolm. "Genius in Disguise." *Newsweek* 21 October 1996: 88.

S659. *Kirkus Reviews* 64 (1 September 1996): 1269.

S660. Lasdun, James. "The Soul's History." *Village Voice* 29 October 1996: 63, 65.

S661. MacCann, Philip. "First, Sew Up His Flies . . ." *Observer* 24 November 1996: Observer Review 17.

S662. Mallon, Thomas. "Where the Past Is Prologue." *Book World* [*Washington Post*] 10 November 1996: 1, 13.

S663. Mars-Jones, Adam. "Histories of American Marriage." *TLS: The Times Literary Supplement* 8 November 1996: 26.

S664. Messud, Claire. "Her Small but Perfect Worlds." *Times* [London] 5 December 1996: 41.

S665. Morley, Patricia. *Canadian Book Review Annual* 1996: 3117.

S666. Phillips, Kate. "An Entire Life History in a Page." *Los Angeles Times Book Review* 13 October 1996, home ed.: 3.

S667. Phillips, Kate. "The Best Books of 1996: Fiction." *Los Angeles Times Book Review* 29 December 1996, home ed.: 5.

S668. Philpott, Joan. *Ms* 7.3 (November/December 1996): 81-82.

S669. *Publishers Weekly* 243.33 (12 August 1996): 61.

S670. "PW's Best Books 96." *Publishers Weekly* 243.45 (4 November 1996): 38.

S671. Reid, Robert. "Canadian Short-Storytellers Rank with the World's Finest." *Kitchener-Waterloo Record* 15 February 1997, final ed.: D5.

S672. Rubin, Merle. "The View from True North and Deep South." *Wall Street Journal* 25 October 1996, eastern ed.: A12.

S673. Seaman, Donna. *Booklist* 92 (August 1996): 1856.

S674. Updike, John. "Magnetic North." *New York Times Book Review* 27 October 1996: 11, 13.

S675. Van Ryzin, Jeanne Claire. *Review of Contemporary Fiction* 17.2 (Summer 1997): 275-276.

S676. Wood, James. "Things Happen All the Time." *London Review of Books* 8 May 1997: 31-32.

S677. Young, Elizabeth. "A Town Called Shame." *Guardian* 5 December 1996, sec. 2: 14.

Something I've Been Meaning to Tell You . . . : Thirteen Stories

S678. Ahrold, Kyle Warren. *Library Journal* 100 (15 January 1975): 146.

S679. Barbour, Douglas. "The Extraordinary Ordinary." *Open Letter* 3rd ser. 3 (Late Fall 1975): 107-110.

S680. Blodgett, E. D. *Canadian Fiction Magazine* 16 (Winter 1975): 99-101.

S681. Busch, Frederick. *New York Times Book Review* 27 October 1974: 54.

S682. *Chatelaine* May 1974: 4.

S683. Dawe, Alan. "Looking at Alice." *Vancouver Sun* 21 June 1974, Leisure sec.: 30a.

S684. Dobbs, Kildare. "New Direction for Alice Munro." *Saturday Night* July 1974: 28.

S685.   Elson, Brigid. *Queen's Quarterly* 82.1 (Spring 1975): 136-137.

S686.   French, William. "Beautiful. Her Talent's Transportable." *Globe and Mail* 25 May 1974: 32.

S687.   Fulford, Robert. "Secrecy Is the Persistent Theme of Alice Munro's Writing." *Toronto Star* 25 May 1974: F5.
Rpt. revised as "Solemn Style" in *Montreal Star* 1 June 1974: D14.

S688.   Fulford, Robert. "'A Superb Analysis of the WASPS.'" *Citizen* [Ottawa] 25 May 1974: 75.

S689.   Garis, Leslie. "At the Mercy of Life." *Ms* January 1975: 42-43.

S690.   Hogg, Carol. "Down Home in Rural Ontario." *Calgary Herald Magazine* [*Calgary Herald*, late city ed.] 23 August 1974: 10.

S691.   Hošek, Chaviva. *Quill & Quire* June 1974: 11.

S692.   Howland, Bette. "Tricks, Trap-Doors, a Writer's Craft." *Chicago Tribune* 6 October 1974: F2.

S693.   Hunt, Russell. "What You Get Is What You See." *Fiddlehead* 102 (Summer 1974): 117-119.

S694.   James, Geoffrey. "Moving Miniaturist." *Time* (Canadian ed.) 17 June 1974: 10.

S695.   Julian, Marilyn. *Tamarack Review* 63 (October 1974): 82-83.

S696.   Kirkwood, Hilda. "Tell Us Again." *Canadian Forum* 55 (June 1975): 42.

S697.   Korstanje, Bas. "Let Alice Munro Dazzle You with Her Great Talent." *Spectator* [Hamilton] 8 June 1974: 34.

S698.   MacMillan, Marionne. *British Columbia Library Quarterly* 38.1/2 (Summer-Autumn 1974): 56-57.

S699.   Naglin, Nancy. "Nel Mezzo Del Cammin . . ." *Books in Canada* 3.4 (June-July 1974): 7-8.

S700.   Nolan, Tom. "Spellbinding Tour of Mind and Heart." *Los Angeles Times* 27 October 1974, Sec. Cal.: 70.

S701.   Noonan, Gerald. *Canadian Book Review Annual* 1978: 3138.

S702.   Oates, Joyce Carol. *Ontario Review* 1 (Fall 1974): 103-104.

S703. Orange, John. "Munro's Magic Weave." *Journal of Canadian Fiction* 4.1 (1975): 194-196.

S704. Powell, Dorothy M. *Canadian Author and Bookman* 50.1 (Fall 1974): 26.

S705. Pritchard, William H. "Novel, Sex and Violence." *Hudson Review* 28 (Spring 1975): 156.

S706. Rix, Beverley. "A Revealing Meeting with a Raconteur." *Citizen* [Ottawa] 24 August 1974: 64.

S707. Rudzik, O. H. T. "Letters in Canada 1974: Fiction." *University of Toronto Quarterly* 44 (Summer 1975): 305.

S708. Stouck, David. *West Coast Review* 10.1 (June 1975): 46-47.

S709. Struthers, J. R. (Tim). "Exciting Collection." *London Free Press* 22 June 1974: 70.

S710. Thomas, Audrey. "Extraordinary Girls and Women." *Canadian Literature* 67 (Winter 1976): 85-87.

S711. Thompson, Richard J. *Best Sellers* 15 October 1974: 323-324.

S712. Tudor, Kathleen. *Atlantis* 1.1 (Fall 1975): 129-130.

S713. Woodcock, George. "Bittersweets for the Short Story Buffs." *Maclean's* June 1974: 94.

Reviews from the following sources are located in the Alice Munro archives at the University of Calgary Library, Special Collections Division:

Albuquerque Journal [NM] December 1974.
Buffalo Evening News 19 October 1974.
Call Enterprise [Downey, CA] 3 October 1974.
Chicago Tribune 6 October 1974.
Dayton Daily News [OH] 6 October 1974.
Evening Telegram [St. John's, NF] 26 October 1974.
Hartford Courant [CT] 29 September 1974.
Houston Post [TX] 6 October 1974.
Los Angeles Times Calendar 27 October 1974.
Minneapolis Star 7 November 1974.
Ottawa Journal 6 July 1974.
St. Catharines Standard 22 June 1974.
Seattle Post-Intelligencer 6 October 1974.
Standard-Times [San Angelo, TX] 30 March 1975.
Star-Phoenix [Saskatoon] 21 June 1974.
Time-News [Erie, PA] 22 September 1974.
Victoria Times 8 June 1974.

Western News [University of Western Ontario] 12 December 1974.
Windsor Star 6 July 1974.

Radio Transcripts

S714.   Carver, Caroline. CKFM. 9 June 1974.

S715.   Jacobs, Ann. *Radio Noon Three*. CBC Maritime. 6 January 1974.

Who Do You Think You Are?: Stories

S716.   Abley, Mark. "Growing Up Sad in Southern Ontario." *Maclean's* 11 December 1978: 62.

S717.   Adachi, Ken. "Turn Off the TV and Read a Story!" *Toronto Star* 4 November 1978: D7.

S718.   Baird, Nora. *Canadian Materials for Schools and Libraries* 7.4 (Autumn 1979): 216.

S719.   Bartlett, Brian. "New Severity: After 10 Years in Print, Alice Munro Reveals an Unusually Painful Bite to Her Work." *Gazette* [Montreal] 13 January 1979, final ed.: 53.

S720.   Bradshaw, Leah. "Portraits in Women's Literature." *Queen's Quarterly* 87.3 (Autumn 1980): 461-462.

S721.   Dewar, Elaine. "FemCanlit." *City Woman* (March-April 1979): 44, 46.

S722.   Earl, Marjorie. "I Read Alice Munro's Book, I Liked It and Told Her So." *Tribune* [Winnipeg] 18 November 1978: 43.

S723.   Edwards, Caterina. "Language and Self." *Branching Out* 6.3 (1979): 43.

S724.   Fallis, Sheila Robinson. *Quill & Quire* October 1978: 43. (Review based on advance proof of original version)

S725.   French, William. "Stamped with the Seal of Quality." *Globe and Mail* 11 November 1978: 40.

S726.   Grady, Wayne. "Alice through a Glass Darkly." *Books in Canada* 7.8 (October 1978): 15-16. (Review based on advance proof of original version)

S727.   Grady, Wayne. "Fiction Chronicle." *Tamarack Review* 77 & 78 (Summer 1979): 98.

S728.   Hofsess, John. "Where Does Munro Go from 'Here and Now'?" *Albertan. Sunday Tab.* 1 April 1979: TO23.

S729.	Josephs, Shirley. *Emergency Librarian* 6.1-2 (September-December 1978): 21.

S730.	Kareda, Urjo. "The War within Alice Munro's Heroine." *Saturday Night* January/February 1979: 62, 64.

S731.	Kilpatrick, Ken. "Alice Munro's Latest Book a Literary Event." *Spectator* [Hamilton] 18 November 1978, city ed.: 29.

S732.	Mallet, Gina. "Alice Munro: The Mud Underneath the Manicure." *Toronto Star* 18 November 1978: D7.

S733.	Morrison, Ray. "Top Writer's Stories Deep, Complex." *Citizen* [Ottawa] 17 February 1979: 40.

S734.	Noonan, Gerald. *Canadian Book Review Annual* 1978: 150-151.

S735.	Off, Carol. "Munro's Kaleidoscopic Impressions." *Gazette* [University of Western Ontario] 5 January 1979: 10.

S736.	Rowe, Percy. *Sunday Sun* [*Toronto Sun*] 17 December 1978: S23.

S737.	Smith, Elaine. "Gifted Author Writes with Humor, Empathy." *Calgary Herald* 30 December 1978: D10.

S738.	Solecki, Sam. "Letters in Canada 1978: Fiction." *University of Toronto Quarterly* 48 (Summer 1979): 319-320.

S739.	Stevens, Peter. "Stories Searching for the Self." *Windsor Star* 3 March 1979, final ed.: 35.

S740.	Struthers, J. R. (Tim). "Munro's Latest Shows Astonishing Maturity." *London Free Press* 16 December 1978: B5.

S741.	Stuewe, Paul. "On the Racks: Gentle Readers . . ." *Books in Canada* 9.1 (January 1980): 20.

S742.	Taylor, Michael. *Fiddlehead* 121 (Spring 1979): 125-127.

S743.	Twigg, Alan. "Alice Munro: Book Impeccably Styled 'Super-Realism.'" *Georgia Straight* 12 (27 April-2 May 1979): 31.

S744.	Whiteway, Doug. "Glimpses into a Life." *Winnipeg Tribune* 5 February 1979, final ed.: 12.

S745.	Whiteway, Doug. "Who Do You Think You Are?" *Canadian Reader* 20.4 (May 1979): [3-4].

S746.   Wiggins, Lee. "Escape into Story." *Ontario Report* 3.5 (August 1979): 33-34.

S747.   Williamson, David. "Alice Munro: Is She the Best Canadian Writer?" *Winnipeg Free Press* 17 February 1979, Leisure/Books: 13.

Reviews from the following sources are located in the Alice Munro archives at the University of Calgary Library, Special Collections Division (C) and in Mills Memorial Library, McMaster University, Archives and Research Collections (M):

Edmonton Journal 18 November 1978. (C)
Edmonton Sun 31 December 1978. (C, M)
Kamloops News 16 March 1979. (M)
Lethbridge Herald 30 December 1978. (C, M)
Newfoundland Evening Telegram 24 March 1979. (C, M)
Ontarion [University of Guelph] 16 January 1979. (C, M)
Ottawa Journal 16 December 1978. (C, M)
Ottawa Revue 8-14 February 1979. (C, M)
Peterborough Examiner December 1978. (C, M)
Saskatoon Star Phoenix 10 February 1979. (M)
Vancouver Express December 1978. (C, M)
Whig-Standard [Kingston, ON] 10 March 1979. (C, M)

Radio Transcripts

S748.   Jacobs-Munton, Ann. *CBC Radio Noon Three*. CBC Radio, Halifax. 28 June 1979.

S749.   Zilm, Glennis. CHQM Radio, Vancouver, BC 28 February 1979.

Books about Alice Munro

S750.   *Alice Munro: Selected Stories: A Tribute.* [Toronto]: McClelland and Stewart, n.d.
"To accompany the 560-page volume published by McClelland and Stewart, this tribute includes an introduction to her work by the author."

This 17 page booklet was issued to accompany the first edition of *Selected Stories* published by McClelland and Stewart. It contains a section by Munro, who explains her writing process and her methods of reading and writing stories. In another section, the publisher Douglas Gibson comments on the stories in the collection. The booklet also contains a brief biography of Munro, excerpts from reviews of her books by country, and an excerpt from an interview by Peter Gzowski published in *The Morningside Years*.

S751.   Besner, Neil Kalman. *Introducing Alice Munro's "Lives of Girls and Women": A Reader's Guide.* Toronto: ECW Press, 1990.

In the beginning pages, Besner gives a brief chronology of Munro's life and career, and outlines the critical reception of Munro's book with the inclusion of excerpts from reviews. Besner divides the criticism into the following groupings: Initiation, Bildungsroman, and Künstlerroman; paradox, parallel, and double vision; regionalism; narration; autobiographical fiction; photography; fictional surfaces and forms of realism; feminism; texts and textuality. The rest of the book contains Besner's interpretation, beginning with a consideration of the novel as a collection of short stories, then continuing with a chapter-by-chapter examination, with a concentration on the themes.

Reviews:

Somerville, Christine. "Ringing the Changes." *Canadian Literature* 140 (Spring 1994): 130-132.

Thacker, Robert. "What's 'Material'? The Progress of Munro Criticism, Part 2." *Journal of Canadian Studies/Revue d'études canadiennes* 33.2 (1998): 196-210.

S752.   Blodgett, E. D. *Alice Munro.* Twayne's World Authors Series TWAS800, Canadian Literature. Boston: Twayne Publishers, 1988.

Blodgett's book covers the span of Munro's writing, from *Dance* to *Progress*, and pays special attention to focalization and narration in the works. The introductory pages review Munro's early life and writing career, and consider the autobiographical aspects of her writing. *Dance* is described as having an intense preoccupation with time and its passing. While examining the themes of each story in the collection, Blodgett also looks at narration, noting the relationship between the narrator and protagonist, and the focalization. In a similar study of *Lives*, Blodgett notes several powerful themes, including the main theme of the protagonist's quest for reality. He also examines death as a theme, the metaphor of the body as text, the mother-daughter relationship, and the opposition of fantasy and reality. The protagonist as a narrator and focalization are discussed. The section on *Something* deals with the relationship between the self and other in the stories, between the narrator and narratee, and the general theme of truth and fiction. The themes of *Who*, especially those relating to roleplaying, mimicry, and pretension, make characterization difficult in characters like Flo and Rose, who use these devices to project an outward self and find that, in the process, they lose themselves. The stories in *Moons* centre on the themes of connection, chance, and the quest for knowledge. In the stories, the syntax is dominant, and not the subject or self. The emphasis is not on the teller but on what is not told. The character is discussed as narrator and as process. The stories in *Progress* are preoccupied with the presence of destiny and its crucial role in the utterance of self. Destiny is viewed as a matter of fiction. In the title story, the relationship between narration, truth, and the self is analyzed. The concluding pages look at Munro's aesthetic vision and at her writing process.

Reviews:

Carrington, Ildikó de Papp. *American Review of Canadian Studies* 19.1 (Spring 1989): 121-123.

Savoy, Eric. *Ariel: A Review of International English Literature* 21 (April 1990): 100-102.

Thacker, Robert. "Go Ask Alice: The Progress of Munro Criticism." *Journal of Canadian Studies/Revue d'études canadiennes* 26.2 (Summer 1991): 156-169.

S753.   Carrington, Ildikó de Papp. *Controlling the Uncontrollable: The Fiction of Alice Munro*. Dekalb: Northern Illinois University Press, 1989.

Analysing some 60 stories, collected and uncollected, published between 1950 to 1988, Carrington investigates Munro's approach to the human paradox of trying to control the uncontrollable aspects of life: death, sexuality, love, biological processes, emotions, accidents, violence, and memory. In the first chapter, Carrington notes the recurrence of certain words and images in Munro's writing such as "humiliation," "shame," "watch," "power," "control," "abdicate." She elaborates on these in selected stories, in relation to Munro's techniques and in relation to Munro's vision of life and art. The image of the narrator or protagonist as watcher is considered to be an intrinsic component in the way the point of view is manipulated. Watchers are often the observers of shame and humiliation, either that of others or, more often, of themselves. Hence the split point of view. The point of view is shown to affect the distancing or detachment of the narrator from what is observed, as in the case of death. Power and the abdication of power are discussed in relation to her characters and to Munro's own artistic power. Next, language enters into the discussion—language as it occurs as an element in a number of stories and as an element of Munro's ambivalent views on language in writing. The following chapters discuss stories containing the uncontrollable elements of violence, accidents, sexuality, and death, and a number of key associative metaphors. In another chapter, controlled and controlling characters, grouped as humiliated characters, voyeurs, and alter egos, are discussed for the stories in each collection. A special grouping is made of stories which centre around the uncontrollable nature of memory, espe-

cially obsessive memories related to mother-daughter and father-daughter relationships. Carrington makes concluding comments on point of view, metaphor, and paradox.
Reviews:
Blodgett, E. D. "She Walks on Water." *Canadian Literature* 132 (Spring 1992): 183-184.
Irvine, Lorna. *American Review of Canadian Studies* 20.2 (Summer 1990): 252-254.
McMullen, Lorraine. *University of Toronto Quarterly* 60.1 (Fall 1990): 168-169.
Messenger, Cynthia. "In Search of Munro." *Essays on Canadian Writing* 47 (Fall 1992): 26-35.
Panofsky, Ruth. "Eclectic Views." *Journal of Canadian Studies/Revue d'études canadiennes* 29.2 (Summer 1994): 189-194. [Carrington on pages192-193]
Thacker, Robert. "Go Ask Alice: The Progress of Munro Criticism." *Journal of Canadian Studies/Revue d'études canadiennes* 26.2 (Summer 1991): 156-169.

S754.   Carscallen, James. *The Other Country: Patterns in the Writing of Alice Munro*. Toronto: ECW Press, 1993.

In a highly detailed and intertexual way, Carscallen weaves together a complex picture of parallels and patterns found in Munro's *oeuvre* from the early uncollected stories to *Friend*. Carscallen lays the groundwork for his study by considering Munro's presentation, looking at signs and meanings, epiphany, sensibility, narrative and meditation, and invasion. In the next chapter, names such as Mary and Elizabeth are associated with Biblical characters and in turn with character-types in the stories. Names are also associated with countries. Carscallen then turns to make comparisons of the linear and circular narrative structures of short stories. He carries the discussion of structure further to the books as collections, and classifies the order of stories in the collections into three phase types: initiatory stories, central stories, and terminal phase stories. He draws comparisons between cyclical patterns found in the Bible and in *Lives* and other works. He suggests groupings of stories according to biblical patterns: Genesis, Wilderness, Judges, Kingdom, the Egyptian stories, the Exodus group, the Passion group, and the Apocalypse group. Throughout the book, attention is brought to patterns of biblical, historical, and literary allusions, images and imagery, character types, motifs, colours, and seasons. The book contains a detailed index of titles and characters.
Reviews:
Beran, Carol L. "Review Essay: New Visions of Alice Munro's Stories." *American Review of Canadian Studies* 28.1-2 (Spring-Summer 1998): 177-182.
Canitz, A. E. Christa. *University of Toronto Quarterly* 65.1 (Winter 1995/96): 247-250.
Messenger, Cynthia. "Pressing Lives." *Canadian Forum* 74 (October 1995): 40-43. [Carscallen on pages 41-42]
Moran, Maureen F. *British Journal of Canadian Studies* 11.1 (1996): 145-147.
Noonan, Gerald A. *English Studies in Canada* 22.1 (March 1996): 97-99.
Rasporich, Beverly. *Canadian Book Review Annual* (1993): 3301.
Somerville, Christine. "Monuments and Magpies." *Canadian Literature* 148 (Spring 1996): 180-181.
Thacker, Robert. "What's 'Material'? The Progress of Munro Criticism, Part 2." *Journal of Canadian Studies/Revue d'études canadiennes* 33.2 (1998): 196-210.
Thompson, Elizabeth. "Unravelling Munro's Secrets." *Literary Review of Canada* 4.10 (November 1995): 22-23.

S755.   Cox, Ailsa. *Alice Munro*. Writers and Their Work. Tavistock, Devon, Eng.: Northcote House in association with the British Council, 2004.

In this study, Cox makes connections across Munro's work and gives detailed readings of selected stories in relation to important themes, techniques, and elements. She supports and elucidates the text with quotations from stories and from personal interviews of the author. Cox first examines the development and emergence of the female artist in *Lives* and "My Mother's Dream." The mother-daughter dyad in both works illustrates the shifting subjectivity of women in their relationship with others. In the second chapter, Cox discusses how Munro's life, including her domestic responsibilities, has affected her writing, particularly in "The Peace of Utrecht" and *Who*. She shows how the close identification between mother and daughter affects female subjectivity in the fiction-making process. The third chapter looks at the Joycean epiphany, or single intuition, as the turning point in the short story, specifically, in *Who* and "The Jack Randa Hotel." Chapter four examines double-voiced discourse, carnival elements, and silence in "Pictures of the Ice," while in "The Love of a Good Woman" both male and female silence is discussed. Chapter five focuses on turning points or "queer turns of fate" which result in unpredictable consequences in "Open Secrets" and "The Children Stay." The sixth chapter looks at how memory rewrites the past in "The Progress of Love," and how letters are used as historical forms of discourse in "Carried Away." The final chapter considers the passage of time in *Open* and its effects on characters—aging, decay, and abjection. Julia Kristeva's concepts of the semiotic and symbolic elements in language and her concept of abjection are applied to the study of "Vandals."

S756.   Dahlie, Hallvard. *Alice Munro and Her Works*. Downsview, ON: ECW Press, 1985. Also pub. in *Canadian Writers and Their Works*. Introd. George Woodcock. Ed. Robert Lecker, Jack David, and Ellen Quigley. Fiction Series 7. Toronto: ECW Press, 1985. 213-256.

Dahlie's book provides, for the uninitiated reader, an introduction to Munro's life, her work, and the criticism. Following a brief biography, Dahlie outlines the tradition and milieu in which Munro was writing. He considers the state of Canadian literature after the war and the authors who influenced Munro as a writer. A critical overview of reviews and published criticism shows the reception of Munro's writing. In chronological order, Dahlie provides a critical analysis for *Dance*, *Something*, *Lives*, and *Who*.
Reviews:
Querengesser, Neil. *Canadian Book Review Annual* (1985): 3241.

S757.   Heble, Ajay. *The Tumble of Reason: Alice Munro's Discourse of Absence*. Toronto: University of Toronto Press, 1994.

Paradigmatic discourse is an area of language use in which, as Heble quotes, "the meaning of an item depends on the difference between it and other items which might have filled the same slot in a given sequence." Absent or potential levels of meaning allow for possibilities. This book, a revised and updated version of Heble's dissertation, looks at absent and latent meaning, subtext, implication, irony, and symbol, and the techniques Munro uses to produce them. Heble moves chronologically through the works from *Dance* to *Progress*, and studies the ways in which paradigmatic discourse operates in each work. In *Dance*, he considers the process of memory turning into legend; in *Lives*, the opposition of reality and fiction; in *Something*, power and suspicion and gaps in communication; in *Who*, disruptive patterns, gaps in time, and discourse of absence; in *Moons*, the poetics of surprise manifested through

the collapse or absence of connections; in *Progress*, patterns of complicity and deception to promote and undo reality at the same time; in *Friend*, forms of deception in themes and structure.
Reviews:
Beran, Carol L. "Review Essay: New Visions of Alice Munro's Stories." *American Review of Canadian Studies* 28.1-2 (Spring-Summer 1998): 177-182.
Canitz, A. E. Christa. *University of Toronto Quarterly* 65.1 (Winter 1995): 247-250.
Fu, Li. *Ariel: A Review of International English Literature* 27.3 (July 1996): 181-183.
Godard, Barbara. *Modern Fiction Studies* 42.1 (Spring 1996): 164-167.
MacKendrick, Louis K. *English Studies in Canada* 22.4 (December 1996): 481-483.
Moyles, R. G. *Canadian Book Review Annual* (1995): 3292.
Nicholson, Colin. *Yearbook of English Studies* 27 (1997): 335-336.
Rasporich, Beverly J. "Critical Vantage."*Canadian Literature* 150 (Autumn 1996): 183-185.
Thacker, Robert. "What's 'Material'? The Progress of Munro Criticism, Part 2." *Journal of Canadian Studies/Revue d'études canadiennes* 33.2 (Summer 1998): 196-210.
Thompson, Elizabeth. "Unravelling Munro's Secrets." *Literary Review of Canada* 4.10 (November 1995): 22-23.
Ware, Tracy. *Studies in Short Fiction* 34.2 (Spring 1997): 264-265.

S758.   Hernáez Lerena, María Jesús. *Exploración de un género literario: Los relatos breves de Alice Munro*. Biblioteca de Investigación 18. Logroño: Universidad de La Rioja, Servicio de Publicaciones, 1998.

Working in a chronological progression through Munro's books and selected stories, Hernáez Lerena examines the evolution of Munro's use of time and space in her reiterative stories and in the analeptic organization of her works. In the first chapter, she provides a background to Munro's life and vision, her literary influences, and the critical reception of her work. The next two chapters include a methodological and general discussion of time and space in the narrative and their significance to the short story. The application of the previous discussion to Munro's works begins in chapter 4. She begins with an examination of several stories in *Dance* which display Munro's first use of the iterative method, where the beginning of the story is a repetition of a prior event. The iterative method continues in *Lives*. But in *Something* and *Moons*, new forms evolve. Temporal organization, duration of time of the narrative, and closed time circles are some of the elements discussed. In *Progress*, Hernáez Lerena demonstrates the breaking down of time, and cases of simultaneous futures. In chapter 7, she examines the function of time in the story cycles *Beggar* and *Lives*. She looks at the links between the stories, classifies the story cycles, and considers time as an element of cohesion and characterization. Finally, in *Open*, time restrictions are examined in light of the narrative direction of the story. Concepts of transition and method of indirection are treated.

S759.   Howells, Coral Ann. *Alice Munro*. Contemporary World Writers. Manchester, Eng.: University of Manchester Press, 1998.

Howells uses the imagery of maps and mapping throughout the book. Beginning chronologically with *Dance*, and ending with *Open*, she examines both common and story-specific themes and the methods Munro uses to promote them. Two stories from *Dance* and *Something* are selected as illustrative of the mapping of landscapes, the elements of gothicism, and the vision of the strange in the ordinary. This double vision of reality continues in *Lives*.

Howells focuses on the mapping of text and place or landscape in the novel, while in *Who* she points to the mapping of time and how the past is remembered and reconstructed. In *Moons*, the mapping imagery moves to star maps. The centre and orbiting principle is applied to the structure within the stories and as the stories relate to the collection as a whole. The shifting perspective in *Moons* continues in *Progress*, but the element of indeterminacy is brought into the discussion. Indeterminacy is accomplished through Munro's methods of unsettlement and disarrangements, including multiple stories, gaps in stories, and shifts in time and point of view. Next, using stories in *Friend*, Howells maps out situations of evasion, secrecy, and silence. In the last book, *Open*, she investigates stories in which a multilayered perception of reality is created through shifting narrative perspectives and time frames, multiple voices, and the presence of alternative or parallel realities. In the concluding chapter, "The Love of a Good Woman" and "What Do You Want to Know For?" are used as examples of the current direction of Munro's work in which mystery and dark spaces within the metaphorical house predominate. In this same chapter, Howell provides an overview of Munro criticism from 1982 onward.

Reviews:

Foy, Nathalie. *University of Toronto Quarterly* 69.1 (Winter 1999/2000): 343-345.

Gorjup, Branko. *World Literature Today* 73.4 (Autumn 1999): 746-747.

Hanson, Clare. *Yearbook of English Studies* 31 (2001): 335-336.

Redekop, Magdalene. *English Studies in Canada* 27.3 (September 2001): 396-398.

Stich, Klaus P. *American Review of Canadian Studies* 30.1 (Spring 2000): 100-102.

Thacker, Robert. "Introducing Oeuvres." *Canadian Literature* 167 (Winter 2000): 124-126.

S760.   MacKendrick, Louis King, ed. *Probable Fictions: Alice Munro's Narrative Acts.* Downsview, ON: ECW Press, 1983.

This edited work contains one interview and nine critical essays focussed on different aspects of Munro's writing: narrative perspective, structural elements, style, language, and narrative methods of dislocation and disarrangement. Annotations for the following papers are listed in their respective sections, "Interviews" and "Articles and Chapters in Books":

Struthers, J. R. (Tim). "The Real Material: An Interview with Alice Munro." pp. 5-36.

Thacker, Robert. "'Clear Jelly': Alice Munro's Narrative Dialectics." pp. 37-60.

Osachoff, Margaret Gail. "'Treacheries of the Heart': Memoir, Confession, and Meditation in the Stories of Alice Munro." pp. 61-82.

Orange, John. "Alice Munro and a Maze of Time." pp. 83-98.

Irvine, Lorna. "'Changing Is the Word I Want.'" pp. 99-111.

Ross, Catherine Sheldrick. "'At Least Part Legend': The Fiction of Alice Munro." pp. 112-126.

Taylor, Michael. "The Unimaginable Vancouvers: Alice Munro's Words." pp. 127-143.

McMullen, Lorraine. "'Shameless, Marvellous, Shattering Absurdity': The Humour of Paradox in Alice Munro." pp. 144-162.

Noonan, Gerald. "The Structure of Style in Alice Munro's Fiction." pp. 163-180.

Mathews, Lawrence. "'Who Do You Think You Are?': Alice Munro's Art of Disarrangement." pp. 181-193.

Reviews:

Jirgens, Karl. *Books in Canada* 13.7 (August-September 1984): 26-27.

Keith, W. J. *Canadian Book Review Annual* (1983): 3294.

Kröller, Eva-Marie. "Craft and Criticism." *Canadian Literature* 103 (Winter 1984): 128-129.

Madoff, Mark S. *University of Windsor Review* 19.1 (Fall-Winter 1985): 88-91.

Thacker, Robert. "What's 'Material'? The Progress of Munro Criticism, Part 2." *Journal of Canadian Studies/Revue d'études canadiennes* 33.2 (1998): 196-210.

S761.   MacKendrick, Louis K. *Some Other Reality: Alice Munro's "Something I've Been Meaning to Tell You."* Canadian Fiction Studies no. 25. Toronto: ECW Press, 1993.

Similar to the outline adopted by Besner in his book on *Lives*, MacKendrick begins with a chronology of Munro's personal life, her writing career, and published works. He evaluates the importance of *Something* in terms of Munro's artistic development. An overview of the critical reception of the book is found in the form of summaries of reviews and critical articles published in periodicals and books. However, the major portion of MacKendrick's book is devoted to an examination of the stories, with a detailed analysis of nine out of the thirteen stories. In "Executioner," for example, he stresses the classical allusions, comic elements, images, motifs, and symbolism. In "Memorial," the garden is seen as a central symbol of control and order in a disordered, unpredictable world. The themes, narrative techniques, and devices are thus explored in each story. Concluding the book, MacKendrick considers Munro's writing technique and vision in light of her own claim of not being able to analyse these herself.

Reviews:

Meyer, Bruce. *Canadian Book Review Annual* (1994): 3302.

Thacker, Robert. "What's 'Material'? The Progress of Munro Criticism, Part 2." *Journal of Canadian Studies/Revue d'études canadiennes* 33.2 (Summer 1998): 196-210.

S762.   Martin, W. R. *Alice Munro: Paradox and Parallel.* Edmonton: University of Alberta Press, 1987.

Martin discusses Munro's first 6 books and some 79 stories, including 9 early and 4 later uncollected stories, paying attention to the development of her narrative techniques, mastery of language, themes, and patterns or parallels in her work. His particular focus is on the dialectic that involves paradoxes and parallels. In most of the works, he notes some form of opposition, contradiction, incongruity, or inconsistency. In the first chapter, Martin examines prominent aspects and themes of Munro's writing and her angles of vision, particularly the opposition of the strange and familiar. In the following several chapters, he traces important themes and methods in the early uncollected stories and in the collection *Dance*, examining them in the order in which they were written. "The Peace of Utrecht" is seen as a decisive story in Munro's artistic development. In *Lives*, Martin points out the oppositions and incongruities in Del's world and Munro's use of irony in the novel. Del's self-identity is formulated through an awareness of the difference between herself and others. Martin views *Something* as a further achievement in Munro's art, in that he sees it as a variation of the short-story cycle. He suggests that the story arrangement and groupings form a type of constellation which exerts a dynamism. *Who* is discussed in terms of a novel, with a beginning, middle, and end. Attention is paid to the revisions made by Munro prior to publication. Flo as a character and her storytelling are discussed. Martin then turns to *Moons*, looking at story groupings, organization, and common threads as he did for *Something*, and concludes that the constellation formed in this case is more fully integrated. Martin discusses only some of the stories in *Progress*, which had not been published at the time of his book. He notes the presence of greater complexity in themes and methods. The concluding chapters

summarize Munro's mastery of language and her art, and assess her achievements as a Canadian short story writer.
Reviews:
Holmgren, Michelle. *Malahat Review* 85 (December 1988): 143.
Kinczyk, Bohdan. *CM: A Reviewing Journal of Canadian Materials for Young People* 15.6 (November 1987): 235-236.
McMullen, Lorraine. *University of Toronto Quarterly* 58.1 (Fall 1988): 172-173.
Savoy, Eric. *Ariel: A Review of International English Literature* 20.1 (January 1989): 101-104.
Stone, William B. *Studies in Short Fiction* 25 (Winter 1988): 95-96.
Thieme, John. *British Journal of Canadian Studies* 3.1 (1988): 184-186.
Trehearne, Brian. *Queen's Quarterly* 96.4 (Winter 1989): 973-975.
Ward, Sandra. "Subfusc Critic." *Matrix* 26 (Spring 1988): 79-80.
Warwick, Susan J. *English Studies in Canada* 14.4 (December 1988): 481-486.
York, Lorraine M. "Sipping Munro." *Essays on Canadian Writing* 39 (Fall 1989): 139-143.

S763.   McCaig, JoAnn. *Reading In: Alice Munro's Archives*. Waterloo, ON: Wilfrid Laurier University Press, 2002.

McCaig applies a feminist cultural studies approach to this examination of Munro's authorship. The three factors McCaig has chosen to explore in Munro's evolution as an author of authority are her Canadian nationality, her feminine gender, and the genre of the short story. She uses the Munro archives located at the University of Calgary Library to look at the correspondence of key individuals in the writer's career, including the correspondence of Robert Weaver and Virginia Barber. Robert Weaver's mentorship is viewed within the context of the Canadian literary culture of the 1950s to the 1970s. This is compared with Virginia Barber's role as Munro's American agent. The agent-author relationship is seen not only as one of aesthetic association and friendship, but also as one of economics and gender. The factor of a female agent promoting a female author is considered an important one in Munro's acceptance as an author of authority in the wider market. The short-story genre is considered within the literary cultures of Canada and the United States, and the different attitudes toward the genre are illustrated by the contrast in the production of *Who* in both countries. Finally, McCaig looks at Munro as a cultural product; a public figure, a producer, and a citizen of Wingham, Ontario. She concludes with the observation that authority allows Munro to explore and question sociopolitical issues in her fiction.
Reviews:
Beran, Carol L. "Jabbing Sentences (review article)." *Essays on Canadian Writing* 79 (Spring 2003): 33-40.
Heer, Jeet. "Minding Alice Munro's Business." *National Post* 11 May 2002: SP1, SP4.
Hermansson, Casie. *University of Toronto Quarterly* 73.1 (2003/2004): 345-347.
Hobbs, Catherine. *Archivaria* 55 (Spring 2003): 164-168.
Latta, Ruth. "Canadian, Eh?" *Briarpatch* 32.8 (October 2003): 13-14.
Rasporich, Beverly. *Canadian Book Review Annual* (2002): 3292.
Ready, Kathryn. "Short Fictions." *Canadian Literature* 181 (Summer 2004): 161-163.

S764.   Miller, Judith, ed. *The Art of Alice Munro: Saying the Unsayable*. Papers from the Waterloo Conference. Waterloo, ON: University of Waterloo Press, 1984.

Annotations for the following papers are listed in the section "Articles and Chapters in Books":

Gold, Joseph. "Our Feeling Exactly: The Writing of Alice Munro." pp. 1-13.
Fitzpatrick, Margaret Anne. "'Projection' in Alice Munro's *Something I've Been Meaning to Tell You*." pp. 15-20.
Martin, W. R. "Hanging Pictures Together: 'Something I've Been Meaning to Tell You.'" pp. 21-34.
Tener, Jean F. "The Invisible Iceberg." pp. 37-42.
Godard, Barbara. "'Heirs of the Living Body': Alice Munro and the Question of a Female Aesthetic." pp. 43-71.
Robson, Nora. "Alice Munro and the White American South: The Quest." pp. 73-84.
Carscallen, James. "The Shining House: A Group of Stories." pp. 85-101.
Struthers, J. R. "Alice Munro's Fictive Imagination." pp. 103-112.
Lamont-Stewart, Linda. "Order from Chaos: Writing as Self-Defense in the Fiction of Alice Munro and Clark Blaise." pp. 113-121.
Reviews:
Köster, Patricia. *Canadian Literature* 117 (Summer 1988): 166-167.
Thacker, Robert. "Conferring Munro." *Essays on Canadian Writing* 34 (Spring 1987): 162-169.

S765.   Munro, Sheila. *Lives of Mothers and Daughters: Growing Up with Alice Munro*. Toronto: McClelland and Stewart, 2001.
Excerpts pub. as:
"Lives of Mothers and Daughters. Chatelaine Bookexcerpt." *Chatelaine* May 2001: 139-140, 142, 144.
"The Trouble with Alice." *Globe and Mail* 14 April 2001: F1, F9.
Alternating between objective and subjective viewpoints, Sheila Munro shows how the daughter of a mother who is a famous writer and friend can have ambivalent feelings, both about her mother's fame and about herself as an individual within the environment in which she grew up. This memoir-biography, personalized with numerous photographs, is also significant for the personal background it gives into Munro's childhood, youth, marriage, motherhood, and family history, and the relationships between these and her writing. Sheila Munro provides insight into how personal family incidents are translated into fiction, such as they are in the story, "Miles City, Montana." The history of the Laidlaw and Chamney families contained in the book also have relevance to some of Munro's stories, for example "A Wilderness Station." Within the chronology of the time period being related, the writing and publication of specific stories and collections are mentioned, and in many cases this is accompanied with a commentary.
Reviews:
Aulin, Virginia. *Room of One's Own* 24.2 (2002): 102-104.
Bush, Catherine. "Alice, Through the Looking Glass." *Globe and Mail* 21 April 2001: D6.
Garvie, Maureen. "A Mother-Daughter Duo." *Books in Canada* 30.1 (July 2001): 19.
Harrison, Kathryn. "Go Ask Alice." *New York Times Book Review* 16 June 2002: 29.
Solecki, Sam. "Still Growing Up." *National Post* 21 April 2001: B7.

S766.   Pfaus, B. *Alice Munro*. Ottawa: Golden Dog, 1984.
Pfaus prefaces his interpretation of Munro's first five books with an overview of prevalent features in her writing, such as realism and the narrative viewpoint. He also comments on something which is less often discussed, the element of humour. In *Dance*, commonality

among the stories relates to the images of "the garrison" and "the other country." In *Something*, Pfaus notes the use of paradox in presenting conflicting versions of reality. Stories in the book have themes of unconsummated relationships and problems with communication. The quest for reality or "real life" dominates in *Lives*, along with the theme clearly stated in the title. Pfaus also looks at the subject of women's bodies. *Who*, like *Lives*, is described as a series of linked stories, with the unifying theme of quest for identity in a life inscribed with roleplaying and "true lies." In *Moons*, the stories revolve around themes of human relationships and connections.

Reviews:

York, Lorraine M. "Joyless in Jubilee?" *Essays on Canadian Writing* 34 (Spring 1987): 157-161.

S767. Rasporich, Beverly Jean. *Dance of the Sexes: Art and Gender in the Fiction of Alice Munro*. Edmonton: University of Alberta Press, 1990.

In a book devoted to the feminist aspects of Munro's writing, Rasporich examines themes, female culture, irony, regionalism, and the genre of the short story, as they relate to Munro as a female writer. Beginning with the overarching themes of feminine quest and societal expectations of females, Rasporich shows how aspects of these themes are articulated in each of Munro's works from *Dance* to *Progress*. Recurring themes include those of feminist self-discovery, the quest for self identity and female identity, romantic love-hate relationships, middle-aged women in transformation, and aging women. Following this thematic study, Munro is viewed in the role of a literary folklorist of female culture. In support of this view, Rasporich details various folk elements found in the stories: domestic interiors, food, fashion, storytelling, superstitions, local speech, rhymes, songs, and fairy tales. Irony receives attention not only as a form of humour, but also in the context of incongruity; specifically the incongruity between the female's conception of herself and her sexuality, and the traditional patriarchal view. The regional aspects of Munro's writing are detailed and associated to the general theme of place and its link to identity. Place in the stories appears as natural, metaphorical, or inner landscapes, as town and country tensions, or as the internal spaces of memory or self. In a final section, Rasporich evaluates Munro as a postmodern female short-story writer, and a writer of the female experience. She elaborates on Munro's style and techniques by looking at patterns, time, light, imagery, symbols, and language in her work.

Reviews:

Gentry, Marshall Bruce. *Studies in Short Fiction* 27.4 (Fall 1990): 612-613.

Ross, Catherine Sheldrick. "Taking Sides." *Canadian Literature* 132 (Spring 1992): 216-218.

Thacker, Robert. "Go Ask Alice: The Progress of Munro Criticism." *Journal of Canadian Studies/Revue d'études canadiennes* 26.2 (Summer 1991): 156-169.

York, Lorraine M. *American Review of Canadian Studies* 22.2 (Summer 1992): 298-300.

S768. Redekop, Magdalene. *Mothers and Other Clowns: The Stories of Alice Munro*. London: Routledge, 1992.

As the title indicates, the central concept of Redekop's book is the maternal clown, described in terms of "the mothering clown" or "mock mother." This figure is constructed by Redekop to show Munro's distancing from the image of the "real mother," an image which Munro finds impossible to capture in her writing. While on the one hand, Munro distances herself from the word "mother," she is obsessed with the mother-daughter relationship. Throughout the book, Redekop uses the parodic figures of clowns, harlots, Madonnas, jokesters, fools, puppets, dolls, and orphans all participating in forms of parades, carnivals, and circuses. In the first five chapters, she explains these figure types. She places Madonna and harlot figures in a parade of mothering clowns. She reviews women's positions as mothers and as reproducers. The absurdity of the female subject is described in her inability to construct herself as subject or to form a self-image. Comedy is linked to the absurdity of domesticity. Circus performances, kinship structures, and Munro's role of an artist as a mothering clown are all associated. Women are seen as readers, and storytellers as jokesters. Metaphors, symbols, imagery, and literary allusions all come into the discussion. From chapter 6 onward, each of Munro's books from *Dance* to *Friend* is studied in the contexts of the material presented in the first five chapters. For instance, in *Who*, Redekop discusses the fool in the person of Milton Homer, jokes, jokesters, and victims of jokes. Rose is seen as a reader and public performer.

Reviews:

Irvine, Lorna Marie. "Review Essay: Writing Women's Lives: My Self, Her Self, Our Selves." *American Review of Canadian Studies* 24.2 (Summer 1994): 229-239. [Redekop on pages 232-234]

Miller, Judith. *RFR: Resources for Feminist Research* 23.1-2 (Spring-Summer 1994): 57-58.

Newman, Judie. *Durham University Journal* 85.1 (new ser. 54.1) (January 1993): 163-164.

Noonan, Gerald. *University of Toronto Quarterly* 63.1 (Fall 1993): 222-226.

Rasporich, Beverly. "A Double Life." *Canadian Literature* 138/139 (Fall-Winter 1993): 148-149.

Thacker, Robert. "What's 'Material'? The Progress of Munro Criticism, Part 2." *Journal of Canadian Studies/Revue d'études canadiennes* 33.2 (1998): 196-210.

S769.   Ross, Catherine Sheldrick. *Alice Munro: A Double Life*. Canadian Biography Series 1. Toronto: ECW Press, 1992.

Ross's book, published before Sheila Munro's, and written from a less personal perspective, also details Munro's early life and career. The concept of "double life" found in the subtitle derives from the fact that Munro has always lived parallel and separate lives; the life of the ordinary world and the secret life of the imagination which is manifested by her writing. This began in childhood, with Munro's reading of books such as *Emily of New Moon* and the formulation of stories in her head while performing household chores. Ross describes the lives of Munro's parents and their family history. She discusses her mother's illness and Munro's complex feelings toward her, noting how this is reflected in her writing. The progression of Munro's writing is traced from her early imitative uncollected stories, to the collection *Friend*. Elements from Munro's personal life or from the lives of the people around her are brought out as they relate to the stories.

Reviews:

Adams, Timothy Dow. *American Review of Canadian Studies* 23.3 (Autumn 1993): 456-460. [Ross on pages 457-458]

Burnham, Clint. "Brief Lives." *Books in Canada* 21.9 (December 1992): 43-44.

Djwa, Sandra. *University of Toronto Quarterly* 63.1 (Fall 1993): 214-217.

Messenger, Cynthia. "Pressing Lives." *Canadian Forum* 74 (October 1995): 40-43. [Ross on pages 42-43]

Rasporich, Beverly. "A Double Life." *Canadian Literature* 138/139 (Fall-Winter 1993): 148-149.

Thacker, Robert. *Biography* 17.1 (Winter 1994): 66-68.

Thacker, Robert. "What's 'Material'? The Progress of Munro Criticism, Part 2." *Journal of Canadian Studies/Revue d'études canadiennes* 33.2 (1998): 196-210.

Van Wart, Alice. *Quill & Quire* 59.1 (January 1993): 21.

S770.   Smythe, Karen E. *Figuring Grief: Gallant, Munro, and the Poetics of Elegy*. Montreal: McGill-Queen's University Press, 1992.

In this revised version of her dissertation on fictional elegy, Smythe proposes that the use of realism invokes an "anti-entropic" documentation of life as a way to stop the process of natural decay. She examines Munro's technique of photographic realism in her stories of death, loss, grief, and mourning. The reader's and character's experience of epiphany is compared with that of "photographic shock." Epiphany is seen as a form of consolation. Smythe examines stories containing deaths in families, anticipatory grief, storytelling and mourning, love and loss, sexuality, and human mortality. The chapters on Munro are: "Munro and Modern Elegy" pp.106-128; "Munrovian Melancholy" pp.129-152.

Reviews:

Irvine, Lorna Marie. "Review Essay: Writing Women's Lives: My Self, Her Self, Our Selves." *American Review of Canadian Studies* 24.2 (Summer 1994): 229-239. [Smythe on pages 234-236]

Noonan, Gerald. *University of Toronto Quarterly* 63.1 (Fall 1993): 222-226.

Pollard, Derek. *British Journal of Canadian Studies* 9.2 (1994): 438.

Thacker, Robert. "What's 'Material'? The Progress of Munro Criticism, Part 2." *Journal of Canadian Studies/Revue d'études canadiennes* 33.2 (1998): 196-210.

S771.   Thacker, Robert. *Alice Munro: Writing Her Lives: A Biography*. Toronto: McClelland and Stewart, 2005.

Thacker's book is based on extensive research that included three two-day sessions with Munro, numerous interviews, and the use of manuscripts, letters, and other primary sources in the Munro Fonds at the University of Calgary and other Canadian and American archives. The book is arranged in a three-part chronology. In the first part, containing the most personal and biographical material, Thacker delves into Munro's Scottish and Irish ancestry, the life of her parents, and Munro's formative years in Lower Town, Wingham between 1931-1949. In the second part, Thacker covers the years of Munro's married life in Vancouver and Victoria, and her development as a writer up to 1980. The third part looks at the period from the publication of *Moons* to *Runaway*. Thacker traces the parallel tracks of Munro's life and her writing, particularly in the earlier years, giving personal links to individual stories. He also details Munro's professional and personal relationships with her mentor Robert Weaver, her agent Virginia Barber, her book editors Douglas Gibson and Ann Close, and the editors at *The New Yorker*, Charles McGrath and Daniel Menaker. In looking at the influence of these, and at the personal and other factors that shaped specific collections and stories, Thacker provides insight into Munro's creative process and the evolution of her career. The critical reception following the publication of each of Munro's books is captured through lengthy and numerous quotations from reviews.

Reviews:
Garvie, Maureen. *Quill & Quire* 71.12 (December 2005): 22.
Grainger, James. "Real Life Makes Great Fiction." *Toronto Star* 27 November 2005: D5, D8.
Keefer, Janice Kulyk. "Alice through a Looking Glass." *Globe and Mail* 26 November 2005: D26-D27.
Schiefer, Nancy. "Munro Maintains Mystery." *London Free Press* 26 November 2005, final ed.: D10.
Stoffman, Judy. "Few Open Secrets in Munro's Life." *Toronto Star* 24 December 2005: H4.
Tihanyi, Eva. "Lovers Unnamed. Friendships Unexplored. A Life Unexamined." *National Post* 10 December 2005: WP15.

S772.   Thacker, Robert, ed. *The Rest of the Story: Critical Essays on Alice Munro*. Toronto: ECW Press, 1999.
   Also pub. as *Alice Munro Writing On . . .* Spec. issue of *Essays on Canadian Writing* 66 (Winter 1998).
Contains 11 critical essays. Annotations for the following papers are listed in the section "Articles and Chapters in Books":
Thacker, Robert. "Introduction: Alice Munro, Writing "Home": 'Seeing This Trickle in Time.'" pp. 1-20.
Redekop, Magdalene. "Alice Munro and the Scottish Nostalgic Grotesque." pp. 21-43.
Micros, Marianne. "Et in Ontario Ego: The Pastoral Ideal and the Blazon Tradition in Alice Munro's 'Lichen.'" pp. 44-59.
Heller, Deborah. "Getting Loose: Women and Narration in Alice Munro's *Friend of My Youth*." pp. 60-80.
McCaig, JoAnn. "Alice Munro's Agency: The Virginia Barber Correspondence, 1976-83." pp. 81-102.
Lecker, Robert. "Machines, Readers, Gardens: Alice Munro's 'Carried Away.'" pp. 103-127.
Martin, W. R. and Warren U. Ober. "Alice Munro as Small Town Historian: 'Spaceships Have Landed.'" pp. 128-146.
Foy, Nathalie. "'Darkness Collecting': Reading 'Vandals' as a Coda to *Open Secrets*." pp. 147-168.
Duffy, Dennis. "'A Dark Sort of Mirror': 'The Love of a Good Woman' as Pauline Poetic." pp. 169-190.
Carrington, Ildikó de Papp. "Recasting the Orpheus Myth: Alice Munro's 'The Children Stay' and Jean Anouilh's *Eurydice*." pp. 191-203.
Beran, Carol L. "The Luxury of Excellence: Alice Munro in the *New Yorker*." pp. 204-231.
Reviews:
Stich, Klaus P. *American Review of Canadian Studies* 30.1 (Spring 2000): 100-102.

S773.   Ventura, Héliane and Mary Condé, eds. Introd. Héliane Ventura. *Alice Munro: Writing Secrets*. Special issue of *Open Letter* 11th ser. 9 (Fall 2003)-12th ser. 1 (Winter 2004): 1-275.
Contains 18 papers from the Alice Munro Conference, *Writing Secrets*, May 19-21, 2003, Université d'Orléans. Annotations for the following papers are listed in the section "Articles and Chapters in Books":
Ventura, Héliane. "Introduction." pp. 15-22.

Lecercle, Jean-Jacques. "Alice Munro's Two Secrets." pp. 23-37.

Howells, Coral Ann. "The Telling of Secrets / The Secrets of Telling: An Overview of Alice Munro's Enigma Variations from *Dance of the Happy Shades* to *Hateship, Friendship, Courtship, Loveship, Marriage*." pp. 39-54.

Dvorak, Marta. "Alice Munro's 'Lovely Tricks' from *Dance of the Happy Shades* to *Hateship, Friendship, Courtship, Loveship, Marriage*." pp. 55-77.

Davey, Frank. "Class, 'Family Furnishings,' and Munro's Early Stories." pp. 79-88.

Buchholtz, Mirosawa. "Pseudo-Longinus and the Affective Theory in Alice Munro's Stories about Childhood." pp. 89-102.

Arnason, David. "Losing and Lost Women: The Early Stories of Alice Munro." pp. 103-112.

Wieckowska, Katarzyna. "The Corporeal Unspeakable: The Gothicized Body and Alice Munro's *Who Do You Think You Are?*" pp. 113-120.

Ricciardi, Caterina. "The Secrets of Intertextuality: Alice Munro's 'Pictures of the Ice.'" pp. 121-136.

Ferri, Laura. "Mothers and Other Secrets." pp. 137-149.

Colvile, Georgiana M. M. "Skunking the Reader: Alice Munro's Olfactory Discourse in Four Recent Stories." pp. 151-165.

Scobie, Stephen. "'Lying under the Apple Tree': Alice Munro, Secrets, and Autobiography." pp. 167-175.

Condé, Mary. "Coded Language in 'Runaway.'" pp. 177-183.

Bennett, Donna. "Open. Secret. Telling Time in Alice Munro's Fiction." Brown, Russell Morton. "Open Secrets? Alice Munro and the Mystery Story." pp. 185-209.

Lacombe, Michèle. "'Strips of Rough Linoleum' Revisited: Reconsidering Realism in the Works of Alice Munro." pp. 211-229.

Soto, Cristina Sánchez. "Spaces between Stories: Reading Secrets in *Lives of Girls and Women*." pp. 231-241.

Francesconi, Sabrina. "Writing Secrets as 'Betraying the Past' in Alice Munro's 'What Is Remembered.'" pp. 243-252.

Ventura, Héliane. "Alice Munro's Secret *Ort*." pp. 255-266.

S774.   York, Lorraine M. *"The Other Side of Dailiness": Photography in the Works of Alice Munro, Timothy Findley, Michael Ondaatje and Margaret Laurence.* Toronto: ECW Press, 1988.

This book is a publication of York's dissertation. In a section called "'The Delicate Moment of Exposure': Alice Munro and Photography" (pages 21-50), York examines the photographic qualities of Munro's vision and her narrative technique in *Dance, Something, Who,* and *Lives,* especially "The Epilogue." Munro's writing reflects the paradoxical nature of photography, where the boundaries between the perceived and real are blurred. York points out the juxtaposition of the grotesque and the beautiful, control and helplessness, motion and stillness. Munro's use of photographs and photography as a technique in the treatment of past and present is examined. Her narrative form is seen as a series of snapshots. Munro's appreciation of Edward Hopper, James Agee, Walker Evans, and Diane Arbus is also noted.
Reviews:

Irvine, Lorna. *American Review of Canadian Studies* 18.3 (Autumn 1988): 399-401.

Tausky, Thomas E. *University of Toronto Quarterly* 59.1 (Fall 1989): 161-162.

Audiovisual

S775.   *Alice Munro.* International Historic Enterprises. London, ON: A.V. International, [198?] 1 sound cassette (25 min.)
Criticism, biographical information, and excerpts from interviews and dramatized works.

S776.   *Lives of Girls and Women*. Introduction to Literature. Prod. Fraser Steele. Ed. Bill Grier. Host/writers Catherine Ross and Allan Gedalof. Selections read by Leanna Brodie. TVOntario, Toronto, 1993. Dist. International Tele-Film, Mississauga, ON; Films for the Humanities & Sciences, Princeton, NJ, 1996. 1 videocassette, VHS, ½ in. (28 min.)
Professor Catherine Ross and Gedalof examine the work and show how Munro's personal life and literature experiences shape her fiction. Parallels between Munro and the work's central character are drawn.

Articles and Chapters in Books about Alice Munro

S777.   Adachi, Ken. "Munro Follows Publisher Gibson from Macmillan." *Toronto Star* 30 April 1986, metro ed.: F1.

Munro's reason for leaving Macmillan and giving the Canadian publishing rights for *Progress* to McClelland and Stewart had nothing to do with dissatisfaction with Macmillan. Rather it was her close association with Douglas Gibson, her editor at Macmillan since 1978, that made her decide to move with him to M&S.

S778.   Adams, James. "Age Brings Urge 'To Do Something Great.'" *Edmonton Journal* 6 November 1982: D1.

Based on an interview with Munro, the article briefly covers personal details, the effect of aging on her writing, the writing process, writer's block, happiness and fame, the female perspective in her writing, and the differences in how society views the writing of male and female writers.

S779.   Adams, James. "Small Town Salutes a Big Name." *Globe and Mail* 11 July 2002: A7.

Munro's home town of Wingham, Ontario invited Munro to the dedication of the Alice Munro Literary Park, which was created in her honour.

S780.   Adilman, Sid. "Handling Munro." *Toronto Star* 8 April 2001: D1, D10.

Details the writing and publishing processes involved in the production of Sheila Munro's book *Lives of Mothers and Daughters*.

S781.   "Advice and Dissent (survey of readers)." *Books in Canada* 16.4 (May 1987): 12-14.

A survey of *Books in Canada* readers asked the question, "Who are your favourite Canadian writers?" Munro came at the top of the list. For a similar survey of Canadian literary personalities, see "Writers' Writers" listed below.

S782.   Alaton, Salem. "CanLit Luminaries Stick with Gibson." *Globe and Mail* 1 May 1986: D5.

Munro is listed as one of several authors who moved with Douglas Gibson from Macmillan to McClelland and Stewart.

S783. "Alice Munro." *Canadian Literature in the 70's*. Ed. Paul Denham and Mary Jane Edwards. Toronto: Holt, Rinehart and Winston, 1980. xii, xx, 35-37.
Briefly covers Munro's life, awards, and writing. The commentary on her fiction includes elements such as regional settings and magic realism. The relationship between real life and fiction in "Material" is discussed.

S784. Allentuck, Marcia. "Resolution and Independence in the Work of Alice Munro." *World Literature Written in English* 16.2 (November 1977): 340-343.
Allentuck points out parallels in the way Mary Wollstonecraft, Virginia Woolf, and Munro treat the emotional dependence of women. In *Lives*, the contrast is made between Aunt Moira's resolve to endurance and Del's resolve to independence. This leads to a discussion of the problem of independence and the female writer.

S785. Allison, Paul S. "A Trick of Fiction: The Progress of Memory in the Stories of Alice Munro." *Prairie Journal of Canadian Literature* 15 (1990): 27-38.
Munro uses memory as a narrative technique to promote disarrangement. Allison shows Munro's development by tracing her uses of memory, time, and language through her writing. In *Dance*, the stories conclude with discrepancies between the intent of the story and the intent of the character. In *Something* and *Beggar*, characters are seen to express a deficiency of memory and language, while in *Moons* and *Progress* there is a falseness of memory and language. Through the creation of multiplicity in events, narrative time, and points of view, Munro exposes the tricks of memory and forces the reader to consider everything in the absence of no one true version of the truth or reality.

S786. Alsop, Kay. "Alice Munro: Writing 'Agonizing but Unavoidable' (Women Who Have a Way with Words)." *Province* [Vancouver] 3 December 1971: 32.
Alsop presents a personal profile of the author and her stance toward writing. She observes the intensity of feeling and honesty found in *Lives*. In the interview, Munro says that writing is integral to her identity and describes it as hard work, but a compulsion, a way of coping with life and of communicating. Writing fiction in which the writer creates her own world is a presumptuous and egotistical thing to do. Munro says she is always observing people, but that they are not strictly copied in her characters. Ada Jordan in *Lives* is a strong character but not her mother. Other things mentioned are her respect for women, her husband's support, and her feelings toward awards and recognition.

S787. Anand. "Translating Alice Munro into Hindi Is a Challenge." *Gazette* [Montreal] 24 September 1994: I2.
Anand discusses the difficulties he had translating *Something*. The translation was complicated by the social and cultural differences inherent in the subject matter of the book.

S788. Arnason, David. "Losing and Lost Women: The Early Stories of Alice Munro." *Alice Munro: Writing Secrets*. Ed. Héliane Ventura and Mary Condé. Special issue of *Open Letter* 11th ser. 9 (Fall 2003)-12th ser. 1 (Winter 2004): 103-112.
Arnason begins by saying that the stories found in *Dance* are not short stories in the traditional patterned form, but rather fall closer to the category of sketches and tales. He illustrates this with the tale and sketch structures found in "Walker Brothers Cowboy" and

"Images" respectively, and points out the similarity in structure found in all the stories in *Dance*. The rest of the paper focuses on female characters who are either losing or lost, in some cases simply because they are female. He notes the similarity in the female voice in "An Ounce of Cure," "The Office," and "Postcard" and the male voice in "Thanks For the Ride." In "The Peace of Utrecht," Arnason sees almost all variants of failed women. The title story contains the only example of an ostensibly lost female who in the end triumphs.

S789. Ash, Susan. "Having It Both Ways: Reading Related Short Fiction by Post-Colonial Women Writers." *SPAN: Journal of the South Pacific Association for Commonwealth Literature and Language Studies* 28 (April 1989): 40-55.

The postcolonial writers included are Margaret Laurence, Audrey Thomas, Yvonne du Fresne, and Munro. The article discusses the elements of postmodern writing, and the strategies used by the writers, such as use of the retrospective narrator. Although Munro's *Lives* does not receive detailed treatment, the article contains some quotations from Munro on retrospective revision in her writing.

S790. Atkins, Lucy. "Shock of the True: The Short Story Is Dead?" *Guardian* [London and Manchester] 19 December 1998: 10.

Based on an interview and interspersed with quotations, this article covers a broad spectrum of topics: Munro's early isolation as a short-story writer, the female writer's problem of balancing writing with family responsibilities, ambivalent views of feminism, writing retrospectively and distancing, writing to produce truth, preference for the short-story genre, and feelings about motherhood.

S791. Atwood, Margaret. *Survival: A Thematic Guide to Canadian Literature*. Toronto: Anansi, 1972. 65, 138, 141, 193, 205, 210.

Includes themes in *Lives* and "The Peace of Utrecht."

S792. "Audrey Tiffin." *Wingham Advance-Times* 24 November 1982: 11.

This brief article is about the efforts of Audrey Tiffin, a teacher in Wingham, to change the town's conception of Munro after the author's alleged remarks about the town in Wayne Grady's article in *Today Magazine*, December 5, 1981. Munro, who denied speaking to the author of the article, claimed that she only used real people and events from the town as starting points for her fiction.

S793. "Author Profile: Alice Munro." *World Literature Today* 79.2 (May-August 2005): 61.

This piece gives a brief account of Munro's life, her awards, and a selected listing of her works. It includes short excerpts from two reviews and from the story "Runaway."

S794. Bailey, Nancy I. "The Masculine Image in *Lives of Girls and Women*." *Canadian Literature* 80 (Spring 1979): 113-118, 120.

Bailey uses the Jungian view of self and individuation to study Del's development as a woman and as an artist in *Lives*. The article delves into male and female social roles and relationships in the novel.

S795. Balestra, Gianfranca. "Alice Munro as Historian and Geographer: A Reading of 'Meneseteung.'" *Intersections: La narrativa canadese tra storia e geografia*. Ed. Liana Nissim and Carlo Pagetti. Università degli Studi di Milano. Facoltà di Lettere e Filosofia. Quaderni di Acme 38. Bologna: Cisalpino, 1999. 119-136.

Munro's narrative strategy and the elements of space and time in the story are discussed. Munro uses a first-person unnamed narrator who, much like a historian selects, orders, and narrates the story. The subjective nature of historical inquiry is shown to be relevant to postmodern historiographic metafiction. Space and time are defined in the culture and life of a 19th-century Canadian town. The article goes on to explore the space-time connection, historical accuracy, the situation of the woman writer in the 19th century, women and creativity, and the symbolism of the Meneseteung River and that of other fluids in the text.

S796. "'Bardon Bus.'" *Magill's Survey of World Literature*. Ed. Frank N. Magill. Vol. 4. New York: Marshall Cavendish, 1993. 1345-1346.

Summarizes the story for the student and general reader. Focuses on the narrator.

S797. Batten, Jack. "Progress of Alice Munro: Canada's World-Class Writer Is a Woman Who Happily Helps Out at a Book Sale." *Review* [Imperial Oil Ltd.] 72 [no. 388] (Spring 1988): 22-25.

Interviewed in Blythe, Munro recalls how the family bookstore cured her of writer's block early in her career. Batten sketches Munro's writing path from early childhood writing and storytelling and being "a housewife who, by the way, wrote," to the time when she became recognized as a significant writer. Batten outlines major themes and characteristics of her writing and includes critics' comments about her latest book, *Progress*. Other areas covered are how Munro writes stories, her important and close working relationships with her publisher and agent, the changes made to *Who*, Munro's close ties to the Huron region and her community.

S798. Baum, Rosalie Murphy. "Artist and Woman: Young Lives in Laurence and Munro." *North Dakota Quarterly* 52.3 (Summer 1984): 196-211.

Baum views Margaret Laurence's *A Bird in the House* and Munro's *Lives* as accounts of adolescent experience related through the voice of an adult narrator. In *Lives*, the first-person narrator is a mature person remembering with the understanding of an adult. Baum covers the preadolescent and adolescent stages of Del's development in the novel. She brings into the discussion the similarities between *Lives* and James Joyce's *A Portrait of the Artist as a Young Man*, and points out differences in the portrayal of the personal and artistic development of the protagonists.

S799. Baum, Rosalie Murphy. "Snow as Reality and Trope in Canadian Literature." *American Review of Canadian Studies* 17.3 (Autumn 1987): 323-333.

Three stories, "Snow" by Frederick Philip Grove, "By a Frozen River" by Norman Levine, and "Winter Wind" by Munro, are the subject of this study. Snow in "Winter Wind" is seen as an element that reflects the struggles between different human values: the values of order and cleanliness of the town, and the chaos and dirt of the country. Baum studies Munro's metaphoric use of snow in the story, and her use of snow as a method of achieving insight into her characters.

S800. Becker, Alida. "Sex and Self-Defense." *New York Times Book Review* 11 September 1994: 36.

In this edited interview which occurred soon after the release of *Open Secrets*, Munro comments on two of the stories in the collection. She gives details about the origin and writing of "The Albanian Virgin" and talks about the romantic aspects of the story. She also talks about the male-female relationship in "Vandals." Associated topics discussed are romance, and sex in marriage, particularly as it relates to women of an earlier generation.

S801. Becker, Susanne. "Exploring Gothic Contextualisation: Alice Munro and *Lives of Girls and Women*." *Gothic Forms of Feminine Fictions*. Manchester: Manchester University Press, 1999. 103-150.

A study of self-reflexive neo-Gothicism in *Lives*, "Home," and "The Ferguson Girls Must Never Marry." Concentrating first on the self-reflexive feminine Gothic, Becker looks at the woman-house connection in *Lives*. She then turns to the Gothic strategies used to transform a realistic representation to a Gothic one in which the familiar is made to turn strange as in "Epilogue: The Photographer." Del is examined as a "subject in the making," writing as she does the "gothic (auto)-graph" and inscribing her feminine self. Gothic elements are brought out in the consideration of Del's gender construction. Finally, Becker examines neo-Gothic connectedness in the narrative structure of the novel *Lives* and in "The Ferguson Girls Must Never Marry." She finishes by pointing out the similarities between Margaret Atwood's *Cat's Eye* and Munro's *Lives*.

S802. Beer, Janet. "Short Fiction with Attitude: The Lives of Boys and Men in the *Lives of Girls and Women*." *The Yearbook of English Studies*. Vol. 31. *North American Short Stories and Short Fictions*. Ed. Nicola Bradbury. Leeds, Eng.: Maney Publishing for the Modern Humanities Research Association, 2001. 125-132.

In this rare consideration of the male characters in *Lives*, Beer shows how the episodic structure of the novel highlights the marginality of the male players in the protagonist's life within the context of women's changing social roles. Men are seen as "bit-players" who are featured in single episodes rather than informing the whole book. Their male authority is refuted in terms of the plot and structure; their lives are expressed as secondary. The inability of men to communicate and male silence are contrasted with the powerful voice of Ada Jordan.

S803. "The Beggar Maid." *The Reader's Companion to the Twentieth Century Novel*. Ed. Peter Parker. London: Fourth Estate; Oxford: Helicon, 1994. 529-530.

Essentially a summary of the book and details of its publication history.

S804. Bender, Eric. "Munro Says Artistic Backwater Was Boon to Early Endeavors." *London Free Press* 16 October 1982: A4.

In this edited interview, Munro says that isolation early in her writing career shielded her from an understanding of the competitive nature of the profession and of the difficulty of being accepted as a short-story writer. Being a housewife, rather than continuing in university, made it possible for her to pursue her writing. Now living in the small town of Clinton, Ontario, Munro finds that she has the privacy and isolation she needs to write.

S805. Bennett, Donna. "Open. Secret. Telling Time in Alice Munro's Fiction." Brown, Russell Morton. "Open Secrets? Alice Munro and the Mystery Story." *Alice Munro: Writing Secrets.* Ed. Héliane Ventura and Mary Condé. Special issue of *Open Letter* 11th ser. 9 (Fall 2003)-12th ser. 1 (Winter 2004): 185-209.

This paper, coproduced with Russell Morton Brown, looks at how time and space/place intersect to provide the crucial locus of the story. The stories discussed deal with mystery and secrecy. The combination of mystery, story, and time involves two time sequences and two narratives: the open story of the present and the secret story of the past. This interplay of time, space and mystery/secrecy is examined in "Save the Reaper," "Carried Away," "Open Secrets," and "The Love of a Good Woman."

S806. Beran, Carol L. "Images of Women's Power in Contemporary Canadian Fiction by Women." *Studies in Canadian Literature/Études en littérature canadienne* 15.2 (1990): 55-76. Accessed 24 April 2006. <http://www.lib.unb.ca/Texts/SCL/vol15_2/Contents.htm>

Female power is investigated in the writings of Aritha Van Herk, Margaret Atwood, and Alice Munro. Beran shows the sources of both women's and men's power and powerlessness in selected stories by Munro. In "The Beggar Maid," Rose's power over Patrick's happiness is illusory. After their divorce, her power derives from the fact that she has made him her enemy. In "Simon's Luck," the natural processes of time and change leave Rose powerless over life and love, despite her temporary success in her career. In "Lichen," where aging and time also play a part, Stella's power derives from writing, acceptance of the processes of nature, and nurturing.

S807. Beran, Carol L. "The Luxury of Excellence: Alice Munro in *The New Yorker*." *Alice Munro Writing On . . . .* Ed. Robert Thacker. Special issue of *Essays on Canadian Writing* 66 (Winter 1998): 204-231.
Rpt. in *The Rest of the Story: Critical Essays on Alice Munro.* Ed. Robert Thacker. Toronto: ECW Press, 1999. 204-231.

Beran begins by discussing Munro's early and ongoing relationship with the editors of *The New Yorker*. Beran's main focus in this paper, however, is to analyse the relationship between the publication of a Munro story in *The New Yorker* and the reader experience of the story. Using "The Love of a Good Woman," Beran examines the story in the context of the ads, cartoons, and other marginalia which are published along with it on the pages of *The New Yorker*. She suggests that this juxtaposition of the "lifestyle," presented by the marginalia in the magazine, and "real life," presented by the story, influences the reader's experience of the story and makes it different from the experience of the reader who reads the story in a book.

S808. Beran, Carol L. "The Pursuit of Happiness: A Study of Alice Munro's Fiction." *Social Science Journal* 37.3 (2000): 329-345.

The link of love or marriage, happiness, and closure in stories is one that is embedded in North American culture. Munro's stories, "White Dump" in particular, do not follow this pattern. The story lacks closure, and happiness is seen as momentary and existing at a "legendary level." The story, in its ambiguity, embodies the Canadian values of peace, order, and good government, as opposed to the American values of life, liberty, and pursuit of happiness. Religious and philosophical traditions identify happiness with faith and the

S809. Beran, Carol L. "Thomas Hardy, Alice Munro and the Question of Influence." *American Review of Canadian Studies* 29.2 (Summer 1999): 237-258.

Beran investigates the connections between the writing of Thomas Hardy and Munro. She points out Hardy's gloom and his use of accidents and coincidence. A borrowing from Hardy's "An Imaginative Woman" is seen in Munro's "Carried Away." Her disarrangements in the ending of the story are compared with Hardy's disproportioning, or presentation of different versions of reality.

S810. Besner, Neil. "Beyond Two Solitudes, After Survival: Postmodern Fiction in Canada." *Postmodern Fiction in Canada*. Ed. Theo D'haen and Hans Bertens. Postmodern Studies 6. Amsterdam: Rodopi, 1992. 9-25.

Besner discusses Munro on pages 19 to 21. While Munro's versions of setting can be read as postmodern, they do not demonstrate the traditional Canadian anxiety about nature and place as being a vast, barren, inhospitable physical space. Her settings are profoundly regional and domestic, and at the same time universal. Munro's vision of nature is compared and contrasted with that of Margaret Atwood.

S811. Besner, Neil. "The Bodies of the Texts in *Lives of Girls and Women*: Del Jordan's Reading." *Multiple Voices: Recent Canadian Fiction. Proceedings of the IVth International Symposium of the Brussels Centre for Canadian Studies, 29 November-1 December 1989*. Ed. Jeanne Delbaere. Introd. Anna Rutherford. Sydney, Austral.: Dangaroo, 1990. 131-144.

The significance and nature of Del's activities as a reader are shown through a study of the various texts found in *Lives* and her approach to these texts as bodies to admire. Del's early life and adolescence are filled with the reading of texts: Uncle Benny's newspapers, the body of the dead cow, Uncle Craig's reported death and funeral, Uncle Craig's manuscript, Ada Jordan's books of Tennyson's poetry and her encyclopaedias, Art Chamberlain's sexual performance, Garnet's body, and finally Del's own body.

S812. Beston, John B. "Alice Munro: A Canadian Nobel Laureate in Literature?" *Commonwealth and American Nobel Laureates in Literature: Essays in Criticism*. Ed. A. L. McLeod. New Delhi: Sterling Publishers, 1998. 181-191.

Beston proposes that two of Munro's works, "Friend of My Youth" and *Lives*, make her a likely candidate for the Nobel Peace Prize. To illustrate Munro's achievement, he presents a close reading of "Friend of My Youth," seeing the story in the light of 19th-century attitudes toward sex and their influence on modern women. Flora's rejection of sex is examined. The narrator-daughter and the mother are both perplexed by Flora, but each has differing views of her. Robert Deal is an enigma and archetype. The significance of the mother in the story is also explored.

S813. Beston, John B. "Theme and Technique in Alice Munro's *Hateship, Friendship, Courtship, Loveship, Marriage*." *The Canon of Commonwealth Literature: Essays in Criticism*. Ed. A. L. McLeod. New Delhi: Sterling Publishers Private, 2003. 31-42.

Beginning with the theme of marriage, Beston examines the element of chance in the selection of partners in the title story and in "Nettles." In "Floating Bridge," "Comfort," and "The Bear Came over the Mountain," he considers the position of women within marriages where the husbands are self-centred. Beston observes that Munro's technique has become more refined and simplified, and that rather than centring the story on the story line, she places clues to mysteries early on in the characters themselves, who remain consistent throughout the story. This is illustrated in the title story and in "Floating Bridge" and "Family Furnishings."

S814. Bethune, Brian. "CanLit's Catalyst. [2004 in Review: Canadian of the Year]." *Maclean's* 27 December 2004: 29.

Bethune writes that Munro has "long surpassed the benchmarks for national icon status in CanLit." Most recently, *Runaway* won her a second Giller Prize and appeared on the *New York Times* bestseller list. Bethune gives several examples of the stature of Munro and her writing, both in Canada and in the United States. He also notes the comments made in her Giller acceptance speech about the change in the public attitude toward Canadian literature.

S815. Beyersbergen, Joanna. "No Bitterness or Anxiety for Writer." *London Free Press* 22 June 1974: 70.

Based on an interview, this article appeared shortly after Munro's separation from her first husband and the publication of *Something*. It briefly covers her early life, her family and writing, and the reaction of her hometown of Wingham, Ontario to her writing.

S816. Birbalsingh, Frank. "Women in Alice Munro's *Lives of Girls and Women*." *Canadiana: Studies in Canadian Literature*. Ed. Jørn Carlsen and Knud Larsen. Aarhus: Canadian Studies Conference, Department of English, University of Aarhus, 1984. 131-137.

The paper begins with a look at the restricted and repressed lives of women living in a small Canadian town in the 1940s and 1950s. The conventional aunts, Elspeth and Gracie, are contrasted with Ada Jordan, Del's unconventional mother, whose speech on changing women's lives is seen as central to the stories. Del's quest for life experience and her search for independence, Ada's beliefs about religion and nature, and sexual liberation and love are all briefly covered.

S817. Blatchford, Christie. "Unveiling the Secret Lives of Women: Alice Munro Writes What Women Think about Men." *National Post* 12 December 1998: B9.

Blatchford calls herself "a late convert to Alice Munro." She proceeds to summarize two Munro stories she has recently read, "Wild Swans" and "Simon's Luck." She says that Munro writes about women, but also about men because "that is all that women think about." Considering the relationship between Jerry Story and Del in *Lives*, she observes that women define themselves by the men in their lives.

S818. Blodgett, E. D. "Prisms and Arcs: Structures in Hébert and Munro." *Figures in a Ground: Canadian Essays on Modern Literature Collected in Honor of Sheila Watson*. Ed. Diane Bessai and David Jackel. Saskatoon: Western Producer Prairie Books, 1978. 99-121, 333-334.

Rpt. (revised) in *Configuration: Essays in the Canadian Literatures.* Ed. E. D. Blodgett. Downsview, ON: ECW Press, 1982. 53-84.

Blodgett compares the treatment and use of the house in four works by Anne Hébert and stories by Munro. While Hébert uses the house in a metonymical manner, Munro uses the house metaphorically and as a device in the narrative organization and the revelation of character. The stories examined are "A Trip to the Coast," "Thanks for the Ride," "The Shining Houses," "The Idyllic Summer," "The Time of Death," "Winter Wind," and "The Peace of Utrecht." The structure of the chapters of *Lives* is also discussed.

S819. Bock, Tony. "Celebrating Alice Munro." *Toronto Star* 1 November 1998: D9.

Reports on Munro's reading of "My Mother's Dream" at the 19th International Festival of Authors.

S820. Bowen, Deborah. "In Camera: The Developed Photographs of Margaret Laurence and Alice Munro." *Studies in Canadian Literature* 13.1 (1988): 20-33. Accessed 24 April 2006. <http://www.lib.unb.ca/Texts/SCL/vol13_1/Contents.htm>

Munro's vision of life as a series of discrete moments of experience bears relevance to the photographic elements found in her writing. In "The Turkey Season," Bowen contemplates the tension between the photograph and photographer. In "Epilogue: The Photographer," she points out the relationship between mystery and presence. The artist, like the photographer, cannot unmask the mystery, only perpetuate it. The contrary and paradoxical pictures found in "Changes and Ceremonies" produce an apprehension of the plurality of reality. Margaret Laurence's *The Diviners* is the other work discussed.

S821. Boyles, Mary. "Woman: The Inside Outsider." *Selected Essays from the International Conference on the Outsider, 1988.* Ed. John Michael Crafton. [Carrollton, GA]: West Georgia College International Conference, 1990. 116-125.

This study deals with the subject of women and private or inner space in Doris Lessing's "To Room Nineteen," Charlotte Perkins Gilman's "The Yellow Wallpaper," and Munro's "The Office." The protagonist in Munro's story attempts to escape the confinement of the house, a male-created space, in order to identify and create her own inner, creative space. But the male intrusion of Mr. Malley, who tries to domesticate this space, overwrites the text she is trying to create and she is forced to remove herself from the office.

S822. "'Boys and Girls.'" *Short Stories for Students: Presenting Analysis, Context and Criticism on Commonly Studied Short Stories.* Ed. Tim Akers and Jerry Moore. Vol. 5. Detroit: Gale Group, 1999. 63-81.

Written for high school students, this overview includes an author biography, a plot summary, and a commentary on characters, themes, style, and historical context. Additionally provided is a critical overview of the story, excerpts from criticism, and a bibliography.

Brown, Russell Morton. See Bennett, Donna.

S823. Bruckner, D. J. R. "An Author Travels to Nurture Ideas about Home." *New York Times* 17 April 1990, late ed.: C13, C17.

Rpt. (excerpts) as "Small-Town Writer, Big-Time Author" in *Vancouver Sun* 28 July 1990: D11.

In a telephone interview after her visit to Scotland, the home of her ancestors, Munro tells Bruckner that she finds the people in Scotland not as easy to know or to write about as people in Canada or the American South. She then talks on a number of subjects: the continuing presence of her mother in her stories, the effect of aging on the way she views her parents and her writing, the origins of her stories, characterization, the writing process, and revision.

S824.   Buchholtz, Miros awa. "Pseudo-Longinus and the Affective Theory in Alice Munro's Stories about Childhood." *Alice Munro: Writing Secrets*. Ed. Héliane Ventura and Mary Condé. Special issue of *Open Letter* 11th ser. 9 (Fall 2003)-12th ser. 1 (Winter 2004): 89-102.

The concept of the sublime as found in the treatise by Longinus, "On the Sublime," is applied to an examination of Munro's artistry and style and its affect on her readers. Buchholtz has chosen to study Munro's stories of childhood and concentrates most of her remarks on the story "Images." One of the necessary qualities of the artist, according to Longinus, is the "ambition to reach artistic excellence." This quality is not only found in Munro, but also in her characters. Munro achieves the sublime in her style, with her realism expressed in images, senses, and emotions. The sublime is also found in her striving for the truth. The collection *Dance* is discussed in relation to elements of potential and absent meaning.

S825.   Caldwell, Rebecca. "Arts Person of the Year: Alice Munro." *Globe and Mail* 27 December 2004: R1.

Partly based on a telephone interview, this profile of the author and her latest book, *Runaway*, includes Munro's thoughts on writing and her acclaim as a writer. Munro's ambition to write began at age 11 and since then she never wanted to do anything else. Writing is still hard, and she has thought about stopping, but cannot, believing that the best is still to come. Munro concentrates on each new story as though it is the only one she has worked on. Caldwell includes Munro's comments on some of the stories in *Runaway*, the critical reaction to the book, Munro's public appearances, and her celebrity in New York.

S826.   Cam, Heather. "Learning from the Teacher: Alice Munro's Reworking of Eudora Welty's 'June Recital.'" *SPAN: Journal of the South Pacific Association for Commonwealth Literature and Language Studies* 25 (October 1987): 16-30.

As a model and point of departure, Cam has chosen Eudora Welty's "June Recital" to study Munro's "Dance of the Happy Shades" and "Changes and Ceremonies." The three stories involve music teachers and their pupils. Comparisons are made between the teachers in the stories, between the pupils, and between the teacher-pupil relationships. In Munro's two stories, the teachers are seen to have achieved freedom, while in Welty's story the teacher has not.

S827.   Canitz, A. E. Christa and Roger Seamon. "The Rhetoric of Fictional Realism in the Stories of Alice Munro." *Canadian Literature* 150 (Autumn 1996): 67-80.

This essay explores the dialectic between legend-making and demythologizing in Munro's stories, and discusses the techniques used to create opposition between fiction and reality.

Canitz outlines three rhetorical strategies Munro uses to create "truth" in fiction: shifts in time; improbability and contingency in the narrative as in "Accident"; and the conventionality of the "fictionalizing" of characters. Canitz further discusses the distancing of the narrators from their stories, resistance in the telling of tales, as in "The Stone in the Field," and the pushing aside of mystery and surmise. An unfavourable portrayal of legend-making and those who engage in it is found in stories such as "Day of the Butterfly," "The Peace of Utrecht," and "Friend of My Youth." In "Meneseteung," the narrator recognizes her tendency to fictionalize at the end of the story.

S828.   Carrera Suárez, Isabel and M. S. Suárez Lafuente. "El linaje materno en la narrativo de Alice Munro." *BELLS: Barcelona English Language and Literature Studies* 1989: 37-44.
The maternal inheritance of sweetness and sorrow is explored in the lives of Munro's female characters as they mature and age. Mothers are shown to be witnesses who pass on their inheritance from generation to generation. Adolescent female characters are studied in their relationship with their mothers, and in the way in which they view their mothers. Examples are used from *Lives* and "Red Dress-1946." Adult daughters are seen as reflecting back in time, remembering their mothers. As seen in "The Peace of Utrecht," some of the daughters' memories are associated with death and decay. The function of women, the function of men, and the oral transmission of inheritance, or storytelling, are other aspects covered.

S829.   Carrington, Ildikó de Papp. "Definitions of a Fool: Alice Munro's 'Walking on Water' and Margaret Atwood's 'Two Stories about Emma: The Whirlpool Rapids and Walking on Water.'" *Studies in Short Fiction* 28.2 (Spring 1991): 135-149.
In her comparison, Carrington looks at synecdoche and stylistic, narrative, and thematic differences between the two stories that bear the same title. She elaborates on Munro's narrative methods: her use of the third-person point of view, discontinuous narration, and dislocation created by flashbacks in memory. A "fool" is defined as one who is hidden and carried within. This ties into the view of reality as something hidden beneath real surfaces.

S830.   Carrington, Ildikó de Papp. "'Don't Tell (on) Daddy': Narrative Complexity in Alice Munro's 'The Love of a Good Woman.'" *Studies in Short Fiction* 34.2 (Spring 1997): 159-170.
The article gives a detailed analysis of the multiple-voiced narration in the story and the resulting narrative complexity. Enid is a focaliser who alternately, and sometimes simultaneously, is a character-narrator and a character-narratee. The boys are character-narrators who tacitly collude not to tell. Jeanette is an unreliable narrator and Enid is a good woman who collaborates in silence. Also included in the discussion are Munro's techniques of time shifts and disarrangement, the presence of voyeur scenes, the circular structure of the narrative, and the significance of the box as a metafictional metaphor.

S831.   Carrington, Ildikó de Papp. "Double-Talking Devils: Alice Munro's 'A Wilderness Station.'" *Essays on Canadian Writing* 58 (Spring 1996): 71-92.
Carrington discusses the narrative techniques used in the discontinuously-narrated mystery plot. The techniques create confusion in perception. As a consequence, the question of guilt cannot be answered. The article includes allusions to the Bible and to *The Private Memoirs and Confessions of a Justified Sinner* by James Hogg, an ancestor of Munro.

S832. Carrington, Ildikó de Papp. "Other Rooms, Other Texts, Other Selves: Alice Munro's 'Sunday Afternoon' and 'Hired Girl.'" *Journal of the Short Story in English* 30 (1998): 33-44.

Two stories ("Sunday Afternoon," published in 1957, and a sequel story, "Hired Girl," published in 1994) are compared in order to illustrate Munro's maturity as a writer both in the evolution of her narrative technique and in the complexity of the text. After pointing out the differences in the point of view of the narrators, Carrington considers the more recent story and the textual and tonal complexity created by the significance of literature, reading, and storytelling to the narrator's definition of her identity. Complex levels of intertexuality are present. A comparison is made between similar scenes in each story.

S833. Carrington, Ildikó de Papp. "Recasting the Orpheus Myth: Alice Munro's 'The Children Stay' and Jean Anouilh's *Eurydice*." *Alice Munro Writing On . . . .* Ed. Robert Thacker. Special issue of *Essays on Canadian Writing* 66 (Winter 1998): 191-203.
Rpt. in *The Rest of the Story: Critical Essays on Alice Munro*. Ed. Robert Thacker. Toronto: ECW Press, 1999. 191-203.

Munro creates ironic intertextualization in the story by recasting the roles of Anouilh's characters, Orphée and Eurydice. She complicates, combines, and multiplies them, thus defining the paradoxical meanings of the title and rejecting Anouilh's conception of a pure, fated love. The protagonist, in giving up her children for her lover, chooses "death" and, in doing so, becomes both Orphée and Eurydice.

S834. Carrington, Ildikó de Papp. "Review Essay: A Borderline Case: The Fiction of Alice Munro. [*Friend of My Youth*]." *American Review of Canadian Studies* 21.4 (Winter 1991): 459-469.

An extended review of *Friend*, with a discussion of each story in the collection. The review also makes reference to earlier works, considers Munro's influence on other writers, and looks at the metafictional dimensions of her work.

S835. Carrington, Ildikó de Papp. "Talking Dirty: Alice Munro's 'Open Secrets' and John Steinbeck's *Of Mice and Men*." *Studies in Short Fiction* 31 (1994): 595-606.

By "talking dirty," Carrington means both rude verbal and rude body language. She examines instances of such speech in the story. Carrington further looks at the unintelligible speech of two of the characters in the story, Alvin Stephens and Mr. Siddicup. She notes the repeated references to language in its spoken, written, and bodily forms. She makes the connection between detective plots and language, and considers Munro's language of silence. Allusions are made to *Of Mice and Men*.

S836. Carrington, Ildikó de Papp. "What's in a Title: Alice Munro's 'Carried Away.'" *Studies in Short Fiction* 30.4 (Fall 1993): 555-564.

While some attention is paid to the pun in the title and its various interpretive meanings, much of the article is taken up with other considerations, namely the narrative structure of the story, the narrative methods used, and the point of view. Parallels are drawn between the fiction of Munro and Thomas Hardy, especially the common elements of chance and accidents. Mourning, biblical allusions, and the epilogue of the story are also examined.

S837. Carrington, Ildikó de Papp. "Where Are You, Mother? Alice Munro's 'Save the Reaper.'" *Canadian Literature* 173 (Summer 2002): 34-51.

In researching this essay, Carrington used the unedited and original version of "Save the Reaper," located in the Munro Archives at the University of Calgary Library. She begins by examining the mother-daughter theme and the cross-generational aspects of this relationship. Carrington goes on to discuss Munro's use of ironic intertextuality, with regard to the underlying Greek myth of Demeter and Persephone. The element of aliens and alienation, particularly alienation between daughter and mother, is examined. Greek mythology is also present in "Vandals," and Carrington points out similarities between the two stories.

S838. Carscallen, James. "Alice Munro." *Profiles in Canadian Literature 2*. Ed. Jeffrey M. Heath. Toronto: Dundurn, [1980]. 73-80.

This profile of Munro's writing relates mainly to *Lives* and *Who*, and to the epilogue stories. Carscallen notes the noncontinuous form of narrative, the use of memory, the characters, surface details, language, epiphany, and the joining of reality and truth. The article contains excerpts from published sources of Munro's own thoughts on her writing process and vision.

S839. Carscallen, James. "The Shining House: A Group of Stories." *The Art of Alice Munro: Saying the Unsayable*. Papers from the Waterloo Conference. Ed. Judith Miller. Waterloo, ON: University of Waterloo Press, 1984. 85-101.

The article focuses on the stories "The Shining Houses," "Wood," "Material," "Images," and "Privilege," and selected chapters in *Lives*, all of which display a commonality in their perspective and interconnections with each other. Carscallen interprets "The Flats Road" in terms of symbolism and metaphors related to biblical Egypt. For the stories, he further discusses common characters and character types, such as barbarians, gypsies, and invaders. He analyzes circular cycles of life and death, the quest for home, questing and knowledge, doubt and truth.

S840. Carscallen, James. "Three Jokers: The Shape of Alice Munro's Stories." *Centre and Labyrinth: Essays in Honour of Northrop Frye*. Ed. Eleanor Cook, et al. Toronto: University of Toronto Press, 1983. 128-146.

Carscallen identifies ternary or three-phase cycles or patterns in a number of Munro's stories. He looks at the ternary cycles in "Baptizing" and "Princess Ida" from *Lives*, then at a series of cycles in the novel which show similarity to the pattern of cycles in the Bible. Allusions are made to the biblical Egypt and associated images. Cycles within cycles are studied in the stories "The Executioners," "Images," "Walker Brothers Cowboy," "Day of the Butterfly," "Who Do You Think You Are?," and "Marrakesh." The characters Nora Cronin, in "Walker Brothers Cowboy," and Char Desmond, in "Something I've Been Meaning to Tell You," and character types such as jokers are included in the analysis.

S841. Cencig, Elisabeth. "The Jordans: Remembered and Invented Past in Christa Wolf's *Kindheitsmuster* and Alice Munro's *Lives of Girls and Women*." *International Journal of Canadian Studies* 6 (Fall 1992): 63-85.

An examination of the thematic, narratological, and structural parallels between the two books. Both books depict small-town life in the 1930s and 1940s. Both themes revolve around the growth of a young girl into womanhood, the growth of the artist, and the complex mother-daughter relationship. The narrations are told from a retrospective adult perspective. Structural parallels are found in the form of the novel, both being first-person narrated and quasi-autobiographical artist novels. Differences in tone, texture, and style are analysed. The river as a symbol is compared in the two books.

S842. Chu, Chung-yi. "Munro's 'Friend of My Youth': A Mediated-Daughter Relationship." *Canadian Culture and Literature and a Taiwan Perspective*. Ed. Steven Tötösy de Zepetnek and Yiu-nam Leung. Edmonton: Research Institute for Comparative Literature, University of Alberta; Hsinchu, Taiwan: Department of Foreign Languages and Literature, National Tsing Hua University, 1998. 187-193.

Luce Irigaray's interpretation of the mother-daughter relationship is described. In her analysis of the story, Chu notes that the first-person narrator reconstructs the story from her mother's story. She elaborates on the fact that the story is framed by the narrator's dream of her dead mother, and that the dream is significant in her reconciliation with her mother. The open-endedness of the story is discussed.

S843. Clark, Miriam Marty. "Allegories of Reading in Alice Munro's 'Carried Away.'" *Contemporary Literature* 37.1 (Spring 1996): 49-61.

Clark sees the two threads found in the story not as parallel stories but as two irreconcilable allegories of reading. The first allegory revolves around the figure of the reader found in Jack Agnew, then later Arthur Doud. The second allegory is seen in the sign of the book and its related metaphor, the library. The ending lays bare the nature of the library and all the acts of reading represented and contained in it.

S844. Clery, Val. "Private Landscapes: Leo Simpson . . . and Alice Munro." *Quill & Quire* March 1974: 3, 15.

Rpt. in *Authors in the News*. Ed. Barbara Nykoruk. Vol. 2. Detroit: Gale Research, 1976. 210.

Briefly covers Munro's writing career, Munro and the short-story form, feminism and her fiction, and gives a general commentary on her writing.

S845. Coe, Clellan and Gerry Brenner. "Dialogizing a Narrative's Nativity: Alice Munro's 'Chaddeleys and Flemings.'" *North Dakota Quarterly* 64.2 (1997): 125-141.

This analysis of the two stories "Connection" and "The Stone in the Field" sheds light on Munro's narrative strategies and the function of the triggering event in the stories. Munro creates alternative locations for triggering events by the blurring or obfuscation of time in the narrator's story. Coexisting meaning is created through multiple narrational desires. These strategies are considered in the context of the themes of the mother-daughter relationship in "Connection" and the father-daughter relationship in "The Stone in the Field."

S846. Colvile, Georgiana M. M. "Relating (to) the Spec(tac)ular Other: Alice Munro's 'The Albanian Virgin.'" *Commonwealth Essays and Studies* 21.1 (Autumn 1998): 83-91.

Colvile shows how the two alternate and sometimes parallel stories of Lottar and Claire within the narrative are linked through linguistic play, complex narrative structures, and the converging elements of travel and transformation, language, literature, and communication. The stories are also linked through the use of sexual-textual language of the body and the senses, and through feminine desire. The three female characters (Lottar, Claire, and Charlotte) are categorized into the two categories of physical/animal and Puritan/antiseptic. In the beginning, all three are located in the second category, but shift into the first and in the process, find their true identity.

S847.   Colvile, Georgiana M. M. "Skunking the Reader: Alice Munro's Olfactory Discourse in Four Recent Stories." *Alice Munro: Writing Secrets*. Ed. Héliane Ventura and Mary Condé. Special issue of *Open Letter* 11th ser. 9 (Fall 2003)-12th ser. 1 (Winter 2004): 151-165.

Colvile examines Munro's use of smells to manipulate reader-response—in other words to "skunk" the reader. In "The Children Stay," erotic odour serves to awaken the "life-drive" of the protagonist. Smells in "Nettles" are used as a device that stimulates the narrator's flow of memories in a series of time shifts. In "The Albanian Virgin," bodily sensations and smell link the multiple narrative levels. The olfactory is a means of expression in this self-quest narrative. In "The Love of a Good Woman," smells are shown to reveal hidden desires.

S848.   Condé, Mary. "The Ambiguities of History in Alice Munro's 'The Love of a Good Woman.'" *Études canadiennes/Canadian Studies* 46 (1999): 123-130.

The story is preoccupied with the view of history as a shifting and elusive reality. Beginning with the ambiguity of the subtitle, "A Murder, A Mystery, A Romance," and continuing with a close reading of the story from beginning to end, Condé shows how the ambiguity and ambivalence found in the story makes it possible for it to be labelled with the three words.

S849.   Condé, Mary. "Coded Language in 'Runaway.'" *Alice Munro: Writing Secrets*. Ed. Héliane Ventura and Mary Condé. Special issue of *Open Letter* 11th ser. 9 (Fall 2003)-12th ser. 1 (Winter 2004): 177-183.

Condé studies the power of names and naming in the story, and analyses the names of people, animals, places, and events. She also explores the politics of language. She looks at how physical actions are made to yield an explicit message. She explains how the politics of language turns on the tensions between objects, people, and their names, between the public and private, indirect and direct use of language, what is spoken and what must remain unspoken.

S850.   Condé, Mary. "Fathers in Alice Munro's 'Fathers.'" *Cahiers de la nouvelle en anglaise/Journal of the Short Story in English* 41 (2003): 93-101.

In the story "Fathers," the attitudes of the three daughters to their fathers range from love and ambivalence to hatred. The narrator returns to the past and to her troubled feelings of betrayal, imagined and actual, of her two friends. She feels humiliation both at the hands of her own father and in the presence of the father of Frances Wainwright. Condé compares the effects of each of the three fathers on their daughters. The most brutal father is seen as the most straightforward and least unsettling in the context of the times of the Second World War. The father of the narrator and that of Frances Wainwright are unsettling because they provoke a feeling of guilt and complicity in their daughters. Condé also introduces the sexual implications of the father-daughter relationship and the significance of audience in the story.

S851.   Condé, Mary. "'True Lies': Photographs in the Short Stories of Alice Munro." *Études canadiennes/Canadian Studies* 32 (1992): 97-110.

The "true lies" are revealed in this article to be photographs that transform a recognizable reality into a different kind of truth. In Munro's stories, photographs can be used not only to preserve memories, but also to transmit subversive messages or to reveal unsuspected truths. Parallels are drawn between photography and storytelling. Condé reviews the use of photographs in many stories such as "Pictures of the Ice," "The Turkey Season," and "Something I've Been Meaning to Tell You."

S852.   Condé, Mary. "Visible Immigrants in Three Canadian Women's Fictions of the Nineties." *Études canadiennes/Canadian Studies* 34 (1993): 91-100.

The three works covered are Sky Lee's *Disappearing Moon Café*, Margaret Atwood's "Wilderness Tips," and Munro's "Oranges and Apples." Victor in Munro's story is presented as a stereotypical visible immigrant to readers who are "established settlers." But Munro, in the Canadian tradition of disarrangement, cheats the readers' expectations of political correctness in the text.

S853.   Condé, Mary. "Voyage towards an Ending: Alice Munro's 'Goodness and Mercy.'" *Telling Stories: Postcolonial Short Fiction in English*. Ed. Jacqueline Bardolph. Finalized for publication by André Viola with Jean-Pierre Durix. Introd. André Viola. Cross/Cultures: Readings in the Post/Colonial Literatures in English 47. Amsterdam: Rodopi, 2001. 59-66.

"Goodness and Mercy" is viewed by Condé as a death-centred story about an ambiguous mother-daughter relationship. The framework of the story is a sea voyage which is seen as a link between the Old World and the new. Condé points out the significance of the symbolism and the allusions to music and literature in the story.

S854.   [Conron, Brandon.] "Alice Laidlaw Munro." *They Passed This Way: A Selection of Citations 1878-1978*. Ed. Robert N. Shervill. Foreword D. Carlton Williams. London, ON: University of Western Ontario, 1978. 113.

This speech was delivered upon the conferring of a Doctor of Letters degree upon Munro at the University of Western Ontario. Beginning with a brief excerpt from *Dance*, Conron gives a short biography of Munro and a history of her writing career, and then he comments briefly on her writing.

S855.   Conron, Brandon. "Munro's Wonderland." *Canadian Literature* 78 (Autumn 1978): 109-112, 114-118, 120-123.

Conron considers Munro's influences, talent, and developing technique. He outlines the qualities of regionalism, magic realism, tone, and texture in her writing, and looks at the influence of writers of the American South such as James Agee and Walker Evans, and the painter Edward Hopper. The stories in *Dance* are briefly discussed, followed by a discussion of the work as a whole. Conron also analyses characters, point of view, themes, settings, and structure in stories and collections published after *Dance*.

S856. Cooke, John. "Alice Munro." *The Influence of Painting on Five Canadian Writers: Alice Munro, Hugh Hood, Timothy Findley, Margaret Atwood and Michael Ondaatje.* Canadian Studies 10. Lewiston, NY: Mellen, 1996. 69-85.

Cooke points out commonality between the documentary photographs of Walker Evans, the grotesque photographs of Diane Arbus, and the writing of Alice Munro. Munro, like Arbus, moves from the "comfortable details" of the physical world to the grotesque. Cooke explores photography, photographers, and photographic images found in *Lives*. He follows with a study of stories which contain references to art or photography: "The Ottawa Valley," "Privilege," "The Turkey Season," "Lichen," and "Monsieur les Deux Chapeaux." Other topics discussed relating to Munro's writing include regionalism, the sense of place, and disarrangement.

S857. Cornacchia, Cheryl. "A Life in the Writing Trade." *Calgary Sun* 6 December 1982: 16.

This edited version of an interview includes Munro's thoughts on her need to write, the difficulties of being a writer with family responsibilities, the maturing of her writing in terms of point of view, and the effect of aging on her life and writing.

S858. Craig, Jamie. "The Pain of Getting It Out: Writers Explain Their Agony." *Vancouver Sun* 27 October 1972: 30.

This article includes brief comments by Munro and two other female writers on the dilemmas associated with being a woman and a writer. Munro points out the opposition between the image of the woman as giving and nurturing and that of the woman writer as detached and outside the normal female roles. This causes conflict for the female writer, who still wants acceptance from men. Munro also comments briefly on writer's block.

S859. Creighton, David. "In Search of Alice Munro." *Books in Canada* 23.4 (May 1994): 19-25.

Creighton toured "Munrovia," Munro's home town of Wingham, Ontario, and the surrounding vicinity. In this article, he links actual physical places, such as buildings, stores, and theatres, to Munro's life and to the events and physical places that appear in her stories.

S860. Crisafulli Jones, Lilla Maria. "Il doppio femminile nella narrativa di Alice Munro." *Canada: Testi e contesti.* Ed. Alfredo Rizzardi. Saggi e ricerche di lingue e letterature straniere 11. Abano Terme: Piovan Editore, 1983. 125-137.

Duality, for women in general and for female writers in particular, exists in the contradiction within themselves between their personal ambitions and their femininity and passivity. Crisafulli examines the emancipated female writer and her guilt at being freed from her mother's destiny and at killing her image. The self-definition of the female artist is complicated by patriarchal definitions that intervene between her two selves. In "The Peace of Utrecht," the two sisters in the story represent the two aspects of female duality. Female duality is also found in the protagonist in "Providence." The twin identity of daughter/mother is examined in "The Ottawa Valley."

S861. Crouse, David. "Resisting Reduction: Closure in Richard Ford's *Rock Springs* and Alice Munro's *Friend of My Youth.*" *Canadian Literature* 146 (Autumn 1995): 51-64.

Crouse looks at time manipulation as a technique in realist closure and character growth in the two books. The framing technique used in "Differently" and "Five Points" involves radical time shifts, where a fixed point in the present acts as a locus from which the past can be viewed. The technique conveys complexities of closure, without jarring. Closure in stories such as "Goodness and Mercy" or "Wigtime" opens up, rather than closes down, possibilities. The responsibility for interpretation is placed on the reader. Epiphanic techniques and time manipulation are discussed in "Friend of My Youth."

S862.   Dahlie, Hallvard. "The Fiction of Alice Munro." *Ploughshares* 4.3 (1978): 56-71.
Munro sees the social world with the same double vision as the physical world—as an external reality beneath which there lies something that is unknown or irrational. With reference to selected stories, Dahlie explores this social world in unconsummated relationships, in abnormal or irrational situations, in the struggle of the elderly to understand the young, and in social and literary protest. Irony and ambiguity are examined in "Characters." Here one finds existential terror or desperation conjoined with existential possibility. Del in *Lives* is studied as a comic protagonist who is "saved in spite of herself."

S863.   Dahlie, Hallvard. "Unconsummated Relationships: Isolation and Rejection in Alice Munro's Stories." *World Literature Written in English* 11.1 (April 1972): 43-48.
　　　　Rpt. (excluding footnotes and textual refs.) in *Short Story Criticism: Excerpts from Criticism of the Works of Short Fiction Writers*. Ed. Sheila Fitzgerald. Vol. 3. Detroit: Gale Research, 1989. 320-322.
The characters in the stories of *Dance* are seen to live lives of isolation, rejection, insecurity, and emptiness, regardless of whether their relationships are consummated or unconsummated. Isolation in the stories "Walker Brothers Cowboy," "Boys and Girls," and "The Shining Houses" is explored. Unconsummated human and sexual relationships are discussed for the stories "The Office," "Thanks for the Ride," and "Postcard."

S864.   Davey, Frank. "Class, 'Family Furnishings,' and Munro's Early Stories." *Alice Munro: Writing Secrets*. Ed. Héliane Ventura and Mary Condé. Special issue of *Open Letter* 11th ser. 9 (Fall 2003)-12th ser. 1 (Winter 2004): 79-88.
Davey challenges Roxanne Rimstead's analysis in *Remnants of Nation* of Munro's distanced approach to class and poverty. He sets out to show how, in Munro's writing, poverty issues are not only ones of class but, more importantly, ones of gender and have more complexity than Rimstead's discussion shows. In Rimstead's analysis, Munro's female characters view their poverty as something from which they desire to escape. But Davey asserts that Munro shifts the focus from poverty and cultural values to the characters themselves, who are "defiant, self-possessed and out of reach." Davey discusses "Family Furnishings," "Thanks for the Ride," and *Lives*.

S865.   Dawson, Anthony B. "Coming of Age in Canada." *Mosaic* 11.3 (Spring 1978): 47-62.
Lives and four other Canadian coming-of-age novels are the focus of this study. In *Lives*, the maturation process involves the tension between transcendence through reading and writing, and sexual awakening and desire. Dawson traces Del's journey to maturity, from her first experience with death in "Heirs" to her sexual maturation in "Baptizing" and finally to her coming-of-age as a writer in "Epilogue: The Photographer."

S866.   Dawson, Carrie. "Skinned: Taxidermy and Pedophilia in Alice Munro's 'Vandals.'" *Canadian Literature* 184 (Spring 2005): 69-83.

Dawson shows how Munro challenges society's naive view of nature as an innocent place through an analysis of the violence toward animals and children found present in Ladner's taxidermic garden. Willing self-deception is practiced by the taxidermist, who attempts to "tell the truth of nature" through a simulation of the natural world. His partner deceives herself by her referral to the natural to explain her partner's behaviour. The question of her "knowingness" is raised. Dawson says that the child victims, who are violated like the stuffed animals, are represented by Munro not as innocent and natural but as sexual and complex beings. The violence premised by the simulated garden demonstrates the consequences of failing to scrutinize the "natural."

S867. Daziron, Héliane. "Alice Munro's 'The Flats Road.'" *Canadian Woman Studies* 6.1 (1984): 103-104.

This study looks at the place of outsiders, or people from "the other country," and their influence on the normal world. This influence is viewed in terms of oppositional archetypes. Uncle Benny is a Jonah figure who embodies the concepts of swallowing, imprisonment, and eventual freedom. Madeleine is the opposing archetype of a devouring ogress who tears apart. These figures, and Del's "devouring" of Uncle Benny's tabloids, are shown to influence her development as a writer.

S868. Daziron, Héliane. "The Anatomy of Embedding in Alice Munro's 'Half a Grapefruit.'" *Recherches anglaises et nord-américaines* 20 (1987): 103-107.

"Half a Grapefruit" contains seven stories and four allusions to other literary works. Daziron says that by the play of juxtaposition and embedding, Munro creates a network of associations and thereby achieves unity in the story. She goes on to examine the device of embedding, embedded stories, and storytelling, and the link between the embedded stories and Rose's main story. She finishes by noting the common theme of passage in all the stories.

S869. Daziron, Héliane. "The Camera Eye and the De-Stabilization of Reality in 'Lichen' from *The Progress of Love* by Alice Munro." *La nouvelle de langue anglaise: The Short Story V: Rencontres internationales.* Ed. Claire Larrière. Paris: Service des Publications de la Sorbonne Nouvelle, [1988]. 29-30.

(Item not seen.)

S870. Daziron, Héliane. "The Dialectics of Separation and Distance: A Differential Approach to A. Munro's 'Dulse.'" *Études canadiennes/Canadian Studies* 18 (1985): 69-82.

Daziron first engages in an analysis of the narrative structure of the story. She explains that the surface structure rests in the transformation from isolation to a form of communication for the protagonist. The deep structure consists of absence in presence, isolation in connection, and separation in union. She elaborates on the isolation and estrangement of the protagonist.

S871. Daziron, Héliane. "Heresie et orthodoxie dans 'Memorial' d'Alice Munro." *Études canadiennes/Canadian Studies* 24 (1988): 99-107.

This is an examination of the narrative techniques Munro uses in the story. Daziron shows that the story is built on a pattern of actantial relations which constructs semantic oppositions. The story consists in the paradoxical and unexpected reversal of these relations. She also points out the irony in the story and reader response to it. The narrator is described as detached.

S872. Daziron, Héliane. "Of Beasts and Stones: 'Mrs. Cross and Mrs. Kidd.'" *Commonwealth Essays and Studies* 11.2 (Spring 1989): 75-82.

Daziron defines the narrative structure of the story as being circular, beginning with conjunction in the characters' relationship, transforming to disjunction, then returning to conjunction. Language and allusions related to animality are linked to Mrs. Cross, while those of minerals are linked to Mrs. Kidd. Sometimes these links overlap between the characters, and their names have cross-meanings. The imagery, archetypes, and religious symbolism contained in the story are analysed.

S873. Daziron, Héliane. "The Pattern of Exclusion in Alice Munro's 'Day of the Butterfly.'" *Cahiers de la nouvelle* 5 (1985): 9-21.

The theory, theme, process, and symbolism of persecution are discussed by Daziron. She describes Myra and her brother as archetypical scapegoats. Their persecution and scapegoating in school are opposed by the narrator. But the narrator's rejection of Myra's gift signals her refusal to become a victim like Myra. Like her classmates, she deals with the tragedy of Myra's impending death by trivializing it.

S874. Daziron, Héliane Catherine. "The Preposterous Oxymoron: A Study of Alice Munro's 'Dance of the Happy Shades.'" *Literary Half Yearly* 24.2 (July 1983): 116-124.

The structural pattern in the story begins with a system of oppositions—past and present, spinster and mother. When the opposites are eventually fused, or yoked together, the resulting movement in the narrative transforms the position of the protagonist from one of degradation to one of triumph. In the analysis, Daziron also looks at the way Munro builds up the reader's expectations and how she uses opposition in the language of the story.

S875. Daziron, Héliane. "Symbols of Transformation: Alice Munro's 'Mrs. Cross and Mrs. Kidd.'" *Open Letter* 6th ser. 8 (Summer 1987): 15-24.

Daziron applies a structural, archetypal, and symbolic approach to the examination of the story. Mrs. Cross and Mrs. Kidd are described as archetypal heroines. Their idiosyncrasies are interpreted as a series of narrative units which echo or oppose each other. The narrative structure follows the circular movement of conjunction, transformation to disjunction, and a return to conjunction or union between the two characters. Connecting devices, imagery, and symbolism are also discussed.

S876. DeSalvo, Louise. "Literature and Sexuality: Teaching the Truth about the Body." *Media and Methods* 15.10 (September 1979): 33, 64-67.

DeSalvo argues her case for using *Lives* in schools to teach young adults about the body, even though it is sexually explicit. Del is portrayed as a young heroine who takes control over her life. She gradually learns about sexuality through her observations and interactions with the people around her. Despite some negative sexual encounters, and after her sexual awakening, Del still affirms her dignity as a human being.

S877. "Despite Awards, Alice Munro Doubts." *Expositor* [Brantford, ON] 28 April 1979: 15.
The article gives details obtained from an interview with Munro. It mentions her personal appearance, awards, and books, then gives her comments on a number of topics: her doubts on her ability to write, the character of Rose in *Who*, self-knowledge, and the early ambition to write.

S878. Di Stefano, Katherine. "Be Proud of Alice Munro." Letter. *Wingham Advance-Times* 13 October 1982: 4.
This resident of Wingham, Ontario, cites the universality and quality of Munro's writing as a reason for the town to be proud of Munro. The letter appeared after the *Books in Canada* article of October 1982, in which Joyce Wayne wrote about the townspeoples' negative reaction to their portrayal in her writing.

S879. Ditsky, John. "The Figure in the Linoleum: The Fictions of Alice Munro." *Hollins Critic* 22.3 (June 1985): 1-10.
Rpt. updated in *Twayne Companion to Contemporary Literature in English: From the Editors of The Hollins Critic*. Ed. R. H. W. Dillard and Amanda Cockrell. Vol 2. New York: Twayne Publishers, 2003. 109-118.
Ditsky considers Munro's realism and how her use of surface detail is accompanied by artistic balance. He discusses the regional and feminine elements in her writing, and her artistic and life visions. For Munro, plot is secondary to the evolution of character. Disconnections in narrative reflect her vision of life as a series of snapshots. Turning to *Lives*, Ditsky looks at the structure and unity of the novel, and the evidence of the literary influences of Agee, Faulkner, and O'Connor. In the books *Something*, *Who*, *Beggar*, and *Moons*, the function of the artist to search for meanings is examined. The heightened realism distracts readers from the presence of the search. The meaning of "the figure in the linoleum" is discussed.

S880. Djwa, Sandra. "Deep Caves and Kitchen Linoleum: Psychological Violence in the Fiction of Alice Munro." *Actes du colloque sur la violence dans le roman canadien depuis 1960/Papers from the Conference on Violence in the Canadian Novel since 1960*. Ed. Virginia Harger-Grinling and Terry Goldie. [St. John's, NF: Memorial University Press, 1981]. 177-190.
In Munro's writing, the element of the Gothic veers from the bizarre to the violent. The violence is not enacted, but is found in the perception of violence or in the psychological response to it, whether the violence is real or imagined. Djwa compares Faulkner's "Rose for Emily" and Munro's "Thanks for the Ride." The connection between the melodrama of the Southern Gothics and psychological truth is explored. The possibility or perception of violence and manifestations of sexual or psychological violence are examined in *Lives* and a number of other books and stories.

S881. Dombrowski, Eileen. "'Down to Death': Alice Munro and Transcience [sic]." *University of Windsor Review* 14.1 (Fall-Winter 1978): 21-29.
In her analysis, Dombrowski focuses on transience and death in Munro's fiction. She begins by saying that the transience of life is central to Munro's worldview and to her motivation as a writer. Mortality, change with the passing of time, and death as a part of a background to life

are discussed for stories in *Dance*, *Lives* and *Something*. Dombrowski examines death as a narrative device and as a theme. She also looks at time shifts as a narrative technique.

S882.   Donovan, Katie. "Tales of Love and Slaughter." *Irish Times* 2 March 1995, city ed.: Arts 12.

Interviewed in Ireland after the publication of *Open* in Britain, Munro comments on the similarities in speech and dialect between Ireland and Huron County, and the stifling atmosphere of small rural communities. She goes on to talk about her early writing and stories of adolescence, her poverty in childhood, her mother's illness, and her relationship with her mother. She describes *Open* and her current work as becoming more fantastic, reflecting her changing vision of life and reality as she ages.

S883.   Duffy, Dennis. "'A Dark Sort of Mirror': 'The Love of a Good Woman' as Pauline Poetic." *Alice Munro Writing On . . . .* Ed. Robert Thacker. Special issue of *Essays on Canadian Writing* 66 (Winter 1998): 169-190.
   Rpt. in *The Rest of the Story: Critical Essays on Alice Munro*. Ed. Robert Thacker. Toronto: ECW Press, 1999. 169-190.

Duffy sees the story as a touchstone work, a Munro poetic. He points out parallels with earlier stories in themes, style, and in the handling of the human body. He compares readers' complicity in this story with that in "Who Do You Think You Are?" Duffy goes on to examine the paradoxical nature of experience, as found in the puzzling opening and the uncertain ending. Pauline duality is identified in the character of Mr. Willens. The function of the boys in the story is explored. The tone is labelled as Pauline Gothic in the treatment of the corrupt and decaying body.

S884.   Duncan, Isla J. "An Examination of the 'Double Distancing' Narrative Perspective in Munro." *British Journal of Canadian Studies* 8.1 (1993): 53-70.

Duncan studies the unique treatment of "double distancing" in "Fits." Munro uses the third-person viewpoint, which combines features of omniscient narration and character focalization. The distancing offers diluted versions of a dramatic experience and, in doing so, presents the reader with new and disturbing revelations about the female character. The story illustrates the dichotomy between the calm surface of life and the secret passions beneath the surface.

S885.   Duncan, Isla J. "'It Seems So Much the Truth It Is the Truth': Persuasive Testimony in Alice Munro's 'A Wilderness Station.'" *Studies in Canadian Literature/Études en littérature canadienne* 28.2 (2003): 98-110.

The subject of letter-writing and public and private narration is treated in this article. Duncan shows how Munro elevates the truth of Annie's testimony over that of the other characters by her narrative strategies of arrangement and transmission. The interaction of the protagonist, epistolary narrative, and the reader is examined. The question of truth and fiction is raised.

S886.   Dvorak, Marta. "Alice Munro's 'Lovely Tricks' from *Dance of the Happy Shades* to *Hateship, Friendship, Courtship, Loveship, Marriage*." *Alice Munro: Writing Secrets*. Ed. Héliane Ventura and Mary Condé. Special issue of *Open Letter* 11th ser. 9 (Fall 2003)-12th ser. 1 (Winter 2004): 55-77.

Dvorak delves into Munro's narrative technique and her aesthetic of indirection, using as illustrations stories such as "An Ounce of Cure," "Postcard," "The Shining Houses," and "The Office." The overlapping of restricted vision and knowledgeable voice is the core of Munro's poetics. "Dance of the Happy Shades" and "What Is Remembered" are two examples chosen for discussion of this aspect.

S887. Dyer, Klay. "'The Albanian Virgin': Short Story 1994." *Beacham's Encyclopedia of Popular Fiction. Analyses Series*. Ed. Kirk H. Beetz. Vol. 1. Osprey, FL: Beacham, 1996. 73-79.

The framework for this critical interpretation of the story is: Characters, Social Concerns, Themes, Techniques, Literary Precedents, Related Titles, Ideas for Group Discussion.

S888. Dyer, Klay. "*The Beggar Maid: Stories of Flo and Rose* [Who Do You Think You Are?]: Story Cycle 1978." *Beacham's Encyclopedia of Popular Fiction. Analyses Series*. Ed. Kirk H. Beetz. Vol. 1. Osprey, FL: Beacham, 1996. 305-312.

The framework for this critical overview of the book is: Characters, Social Concerns, Themes, Techniques, Literary Precedents, Related Titles.

S889. Dyer, Klay. "*Lives of Girls and Women*: Novel/Story Cycle 1971." *Beacham's Encyclopedia of Popular Fiction. Analyses Series*. Ed. Kirk H. Beetz. Vol. 4. Osprey, FL: Beacham, 1996. 2455-2462.

The framework for this critical overview of the novel is: Characters, Social Concerns, Themes, Techniques, Literary Precedents, Related Titles, Adaptations.

S890. Edemariam, Aida. "Riches of a Double Life." *Guardian* [London] 4 October 2003, final ed.: 20-23.

In this extended profile of Munro's life, career, and writing, Edemariam uses quotations from a variety of sources including Munro herself, her writings, her friends Margaret Atwood and Audrey Thomas, and her two *New Yorker* fiction editors Charles McGrath and Daniel Menaker. She moves chronologically through important phases of Munro's life and career. Among other details, she touches on the effect of Munro's relationship with her mother on her writing, the difficult publishing situation in Canada in the 1960s, Munro's ability to portray female sexuality, the evolving complexity of her work, and the effect of illness and aging on her writing.

S891. Edwards, Bruce L. "*Lives of Girls and Women*." *Masterplots II: British and Commonwealth Fiction Series*. Ed. Frank N. Magill. Vol. 2. Pasadena, CA: Salem, 1987. 980-983.

The outline for this critical overview of the novel is: The Novel, The Characters, Themes and Meanings, Critical Content.

S892. Eldredge, L. M. "A Sense of Ending in *Lives of Girls and Women*." *Studies in Canadian Literature* 9.1 (1984): 110-115. Accessed 24 April 2006. <http: www.lib.unb.ca/Texts/SCL/vol9_1/Contents.htm>

Eldredge focuses on the unconventional structure of the novel. Rather than having the structure of a conventional plot and conclusion, *Lives* is constructed as a series of events linked by characters and theme. The conclusion consists of an epilogue in which a shift occurs in the protagonist's point of view. Del at the end becomes the author of her own realistic story. Bobby Sherriff and the themes of madness, truth, and reality are also discussed.

S893.   Elliott, Gayle. "'A Different Tack': Feminist Meta-Narrative in Alice Munro's 'Friend of My Youth.'" *Journal of Modern Literature* 20.1 (Summer 1996): 75-84.

Following a look at women writers and the structures of narrative, Elliott turns to an examination of metonymic meaning and meta-narrative in the story "Friend of My Youth." The interconnecting stories of the mother and daughter and the stories of the other characters challenge the reader to recognize the interconnections and to discover the truth. In the daughter's re-visioning of her mother's version of Flora, she comes closest to the truth and experiences the epiphany of seeing her mother in a new light.

S894.   Farrow, Moira. "Least Praised Good Writer: Housewife Finds Time to Write Short Stories." *Citizen* 10 August 1961: 3.

The article is based on an interview with Munro and begins with biographical details of Munro and her writing career. Munro's comments include the fact that she is presently writing less because of family responsibilities, and that she writes about southern Ontario, where she spent her childhood.

S895.   Fawcett, Brian. "Provocations." *Capilano Review* 2nd ser. 2 (Spring 1990): 111-116.

Fawcett's article on modern fiction mentions Munro as a master of the modernist short story or the 19th-century fictional narrative. He suggests that the short story is limited in the climate of the modern world, and even perhaps obsolete. He argues that writers should be intellectual generalists and conceptualists.

S896.   Ferri, Laura. "Mothers and Other Secrets." *Alice Munro: Writing Secrets*. Ed. Héliane Ventura and Mary Condé. Special issue of *Open Letter* 11th ser. 9 (Fall 2003)-12th ser. 1 (Winter 2004): 137-149.

After reviewing the various images of liberated and unliberated mothers in Munro's fiction, Ferri says that almost all of them have one thing in common—they carry secrets. While focussing on the impossibility of reaching the mother, Munro exposes the silence, mystery, indeterminacy, and gap in the mother-daughter relationship. This relationship is studied in "The Progress of Love" and "The Ottawa Valley." Fathers also present a mystery for daughters. In the similar quest "to get at" or "to get rid of" the father, the daughter reveals secrets about herself. These relationships are explored in "Before the Change" and "Fathers."

S897.   Findley, Timothy. "Weaver a Class Act." Letter. *National Post* 24 June 2000: B11.

In response to Metcalf's article in the *National Post* of June 17, Findley says that Robert Weaver cannot be faulted for not furthering Munro's career in the United States, because he did not act as her agent. However, he did bring Munro to national attention in Canada.

S898.   Fitzpatrick, Margaret Anne. "'Projection' in Alice Munro's *Something I've Been Meaning to Tell You*." *The Art of Alice Munro: Saying the Unsayable*. Papers from the

Waterloo Conference. Ed. Judith Miller. Waterloo, ON: University of Waterloo Press, 1984. 15-20.

Fitzpatrick studies the psychoanalytical concept of projection in the book and how Munro uses it as a method to construct characters and plot. He elucidates various instances of projection in many of the stories. For example in the title story, one finds the projection of aggressive management. In "Material," there is the projection of a degraded self-image, while in "Memorial," the projection is one of hidden coldness. Defense mechanisms in characters are seen as an aspect of narrative irony.

S899.   Fleenor, Juliann E. "Rape Fantasies as Initiation Rite: Female Imagination in *Lives of Girls and Women*." *Room of One's Own* 4.4 (1979): 35-49.

The article begins with an examination of the female imagination and the female-defining characteristics of passivity, powerlessness, and masochism which are evident in rape. Fleenor then makes the distinction between the patriarchal rape myth and the female rape fantasy. Rape fantasy is defined as a means by which a woman transforms her state of powerlessness into one of control. Rape fantasy is the underlying element in the structure of *Lives*. In Del's first sexual encounter with Garnet French, the rape fantasy is a ceremony of rebirth, and a female initiation rite.

S900.   Forceville, Charles. "Alice Munro's Layered Structures." *Shades of Empire in Colonial and Post-Colonial Literatures*. Ed. C. C. Barfoot and Theo D'haen. Intro. Theo D'haen. Amsterdam: Rodopi, 1993. 301-310.

Forceville examines the recurring image of layered structures in Munro's fiction. He analyses the physical layering of objects and landscapes in stories such as "A Queer Streak" and "Walker Brothers Cowboy." Layering is also found in individual persons, when the present self is layered with an earlier self, as Forceville identifies in stories such as "Bardon Bus." Finally, the layering of experience occurs when the experience of one character is mediated by that of another, as is the case in "Friend of My Youth."

S901.   Forceville, Charles. "Language, Time and Reality: The Stories of Alice Munro." *External and Detached: Dutch Essays on Contemporary Canadian Literature*. Ed. Charles Forceville, August J. Fry, and Peter J. De Voogd. Canada Cahiers no. 4. Amsterdam: Free University Press, 1988. 37-44.

Slightly adapted version of an article originally pub. as "Taal tijd en werkelijkheid—over de verhalen van Alice Munro." *Bzzlletin* 152 (January 1988).

According to Forceville, the discrepancy between outward appearance and hidden reality creates a schizothymia in characters such as Rose in *Who* and Del in *Lives*, who uphold an appearance of acceptance by pretending and withholding information. Rose becomes an actress; Del is both a participant and an observer. She becomes a writer but discovers that reality, in its elusiveness, cannot be captured in language. Forceville goes on to say that the tension between the past and the present is directly connected to the contrast between fiction and reality. The double perspective of the retrospective narrator and the multiple point of view are also considered.

S902.   Fortunato, Mario. "Scrittrici/Alice Munro—Proust dell'Ontario." *L'Espresso* (4 agosto 1995): 82.

The article announces the publication of the Italian translation of *Who* and comments on the critical reception of the original English version in the United States and England.

S903. Fowler, Rowena. "The Art of Alice Munro: *The Beggar Maid* and *Lives of Girls and Women*." *Critique: Studies in Modern Fiction* 25.4 (Summer 1984): 189-198.
Rpt. (excerpts) in *Short Story Criticism: Excerpts from Criticism of the Works of Short Fiction Writers*. Ed. Sheila Fitzgerald. Vol. 3. Detroit: Gale Research, 1989. 341-343.

Fowler says that the art of Munro's fiction is to discover an "overall design" for a "conglomeration of stories." Del Jordan in *Lives* and Rose in *Beggar* are both artists who learn the art of narrative in the process of telling their stories. Fowler looks at Del as a writer and at the elements that shaped her as an artist: the handing-down of stories from mother to daughter, chroniclers and storytellers, myths and memories, literature and life. Fowler notes that re-interpretation and testing against experience are important structural principles of *Lives*. In *Beggar*, storytellers like Rose are survivors. In the end, Rose is shamed by broadcasting the "old mythology" of her life story. Both artists reject false ways of writing and determine to be more faithful to the past.

S904. Foy, Nathalie. "'Darkness Collecting': Reading 'Vandals' as a Coda to *Open Secrets*." *Alice Munro Writing On . . . .* Ed. Robert Thacker. Special issue of *Essays on Canadian Writing* 66 (Winter 1998): 147-168.
Rpt. in *The Rest of the Story: Critical Essays on Alice Munro*. Ed. Robert Thacker. Toronto: ECW Press, 1999. 147-168.

Despite the darkness of the story, Foy believes that it illustrates Munro's reverential stance toward fiction. She also sees the story as having important links and parallels with other stories in the collection. Using "Open Secrets" and "Carried Away" as examples, Foy examines the parallel stories found in the narratives. "Vandals" resembles these stories in its multiple layers of narrative. It also picks up narrative threads from the stories which precede it. This layering of parallel and intersecting narratives makes the stories in the collection "hang together."

S905. France, Louise. "Mistress of All She Surveys." *Observer* 6 February 2005, Review: 15.

Munro's life and writing are profiled by France, who interviewed Munro in New York. Munro's early career is set in the social and literary context of Canada in the 1950s and in the early years of her first marriage when she experienced writer's block. Munro's childhood environment in Wingham, her feelings for her mother, and her two marriages are also touched on. Of the present Munro says, "I just wish there could be more of this stage." Age has not lessened the drive to write. She briefly explains how she writes. Her latest project is a memoir of her family.

S906. Francesconi, Sabrina. "Writing Secrets as 'Betraying the Past' in Alice Munro's 'What Is Remembered.'" *Alice Munro: Writing Secrets*. Ed. Héliane Ventura and Mary Condé. Special issue of *Open Letter* 11th ser. 9 (Fall 2003)-12th ser. 1 (Winter 2004): 243-253.

Francesconi presents three levels by which Munro's writing of secrets may be read: as a means of introducing an invisible layer of the ungraspable under the surface of ordinary domestic life; as a denouncement and subversion of the Puritan code of behaviour and silence; and as a codification of meaning. The balance of the paper is taken up with an analysis of the untold secret in "What Is Remembered." Meriel's secret is one which is fluid and unreachable, changing with her imagination, selective memory, and time. It is something she cannot tell without having it dissolve. Francesconi concludes by saying, "The writing of a secret enacts a never ending cycle of re/reading, re/codification, and re/semantification."

S907. Franzen, Jonathan. "Alice's Wonderland." *New York Times* 14 November 2004, late ed., final: Sec. 7: 1.

Franzen feels that Munro has not received the recognition and fame she deserves. He presents his argument by saying that Munro is a pure short-story writer, that her material is personal and has personal relevance for the reader. Her writing has the qualities of purity, suspense, and complexity. He uses "The Bear Came Over the Mountain" as an example to show the complexity of her work.

S908. French, William. "In Alice Land." *Globe and Mail* 19 June 1973: 12.

French's article talks about Munro's Book Store in Victoria, B.C. and the sales of Munro's books *Dance* and *Lives* in it. He traces the progression of her writing from the early years when Munro wrote for small magazines to the present, 20 years later. He remarks that she wrote in relative obscurity all this time and even now is a very private writer, not even discussing her work with her husband.

S909. French, William. "Women in Our Literary Life." *Imperial Oil Review* 59.1 [no. 322] (1975): 2-7. [Munro on page 7]
    Rpt. in *Canadian Author and Bookman* 51.3 (Spring 1976): 1-6.

In his discussion of the current popularity of Canadian women writers, French notes that Munro's work is concerned with women whose problems, though individual, are at the same time universal. He comments briefly on *Lives* and *Something*.

S910. Frye, Joanne S. "Growing Up Female: *Lives of Girls and Women* and *The Bluest Eye*." *Living Stories, Telling Lives: Women and the Novel in Contemporary Experience*. Ann Arbor: University of Michigan Press, 1986. 77-108.

The two books are discussed as *Bildungsroman*. Frye looks at the narrative technique used in developing the protagonists' identities. In *Lives*, she focuses on Del's growth to selfhood and how Del develops as an artist without giving up her female identity or giving in to culturally imposed femininity. Frye also considers the relationship of language to Del's sense of being female and the act of naming to control experience.

S911. Gadpaille, Michelle. "Alice Munro." *The Canadian Short Story*. Toronto: Oxford University Press, 1988. 57-81.

In this broad examination of Munro's writing and works, Gadpaille describes the structure of her stories as being spatial, her strategy as digressive, and her narrative as discontinuous. She further discusses the relationship of art to reality, storytelling and storytellers, and the prime importance of feeling rather than events in Munro's writing. Gadpaille provides not only a collective commentary on the stories in *Something*, *Who*, *Moons*, and *Progress*, but also comments on a number of individual stories and groups of stories.

S912. Gane, Margaret Drury. "Do You Use Real People in Your Fiction?" *Saturday Night* November 1975: 39-43. [Munro on page 41]

The question "Do you use real people in your fiction?" was posed to a number of Canada's well-known authors, including Munro. She replies, "Mostly I use composites, but I have used real people in a few stories." Then she says, "I have tried to write about myself seeing them, as well as about them. This seems to make it less dishonourable." She calls fiction "a serious adventure," a necessary thing to deal with strong feelings. In the process, she says, you will do almost anything required; audience and consequences are forgotten. Family and friends who love you understand that in your writing you "use things out of faith and necessity, not for diversion."

S913. Garner, Hugh. "Foreword." *Dance of the Happy Shades: Stories*. Toronto: McGraw-Hill Ryerson, 1968. vii-ix.

Garner praises Munro's craftsmanship and skill as a short-story writer. He points out the truth in her portrayal of ordinary characters and their emotions, saying that readers can identify with them and relate their problems to their own lives. Although Munro writes about women, Garner believes that her writing is universal and can be enjoyed by both men and women. He mentions the important role of Robert Weaver and the Canadian Broadcasting Corporation in promoting Munro's stories.

S914. Garson, Marjorie. "Alice Munro and Charlotte Brontë." *University of Toronto Quarterly* 69.4 (Fall 2000): 783-825.

Brontë's *Jane Eyre*, and secondarily *Villette* and *The Professor*, are examined as influences in Munro's writing. Garson identifies three motifs common to the works of both authors. The motif of the alien bride, or an unconventional female figure wearing a bridal costume, is discussed for five stories, including "Cortes Island." The second motif, the intrusive governess, a woman who brings order into a home and cares for children but has self-interest in mind, is studied in 4 stories, notably in "The Love of a Good Woman." The third motif, the damaged consort, or a man who is wounded or handicapped and controlled by a powerful woman, is applied to "Cortes Island," "The Love of a Good Woman," and "Rich as Stink." Parallels are drawn with *Jane Eyre*.

S915. Garson, Marjorie. "I Would Try to Make Lists: The Catalogue in *Lives of Girls and Women*." *Canadian Literature* 150 (Autumn 1996): 45-63.

Garson catalogues and assigns meaning to the various types of lists found in *Lives*. Lists of street names symbolize historical permanence in the presence of evanescence; lists of food suggest a hunger or greed for life; lists of women's chores stand as an indictment of the definition of real work as masculine; lists of things relating to the female body show ambivalence about excess. Garson also examines the process of list-making by Del Jordan, Jerry Story, and Garnet French.

S916. Garson, Marjorie. "Synecdoche and the Munrovian Sublime: Parts and Wholes in *Lives of Girls and Women*." *English Studies in Canada* 20.4 (December 1994): 413-429.

Garson identifies two parts in *Lives*: one that is corporeal or relating to the body and its associated members, organs, and fluids; and a second that is social, or which encompasses the family, the small town, and mankind. Combining and connecting these two parts is the image of "The Living Body." The study then turns to Munro's synecdochal technique and the functional dynamics between the parts and the whole. Synecdoche is shown to operate at all levels of the text: story and character, language and imagery. The influence of James Joyce's *A Portrait of the Artist as a Young Man* is found in *Lives*.

S917.   Gervais, Marty. "She's a Person First." *Windsor Star* 16 October 1982: C9.
Gervais reports on an interview with Munro in which she gives her thoughts on book promotion tours. Using "The Turkey Season" as an example, Munro talks about writing that combines autobiography, fiction, and research.

S918.   Gibson, Douglas M. "Canadian Literature Strong and Free: U.S. Role Exaggerated." Letter. *National Post* 24 June 2000: B2.
Responding to an article written by John Metcalf in the *National Post* on June 17, Gibson refutes Metcalf's claim that Munro's career is an American construct.

S919.   Gibson, Douglas. "A Very Canadian Celebrity: A Profile of Alice Munro." *Read: Life with Books* 2.2 (2001): 8-10.
    Also online. Accessed 24 April 2006. <http://www.randomhouse.ca/readmag/page8.htm>
This article gives some insight into Gibson's editorial and personal relations with Munro. He describes Munro as a person who is down-to-earth and unaffected by her celebrity. He comments on the polished state of her stories prior to publication and the quality of her interviews. Gibson recalls his reaction to Munro's requests for press-stage changes that involved major revisions to *Who*, and for the printing of *Hateship* on recycled paper.

S920.   Gilbert, Paula Ruth. "All Roads Pass through Jubilee: Gabrielle Roy's *La Route d'Altamont* and Alice Munro's *Lives of Girls and Women*." *Colby Quarterly* 29.2 (June 1993): 136-148.
By examining the narrative structure and strategy used in the two works, Gilbert sets out to show the differences in the approach of the two writers and, by inference, the differences between French and English Canadian literature. In *Lives*, Gilbert examines Del, the narrator, and her point of view. She discusses Del as a double or split narrator who is both participant and observer and as a narrator who is remembering the past. The use of narrative interventions causes temporal confusion. Del's desire for narrative control is evident. The elements of time and space in the novel and the blurring of the boundaries between reality and fiction are other aspects discussed.

S921.   Gingerich, Judy. "Alice Munro, Great Inspiration." *Cord Weekly* [Wilfred Laurier University] 28 October 1982: 11.
Gingerich reports on a talk given by Munro for "Meet the Author Series" at Wilfred Laurier University. In her comments about writing short stories, Munro tells her audience how her stories originate and provides an example based on a scene she viewed from a window in the Wingham Public Library.

S922.   Giordani, Maria Rosa. "Gustave Flaubert, Alice Munro: Due microcosmi a confronto." *Revista di studi canadesi* 8 (1995): 187-194.
In her comparison between Gustav Flaubert's *Madame Bovary* and Munro's *Who*, specifi-

cally the story "Mischief," Giordani sees the influence of the French writer on Munro's work. The story of adultery committed by women dissatisfied in marriage is common to both works. The associated scandal does not affect Munro's protagonist, Rose, as much as Flaubert's Emma since women in Flaubert's time were not so free. Giordani compares the portrayal and situations of both women. Munro's style of documentary and heightened realism is compared with Flaubert's realism. Munro distances herself from her character, while Flaubert identifies himself with his.

S923. Gironnay, Sophie. "Adulée, primée, mais toujours inquiète . . . ." *Actualité* 15 décembre 1998: 105.

This article reports on Munro's reading of "My Mother's Dream" at the 19th International Festival of Authors in Toronto on 31 October 1998, and comments on the critical acclaim of her work and the awarding of the Giller Prize for *The Love of a Good Woman*.

S924. Gittings, Christopher E. "Constructing a Scots-Canadian Ground: Family History and Cultural Translation in Alice Munro." *Studies in Short Fiction* 34.1 (Winter 1997): 27-37.

Gittings presents Annie in "A Wilderness Station" as a descendant of Scottish immigrants who has translated herself into the New World and the Canadian ground. The story has its origins in Munro's own family history. Gittings begins his analysis by considering the various epistolary recountings of the death that occurs in the story. He then presents the contrasting views of Annie and Reverend McBain toward the wilderness, God, and the moral code. Through the multiple construction of past events, Munro introduces a multiplicity of alternatives to the single, Old World narrative of Scots-Calvinist–based truth.

S925. Givner, Joan. "Running in the Family." *Toronto Star* 29 April 2001: D15.

Givner summarizes some of the highlights from Sheila Munro's book, *Lives of Mothers and Daughters*. She suggests that, by writing the book, Sheila Munro shows a need to establish her own identity.

S926. Godard, Barbara. "'Heirs of the Living Body': Alice Munro and the Question of a Female Aesthetic." *The Art of Alice Munro: Saying the Unsayable*. Papers from the Waterloo Conference. Ed. Judith Miller. Waterloo, ON: University of Waterloo Press, 1984. 43-72.

Godard writes from a feminist perspective about women as writers, and about the woman's self coming into being in language. Writing as a woman is a central issue in Munro's *Lives*. Godard examines the male literary tradition in *Who* and *Lives*, and the female oral narratives found in women's storytelling. She notes the double-talk and the subjective elements in women's stories of themselves in *Lives*, as for example in Ada's story. Ada is examined as a writer, a feminist, and as a model of Tennyson's Ida. The link between women's sexuality and language is shown in Del, who discovers a new language through her sexual body and is free to pursue her own life and writing.

S927. Gold, Joseph. "Our Feeling Exactly: The Writing of Alice Munro." *The Art of Alice Munro: Saying the Unsayable*. Papers from the Waterloo Conference. Ed. Judith Miller. Waterloo, ON: University of Waterloo Press, 1984. 1-13.

In Munro's characters, female consciousness is created through the movement between feeling and language. Gold first considers the limitations of language to express feeling. He examines not-telling and feeling in "Who Do You Think You Are?" He describes, as a mystery, the shift from perception and felt experience to writing. In *Lives*, Del discovers language as a means of ordering the chaos associated with sex. In "Wild Swans," Gold points out the double entendre where the familiar Victorian surface is destroyed by the power of an individual female sexual experience.

S928. Goldman, Marlene. "Penning in the Bodies: The Construction of Gendered Subjects in Alice Munro's 'Boys and Girls.'" *Studies in Canadian Literature/Études en littérature canadienne* 15.1 (1990): 62-75. Accessed 24 April 2006. <http://www.lib.unb.ca/Texts/SCL/vol15_1/Contents.htm>

The patriarchal division and control of space is examined as it relates to the creation of the gendered person. In the story, the concept of the pens in which the father raises his foxes is translated by Goldman into a metaphor for the house which encloses and controls bodies. Goldman looks at the father-daughter and mother-daughter relationships in the context of the behaviours and roles traditionally connected with males and females. She comments on the symbolism found in the story. By the end of the story, the young narrator's gender role has been established.

S929. Goodman, Charlotte. "Cinderella in the Classroom: (Mis)Reading Alice Munro's 'Red Dress—1946.'" *Reader: Essays in Reader Oriented Theory, Criticism, and Pedagogy* 30 (Fall 1993): 49-64.

Goodman considers student development theory, reader-response theories, and gender reading theories in her discussion of students' misreading of the story. Students interpret the story as a Cinderella tale, and fail to see that Munro has subverted the classical tale by including two key issues of female development: the mother-daughter relationship and female bonding. They also fail to consider the story's time frame and overlook the significance of the beginning and ending.

S930. Grabes, Herbert. "Creating to Dissect: Strategies of Character Portrayal and Evaluation in Short Stories by Margaret Laurence, Alice Munro and Mavis Gallant." *Modes of Narrative: Approaches to American, Canadian and British Fiction*. Ed. Reingard M. Nischik and Barbara Korte. Würzburg: Königshausen & Neumann, 1990. 119-128.

Grabes's analysis includes Margaret Laurence's "To Set Our House in Order," Mavis Gallant's "Acceptance of Their Ways," and Munro's "Who Do You Think You Are?" In Munro's story, the third-person narrative perspective is used. All information about the other six characters is filtered through Rose's mind. Her selection of information reveals her predilections and her bias toward the uninhibited character, Milton Homer. The sequencing of the information from the long time span of memory conveys changes in the characters, particularly in Rose herself, who is seen to acquire a heightened self-knowledge.

S931. Grady, Wayne. "Story Tellers to the World." *Today Magazine* 5 December 1981: 10-12.

Grady's article mentions five Canadian short-story writers, including Munro. He briefly covers Munro's life and career and notes the use of the town in her fiction, linking the fictional Jubilee and Hanratty to Wingham. He includes a quote from a recent interview in which Munro describes Lower Town where she lived as a kind of ghetto, "outside the whole social structure." The article characterizes the town as "stultifyingly provincial." More broadly, Grady comments on the international status of the Canadian short story and the history and importance of the genre in Canada. The Canadian short story is dominated by the feeling of exile and displacement.

S932.   Groen, Rick. "Author's Fragility Blends with Undeniable Strength." *Globe and Mail* 22 October 1986: C7.

Munro was interviewed by Groen after a reading at the International Festival of Authors in Toronto. He reports on subjects discussed by Munro during the interview: the importance of women's physical appearance, the writing process, her fictional aesthetic, reader response, and being a short-story writer with a family.

S933.   Gros-Louis, Dolores. "Pens and Needles: Daughters and Mothers in Recent Canadian Literature." *Kate Chopin Newsletter* 2.3 (Winter 1976-77): 8-15.

The four books Gros-Louis discusses are Margaret Laurence's *A Bird in the House*, Fredelle Bruser Maynard's *Raisins and Almonds*, Audrey Thomas's *Songs My Mother Taught Me*, and Munro's *Lives*. In *Lives,* Ada Jordan tries to break out of the traditional role model associated with the mother of the 1930s and 1940s, but is prevented from doing so because of her lack of education. She encourages Del to get educated and thus escape a stifled life in Jubilee. Del's liberation, however, evolves from observing the unliberated lives of the women around her. Gros-Louis comments on the novel as a female *Künstlerroman* and a *Bildungsroman*, and she notes the autobiographical aspects of all four books.

S934.   "'Half a Grapefruit.'" *Magill's Survey of World Literature*. Ed. Frank N. Magill. Vol. 4. New York: Marshall Cavendish, 1993. 1344-1345.

Written for the student and general reader, this brief introduction to "Half a Grapefruit" places it within the context of the *Bildungsroman, Who,* and summarizes the situation of the protagonist in a stage of her quest for self-identity. Preliminary pages give biographical information on Munro, her career, publications, and awards.

S935.   Hampson, Robert. "Johnny Panic and the Pleasures of Disruption." *Re-Reading the Short Story*. Ed. Clare Hanson. Basingstoke, Eng.: Macmillan, 1989. 69-85.

Munro's narrative strategy of disruption and the associated concepts of reader expectations and conflict resolution or non-resolution are examined in a number of stories. In "How I Met My Husband" and "Walking on Water," for example, reader expectation is disrupted in the non-resolution and ambiguities of the stories. The conflict between fiction and truth in "Material" and the evasion of disruptive experiences in "Memorial" are also examined.

S936.   Hanly, Charles. "Autobiography and Creativity: Alice Munro's Story 'Fits.'" *Reflections: Autobiography and Canadian Literature*. Ed. and introd. K. P. Stich. Ottawa: University of Ottawa Press, 1988. 163-174.

Using dream psychology and Freudian psychoanalysis in his discussion, Hanly begins by emphasizing the role of "primary process thought activity" in the imaginative process, and the creation of a more convincing reality than one that is guided by conscious memories and perceptions. In modifying real experiences, Munro makes them her own by bringing them into the realm of her own character and life-shaping unconscious memories and fantasies. Inherent in the creative process then is the element of autobiography. While the protagonist of "Fits" cannot be said to be Munro, she disguises her inner life just as Munro does unconsciously through her creative imagination.

S937. Harris, Margaret. "Authors and Authority in *Lives of Girls and Women.*" *Sydney Studies in English* 12 (1986-1987): 101-113.

Harris explores Del's artistic development and her search for "real life." She makes comparisons between Del and the protagonist of James Joyce's *A Portrait of the Artist as a Young Man*. Del's intense relationship to her experience and her narrative suggest elements of autobiography in the novel. Del challenges and rejects a number of authors and authority figures in the course of her development, among them Tennyson and the Tennysonian heroine admired by her mother, and Uncle Craig and his factual accounts. The mother-daughter relationship and Del's challenge to her mother's authority are discussed.

S938. Harveit, Lars. "Alice Munro and the Canadian Imagination." *A Sense of Place: Essays in Post-Colonial Literatures: The Proceedings of the Gothenburg University Congress of Commonwealth Language and Literature, September 1982.* Ed. Britta Olinder. Gothenburg University Commonwealth Studies. Göteborg: The English Department, Gothenburg University, 1984. 85-90.

Viewing survival as a central concern in Munro's writing, Harveit examines the protagonists in *Lives* and *Who* and their lives in the isolated Canadian towns of Jubilee and Hanratty. Each character lives both inside the town and in its less respectable outer fringes. "The Flats Road" in *Lives* shows Del Jordan's conflicting loyalties to her two homes. Flo in *Who* rejects the social pretense of the town in which Rose lives and goes to school. Despite the negative attitudes held toward education in their restrictive environments, the protagonists see education as a means of escape. For them, survival is a result of adaptation, rebellion, and reconciliation. Harveit comments also on the memoir technique, humour, and storytelling in the two works.

S939. Harvor, Beth. "'My Craft and Sullen Art': The Writers Speak." *Atlantis* 4.1 (Fall 1978): 147-150.

Harvor names twelve women writers she admires, saying she likes "almost all of Alice Munro." She compares two coming-of-age novels, *In an Iron Glove* by Claire Martin and *Lives* by Munro. Contrasting Martin's repressed upbringing with Munro's more liberal one, Harvor concludes that it is because of Munro's more relaxed early environment that she can write so convincingly and in a celebratory way about sex.

S940. He, Miao-bo. "A Pragmatic Perspective of Analyzing Stories—Narrative Implication." *Haerbin Gongye Daxue Xuebao (Shehui Kexue Ban)/Journal of the Harbin Institute of Technology (Social Sciences Edition)* 6.4 July 2004):119-122.

Using as a point of reference the cooperative principle in conversation, Miao-bo He examines how the violation of the cooperative principle produces the narrative implication in "Open Secrets." The analysis of narrative implication provides a pragmatic perspective for understanding the structure and theme of the story. (Based on abstract)

S941. Hedenstrom, Joanne. "Puzzled Patriarchs and Free Women: Patterns in the Canadian Novel." *Atlantis* 4.1 (Fall 1978): 2-9.

By writing about heroines, female Canadian writers are freeing and expanding the roles of women. Hedenstrom illustrates her point by referring to Ada Jordan's rousing speech in *Lives* in which she predicts a change in women's repressed lives.

S942. Heller, Deborah. "Getting Loose: Women and Narration in Alice Munro's *Friend of My Youth*." *Alice Munro Writing On* . . . . Ed. Robert Thacker. Special issue of *Essays on Canadian Writing* 66 (Winter 1998): 60-80.

Rpt. in *The Rest of the Story: Critical Essays on Alice Munro*. Ed. Robert Thacker. Toronto: ECW Press, 1999. 60-80.

Rpt. with minor revisions in *Literary Sisterhoods: Imagining Women Artists*. Montreal: McGill-Queen's University Press, 2005. 69-87.

Heller views the collection as stories about women who "get loose" from the roles expected of them by other characters and by readers. Additionally, some stories "get loose" from the female narrator's knowledge and control. In "Friend of My Youth" for example, both Flora and the narrator's mother escape from the roles expected of them by other characters. Characters like Almeda in "Meneseteung" are freed from the roles readers expect of them in predictable plots. In "Goodness and Mercy," Averill, the narrator, is "let loose" from her own knowledge and control, and thus her story itself "gets loose."

S943. Henderson, Scott. "The Lives of Cousins, Once-Removed: The Strong Familiarity of Being Alice Munro's Relative." *Toronto Star* 6 May 2001: D6.

As the son of Munro's first cousin, Henderson was prompted to write about his personal connection and meeting with Munro after the publication of Sheila Munro's book, *Lives of Mothers and Daughters*. He says that when he reads Alice Munro's fiction, he looks for personal and ancestral landmarks and hidden meaning. "The Progress of Love" and "The Ottawa Valley" both relate to his family past.

S944. Hernáez Lerena, María Jesús. "Fiction as Short-Storyness: Some Textual Strategies in Alice Munro's Narratives." *Revista canaria de estudios ingleses* 36 (1998): 215-229.

Hernáez Lerena examines the elements which distinguish the short story from the novel and ties these to Munro's strategies. Much like the view of life held by Munro, the lives of characters are presented as separate pictures with no interrelating causes or circumstances. Time is evident only in the contrast seen in the character's evolution, as for example in Del, Uncle Craig, and Miss Farris in *Lives*, and Rose and Flo in *Beggar*. Epiphany, another important element in Munro's stories, is discussed for "Material" and several other stories. The last element, the single incident or emotion upon which a story is built, is illustrated in "Carried Away" and "A Wilderness Station."

S945. Hernáez Lerena, María Jesús. "Modulación de mundos imaginarios a través de dos técnicas de presentación del tiempo en *Dance of the Happy Shades*." *Miscelánea: A Journal of English and American Studies* 19 (1998): 57-87.

Hernáez Lerena characterizes the techniques by which Munro presents time in *Dance* as the first-person iterative narrative, alternating with the singular narrative. The iterative technique is found in "Walker Brothers Cowboy," where the adult narrator, speaking in the present tense, talks about the past. Verbal time in the story is discussed. "Images" contains a similar iterative organization, but the verbal time is more complex and contradictory. Other reoccurring characteristics include incidents as repetitions of former events, memory as a synchronous act, and the emphasis on character types. Finally the implication of the iterative mode in Munro's work is considered.

S946. Heward, Burt. "The Enigmatic Alice Munro: Literary Paradox with a Purpose." *Citizen* [Ottawa] 22 November 1982, capital ed.: 41.

After a promotional tour of *Moons*, Munro tells Heward that she likes reading stories that are paradoxical and complex and leading in many directions. She counters the criticism that her new book is gloomy. While Munro admits writing to be exhausting, she continues to write. At public readings, she enjoys the feedback from readers after writing in isolation. Writing a story is not a planned process but based on an evolving vision of the story and its ending. She eschews "fancy prose" and including morals in her writing.

S947. Hill, Heather. "Awards and Acclaim Can't Dull Munro's Charm of Familiarity." *Gazette* [Montreal] 25 September 1986: E1.

Meeting Munro for the first time, Hill finds her comfortably familiar. During the meeting, Munro shares personal thoughts on her writing, describing her anxiety and apprehension after the publication of her books and the fact that she cannot bring herself to read her stories until some time after publication. When reading one of her stories publicly, Munro says she feels personally exposed. Other topics touched on are her writing routine, her compulsion to write, and the importance of writing to her life.

S948. Hiscock, Andrew. "'Longing for a Human Climate': Alice Munro's *Friend of My Youth* and the Culture of Loss." *Journal of Commonwealth Literature* 32.2 (1997): 17-34.

Hiscock studies the dynamic nature of human silences in loss, transience, gaps in knowledge, cultural gaps, discrepancies, and nonfulfillment. These gaps and deficiencies manifest themselves in the many stories examined by Hiscock in *Friend*. Characters are engaged in an abiding quest for order, self-repossession, emancipation, knowledge, and rootedness. In his examination of "Friend of My Youth," for example, Hiscock looks at the mother-daughter relationship and the recognition of loss which is promoted in epiphanic terms in the story. He also considers the silences or the gaps in the mother's past which the narrator-daughter tries to fill.

S949. Hluchy, Patricia. "Maclean's Honour Roll 1998: Alice Munro." *Maclean's* 21 December 1998: 66-67.

Munro describes her method of creating a story as a process of "woolgathering." Hluchy includes biographical details about Munro and information about her Governor General's awards and her recent Giller Prize for *The Love of a Good Woman*.

S950. Horwood, Harold. *Among the Lions: A Lamb in the Literary Jungle*. St. John's, NF: Killick, 2000. 127-132.

Briefly detailing Munro's life, her beginnings as a writer at the age of 11, and her first literary influences, Horwood goes on to outline the publication of her early work, including that of *Dance* by Ryerson. He attributes the book's poor sales to Ryerson's lack of promotion. He also describes Munro's writing habits, her roots in the puritanical and conservative environment of Wingham, and her lack of popularity with the townspeople there.

S951.   Houston, Pam. "A Hopeful Sign: The Making of Metonymic Meaning in Munro's 'Meneseteung.'" *Kenyon Review* 14.4 (Fall 1992): 79-92.

Houston begins by looking at the differences between men and women in their processes of thinking and use of language. She associates with men the metaphoric relationship based on a narrative within a closed and complete system; and with women, the metonymic relationship based on association, proximity, contiguity, and context. In "Meneseteung," Houston examines the metonymic significance of female bodily fluids in relation to human and narrative desire.

S952.   Howells, Coral Ann. "Alice Munro: *Lives of Girls and Women, The Beggar Maid.*" *Private and Fictional Words: Canadian Women Novelists of the 1970s and 1980s.* London: Methuen, 1987. 71-88.

Howells investigates Munro's use of fantasy in these two realistic works. While the framework of the stories remains realistic, the emphasis drifts into fantasy and challenges realism. Munro manages to make the strange coexist with the ordinary, and to make connections between disparate and conflicting events and perceptions. Howells also notes the relationships between female fantasy and love, sexuality, and Gothic romance.

S953.   Howells, Coral Ann. "Alice Munro's Art of Indeterminacy: *The Progress of Love.*" *Modes of Narrative: Approaches to American, Canadian and British Fiction.* Ed. Reingard M. Nischik and Barbara Korte. Würzburg: Königshausen & Neumann, 1990. 141-152.

Munro's narrative method has developed into one of indeterminacy, where multiple contradictory meanings produce unaccounted-for gaps or uncertainties. Instead of the framework of plot, Munro's narratives are composed of spaces and connections, centring around time shifts and shifts in point of view. They re-cover the same ground from different angles. Stories are thus never independent of the teller's interpretation. Howells focuses on "The Progress of Love," "Fits," and "White Dump."

S954.   Howells, Coral Ann. "Alice Munro's Heritage Narratives." *Where Are the Voices Coming From? Canadian Culture and the Legacies of History.* Ed. and introd. Coral Ann Howells. Amsterdam: Rodopi, 2004. 5-14.

Howells looks at Munro's treatment of the Anglo-Canadian colonial inheritance from the feminine perspective. Her analysis highlights the way Munro, through her female characters, explores the indeterminate boundaries between history and fiction, and the impossibility of ever knowing the truth about the past. Family history, local history, the passing of generations, and what they have left behind are examined in "Heirs of the Living Body," "Chaddeleys and Flemings: The Stone in the Field," and "A Wilderness Station."

S955.   Howells, Coral Ann. "Intimate Dislocations: Alice Munro, *Hateship, Friendship, Courtship, Loveship, Marriage.*" *Contemporary Canadian Women's Fiction: Refiguring Identities.* New York: Palgrave Macmillan, 2003. 53-78.

Using Henri Lefebvre's concepts of space, Howells discusses how dislocations in personal space are related to dualities or multiplicities within the individual identity. Personal space, composed of time and place, and identity are discussed in the title story and in "Floating Bridge." In "What Is Remembered," female romantic fantasy is seen as a space which is shut out of reality, and female sexuality and desire as integral to a woman's sense of identity. In "The Bear Came Over the Mountain," the multiplicities of self seen in Fiona combine with shifting subjective locations. The link between jokes, dislocation, and double vision of identity is also discussed.

S956.   Howells, Coral A. "Intimate Dislocations: Buried History and Geography in Alice Munro's Sowesto Stories." *British Journal of Canadian Studies* 14.1 (1999): 7-16.
See associated article by Ingram, David R.

In her spatial and historical discourse of region, Munro writes narrative maps of alternative worlds. In Munro's fiction, Howells discusses geographical place and individual psychic space, a space of enigma, one of fact and fiction. She looks at historical geography, private secret worlds, layering, imagination, and fictive artifice. In her examination of geography, history, and subjective dislocation, Howells refers to "Walker Brothers Cowboy," "Chaddeleys and Flemings," and "What Do You Want to Know For?"

S957.   Howells, Coral Ann. "No Transcendental Image: Canadianness in Contemporary Women's Fictions in English." *British Journal of Canadian Studies* 6.1 (1991): 110-117.

Aritha Van Herk in *No Fixed Address*, Margaret Atwood in *Cat's Eye*, and Munro in "The Progress of Love" show a distinctively Canadian approach by defamiliarizing their characters' relations to culture and landscape. In Munro's story, Howells notes the lack of distinction between the real and the fictional in the documentary surfaces of the story. The narrative contains multiple, shifting meanings and interpretations. The narrator stands on marginal and unfamiliar ground in relation to all the other stories.

S958.   Howells, Coral Ann. "A Question of Inheritance: Canadian Women's Short Stories." *Determined Women: Studies in the Construction of the Female Subject, 1900-90*. Ed. and introd. Jennifer Birkett and Elizabeth Harvey. Savage, MD: Barnes & Noble Books, 1991. 108-120.

Howells examines cultural and literary inheritance in Audrey Thomas's "Crossing the Rubicon," Margaret Atwood's "Bluebeard's Egg," and Munro's "Heirs of the Living Body." In Munro's work, Del, the protagonist, resists and revises her patriarchal inheritance from Uncle Craig and his county history. She tells the stories of women's secret lives within the body of social history, and the dark secrets hidden within the official history written by men.

S959.   Howells, Coral Ann. "Star Maps and Shifting Perspectives: Alice Munro's *The Moons of Jupiter*." *"Union in Partition": Essays in Honour of Jeanne Delbaere*. Ed. and biography Gilbert Debusscher. Ed. Marc Maufort. Liège, Belgium: Université de Liège, English Dept., 1997. 173-180.

Howells says that *Moons* marks a change in Munro's evolving narrative methods. In the new mobility which is seen in the structure, an instability of meaning in a story is complemented by the mobile arrangement of the collection as a whole. Each story structure is based on a centre and orbiting principle. Within an endless process of change in women's lives, there is an image, not of chaos but of order, which is centred on human relationships and connections. Howells discusses "Connection," "The Stone in the Field," and "The Moons of Jupiter."

S960. Howells, Coral Ann. "The Telling of Secrets / The Secrets of Telling: An Overview of Alice Munro's Enigma Variations from *Dance of the Happy Shades* to *Hateship, Friendship, Courtship, Loveship, Marriage*." *Alice Munro: Writing Secrets*. Ed. Héliane Ventura and Mary Condé. Special issue of *Open Letter* 11th ser. 9 (Fall 2003)-12th ser. 1 (Winter 2004): 39-54.

For Munro, secrecy is a way of generating her feminine mode of storytelling and re-discovering a space for the feminine imaginary, a space where women can escape from their gendered roles and expected behaviours. Munro's writing explores the limits of knowledge, glimpses of secrets, and the gaps between the familiar and the unknown and inaccessible. Howells examines Munro's discourse of secrecy in "Oranges and Apples," "Walker Brothers Cowboy," "What Do You Want to Know For?," "Open Secrets," and "Floating Bridge." In the last story, she points out that the secret discourse of resistance is disguised in the form of jokes.

S961. Howells, Coral Ann. "Worlds Alongside: Contradictory Discourses in the Fiction of Alice Munro and Margaret Atwood." *Gaining Ground: European Critics on Canadian Literature*. Ed. Robert Kroetsch and Reingard M. Nischik. Preface Robert Kroetsch. Edmonton: NeWest, 1985. 121-136.

In Margaret Atwood's *Surfacing* and *Bodily Harm* and in Munro's *Lives* and *Who*, the contradictory discourses of fantasy and reality coexist. Fantastic discourse focuses on the accidental, unpredictable, and inexplicable, while realistic discourse focuses on the describable and the intelligible. The protagonists of Munro's books secretly resist female repression while displaying outward conformity. Del and Rose both live in the real world, but also in worlds of fictional fantasy—the Gothic in Del's case and the theatrical in Rose's. This creates tensions for each of them. The female fantasy of falling in love is also discussed in the two works and in "Bardon Bus."

S962. Hoy, Helen. "Alice Munro: 'Unforgettable, Indigestible Messages.'" *Journal of Canadian Studies/Revue d'études canadiennes* 26.1 (Spring 1991): 5-21.

Munro's view of reality is one of multiplicity, indeterminacy, and flux; and one which accommodates all that is contradictory and incongruous about life. She dwells on unresolved contradictions in the lives of her characters who use pretensions, stratagems, concealments, self-deceptions, and evasions. Love is discussed as a means of side-stepping reality, and death as a means to discover another reality. Hoy also looks at Munro's narrative methods and her art of disarrangement. Among the works she examines are *Lives*, *Who*, and "Accident."

S963. Hoy, Helen. "'Dull, Simple, Amazing, and Unfathomable': Paradox and Double Vision in Alice Munro's Fiction." *Studies in Canadian Literature* 5.1 (Spring 1980): 100-115. Accessed 24 April 2006. <http://www.lib.unb.ca/Texts/SCL/vol5_1/Contents.htm>

Rpt. (excluding footnotes and textual refs.) in *Contemporary Literary Criticism*. Ed. Brigham Narins and Deborah A. Stanley. Vol. 95. Detroit: Gale, 1997. 283-289.

Rpt. (excerpt) in *Short Story Criticism: Excerpts from Criticism of the Works of Short Fiction Writers*. Ed. Sheila Fitzgerald. Vol. 3. Detroit: Gale Research, 1989. 335-337.

Hoy sees Munro's method of rhetorical opposition and paradox as a tool in sustaining the theme of the duality of reality. She examines the use of verbal paradox or oxymorons. Hoy also looks at Munro's portrayal of character and emotions, saying that emotions are shown with greater precision and complexity when opposition and paradox are used. The juxtaposition of conflicting realities, such as the real against the romantic, mythic, or illusory worlds, produces a vision where the strange is familiar and the familiar strange. Thus a clearer picture of reality is perceived. *Lives*, *Who*, and stories in *Dance* and *Something* are discussed.

S964. Hoy, Helen. "'Rose and Janet': Alice Munro's Metafiction." *Canadian Literature* 121 (Summer 1989): 59-83.

In a detailed examination of the manuscript of *Who* at Macmillan and the Munro papers at the University of Calgary Library, Hoy traces the extensive revisions made to the book prior to publication. She points out the changes to the arrangement of the stories, the change from the first-person to the third-person point of view, and the addition or exclusion of stories. Hoy illustrates the extent and nature of the revision by comparing the Rose and Janet versions of "Who Do You Think You Are?" She also looks at the American and Canadian publishers' involvement.

S965. Hunter, Adrian. "Story into History: Alice Munro's Minor Literature." *English: The Journal of the English Association* 53 [no. 207] (Autumn 2004): 219-238.

Using concepts from Hélène Cixous, Gilles Deleuze, and Felix Guattari, Hunter examines several stories dealing with female colonial experience to demonstrate Munro's art that places her writing in the category of "minor" literature, or that type of revolutionary and creative writing "which a minority constructs within a major language." Hunter discusses the development of Munro's elliptical and interrogative narrational style and shows how she uses the short story as a counter-narrative to the novel, the historical record, and the feminist revisionary project of reconstructing a female literary tradition in "Heirs of the Living Body," "The Stone in the Field," "Friend of My Youth," and "Meneseteung."

S966. Ingram, David R. "Contemplations on a Set of Maps: A Response to Howell's 'Intimate Dislocations.'" *British Journal of Canadian Studies* 14.1 (1999): 17-20.

Ingram responds to Howell's article by elaborating on the mapping in "What Do You Want to Know For?" He discusses historical geography and the human landscape in terms of settlement in Southwestern Ontario. He looks at the hidden and ignored landscapes in the story.

S967. Irvine, Lorna. "'Changing Is the Word I Want.'" *Probable Fictions: Alice Munro's Narrative Acts*. Ed. Louis MacKendrick. Downsview, ON: ECW Press, 1983. 99-111.

Change and fluidity in Munro's narration are noted in the fluid relationship between order and disorder, stillness and movement, revelation and secrecy. Irvine's discussion focuses on women who are in the process of physical or social transformation and uses examples from *Lives*, "The Ottawa Valley," and "Memorial." Secrecy in women's lives, found in secrets about their bodies, ego boundaries, and social status, is explored in *Lives*, *Dance*, and *Something*. Social transformation and women's bodies are explored in *Who*.

S968. Irvine, Lorna. "Hostility and Reconciliation: The Mother in English Canadian Fiction." *American Review of Canadian Studies* 8.1 (Spring 1978): 56-64.
Irvine studies the maternal past and women's quest for autonomy in the writing of Margaret Laurence, Margaret Atwood, Sylvia Fraser, Marian Engel, and Alice Munro. The article includes one paragraph on the daughter's guilt in Munro's "The Peace of Utrecht."

S969. Irvine, Lorna. "A Psychological Journey: Mothers and Daughters in English-Canadian Fiction." *The Lost Tradition: Mothers and Daughters in Literature*. Ed. Cathy N. Davidson and E. M. Broner. New York: Ungar, 1980. 242-252.
Along with works by Margaret Atwood, Margaret Laurence, and Sylvia Fraser, Irvine examines Munro's "Red Dress—1946," *Lives*, "Boys and Girls," and "The Ottawa Valley." In her study of the psychological aspects of the mother-daughter relationship, Irvine looks at the daughter's struggle for autonomy, her search for female identity, and her ambivalent feelings of anger, guilt, and affection toward her mother.

S970. Irvine, Lorna. "Questioning Authority: Alice Munro's Fiction." *CEA Critic: An Official Journal of the College English Association* 50.1 (Fall 1987): 57-66.
Irvine's article deals with the relationship between gender, authority, and art. Saying that Canada has not been culturally dominated by male ideologies, Irvine looks at the subject of feminism in relation to Canadian nationalism. Turning to the narrators in "Material" and "Memorial," she points out that both women believe art should be "at the mercy" of experience and not an exercise in authority. The first story illustrates the psychological and historical reasons for women's attitude toward authority. In the second story, Irvine concentrates on Eileen's observation of her sister's carefully constructed life.

S971. Irvine, Lorna. "Women's Desire/Women's Power: *The Moons of Jupiter*." *Sub/Version*. Toronto: ECW Press, 1986. 91-110.
Female desire, including sexual desire, is bound up with women's power or lack of it, as Irvine demonstrates in selected stories from *Moons*. In "Connection," the consequence of female desire and independence is loneliness, while in "The Stone in the Field" the loss of desire results in silence. Distancing in love produces power in "Labor Day Dinner," and in "Dulse" the surrender of power to love means the surrender of authority as an author. The narrator of "Bardon Bus" takes pleasure in suffering after the loss of love and power. "Hard-Luck Stories" and "The Moons of Jupiter" display the connections between desire and storytelling or writing.

S972. Jakobsen, Linda. "Alice Munro Prefers the Risk of a Life Filled with Choice." *Post* [Burlington, ON] 24 November 1982: C1.
After the publication of *Moons*, Jacobsen met with Munro on a book promotion tour. Her article includes an overview of the new book and Munro's thoughts on book tours and on the general problems of modern women which are reflected in the book.

S973. Jamieson, Sara. "The Fiction of Agelessness: Work, Leisure, and Aging in Alice Munro's 'Pictures of the Ice.'" *Studies in Canadian Literature* 29.1 (2004): 106-126.
In "Pictures of the Ice," Jamieson explores the problems of physical, social, and economic decline associated with aging, in the context of a contemporary consumptive society. The

ideal of "positive aging" emphasizes self-reliance and the pursuit of personal pleasure and fulfillment in retirement. Jamieson shows how Austin, the aging character in the story, has difficulty forging an identity for himself in old age that is separate from the expectations of modern culture. She points out the significance of visual representations such as photographs, mirrors, and acts of seeing by the younger characters to the way the elderly are perceived. Through the emphasis on deception and surprise, Munro shows the power of visual impressions but at the same time she destabilizes that power.

S974. Jansen, Reamy. "Being Lonely—Dimensions of the Short Story." *Cross Currents* 39.4 (Winter 1989-90): 391-401, 419.

Jansen's article examines male loneliness and isolation in the work of Raymond Carver and in Munro's "Wood." First commenting on the effect of male isolation on the female, Jansen says that men, by their illusory isolation, produce both an attraction for women and at the same time an unhappiness and loneliness in them. "Wood" presents a sustained look into male loneliness. The narrator is a male whose narrative is unmediated by a female observer. Jansen discusses the themes in the story.

S975. Jarrett, Mary. "Women's Bodies in Alice Munro's *The Progress of Love*." *Recherches anglaises et nord-américaines* 22 (1989): 83-88.

Jarrett talks about a number of the stories in the book featuring aging women and their bodies. Aging bodies are often juxtaposed or contrasted with the bodies of younger women, either their own bodies as younger women or those of other characters. Appearing in Jarrett's study are "Lichen," "White Dump," "The Moon in the Orange Street Skating Rink," "A Queer Streak," "Circle of Prayer," and "Fits." Jarrett discusses the male assessment of women's bodies, the significance of interior decoration in the expression of female sensuality, and clothing as a method of concealment of the female body.

S976. Johnson, Brian. "Private Scandals/Public Selves: The Education of a Gossip in *Who Do You Think You Are?*" *Dalhousie Review* 78.3 (Autumn 1998): 415-435.

Johnson considers the book as a *Klatchmaulroman*, or a novel of the education of a gossip. For Rose, the practice of gossip learned from her mother is essential to her self-invention and identity. Gossip gives her power but also promotes self-deception and hypocrisy. "Simon's Luck" is seen as being crucial to the design of the book, because it is a turning point in Rose's development and her dependency on gossip. In the end, Rose finds her power in the rejection of gossip and in her acceptance of the ethic of privacy.

S977. Jones, Michelle. "*Lives of Girls and Women*." *Masterplots II: Women's Literature Series*. Ed. Frank N. Magill. Vol. 4. Pasadena, CA: Salem, 1995. 1335-1339.

In a format and level designed for the reference needs of upper-level students, *Lives of Girls and Women* is discussed under the following headings: "Form and Content" giving an overview of the subject matter; "Analysis" of the themes and ideas; "Context" or the influence of the work and major ideas conveyed. This is followed by a short bibliography, "Sources for Further Reading."

S978. Jones, Michelle. "*The Progress of Love*." *Masterplots II: Women's Literature Series*. Ed. Frank N. Magill. Vol. 5. Pasadena, CA: Salem, 1995. 1896-1899.

In a format and level designed for the reference needs of upper-level students, *The Progress of Love* is discussed under the following headings: "Form and Content" giving an overview of the subject matter; "Analysis" of the themes and ideas; "Context" or the influence of the work and major ideas conveyed. This is followed by a short bibliography, "Sources for Further Reading."

S979.   Kamboureli, Smaro. "The Body as Audience and Performance in the Writing of Alice Munro." *A Mazing Space: Writing Canadian Women Writing*. Ed. Shirley Neuman and Smaro Kamboureli. Edmonton: Longspoon, 1986. 31-38.

Feminine language and discourse speak in the plurality of the female body rather than in the monologue of the male body. Kamboureli examines female body images in "Connections." In *Lives*, she establishes that the female body, as both audience and performer, is the undoing of sexual opposition. Del emerges from her sexual encounters with men with a new language that is feminine.

S980.   Keegan, Alex. "Alice Munro: The Short Answer." *Eclectica Magazine* 2.5 (August/September 1998). 7 pp. Accessed 24 April 2006. <http://www.eclectica.org/v2n5/keegan_munro.html>

Keegan begins by saying that Munro's stories and collections have the range, depth, and elements that are found in novels. Munro achieves this through reduction and compression. He goes on to examine eight qualities in Munro's writing: looseness, separateness, and also interconnectedness in stories, strong autobiographical threads, challenge to the reader's expectations, literary teases, compression, and precision in language. Keegan concludes by saying Munro's work in its totality has an organic wholeness. *Lives*, *Beggar*, and "Differently" are used in the discussion.

S981.   Keith, W. J. "Alice Munro." *A Sense of Style: Studies in the Art of Fiction in English-Speaking Canada*. Toronto: ECW Press, 1989. 155-174.

Munro's style and her paring down of style are examined in stories from *Dance*, *Lives*, *Something*, *Who*, *Moons*, and *Progress*, and in "Working for a Living." Keith notes Munro's movement away from extreme Gothic effects and a shift in the subject matter of the stories. In relation to stories such as "Mischief" and "Royal Beatings," Munro's ambivalence toward making moral judgements is mentioned. The autobiographical aspects of Munro's work are brought out. Keith also examines Munro's stance toward fiction, the artifice of fiction, and fictive reality.

S982.   Keith, W. J. "'Criticism in Practice': John Metcalf's Private Part." *An Independent Stance: Essays on English-Canadian Criticism and Fiction*. Critical Directions. Erin, ON: Porcupine's Quill, 1991. 107-127.

On pages 122 and 123, Keith looks at Munro's influence on Metcalf in the transformation of his autobiographical memoir into the story "The Teeth of My Father." He mentions three of Munro's stories: "The Ottawa Valley," "Winter Wind," and "Home."

S983.   Keith, W. J. "The Post-Modernist Phenomenon and Canadian Literature." *An Independent Stance: Essays on English-Canadian Criticism and Fiction*. Critical Directions. Erin, ON: Porcupine's Quill, 1991. 92-106.

On pages 104 and 105, Keith considers the evolution of the postmodernist elements in Munro's endings. In her early writing, Munro ended her stories neatly with concluding paragraphs. In the 1970s, neat endings were replaced with reflective conclusions on the part of the narrators, as in "The Ottawa Valley" and "Home." Munro progressed to de-constructed stories and endings, and more recently, backs off even this.

S984.   Kelly, Darlene. "Alice Munro's 'Day of the Butterfly': An American Source." *Ariel: A Review of International English Literature* 29.2 (April 1998): 115-128.

Munro's story has many parallels in *The Hundred Dresses* by Eleanor Estes. Kelly begins by looking at Munro's early reading and her imitative writing. She then turns to a discussion of the similarities between the two works in their themes, narrative perspective, and characters.

S985.   Kilpatrick, Ken. "Alice Munro Talks about Her Life." *Hamilton Spectator* 9 December 1978, city ed.: 74.

In this edited interview, Munro briefly talks about her early life in Wingham, her father and his book, the beginnings of her writing at age 11, her writing schedule, the prepublication changes to *Who*, her income as a writer, her work in Munro's Book Store, classism in the small town, and publication in *The New Yorker*.

S986.   Kirchhoff, H. J. "Alice Munro: Her Unadorned but Rich Portraits of Small-Town Ontario Allow Plenty of Room for Reading between the Lines." *Globe and Mail* 28 April 1990: C1.

This piece includes brief quotes from an interview covering Munro's feelings about success and publicity, her writing and revision process, honesty in writing, the short-story genre, and the Huron County setting.

S987.   Kloss, Robert J. "The Problem of Who One Really Is: The Functions of Sexual Fantasy in Stories of Atwood, Lispector, and Munro." *Journal of Evolutionary Psychology* 20: 3 & 4 (August 1999): 227-234.

Referring to Clarice Lispector's "Pig Latin," Margaret Atwood's "Rape Fantasies," and Munro's "Wild Swans," Kloss asserts that the rape or sexual fantasies of the female characters reveal depths of character previously undisclosed. In Munro's story, he points out the swan as a symbol of sexual desire and the tendency of women to imagine themselves as objects in sexual fantasy. Rose's ambivalence, in her desire to be both victim and accomplice in the fantasy, is seen to have a positive, lasting effect. In distancing herself in the sexual encounter and abandoning herself to the experience, Rose achieves power and independence from Victorian suppression.

S988.   Knelman, Martin. "The Past, the Present and Alice Munro." *Saturday Night* November 1979: 16-18, 20, 22.

Knelman describes Munro's changes to *Who* at the press stage. He mentions the use of southwestern Ontario in Munro's settings and the relationship of the urban present to Munro's rural past. He notes the development of her writing from youth to the present.

S989.   Kröller, Eva-Marie. "The Eye in the Text: Timothy Findley's *The Last of the Crazy People* and Alice Munro's *Lives of Girls and Women*." *World Literature Written in*

English 23.2 (Spring 1984): 366-374.

Various forms of seeing have the effect of undermining the realistic surface in the narratives of the two books. Both deal with the I/eye of the adolescent character whose perception impacts on her personal growth. In *Lives*, where the realistic surface is seen to constantly reassemble itself, Del attempts to translate her visual perception into writing. Kröller also examines words as the representation of objects, and the worlds of words that are found in the homes of Uncle Benny and Uncle Craig.

S990. Kustec, Aleksander. "Unravelling the Mystery of Reality: Typical Canadian Elements in the Short Stories of Alice Munro." *Acta Neophilologica* 31 (1998): 105-114.

Kustec begins with Munro's style and her heightened realism. He then looks at the unconventional structure of her stories, and at the short-story cycles in *Lives* and *Who*. Rather than concentrating on plot, Munro focuses her attention on characters which Kustec categorizes as round, flat, dynamic, and static. He also examines Munro's techniques of direct and indirect characterization and her retrospective narrative technique. Other elements in Munro's writing which Kustec discusses are the presence of absurdity, Canadian subjects and themes, regionalism, local speech, and elements of realism and fantasy.

S991. Lacombe, Michèle. "'Strips of Rough Linoleum' Revisited: Reconsidering Realism in the Works of Alice Munro." *Alice Munro: Writing Secrets*. Ed. Héliane Ventura and Mary Condé. Special issue of *Open Letter* 11th ser. 9 (Fall 2003)-12th ser. 1 (Winter 2004): 211-229.

Lacombe uses feminist psychoanalytical theory to examine the working-class perspective in Munro's work, particularly in "Heirs of the Living Body" and "Post and Beam." The discussion begins with a look at post-structuralism and the metafictional elements in the stories. In "Heirs of the Living Body," Lacombe studies women's secrecy, identity, power or lack of it, and the attainment of power through language. In "Post and Beam," the discussion centres around family secrets, sexuality, and female sexual identity.

S992. Lamont-Stewart, Linda. "Order from Chaos: Writing as Self-Defense in the Fiction of Alice Munro and Clark Blaise." *The Art of Alice Munro: Saying the Unsayable*. Papers from the Waterloo Conference. Ed. Judith Miller. Waterloo, ON: University of Waterloo Press, 1984. 113-121.

The two authors are very similar in their perception and approach to reality. In examining the texture of reality through their realistic presentation of surface details, they uncover the absurdity and horror beneath the surface of life. The only protection from these is irony. Lamont-Stewart examines ironic distancing found in "An Ounce of Cure." She also discusses *Lives*, "The Ottawa Valley" and "Winter Wind," and points out the use of writing and fiction in these works as a means of understanding, managing, or controlling life. The irony rests in the inadequacy of fiction to do these things.

S993. Laurence, Jocelyn. "Munro, Exploring Disguises." *Chatelaine* November 1978: 67, 116.

Munro tells Jocelyn Laurence that she believes the complexities in people's lives are revealed in the ordinary. Women use disguises in life so often that they become commonplace. Munro says that her work is personal, but that she is essentially a private person.

S994. Laurence, Margaret. Letter to Alice Munro dated 29 January 1981. *A Very Large Soul: Selected Letters from Margaret Laurence to Canadian Writers*. Ed., pref. and introd. J. A. Wainwright. Dunvegan, ON: Cormorant Books, 1995. 142-143.

Laurence bemoans the poor treatment Canadian women writers (including herself and Munro) received in an article published in an English magazine. Following the letter, Munro contrasts Laurence's wounded reaction to the censorship of her books with her own, which is more detached.

S995. Laurence, Margaret. Letter to Alice Munro dated 26 March 1981. *A Very Large Soul: Selected Letters from Margaret Laurence to Canadian Writers*. Ed., pref. and introd. J. A. Wainwright. Dunvegan, ON: Cormorant Books, 1995. 144.

Laurence tells Munro that she is beginning a new novel and gives details about her writing regime. Following the letter, Munro comments on Laurence's strong sense of public obligation.

S996. Lawson, Neroli. "Putting the Picture Straight." *Times* [London] 15 October 1990: 17.

Basing her article on an interview with Munro, Lawson begins with general comments on Munro's writing and then gives details about her life and her writing career. Munro briefly shares her thoughts on relationships with men, motherhood, multiple viewpoints, and her process of writing.

S997. Lecercle, Jean-Jacques. "Alice Munro's Two Secrets." *Alice Munro: Writing Secrets*. Ed. Héliane Ventura and Mary Condé. Special issue of *Open Letter* 11th ser. 9 (Fall 2003)-12th ser. 1 (Winter 2004): 23-37.

Lecercle defines two types of secrets in modern literature: one which is concealed and provokes a strong impulse to discover and one which is indifferent to revelation. In "Hateship, Friendship, Loveship, Courtship, Marriage," he looks at the temporality of secrecy. In "Miles City, Montana," the temporal structure of the story is also examined, but Lecercle sees the secret in this story lying in the mystery of otherness. In "Fits," the two types of secrets are present, the first being embodied in the main character. The meaning is elusive and does not provide any form of closure.

S998. Lecker, Robert. "Machines, Readers, Gardens: Alice Munro's 'Carried Away.'" *Alice Munro Writing On . . . .* Ed. Robert Thacker. Special issue of *Essays on Canadian Writing* 66 (1998): 103-127.

Rpt. in *The Rest of the Story: Critical Essays on Alice Munro*. Ed. Robert Thacker. Toronto: ECW Press, 1999. 103-127.

Reading and writing, the dominant features of the story, are historically conditioned acts that help people define themselves in their communities and in their particular time. Lecker examines the four parts of the story and the situations of the three main characters. He comments on the historical circumstances during the time covered in the story, showing how postwar industrialism destroyed the sense of community and identity and created a machine-conscious and commodity-based system of values. It also produced a literary consciousness.

S999. Levene, Mark. "'It Was about Vanishing': A Glimpse of Alice Munro's Stories." *University of Toronto Quarterly* 68.4 (Fall 1999): 841-860.

Levene notes a change in Munro's later stories which are marked by the connection between "vanishing" and the spatial, rather than temporal, character of the narrative. He discusses narrative space in relation to survival and vanishing, the possibility and habitation of space, the appearance, disappearance, and reappearance of re-formed figures, and spaces filled with familiar objects and open secrets. Levene examines Munro's books and many of her stories in chronological order from "Walker Brother's Cowboy" to "My Mother's Dream." He also discusses the structure of *Lives* and *Something*, and the change in Munro's writing found in her sombreness of mood and in the introduction of gaps, complexity, and multiplicity.

S1000. Lilienfeld, Jane. "Shirking the Imperial Shadow: Virginia Woolf and Alice Munro." *Woolf Studies Annual* 10 (2004): 253-274.

In an examination of the similarities in the lives and the writing of Woolf and Munro, Lilienfeld shows how Munro, a "dominion/ated writer," continues the legacy of Virginia Woolf, the British anti-imperialist. Looking first at commonalities between the writers, Lilienfeld details their social backgrounds, their family structures, and their relationships with their sick mothers. Lilienfeld then suggests that Munro has been influenced by Woolf's "Modern Fiction," specifically in her focus on consciousness rather than plot, the multilayering of narrative voices, the feminist critique of the "marriage plot," and the random event. She looks at two of Munro's stories, "How I Met My Husband" and "Accident."

S1001. Lilienfeld, Jane. "'Something I've Been Meaning To Tell You': Alice Munro as Unlikely Heir to Virginia Woolf." *Virginia Woolf Out of Bounds: Selected Papers from the Tenth Annual Conference on Virginia Woolf*. Ed. Jessica Berman and Jane Goldman. New York: Pace University Press, 2001. 92-96.

Lilienfeld looks at Virginia Woolf's influence on Munro in the story "How I Met My Husband." Munro, like Woolf, uses the polyvocal voice in the narrator, and multilayering in the discourse. The story is one of the female experience and is a feminist critique of the romantic view of marriage.

S1002. Lostanlen, Claire. "Le défi dans *The Progress of Love* d'Alice Munro." *Défi/challenge dans le roman canadien de langue française et de langue anglaise*. Comp. Jacques Leclaire. Cahiers de l'I.P.E.C. 4; Collection de l'A.F.E.C. 4. Rouen: Université de Rouen, 1994. 155-161.

Many of the protagonists in the stories discussed take stock of their lives by looking back at the past. But they must defy the past in order to better face the future. The notion of strong will and determination is a dominant thread. In the title story, for example, Lostanlen looks at how the protagonist adjusts her memories to support what she wishes to believe is the truth. Her defiance is in maintaining this new truth.

S1003. "*The Love of a Good Woman* (Discussion guide)." *Reading Group Center*. n.d. Vintage Books-Random House. Accessed 24 April 2006. <http://www.randomhouse.com/vintage/read/goodwoman/>

A general overview of the collection is provided, along with a discussion guide for educators and students. The discussion guide contains questions to stimulate discussion for each story.

S1004. Lozar, Tomaz. "Alice Munro's *Friend of My Youth* Read on the Sly." *Literature, Culture and Ethnicity: Studies on Medieval, Renaissance and Modern Literatures*. A Festschrift for Janez Stanonik. Ed. Mirko Jurak. Ljubljana: Dept. of English, Filozofska Fakulteta, Znanstveni Inštitut, 1992. 133-139.

Through the lenses of feminism and puritanism, Lo•ar looks at political correctness in Munro's treatment of sex in three of the stories in the collection. In the title story, Lo•ar makes the contrast between the mother's sexually repressed version of Flora's story and the daughter's more vital sexual interpretation. At a time when it was politically incorrect to do so, Munro celebrates men in the person of Robert Deal. Political correctness and the sexual aspects of "Oranges and Apples" and "Differently" are also discussed. Lo•ar says that sexual repression is the product of patriarchal authoritarian societies.

S1005. Lynch, Gerald. "No Honey, I'm Home: Place Over Love in Alice Munro's Short Story Cycle, *Who Do You Think You Are?*" *Canadian Literature* 160 (Spring 1999): 73-98. Rpt. (revised) as "No Honey, I'm Home: Alice Munro's *Who Do You Think You Are?*" in *The One and the Many: English-Canadian Short Story Cycles*. Toronto: University of Toronto Press, 2001. 159-181.

Lynch examines the connection between identity formation, place, and love. The role of love in Rose's search for identity is explored in her relationships with men, particularly in "Mischief." Rather than finding her identity in love, Rose discovers herself through Ralph Gillespie, who brings her back to her place of origin. In his analysis, Lynch elaborates on the symbolism and motifs of honey and sweets found throughout the book. He examines the structure of *Who* as a short-story cycle, noting dynamic patterns of recurrence and development that link the stories together, and individual stories which mimic the shape and movement of the whole cycle.

S1006. Lynch, Gerald. "The One and the Many: English-Canadian Short Story Cycles." *Canadian Literature* 130 (Autumn 1991): 91-104.
Rpt. (revised) as "The One and the Many: Canadian Short Story Cycles" in *The Tales We Tell: Perspectives on the Short Story*. Ed. Barbara Lounsberry, et al. Westport, CT: Greenwood Press, 1998. 35-45.

Munro's *Who* is discussed within the context of other important Canadian short-story cycles. Lynch believes that the cycle form is geopolitically appropriate to Canadian writing. On pages 100 and 101, he examines the cumulative function of the concluding stories in Rose's quest for self and identity.

S1007. MacDonald, Rae McCarthy. "A Madman Loose in the World: The Vision of Alice Munro." *Modern Fiction Studies* 22.3 (Autumn 1976): 365-374.
Rpt. (with minor omission and excluding footnotes and textual refs.) in *Short Story Criticism: Excerpts from Criticism of the Works of Short Fiction Writers*. Ed. Sheila Fitzgerald. Vol. 3. Detroit: Gale Research, 1989. 328-331.

MacDonald discusses the double vision found in Munro's first three books, *Dance*, *Lives*, and *Something*. This vision is seen in the tensions between two sets of values, two ways of seeing, and two worlds in the stories "Dance of the Happy Shades," "Day of the Butterfly," "Thanks for the Ride," and "The Time of Death." In *Lives*, the distinction between the world and "the other country" is central. MacDonald identifies Et in "Something I've Been Meaning to Tell You" as a guilty garrison figure. "Winter Wind" is a story which illustrates the price of social conformity.

S1008. MacDonald, Rae McCarthy. "Structure and Detail in *Lives of Girls and Women*." *Studies in Canadian Literature* 3.2 (Summer 1978): 199-210. Accessed 10 May 2006. <http://www.lib.unb.ca/Texts/SCL/vol3_2/Contents.htm>
Rpt. in *Modern Canadian Fiction*. Comp. Carole Gerson. 2nd rev. ed. Richmond, BC: Open Learning Institute, 1980. 175-182.

In a chapter-by-chapter analysis of the book, MacDonald follows Del's search for a livable compromise between the "normal" world which she labels the "garrison of survivors," and the world of misfits and eccentrics, or "the other country." She focuses on the series of parallel crises Del experiences from chapter to chapter, and on the mass of details surrounding them. The crises divert Del's attention away from the details of everyday life which are the real threat to her goal of achieving selfhood and identity.

S1009. Macfarlane, David. "Writer in Residence." *Saturday Night* 101 (December 1986): 51-52, 54, 56.

Macfarlane profiles Munro's life, career, and writing, after personal and telephone interviews with the author. He notes concealment as an integral part of her writing and life, particularly as a female writer with family obligations. Also discussed are the use of time and the growing complexity of Munro's work, specifically in *Progress*. Munro comments on several stories in the book, and explains her current preference for writing personal rather than objective stories.

S1010. Macpherson, Heidi Slettedahl. "Escaping the Home of Youth." *Escape as Transgression in North American Feminist Fiction*. Amsterdam; Atlanta, GA: Rodopi, 2000. 103-105.

Both protagonists in *Lives* and *Who* seek to escape the stifling atmosphere of the isolated Ontario communities in which they live. In *Lives*, Del observes both the female and male characters around her who are trapped, for example Uncle Benny, Madeleine, and Ada Jordan, who cannot escape the role of outsider in the town. Del seeks escape through religion, education, and sex. Rose also has the urge to escape from Hanratty, but is also drawn back. The significance of storytelling, education, and marriage as forms of escape for females is covered.

S1011. Mallet, Gina. "A Good Time to Be a Canadian Writer." *Toronto Star* 20 October 1981: F1, F3.

Mallet gives a personality profile of Munro. In her interview with Mallet, Munro talks about the short story as a genre, about being a female writer, getting published in *The New Yorker*, and being recognized as a Canadian writer.

S1012. Mallinson, Jean. "Alice Munro's *The Progress of Love*." *West Coast Review* 21.3 (Winter 1987): 52-58.

In this review essay, Mallinson examines the stories and their narrative structure and patterns. She also looks at the strategies and devices used by Munro, including ellipsis, embedding, and layering of perspectives. Ellipsis is found in "The Moon in the Orange Street

Skating Rink" and "A Queer Streak." Analogy is used as a structural basis in "Miles City, Montana" and "Eskimo." Mallinson goes on to discuss the use of the metaphor in "Lichen," double-meaning and image in "Monsieur les Deux Chapeaux," imagery in "White Dump," patterns in "Circle of Prayer," and the strange and familiar in "Fits."

S1013.   Martin, Peggy. "'What a Pathetic Old Tart': Alice Munro's Older Women." *English Studies in Canada* 24.1 (March 1998): 83-92.

Martin says that Munro resists the social norms which place value on women according to their age and class, and that she revalues middle-aged women in her stories. The stories chosen for this study centre around the female experience from the perspective of middle age. Martin considers how sensory perception, language, and memory establish community between these women in "Connection," "The Stone in the Field," "Hold Me Fast, Don't Let Me Pass," and "The Jack Randa Hotel." For the last story, Martin provides a detailed dictional analysis.

S1014.   Martin, W. R. "Alice Munro and James Joyce." *Journal of Canadian Fiction* 24 (1979): 120-126.

Similarities between Joyce's *The Dubliners* and Munro's *Dance* are used by Martin to show the influence of the Irish writer on Munro. He compares their common intents to recreate their places of origin, Dublin and Jubilee (Wingham, Ont.). Martin also examines the Joycean influence on the structure, theme, and style in *Dance*. He points out the external and emotional similarities between Joyce's "The Dead" and Munro's "Dance of the Happy Shades," and shows parallels in the juxtaposition of the last two stories in each collection. Turning to Munro's *Lives*, Martin says that the novel is a *Bildungsroman* much like Joyce's *A Portrait of the Artist as a Young Man*, but that the Joycean influence is not as obvious. This shows Munro coming into her own as a writer.

S1015.   Martin, W. R. "Family Relations in Alice Munro's Fiction." *New Quarterly: New Directions in Canadian Writing* 7.1-2 (Spring-Summer 1987): 247-254.

Martin looks at the different types of relationships in families. He begins with family division in one of Munro's early stories, "At the Other Place." He proceeds by examining the relationships between sisters in "The Peace of Utrecht," between cousins in "The Moon in the Orange Street Skating Rink," and between husband and wife in "Labor Day Dinner." The complex family relationships found in *Lives* and *Who* are also examined.

S1016.   Martin, W. R. "Hanging Pictures Together: *Something I've Been Meaning to Tell You*." *The Art of Alice Munro: Saying the Unsayable.* Papers from Waterloo Conference. Ed. Judith Miller. Waterloo, ON: University of Waterloo Press, 1984. 21-34. Rpt. revised and expanded in *Alice Munro: Paradox and Parallel*. W. R. Martin. Edmonton: University of Alberta Press, 1987. 1-13.

The double vision that informs Munro's narrative method can also be seen in the arrangement of the stories in *Something*. The groupings and patterns that are a part of Munro's method and style are characterized by contrasts and paradoxes which are interwoven with similarities and parallels. Martin analyses the juxtaposition of the stories, the contrapuntal structure, and the interplay of similarities and differences. He concludes with comments on Munro's skills and her preference for the short-story genre.

S1017. Martin, W. R. "The Strange and the Familiar in Alice Munro." *Studies in Canadian Literature* 7.2 (1982): 214-226. Accessed 24 April 2006. <http://www.lib.unb.ca/Texts/SCL/vol7_2/Contents.htm>

Martin explains the concepts of the strange and familiar in Munro's writing. By the use of vivid images and scenes, Munro makes concepts which are cloudy or "strange" seem familiar and real. On the other hand, common and familiar incidents are invested with surprise meanings and insights which make them appear less familiar and even strange. Martin examines these features in "Walker Brothers Cowboy," "The Flats Road," "Heirs of the Living Body," and "Royal Beatings."

S1018. Martin, W. R. and Warren U. Ober. "Alice Munro as Small Town Historian: 'Spaceships Have Landed.'" *Alice Munro Writing On....* Ed. Robert Thacker. Special issue of *Essays on Canadian Writing* 66 (Winter 1998): 128-146.
Rpt. in *The Rest of the Story: Critical Essays on Alice Munro*. Ed. Robert Thacker. Toronto: ECW Press, 1999. 128-146.

Martin and Warren explore the method by which Munro is able to transform a small fictional town in Ontario to a universal archetype. They point out the various classical literary allusions found in the stories of *Friend* and *Open*, and say that these place the small-town settings in a world context. Carstairs, the setting of most of the stories in *Open*, is seen to change over time. However, despite these changes, the town retains its mythical and archetypal status, especially in the story "Spaceships Have Landed." The revisions made to the story before publication in *Paris Review* are described. The authors analyse the archetypal images, figures, and themes in the story.

S1019. Martin, W. R. and Warren U. Ober. "Alice Munro's 'Hold Me Fast, Don't Let Me Pass' and 'Tam Lin.'" *ANQ: A Quarterly Journal of Short Articles, Notes, and Reviews* 13.3 (Summer 2000): 44-48.

While the authors see parallels between Munro's story and the old Scottish ballad "Tam Lin," they say that Munro turns the ballad upside down. Whereas the ballad is the story of a fairy who moves into the human world, Munro's narrative involves the transition from the mundane human world of the town to the world of the fairies in the remote Scottish highlands.

S1020. Martin, W. R. and Warren U. Ober. "The Comic Spirit in Alice Munro's *Open Secrets*: 'A Real Life' and 'The Jack Randa Hotel.'" *Studies in Short Fiction* 35.1 (Winter 1998): 41-47.

The comedy in the two stories comes in the form of satire, irony, and humour. In "A Real Life," satire and irony are directed at the characters of Muriel and Millicent. The comedy is based on the contrast between bourgeois and rural life. "The Jack Randa Hotel" contains high comedy. A farcical comedy is seen on the surface but operates on a deeper level. Martin and Warren conclude the article with a look at the farcical elements of the story's title.

S1021. Martin, W. R. and Warren U. Ober. "A Misreading Corrected." *Canadian Notes & Queries* 53.1 (1998): 26-29.

Martin and Warren disagree with Carrington's view, in her article "Double-Talking Devils," that Annie is a double-talking devil who consciously lies and confuses the perception of others and is, in a sense, Munro's alter ego. They argue that the murder in the story is based on historical facts from the social history of Huron County and Munro's own family history. They conclude that Annie is not a liar, but a genuine Canadian pioneer woman.

S1022.   Matchan, Linda. "Alice Munro: From the Ontario Hinterlands to The Moons of Jupiter." *Boston Globe* 25 May 1983: 69, 73.
   Reprinted as "Canadian Applauded in U.S. but Munro Shuns 'Literary Life'" in *Gazette* [Montreal] 4 June 1983: I1.

Reporting on an interview with Munro, Matchan gives her impressions of Munro as a person and talks of the style and subject matter of her writing. In the interview, Munro describes the conservative Presbyterian environment in which she grew up in Huron County. Speaking about her writing, she says that some aspects of herself can be found in her characters. She says that with age writing becomes more difficult, but that there is greater freedom. She is no longer obsessed with being a first-rank author.

S1023.   Mathews, Lawrence. "'Who Do You Think You Are?': Alice Munro's Art of Disarrangement." *Probable Fictions: Alice Munro's Narrative Acts*. Ed. Louis K. MacKendrick. Downsview, ON: ECW Press, 1983. 181-193.

Mathews demonstrates Munro's distrust of aesthetic pattern in this examination of her use of disarrangement. Using three stories from *Who* ("Royal Beatings," "Mischief," and "Who Do You Think You Are?"), Mathews shows how disruptions in the pattern of Rose's narrative are accomplished by the insertion of "new chunks of information" in the story epilogues, and in characters, situations, and anecdotes which are not necessary to the development of the narrative but bear a thematic relation to it. The balance of surface detail and disarrangement reflects Munro's vision of reality, in which truth can only be partial and provisional.

S1024.   May, Charles E. "Why Does Alice Munro Write Short Stories?" *Wascana Review of Contemporary Poetry and Short Fiction* 38.1 (Spring 2003): 16-28.

Munro's notion that there is "a short-story way" of seeing reality leads May to investigate why Munro chose the historically underrated genre of short fiction. He distills from Munro's remarks in various interviews her poetic of short fiction. Her work is characterized by the elements of tension, control, mood, emotion, mystery, secret self, and the refusal to explain. Focusing on *Love* and *Hateship*, May shows how complexity is achieved through Munro's way of seeing the world in "a short-story way" rather than through multiplicity of characters, context, and plots as in novels.

S1025.   Mayberry, Katherine J. "'Every Last Thing . . . Everlasting': Alice Munro and the Limits of Narrative." *Studies in Short Fiction* 29.4 (Fall 1992): 531-541.
   Rpt. (excluding footnotes, textual refs. and works cited) in *Contemporary Literary Criticism*. Ed. Brigham Narins and Deborah A. Stanley. Vol. 95. Detroit: Gale, 1997. 315-319.

The storytelling of the narrators in Munro's fiction is always inadequate because of the incongruence between their experiences and their narratives. Their storytelling is further complicated by the mediation of their memories. Mayberry discusses the relationship between truth and narrative, and between knowing and telling. She characterizes the narrators in *Moons* as women who are groping for the knowledge of "an unknowable male other" through their stories. "Hard-Luck Stories" and "Visitors" are discussed.

S1026. Mayberry, Katherine J. "Narrative Strategies of Liberation in Alice Munro." *Studies in Canadian Literature/Études en littérature canadienne* 19.2 (1994): 57-66. Accessed 10 May 2006. <http://www.lib.unb.ca/Texts/SCL/vol19_2/Contents.htm>

Mayberry studies the narrative methods used by Munro's female characters in *Moons* in their effort to arrive at the truth and thus reconstitute themselves within relationships. The successful narratives are often multivoiced and reach a consensual version of the truth. In "Dulse," Mayberry examines the misuse of narrative by the protagonist who does not gain the truth about her failed relationship. The two narrators in "Hard-Luck Stories" have different motives; one tells her story to fend off experience, the second to truthfully render experience. In "The Moons of Jupiter," father and daughter jointly participate in the narrative to arrive at the truth.

S1027. McCaig, JoAnn. "Alice Munro's Agency: The Virginia Barber Correspondence, 1976-83." *Alice Munro Writing On....* Ed. Robert Thacker. Special issue of *Essays on Canadian Writing* 66 (Winter 1998): 81-102.
Rpt. in *The Rest of the Story: Critical Essays on Alice Munro*. Ed. Robert Thacker. Toronto: ECW Press, 1999. 81-102.

McCaig used the correspondence of Munro's literary agent, Virginia Barber, to study the development of Munro's authorship and authority. She notes Munro's early career in Canada, where Robert Weaver acted as her literary mentor. Munro's career in the United States was promoted by the Virginia Barber Agency. The female author/literary agent relationship of Munro and Barber is discussed, along with their financial and fiduciary association. McCaig considers the handicaps of gender and nationality within the patriarchal literary culture. She looks at Munro's publication in *The New Yorker* and gives details of the publication history of *Who*, showing that the novel is a more popular genre in the United States than the short story.

S1028. McCaig, JoAnn. "Obscure Canadian Essayist Responds: CanLit Controversy." Letter. *National Post* 1 July 2000: B8, B12.

McCaig responds to the controversy initiated by John Metcalf's article in which he quotes from her essay regarding Robert Weaver's role in Munro's career. She clarifies and defends her position, maintaining that while Robert Weaver played a very important part in Munro's career in Canada, he was much less effective than Virginia Barber in promoting her work in the United States. She also responds to Munro's criticism of her essay (see entries P656 and S1045).

S1029. McCaig, JoAnn. "The Uses of Disenchantment." *Relocating Praise: Literary Modalities and Rhetorical Contexts*. Ed. Alice G. den Otter. Toronto: Canadian Scholars' Press, 2000. 145-151.

McCaig claims that the aim of her doctoral thesis was not to praise Munro, but to demonstrate her career as a sociohistorical, cultural phenomenon. Her original thesis concluded with praise for Munro, but McCaig says that she received negative reaction from her colleagues, both for the inclusion of praise and for situating the author as a sociohistorical entity. McCaig disagrees and argues that there should be room in the academic world for praise that is "educated."

S1030. McCarthy, Dermot. "The Woman Out Back: Alice Munro's 'Meneseteung.'" *Studies in Canadian Literature/Études en littérature canadienne* 19.1 (1994): 1-19. Accessed 10 May 2006. <http://www.lib.unb.ca/Texts/SCL/vol19_1/Contents.htm>

The protagonist of the story is situated in a Victorian patriarchal society. But she rejects a place in that society and chooses instead to live a life of marginality, viewed as an eccentric female. By the end of the story, a disarrangement occurs which puts into question everything that comes before. In the process of rewriting Almeda's story, the narrator of the present gradually merges with the character of the past. McCarthy elaborates on the symbolism in the story and on the use of the poetic, journalistic, and photographic texts of the past. She interprets Almeda's breakdown as a liberation and a triumph.

S1031. McCombs, Judith. "'From Listening to the Stories of Others, We Learn to Tell Our Own': Southern Ontario Gothic in Alice Munro's 'Wilderness Station' and *Alias Grace*." *Margaret Atwood Society Newsletter* Fall-Winter 1999: 32-33.

McCombs views Munro's story as an influence on Atwood's novel. The works bear striking similarities. Both are set in the southern Ontario Gothic; murders occur; their structures are epistolary; multiple and simultaneously true and false testimonies are given; the stories remain unsolved; and Bluebeard archetypes are used.

S1032. McCombs, Judith. "Searching Bluebeard's Chambers: Grimm, Gothic, and Bible Mysteries in Alice Munro's 'The Love of a Good Woman.'" *American Review of Canadian Studies* 30.3 (Autumn 2000): 327-348.

McCombs associates Bluebeard archetypes from Grimm's tales "Fitcher's Bird" and "The Robber Bridegroom" with the four main characters of the story. She studies the symbolism, imagery, and the themes of sex and death in the story. Gothic elements are shown to share similarities with those in the Gothic story of *Jane Eyre*. Elements from the biblical myth of Saul are also found in the story. Munro's techniques and elusive clues involve the reader in a search to solve a mystery.

S1033. McDougall, Joyce. "The Truth behind Alice Munro's Tales." Letter. *Wingham Advance-Times* 22 December 1981: 9.

The writer of this letter says she is one of Munro's former friends and neighbours in the town of Wingham, Ontario. She is upset about the comments attributed to Munro in an article by Wayne Grady published on December 5th in *Today Magazine*. Unlike the community of "bootleggers, prostitutes and hangers-on" described by Munro, McDougall says that Wingham is a town made up of hardworking, moral, and respectable people.

S1034. McGill, Robert. "Somewhere I've Been Meaning To Tell You: Alice Munro's Fiction of Distance." *Journal of Commonwealth Literature* 37.1 (April 2002): 9-29.

Munro writes stories of rural Ontario for a distant audience. McGill discusses Munro's geographic metafiction and "the fiction of distance," which calls attention to spatial difference. Using "Something I've Been Meaning to Tell You" and a number of different stories to illustrate his discussion, McGill examines rural-urban relations and the performance of place. He also discusses the learning of place, the relationships between author, reading, and text, real and fictional places, and familiar places turned foreign or unfamiliar.

S1035. McGill, Robert. "Where Do You Think You Are? Alice Munro's Open Houses." *Mosaic* 35.4 (December 2002): 103-119.
In this study of fictional space in "Vandals," McGill first begins with a consideration of geographical metafiction and the concepts of geography or place, and space. He looks at the house as a metonym for fiction. Space is considered in terms of gender: male power and female marginalization. The house is a place where women are confined. McGill also discusses the reading of landscape as text, stasis, and mobility in space, and the process of deterritorialization by the reader. Munro's narrative techniques in relation to these are examined.

S1036. McGoogan, Kenneth. "Munro Remains Nation's Short-Story Queen." *Calgary Herald* 19 November 1986: C1.
Writing this article shortly after the publication of *Progress*, McGoogan discusses Munro's status as a short-story writer, gives biographical information on the author and mentions *Lives* as being the most appealing of Munro's books. He comments on her latest book.

S1037. McKinnon, Jean D. "Munro's Books Are Unfair to Wingham." Letter. *Wingham Advance-Times* 9 March 1983: 4.
The writer of this letter says she was born and educated in Wingham and is proud of the town, which produced many professional people. She claims that she can identify many local people in Munro's stories, although their names are fictitious. She questions why Munro cannot write more positively about the town and its people.

S1038. McMullen, Lorraine. "'Shameless, Marvellous, Shattering Absurdity': The Humour of Paradox in Alice Munro." *Probable Fictions: Alice Munro's Narrative Acts*. Ed. Louis MacKendrick. Downsview, ON: ECW Press, 1983. 144-162.
McMullen shows paradox to be central to the structural, technical, or linguistic attitude in Munro's writing. Humour and wit are found in the form of bizarre or grotesque characters, or in farcical situations. Munro, however, goes beyond the superficiality of the humourous or comedic to show a doubling of perspective. She examines the comic devices of verbal wit, satire, and irony, along with the coexistence of the bizarre and farcical with the ordinary, in characters and situations in *Lives*, *Who*, and "An Ounce of Cure."

S1039. McNeilly, Anne. "Happiness Depends on Viewpoint." *Kitchener-Waterloo Record* 17 February 1979: 74.
Canadian Press article reprinted in many Canadian newspapers under different titles. McNeilly interviewed Munro and, in this article, records Munro's thoughts on a number of topics: writing as a "leap of faith"; Rose, the protagonist of *Who*, as a composite of real people; curiosity as the key to happiness; her ambition as a child to become a famous actress; the start of writing in her teenage years; the concealment of her love for books; and happiness in middle age.

S1040. Mechling, Lauren. "Canada Didn't Get Me, Munro Tells *New Yorker*: Web Site Interview." *National Post* 14 February 2001: B10.
Mechling reports on an online interview of Munro by Alice Quinn, Munro's editor at *The New Yorker*. In the interview, Munro says that in Canada in the 1970s she was viewed as a

slightly outmoded writer whose writing was regional and old-fashioned in the sense that her subject matter was not in the forefront. She feels her stories were accepted by *The New Yorker* because its readers were a more discerning audience.

S1041. Meindl, Dieter. "Modernism and the English Canadian Short Story Cycle." *Recherches anglaises et nord-américaines* 20 (1987): 17-22.

On pages 20 and 21, Meindl discusses *Lives* as an illustration of the modernist view of a short-story cycle which presents "cross-cuts of life," and is made up of self-contained, yet related, stories. He says that the book does not simply show Del's development as an artist, but that it provides proof of it. He comments also on the richness of detail in the work.

S1042. Melnyk, Helen. "Rigid Schedule for Writing a Must: Author." *Victoria Times* 12 January 1972: 23.

Melnyk's interview with Munro ranges over a number of topics: her writing process and writing routine; the dual role of writer and housewife; the financial aspects of writing; and doubt in her abilities as a writer and in the profession of writing. Munro's writing process begins with a period of thought, followed by the writing of a first draft and numerous revisions. In the beginning, Munro's career developed slowly and she did not finish many stories she had begun. Ego and inner confidence are a necessary defense against discouragement, Munro says. Self-discipline and a rigid writing schedule are requirements for the writer. Her writing routine is fitted around her family life, and both are kept separate from each other. Despite the frustration of never achieving her original intent, the draining nature of the work, and the realization that her talents fall short of her youthful ambitions, Munro continues to write.

S1043. Merkin, Daphne. "Northern Exposures." *New York Times Magazine* 24 October 2004: 58-62.

Merkin describes Munro as a private person in whom self-effacing reticence competes with a "strong impulse to strip away the curtains." Munro talks to Merkin about her personal life: her two marriages, her assessment of herself as a mother, her feelings about her own mother, and the restrictive farming community where she grew up. As a writer, Munro says she is "frightened of being overvalued" because "someone will shoot you down." She further states that "being a writer is a shameful thing. It's always pushing out your version. I try to correct for this." Later, in talking about her writing Munro says, "I write the story I want to read." But it is difficult to get out what she wants to say. Comparing the short story to the novel, she says that some novels could be written as short stories.

S1044. Metcalf, John. "Alice Munro." *Canadian Classics: An Anthology of Short Stories*. Critical commentary John Metcalf. Bibliographical and textual research J. R. (Tim) Struthers. Toronto: McGraw-Hill Ryerson, 1993. 101-103.

Metcalf considers the progression of Munro's skill as a writer, from the more conventional stories in *Dance*, to the more intense and mysterious stories in *Friend* which challenge the boundaries between "fact" and "fiction." However, what remains constant throughout is Munro's love of surface detail.

S1045. Metcalf, John. "Canada's Successful Writers Must Rely on Blessings from U.S. First." *National Post* 17 June 2000: E4-E5.

Metcalf contends that it was only after Munro was published in *The New Yorker* that she became better known in Canada and around the world. He talks about Robert Weaver's role in Munro's career, and points out his limitations as an agent in promoting Canadian culture in the United States. For responses to this article, see entries under Timothy Findley, Douglas M. Gibson, and JoAnn McCaig. For a response by Alice Munro, see entry P656.

S1046. Metcalf, John. [Maitland, James A. (pseud.)] "Casting Sad Spells: Alice Munro's 'Walker Brothers Cowboy.'" *Writers in Aspic*. Ed. John Metcalf. Montreal: Véhicule, 1988. 186-200.
   Rpt. in *Freedom from Culture: Selected Essays 1982-92*. Ed. John Metcalf. Toronto: ECW Press, 1994. 173-187.

Metcalf begins with a discussion of the primacy of the image in "Images" and "Walker Brothers Cowboy." He then considers the structure of the latter story, seeing in it three sections, the first of which contains the essence of the other two. He says that the adult narrator's voice suggests the voice of a young girl and her sensibilities. Following a detailed analysis of the three sections, Metcalf comments on the undertones of sexuality in both this story and in "Images." He speculates on why Munro included the penultimate paragraph, which he considers vague and ambiguous and "slightly pretentious."

S1047. Metcalf, John. Introduction. *New Worlds: A Canadian Collection of Stories with Notes*. Ed. and introd. John Metcalf. Toronto: McGraw-Hill Ryerson, 1980. 7-9.

In his introduction to "Boys and Girls," Metcalf points out the style, the use of language, and the theme of gender roles.

S1048. Metcalf, John. "Questions about the Stories." *New Worlds: A Canadian Collection of Stories with Notes*. Ed. and introd. John Metcalf. Toronto: McGraw-Hill Ryerson, 1980. 162-164.

Metcalf provides a point of departure for student discussion of "Boys and Girls," by presenting a series of questions about how emotions are shown in the story.

S1049. Micros, Marianne. "Et in Ontario Ego: The Pastoral Ideal and the Blazon Tradition in Alice Munro's 'Lichen.'" *Alice Munro Writing On . . . .* Ed. Robert Thacker. Special issue of *Essays on Canadian Writing* 66 (1998): 44-59.
   Rpt. in *The Rest of the Story: Critical Essays on Alice Munro*. Ed. Robert Thacker. Toronto: ECW Press, 1999. 44-59.

In the story "Lichen," Micros identifies allusions to, and the use of, 16th-century conventions of pastoral poetry, love sonnets, and the blazon. The blazon is a poetic catalogue of women's body parts that idealizes, yet fragments, the woman's body. Micros looks at the male view of the female body, at women's views of themselves, and at their relations with men. She outlines the difficulties of image-making through metaphor, simile, photography, and language.

S1050. "Middle Age Set Her Free." *Victorian* 4 April 1973: 32-33.
(Item not seen.)

S1051. Miller, Judith Maclean. "Deconstructing Silence: The Mystery of Alice Munro." *Antigonish Review* 129 (Spring 2002): 43-52.

Miller looks at silences and mystery in "Something I've Been Meaning to Tell You" and "Save the Reaper." She begins by analysing the language of silence, which is defined as not saying, but communicating. In the first story, the narrator withholds information as a method of control. Within the spaces of the told and untold there may be answers to the mystery of the story. In "Save the Reaper," the ugly parts of the story are left out. Miller presents similarities between this story, *Lives*, and "Walker Brothers Cowboy."

S1052. Miller, Judith M. "An Inner Bell That Rings: The Craft of Alice Munro." *Antigonish Review* 115 (Fall 1998): 157-176.

In conversations with Geoff Hancock, Beverly Rasporich, and John Metcalf, Munro spoke of her fictional aesthetics and writing process. Miller includes excerpts from these interviews in her examination of Munro's style, her angle of vision, her photographic composition, poeticism, language, and the narrative structure of her work. She discusses the realism of Munro's writing and the importance paid to surface details.

S1053. Miller, Judith Maclean. "On Looking into Rifts and Crannies: Alice Munro's *Friend of My Youth*." *Antigonish Review* 120 (Winter 2000): 205-226.

In this review essay, Miller provides commentaries on each of the stories in the collection. Prefacing these are elements of the writing process described by Munro in interviews. She explains how images form into stories through a preliminary process of reverie. She describes a layeredness of feeling, comprised of layers of speech, thought, dream, and sense impression.

S1054. Miller, Karl. "What's Difficult, and What Isn't: Two Books Published in the 1960s." *Changing English* 11.2 (October 2004): 183-188.

The postmodern bias toward difficulty or obscurity has placed greater value on difficult literary texts than it has on popular literature. Miller's article is indicative of a trend away from "dysfunctional or fashionable difficulty." He compares Iris Murdoch's novel *An Unofficial Rose* with two stories from Munro's *Dance*, "Walker Brothers Cowboy" and "Thanks for the Ride." He places Murdoch's writing in the category of "difficult" for readers because of its preoccupation with gentility and the fantastic. Munro, on the other hand, writes popular literature for adults which is real and persuasive. For readers, her stories are "fictions that can be lived as lives are lived." They give good reason to question the popularity of "difficulty, alienation, pretension" in literature.

S1055. Miller, Lori. "'I Know Where the Rope Is Attached.'" *New York Times Book Review* 14 September 1986: 7.

Miller interviewed Munro shortly after the publication of *Progress*. She records Munro as saying that, in her writing, she is interested in the present but wants to tie the present to the past. Munro explains her preference for the short story over the novel. In the writing of a story she says, "I get a kind of tension when I'm writing a short story, like I'm pulling a rope and I know where the rope is attached."

S1056. Mitchell, Reid. "Imaginary Evidence: The Historical Fiction of Alice Munro." *Writing History/Writing Fiction: A Virtual Conference Session.* Accessed 18 October 2002. <http://www.albany.edu/history/hist_fict/Mitchell/Mitchelles.htm>

Mitchell uses "The Wilderness Station" as an example of how historical method can be used to write modern fiction, or the literature of uncertainty. In the story, imaginary evidence is delivered in the form of "documents," that is in letters and newspaper articles. However, like the imprecision of written history, there is no guarantee that what the reader thinks has happened really happened. Munro denies conclusive evidence.

S1057. Monaghan, David. "Confinement and Escape in Alice Munro's 'The Flats Road.'" *Studies in Short Fiction* 14 (Spring 1977): 165-168.
Rpt. (with minor omissions and excluding footnotes and textual refs.) in *Short Story Criticism: Excerpts from Criticism of the Works of Short Fiction Writers.* Ed. Sheila Fitzgerald. Vol. 3. Detroit: Gale Research, 1989. 331-333.

In *Lives*, Del's crucial life experiences with death, family, religion, love, and sex erode her sense of freedom, and progressively increase her feeling of confinement. Monaghan shows how "The Flats Road" gives intimations of Del's final awareness. Uncle Benny, unlike Del, is a man who is free to step outside "the cave." Imagery in "The Flats Road" is also discussed.

S1058. Moore, Lorrie. "Introduction ['Save the Reaper']." *Prize Stories, 1999: The O. Henry Awards.* Ed. and introd. Larry Dark. 1st Anchor Books original ed. New York: Anchor Books, 1999. 60.

In her introduction to the story, Moore compares "Save the Reaper" to Flannery O'Connor's "A Good Man Is Hard to Find."

S1059. Morrell, Stuart. "Alice Munro." *Overland* 80 (July 1980): 48.

Morrell talks to Munro during her tour of Australia. He notes first that she won the Canada-Australia Literary Prize in 1977. In the course of the interview, Munro discusses different aspects of her writing: the use of factual and personal material; truth and convincing details; her female characters; the female perspective; and the use of crudity. Munro confesses that she does not like publicity and dislikes speaking on certain subjects, such as the state of Canadian art.

S1060. Moss, John. "Alice in the Looking Glass: Munro's *Lives of Girls and Women*." *Sex and Violence in the Canadian Novel: The Ancestral Present.* Toronto: McClelland and Stewart, 1977. 54-68.

The novel is considered as a portrait of the artist as a girl and a young woman. The protagonist passes through a series of phases in the making of her creative sensibility. Moss focuses on Del's double vision across time. He further considers point of view in the multiple consciousness of Del as a protagonist, adult narrator, and persona of Munro. The point of view is also discussed in "How I Met My Husband," "An Ounce of Cure," "The Found Boat," and "Thanks for the Ride."

S1061. Moss, John. Introduction. *Here and Now: A Critical Anthology.* Vol. 1 of *The Canadian Novel.* Ed. and introd. John Moss. Toronto: NC Press, 1978. 7-10, 12-13.

Moss summarizes heightened or magic realism in Munro's writing, her use of language, and her narrative techniques.

S1062. Murphy, Georgeann. "The Art of Alice Munro: Memory, Identity, and the Aesthetics of Connection." *Canadian Women Writing Fiction*. Ed. Mickey Pearlman. Jackson: University Press of Mississippi, 1993. 12-27.

Using stories from *Dance, Lives, Something, Beggar,* and *Friend,* Murphy focuses on the characters and on the connections between what went on before a change in their lives and what comes after. The characters discussed include fathers and mothers, first-person narrators, and third-person protagonists who are writers or artists. Murphy looks at various human situations: the familial connection, death as change, sexual love as dangerous, and the longing for sexual connection. Narrative technique and point of view are included in the discussion.

S1063. New, W. H. "Pronouns and Propositions: Alice Munro's Stories." *Open Letter, 3rd ser.* 5 (Summer 1976): 40-49.
Rpt. as "Pronouns and Propositions: Alice Munro's *Something I've Been Meaning to Tell You*" in *Dreams of Speech and Violence: The Art of the Short Story in Canada and New Zealand.* Toronto: University of Toronto Press, 1987. 201-210.

New demonstrates how Munro's style, particularly her language, causes the reader to see that beyond the apparent meaning in *Something*, that is the failure of communication, there is another meaning that is deeper and beyond the words of the teller. He focuses on Munro's use of pronouns and how they are used to establish personal relationships and also on the point of view. He further shows how the stories are linked in their themes of frustrated communication, in phrases and in recurrent flashback techniques that link past and present. Among the stories discussed are "Material," "Something I've Been Meaning to Tell You," and "Walking on Water."

S1064. New, W. H. "The Rowboat, The Wheel, and the Galloping Oilcan." *Australian and New Zealand Studies in Canada* 12 (December 1994): 64-72.

Moons repeatedly concerns itself with memory. The stories involve characters who live in Ontario and travel "away," that is they move from the familiar. The characters all have the need to discover why this changes them. New briefly discusses a number of stories in this regard. He then turns to the theme of human connections and separations. He looks at the "fictions of recognition" or the indeterminacy of "truth" in stories and story-making. The relationship between language, human connection, and uncertainty is discussed.

S1065. Nischik, Reingard M. "'Pen Photographs': Zum Phanomen des (kanadischen) Kurzgeschichtenzyklus." *Deutsche Vierteljahrsschrift fur Literaturwissenschaft und Geistesgeschichte* 66.1 (märz 1992): 192-204.

Nischik looks at the short-story cycle as a national literary genre of Canada. He situates the phenomenon of the short-story cycle in the Canadian context of historical and social development. Munro's *Lives* and *Beggar* serve as examples for discussion.

S1066. Noonan, Gerald. "Alice Munro's Short Stories and the Art-That-Distrusts-Art." *Short Fiction in the New Literatures in English: Proceedings of the Nice Conference of the European Association for Commonwealth Literature and Language Studies.* Ed. and introd. J. Bardolph. Nice: Faculté des Lettres et Sciences Humaines de Nice, 1989. 141-146.

Noonan bases his discussion on Munro's distrust of art and on the illusions of art. Fiction, or art, is seen to be in conflict with real life, in which disarrangements occur as demonstrated in "Simon's Luck." In *Something,* art is seen to be a doubtful means of controlling reality. The conventions of fiction are an illusion, but characters pretend that the illusion is real, as in "White Dump." Noonan concludes by saying that Munro disrupts our conventional expectations of art, to show that the therapeutic and mysterious are not found in art but in our subjective selves.

S1067.   Noonan, Gerald. "The Structure of Style in Alice Munro's Fiction." *Probable Fictions: Alice Munro's Narrative Acts.* Ed. Louis K. MacKendrick. Downsview, ON: ECW Press, 1983. 163-180.

Through a study of Munro's first four books, *Dance, Lives, Something,* and *Who,* Noonan examines Munro's style in relation to the content and structure of her work. He traces the development of her style, beginning with the use of detail and verbal paradox in the early works through to the paradox of event and structure in the later books. Noonan looks at shifts in technique, the use of literary devices, and language.

S1068.   "Novelist Fights Book Banning." *Montreal Star* 25 May 1978: B11.

This article reports on Munro's concern for the banning of books such as Margaret Laurence's *The Diviners* from high school reading lists. She says that writers, represented by the Canadian Writers' Union, must fight against the conservative backlash that has caused this situation.

S1069.   Nunes, Mark. "Postmodern 'Piecing': Alice Munro's Contingent Ontologies." *Studies in Short Fiction* 34.1 (Winter 1997): 11-26.

Instead of showing the unravelling of a narrative, Munro's writing concentrates on what holds a story together. Nunes looks at Munro's aesthetic of contingent arrangements of pieces and discusses the narrative strategies which allow the pieces of the narrative to come together. In *Friend,* Nunes points out a wide array of references to the textile crafts. Piecing is seen as a metaphor for the narrative process. The stories "Goodness and Mercy," "Friend of My Youth," "Differently," and "Meneseteung" are examined.

S1070.   O'Connor, Mary. "Chronotopes for Women under Capital: An Investigation into the Relation of Women to Objects." *Critical Studies: A Journal of Critical Theory, Literature and Culture* 2.1-2 (1990): 137-151.

O'Connor looks at the question of how women writers present objects, and links this to the position of women in a patriarchal society in which women are relegated to interior, private space. She then turns to examine Munro's treatment of objects in "Fits," a story which is underscored with violence. Tension in the story is produced by shifts from sameness to otherness, and a movement back and forth from the ordinary and the horrific. O'Connor refers to Bakhtin's essay on the chronotope.

S1071.   Off, Carol. "Author Munro Speaks Out on Rights." *Gazette* [University of Western Ontario] 5 January 1979: 10.

Off reports on an interview in which Munro expresses her feelings about the lobby to have certain books banned in Huron County high schools, among them Margaret Laurence's *The*

Diviners. She mentions the puritanism and narrow-mindedness of the lobby group, saying that they are religiously motivated and have no interest in reading or in books. Munro says that she is actively involved, through the Canadian Writers' Union, in promoting and defending Canadian literature.

S1072.   Ohm, Viveca. "'In the '50's You Got Married.'" *Vancouver Sun* 3 December 1971: 35.
Soon after the publication of *Lives*, Munro speaks to Ohm and touches on a number of topics relating to her writing: the place of autobiography in fiction, her doubts as a writer, writer's block, and the need for discipline. She says that writing is the only thing she wanted to do. Women writers who are housewives, like her, are limited to their experience. She mentions the support of her husband.

S1073.   "*Open Secrets* (Discussion guide)." *Reading Group Center*. n.d. Vintage Books-Random House. Accessed 24 April 2006. <http://www.randomhouse.com/vintage/read/secrets/>
A general overview of the collection is given. Questions are included for each of the stories to initiate discussion.

S1074.   Orange, John. "Alice Munro and a Maze of Time." *Probable Fictions: Alice Munro's Narrative Acts*. Ed. Louis K. MacKendrick. Downsview, ON: ECW Press, 1983. 83-98.
Orange studies the development of Munro's narrative technique over the course of her first five books. He notes that in *Dance* and *Lives* Munro uses a first-person narrator, a chronological ordering of the narrative, and the double perspective of the narrator as adult and child. Beginning with *Something*, and subsequently in *Who* and *Moons*, Munro shifts to the third-person limited narrator. As structural devices, she uses disruptions in time and abrupt shifts in setting.

S1075.   Osachoff, Margaret Gail. "'Treacheries of the Heart': Memoir, Confession, and Meditation in the Stories of Alice Munro." *Probable Fictions: Alice Munro's Narrative Acts*. Ed. Louis K. MacKendrick. Downsview, ON: ECW Press, 1983. 61-82.
Osachoff examines how the narrator's relationship or attitude toward the autobiographical material in her story affects her voice. A memoir is usually told in the first person from the point of view of an adult who looks back at a memorable childhood event. A confession is made in a confiding voice to a listener in order to share or absolve a past burden or guilt. A meditation is an effort to find clarity or truth and occurs in the speaker's head to an imaginary listener. A "treachery of the heart" occurs in the wrong use of autobiographical material. Osachoff studies memoir in *Dance*, confession and meditation in *Something*, and meditation in "Home."

S1076.   Osmond, Rosalie. "Arrangements, 'Disarrangements,' and 'Earnest Deceptions.'" *Narrative Strategies in Canadian Literature: Feminism and Postcolonialism*. Ed. Coral Ann Howells and Lynette Hunter. Introd. Lynette Hunter. Milton Keynes, Eng.: Open University Press, 1991. 82-92.
Munro's writing has evolved from "arranged" stories in *Dance* and *Something* to stories containing disarrangements and "earnest deceptions" in *Who* and *Moons*. Osmond defines

an "arranged" story, such as "Something I've Been Meaning to Tell You," as one which takes an event and distills from it a changed perception and a new layer of reality. When unexpected events or "disarrangements" occur, as they do in "Labor Day Dinner," they cause an epiphanic shock, then a rearrangement. Too complacent arrangements, as in "Dulse," produce "earnest deceptions." Order and disorder are discussed in "Bardon Bus" and "The Moons of Jupiter." *Progress* moves away from these strategies to a more pessimistic and complex approach.

S1077.   Packer, Miriam. "*Lives of Girls and Women*: A Creative Search for Completion." *Here and Now: A Critical Anthology*. Vol. 1 of *The Canadian Novel*. Ed. and introd. John Moss. Toronto: NC Press, 1978. 134-144.

Del's personal and artistic growth are examined by Packer. She makes the observation that Del learns what she does not want to be from the others around her. The novel is the story of a female who is growing up in an oppressive environment. It is also about the development of Del's artistic vision. Packer outlines how each of the eight chapters corresponds to a phase in Del's life.

S1078.   Palusci, Oriana. "Danzando con le ombre." *La danza delle ombre felici*. Trans. Gina Maneri. Milano: La Tartaruga, 1994. 241-248.

In this introduction to the Italian translation of *Dance*, Palusci briefly presents Munro's aesthetics of short-story writing, her place in Canadian literature, her literary influences, settings, characters, and important elements in her writing such as memory, retrospective narration, and regionalism. She gives an overview of *Dance*, elaborating on setting, point of view, characters, and important elements. The stories discussed are "Walker Brothers Cowboy," "Boys and Girls," "The Office," "The Peace of Utrecht," and "Dance of the Happy Shades."

S1079.   Perrakis, Phyllis Sternberg. "Portrait of the Artist as a Young Girl: Alice Munro's *Lives of Girls and Women*." *Atlantis: A Women's Studies Journal/Journal d'études sur la femme* 7.2 (Spring 1982): 61-67.

Perrakis says that the emphasis in the novel is on Del's growth and development as a woman; in other words that *Lives* is a *Bildungsroman*. There is, however, a crucial relationship between Del's growth to womanhood and her development as an artist. Perrakis reviews these two elements in the novel and concludes by saying that Del finally accepts and transcends the limitations placed on her by "real life." She discusses also the theme of reality found beneath the surface of life.

S1080.   Peterson, Leslie. "Munro Blows Her Horn—But Very Quietly." *Vancouver Sun* 12 November 1986: C5.

Mentioning Munro's book tours after the publication of *Progress*, Peterson says that Munro is reticent to give interviews. The article includes personal information on Munro, a general commentary on her writing, and brief quotes by Munro about her writing.

S1081.   Peterson, Leslie. "Nothing to Tell Us." *Vancouver Sun* 13 February 1976, Leisure and TV Week: 30A.

Peterson came away from a public reading by Munro at Simon Fraser University feeling dissatisfied and disappointed. Rather than reading from a work in progress, Munro read from

Something I've Been Meaning to Tell You, which was published several years before. Saying that the question and answer period was very brief, with Munro giving little elaboration in her answers, Peterson concluded that, as an author receiving money from the Canada Council, a publicly supported agency, Munro should have offered the audience something more.

S1082. Porteus, Neil. "Munro National in Scope." Letter. *Globe and Mail* 18 December 1982: 7.

As a reader of Munro's fiction, Porteus says that the local detail in Munro's writing expresses the national temperament, which is created and sustained by the landscape. He mentions the story "Providence," which is set in British Columbia, not in small-town Ontario.

S1083. "Postscript Notes, Questions, and Projects." *The Play's the Thing: Four Original Television Dramas*. Ed. Tony Gifford. Toronto: Macmillan of Canada, 1976. 167-169, 171, 174, 181.

The notes comment on the dramatized version of "How I Met My Husband." Questions for student discussion are also included.

S1084. Prentice, Christine. "Storytelling in Alice Munro's *Lives of Girls and Women* and Patricia Grace's *Potiki*." *Australian-Canadian Studies* 8.2 (1991): 27-40.

Del's narration of her own story provides a common meeting place for all the stories that went before and were instrumental in her development as a woman and artist. Prentice gives examples from the two traditions of oral storytelling and written history found in the novel. These are Ada Jordan's stories of her brother Bill, Uncle Craig's version of Madeleine, the legendary story of Miss Farris, the storytelling of the aunts, and the family history recorded by Uncle Craig. Del, in the end, rebels against the male voice of authority in their writings about women and determines to write her own stories using the legacies of storytelling among women.

S1085. Prose, Francine. "Friend of Our Youth." *Real Simple* (February 2001): 120-122. Rpt. as "A Smart and Important Friend: Her Stories Have Guided a Generation of Women." *National Post* 3 April 2001: B1, B5.

Prose has a great appreciation for Munro as a female writer, and says that all women identify with the situations and relationships she writes about. She gives a background to Munro's life and writing career. The juggling between Munro's early family responsibilities and writing is mentioned. A brief synopsis is provided for *Beggar* and *Lives*. The article is based on an interview and includes some quotations.

S1086. Pruitt, Virginia D. "Gender Relations: Alice Munro's 'Differently' and 'Carried Away.'" *Bulletin of the Menninger Clinic* 64.4 (Fall 2000): 494-508.

Using a psychiatric and psychological approach, Pruitt looks at erotic relationships between heterosexual couples which involve passion and romantic love, linking these intimate relationships to personal fulfilment. In "Differently," Georgia finds her essential self as a result of romantic love and passion. Arthur, in "Carried Away," finds self-realization in a love in which he loses himself.

S1087. Quartermaine, Peter. "'Living on the Surface': Versions of Real Life in Alice Munro's *Lives of Girls and Women*." *Recherches anglaises et nord-américaines* 20 (1987): 117-126.

In "The Flats Road" and "Epilogue: The Photographer," Munro portrays human life as walking on a fragile surface. In the first chapter, the ordinary coexists with the extraordinary and the surface details conceal hidden truths. Uncle Benny, in his world of tabloids and with his simplistic approach to life, is like a world living alongside of Del, close yet separate. In "Epilogue," Quartermaine discusses the terrors and pleasures of sex, the Sherriffs, the inscrutability of the photographic image, and real life.

S1088. Quinn, Alice. "The Genius of Alice Munro." *New Quarterly: New Directions in Canadian Writing* 21.2 & 3 (Summer-Fall) 2001: 201-204.
 Slightly revised and expanded version of "The 'Wholly Original' Alice Munro." *National Post* 18 November 2000: B11.

Quinn, Munro's editor at *The New Yorker*, praises Munro's skill as a writer. She describes the excitement and comments made in the editorial office when Munro's submission "Royal Beatings" first appeared. Despite the editors' concerns about the crude words and non-chronological arrangement, the story was published unrevised. As an illustration of Munro's talent, Quinn details how, in "The Children Stay," Munro uses the play in the story to further the situation of the young wife.

S1089. Raabe, David. "Alice Munro: 'Wild Swans' and Things." *Eureka: Studies in Teaching Short Fiction* 1.2 (Spring 2001): 43-52.

In a pedagogical approach, Raabe uses Munro's story to examine the treatment of objects in literature. He focuses on the surprise ending. (Based on abstract)

S1090. Ramraj, Victor J. "'Wild Swans.'" *Masterplots II: Short Story Series*. Ed. Frank N. Magill. Vol. 6. Pasadena, CA: Salem, 1986. 2619-2622.

Provides a student guide to "Wild Swans" under the following headings: The Story; Themes and Meanings; Style and Technique.

S1091. Rasporich, Beverly. "Child-Women and Primitives in the Fiction of Alice Munro." *Atlantis: A Women's Studies Journal* 1.2 (Spring 1976): 4-14.

Rasporich examines two types of female characters in *Dance*, *Lives*, and *Something*. She labels them as "child-women" and "primitives." The child-women are defined as alienated, repressed, and discontented Victorian women who hide their true identity beneath social faces. The primitives are poor white women of rural Ontario who lash out with gestures of frustrated aggression. These two types of women illustrate the feminine dilemma of being trapped in past memory and value systems while living in the present.

S1092. Rasporich, Beverly Matson. "Locating the Artist's Muse: The Paradox of Femininity in Mary Pratt and Alice Munro." *Woman as Artist: Papers in Honour of Marsha Hanen*. Ed. Christine Mason Sutherland and Beverly Matson Rasporich. Calgary: University of Calgary Press, [1993]. 121-143.

Both artists interpret femininity as an unresolvable and aesthetic paradox. Rasporich sees this as impacting on their choices of subjects, techniques, and their visions. Their female characters are feminine and domestic artists, but the art of being feminine inhibits their power as females and limits them as artists. Almeda Roth, in "Meneseteung," is one such character. Rasporich further elaborates on the status of the female artist and the relationship between gender and art. The attention to surface details, the portrayal of the female body, and the photographic realism in their works reflect the femininity of both Pratt and Munro.

S1093. Reaney, James. "Stellar Writer a Class Actor: Alice Munro Kicks Up Her Heels." *London Free Press* 24 June 2000, final ed.: 4.

Reaney reports on Munro as an actor playing in a Huron County amateur theatre performance in the Livery Theatre. He comments on her participation in the community spirit.

S1094. Redekop, Magdalene. "Alice Munro and the Scottish Nostalgic Grotesque." *Alice Munro Writing On . . . .* Ed. Robert Thacker. Special issue of *Essays on Canadian Writing* 66 (1998): 21-43.
Rpt. in *The Rest of the Story: Critical Essays on Alice Munro*. Ed. Robert Thacker. Toronto: ECW Press, 1999. 21-43.

The influence of the Scottish oral tradition and Munro's Scottish ancestors, James Hogg and Margaret Laidlaw, are demonstrated in her writing, particularly in her construction of nostalgia as the grotesque. Redekop studies Milton Homer in *Who* as the embodiment of the Scottish nostalgic grotesque. She also examines the Scottish influence in "Friend of My Youth," "A Wilderness Station," "Hold Me Fast, Don't Let Me Pass," and "Carried Away." In the last story, she focuses on the epilogue. Redekop concludes with a consideration of Munro as a storyteller in the tradition of her ancestors.

S1095. Redekop, Magdalene. "Alice Munro's Tilting Fields." *New Worlds: Discovering and Constructing the Unknown in Anglophone Literature*. Presented to Walter Pache on Occasion of His 60th Birthday. Ed. Martin Kuester, Gabriele Christ, and Rudolf Beck. Schriften der Philosophischen Fakultäten der Universität Augsburg no. 59: Literatur- und sprachwissenschaftliche Reihe. München: Ernst Vögel, 2000. 343-362.

Redekop observes that Munro's writing does not fall into the category of magic realism, which is eye-dominated. Her technique involves the interplay of eye and ear, and is thus closer to the cinematic than the photographic technique. She looks at the use of ekphrasis, a rhetorical figure in which verbal representation is made of visual representation, as in "Simon's Luck." In the hyperrealist and deictic description of objects in "The Love of a Good Woman," Redekop shows how the power to see is limited by external forces, and looking and listening are separated. In "The Children Stay," the mother's position of "watcher" and "keeper" tilts the fields of vision and unleashes other texts such as Anouilth's Eurydice and Orpheus stories.

S1096. Regan, Stephen. "'The Presence of the Past': Modernism and Postmodernism in Canadian Short Fiction." *Narrative Strategies in Canadian Literature*. Ed. Coral A. Howells and Lynette Hunter. Introd. Lynette Hunter. Milton Keynes, Eng.: Open University Press, 1991. 108-134.

Regan describes Munro's fiction as "concerned with its own historicity." It is rooted in southwestern Ontario and involves girls and women in the postwar society. "Red Dress—1946" is an example. Regan goes on to look at the interrelationships between the past and present, and how characters try to understand or reconcile themselves to the past in order to give meaning to the present. In *Something*, *Moons*, and *Progress*, discrepancies occur between public and private versions of history. The stories discussed are "The Peace of Utrecht," "Winter Wind," "The Ottawa Valley," and "The Progress of Love."

S1097.   Reid, Verna. "The Small Town in Canadian Fiction." *English Quarterly* 6 (Summer 1973). 171-181.

Reid describes the small town in Canadian literature as an emotional force that shapes the characters and their actions. *Lives* is one of several Canadian works included in the study. Reid points out the strong love/hate relationship of the characters toward Jubilee. The marginal no-man's-land of Flats Road is contrasted with the town, which women like Ada Jordan view as a defense against loneliness.

S1098.   Reisman, Rosemary M. Canfield. "*Friend of My Youth.*" *Masterplots II: Women's Literature Series*. Ed. Frank N. Magill. Vol. 2. Pasadena, CA: Salem, 1995. 849-853.

In a format and level designed for the reference needs of upper-level students, *Friend of My Youth* is discussed under the following headings: "Form and Content" giving an overview of the subject matter; "Analysis" of the themes and ideas; "Context" or the influence of the work and major ideas conveyed. This is followed by a short bibliography, "Sources for Further Reading."

S1099.   Relke, Diana. "Models, Muses, and Mothers of the Mind: Mentrix Figures in the Early Lives of Artist-Heroines." *Woman as Artist: Papers in Honour of Marsha Hanen*. Ed. Christine Mason Sutherland and Beverly Matson Rasporich. Calgary: University of Calgary Press, [1993]. 19-39.

On pages 30 to 37, Relke discusses mentrix figures in Munro's *Lives* and *Who*. She defines mentrix figures as characters who facilitate female artistic development through their behaviour early in the artist's life. Such a figure is seen in Ada Jordan in *Lives*, who encourages Del in her literary and educational aspirations. Relke examines Ada Jordan's early mentors and role models, then points out the differences between Ada and her daughter. Del's other literary role models are mentioned. In *Who*, Dr. Henshawe appoints herself to the role of mentrix to Rose.

S1100.   Ricciardi, Caterina. "The Secrets of Intertextuality: Alice Munro's 'Pictures of the Ice.'" *Alice Munro: Writing Secrets*. Ed. Héliane Ventura and Mary Condé. Special issue of *Open Letter* 11th ser. 9 (Fall 2003)-12th ser. 1 (Winter 2004): 121-136.

Betrayal, secrecy, deception, and change from the old order to the new are motifs which Ricciardi links to the fragments of literary works which are embedded in the text of the story. Looking at allusions to Francis Bacon's "Of Parents and Children," she explores the role of secrecy and deception in Austin's relationship with his children. Continuing with deception in the parent-child relationship, Ricciardi draws attention to a paraphrase from Walter Scott's *Marmion*. Another phrase, a direct quote from Alfred Lord Tennyson's *The Passing of Authur*, is shown to be relevant to Austin's situation as a retiring minister. Ultimately, however, neither the pictures nor the texts found in the story change the elusive nature of reality.

S1101. Ricou, Laurie. "The Language of Childhood Remembered: Alice Munro and Margaret Laurence." *Everyday Magic: Child Languages in Canadian Literature*. Vancouver: University of British Columbia Press, 1987. 14-34.

In Munro's *Lives* and Margaret Laurence's *A Bird in the House*, Ricou examines how the adult narrator tells the story of her remembered childhood. The narrative angle in *Lives* is one of double vision, where the adult narrator watches her younger self as she is watching and suffering. Del's story is about all the stories she remembers from childhood, with little nostalgia and with the language of the child telling a story. The structure and style of the novel are also discussed. Ricou looks at Del's childhood grammars of local history, operettas, and tabloids. She notes the long passages of direct speech.

S1102. Riddell, Elizabeth. "To Alice Short Is Beautiful." *Bulletin* [Sydney, Austral.] 100 (17 April 1979): 52.

Riddell interviewed Munro during her visit to Australia to receive the Canada-Australia Literary Prize. In the interview, Munro gives her impressions of Australia, and then talks of her home town of Clinton, Ontario, which she says is very conservative. She mentions the banning of certain books in the high schools of that area. On the subject of her writing and career as a writer, she says that it is difficult to write about sexual love. Only recently has she started earning income from her books and become known in Canada. Munro further observes that Canadians have an inborn doubt about themselves in the world.

S1103. Rimstead, Roxanne. "'We Live in a Rickety House': Social Boundaries and Poor Housing. 3.2 Alice Munro's Gaze—From a Distance." *Remnants of Nation: On Poverty Narratives by Women*. Toronto: University of Toronto Press, 2001. 104-111.

Rimstead proposes that Munro's view of poverty is based on a bourgeois ethos. She argues that Munro's style and perspective give a distanced view of poverty. In "The Shining Houses," for example, the middle-classed protagonist displays moral paralysis in the clash between the social classes. In *Beggar*, the narrative moves between rich and poor homes, and there is a distancing from both. The narrative itself contains a bourgeois sense of order and modulation, and a detachment on the part of Rose, who has moved into a position of power. For a dissenting view, see the article by Frank Davey.

S1104. Rizzardi, Biancamaria. "Alice (Munro) nel paese delle meraviglie." *Moderni e post moderni: Studi sul racconto canadese del Novecento*. Ed. Alfredo Rizzardi. Saggi e ricerche di lingue e letterature straniere 39. Abano Terme: Piovan Editore, 1994. 165-176.

Much like Lewis Carroll in *Alice in Wonderland*, Munro creates magic in a "dimension of great limitedness," that is, in a domestic setting in small-town Ontario. She uses the ordinary to reveal the extraordinary; makes the familiar strange and the strange familiar; and the mysterious touchable and the touchable mysterious. Rizzardi discusses these qualities in Munro's writing and also examines magic realism, language, and techniques, particularly the use of paradox, verbal humour, and wit in *Lives* and *Who*. She also comments on recurring examples of oxymoron, the dichotomies in *Lives*, and on the bizarre and farcical humour in "An Ounce of Cure."

S1105. Robson, Nora. "Alice Munro and the White American South: The Quest." *The Art of Alice Munro: Saying the Unsayable*. Papers from the Waterloo Conference. Ed.

Judith Miller. Waterloo, ON: University of Waterloo Press, 1984. 73-84.
Robson sees parallels between Del's search for "real life" in *Lives* through religion, sex, and education and the quest themes found in the writing of the white American South. She compares the death imagery at Uncle Craig's funeral with the treatment of the Faulknerian school. Parallels are also seen in sex, where erotica is mixed with grotesquerie. Del's quest for religion is discussed. Robson compares Munro's treatment of religion with that of Flannery O'Connor. Munro's story "Home," in which deformity is linked with the biblical sense of sin, is compared with O'Connor's *Wise Blood*.

S1106. Robson, Nora. "Sense of Place in Alice Munro's Fiction." *Literary Criterion* [India] 19.3-4 (1984): 138-146.
Robson studies the rural and urban landscapes in Munro's work, beginning with a discussion of Del's ambivalent relationship to Flats Road and Jubilee in *Lives*. She then links the depiction of the seasons to these landscapes. Winter is linked with the country in "Winter Wind" and summer is linked with the town in "A Trip to the Coast." Houses are also connected with urban and rural landscapes, the urban in "Winter Wind" and the rural in "Royal Beatings." Robson comments on the sensuous details which contribute to the realism of place and on the mythical landscape of Wawanash County.

S1107. Rocard, Marcienne. "Alice Munro: A Mi-chemin entre la nouvelle et le roman." *Cahiers de la nouvelle: Journal of the Short Story in English* 1 (1983): 103-112.
Rocard believes that the reader can view *Lives* and *Who* as either long novels or as a series of separate linked stories. She proceeds to analyse specific elements in the two books that support her argument: the unity of impression, time shifts and flashbacks, and the unconventional plot. Rocard concludes with the suggestion that the books may be considered as a new kind of novel.

S1108. Rocard, Marcienne. "L'art et la nécessité de la connexion dans 'Connexion' d'Alice Munro." *Recherches anglaises et nord-américaines* 20 (1987): 109-115.
Prefacing her study of the story "Connection," Rocard speaks of connection as a common theme which structurally links all the stories in *Moons*. In the story, family connections are discussed as an impossible connection. Rocard examines the narrative techniques used in the story, and its structure, noting the circular movement of the text, with convergence and epiphany at the end.

S1109. Rocard, Marcienne. "'Who Do You Think You Are?' d'Alice Munro: Un titre unifiant." *Recherches anglaises et nord-américaines* 16 (1983): 45-55.
Rocard examines the methods by which Munro achieves unity in *Who*. First, the title gives the unifying vision and theme of the book, that is, the fundamental problem of identity for Rose. The stories are all third-person narratives and told from the point of view of the heroine. Structural techniques relating to the reoccurrence of details and themes in different settings, and the correspondences between incidents and persons in the same story, bring unity between the stories and within the stories. Rocard discusses individual stories in the book, commenting, for example, on the parallel stories in "Half a Grapefruit," and the structural significance of the double image of the swan in "Wild Swans."

S1110.   Rooke, Constance. "Fear of the Open Heart." *A Mazing Space: Writing Canadian Women Writing*. Ed. Shirley Neuman and Smaro Kamboureli. Edmonton: Longspoon, 1986. 256-269.

Rooke associates fear with Scottish Presbyterianism and the Canadian "garrison mentality," and applies the concept to works by Mavis Gallant, Margaret Laurence, and Munro. Rooke considers Rose in *Who* as a "quintessential Munro heroine." She lives inside the garrison but prefers to live outside of it. Through art, she manages to synthesize the two. Her fear and need for love are discussed. Milton Homer is another artistic character in the book, who both moves through society and is outside of it.

S1111.   Rooke, Constance. "Munro's Food." *Fear of the Open Heart: Essays on Contemporary Canadian Writing*. Toronto: Coach House, 1989. 41-53.

The symbolism, imagery, and language of food are examined by Rooke in selected Munro stories. For example, in "Heirs of the Living Body" and "Princess Ida," food is connected with death; in "Images" with poisoning; in "Providence" and "Something I've Been Meaning to Tell You" with fairy tale princesses; in "Bardon Bus," "Providence," and "Simon's Luck" with sex. The image and symbolism of food are also discussed in "Labor Day Dinner," "White Dump," and "Spelling."

S1112.   Ross, Catherine Sheldrick. "Alice Munro: A Double Life (excerpt)." *Books in Canada* 21.3 (April 1992): 16-21.

This excerpt from Ross's book, *Alice Munro: A Double Life*, includes early details of the Laidlaw family, Munro's parents, and Munro's life from birth to youth. Ross covers Munro's schooling, her relationship with her mother, the effect of her mother's illness, her early reading, and her imitative writing.

S1113.   Ross, Catherine Sheldrick. "'At Least Part Legend': The Fiction of Alice Munro." *Probable Fictions: Alice Munro's Narrative Acts*. Ed. Louis K. MacKendrick. Downsview, ON: ECW Press, 1983. 112-126.

In her analysis, Ross looks at how Munro translates ordinary experience into something that is extraordinary, and presents for the reader powerful legendary shapes behind the ordinary lives of characters. She examines this in *Lives* and in selected stories from *Dance*, *Something*, and *Who*. Ross says that myths, legends, rituals, and ceremonies help in the arrangement of details and in the organization of story design. Ritualized events, such as death and initiation into sexual roles, form the centres of stories. Shifts in perception cause characters to see the ordinary as extraordinary. Discussing many stories, Ross compares the luminous upper world of ordinary life in these stories with the "deep holes" or the shadowy world of legends and myths below the surface.

S1114.   Ross, Catherine Sheldrick. "Calling Back the Ghost of the Old-Time Heroine: Duncan, Montgomery, Atwood, Laurence, and Munro." *Studies in Canadian Literature* 4.1 (Winter 1979): 43-58. Accessed 24 April 2006. <http://www.lib.unb.ca/Texts/SCL/vol4_1/Contents.htm>

Rpt. in *Such a Simple Little Tale: Critical Responses to L. M. Montgomery's Anne of Green Gables*. Ed. Mavis Reimer. Metuchen, NJ: Children's Literature Association and Scarecrow, 1992. 39-55.

Ross studies the use of the old-time romantic heroine in the works of five Canadian authors, including a brief section on Munro's *Lives*. Del lives in a world of romance and sees herself in the role of the romantic heroine. In "Epilogue: The Photographer," however, she abandons her plan to write a Gothic romance and decides to write about real life. Even so, the real life she plans to write about is underlined with myths and fairy tales.

S1115.   Ross, Catherine Sheldrick. "The Progress of Alice. Excerpt." *Quill & Quire* 58.2 February 1992: 25.

This excerpt from Ross's *Alice Munro: A Double Life* concentrates on the period between Munro's depression and writer's block and her winning of the Governor General's Award for *Dance*. Her life in Victoria was the happiest in her marriage. But later, when Munro became overwhelmed with her children, housework, and work in Munro's Book Store, her marriage suffered. In the meantime, *Dance* was produced and published by Ryerson, but experienced low sales because of poor promotion. Winning the Governor General's Award confirmed Munro's profession as a writer and gave her an enormous boost.

S1116.   Ross, Catherine Sheldrick. "'Too Many Things': Reading Alice Munro's 'The Love of a Good Woman.'" *University of Toronto Quarterly* 71.3 (Summer 2002): 786-810.

In her beginning remarks, Ross talks about Munro's current writing, saying that it is more complex and multilayered. It includes disruptions, resistance to closure, double meanings, symbolism, and imagery. Reader interpretation and reaction to the narrative techniques are also brought up. In "The Love of a Good Woman," Ross maintains that the complexity arises from the inclusion of details that do not fit the patterns, and that often subvert them. She examines in detail the symbolism and significance of the red box, the forsythia, the "good woman," the dream, and the little hatchet.

S1117.   Ross, Cecily. "Sheila and Alice." *Globe and Mail* 21 April 2001: D6.

In this interview with Ross, Sheila Munro talks about her relationship with her mother and the writing of her memoir, *Lives of Mothers and Daughters*.

S1118.   Ross, Val. "A Writer Called Alice." *Globe and Mail* 1 October 1994: C1, C21.

Speaking with Ross about her latest book, *Open Secrets*, Munro says that the stories originated from those she heard from people around her. Munro comments on three stories in the collection and reacts to reader and literary assessments that her stories are bleak. In her general comments about assessing one's life, Munro worries that being a writer has affected her daughters.

S1119.   Rothstein, Mervyn. "Canada's Alice Munro Finds Excitement in Short-Story Form." *New York Times* 10 November 1986, late ed.: C17.

Rothstein interviewed Munro after the publication of *The Progress of Love*. Munro tells Rothstein that she began writing short stories out of the necessity of time. She says that short stories, unlike novels, turn on pivotal moments which she finds exciting. Her stories have to do with self-deception. While Munro sees herself essentially as an outsider, she assumes a disguise in order to fit in. She learned this when growing up in a rural community in Huron County. She describes the community and region.

S1120.   Rubio, Jennie. "'Escaping her Carapace': Calvinism and the Body in Alice Munro and Elspeth Barker." *Scotlands* (1995): 74-87.

Rubio discusses Barker's *O Caledonia* and Munro's "Friend of My Youth." She first draws connections between the Calvanist legacy, women's identities, and the female body. In Munro's story, Rubio examines the mother-daughter relationship and outlines their contrasting views of the mother's body. The daughter's view is closer to the Calvanist view of the abject body as a prison from which the spirit cannot escape. The mother sees herself as spiritually distanced from her body. Rubio points out the presence of Calvanist predestination in the mother's story. The mother's puritanism in her notions about female desire and sexuality are contrasted with those of the daughter.

S1121.   Rutledge, Margie. "Motherhood and the Muse." *Globe and Mail* 7 November 1998, weekend ed.: D1-D2.

Rutledge asks a number of female Canadian writers whether mothering has affected their writing. Reconciling the demands of writing and motherhood, Munro says, is "the most insoluble problem in a woman's life." Children compete with writing for "the space of heart, soul and mind." Idleness spent in gathering ideas for writing is viewed as self-indulgence and contrary to what society expects from mothers.

S1122.   Saggini, Francesca. "Attraverso lo specchio: *Lives of Girls and Women* come Bildungsroman femminile." *Confronto letterario: Quaderni del Dipartimento di Lingue e Letterature Straniere Moderne dell'Università di Pavia e del Dipartimento di Linguistica e Letterature Comparate dell'Universita di Bergamo* 13.26 (November 1996): 815-833.

Saggini examines *Lives* as a *Bildungsroman*. She traces the formative factors in Del's development, looking at Ada Jordan and her feminist ideas, and the two aunts Elspeth and Grace, whom she discusses as opposites. Saggini also explores the differences between the female and male views of the world and life, Del's relationships with males, her coming to terms with reality, and the development of her identity in the novel.

S1123.   Sallot, Jeff. "Students 'Overwhelmingly Against' High School Principal Who Opposes Munro Novel." *Globe and Mail* 14 February 1976, metro ed.: 3.

The article reports on the removal of *Lives* from a Grade 13 English course list in a high school in Peterborough, Ontario, based on the principal's objection to its sexual content. The students protested the banning. The removal of Margaret Laurence's *The Diviners* is also covered.

S1124.   Scobie, Stephen. "Amelia, or: Who Do You Think You Are? Documentary and Identity in Canadian Literature." *Canadian Writers in 1984*. Ed. W. H. New. Vancouver: University of British Columbia Press, 1984. 264-285.

On pages 264 to 266, Scobie discusses *Who* and the problem of Rose's identity. He shows how Munro uses the documentary image of Frances Farmer to define Rose's predicament and identity.

S1125.   Scobie, Stephen. "'Lying under the Apple Tree': Alice Munro, Secrets, and Autobiography." *Alice Munro: Writing Secrets*. Ed. Héliane Ventura and Mary Condé.

Special issue of *Open Letter* 11th ser. 9 (Fall 2003)-12th ser. 1 (Winter 2004): 167-175. Scobie's paper is taken up with the question of whether Munro's story is a short story or a memoir. He begins with a detailed look at the textual presentation of the story in *The New Yorker*, noting that it appeared under the classification of "Memoir," presumably with Munro's approval. Scobie looks at the details in the story that bring out the double meaning of the word "lying." He discusses the problem of truthfulness and invention in autobiography and memoir, and examines the "tangled web of self-references" in the story. While Scobie arrives at the tentative conclusion that the story is not a memoir, he says this cannot be fully resolved.

S1126. Sellwood, Jane. "'Certain Vague Hopes of Disaster': A Psychosemiotic Reading of Alice Munro's 'The Found Boat' as the Flooding Text." *Studies in Canadian Literature/Études en littérature canadienne* 17.1 (1992): 1-16. Accessed 24 April 2006. <http://www.lib.unb.ca/Texts/SCL/vol17_1/Contents.htm>

Sellwood applies Julia Kristeva's psychosemiotic concepts to her study of "The Found Boat." In her analysis, Sellwood says that the story "draws attention to its paradoxical use of structure, technique and language, thus drawing attention to itself as a 'lie.'" She says that the "lie" mimics realist narrative and the psychoanalytic tradition of gender construction. Paradox subverts and destabilizes the authority of both. Within her discussion, Sellwood makes connections between gender construction by a phallocentric society, the division of space, and the double vision or "split image" of the female subject.

S1127. Seyersted, Per. "'Who Do You Think You Are?': Alice Munro and the Place of Origin." *American Studies in Scandinavia* 24.1 (1992): 17-23.

The title of *Who* illustrates the differences between the national characteristics of Canada and the United States, which have their origins in history. Americans admire ambition, independence, and individualism, qualities which are reflected in the American frontier society. Canadians, on the other hand, shaped by the British tradition, value law and order and the collective good. Seyersted briefly discusses the two protagonists in *Lives* and *Who*. Both are ambitious and trying to find their true selves, but they live in small towns which frown on individual aspiration and pretension.

S1128. Sheckels, Theodore F. "Small-Town Traps: Margaret Laurence's *A Jest of God*; Alice Munro's *Lives of Girls and Women*." *The Island Motif in the Fiction of L. M. Montgomery, Margaret Laurence, Margaret Atwood, and Other Canadian Women Novelists*. Studies on Themes and Motifs in Literature 68. New York: Peter Lang, 2003. 107-132.

In separate analyses of the works of Laurence and Munro, Sheckels looks at the towns of Manawaka and Jubilee as islands-of-the-mind which entrap the protagonists. Sheckels follows the steps of Del's development that lead to her escape from Jubilee. Del's education begins by observing the women around her. Later she chooses not to follow her mother's model, and looks for answers in religion, then in sexual experience. After confronting male power and control in Garnet, Del determines to follow her own path and become a writer. Sheckels comments on the epilogue as contributing a more positive ending to the novel.

S1129. Shih, Elizabeth A. "Phallicism and Ambivalence in Alice Munro's 'Bardon Bus.'" *Contemporary Literature* 44.1 (Spring 2003): 73-105.

Shih applies Freuds's theory of phallicism to the psychosexual identity crisis experienced by the narrator, and her obsession with character X who is seen as a replacement for her absent idealized mother. X's reliance on women as phallic mothers is also considered. Shih speculates that the ambivalence of the characters toward the lost mother could just as likely be channeled into homosexual as heterosexual love and that this is what motivates the two love triangles in the story. Also considered are the narrator's ambivalence between "hysterical eroticism" and common sense, elements of the Freudian concept of "the uncanny," and the image of the "pretty boy" which exposes the phallocentric fallacy of heterosexual gender identity.

S1130. Simpson, Mona. "Alice Munro: Conveying Our Dreams." [Time 100: The 2005 List of the World's Most Influential People . . .] *Time* 18 April 2005 (Canadian ed.): 92; (American ed.): 116.

In this largely laudatory short piece, Simpson points out Munro's skill in conveying the complexity of reality, in creating characters of "mythic resonance," and in writing "with a lucidity equal to Chekhov's." During the past fifteen years, "Munro's stories have broken out of their forms, expanding the genre." Simpson ends by saying that Munro deserves the Nobel Prize.

S1131. Simpson, Mona. "A Quiet Genius." *Atlantic Monthly* December 2001: 126, 128-132, 134-136.

The head note for this article reads "Alice Munro is the living writer most likely to be read in a hundred years." In this review article of *Hateship*, Simpson provides an overview of Munro's work and gives the reasons why the qualities of her writing make her a great, but under-appreciated, writer. Much of the article is taken up with Simpson's account of her interview with Munro for *Paris Review*.

S1132. Simpson, Mona. "Special Award for Continuing Achievement. ['Floating Bridge' by Alice Munro. Introduced by Mona Simpson]." *Prize Stories, 2001: The O. Henry Awards*. Ed. and introd. Larry Dark. New York: Anchor Books, 2001. 81, 83-84.

Simpson remarks on Munro's talents as a writer and gives a commentary on the story "Floating Bridge."

S1133. Sims, Peter. "Photography 'In Camera.'" *Canadian Literature* 113-114 (Summer-Fall 1987): 145-166.

The theme of this article is enclosure and re-enclosure of photography in Canadian novels published between 1970 and 1980. Munro's "Epilogue: The Photographer" and a passage at the end of "Who Do You Think You Are?" are among the works discussed. Sims says that photography is metaphorically "eaten by this writing, absorbed into a process which both destroys and redeems it." Digestion of these photographic images "reconnects them with life and sensation."

S1134. Slopen, Beverley. "Paper Clips." *Quill & Quire* 44.15 (November 1978): 24.

Slopen details the costly last-minute changes Munro made to the manuscript of *Who* just prior to its publication by Macmillan. She describes the changes made to the second half of the book, the alteration of the protagonist's name from Janet to Rose, and the addition of a new story.

S1135.   Slung, Michele. "Book Report: Alice Munro on Writing and Herself." *Book World* [*Washington Post*] 8 May 1983: 23.

In this brief article, Slung reports on an interview with Munro after a reading in Washington, D.C. Munro talks mainly about her isolation as a writer, beginning in youth when she kept her writing secret and in the early years of her career when she wrote without any connections with other authors. Even now she does not like to discuss her writing.

S1136.   Smiley, Jane. "Canada's Best. Cameo Artist: Alice Munro." *Time* (Canadian ed.) 16 December 2002: 49.

Smiley praises Munro's gifts as a writer: the truth of her voice; her inventiveness in producing a variety of interesting stories; the way in which she gives ordinary characters deep insight; and the hope and surprise always found in her gaze. But Munro's greatest accomplishment, Smiley says, is the way in which she has transformed the short story so that it has "gained the capaciousness and fluidity of great novels." To American readers, Smiley adds, her writing gives the feeling of "a slightly foreign country."

S1137.   Smith, Dinita. "Forsaking Her Lair Only in Stories." *New York Times* 30 November 1998, late ed.: E1, E5.
   Rpt. (in part) as "Into the Writer's Lair: Munro Won't Leave Home Unless She Has To." *Sunday Herald* [Halifax] 13 December 1998: C8.

Munro's skill and quality as a writer are praised by Smith. She gives a summary of some of the stories in *Love*, and reports on details from an interview with Munro. Munro talks about her personal life and her writing. She speaks briefly about the progression of her writing, from writing secretly in youth, early rejections by *The New Yorker*, the publication of *Dance*, writer's block, the conflicting demands of family and writing, and the support of her husband. On the subject of femininity and sexuality, Munro says that she camouflages her seriousness behind her sexuality.

S1138.   Smith, Margaret. "Telling Life As It Is." *Weekend Australian Magazine* 14-15 February 1981: 12.

Smith notes that *Beggar* was among the six finalists for the Booker Prize. She reviews *Beggar* and *Lives*, and includes brief excerpts of Munro's own comments on the books.

S1139.   Smith, Rebecca. "'The Only Flying Turtle under the Sun': The Bildungsroman in Contemporary Women's Fiction." *Atlantis* 2.2, Pt. 2 (Spring 1977): 124-132.

On pages 126 to 127 and 129 to 132, Smith discusses *Lives*, saying that the protagonist is both intelligent and perceptive. She traces Del's development, noting her inner conflict between her public role and her authentic self, her spiritual crisis, and final self-affirmation.

S1140.   Smith, Rowland. "Rewriting the Frontier: Wilderness and Social Code in the Fiction of Alice Munro." *Telling Stories: Postcolonial Short Fiction in English*. Ed. Jacqueline Bardolph. Finalized for publication by André Viola with Jean-Pierre Durix.

Introd. André Viola. Cross/Cultures: Readings in the Post/Colonial Literatures in English 47. Amsterdam: Rodopi, 2001. 77-90.

Smith examines how the ethos of the past, associated with the frontier town or garrison, impacts on the attitudes of the protagonists in Munro's fiction. He explores the extent to which the memories of the past create a mythologized experience of wilderness life in order to emotionally manage and tame it. The relationship between women and the frontier or wilderness settlement is discussed. In "Meneseteung" and "A Wilderness Station," the protagonists find refuge in the Canadian wilderness. In "Hard-Luck Stories," the frontier/colonial past is juxtaposed with the "swinging present." There is a need to break away from traditional cultural expectation by indulging in passion. In *Friend*, the yearning for the dangerous and prodigal is related to the reaction against the proprieties and restraints of the past.

S1141. Smythe, Karen. "Sad Stories: The Ethics of Epiphany in Munrovian Elegy." *University of Toronto Quarterly* 60.4 (Summer 1991): 493-506.

Smythe looks at photographic elegism and the elements of realism, magic realism, filmic shock and knowledge, and epiphany and consolation in Munro's stories of elegy. She explains how the perception of a paradox creates an epiphanic understanding of reality in which there is elegiac consolation. Mourning, loss, grief, epiphany, ethics, and consolation are discussed in "The Peace of Utrecht," "The Ottawa Valley," "The Progress of Love," "Friend of My Youth," and "Goodness and Mercy."

S1142. Smythe, Karen. "Shapes and Shades of Death: The Meaning of Loss in Munro's Early Stories." *Wascana Review* 25.1 (Spring 1990): 41-52.

Familial death, grief, elegy, and loss are examined in selected stories from *Dance* and *Something*. Smythe discusses how characters respond to the loss of love and the sense of loss in the passage of time in stories such as "Walker Brothers Cowboy." In stories relating to death, Smythe points out the narrative techniques used to portray the characters' response to death and their recovery. Besides "Walker Brothers Cowboy," Smythe discusses "Images," "Memorial," "The Time of Death," "Day of the Butterfly," "Winter Wind," "Material," and "Tell Me Yes or No."

S1143. Somacarrera, Pilar. "The Codification of Uncertainty: Modality in English-Canadian Fiction." *Aspects of Discourse Analysis*. Ed. Pilar Alonso, et al. Salamanca, Spain: Universidad de Salamanca, 2002. 119-129.

Somacarrera compares the modality of uncertainty in "Something I've Been Meaning to Tell You" and Mavis Gallant's "The Pengnitz Junction." (Based on abstract)

S1144. Somacarrera, Pilar. "Exploring the Impenetrability of Narrative: A Study of Linguistic Modality in Alice Munro's Early Fiction." *Studies in Canadian Literature/ Études en littérature canadienne* 21.1 (1996): 79-91. Accessed 10 May 2006. <http://www.lib.unb.ca/Texts/SCL/vol21_1/Contents.htm>

In her stylistic examination of modality, Somacarrera reveals knowledge to be the main theme in the stories "Something I've Been Meaning to Tell You," "Royal Beatings," and "Half a Grapefruit." In reviewing Munro's style, Somacarrera brings attention to the linguistic aspects of the narrative complexity of her writing. She looks at the modalized statements which convey the narrator's attitude toward the reliability of narrated events, for example the use of the word "know." In "Royal Beatings," possibility, reality and acting, and gossip are discussed.

S1145. Somacarrera, Pilar. "Speech Presentation and 'Coloured' Narrative in Alice Munro's *Who Do You Think You Are?*" *Textual Studies in Canada* 10.11 (1998): 69-79.
"Coloured" narrative is defined as a narrative discourse which suggests the speech of characters without the framework of direct or indirect speech. Somacarrera examines these forms of narrative discourse in *Who*. In "Royal Beatings," free direct speech and free speech are used for parody and objectification. In "Half a Grapefruit," indirect speech is used. "Wild Swans" contains "coloured" speech where the narrative has an oral flavour of storytelling. Somacerrera points out that the idiosyncratic linguistic features reflect the way in which the character's mind is organized, for example the mind of Rose as a child in "Royal Beatings."

S1146. Soper-Jones, Ella. "Wilderness Stations: Peregrination and Homesickness in Alice Munro's *Open Secrets*." *Wascana Review of Contemporary Poetry and Short Fiction* 38.1 (Spring 2003): 29-50.
In *Open Secrets*, three stories ("Spaceships Have Landed," "A Real Life," and "Open Secrets") involve "psuedo-wilderness" settings on the outskirts of the fictional town of Carstairs. These settings represent "wilderness stations" or environments through which the protagonists pass in their evolution through time to another status. The "wildernesses" through which the females travel are socially devalued or environmentally degraded, and reflect the devaluation and victimization of the female travellers. Soper-Jones's article shows how the female characters respond to their situations and how the protagonists are transformed when they exchange one "station" in life for another. In their wanderings and in their search for viable homes and identities, however, they are confronted by the societal belief that women's independence is untenable.

S1147. Soto, Cristina Sánchez. "Spaces between Stories: Reading Secrets in *Lives of Girls and Women*." *Alice Munro: Writing Secrets*. Ed. Héliane Ventura and Mary Condé. Special issue of *Open Letter* 11th ser. 9 (Fall 2003)-12th ser. 1 (Winter 2004): 231-241.
Soto views *Lives* as a short-story composite or a short-story cycle. With this form, Munro achieves coherence, closure, and wholeness. It also allows Munro to keep narrative secrets from the reader by means of discontinuity, gaps, and spaces between the stories. The reader is encouraged to think about these secrets, which are hidden in the "white spaces" between the stories and which also inform them. Soto devotes much of her paper to an examination of the significance of these spaces between the chapters and the part they play in giving coherent meaning in the novel. Secrets inscribed within stories, such as in "Changes and Ceremonies," are also discussed.

S1148. Spettigue, Doug. "Alice Laidlaw Munro: A Portrait of the Artist." *Alumni Gazette* [University of Western Ontario] 45.3 (July 1969): 4-5.
Reissued online *Western Alumni Gazette. Archives. Features.* 21 July 2005. Accessed 29 April 2006. <www.alumnigazette.ca>
The article is written as a tribute to Munro, who won the Governor General's award for *Dance*. Spettigue recalls literary life at the university during the time Munro was a student there, and says that Munro was just outside the circle but contributed to the literary periodi-

cal *Folio*. Robert Weaver's role in Munro's early career is mentioned. Spettigue calls Munro's writing regional and, at the same time, universal. *Dance*, he says, displays a broad range of experience and understanding.

S1149.   Stanley, Don. "On Line: Alice Doesn't Live There Anymore." *Vancouver Magazine* December 1982: 20, 22.

In her interview with Stanley, Munro talks of her early life as a housewife and writer in Vancouver, British Columbia. In those days, the support of her husband was a major factor in her perseverence as a writer. While living in North Vancouver, Munro kept her writing secret from her friends, because she wanted to live a normal life and not that of a literary person outside society. She describes the closely knit community of housewives and the petition about a house in her neighbourhood on which the story "The Shining Houses" was based.

S1150.   Stapleton, Margaret. "Alice Munro—Friend of Our Youth." *Wingham Advance-Times* 16 December 1998: 10-11.

Under the series caption "Glimpses of Our Past: A Look at Wingham of the 1940s," this article contains the personal memories of friends, classmates, and teachers of Munro when she was a girl in the elementary and secondary schools in Wingham. She is described as being gentle, shy, a good listener, studious, isolated, and not greatly involved in social activities. Other qualities mentioned are her intelligence, powers of observation, interest in detail, and gifts as a reader and writer. Family details include her mother's illness, the value her mother placed on education and literature, and the family's attendance at the Wingham United Church.

S1151.   Stead, Kit. "The Twinkling of an 'I': Alice Munro's *Friend of My Youth*." *The Guises of Canadian Diversity/Les masques de la diversité canadienne*. Ed. Serge Jaumain and Marc Maufort. Amsterdam: Rodopi, 1995. 151-164.

Using Jacques Lacan's theory of the split self, the subject "I" who speaks and the "I" who appears as a subject within what is spoken, Stead examines how Munro manages to make coherent, in a moment of time, the endlessly transforming selves of the characters in *Friend of My Youth*. In her examination, Stead looks at the plurality of reality and at the dichotomy between fact and fiction. Photography is discussed as a metaphor for writing fictions and for the ever-changing "I" in "Friend of My Youth" and "Meneseteung." Stead also analyses the metaphorical significance of the house in "Friend of My Youth" and "Wigtime," and the use of clothes in creating a new self in "Pictures of the Ice." Other aspects considered are the mother-daughter relationship, imagery, symbols, and Munro's autobiographical influences.

S1152.   Stewart, Ralph. "A Note on Munro's 'Executioners' and the Fall of Troy." *Journal of the Short Story in English/Les Cahiers de la nouvelle* 42 (2004): 159-165.

Contrary to Munro's opinion of "Executioners," Stewart feels the story is very successful. His article defends this judgement by focusing on the parallels between this story and the classical story of the Trojan War found in Homer's *Iliad*. Stewart draws links between plots, characters, and images and makes historical associations with the wider theme of a changing rural way of life and view of the world. The attributes of Robina and her brothers, their tenacity, beliefs in the supernatural, and determination for revenge seem to have more in common with the Myceneans than modern Ontario. Their disappearing world belongs to the historical past which survives in narrative.

S1153.   Stich, Klaus P. "The Cather Connection in Alice Munro's 'Dulse.'" *Modern Language Studies* 19.4 (Fall 1989): 102-111.

More than a quarter of the story "Dulse" is about the writer Willa Cather. In his examination of the Cather connection in the story, Stich points out that the theme of Cather's book, *A Lost Lady*, reflects Lydia's situation—the decline of dignity, love, and faith in human relations. Like Lydia, Cather spent time on Grand Manan Island. Stich discusses the portrayal of Mr. Stanley and his relationship with Lydia, which he compares to the father-daughter relationship in "The Stone in the Field." Mr. Stanley, Cather, and the island all dramatize Lydia's transition from deception to healing. Stich points out the importance of connections in the story.

S1154.   Stich, Klaus P. "Letting Go with the Mind: Dionysus and Medusa in Alice Munro's 'Meneseteung.'" *Canadian Literature* 169 (Summer 2001): 106-125.

The mythic and psychological allusions to the Greek archetypal figures of Dionysus and Medusa are examined by Stich. Dionysus, the god of wine, is alluded to in the emphasis on grapes and alcohol. The Medusa archetype, especially in relation to thwarted creativity, is seen in Almeda. In his study of the story, Stich also discusses the symbolism of Pearl Street, the image of the Greek classical theatre, and the mythical background to Almeda's rejection of her suitor.

S1155.   Stoffman, Judy. "Celebrating Alice Munro." *Toronto Star* 1 November 1998: D9.
Stoffman reports on what was described as Munro's last public reading at The International Festival of Authors at Harbourfront in Toronto, Ontario, where she read "My Mother's Dream."

S1156.   Stoffman, Judy. "Jubilation in Jubilee." *Toronto Star* 11 July 2002, Ont. ed.: A28.
Stoffman writes about the dedication of the Alice Munro Literary Garden in Munro's home town of Wingham, Ontario. The garden was created by the town to honour Munro, and to show its appreciation for her as a writer and for what she has done for the town.

S1157.   Stoffman, Judy. "A Munro Motherlode: One More Famous Mother, Angry Daughter Memoir." *Toronto Star* 24 April 2001: D5-D6.

Sheila Munro's "surprisingly angry book," as Stoffman calls it, is described by Sheila Munro as something that was necessary for her to write in order to deal with the burden of being the daughter of a literary icon. Stoffman mentions some of the details included in the book, but remarks upon what has not been included, such as details about Munro's siblings. In the article, Sheila Munro is reported as saying that she is interested in self-discovery and needs esteem from others to build her own self-esteem.

S1158.   Stovel, Nora Foster. "Temples and Tabernacles: Alternative Religions in the Fictional Microcosms of Robertson Davies, Margaret Laurence, and Alice Munro." *International Fiction Review* 31.1-2 (2004): 65-77.

The "fictional microcosms" created by Davies, Laurence, and Munro are typical Canadian small towns whose social hierarchies are portrayed through the various religious denominations found in them. In Munro's *Lives*, Del explores the various churches of Jubilee in her search for faith and God. She characterizes each denomination in terms of social status, rather than religious faith. In the end, she rejects the most prosperous of the churches, the

United Church, and the extremist churches of the Baptists and Catholics, in favour of the Anglican Church, a church of the marginalized and one which embodies "the theatrical in religion."

S1159. Stratford, Philip. "Portraits of the Artist: Alice Munro and Marie-Claire Blais." *All the Polarities: Comparative Studies in Contemporary Canadian Novels in French and English*. Toronto: ECW Press, 1986. 56-70.

Munro's *Lives* and Blais's *Une saison dans la vie d'Emmanuel* are compared and contrasted as *Künstlerromans*. In Munro's work, Stratford points out the preciseness of time and place, character and detail. He says that Munro's style is one in which she details Del's emotions and thoughts all through her development until the final statement of artistic ambition at the end of the book. Del sees with two levels of observation—ordinariness and order, and chaos. Stratford also discusses the elements of Gothicism, storytelling, the creative dualism of watching and suffering, and the connection between the surface of life and the grotesque beneath.

S1160. Strauss, Jennifer. "Portrait of the Artist as a Young Woman: Cultural Contexts and the Quest for Identity in Alice Munro's *Lives of Girls and Women* and in Miles Franklin's *My Brilliant Career* and *My Career Goes Bung*." *Australian-Canadian Studies* 8.2 (1991): 41-55.

Strauss compares the three books, labelling them as *Bildungsromans*. All three are fictive autobiographies of a female writer's development as an artist and all have a similar social, cultural, and historical context. The period of time in which the books are set is marked by a search to define the national identity and the role of women in society. *Lives* shows the importance of the past in understanding the roots of the contemporary Canadian. In the novel, Strauss looks at the representative role of the mother and the connection between the small town, national identity, and Del's artistic development. She also elaborates on the place of schooling in Del's ambitions, the representation of sexuality, and Del's development as a novelist.

S1161. Strickland, Nicole. "Lonely Enough to Write." *Vancouver Sun* 3 January 1973: 69.

Strickland bases this article on an interview with Munro. Munro describes her childhood as the classic lonely one of a writer. She talks on a variety of topics related to her writing, among them how she began to write, the multiple roles of wife, mother, and writer, and the publication of *Dance* and *Lives*. She says that women have more interesting personal identities than men, because men have social images to maintain while women do not.

S1162. Struthers, J. R. (Tim). "Alice Munro and the American South." *Canadian Review of American Studies* 6 (1975): 196-204.
    Rpt. revised in *Here and Now: A Critical Anthology*. Vol. 1 of *The Canadian Novel*. Ed. and introd. John Moss. Toronto: NC Press, 1978. 121-133.
    Rpt. in *A Reader's Guide to Canadian Literature*. Toronto: McClelland and Stewart, 1981. 215-219.

The Scots-Irish Protestant ethos produces similarities between Munro and the writers of the American South in character and treatment. Struthers illustrates both the similarities and differences in Munro's writing. While *Lives* follows the open form structure found in Eudora

Welty's *The Golden Apples*, it is not an imitation. The single character point of view is closer to some of the works of Joyce. Munro shows distinctness from all these authors in her first-person feminine point of view. Struthers attributes the effect of documentary photography in her fiction to the influence of James Agee and Walker Evans. Munro's camera-eye technique produces an emotional response to surface details.

S1163. Struthers, J. R. "Alice Munro's Fictive Imagination." *The Art of Alice Munro: Saying the Unsayable*. Papers from the Waterloo Conference. Ed. Judith Miller. Waterloo, ON: University of Waterloo Press, 1984. 103-112.

Munro's fiction is metafiction or self-referring fiction. Her stories are about storytelling or the "fictive imagination." Struthers examines storytelling and mystery in "Something I've Been Meaning to Tell You." He also looks at Munro's use of the epilogue to handle narrative time and structure in *Who*. The development of Munro's skill is seen in later stories, where the stories are internalized in the mental world of the character. Struthers says that imagination plays an important role in Munro's work, serving as theatre, subject, and form. He ends with an analysis of the structure of "Spelling," and its theme of language and the desire to make up stories.

S1164. Struthers, J. R. (Tim). "Myth and Reality: A Regional Approach to the Canadian Short Story." *Laurentian University Review/Revue de l'Université Laurentienne* 8:1 (November 1975): 28-48.

On pages 28 and 30, Struthers mentions three of Munro's stories in terms of the links between historic-geographical environment, personal identity, and art. The geographic landscape is quoted from "Walker Brothers Cowboy." In "The Peace of Utrecht," art takes fragments of the world and unites them in "the other country." In "Winter Wind," where people carry stories within themselves, art is seen as a country.

S1165. Struthers, J. R. (Tim). "Reality and Ordering: The Growth of a Young Artist in *Lives of Girls and Women*." *Essays on Canadian Writing* 3 (Fall 1975): 32-46.
   Rpt. (revised) in *Modern Canadian Fiction*. Ed. Carole Gerson. 2nd rev. ed. Richmond, BC: Open Learning Institute, 1980. 166-174.

James Joyce's *Portrait of an Artist as a Young Man* and Munro's *Lives* are considered as forms of the *Künstlerroman*, or the story of the developing artist. Struthers draws parallels between the two books and their protagonists. He notes Del's distancing from the events in her life with the artist's detached vision as an observer of herself. He also briefly points out similarities between *Lives* and Joyce's *Ulysses*.

S1166. Struthers, J. R. (Tim). "Some Highly Subversive Activities: A Brief Polemic and a Checklist of Works on Alice Munro." *Studies in Canadian Literature* [6.1] (1981): 140-150. Accessed 24 April 2006. <http://www.lib.unb.ca/Texts/SCL/vol6_1/Contents.htm>

In this polemic, Struthers examines the published criticism of Munro and points out its failure to quote or to comment on the work of other critics. He provides a checklist of criticism as a guide to editors and future critics.

S1167. Stubbs, Andrew. "Fictional Landscape: Mythology and Dialectic in the Fiction of Alice Munro." *World Literature Written in English* 23.1 (Winter 1984): 53-62.

In Stubbs's words, "Munro's communities always exist at some primary level as a myth, the outcome of the writer's descent into and emergence from the underworld of the concrete." He says there is a pervasive dialectic tension in her writing, the sense that the surface can open to reveal hidden depths, as in Uncle Benny's world in *Lives*. He describes as poetic the way in which Munro blurs the distinctions between the fictional and factual, and makes the inexplicable seem true. Munro's fiction "symbolizes the eye's collision with surfaces and dramatizes its descent into empty space." Stubbs discusses images of descent and disappearance in "Changes and Ceremonies," the strange and familiar, magic realism, and human relationships located beneath the surfaces in "Hard Luck Stories" and "The Moons of Jupiter."

S1168. Sturgess, Charlotte. "Alice Munro's Fiction: Feminine Identities as Postcolonial Discourses." *La création biographique/Biographical Creation*. Ed. and introd. Marta Dvorak. Collection de L'AFEC 5. Rennes, Fr.: Presses Universitaires de Rennes, 1997. 85-90.

Sturgess examines the emergence of self-knowledge and feminine identity in the context of historical continuity and discontinuity in *Lives* and *Who*. In *Lives*, Del's development takes place within the framework of displaced origins seen in the topographical complexities of Jubilee and Flats Road. In the book, Sturgess notes a retreat from historical continuity and resistance to the closure of secured meaning. For Rose in *Who*, the noncontinuity of self in time involves both a falling away of identity and its constant restaging in a "re-presentation" of self. Indeterminacy is Rose's narrative mode. "Royal Beatings" and "Spelling" are specifically discussed.

S1169. Sturgess, Charlotte. "Alice Munro's 'Progress of Love': Secrets, Continuity and Closure." *Études canadiennes/Canadian Studies* 30 (1991): 105-112.

Sturgess explores how Munro "negotiates the thread of sequence (continuity) and closure against the theme of family secrets that are 'unsaid.'" While the repressed and distorted secrets are contained and maintained in the process of sequence, their energy is displaced across the narrative through constant reinterpretation. This permeates the sequence and colours the events. Sturgess continues with a discussion of locating the self as space, and female narrative desire as it relates to the story. The multiple feminine narratives in the story converge with time. There is a constant movement toward, and deferral of, final closure.

S1170. Sturgess, Charlotte. "La représentation féminine et la mise en scène dans *The Beggar Maid: Stories of Flo and Rose* d'Alice Munro." *Commonwealth Essays and Studies* 17.2 (Spring 1995): 44-49.

The narratological significance of staging, or the theatrical, is examined in *Beggar*. Sturgess says that the double system of codes, patriarchal codes and personal conscience, creates ambivalence in the feminine identity and causes women to play roles where they achieve a conceptual level of language. Sturgess looks at the mimetic field of language, the feminine playing of roles, the ruptured identities and mimicry of Rose and Flo, theatrical performance, gossip, and silence.

S1171. Suárez Lafuente, M. S. "Fiction and Reality in Alice Munro's Short Stories." *Short Fiction in the New Literatures in English: Proceedings of the Nice Conference of the European Association for Commonwealth Literature and Language Studies*. Ed. and introd. J. Bardolph. Nice: Faculté des Lettres et Sciences Humaines de Nice, 1989. 147-151.

Suárez Lafuente studies Munro's strategy of the two-faced narrative, where she describes the occurrences of the everyday world and the account of them as seen and told from the internal point of view of the narrator. For a number of stories, she briefly discusses the points of view of the characters, the passing of time, the theme of death, and the significance of the house.

S1172.   Sutton, Brian. "Munro's 'How I Met My Husband.'" *Explicator* 63.2 (Winter 2005): 107-110.

Sutton shows how the narrator's awareness of the value of secrets and her ability to keep them works in her favour. He contrasts her behaviour of withholding information with that of other characters in the story who lack the same sense of privacy or discretion. These characters are viewed unsympathetically by others. In the concluding paragraph, the narrator's secrecy is rewarded and results in a relationship with her future husband.

S1173.   Szalay, Edina. "The Gothic as Adolescent Fantasy: Alice Munro's *Lives of Girls and Women*." *Central European Journal of Canadian Studies* 1 (2001): 5-17.

The interrelationships of Gothic fantasy and female fantasy are discussed. The Gothic patterns of Del's fantasy are the result of the reading of Gothic novels. These are shown to influence her relationships with men and her sexuality. However, in tracing Del's growing sense of independence, Munro undermines the validity of the Gothic discourse in her revisionary study of the Gothic genre. Szalay looks at the Gothic elements in the novel and discusses female sexual desire and Gothic heroines.

S1174.   Tausky, Thomas E. "Biocritical Essay." *The Alice Munro Papers, First Accession: An Inventory of the Archive at the University of Calgary Libraries*. Comp. Jean M. Moore and Jean F. Tener. Ed. Apollonia Steele and Jean F. Tener. Canadian Archival Inventory Series: Literary Papers 7. Calgary: University of Calgary Press, 1986. ix-xxiv. Also online. Accessed 24 April 2006. <http://www.ucalgary.ca/lib-old/SpecColl/munrobioc.htm>

Using quotations from a private interview with Munro, Tausky covers the author's early life in the conservative environment of Wingham, Ontario. Munro tells Tausky that when she was growing up she felt like an outsider. She began writing at the age of 12. Her feelings of excitement in writing and the fact that her early writing was largely imitative are discussed. Tausky follows the evolution of Munro's writing career, including a period in which she lost confidence in her writing. He details the chronology in which the stories in *Dance* were written, and follows this with a critical analysis of *Dance*, *Lives*, *Something*, *Who*, and *Moons*. Autobiographical elements in "The Peace of Utrecht" and "Walker Brothers Cowboy" are presented.

S1175.   Tausky, Thomas E. "'What Happened to Marion?': Art and Reality in *Lives of Girls and Women*." *Studies in Canadian Literature* 11.1 (Spring 1986): 52-76. Accessed 24 April 2006. <http://www.lib.unb.ca/Texts/SCL/vol11_1/Contents.htm>

In the novel, Tausky explores the artificiality and limitations of art in dealing with reality. He begins with a look at Munro's fictional aesthetic and at the characters, Miss Farris and Uncle Craig, as models of the committed artist and realist (historian). Comparing the drafts and final versions of "Epilogue: The Photographer," Tausky discloses Munro's artistic crisis in writing the chapter. The motifs in the chapter provide insight: the failed artistic effort, the awareness of inadequacy, and passion in the creative impulse. Other stories of art and artists discussed are "The Ottawa Valley," "Home," and "Material."

S1176. Taylor, Michael. "The Unimaginable Vancouvers: Alice Munro's Words." *Probable Fictions: Alice Munro's Narrative Acts*. Ed. Louis K. MacKendrick. Downsview, ON: ECW Press, 1983. 127-143.

Munro's fiction, which often repeats words, encourages the reader to see these words almost as objects, with properties of their own. In *Lives*, Taylor points out Del's passion for the surfaces of words such as "mistress," and her imaginative response to words such as "attack," as in heart attack. Dull, clichéd words are given new life, originality, and the possibility of beauty by Rose in "Royal Beatings." Both Del and Rose group words together for the sheer pleasure of reciting them. Both, in their environments of poverty, are sustained by the richness of printed words. Taylor also examines the effects of words expressing nonconformity, words of eccentrics, the lack of words, and pretentious language. A distrust of language and art, and scepticism about words, found in stories such as "Material" and "Spelling," may be evidence of the sentiment held by Munro herself.

S1177. Tener, Jean F. "The Invisible Iceberg." *The Art of Alice Munro: Saying the Unsayable*. Papers from the Waterloo Conference. Ed. Judith Miller. Waterloo, ON: University of Waterloo Press, 1984. 37-42.

Tener details the arrangement and description of the Alice Munro papers at the University of Calgary Library, prior to the publication of a preliminary inventory of the collection. The principles used to assemble the trunk and suitcase of papers received from Munro were based on provenance and original order. The complicated task of sorting and arranging in chronological order the different drafts, revisions, and aborted versions of the same work, of identifying fragments, and piecing together manuscripts is described. The collection was sorted into a correspondence file of over 200 letters, literary papers, individual stories, exercise notebooks, and an unfinished novel. Several draft manuscripts of *Lives* and *Something* were identified.

S1178. Thacker, Robert. "Alice Munro and the Anxiety of American Influence." *Context North America: Canadian/U.S. Literary Relations*. Ed. Camille R. La Bossière. Ottawa: University of Ottawa Press, 1994. 133-144.

Thacker questions why Canadian literary critics focus on British and European writers as influences on Munro, while Munro herself acknowledges being affected by the visions of a number of American writers, particularly Eudora Welty. He sees Willa Cather as a forerunner to both Welty and Munro, in practicing the "art of connection" in her community stories. He examines Cather's influence on Munro's story "Dulse." Briefly commenting on the criticism of W. R. Martin and Klaus P. Stich, Thacker concludes that, while such studies deal with the question of Munro's American influences, further and deeper analysis is needed and other American writers need to be explored in this regard.

S1179. Thacker, Robert. "Alice Munro's Willa Cather." *Canadian Literature* 134 (Autumn 1992): 42-57.

Cather's influence on Munro and their shared views are demonstrated in Thacker's comparative analysis of Cather's "Before Breakfast" and Munro's "Dulse." His study is based on the differences between drafts of Munro's story. Thacker makes a comparison between the protagonists of the two stories. In "Dulse," he further examines the characters of Lydia and Stanley and the characterization of Cather herself. The distancing resulting from the third-person point of view is also discussed.

S1180. Thacker, Robert. "(Auto)biographical Home Places in Carr, Laurence, and Munro." *La création biographique/Biographical Creation*. Ed. and introd. Marta Dvorak. Collection de L'AFEC 5. Rennes, Fr.: Presses Universitaires de Rennes, 1997. 135-142.

Thacker looks at the three authors' personal connections to their geographic home places, and their conscious autobiographical creation of these places in their writing. First looking at the female empathetic connection to place and women's autobiography, Thacker includes an excerpt from Eudora Welty's theory of place in fiction. In the case of Munro, he discusses her autobiographical attachment to her home place, Wingham, Ontario, fictionalized as Jubilee in stories such as "The Peace of Utrecht." He emphasizes the mother-daughter connection and the physical and material details of the home place written into the story.

S1181. Thacker, Robert. "Canadian Literature's 'America.'" *Essays on Canadian Writing* 71 (2000): 128-139.

Thacker discusses the importance of foreign markets to Canadian writers and, on pages 134 to 137, explains how Munro's career took off when Virginia Barber became her American literary agent in 1976. He also refers to a talk given by John Metcalf, in which Metcalf asserted that Munro's high reputation in Canada was a result of having been published in *The New Yorker*. This talk was later revised and published in the *National Post*. Thacker comments on the reaction in Canada to Metcalf's article.

S1182. Thacker, Robert. "'Clear Jelly': Alice Munro's Narrative Dialectics." *Probable Fictions: Alice Munro's Narrative Acts*. Ed. Louis K. MacKendrick. Downsview, ON: ECW Press, 1983. 37-60.

Thacker examines the development of Munro's technique of narrative dialectics, by which she balances one point of view against another in order to make things clear. He follows her stories chronologically and discusses the first- and third-person points of view, retrospective narration, and the presentation of character. In "Good-By Myra," he considers the retrospective first-person narrator and the revisions to the story. In "Thanks for the Ride," Munro uses a protagonist who is a first-person participant and a third-person observer. Munro's development culminates with the dual-voiced retrospective technique to which she makes subtle adjustments.

S1183. Thacker, Robert. "Connection: Alice Munro and Ontario." *American Review of Canadian Studies* 14.2 (Summer 1984): 213-226.

In Munro's fiction, the characters define themselves through their connection with rural Ontario. Their identity is dependent on memory, association, and connection with the past and present. Thacker elaborates on these connections. He notes the importance of setting in several early stories and the reflexive use of Ontario in "The Ottawa Valley," "The Peace of

Utrecht" is cited as the first story to establish Munro's use of place. The significance of the town of Jubilee in the story is outlined. Thacker also briefly discusses "Connection."

S1184.   Thacker, Robert. "Go Ask Alice: The Progress of Munro Criticism (Review article)." *Journal of Canadian Studies/Revue d'études canadiennes* 26.2 (Summer 1991): 156-169.
In this review article, Thacker talks about the growing body of Munro literary criticism. He reviews six critical books which are either entirely devoted to Munro's fiction or which contain chapters on it. The books he discusses are by E. D. Blodgett, Linda Hutcheon, Michele Gadpaille, Ildikó de Papp Carrington, Beverly Rasporich, and Coral Ann Howells. (For Part 2, see entry S1188.)

S1185.   Thacker, Robert. "Introduction: Alice Munro, Writing 'Home': 'Seeing This Trickle in Time.'" *Alice Munro Writing On . . . .* Ed. Robert Thacker. Special issue of *Essays on Canadian Writing* 66 (Winter 1998): 1-20.
   Rpt. in *The Rest of the Story: Critical Essays on Alice Munro*. Ed. Robert Thacker. Toronto: ECW Press, 1999. 1-20.
Thacker's introduction includes a commentary on the essays in the volume, but focuses mainly on the uncollected story "Home." He sees the story as being at the centre of Munro's work, illustrating the ongoing connections in her art. "Home" forecasts a relationship with the later stories "The Progress of Love" and "Friend of My Youth." It looks forward and backward to stories, such as "Friend of My Youth," "My Mother's Dream," "The Peace of Utrecht," and "The Ottawa Valley," in which Munro has fictionalized her relationship with her mother. Besides the mother-daughter relationship, Thacker brings up other continuing elements in Munro's fiction such as the Huron County setting, autobiography, and gender roles.

S1186.   Thacker, Robert. "Mapping Munro: Reading the 'Clues.'" *Dominant Impressions: Essays on the Canadian Short Story*. Ed. Gerald Lynch and Angela Arnold Robbeson. Reappraisals: Canadian Writers 22. Ottawa: University of Ottawa Press, 1999. 127-135.
At the beginning of the article, Thacker describes the relationship between Munro's work and its critics, calling them an "empathetic union of readers." He relates Munro's vision of life to her fiction. "The Peace of Utrecht" stands out as an important demonstration of Munro's autobiographical connection to her home and mother. Thacker uses information from the manuscripts in the Munro Archives at the University of Calgary Library to map details from Munro's past or home place and link them to details in her work, specifically in "Miles City, Montana." Secondly, he studies the recurrences of images or incidents in her work.

S1187.   Thacker, Robert. "'So Shocking a Verdict in Real Life': Autobiography in Alice Munro's Stories." *Reflections: Autobiography and Canadian Literature*. Ed. and introd. K. P. Stich. Ottawa: University of Ottawa Press, 1988. 153-161.
Thacker notes that the narrative perspective in Munro's fiction has gradually grown older and that this reflects Munro's changing perspective of life with age. As in autobiography, the main concern of her stories is a definition of self. Self-definition is accompanied by increasing uncertainties about what is real. The underpinning of autobiography, Thacker says, gives fictional stories validity. Discussed are "The Ottawa Valley," "The Peace of Utrecht," "Connection," "The Stone in the Field," "The Moons of Jupiter," and "Dulse."

S1188. Thacker, Robert. "What's 'Material'? The Progress of Munro Criticism, Part 2 (Review article)." *Journal of Canadian Studies/Revue d'études canadiennes* 33.2 (1998): 196-210.

This is the second part of Thacker's evaluation of the literary criticism on Munro's work. In this part, he reviews critical books published since 1990. They include works by Neil Besner, James Carscallen, Ajay Heble, Louis King MacKendrick, Magdalene Redekop, Catherine Ross, and Karen Smythe. (For Part 1, seen entry S1184.)

S1189. Thomas, Sue. "Reading Female Sexual Desire in Alice Munro's *Lives of Girls and Women*." *Critique: Studies in Contemporary Fiction* 36.2 (Winter 1995): 107-120.

Thomas begins by reviewing the feminist interpretations of Coral Ann Howells, Barbara Godard, and Smaro Kambourali. She moves to a discussion of Ada Jordan's view of romantic sexual desire as a cause of women's dependency on men. Ada's views are contrasted with Del's desire for passion, something that is lacking in her relationship with Jerry Story. Del has difficulty reconciling passion with reason, and her sexual desires with her ambitions. Her psychological anxieties and ambiguities give emotional intensity to Del's sexual desire, and complicate her attempt to live as a female sexual subject.

S1190. Thompson, Elizabeth. "Foreword." *Friend of My Youth*. By Alice Munro. Canadian Literary Classics. Large Print Library. Markham, ON: Fitzhenry & Whiteside, 1997. ix-xiv.

Thompson provides commentaries on the stories "Five Points," "Oh, What Avails," "Hold Me Fast, Don't Let Me Pass," "Pictures of the Ice," "Goodness and Mercy," "Meneseteung," and "Friend of My Youth."

S1191. Tiffin, Audrey. "Join in Praise for Work of Alice Munro." Letter. *Wingham Advance-Times* 20 October 1982: 4.

Tiffin, a teacher in Wingham, responds to Joyce Wayne's article published in *Books in Canada* which refers to the negative reaction of Wingham residents to the portrayal of their town in Munro's writing and remarks. Tiffin defends Munro by praising her work. She says that her success still "fuels Wingham's ire." Because of her, Tiffin says, Wingham has become famous and the town should praise Munro, along with the rest of the world.

S1192. Timson, Judith. "Merciful Light: Alice Munro's New Stories Are Luminous." *Maclean's* 7 May 1990: 66-67.
   Rpt. (excluding photographs) in *Contemporary Literary Criticism*. Ed. Brigham Narins and Deborah A. Stanley. Vol. 95. Detroit: Gale, 1997. 306-308.

Timson combines a review of *Friend* with a brief report on an interview she had with Munro. In the interview, Munro talks about fame, book tours, and publicity as taking the focus away from writing. She feels guilty dividing her time between family and writing, and says society expects women to be nurturing. Writing is of primary importance to her.

S1193. Timson, Judith. "The Prime of Alice Munro: No One Reveals the Inner Lives of Women Like Our Greatest Short Story Writer." *Chatelaine* October 1998: 42.

In this short article, Timson mentions Munro's latest collection, *Love*, and the story "Miles City, Montana." She praises Munro's work and raises the themes of women, their self-discovery, and their duplicity when involved in adultery.

S1194. Toolan, Michael. "Values Are Descriptions: Or, From Literature to Linguistics and Back Again by Way of Keywords." *BELL: Belgian Journal of English Language and Literature* ns 2 (2004): 11-30.

(Item not seen. Keywords: "The Love of a Good Woman"; corpus analysis; lexicology; reader response)

S1195. Tracy, Laura. "Culture and Transference." *"Catching the Drift": Authority, Gender and Narrative Strategy in Fiction*. New Brunswick, NJ: Rutgers University Press, 1988. 188-206.

On pages 193 to 200, Tracy discusses female desire in the story "Labor Day Dinner." The protagonist, Roberta, is examined as a woman in whom female desire is absent. She is located in the cultural prison in which society places autonomous women with desires. Roberta connects passivity, or the refraining from the exercise of desire, to power and autonomy of being. Tracy says that Munro writes with didactic purpose and with narrative authority, and engages the reader by subverting the narration itself. The absence in her stories implies the cultural suppression of female desire.

S1196. Truss, Lynne. "Alice in Memory's Looking Glass." *Independent, Sunday Review* [London] 14 October 1990: 33.

Truss bases her article on an interview with Munro. In it, Munro talks about how the titles of her collections are decided and how she feels about her work being labelled as depressing. Speaking of her return to Huron County, Munro says that she felt a disjunction between the person she was in the past and the person she is now. She says she has less time for writing now, and talks about the differences in time available to men and women writers. Mentioning her Scottish ancestor James Hogg, Munro says that modesty, self-denigration, and guilt originate from Calvinist teachings.

S1197. Twigg, Alan. "Alice Doesn't Live Here Any More—But She's a Distinguished Visitor." *Vancouver Province, The Magazine* 9 March 1980: 12.

Twigg interviews Munro, who is the University of British Columbia's first writer-in-residence. Twigg's article begins with her biographical background and a general commentary on her writing. Twigg points out its documentary realism and calls Munro a "Vermeer of emotions." Munro talks about her preference for the short story and her need to work out a design before writing. She shies away from being called a feminist, and sees the injustices toward women as complicated, not black and white. The removal of *Lives* from the school library in Huron County, and the fundamentalist attitude of the community, bothers her.

S1198. Urquhart, Jane. Afterword. *No Love Lost*. New Canadian Library. Toronto: McClelland & Stewart, 2003. 416-421.

Urquhart writes about the theme of love in the collection of stories she has assembled: "The Albanian Virgin," "Bardon Bus," "The Bear Came Over the Mountain," "Carried Away," "The Children Stay," "Hateship, Friendship, Courtship, Loveship, Marriage," "The Love of a Good Woman," "Meneseteung," "Mischief," and "Simon's Luck." She says that Munro is interested in the singularity of the experience of love and with the secrecy associated with it. Munro conveys situations of suffering women with a perfect balance of honesty and empathy. Urquhart discusses how love brings about a transformation of self in some of the stories.

S1199. Van Rys, John C. "Reclaiming Marginalia: The Grotesque and the Christian Reader." *Christianity and Literature* 44.3-4 (Spring-Summer 1995): 345-357.

Unlike the relationship between the grotesque and grace in Flannery O'Connor's writing, the grotesque in Munro's work is used as a disruptive strategy. Munro uses the grotesque in graphic descriptions of the body, in patterns of inflation and deflation, and in exposing the bizarre beneath the ordinary surface of life. Van Rys studies the grotesque in "Meneseteung," where it is seen to counter the protagonist's life and art. The grotesque reduces the conventional Christianity that has defined Almeda's life to polite superficiality which breaks apart in the face of "the other." Van Rys suggests that Christian readers must become dialogically open to the voice of the grotesque.

S1200. Vanstone, Ellen. "*Saturday Night* Scores Coup with Munro Tale ['Jakarta']." *Globe and Mail* 12 January 1998: C5.

Vanstone reviews the story "Jakarta," which was published in the January 1998 issue of *Saturday Night*.

S1201. Vasey, Paul. "Alice Has a Lot of Reasons to Be Happy." *Windsor Star* 27 September 1974: 34.

Vasey interviewed Munro after her move to London, Ontario, where she took up the position of writer-in-residence at the University of Western Ontario. Munro tells Vasey she is happy. She talks about how she began to write and describes her writing habits and process. Relating to her personal life, Munro talks about marrying when she was quite young, her recent divorce, and her move back to Ontario.

S1202. Ventura, Héliane. "Alice Munro's 'Boys and Girls': Mapping Out Boundaries." *Commonwealth Essays and Studies* 15.1 (Autumn 1992): 80-87.

The theme of the story centres around the female passage into adolescence and a girl's rebellion against her resulting deflation of status. Ventura concentrates on gender roles and links these to the topography inside and outside the house. She associates the inside with female gender roles, which are viewed negatively. The outside of the house is the male domain, where male activities are viewed positively, even valorized. Ventura goes on to examine the inverted topography of the house, which is mirrored in the barn scene. She carries the inside-outside dichotomy to the space in the children's bedroom, which in turn mirrors the layout of the fox pens.

S1203. Ventura, Héliane. "Alice Munro's 'Forgiveness in Families': The Story of a Parasite." *Recherches anglaises et nord américaines* 24 (1991): 137-142.

Ventura examines the strategies used by the narrator of the story to indict her brother and portray him as a pseudo-criminal, a pseudo-psychotic, and a pseudo-religious person. She looks also at the brother and sister rivalry and their reciprocal accusations.

S1204. Ventura, Héliane. "Alice Munro's Secret *Ort*." *Alice Munro: Writing Secrets*. Ed. Héliane Ventura and Mary Condé. Special issue of *Open Letter* 11th ser. 9 (Fall 2003)-12th ser. 1 (Winter 2004): 255-266.

"Ort," Heidegger's term for an epiphanic site, is a concept which Ventura links to traces, or secrets, in three stories. In "Pictures of the Ice," "ort" is a snow-covered landscape and the trace is the sediment or the build-up of ice or snow that both conceals traces and exposes other traces, thus making room for recovery. In "The Children Stay," the imprint of the footprint in the sand is the trace which provides the female character a sense of recurrence, and thus recovery, after the loss of her children. In "Floating Bridge," the "ort" is the bridge on which the secret trace of the kiss redeems the female character from her abject state.

S1205.   Ventura, Héliane. "Country Girls and City Girls in Alice Munro's 'The Progress of Love.'" *Études canadiennes/Canadian Studies* 29 (1990): 222-233.
In the story, Ventura identifies two geographical poles: the countryside (associated with good country people) and the city (associated with people of looser morals and a faster lifestyle). The latter are represented by the narrator's grandfather and visiting aunt. The two sides become fused and entangled, much like the moral attitudes and feelings that were first attached to them. The removal of the layers of wallpaper is examined as a metaphor for the complex texture of the past, with its fused patterns and meanings. In rearranging the reality and getting to the essence, the narrator is defining her goal as an artist.

S1206.   Ventura, Héliane. "Delusion, Deception and Disillusionment in the Mountains: Alice Munro's 'Providence.'" *Études canadiennes/Canadian Studies* 31 (1991): 107-114.
The mountain environment which dominates the story is shown to be symbolic of both shelter to the run-away wife and her daughter and of an obstacle that blocks the path to further adventures. The environment causes the narrator to discover a world of delusions and deceptions. Ventura shows how ambivalence, irony, and contradiction are inscribed within the text. She discusses the concept of deception and "true lies."

S1207.   Ventura, Héliane. "'Fits': A Baroque Tale." *Recherches anglaises et nord-américaines* 22 (1989): 89-97.
Ventura applies a version of distortion, called baroque anamorphosis, to her examination of the story "Fits." The method of anamorphosis involves setting surface appearance or truth in strong relief against illusion, camouflage, and deception. This results in a sense of instability and alienation in the story. Ventura looks at the narrative strategy of omission, and the internal focalization of the outsider whose knowledge is restricted. The traits of baroque anamorphosis are applied to the treatment of the main character and to the landscape as seen through the eyes of her husband.

S1208.   Ventura, Héliane. "The Ordinary As Subterfuge: Alice Munro's 'Pictures of the Ice.'" *Journal of the Short Story in English* 38 (Spring 2002): 73-84.
Ventura uses Louis Marin's theoretical framework of entrapment in her examination of the devices used for deception in "Pictures of the Ice." According to Marin, the art of entrapment relies on the ordinary; and the art of deconstructing artifice relies on finding the strange in the ordinary. Marin's three types of entrapment (fantasy, appetite, and movement) are applied in Ventura's analysis, which considers the two story lines of Austin Cobbett and Karin Duprey. She links double images to duplicity and duplicitous transformation. The forms of entrapment are shown to involve both characters and readers who are lured by baits such as photographs. Ventura discusses devices such as polysemy, metaphors, and semantic and stylistic parallelisms.

S1209. Ventura, Héliane. "The Setting Up of Unsettlement in Alice Munro's 'Tell Me Yes or No.'" *Postmodern Fiction in Canada*. Ed. Theo D'haen and Hans Bertens. Postmodern Studies 6. Amsterdam: Rodopi, 1992. 105-123.

Throughout the story, Munro maintains a dialectic tension between fact and fantasy as a prelude to the unsettlement that occurs at the end of the story, where fact and fantasy crumble. The two different planes or narratives of the story are differentiated by tense. The facts of the past are represented by the past tense, while the fantasy of the present is represented by the present tense. Ventura examines the methods of entanglement between the two narratives. She finds that dialectic proximity and distance in the relationship are inscribed both in the theme and the language of the story.

S1210. Vickers, Reg. "The Pain and Joys of Writing." *Herald Magazine* [*Calgary Herald*] 2 June 1972: 8.

Vickers interviewed Munro after she won the Canadian Booksellers' Association Award for *Lives*. He records her remarks about the adjustments women make to obtain power and satisfaction in their lives. Munro talks also about revision of her work, mentioning *Lives* in this regard, and says she is working on a new novel. She gives her thoughts about being a woman writer.

S1211. Wainwright, J. A. "Deep Caves and Kitchen Linoleum: The Tale within the Tale in Alice Munro's Fiction." *Journal of the Short Story in English/Les Cahiers de la nouvelle* 4 (Spring 1985): 141-149.

Wainwright observes that in Munro's fiction, women narrators select material from their past and tell stories about themselves to help reveal their present condition and to shape themselves. He goes on to examine examples of tales within tales in "Images," "The Shining Houses," *Lives* ("Changes and Ceremonies" and "Epilogue: The Photographer"), *Something* ("Executioners," "Winter Wind," and "The Ottawa Valley"), *Who* ("Royal Beatings"), and *Moons* ("The Stone in the Field" and "Visitors").

S1212. Wainwright, J. A. "The Gate in Her Head." *International Literature in English: Essays on the Major Writers*. Ed. Robert L. Ross. New York: Garland, 1991. 303-314.

In a section entitled "De-Colonizing Patriarchy," Wainwright examines gender gaps, the differences between males and females, and women's responses to these. He begins with the story "Red Dress—1946" and looks at the shaping of female consciousness by society and the female resistance to it. In *Lives*, the gender gap is bridged through the assertion of female differences. The female creative voice is brought forward in "Tell Me Yes or No." The opposition of female and male voices, and male and female acceptance of differences, is found in *Who*. Other stories discussed are "White Dump," "Hold Me Fast, Don't Let Me Pass," and "Meneseteung."

S1213. "Walker Brothers Cowboy." *Short Stories for Students: Presenting Analysis, Context, and Criticism on Commonly Studied Short Stories*. Ed. Jennifer Smith. Detroit: Gale Group, 2001. 282-299.

This guide for students gives an overview of the story under the following headings: plot summary, characters, themes, style, historical context, and critical overview. It also includes excerpts from criticism and sources for further reading.

S1214. Wall, Kathleen. "Representing the Other Body: Frame Narratives in Margaret Atwood's 'Giving Birth' and Alice Munro's 'Meneseteung.'" *Canadian Literature* 154 (1997): 74-90.

Wall looks at the framed representation of women and their bodies. The frame, she says, presents the woman as a divided self, as both object and subject. The two stories "de-romanticize" and "de-reify" the female body. The frame and the framed bodies interact to call attention to the margin and marginal. Wall examines the narrative construction of the stories of Atwood and Munro, and notes similarities in the doubled and mirrored structure. She also examines the narrator and narrative techniques used. The article concludes with a consideration of women as writers writing about the body, and language as a means of articulation between body and mind, and body and society.

S1215. Wallace, Bronwen. "Women's Lives: Alice Munro." *The Human Elements: Critical Essays*. Ed. David Helwig. Ottawa: Oberon, 1978. 52-67.
Rpt. (excerpt) as "Men, Women and Body English in Alice Munro" in *Books in Canada* 7.7 (August-September 1978): 13.

Using a feminist perspective, Wallace studies the way in which Munro presents the experiences and perceptions of women. Munro's fiction demonstrates the differences in how men and women deal with life. Women gain strength through their limitations, weaknesses, and the oppositions in their lives. Men tend to deny, control, and fear that which they cannot understand or do not like in themselves. Wallace discusses the feminine experience in *Lives*, "Boys and Girls," "Material," "Tell Me Yes or No," "The Peace of Utrecht," and "The Ottawa Valley."

S1216. Walsh, Nancy. "The Progress of Alice Munro: 1995 CBA Author of the Year." *Canadian Bookseller* 18.5 (June-July 1996): 46-48.

The Canadian Booksellers' Association presented Munro with the 1995 Author of the Year Award for *Open Secrets*. Walsh outlines Munro's publishing history and awards, and comments on her writing, saying that as Munro progresses "she keeps getting better."

S1217. Ward, Audrey. "Betwixt and Between: The Suspended Women of Alice Munro." *Gender and Domination: The Problem of Patriarchal Power in the Narratives of Alice Walker, Alice Munro, Gloria Naylor and Toni Morrison*. Owings Mills, MD: Watermark, 1990. 16-25.

In a nonacademic treatment, Ward describes the theme of male domination in "How I Met My Husband," "Walking on Water," "Marrakesh," and "Material."

S1218. Ward, Olivia. "Men Are Suffering, Too." *Sunday Star* [*Toronto Star*] 6 May 1979: D5.

Ward's article reports on an interview with Munro. She quotes Munro as saying, "People mistake my point of view. My stories show how women suffer, but not all pain is on one side, men are suffering too." Her view of feminism is not political, but one of women telling the truth about themselves. The duality in her roles of mother and writer is mentioned. The article also includes some details of her life, writing career and awards.

S1219. Ware, Tracy. "Knowing Our Place." Letter. *Globe and Mail* 4 January 1997: D12.

To gain literary power in Canada, Canadian writers must be internationally acclaimed. Ware cites as an example Munro's international exposure after being published in *The New Yorker*.

S1220. Warwick, Susan J. "Growing Up: The Novels of Alice Munro." *Essays on Canadian Writing* 29 (Summer 1984): 204-225.

Warwick compares the narrative techniques used to portray the development of the two protagonists in *Lives* and *Beggar*. Both novels show commonality in their "open-form" structure. In both, the manipulation of time creates a sense of loss and optimism. The stories are ordered chronologically. Warwick describes *Lives* as a retrospective account of childhood through to adolescence from the perspective of an adult. *Who* is an account of remembered childhood, adolescence, and adulthood, with a backward and forward movement in time. A comparison is also made between the characters of the protagonists.

S1221. Waterston, Elizabeth. "Duncan, Munro, and the Vistas of Memory." *Rapt in Plaid: Canadian Literature and Scottish Tradition*. Toronto: University of Toronto Press, 2001. 249-265.

Jane Duncan, the pseudonym for Elizabeth Jane Cameron, and Alice Munro share similarities in the complex way in which they link female experience through the female narrator's memory. Waterson explores both authors' personal backgrounds and writing styles. In Munro's "Friend of My Youth," Waterson notes the Scottish allusions and undertone, the narrative technique and the mother-daughter relationship. She also summarizes the story "Hold Me Fast, Don't Let Me Pass." Munro's narrative method resembles the rhythm of Scottish women's gossip and storytelling.

S1222. Watmough, David. "Confessionalism and the First Person, or the Future of Fiction." *Canadian Fiction Magazine* 32/33 (1979-1980): 135-139.

On page 137, Watmough explains how Munro's fiction demonstrates the trend toward the expression of individual experience through a new literature of confessionalism. The quietness and reticence of the stories in *Dance* are contrasted with the strong personal fiction of "Tell Me Yes or No." Watmough warns of the dangers of confessionalism.

S1223. Watts, Janet. "A Long Training in Duplicity." *Observer* [London] 1 Feb. 1987: 58.

In this reported interview with Watts, Munro explains that, although her vision as a writer may be getting bleaker, there is still optimism in her view of life and in her stories, and that an enormous amount of faith goes into the writing of fiction. Moving from childhood to her first marriage, Munro says that she always had the desire to write, but the expectations of others caused her to live a life of duplicity, carrying out the expected roles while continuing to write. In explaining her writing process and fictional aesthetics, Munro says that the most difficult part is building a story around a pivotal moment. If the story is written well, it will show mystery in the moment and this negates the negative aspects in the story.

S1224. Wayne, Joyce. "Huron County Blues." *Books in Canada* 11.8 (October 1982): 9-12.

Wayne's article is partly based on an interview with Munro. The topics first covered are Munro's early writing, marriage, children, writer's block, and separation from her husband. Wayne then focuses on Munro's close relationship with Huron County, and the antagonistic feelings of the people in Wingham toward her and her writing. Alleged negative remarks she made about the town in an article published in *Today Magazine* caused the editor of the *Wingham-Advance Times* to write a stinging response in the paper. Wayne studies the role of this tension in Munro's fiction. Speaking in the context of "Chaddeleys and Flemings,"

Munro says that "there is a good deal of [her] father's family" in herself. She also identifies with her conservative rural heritage, which views ambition as something that "will catch up to you."

S1225. Weaver, John. "Society and Culture in Rural and Small-Town Ontario: Alice Munro's Testimony on the Last Forty Years." *Patterns of the Past: Interpreting Ontario's History*. Ed. Roger Hall, William Westfall, and Laurel Sefton MacDowell. Toronto: Dundurn, 1988. 381-402.

Weaver examines Munro as an interpreter of Ontario's cultural and social history in *Lives*, *Who*, *Moons*, and *Something*. His study begins with a look at characters, such as Uncle Craig in *Lives*, who are historians and archivists. Moving on to Munro's treatment of the small town, Weaver shows how the demographic and social traits of the population of Jubilee and its geographical details correspond accurately with the town of Wingham, Ontario. He further examines the mental mapping of places in *Lives*, and considers in detail the various aspects of small-town life that are reflected in Munro's fiction.

S1226. Weinhouse, Linda. "Alice Munro: Hard-Luck Stories or There Is No Sexual Relation." *Critique: Studies in Contemporary Fiction* 36.2 (Winter 1995): 121-129.

As frames of reference, Weinhouse uses Jacques Lucan's theories of love in the analytical discourse, and Sigmund Freud's description of the joke as a triangular love story, to study "Hard-Luck Stories." The women in the story are seen as jokers who, through story-telling, as in a good joke, overcome adverse romantic encounters and control their own destinies. The two narrators and their three stories of hard-luck in romance are shown by Weinhouse to demonstrate different approaches in their analysis, but similarities in their approach to their lovers.

S1227. Weiss, Allan. "'How I Met My Husband,' by Alice Munro, 1974." *Reference Guide to Short Fiction*. Ed. Noelle Watson. Detroit: St. James, 1994. 1002-1003. 2nd ed. Ed. Thomas Riggs. Detroit: St. James Press, 1999. 866-867.

A summary of the story is followed by a commentary on the narrator's voice, and on the strong consciousness of social class in the story.

S1228. [Wenger, Barry.] "A Genius of Sour Grapes." Editorial. *Wingham Advance-Times* 16 December 1981: 4.

This editorial in Wingham's local newspaper expresses strong exception to Munro's remarks about Lower Town and the portrayal of the town in Wayne Grady's article in *Today Magazine* in which it was characterized as being "stultifyingly provincial." (See under Grady, Wayne above.) Wenger does not deny that Munro is a gifted writer, but questions the accuracy of her statements about Lower Town and asks why she returned to live in the area and dwell on past real or "imagined injuries" in her writing.

S1229. Whiteway, Doug. "Munro Battles Huron County." *Winnipeg Free Press* 27 October 1982: 17.

In this account of an interview with Munro, Whiteway records that Munro had a youthful ambition to become famous. But in Huron County where she spent her youth, the striving for fame was frowned upon because it invoked the sin of pride. Local people were offended by

S1230. Wieckowska, Katarzyna. "The Corporeal Unspeakable: The Gothicized Body and Alice Munro's *Who Do You Think You Are?*" *Alice Munro: Writing Secrets*. Ed. Héliane Ventura and Mary Condé. Special issue of *Open Letter* 11th ser. 9 (Fall 2003)-12th ser. 1 (Winter 2004): 113-120.

Wieckowska examines the "Gothicized" body in *Who* as a space of social inscription; a space threatened by the breakdown of language and abjection. The deformed and disfigured bodies of Becky Tyde and Franny McGill serve as examples of such bodies which are associated in Gothic fiction with the violation of the basic social convention of incest. Seeing the social response to this difference or "otherness," the protagonist learns to fit into society through mimicry. In youth, she learns language through bodily inscription, but later questions the validity of language and whether it is "an evasion, a questionable trick."

S1231. Wiedemann, Margaret Anne. "Alice Munro's 'The Stone In the Field': Assimilation or Deviance?" *Contest Essays by Canadian Students*. Ed. Robert Hookey and Joan Pilz. Toronto: Holt, Rinehart and Winston of Canada, 1991. 215-217.

In this student essay, Wiedemann says that human contact demands change and assimilation in order to be socially compliant. Noncompliance results in social exclusion and isolation. The situations of the Fleming sisters and Poppy Cullender are examined in the story as an illustration.

S1232. Wigod, Rebecca. "The Munro Doctrine Glistens." *Times Colonist* [Victoria, BC] 9 November 1982: CP1.

Basing her article on an interview with Munro, Wigod notes that most of Munro's fiction is about women or about men as seen through women's eyes. Munro says that men have a built-in obtuseness when writing about women. Small-town life is an integral part of Munro's writing. She says that she is attracted to the writers of the American South because of their depiction of rural people and rural life. The reception of Munro's writing in her home town of Wingham is mentioned.

S1233. Williams, David. "Beyond Photography: Parody as Metafiction in the Novels of Alice Munro." *Confessional Fictions: A Portrait of the Artist in the Canadian Novel*. Toronto: University of Toronto Press, 1991. 193-218.

Williams begins with a look at the photographic aspects of *Lives*. In "Epilogue: The Photographer," he discusses photographic truth, the paradox of photographic vision, and the photographic doubling of reality. *Who* marks a major transformation in Munro's writing, according to Williams. It shows the process by which "reality" is imagined. The discontinuous ways of seeing, the technique of disarrangement, and the use of parody as a social strategy and literary device are pointed out.

S1234. Wilson, Trish. "Alice Munro Takes Success in Her Stride: A Writer's Uncertain Life." *Upbeat* [*Kitchener-Waterloo Record*] 21 October 1982: 1, 3.

Visiting Sir Wilfrid Laurier University for a reading, Munro speaks briefly with Wilson on a number of topics: her anxieties about writing, the compulsion to write, how details of her stories grow from remembered things, and her love-hate relationship with Southwestern Ontario. Her new book *Moons* prompts comments on emotional relationships. She states how she feels about the academic study of her work and how important the library and books were to her in early life.

S1235.   "Women in the News: Alice Munro—Award Winner." *Record News* [Oakville, ON] 29 May 1969: 12.

Not long after the announcement of her first Governor-General's Award, Munro spoke to a reporter about her writing process and how she gets ideas for her stories. Her material is taken from memories of her youth. She talks about the two roles of writing and being a mother. Speaking about working in Munro's Book Store, Munro says that the customers prefer reading novels to short stories. She says that she is currently working on a book-length project.

S1236.   Woodcock, George. "One's Own Vision and Experience: Clark Blaise, Hugh Hood, John Metcalf, Alice Munro, Sheila Watson." *George Woodcock's Introduction to Canadian Fiction*. Toronto: ECW Press, 1993. 100-116.

On pages 111 and 112, Woodcock places Munro's fiction in the tradition of modernism. He says that Munro has two roles, one as a popular short-story writer, and one as a writer's writer. She is appreciated for her depiction of surface realism and for what lies below the surface, the unsaid, and the silences. In Munro's fiction, morality is seen to be an elusive aspect of reality.

S1237.   Woodcock, George. "The Plots of Life: The Realism of Alice Munro." *Queen's Quarterly* 93.2 (Summer 1986): 235-250.
Rpt. (with minor rev.) in *Northern Spring: The Flowering of Canadian Literature*. Vancouver: Douglas & McIntyre, 1987. 132-146.
Rpt. in *Contemporary Literary Criticism*. Ed. Brigham Narins and Deborah A. Stanley. Vol. 95. Detroit: Gale, 1997. 295-302.
Rpt. (excerpts) in *Short Story Criticism*. Ed. Sheila Fitzgerald. Vol. 3. Detroit: Gale Research, 1989. 343-346.

Woodcock says that the richness and tension in Munro's writing is created through the fluctuation between autobiography and invention. He examines her affinities in technique and style to those of superrealist painters. Munro combines documentary methods with a clarity of vision and of voice. The photographic element in scenes and characters is an essential factor in her writing. Her approach has commonality with European realism of the early 1900s. Woodcock looks at some of the stories about childhood in *Dance*, and at the theme and form of *Lives*. He does not find the later works, such as *Who*, as convincing as childhood and adolescent stories in both emotional and aesthetic terms. Munro's writing, in terms of skill and realistic technique, has not fundamentally changed. Woodcock concludes that Munro has not achieved her potentialities, because she has not mastered transformation of form.

S1238.   Wray, John. "Proud of Success of Wingham Writer." Letter. *Wingham Advance-Times* 10 November 1982: 4.

Responding to Audrey Tiffin's letter published on October 20, 1982, Wray says that he also grew up in the area. He hopes that more local people will show their support for Munro's accomplishments.

S1239.   "Writer Uses Bible in Bid to Thwart Banning of Books." *Globe and Mail* 14 June 1978, metro ed.: 9.

This article includes a brief section on Munro's defense of three novels that a group of Huron residents requested to have removed from the Grade 12 reading lists, including Margaret Laurence's *The Diviners*. Munro referred to the Bible to support her argument that certain language is needed to humanize characters and prove a moral point.

S1240.   "Writers' Writers." *Books in Canada* 16.1 (January-February 1987): 8-11.

Books in Canada magazine surveyed 25 literary personalities in Canada to find out their thoughts on the current state of Canadian literature, and what they were currently reading. "Almost everyone is reading *The Progress of Love* by Alice Munro." For a similar survey of readers, see "Advice and Dissent."

S1241.   "'Writing's Something I Did, Like the Ironing.'" *Globe and Mail* 11 December 1982: E1.

Based on an interview, this article gives a background to Munro's life and writing. Mentioning the careers of Munro's father and her mother's illness, the writer of the article says that poverty did not affect Munro's early ambitions. Munro comments on her roles as writer, mother, and wife. She compares the writing of novels and of short stories, and discusses the differences in the situations of male and female writers. Munro calls writing a vocation. In writing, honesty and language are important. The reaction of the people in Wingham to her writing is mentioned. Munro also reveals her thoughts on sex and obsessive love, and the importance of personal attractiveness.

S1242.   York, Lorraine. "Alice Munro 1931- ." *The New Canadian Anthology: Poetry and Short Fiction in English*. Ed. Robert Lecker and Jack David. Scarborough, ON: Nelson Canada, 1988. 360-361.

York provides a short biography of Munro, then briefly discusses her fiction in terms of themes, form, and narrative techniques.

S1243.   York, Lorraine M. "'Distant Parts of Myself': The Topography of Alice Munro's Fiction." *American Review of Canadian Studies* 18.1 (Spring 1988): 33-38.

The crossing of a terrain, or a journey, mirrors the narrative movement of fiction. It is the process of this journey or movement in fiction that fascinates Munro and is the focus of this study. York explores the mediation on routes and the detours of life's narratives in "Walker Brothers Cowboy" and "Miles City, Montana"; maps and mapping in "The Flats Road," "Tell Me Yes or No," and "Miles City, Montana"; fictionalized terrain in "The Shining Houses" and "Something I've Been Meaning to Tell You"; and the merging of fantasy and fictional geography in "Changes and Ceremonies" and "Wild Swans."

S1244.   York, Lorraine M. "'Gulfs' and 'Connections': The Fiction of Alice Munro." *Essays on Canadian Writing* 35 (Winter 1987): 135-146.

Rpt. (excluding footnotes, textual refs. and references) in *Contemporary Literary Criticism*. Ed. Brigham Narins and Deborah A. Stanley. Vol. 95. Detroit: Gale, 1997. 302-306.

York says, "Connection sums up the fundamental vision of Munro's fiction." She traces the growing importance of connection through *Lives, Something, Who,* and *Moons.* In *Lives,* connection is the substance and aim of Del's search, both on a personal and an artistic level. In *Who,* Rose's search for connection leads her to the discovery that the most important connections are between herself and her past. The story "Material" in *Something* shows how the connection between the artist and the world involves connection between the self and others. Other stories in the book show an absence of connection. *Moons* contains the deepest study of the problem, and demonstrates how the process of working toward connections can be more valuable than the connections themselves.

S1245.   York, Lorraine M. "Lives of Joan and Del: Separate Paths to Transformation in *Lives of Girls and Women* and *Lady Oracle.*" *University of Windsor Review* 19.2 (Spring-Summer 1986): 1-10.

Both heroines in the novels of Munro and Atwood achieve their freedom by following joint paths of fantasy and reality. York compares the two heroines, noting that at a crucial moment in their personal or artistic development they identify with the isolated Tennysonian heroine, but ultimately reject the analogy. They share the paradoxical problem of the need for human connection and the need for solitude. They undergo traumatic experiences related to theatrical fantasy and this leads to the dichotomy of the real and the ideal, or fantasy, in their lives. After her investigation of religion, experiences with death and sex, and a meeting with Bobby Sherriff, Del abandons her Gothic melodrama and chooses "real life."

S1246.   York, Lorraine M. "'The Other Side of Dailiness': The Paradox of Photography in Alice Munro's Fiction." *Studies in Canadian Literature* 8.1 (1983): 49-60. Accessed 24 April 2006. <http://www.lib.unb.ca/Texts/SCL/vol8_1/Contents.htm>
Rpt. (excluding footnotes and textual refs.) in *Contemporary Literary Criticism.* Ed. Brigham Narins and Deborah A. Stanley. Vol. 95. Detroit: Gale, 1997. 291-295.
Rpt. (with minor omissions and excluding footnotes and textual refs.) in *Short Story Criticism.* Ed. Sheila Fitzgerald. Vol. 3. Detroit: Gale Research, 1989. 337-340.

York uses the paradox of photography as a point of reference in her study. As in photography, the familiar becomes strange, and the strange familiar as, for example, in "Epilogue: The Photographer." Truth and illusion, fact and fiction are dominant themes in *Who.* York applies the concepts of photographic stillness and motion to the interconnected stories in *Lives* and *Who,* and to the imagery in "The Spanish Lady." Photography and fiction as a means of capturing and exorcizing experience, of gaining control of experience, or of ordering chaos, prove to be inadequate.

S1247.   York, Lorraine M. "The Rival Bards: Alice Munro's *Lives of Girls and Women* and Victorian Poetry." *Canadian Literature* 112 (Spring 1987): 211-216.

The clash in sensibilities between Alfred Lord Tennyson and Robert Browning reflects the conflict between tradition and innovation and the mother-daughter relationship in *Lives.* Ada Jordan is an admirer of Tennyson, while Del is drawn to Robert Browning. York discusses Ada as the heroine figure in "The Princess." Del, while briefly identifying with Tennyson's Marianna figure, ultimately rejects the Tennysonian, and her mother's image of the female who is a half-woman in the world of men.

S1248. York, Lorraine M. "'Royal Beatings,' by Alice Munro, 1978." *Reference Guide to Short Fiction*. Ed. Noelle Watson. Detroit: St. James, 1994. 878-879. 2nd ed. Ed. Thomas Riggs. Detroit: St. James, 1999. 1002-1003.

York begins with a short summary of the story. She then examines some of the characters. Rose is a verbally imaginative and artistically minded girl who, though surrounding by poverty, derives creative energy from her surroundings. Becky Tyde is described as a grotesque character and Flo as a hidden artist. The pairing of ceremony with grimy detail in the beating scene is discussed.

S1249. Zagratzki, Uwe. "Ralph Connor, Hugh MacLennan and Alice Munro: Three Scottish-Canadian Authors." *Zeitschrift für Kanada-Studien* 19.1 (1999): 97-116.

Selected fiction of the three writers are narratives of the Scottish heritage on Canadian soil. But unlike Connor and MacLennan, Munro individualizes the Scottish heritage. Her stories include women racked with chauvinist discourses, especially Scottish Calvinism. Using "Friend of My Youth" as an example, Zagratzki discusses how Munro rewrites the colonizing Scottish discourse about women, texts, and history and in doing so, shows how a new individual identity can be created within the Canadian present.

Bibliographies

S1250. "Alice Munro: Bibliography." *Author Profile: Alice Munro. Northwest Passages: Canadian Literature Online.* Updated to 1999. Accessed 24 April 2006. <http://www.nwpassages.com/bios/munro2.asp/>

S1251. Cook, D. E. "Alice Munro: A Checklist (to December 31, 1974)." *Journal of Canadian Fiction* 16 (1976): 131-136.

S1252. Gnarowski, Michael. "Munro, Alice 1931- ." *A Concise Bibliography of English-Canadian Literature.* Rev. ed. Toronto: McClelland and Stewart, 1978. 100-101.

S1253. Hoy, Helen. "Munro, Alice (1931-)." *Modern English-Canadian Prose: A Guide to Information Sources.* American Literature, English Literature, and World Literatures in English Information Guide Series 38. Detroit: Gale Research, 1983. 346-351.

S1254. Moore, Jean M. and Jean F. Tener, comps.; Steele, Apollonia and Jean F. Tener, eds. *The Alice Munro Papers: First Accession: An Inventory of the Archive at the University of Calgary Libraries.* Canadian Archival Inventory Series: Literary Papers 7. Calgary: University of Calgary Press, 1986.
Reviews:
Cairns, A. T. J. *Canadian Book Review Annual* (1986): 1001.
Hoy, Helen. "Archives." *Canadian Literature* 116 (Spring 1988): 203-205.
Thieme, John. *British Journal of Canadian Studies* 3.1 (1988): 184-186.

S1255. Moore, Jean M., comp.; Steele, Apollonia and Jean F. Tener, eds. *The Alice Munro Papers: Second Accession: An Inventory of the Archive at the University of Calgary Libraries.* Canadian Archival Inventory Series: Literary Papers 12. Calgary: University of Calgary Press, 1987.

S1256. "Munro, Alice 1931- ." *Canadian Fiction: An Annotated Bibliography.* Ed. Margery Fee and Ruth Cawker. Toronto: Peter Martin Associates, 1976. 85.

S1257. Schwartz, Narda Lacey. "Alice Munro (1931-)." *Articles on Women Writers: Volume 2, 1976-1984: A Bibliography*. Santa Barbara, CA: ABC-CLIO, 1986. 171.

S1258. Struthers, J. R. (Tim). "Some Highly Subversive Activities: A Brief Polemic and a Checklist of Works on Alice Munro." *Studies in Canadian Literature* [6] (1981): 140-150. Accessed 24 April 2006. <http://www.lib.unb.ca/Texts/SCL/vol6_1/Contents.htm>

S1259. Thacker, Robert. "Alice Munro: An Annotated Bibliography." *The Annotated Bibliography of Canada's Major Authors*. Ed. Robert Lecker and Jack David. Vol. 5. Downsview, ON: ECW Press, 1984. 354-414.

S1260. Weiss, Allan, comp. "Munro, Alice (1931)." *A Comprehensive Bibliography of English-Canadian Short Stories, 1950-1983*. Toronto: ECW Press, 1988. 472-476.

Reference Works

S1261. "Alice (Laidlaw) Munro: *The Progress of Love*. Governor General's Literary Award: Fiction." *Contemporary Literary Criticism. Yearbook 1987: One Year in Fiction, Poetry, Drama, and World Literature and the Year's New Authors, Prizewinners, Obituaries, and Works of Literary Biography*. Ed. Sharon K. Hall. Vol. 50. Detroit: Gale Research, 1988. 207-222.
Reprints of reviews.

S1262. "Alice Munro." *AOL.Hometown*. 15 September 2001. America Online. Accessed 24 April 2006. <http://hometown.aol.com/MunroAlice>

S1263. "Alice Munro." *Great Women Writers: The Lives and Works of 135 of the World's Most Important Women Writers, From Antiquity to the Present*. Ed. Frank N. Magill. Introd. Rosemary Canfield Reisman. New York: Holt, 1994.

S1264. "Alice Munro." *The Reader's Companion to Twentieth-Century Writers*. Ed. Peter Parker. Consultant ed. Frank Kermode. London: Fourth Estate, 1995. 531-532.
American ed.: *A Reader's Guide to Twentieth-Century Writers*. Ed. Peter Parker. Consultant ed. Frank Kermode. New York: Oxford University Press, 1996. 531-532.

S1265. "Alice Munro." *Wikipedia: The Free Encyclopedia*. 16 May 2006. Wikimedia Foundation. Accessed 24 May 2006. <http://en.wikipedia.org/wiki/Alice_Munro>

S1266. "Alice Munro 1931- ." *Characters in 20th Century Literature. Book 2*. Kely King Howes. New York: Gale Research, 1995. 332-335.

S1267. "Alice Munro, 1931- ." *Short Story Criticism: Excerpts from Criticism of the Works of Short Fiction Writers*. Ed. Sheila Fitzgerald. Vol. 3. Detroit: Gale Research, 1989. 319-350.

S1268. "Alice Munro (1931-)." *The Internet Public Library: Online Literary Criticism Collection*. Updated 28 February 2006. Accessed 24 April 2006. <http://www.ipl.org/div/litcrit/bin/litcrit.out.pl?au=mun-293>

S1269. "Alice Munro (1931-)." *World Literature Criticism. Supplement: A Selection of Major Authors from Gale's Literary Criticism Series*. Ed. Polly Vedder. Vol. 2. Detroit: Gale, 1997. 673-688.

S1270. "Alice Munro: Biography, Chronology." *Meyer Literature. Authors in Depth: Fiction in Depth*. n.d.: Bedford/St. Martin's Publishers. Accessed 24 April 2006. <http://www.bedfordstmartins.com/literature/bedlit/authors_depth/munro.htm>

S1271. "Author Profile: Alice Munro." *Northwest Passages: Canadian Literature Online*. Accessed 24 April 2006. <http://www.nwpassages.com/bios/munro1.asp/>

S1272. Biblowitz, Iris, et al., comps. *Women and Literature: An Annotated Bibliography of Women Writers*. 3rd ed. Cambridge, MA: Women and Literature Collective, 1976. 151-152, 181.

S1273. Bright, Juliette. "Munro, Alice (Anne, neé Laidlaw)." *Contemporary Novelists*. Ed. Lesley Henderson. 5th edition. Chicago: St. James Press, 1991. 672-674. 6th ed. Ed. Susan Windisch Brown. New York: St. James Press, 1996. 741-744. 7th ed. Ed. Neil Schlager and Josh Lauer. Detroit: St. James Press, 2001. 738-742.
6th and 7th eds. updated by J. R. Struthers.

S1274. Brunsdale, Mitzi M. "Alice Munro." *Critical Survey of Short Fiction: Current Writers*. Ed. Frank N. Magill. Vol. 7. Englewood Cliffs, NJ: Salem, 1981. 2738.

S1275. Clancy, Laurie. "Munro, Alice (Anne)." *Reference Guide to Short Fiction*. Ed. Thomas Riggs. 2nd ed. Detroit: St. James Press, 1999. 447-449.
See under Woodcock, George for 1st ed.

S1276. Coldwell, Joan. "Munro, Alice." *The Oxford Companion to Canadian Literature*. Gen. ed. William Toye. Toronto: Oxford University Press, 1983. 536-538. 2nd ed. Gen. eds. Eugene Benson and William Toye. Toronto: Oxford University Press, 1997. 777-778.

S1277. Dahlie, Hallvard. "Alice Munro." *Canadian Writers and Their Works*. Ed. Robert Lecker, Jack David and Ellen Quigley. Introd. George Woodcock. Fiction Series 7. Toronto: ECW Press, 1985. 215-256.
Rpt. as *Alice Munro and Her Works*. By Hallvard Dahlie. Toronto: ECW Press, 1985.

S1278. Dahlie, Hallvard. " Alice Munro (1931-)." *ECW's Biographical Guide to Canadian Novelists*. Ed. Robert Lecker, Jack David, and Ellen Quigley. Toronto: ECW Press, 1993. 188-191.

S1279. Dahlie, Hallvard. "Munro, Alice." *Contemporary Novelists*. Ed. James Vinson. 1st ed. London: St. James Press, 1972. 910-911. 2nd ed. London: St. James Press, 1976. 988-990. 3rd ed. New York: St. Martin's Press, 1982. 478. 4th ed. New York: St. Martin's Press, 1986. 625-627.
See under Bright, Juliette for 5th ed.

S1280. Davey, Frank. "Alice Munro (1931-)." *From There to Here: A Guide to English-Canadian Literature Since 1960*. Vol. 2 of *Our Nature—Our Voices*. Erin, ON: Press Porcepic, 1974. 201-204.

S1281. Dyer, Klay. "Alice Munro 1931." *Beacham's Encyclopedia of Popular Fiction*. Ed. Kirk H. Beetz. Biography Series 2. Osprey, FL: Beacham, 1996. 1324-1330.

S1282. Forceville, Charles. "Alice Munro." *Post-War Literatures in English: A Lexicon of Contemporary Writers*. Ed. Hans Bertens. Houten, Neth.: Bohn Staflen van Loghum; Groningen, Neth.: Wolters-Noordhoff, 13 Sept. 1991. 1-13. A1-A2. B1-B2.

S1283. Freake, Douglas. "Munro, Alice (1931-)." *Encyclopedia of Folklore and Literature*. Ed. Mary Ellen Brown and Bruce A. Rosenberg. Santa Barbara, CA: ABC-CLIO, 1998. 429-430.

S1284. Holland, Patrick. "Munro, Alice 1931-." *Reader's Guide to Literature in English*. Ed. Mark Hawkins-Dady. London; Chicago: Fitzroy Dearborn, 1996. 501-503.
Summary of major critical studies of Munro's writing: Carrington, Carscallen, Dahlie, Heble, Redekop, Smythe.

S1285. Howells, Coral Ann. "Munro, Alice." *Encyclopedia of Literature in Canada*. Ed. William H. New. Toronto: University of Toronto Press, 2002. 769-772.

S1286. Jackel, David. "Short Fiction." *Literary History of Canada: Canadian Literature in English*. Gen ed. W. H. New. Ed. Carl Berger, et al. 2nd ed. Vol. 4. Toronto: University of Toronto Press, 1990. 46-72.

S1287. Keith, W. J. *Canadian Literature in English*. London: Longman, 1985. 6, 7, 8, 157, 161-162, 170, 176, 265.

S1288. Kildahl, Karen A.; revised by Kenneth W. Meadwell. "Alice Munro." *Short Story Writers*. Ed. Frank N. Magill. Vol. 2. Pasadena, CA: Salem Press, 1997. 641-649.

S1289. McClung, M. G. *Women in Canadian Literature*. Pref. George Woodcock. Women in Canadian Life. Toronto: Fitzhenry & Whiteside, 1977. 59-60.

S1290. McGill, Robert James. "Alice Munro (1931-)." *The Literary Encyclopedia*. 24 June 2004. Accessed 24 April 2006. <http://www.litencyc.com/php/speople.php?rec=true&UID=5050>

S1291. Moss, John. *A Reader's Guide to the Canadian Novel*. Toronto: McClelland, 1981. 215-219, 354-355, 358, 362-363, 372, 375, 377-378. 2nd ed. Toronto: McClelland and Stewart, 1987. 276-280.

S1292. "Munro, Alice." *Benét's Reader's Encyclopedia*. 3rd ed. New York: Harper & Row, 1987. 674. 4th ed. Ed. Bruce Murphy. New York: HarperCollins, 1996. 710.

S1293. "Munro, Alice." *Biographical Companion to Literature in English*. Antony Kamm. Lanham, MD: Scarecrow, 1997. 388.

S1294. "Munro, Alice." *Bloomsbury Guide to Women's Literature*. Ed. Claire Buck. London: Bloomsbury, 1992. 840-841.

S1295. "Munro, Alice." *Current Biography Yearbook, 1990*. Ed. Charles Moritz. New York: H. W. Wilson, 1991. 454-458.

S1296. "Munro, Alice." *International Who's Who of Authors and Writers, 2006*. 21st ed. London: Routledge, 2005. 550.

S1297. "Munro, Alice 1931- ." *Contemporary Authors: A Bio-Bibliographic Guide to Current Authors and Their Works*. Rev. ed. Vols. 33-36. Detroit: Gale Research, 1978. 588-589.

S1298. "Munro, Alice 1931- ." *Contemporary Authors: A Bio-Bibliographical Guide to Current Writers in Fiction . . . .* New rev. series. Vol. 33. Detroit: Gale Research, 1991. 322-323. Vol. 53. Detroit: Gale, 1997. 360-363. Vol. 75. Detroit: Gale Group, 1999. 325-328. Vol. 114. Detroit: Gale Group, 2003. 324-330.

S1299. "Munro, Alice 1931- ." *Contemporary Canadian Authors: A Bio-Bibliographical Guide to Current Canadian Writers in Fiction . . . .* Coordinating ed. Robert Lang. Project ed. Pamela Willwerth Aue and David M. Galens. Vol. 1. New York; Toronto: Gale Canada, 1996. 346-349.

S1300. "Munro, Alice 1931- ." *Contemporary Literary Criticism: Excerpts from Criticism of the Works of Today's Novelists, Poets, Playwrights . . . .* Vol. 6. Detroit: Gale Research, 1976. 341-342. Vol. 10. 1979. 356-359. Vol. 19. 1981. 343-347. Vol. 50. 1988. 207-221. Vol. 95. 1997. 282-326.

S1301. "Munro, Alice (1931-)." *The Oxford Companion to Twentieth-Century Literature in English*. Ed. Jenny Stringer. Oxford, Eng.: Oxford University Press, 1996. 472.

S1302. "Munro, Alice (Anne)." *Reference Guide to Short Fiction*. 2nd ed. Ed. Thomas Riggs. Detroit: St. James Press, 1999. 447-449.

S1303. "Munro, Alice (Anne Laidlaw)." *World Authors, 1980-1985*. Ed. Vinetta Colby. New York: H. W. Wilson, 1991. 621-627.

S1304. "Munro, Alice Anne Laidlaw 1931- ." *Creative Canada: A Biographical Dictionary of Twentieth Century Creative and Performing Artists*. Vol. 1. Toronto: University of Toronto Press, 1971. 228.

S1305. "Munro, Alice (Canada) 1931- ." *Modern Women Writers*. Comp. and ed. Lillian S. Robinson. Vol. 3. Library of Literary Criticism. New York: Continuum, 1996. 299-307.

S1306. "Munro, Alice (Laidlaw)." *The Feminist Companion to Literature in English: Women Writers from the Middle Ages to the Present.* Ed. Virginia Blain, Patricia Clements, and Isobel Grundy. New Haven: Yale University Press, 1990. 775-776.

S1307. "Munro, Alice (Laidlaw). 1931- ." *The Reader's Adviser.* Vol. 2. *The Best in World Literature.* Ed. Robert DiYanni. 14th ed. New Providence, NJ: Bowker, 1994. 921-922.

S1308. New, W. H. *A History of Canadian Literature.* Gen. ed. Norman Jeffares. New York: New Amsterdam, 1989. 250-252.

S1309. New, William H. "Fiction." *Literary History of Canada: Canadian Literature in English.* Gen. ed. Carl F. Klinck. Ed. Alfred G. Bailey, et al. 2nd ed. Vol. 3. Toronto: University of Toronto Press, 1976. 233-283.

S1310. Quartermaine, Peter. "Munro, Alice (1931-)." *A Guide to Twentieth Century Literature in English.* Ed. Harry Blamires. London: Methuen, 1983. 190.

S1311. Reisman, Rosemary M. Canfield. Revised by Joanne McCarthy. "Alice Munro." *Cyclopedia of World Authors.* Ed. Frank N. Magill. Rev. 3rd ed. Vol. 4. Pasadena, CA: Salem Press, 1997. 1463-1464.

S1312. Rogers, Jane. "Munro, Alice." *Good Fiction Guide.* Ed. Jane Rogers. Oxford: Oxford University Press, 2001. 370.

S1313. Ross, Catherine Sheldrick. "Alice Munro." *Dictionary of Literary Biography, Vol. 53. Canadian Writers since 1960, First Series.* Ed. W. H. New. Detroit: Gale Research, 1986. 297-306.

S1314. Story, Norah. "Munro, Alice (1931-)." *Supplement to the Oxford Companion to Canadian History and Literature.* Gen. ed. William Toye. Toronto: Oxford University Press, 1973. 235.

S1315. Stouck, David. "Alice Munro." *Major Canadian Authors: A Critical Introduction to Canadian Literature in English.* 2nd ed., rev. and expanded. Lincoln: University of Nebraska Press, 1988. 257-272.

S1316. Stouck, David. "Munro, Alice [Laidlaw]." *Benét's Reader's Encyclopedia of American Literature.* Ed. George Perkins, Barbara Perkins, and Phillip Leininger. New York: HarperCollins, 1991. 742.

S1317. Struthers, J. R. (Tim). "Alice Munro (July 10, 1931-)." *A Reader's Companion to the Short Story in English.* Ed. Erin Fallon, et al. Westport, CT: Greenwood Press, 2001. 288-299.

S1318. Thacker, Robert. "Munro, Alice." *Encyclopedia of World Literature in the 20th Century*. Gen. ed. Steven R. Serafin. Vol. 3. Farmington Hills, MI: St. James Press, 1999. 323-324.

S1319. Trumpener, Katie and Deidre Lynch. "Alice Munro 1931- ." *Encyclopedia of the Novel*. Ed. Paul Schellinger. Vol. 2. Chicago: Fitzroy Dearborn Publishers, 1998. 876-877.

S1320. Watson, Dana Cairns. "Alice Munro (1931-)." *World Writers in English*. Ed. Jay Parini. Vol. 1. New York: Scribner's, 2004. 343-365.

S1321. Weil, Herb. "Munro, Alice (1931-)." *Encyclopedia of Post-Colonial Literatures in English*. Ed. Eugene Benson and L. W. Conolly. Vol. 2. London: Routledge, 1994. 1056-1058.

S1322. Wiedemann, Barbara. "Alice Munro." *Magill's Survey of World Literature*. Ed. Frank N. Magill. Vol. 4. North Bellmore, NY: Marshall Cavendish, 1993. 1339-1346.

S1323. Woodcock, George. "Munro, Alice (Anne, née Laidlaw)." *Reference Guide to English Literature*. Ed. D. L. Kirkpatrick. 2nd ed. Vol. 2. Chicago: St. James, 1991. 1006-1008.

S1324. Woodcock, George. "Munro, Alice (Anne, née Laidlaw)." *Reference Guide to Short Fiction*. Ed. Noelle Watson. Detroit: St. James, 1994. 375-377.

Awards

Academy Award

"Boys and Girls"—best Short Film (Live-Action) 1984

Aer Lingus Fiction Prize (*Irish Times*)

Friend of My Youth—short listed

S1325. "Munro Collection on Short List: Literary Prize Worth $50,000." *Globe and Mail* 14 September 1990, metro ed.: C13.

Open Secrets—short listed 1995

Booker Prize for Fiction (U.K.)

Who Do You Think You Are?—short listed

S1326. *Sunday Times* [London] 26 October 1980: 13.

S1327. Dafoe, Christopher. "Making the Grade." *Vancouver Sun* 31 October 1980: C6.

Canada-Australia Literary Prize

S1328. "Munro Awarded Literary Prize." *Globe and Mail* 23 January 1978: 13.

S1329. "Munro is Literary Prizewinner." *Toronto Star* 23 January 1978: D1.

S1330. "Literary Ambassadors to Commonwealth." *Quill & Quire Update* 44.3 (16 February 1978): 1.

Canada Council Molson Prize
(Lifetime Contribution to Canadian Cultural Life)

S1331. "Alice Munro, Jean Jacques Nattiez Win $50,000 Cultural Awards." *Toronto Star* 10 January 1991: D1.

S1332. "Munro, Nattiez Honoured." *Globe and Mail* 10 January 1991: C5.

S1333. "Munro, Nattiez Receive Awards." *Kitchener-Waterloo Record* 10 January 1991: C7.

S1334. "Writer and Musicologist Win $50,000 Prizes." *Calgary Herald* 11 January 1991: C5.

S1335. "Canada Council Awards." *Feliciter* February 1991: 14.

S1336. "Cultural Award Winner." *Toronto Star* 4 April 1991, metro ed.: C4.

S1337. "1990 Canada Council Molson Prizes Awarded to Alice Munro and Jean-Jacques Nattiez." *Canada Council Bulletin* Spring 1991: 8.

Canadian Authors Association. Jubilee Award for Short Stories

Selected Stories

S1338. "7 Writers Win Prizes." *Globe and Mail* 9 May 1997, metro ed.: D2.

Canadian Booksellers' Association. Libris Award. Author of the Year

Lives of Girls and Women

S1339. "Alice Munro Wins CBA Award." *Quill & Quire* June 1972: 8.

S1340. Carter, Alixe. "Alice Munro Probes Lives of Girls and Women." *Ottawa Journal* 17 May 1972: 54.

S1341. Dobbs, Kildare. "Book on the Way Up." *Toronto Star* 4 April 1973: 32.

Who Do You Think You Are?

S1342. "Booksellers Group Presents 4 Awards." *Globe and Mail* 30 July 1979, metro ed.: 13.

Open Secrets

S1343. "Munro Named Author of the Year." *Gazette* [Montreal] 16 June 1995, early ed.: D5.

S1344. "Munro Named Author of the Year." *Toronto Star* 16 June 1995, metro ed.: E15.

S1345. "Munro Named: Author of the Year." *Calgary Herald* 16 June 1995, city ed.: D2.

S1346. "Munro Named Author of Year for *Open Secrets*." *Hamilton Spectator* 16 June 1995, final ed.: A3.

S1347. "Munro Takes Prize." *Globe and Mail* 16 June 1995, metro ed.: C1.

The Love of a Good Woman

S1348. "Entertainment Buzz: Alice Munro Triple Winner." *London Free Press* 19 June 1999, final ed.: C2.

S1349. "Munro and Barber Are Triple Winners at '99 Libris Awards." *Kitchener-Waterloo Record* 19 June 1999, final ed.: F02.

S1350. Ross, Val. "Munro Honoured by Booksellers with Three Awards." *Globe and Mail* 21 June 1999: D3.

Commonwealth Writers' Prize (Caribbean and Canada Region), Best Book

Friend of My Youth

S1351. "Alice Munro wins $10,000 authors prize." *Globe and Mail* 28 August 1991, metro ed.: C3.

S1352. "Canadian Takes Writer's Prize: Commonwealth Grants Award to B.C.'s Alice Munro." *Calgary Herald* 29 August 1991, city ed.: D3.

S1353. "Munro Regional Winner in Commonwealth Competition." *Chronicle-Herald* [Halifax] 30 August 1991, provincial ed.: B3.

Giller Prize

The Love of a Good Woman

S1354. Edemariam, Aida and Kate Fillion. "Short Stories Win Prestigious Literary Prize." *National Post* 4 November 1998: A1, A3.

S1355. Goddard, John. "Giller Prize Goes to Munro." *Calgary Herald* 4 November 1998: E1. Rpt. (with omissions) in *Gazette* [Montreal] 4 November 1998, first ed.: E1. Rpt. (with omissions) in *Vancouver Sun* 4 November 1998: C5.

S1356. "Munro Gets Giller." *Fredericton Daily Gleaner* 4 November 1998: A12.

S1357. "Munro Wins Giller: Prestigious Literary Award Honours Go to Writer's Collection of Short Stories." *Toronto Star* 4 November 1998: D1, D4.

S1358. "Munro Wins Giller Prize." *Toronto Sun* 4 November 1998, final ed.: 56.

S1359. Renzetti, Elizabeth. "Alice Munro Celebrates 'Wonderful' Giller Prize: Short-Story Writer Wins $25,000 Award." *Globe and Mail* 4 November 1998, metro ed.: A1, A11.

S1360. Tobin, Anne-Marie. "Munro Wins Giller Prize." *Kitchener Waterloo Record* 4 November 1998, final ed.: E8.

S1361. Tobin, Anne-Marie. "Munro's 'Habit' Nets Her Giller." *London Free Press* [London, ON] 4 November 1998, early and final eds.: C3.

S1362. "Alice Munro remporte le Prix Giller." *Droit* 5 novembre 1998: 39.

S1363. "Le Giller Prize à Alice Munro." *Devoir* 5 novembre 1998: B8.

S1364. "A Good Woman: A Great Writer." *London Free Press* [London, ON] 5 November 1998, final ed.: A12.

S1365. "Munro Wins Giller Prize." *Moncton Times and Transcript* 5 November 1998: B5.

1366. Teahen, Kelley. "Our Lives Revealed in 'True Lies.'" *London Free Press* 5 November 1998, final ed.: A3.

S1367. Tobin, Anne-Marie. "Munro's Short Story Collection Wins Giller Prize." *Chronicle-Herald* [Halifax] 5 November 1998, provincial ed.: B7.

S1368. Mallick, Heather. "The Giller Guide: Alice Munro Grabbed Canada's Most Prestigious Literary Award, But the Other Nominees Are Definitely Worth a Read." *Ottawa Sun* 8 November 1998, final ed.: S14.

S1369. "The Love of a Great Author." *Maclean's* 16 November 1998: 82.

S1370. "Munro Wins Giller." *Quill & Quire* December 1998: 5.

Runaway

S1371. Caldwell, Rebecca. "Alice Munro Snaps up Second Giller Prize." *Globe and Mail* 12 November 2004: A8.

S1372. "Munro Grabs $25,000 Giller Prize." *Record* [Kitchener-Waterloo] 12 November 2004, final ed.: B8.

S1373. Stoffman, Judy. "Munro Awarded Second Giller." *Toronto Star* 12 November 2004: A03.

Governor General's Literary Award

Dance of the Happy Shades

S1374. "B.C. Mother of Three Wins Top Literary Award." *Vancouver Sun* 22 April 1969: 1.

S1375. French, William. "The Establishment Beware! These Awards Are With It." *Globe and Mail* 22 April 1969, metro ed.: 13.

S1376. "Victoria Woman's Book Wins Literary Award." *Daily Colonist* [Victoria, BC] 22 April 1969: 1-2.

Who Do You Think You Are?

S1377. "Alice Munro Wins 2nd Book Award." *Globe and Mail* 21 March 1979, metro ed.: 14.

S1378. "Munro Wins 2nd G-G's Award." *Montreal Star* 21 March 1979: D2.

The Progress of Love

S1379. Portman, Jamie. "Third Governor-General's Award for Munro." *Vancouver Sun* 27 May 1987: D10.

S1380. "Governor General's Award to Munro Amid Poetry Protest." *Gazette* [Montreal] 28 May 1987: C1.

S1381. Portman, Jamie. "Munro Wins Third Governor-General's Award." *Calgary Herald* 28 May 1987, home ed.: C9.

S1382. Rochon, Lisa. "Munro Wins Top Literary Prize." *Globe and Mail* 28 May 1987, final metro. ed.: D1.

S1383. "Munro Short Story Collection Wins Award." *Winnipeg Free Press* 29 May 1987, final ed.: 34.

S1384. Cox, Yvonne. "People." *Maclean's* 8 June 1987: 46.

S1385. "Governor General's Award Winners." *Quill & Quire* July 1987: 53-54.

S1386. "Alice (Laidlaw) Munro: 'The Progress of Love.' Governor General's Literary Award: Fiction." *Contemporary Literary Criticism. Yearbook 1987: One Year in Fiction, Poetry, Drama, and World Literature and the Year's New Authors,*

Prizewinners, Obituaries, and Works of Literary Biography. Ed. Sharon K. Hall. Vol 50. Detroit: Gale Research. 1988. 207-222.

Great Lakes College Association Award

Dance of the Happy Shades—1974

Lannan Literary Award (U.S.)

S1387. "$50,000 for Writer: Munro Wins U.S. Literary Prize. $50,000 for Writer." *Globe and Mail* 19 September 1995, metro ed.: C1.

S1388. "Alice Munro Wins $50,000 Lannan Award." *Hamilton Spectator* 20 September 1995, final ed.: C11.

S1389. "International Honor for Munro." *Kitchener-Waterloo Record* 20 September 1995, final ed.: E6.

Marian Engel Award

The Progress of Love

S1390. "$10,000 Engel Prize Goes to Alice Munro." *Globe and Mail* 11 October 1986: E10.

S1391. McGoogan, Kenneth. "Engel Award to Munro." *Calgary Herald* 19 October 1986, home ed.: C5.

S1392. Adachi, Ken. "Alice Munro Honored with First Marian Engel Award." *Toronto Star* 21 October 1986: H1.

National Arts Club Medal of Honor for Literature (U.S.)
Lifetime Achievement Award

S1393. "Alice Munro Wins Big Honour in New York." *Globe and Mail* 3 February 2005: R2. (Lifetime Achievement Award)

National Book Critics Circle Award (U.S.)

The Love of a Good Woman

S1394. Houpt, Simon R. "Alice Munro Wins Major US Book Prize." *Globe and Mail* 9 March 1999, metro ed.: A1, A17.

S1395. Italie, Hillel. "Alice Munro Wins U.S. Critics' Award." *Vancouver Sun* 9 March 1999: A2.

S1396. "Munro Nails One Prize While Missing Another." *London Free Press* 9 March 1999, final ed.: C6.

S1397. "Munro Wins Book Critics' Fiction Award." *Fredericton Daily Gleaner* 9 March 1999: C7.

S1398. "Munro Wins U.S. Book Critics Circle Prize." *Toronto Star* 9 March 1999: D7.

S1399. *New York Times* 9 March 1999, late ed.: B2.

S1400. "Alice Munro est primée aux États-Unis. *Devoir* 10 mars 1999: B8.

S1401. "Alice Munro primée par les critiques littéraires américains." *Presse* 10 mars 1999: E5.

S1402. "Alice Munro Wins Book Prize." *Calgary Sun* 10 March 1999, final ed.: 56.

S1403. "La Canadienne Alice Munro primée par les critiques littéraires américains." *Soleil* 10 mars 1999: C5.

S1404. "Munro Wins Critics Circle Fiction Award." *Winnipeg Sun* 10 March 1999: 21.

S1405. "Munro Wins U.S. Book Critics' Prize." *Gazette* [Montreal] 10 March 1999: F9.

S1406. "Munro's Newest Honour." *National Post* 10 March 1999: B8.

S1407. "Munro's *The Love of a Good Woman* First Non-U.S. Winner of Critics' Prize." *Hamilton Spectator* 10 March 1999, final ed.: F4.

National Magazine Foundation. Gold Medal Award

"*Accident*"—1977

"*Mrs. Cross and Mrs. Kidd*"—1983

Nobel Prize

Name submitted

S1408. "Medicine Prize Kicks Off Nobel Awards: Alice Munro of Clinton and Margaret Atwood Race for Top Honours in Literature." *London Free Press* 9 October 2000, final ed.: D8.

S1409. "Atwood and Munro Tipped in Nobel Prize." *Toronto Star* 11 October 2000: D4.

O. Henry Award for Continuing Achievement in Short Fiction

S1410.   Simpson, Mona. "Special Award for Continuing Achievement." *Prize Stories, 2001: The O. Henry Awards*. Ed. and introd. Larry Dark. New York: Anchor Books, 2001. 81, 83-84.

Ontario Council of the Arts

1974—shared with Hugh Hood

Order of Ontario

1994—presented 1995

S1411.   MacKinnon, Donna Jean. "19 Awarded Ontario's Top Honor." *Toronto Star* 4 May 1995, final ed.: A12.

PEN-Malamud Award for Excellence in Short Fiction
(For Body of Work)

S1412.   Gessel, Paul. "Munro First Foreigner to Take Top U.S. Award." *Hamilton Spectator* 12 November 1997, final ed.: F3.

S1413.   "Americans Honor Munro." *Kitchener-Waterloo Record* 14 November 1997, final ed.: A18.

S1414.   "Munro Wins Excellence Prize in U.S." *Toronto Star* 14 November 1997: D15.

S1415.   "Alice Munro Wins PEN-Malamud Award." *Globe and Mail* 15 November 1997, metro ed.: C8.

S1416.   Gessell, Paul. "Munro's Win a First for U.S. Award." *Gazette* [Montreal] 15 November 1997: D8.

S1417.   "Le PEN-Malamud: Alice Munro." *Presse* 18 novembre 1997: E4.

Periodical Distributors of Canada Authors' Award

Who Do You Think You Are?—Best English language fiction paperback of the year

S1418.   "Munro, Laurence Net Book Honors." *Globe and Mail* 28 October 1980, metro ed.: 19.

Rea Award (U.S.)

(Lifetime Achievement)

S1419.   "Alice Munro Wins $30,000 Prize." *Toronto Star* 29 March 2001: A33.

S1420.   "Another Prize for Alice Munro." *Globe and Mail* 29 March 2001, final metro ed.: R2.

S1421.   "Munro Wins Rea Award." *Publishers Weekly* 248.14 (2 April 2001): 16.

S1422.   "Passages." *Maclean's* 9 April 2001: 14.

Rogers Writers' Trust Fiction Prize

Runaway

S1423.   Tobin, Anne-Marie. "Munro, Newman Haul in Literary Awards." *London Free Press* 10 March 2005: T17.

Royal Society of Canada: The Academies of Arts, Humanities and Sciences of Canada. Lorne Pierce Medal.

Achievement in critical or imaginative literature—1993
<http://www.rsc.ca/>

Terasen Lifetime Achievement Award

S1424.   "Award Honours Munro for Lifetime of Stories." *Hamilton Spectator* 25 May 2005: A8.

S1425.   Bains, Camille. "Munro Calls Library Fitting Award Venue." *London Free Press* 25 May 2005: D6.

S1426.   "Passages: Honoured." *Maclean's* 6 June 2005: 18.

Time Magazine. Time 100: The 2005 List of the World's Most Influential People . . . : Artists and Entertainers

S1427.   Simpson, Mona. "Alice Munro: Conveying Our Dreams." *Time* (Canadian ed.) 18 April 2005: 92; (American ed.) 116.

Trillium Book Award (Ontario)

Friend of My Youth

S1428. "Alice Munro Wins Trillium Award." *Toronto Star* 17 April 1991: F1.

S1429. "Munro Wins Trillium." *Globe and Mail* 17 April 1991, metro ed.: C1.

S1430. "Never 'Blase' about Awards, Munro Says in Accepting Prize." *Kitchener-Waterloo Record* 17 April 1991: F1.

S1431. Currie, Rod. "Author Munro Wins Ontario Book Award." *Chronicle-Herald* [Halifax] 18 April 1991, provincial ed.: B5.

The Love of a Good Woman

S1432. "Double-Tie for Trillium Award." *Toronto Sun* 16 April 1999, final ed.: 70.

S1433. "Munro, Alexis Split Trillium Award." *London Free Press* 16 April 1999, final ed.: C2.

S1434. Ross, Val. "Alice Munro, Andre Alexis share 1999 Trillium Award." *Globe and Mail* 16 April 1999, final metro ed.: D8.

S1435. Stoffman, Judy. "Duo Shares Trillium Prize." *Toronto Star* 16 April 1999, metro ed.: C8-C9.

S1436. Stoffman, Judy. "Munro and Alexis Share Trillium Literary Award." *Hamilton Spectator* 16 April 1999, final ed.: B8.

S1437. "Trillium Award: Munro, Alexis Creations Get Top Recognition." *Fredericton Daily Gleaner* 16 April 1999: B10.

S1438. "Alice Munro, Andre Alexis Share Award." *Kitchener-Waterloo Record* 17 April 1999, final ed.: F02.

S1439. "Munro and Alexis Split Lit Award." *Gazette* [Montreal] 17 April 1999: D16.

S1440. "Sharing Award." *Fredericton Daily Gleaner* 17 April 1999: C7.

University of Western Ontario. Honorary Doctorate, 1976.

Upper Canada Brewing Company Writers' Craft Award

Hateship, Friendship, Courtship, Loveship, Marriage

S1441. Mahoney, Jeff. "Alice Munro Gets Prize at Gala for Short Stories." *Hamilton Spectator* 17 October 2002, final ed.: D3.

S1442. "Cup Runneth Over for Alice Munro." *Toronto Star* 18 October 2002, Ont. ed.: D13.

W. H. Smith Literary Award (U.K.)

Open Secrets—Best Book in the United Kingdom, 1995

Appendix

Stories in the Collected Works

Dance of the Happy Shades: Stories (1968)
   Walker Brothers Cowboy; The Shining Houses; Images; Thanks for the Ride; The Office; An Ounce of Cure; The Time of Death; Day of the Butterfly; Boys and Girls; Postcard; Red Dress—1946; Sunday Afternoon; A Trip to the Coast; The Peace of Utrecht; Dance of the Happy Shades

Something I've Been Meaning to Tell You . . . : Thirteen Stories (1974)
   Something I've Been Meaning to Tell You; Material; How I Met My Husband; Walking on Water; Forgiveness in Families; Tell Me Yes or No; The Found Boat; Executioners; Marrakesh; The Spanish Lady; Winter Wind; Memorial; The Ottawa Valley

Who Do You Think You Are?: Stories (1978)
(The Beggar Maid: Stories of Flo and Rose) (1979)
   Royal Beatings; Privilege; Half a Grapefruit; Wild Swans; The Beggar Maid; Mischief; Providence; Simon's Luck; Spelling; Who Do You Think You Are?

The Moons of Jupiter: Stories (1982)
   Chaddeleys and Flemings. 1: Connection; Chaddeleys and Flemings. 2: The Stone in the Field; Dulse; The Turkey Season; Accident; Bardon Bus; Prue; Labor Day Dinner; Mrs. Cross and Mrs. Kidd; Hard-Luck Stories; Visitors; The Moons of Jupiter

The Progress of Love: Stories (1986)
   The Progress of Love; Lichen; Monsieur les Deux Chapeaux; Miles City, Montana; Fits; The Moon in the Orange Street Skating Rink; Jesse and Meribeth; Eskimo; A Queer Streak; Circle of Prayer; White Dump

Friend of My Youth: Stories (1990)
   Friend of My Youth; Five Points; Meneseteung; Hold Me Fast, Don't Let Me Pass;

Oranges and Apples: Pictures of the Ice: Goodness and Mercy: Oh, What Avails: Differently: Wigtime

Open Secrets: Stories (1994)
Carried Away: A Real Life: The Albanian Virgin: Open Secrets: The Jack Randa Hotel: A Wilderness Station: Spaceships Have Landed: Vandals

Selected Stories (1996)
Walker Brothers Cowboy: Dance of the Happy Shades: Postcard: Images: Something I've Been Meaning to Tell You: The Ottawa Valley: Material: Royal Beatings: Wild Swans: The Beggar Maid: Simon's Luck: Chaddeleys and Flemings: Dulse: The Turkey Season: Labor Day Dinner: The Moons of Jupiter: The Progress of Love: Lichen: Miles City, Montana: White Dump: Fits: Friend of My Youth: Meneseteung: Differently: Carried Away: The Albanian Virgin: A Wilderness Station: Vandals

The Love of a Good Woman: Stories (1998)
The Love of a Good Woman: Jakarta: Cortes Island: Save the Reaper: The Children Stay: Rich as Stink: Before the Change: My Mother's Dream

Hateship, Friendship, Courtship, Loveship, Marriage: Stories (2001)
Hateship, Friendship, Courtship, Loveship, Marriage: Floating Bridge: Family Furnishings: Comfort: Nettles: Post and Beam: What Is Remembered: Queenie: The Bear Came Over the Mountain

Runaway: Stories (2004)
Runaway: Chance: Soon: Silence: Passion: Trespasses: Tricks: Powers

Chapters in the Novel

Lives of Girls and Women: A Novel (1972)
The Flats Road: Heirs of the Living Body: Princess Ida: Age of Faith: Changes and Ceremonies: Lives of Girls and Women: Baptizing: Epilogue: The Photographer

Unverified Radio Broadcasts

"The Strangers." *Canadian Short Stories*. CBC Radio. October 5, 1951.
"The Liberation." *Canadian Short Stories*. CBC Radio. June 13, 1952.
"The Idyllic Summer." *Anthology*. CBC Radio. March 22, 1954.
"The Green April." *Anthology*. CBC Radio. 1956.
"Dance of the Happy Shades." *CBC Sunday Night*. October 30, 1960.

Archives

Alice Munro Fonds. University of Calgary Library, Special Collections. Calgary, AB
   http://www.ucalgary.ca/lib-old/SpecColl/munroa.htm
   See also entries S1255 and S1256 in this bibliography.

Macmillan Company of Canada Fonds. McMaster University, Mills Memorial Library, William Ready Division of Archives and Research Collections. Hamilton, ON
   http://library.mcmaster.ca/archives/findaids/fonds/m/macmilla.htm

McClelland & Stewart Ltd. Fonds. McMaster University, Mills Memorial Library, William Ready Division of Archives and Research Collections. Hamilton, ON
   http://library.mcmaster.ca/archives/findaids/fonds/m/mcstew.htm

Collections

"Alice Munro/W. R. Martin Reference Materials." University of Waterloo Library, Archives and Rare Books. Waterloo, ON
   http://www.lib.uwaterloo.ca/discipline/SpecColl/archives/munmart.html

The following libraries hold significant collections of Munro's books and their translations:

Library and Archives Canada. Ottawa, ON
Toronto Reference Library (Toronto Public Library). Toronto, ON
University of Calgary Library, Special Collections. Calgary, AB
University of Toronto, Thomas Fisher Rare Book Library. Toronto, ON

Author and Title Index

This index includes names of authors, editors, directors, producers, narrators, and script writers, and titles of works by Alice Munro. All references are to entry numbers: P = Primary Works, S = Secondary Works. Book titles are in italics. Story titles are in quotation marks.

"1847: The Irish"
    Film adaptations. P759
    Television broadcasts. P748

Abcarian, Richard. P261
Abley, Mark. S716
"Accident." P19, P20
Ackerman, Marianne. S639
Adachi, Ken. S392, S522, S717, S777, S1392
Adams, Alice. P211, P671
Adams, James. S778, S779
Adams, Lorraine. S244
Adams, Timothy Dow. S769
Adilman, Sid. P723; S780
Aguilar, Carmen. P11
Aherne, Catherine Lynne. S1
Ahrold, Kyle Warren. S678
Aitken, Lee. S580
Alaton, Salem. S782
"The Albanian Virgin." P15, P21-26
    Radio broadcasts. P707
    Read by Alice Munro. P762
    Sound recordings. P762
    Translations. P26
Alford, Edna. P255

Allardice, Lisa. S245
Allen, Bruce. S246, S462, S581
Allentuck, Marcia. S784
Allison, Paul S., S785
Alsop, Kay. S786
Alvarez, A., S582
Anand, P13, S787
Anderson, Allan. P840
Andrews, Audrey. S463, S524
Andrews, Carol. P835
Angell, Roger. P276
"An Appreciation." P657
Arbing, Susan. S2
Archer, Bert. S640
Arkin, Marian. P203
Armstrong, Carol A., S3
Armstrong, Sean. P98, P700
Arnason, David. S788
Arnold, Sue. S513
Ash, Susan. S789
Assad, Mavis. S4
"At the Other Place." P27
Atkins, Lucy. S790
Attebery, Brian. P429

Atwood, Margaret, P275, P318, P421, P673; S791
Aulin, Virginia, S247, S337, S765
Austin, Allan, S525
Austin, Mauralea, P815, P819
Austin-Smith, Brenda, S526

Babineau, Nicole, S5
Backman, George, P763
Bailey, Nancy I., S794
Bailey, Paul, S192, S248, S583
Baillieul, J. G., S338
Bain, Carl E., P62, P74
Bains, Camille, S1425
Baird, Nora, S718
Balakian, Nona, S135, S136
Balée, Susan, S249, S339
Balestra, Gianfranca, S795
Ballon, Heather M., S6
Balpataky, Elaine, S393
Banville, John, S641
"Baptizing," P28, P29
    Film adaptations, P749
    Television broadcasts, P708
Barbour, Douglas, S679
"Bardon Bus," P15, P30-33
    Radio broadcasts, P709
    Read by Alice Munro, P709
Barlow, Pat, P765, P810
Barnet, Sylvan, P66, P68, P80, P82, P115, P116, P258, P702
Barrett, Mary Ellin, S296
Barrie, Barbara, P770
Bartlett, Brian, S719
Bartsch, Ernst, P85
"A Basket of Strawberries," P34, P35
Basso, Susanna, P4, P6, P11
Batstone, Kathleen, S7, S8
Batten, Jack, S797
Baum, Rosalie Murphy, S798, S799
Bausch, Richard, P461, P500, P702
Bautz, Mark, S584
Baxter, Charles, P691
"The Bear Came Over the Mountain," P15, P36-39

Beattie, Ann, P125, P667; S250
Beatty, Jack, S137
Beatty, Jane N., P482
Beaty, Jerome, P62, P64, P74, P77, P299
Becker, Alida, S800
Becker, Robin, S394
Becker, Susanne, S801
Beddoes, Julie, S395, S527
Beer, Janet, S802
Beer, Patricia, S297
"Before the Change," P40-44
    Translations, P43, P44
"The Beggar Maid," P45-53
    Translations, P53
The Beggar Maid: Stories of Flo and Rose, P1
    Reviews, S135-158
    Sound recordings, P763, P764
    Translations, P1
Bell, Millicent, S642
Bellamy, Connie, S9
Belyea, Andy, S10
Benrose, John, S251, S340
Bender, Elaine, S585
Bender, Eric, S804
Benecke, Karin, P1, P3, P7, P9
Bennett, Donna, P361, P449, P525; S805
Bentley College, P760
Beran, Carol L., S754, S757, S763, S806-809
Berman, Morton, P66, P68
Besner, Neil, P214, P493; S341, S751, S810, S811
Beston, John B., S812, S813
Bethune, Brian, S814
"A Better Place Than Home," P54
Beyersbergen, Joanna, S815
Bezanson, Bridget, S11
Biblowitz, Iris, S1272
Bigsby, Christopher, P894
Birbalsingh, Frank, S816
Black, Barbara, S397
Blaise, Clark, P46, P138, P546
Blake, Patricia, S398
Blatchford, Christie, S817
Blodgett, E. D., S399, S529, S680, S752, S753, S818

Blumberg, Myrna, S159
Blythe, Ronald, S160, S298
Bock, Tony, S819
Boddy, Kasia, S586
Bohner, Charles H., P65, P78, P84, P217
Bolton, Sondra, P796, P799
Bonetti, Kay, P889
Bonnière, René, P734, P735
Borchiver, Richard, P754
Boston, Anne, S193
Bowen, Deborah, S12, S820
Bowering, George, P32
Bowers, Rick, P160, P371
Boyce, Pleuke, P6, P9, P11, P901
Boyle, Harry, P847
Boyles, Mary, S821
Boynton, Danelle Gail, S13
Boynton, Robert W., P140
"Boys and Girls," P55-85, P659
    Film adaptations, P750
    Television broadcasts, P710
    Translations, P85
Boyt, Susie, S645
Bradbury, Patricia, S531
Bradshaw, Leah, S720
Brenner, Gerry, S845
Bright, Juliette, S1273
Brisac, Geneviève, S242, S517
Brockway, James, S162
Brodie, Leanna, P755; S776
Brookner, Anita, S194, S254, S401, S466, S646
Brooks, Sheila A., P598
Broughton, Katheryn Maclean, P192
Brown, Daniel J., S14
Brown, Harry, P856
Brown, Rosellen, S587
Brown, Russell, P361, P449, P525; S805
Brown, Susan Windisch, P702
Broyard, Anatole, S402
Bruckner, D. J. R., S823
Brunsdale, Mitzi M., S1274
Buchholtz, Mirosława, S824
Buell, Masha, P256
Buitenhuis, Peter, S195, S403, S404
Bula, Javier Alfaya, P6
Bulpitt, Mildred, S335

Burnham, Clint, S769
Burroughs, Jackie, P806
Burto, William, P66, P68
Busch, Frederick, S681
Bush, Catherine, S467, S765
Butala, Sharon, S468
Byatt, A. S., S342, S532, S647
Byers, Catherine, P809

Cadogan, Mary, S140
Cahill, Susan N., P120, P379, P447
Cairns, A. T. J., S1254
Caldwell, Gail, S196, S255, S343, S469, S648
Caldwell, Rebecca, S825, S1371
Calisher, Hortense, P648
Callaghan, Barry, S163
Cam, Heather, S826
Cameron, Marsaili, S141
Campbell, Leslie Marion, S15
Campbell, Terry, P854
Canitz, A. E. Christa, S754, S757, S827
Caplan, Brina, S533
Carey, Barbara, S344
Carrera Suárez, Isabel, S828
"Carried Away," P15, P16, P86-95, P665
    Radio broadcasts, P711
    Translations, P93-P95
Carrington, Ildikó de Papp, S197, S752, S753, S829-837
Carscallen, James, S754, S838-840
Cart, Michael, P228
Carter, Alixe, S405, S1340
Carver, Caroline, S714
Carver, Raymond, P354
Carver Taylor, Mary Anne, S16
Casas, Flora, P8, P9, P348
Caskey, Sarah A., S17
Cassill, R. V., P49, P456, P461, P489, P500, P631, P702
Castro, Julio Paredes, P8
Caton, Elizabeth, P773
Causse, Michèle, P14, P226, P501
Caws, Mary Ann, P29
Cencig, Elisabeth, S18, S841
Chabon, Michael, P517, P679

"Chaddeleys and Flemings. 1: Connection," P96-101, P128
   Film adaptations, P751
   Translations, P101
"Chaddeleys and Flemings. 2: The Stone in the Field," P102-108, P545-549
   Radio broadcasts, P740
   Read by Alice Munro, P740
   Translations, P108, P548, P549
Chamney, Anne [pseud.], P650
"Chance," P109, P110
"Changing Places," P663
Chapman, Marilyn, P408
Chaput, Sylvie, S518
"Characters," P111
Charters, Ann, P51, P71, P254, P602, P604
Charters, Samuel, P604
Chase, Thomas, P79
Chatman, Seymour, P429
Chian, Li-chu, P528
"The Children Stay," P15, P112-122, P666
   Translations, P121, P122
Chong, Denise, P342
Chouteau, René, P768, P838
Chu, Chung-yi, S842
Ciabattari, Jane, S256
"Circle of Prayer," P123-125, P667
   Read by Alice Munro, P818
   Sound recordings, P818
Clancy, Laurie, S1275
Clapp, Susannah, S470
Clark, Alex, S257
Clark, Miriam Marty, S843
Clausen, Signe Pihl, P363
Clayton, Gina, P777, P781
Clayton, John J., P491
Clery, Val, S844
Coe, Clellan, S845
Coghill, Joy, P739
Cohen, Marcelo, P4
Coldwell, Joan, S302, S1276
Coles, Joanna, S198
Collier, Michael, P691
Collins, Anne, S406
"The Colonel's Hash Resettled," P664
Colvile, Georgiana M. M., S846, S847

"Comfort," P126, P127
Common, Laura, P720
Condé, Mary, S773, S848-853
Congram, John, S199
"Connection" *see* "Chaddeleys and Flemings 1: Connection"
Connolly, Kevin, P886
Conron, Brandon, S854, S855
Cook, D.E., S1251
Cooke, John, S856
Corbeil, Carole, P98
Cornacchia, Cheryl, S857
"Cortes Island," P129-131
   Radio broadcasts, P712
   Translations, P131
Coupland, Douglas, P613
Cox, Ailsa, S755
Cox, Yvonne, S1384
Craig, Jamie, S858
Craig, Patricia, P326; S200, S534
Creighton, David, S859
Crerar, Tom, S407
Crisafulli Jones, Lilla Maria, S860
Crittenden, Yvonne, S408
Croft, Barbara, S345
Crom, Nathalie, S519
Crosbie, Lynn, S202
Crouse, David, S861
Crowell, Catherine, P827
Curb, Randall, S346
Curnew, Judy, P742
Currie, Rod, S1432
Currie, Sheldon, S303
Curtis, C. Michael, P430, P591
Curtis, Gary, S588
Cusk, Rachel, S589

Dafoe, Christopher, S165, S304, S1327
Dahlie, Hallvard, S756, S862, S863, S1277-1279
Dakin, Kymberly, P775, P776, P822, P823
"Dance of the Happy Shades," P132-143
   Translations, P142, P143
Dance of the Happy Shades: Stories, P2
   Reviews, S159-191
   Sound recordings, P765-768
   Translations, P2, P768

"The Dangerous One," P144
Dark, Larry, P113, P186, P237, P297, P508, P666, P670, P672, P678
Daurio, Beverley, S535
Davey, Frank, S864, S1280
David, Jack, P67, P200, P620; S756
Davidson, Joyce, P855
Davies, Dorothy, P747
Davis, Amanda, S258, S347
Davis, Buffy, P833
Dawe, Alan, S683
Dawson, Anthony B., S865
Dawson, Carrie, S866
"Day of the Butterfly," P145-150
Day, Susan X., P499
Daymond, Douglas, P139, P646
Daziron, Héliane, S19, S867-875
de Vos, P., P14
De Wiel, Alexa, S409
Dean, Nancy, P478
Decision, P362
Deignan, Tom, S259
DeMott, Benjamin, S410
Denham, Paul, P310, P524, P577
DeSalvo, Louise, S876
Devarrieux, Claire, S520
Dewar, Elaine, S721
Dhuibhne, Éilis Ní, S590
Di Stefano, Katherine, S878
Dickman, Amy G., S20
"Differently," P16, P151-154, P668
    Film adaptations, P752
DiLeo, Michael, S21
"The Dimensions of a Shadow," P155
Ditsky, John, S879
DiYanni, Robert, P458
Djwa, Sandra, S769, S880
Dobbs, Kildare, S305, S684, S1341
Dombrowski, Eileen, S881
Donley, Carol, P544
Donovan, Katie, S882
Dooley, D. J., S411
Dougherty, Dean, P78, P217
Doze, Geneviève, P4, P6, P12, P143, P272, P313, P398, P438, P530, P607
Drainie, Bronwyn, S260

Drysdale, Andrea, S22
Dubus, Andre, S471
Duchêne, Anne, S536
Dufault, Roseanna Lewis, S23
Duffy, Dennis, S649, S883
Duguid, Lindsay, S592
"Dulse," P156-161
    Translations, P161
Duncan, Isla J., S24, S884, S885
Durrant, Digby, S537
Duteau, Claire L., S25
Duthie, Bill, S182
Dvorak, Marta, S886
Dyer, Klay, S887-889, S1281
Dyment, Betty J., S26
D'Souza, Irene, S261, S348, S591

Earl, Marjorie, S722
Eckstein, Barbara J., S203
Edemariam, Aida, S890, S1354
"The Edge of Town," P162
Edwards, Bruce L., S891
Edwards, Caterina, S412, S723
Edwards, Harriet, S295
Edwards, Mary Jane, P310, P524
Edwards, Thomas R., S142
Eikli, Ragnhild, P18, P53, P95, P101, P108, P161, P166, P183, P218, P238, P263, P282, P314, P316, P331, P368, P389, P424, P439, P442, P538, P593, P608, P635
Eldredge, L.M., S892
Elliott, Gayle, S893
Elliott, Lesley, P408
Elson, Brigid, S685
"Emily," P163
Enright, Anne, S263
Epps, Garrett, S143
Erdrich, Louise, P469, P675
Eri, Unni, P2
Erskine, Bruce, S593
"Eskimo," P164-167
    Translations, P166, P167
Esmonde de Usabel, Frances M., S144
Etter, Kathryn, S27
Evans, Jennifer, S28

"Everything Here Is Touchable and Mysterious," P682
"Executioners," P168

Fadiman, Clifton, P31
Fallis, Sheila Robinson, S724
"Family Furnishings," P169-172, P669
Farmer, Lesley S. J., S205
Farrow, Moira, S894
"Fathers," P173, P174, P706
Faustmann, John, S413
Fawcett, Brian, S895
Feinberg, Cara, P906
"The Ferguson Girls Must Never Marry," P175
Ferguson, Mary Anne, P488
Ferns, Pat, P748, P759
Ferrari, Margaret, S306
Ferri, Laura, S896
Fertile, Candace, S264, S651
Figes, Kate, P640
Fillion, Bryant, P148, P547
Fillion, Kate, S1354
Findley, Timothy, S897
Finnbogason, Jack, P366
Firth, Suzanne, P252
Fischman, Sheila, S167
Fish, Maria, S594
Fisher, Ann H., S473
Fisher, Don, S29
"Fits," P176-180
Fitzpatrick, Margaret Anne, S898
"Five Points," P181-183
    Translations, P183
Flam, Jack, S206
Flater, Leah, P193
Fleenor, Juliann E., S899
"Floating Bridge," P184-188, P670
Flower, Dean, S414
Foote, Audrey C., S307
Forceville, Charles, P462; S900, S901, S1282
Ford, Richard, P153, P625, P668, P680; S652
Ford, Theresa, P405

"Forgiveness in Families," P189-197, P878
    Film adaptations, P753
    Radio broadcasts, P713
    Sound recordings, P769, P770
Forkash, Diana Grace, S30
"A Form of Marriage," P472
Fortier-Masek, Marie-Odile, P3
Fortunato, Mario, S902
"The Found Boat," P198-208
    Radio broadcasts, P714
Fowler, Beth, P774
Fowler, Lois Josephs, P292
Fowler, Rowena, S903
Foy, Nathalie, S31, S759, S904
France, Louise, S905
Francesconi, Sabrina, S906
Frank, Michael, S350, S595
Franklin, Ruth, S265
Franks, Lucinda, S415
Franzen, Jonathan, S596, S907
Fraser, Marian Botsford, S653
Fraser, Ruth, P722, P787
Freake, Douglas, P886; S1283
Freeman, John, S266, S597
Freeman, Judith, S207
Freeman, Suzanne, S416
French, William, P866, P867; S208, S417, S539, S686, S725, S908, S909, S1375
Friedlander, Mitzi, P772, P795
"Friend of My Youth," P209-218, P671
    Radio broadcasts, P715
    Read by Alice Munro, P715
    Translations, P218
Friend of My Youth: Stories, P3
    Read by Alice Munro, P771
    Reviews, S192-243
    Sound recordings, P771-774
    Translations, P3
Frizzell, John, P733, P756
Frum, Barbara, P844
Frye, Joanne S., S910
Fu, Li, S757
Fulford, Robert, P415; S687, S688
Funk, Robert, P499
Furman, Laura, P174, P706

Gadpaille, Michelle, S911
Galloway, Priscilla, P250
Gamerman, Amy, S474
Gane, Margaret Drury, P850; S912
Gardam, Jane, S351, S579
Gardiner, Jill Marjorie, P845; S32
Garebian, Keith, S352, S353
Garis, Leslie, S689
Garner, Hugh, P2, S913
Garrett, Charlotte K., S33
Garson, Marjorie, S914-916
Garvie, Maureen, S765, S771
Gatti, Tom, S598
Gaunce, Julia, P345
Gedalof, Allan, P755; S776
Geddes, Gary, P293, P514, P699, P702, P864
Gent, Shirley, P831, P832
Gentry, Marshall Bruce, S767
Gerson, Carole, P195, P859
Gersoni-Stavn, Diane, S308
Gervais, Marty, S917
Gervais, Mary, S418
Gessel, Paul, S1412, S1416
Gholamain, Mitra, S34
Giannarelli, Laura, P788
Gibson, Douglas M., S918, S919
Gibson, Flo, P817
Gibson, Graeme, P698, P842
Gifford, Tony, P247, P717; S1083
Gilbert, Paula Ruth, S920
Gilbert, Sandra M., P630
Giles, Jeff, S267
Gingerich, Judy, S921
Gintsburg, 'Adi, P4
Gioia, Dana, P257, P259, P702
Giordani, Maria Rosa, S922
Gironnay, Sophie, S475, S923
Gittings, Christopher E., P899; S35, S924
Givner, Joan, S925
Glover, Douglas, P172, P185, P296
Gnarowski, Michael, S1252
Godard, Barbara, S757, S926
Goddard, John, S1355
Godfrey, Lisa, P909
Godley, Elizabeth, S209
"Going to the Lake," P684

Gold, Joseph, S927
Goldberg, Carole, S599
"Golden Apples," P685
Goldman, Marlene, S928
"Good Woman in Ireland," P686
"Good-By, Myra," P219
Goodman, Charlotte, S929
"Goodness and Mercy," P220-222
Gordon, Giles, P88, P212, P213, P222, P233, P358, P470, P471
Gorjup, Branko, P548; S476, S759
Gorra, Michael, S354, S540
Gorse, Oliver, S541
Gould, Jan, S168
Govier, Katherine, S355
Grabes, Herbert, S930
Grady, Wayne, P158, P563, P618; S419, S726, S727, S931
Graham, Barbara J., S542
Grainger, James, S771
Granatstein, J. L., S514
Grant, Lyman, P84
Gray, Bill, P758
Gray, Paul, S543
Greenstein, Michael, S268
Grier, Bill, P755, S776
Grieve, Meghan, S36
Griffin, Nonnie, P717
Groen, Rick, S932
Gros-Louis, Dolores, S933
Grosskurth, Phyllis, S169, S309
Grove, Chris, P791
Guadagni, Nicky, P738, P746
Gubar, Susan, P630
Guth, Hans P., P75
Gutteridge, Don, P480
Gwynn, R. S., P259, P632, P702
Gzowski, Peter, P869-873, P881-885, P891, P892, P897, P898, P902, P905

Hagen, Anne Marie, S37
Hale, Alice K., P598
"Half a Grapefruit," P223-226
    Translations, P226
Hall, Donald, P201
Halling, Kia, P4, P6

Hamad, José. P6
Hammerstad, Gerd. S38
Hammick, Georgina. P519, P522
Hamon-Hill, Cindy. P751
Hampl, Patricia. P50
Hampson, Robert. S935
Hancock, Geoff. P864, P865
Hanly, Charles. S936
Hansen, Ron. P285
Hanson, Clare. S759
Harcourt, Joan. P239
"Hard-Luck Stories." P227, P228
Harris, Claire. P255
Harris, Gale. S477
Harris, Margaret. S937
Harrison, John Kent. P757
Harrison, Kathryn. S765
Harron, Don. P852, P853
Hartmann, Eva Maria. S39
Harveit, Lars. S938
Harvey, Caroline. S356
Harvor, Beth. S170, S939
Haslund, Ebba. P8, P643
"Hateship, Friendship, Courtship, Loveship, Marriage." P15, P16, P229, P230
Hateship, Friendship, Courtship, Loveship, Marriage: Stories. P4
    Radio broadcasts. P716
    Reviews. S244-295
    Sound recordings. P775-782
    Translations. P4, P782
Haviland, Beverly. S544
Hawthorne, Mary. S600
Hayes, Elizabeth J.. S40
He, Miao-bo. S940
Heaton, Caroline. P441
Heble, Ajay. S41, S654, S757
Hedenstrom, Joanne. S941
Heeger, Susan. S478
Heer, Jeet. S763
Hefferman, Teresa. S479
Heinrich, Karl. P85
Heller, Deborah. S942
Helwig, David. P232, P235, P239, P334, P637; S171, S480
Helwig, Maggie. P235, P637

Henderson, Heather. S545
Henderson, Jim. P148, P547
Henderson, Lynn. P737
Henderson, Scott. S943
Herford, Oliver. S601
Hermann, Judith. P44, P122, P373, P484, P782
Hermansson, Casie. S763
Hernáez Lerena, María Jesús. S758, S944, S945
Hesse, M. G.. P60, P479
Hesse, Nicole Christine. S42
Hestnes, Haege. P363
Heuvelmans, Ton. P7
Heward, Burt. S946
Higgins, Krystyna. S481
Hill, Douglas. S420
Hill, Heather. S947
Hill, Susan. P422
Hill, William B.. S310
Hirano, Keiichi. P252
"Hired Girl." P231-233
Hirsch, Edward. P691
Hirschberg, Stuart. P702
Hirschberg, Terry. P702
Hiscock, Andrew. S948
Hluchy, Patricia. S949
Hobbs, Catherine. S763
Hodgins, Jack. P191
Hoeper, Jeffrey D.. P325, P383
Hoff, Berit. P1
Hoffert, Barbara. S655
Hofsess, John. S728
Hogan, Russell J.. P194
Hogan, Susan. P712
Hogg, Carol. S690
"Hold Me Fast, Don't Let Me Pass." P234-238
    Translations. P238
Holland, Patrick. S1284
Hollinghurst, Alan. S145, S421
Holmebakk, Gordon. P18, P53, P95, P101, P108, P161, P166, P183, P218, P238, P263, P282, P314, P316, P331, P368, P389, P424, P439, P442, P538, P592, P593, P608, P635
Holmgren, Michelle. S762
Holstrom, David. S482
Holton, Danica Lynn. S43
"Home." P239, P240

"The Honeyman's Granddaughter," P241
Hookey, Robert, P105
Hooper, Brad, S210, S602
Hopson, Jeanne, P764, P786, P830
Hornosty, Janina Camille, S44
Horwood, Harold, P879; S950
Hošek, Chaviva, S691
Houpt, Simon R, S1394
Houston, Pam, S951
"How Could I Do That?" P242, P243
    Translations, P243
"How I Met My Husband," P244-263
    Television broadcasts, P717
    Translations, P263
Howard, Irene, S311
Howard, Philip, S546
Howells, Coral Ann, S269, S759, S952-961, S1285
Howland, Bette, S692
Hoy, Helen, S962-964, S1253, S1254
Huang, Shu, S45
Hughes, David, P88, P212, P213, P222, P233, P358, P470, P471
Hughes-Hallett, Lucy, S357, S483, S656
Huisgen, Helga, P9
Hulan, Renée, P340; S46
Hulbert, Ann, S422, S484
Humphreys, Josephine, S485
Hunt, Russell, S693
Hunter, Adrian, S965
Hunter, J. Paul, P62, P74, P77
Hunter, Martin, P723
Hunter, Shaun M., S47, S48
Hutcheon, Linda, P32

Ibáñez, Enrique, P522
"The Idyllic Summer," P264
"Images," P265-272
    Radio broadcasts, P718
    Translations, P271, P272
Ingram, David R., S966
Irvine, Lorna, S49, S753, S768, S770, S774, S967-971
Israel, Charles E., P54
Italie, Hillel, S1395
Iyer, Lalitha, S50

"The Jack Randa Hotel," P273-277
    Sound recordings, P783
Jackel, David, S1286
Jackson, Heather, S312
Jacobs, Henry E., P204, P208, P322
Jacobs, Rita D., S657
Jacobs-Munton, Ann, S715, S748
Jacobus, Lee A., P364
"Jakarta," P278-280
    Translations, P280
Jakobsen, Linda, S972
James, Geoffrey, S694
Jamieson, Sara, S973
Jansen, Ann, P746
Jansen, Reamy, S974
Jarab, Josef, P17, P43, P94, P121, P142, P271, P312, P346, P367, P397, P437, P529, P606
Jarman, Mark Anthony, P409
Jarrett, Mary, S975
Jennings, C. Wade, P251
Jensen, Liz, S358
"Jesse and Meribeth," P281, P282
    Translations, P282
Jindrová-Špilarová, Alena, P17, P43, P94, P121, P142, P271, P312, P346, P367, P397, P437, P529, P606
Jirgens, Karl, S760
Johnson, Andrew, P761
Johnson, Brian R., S51, S976
Johnson, Katherine M., S52
Johnson, Marigold, S313
Johnston, Ingrid, S359
Jonas, George, P717
Jones, D. A. N., S547
Jones, Malcolm, S211, S486, S658
Jones, Michelle, S977, S978
Jones, Raymond E., P160, P371
Josephs, Shirley, S729
Julian, Marilyn, S695

Kakutani, Michiko, S212, S270, S487, S548, S603
Kamboureli, Smaro, S979
Kane, Mary, P826
Kareda, Urjo, S423, S730
Kaveney, Roz, S424

Kazuko, Yokoyama, P7
Keefer, Janice Kulyk, S771
Keegan, Alex, S980
Keith, W. J., S760, S981-983, S1287
Kelly, Darlene, S984
Kelman, Suanne, P868
Kemp, Peter, S213, S425
Kenison, Katrina, P87, P171, P211, P328, P432, P469, P504, P507, P517, P665, P669, P671, P674-677, P679
Kennedy, X. J., P257
Kenyon, Linda, S488
Kephart, Beth, S360
Kerr, Alison Patricia, S53
Kiernan, Kathy, P35
Kildahl, Karen A., S1288
Kilpatrick, Ken, S731, S985
Kim, Helen M., S54
Kinczyk, Bohdan, S762
King, Allan, P708
Kingsolver, Barbara, P432, P674
Kirby, Blaik, P748
Kirchhoff, H. J., S986
Kirkwood, Hilda, S172, S696
Kirszner, Laurie G., P70, P81
Klein, Norma, S315
Klinck, Carl F., P512
Klinkenborg, Verlyn, P762
Kloss, Robert J., S987
Klotz, Marvin, P261
Knapp, Mona, S271, S362
Knelman, Martin, S988
Knox, Rita, P802
Koenig, Wolf, P751
Kohn, Martin, P544
Komisar, Elizabeth, P846
Korstanje, Bas, S697
Köster, Patricia, S764
Kostov, Velimir, P167, P290, P291
Kramer, John, P757
Kritenbrink, Angie, S605
Kroll, Jeri, P860
Kröller, Eva-Marie, S760, S989
Kustec, Aleksander, S990

LaBarge, Dorothy, S427
"Labor Day Dinner," P283-286
Lacayo, Richard, S606
Lacombe, Michèle, S991
LaHood, Marvin J., S550
Laidlaw, Alice. *See* Munro, Alice
Lallier, Lily Marie, S55
Lalonde, Jeremy, S607
Lamont-Stewart, Linda, S56, S992
Lampe, David, P324
Lane, Bill, P742
Langley, Sandra Wynne, S57
Langston, Corinne, P744
Laniel, Carole-Andrée, S575
Larson, Charles R., P382
Lasdun, James, S660
Latta, Ruth, P763
Laurence, Jocelyn, S993
Laurence, Margaret, S994, S995
Lawson, Neroli, S996
Lecercle, Jean-Jacques, S997
Lecker, Robert, P67, P200, P620; S756, S998
Lee, Hermione, P337, P571; S363
Lehman, David, S428
Leitch, Linda, S58
Leite, Cássio de Arantes, P4
Lesser, Wendy, S490
Levene, Mark, P180; S551, S999
Levin, Martin, S173
Levine, Norman, S552
Lewis, Trevor, S272
Lewochko, Mary, S59
"Lichen," P287-291
    Translations, P290, P291
Lilienfeld, Jane, S1000, S1001
Litzinger, Boyd, P542
Liu, Xiujie, S60
"Lives of Girls and Women," P292-294
    Film adaptations, P754, P755
Lives of Girls and Women: A Novel, P5; S776
    Radio broadcasts, P719-723
    Read by Alice Munro, P719, P721
    Reviews, S296-336
    Sound recordings, P784-793
    Television broadcasts, P724
    Translations, P5

Lockerbie, Catherine, S273
London, Joan, S491
Lostanlen, Claire, S1002
Lothian, Andrew, S147
"Lottar," P22
Loughery, John, P583
"The Love of a Good Woman," P15, P295-301, P672
   Translations, P301
The Love of a Good Woman: Stories, P6
   Reviews, S337-391
   Sound recordings, P794-799
   Translations, P6
Love, Barbara, S365
Lovrinèeviæ Ljiljanka, P548
Lowery, Adrien Jeanette, S61
Lowry, Elizabeth, S366
Lozar, Tomaz, S1004
Lucas, Alec, P378; S215
Lumsden, Susan, P737
"Lying under the Apple Tree," P302
Lynch, Deidre, S1319
Lynch, Gerald, P215, P621; S1005, S1006
Lynch, Kate, P711
Lynch, Paul, P743
Lynn, Steven, P262

MacCann, Philip, S661
Macdonald, Jenny, S367
MacDonald, Rae McCarthy, S1007, S1008
Macfarlane, David, S553, S1009
Mack, Maynard, P140
MacKendrick, Louis King, S757, S760, S761
MacKinnon, Donna Jean, S1411
MacMillan, Marionne, S698
MacMillan, Michael, P733, P750, P756
MacNeill, James A., P404
MacPherson, Cheryl S., S62
Macpherson, Heidi Slettedahl, S1010
Madden, David, P206
Madoff, Mark S., S760
Mahbey, Judy, P722, P787, P789, P793
Mahoney, Jeff, S1442
Maitland, James A. (pseud.). *See* Metcalf, John, S1046
Mallet, Gina, S732, S1011

Mallick, Heather, S368, S1368
Mallinson, Jean, S554, S1012
Mallon, Thomas, S662
Mandell, Stephen R., P70, P81
Maneri, Gina, P2, P3; S1078
Manguel, Alberto, P178, P582, P725
Marchand, Philip, S216, S274, S492, S608
Markovits, Benjamin, S275
"Marrakesh," P303
Mars-Jones, Adam, S663
Martin, Betty Ann, S63
Martin, Margaret Kathleen, S64
Martin, Peggy, S1013
Martin, Sandra, P334; S217, S369
Martin, W. R. [Walter Rintoul], S762, S1014-1021
Martin, Wendy, P188, P492
Martineau, Barbara, P848
Martone, Michael, P329
Matchan, Linda, S1022
"Material," P304-314
   Translations, P312-314
Mathews, Lawrence, S1023
Matsell, Ruth, S65
Matthews, Carol Anne, S66
Matthews, Mike, S218, S609
Max, B. Delores, P537
May, Charles E., S1024
Mayberry, Katherine J., S1025, S1026
Mayr, Suzette, P345
McAlpine, Mary, S317
McBrearty, Don, P733, P750, P756
McCaig, JoAnn Elizabeth, S67, S763, S1027-1029
McCarthy, Dermot, S1030
McCarthy, Joanne, S1311
McClay, Jill Kedersha, S276
McClung, M.G., S1289
McCombs, Judith, S1031, S1032
McCormick, Kathleen, P292
McCulloch, Jeanne, P895
McCullough, Elizabeth, P199
McDonnell, Helen, P194
McDougall, Joyce, S1033
McDowell, Lesley, S610
McElheny, Kenneth R., P639

McEwen, Christian, P294
McGahern, John, S277
McGill, Robert James, S68, S1034, S1035, S1290
McGoogan, Kenneth, S370, S1036, S1391
McGovern, Clare, S611
McGowan, Martha, P202
McGraw, Erin, S493
McHaney, Pearl Amelia, P685
McKenzie, Sandra, S494
McKinnon, Jean D., S1037
McLatchie, Ian B., S69
McLean, Seaton, P733, P750, P756
McLennan McCue, Sharon A., S219
McLoughlin, Pat, P627
McMahan, Elizabeth, P499
McMullen, Lorraine, S318, S429, S753, S762, S1038
McNeilly, Anne, S1039
McShane, Javier Alfaya, P6
Mead, Catherine, P800, P811, P816
Meadwell, Kenneth W., S1288
Mechling, Lauren, S1040
Meek, Jim, S495
Meindl, Dieter, S1041
Mellor, Susan, P803
Mellors, John, S430
Melnyk, Helen, S1042
"Memorial," P315, P316
   Translations, P316
"Meneseteung," P15, P317-331, P673
   Translations, P331
Mercier, Christophe, S521
Merkin, Daphne, S1043
Mersereau, M. Grace, P403
Messenger, Cynthia, S753, S754, S769
Messenger, W. E., P63
Messud, Claire, S612, S664
Metcalf, John, P46, P57, P61, P135, P138, P146, P266, P323, P353, P386, P393, P401, P454, P490, P494, P546, P601, P619, P649, P659, P664, P694, P702, P841; S319, S1044-1048
Meyer, Bruce, P207; S761
Meyer, Michael, P253, P343, P344, P410, P411, P459, P460

Mi-gyong, Pak, P5
Micros, Marianne, S1049
"Miles City, Montana," P332-348
   Radio broadcasts, P725
   Read by Alice Munro, P818
   Translations, P346-348
Millar, Mary, S555
Miller, James E., P194
Miller, Judith, S371, S764, S768, S1051-1053
Miller, Karl, S613, S1054
Miller, Lori, S1055
Miller, Sue, P171, P669
Milne, Kirsty, S556
Miner, Valerie, S614
Minow, Martha, P495
"Mischief," P15, P349-351
Mitchell, Ken, P79
Mitchell, Reid, S1056
Moffett, James, P639
Mokros, Anne, S70
Moller-Madsen, Lisbeth, P3, P5, P6, P8, P9
Monaghan, David, S1057
Monkman, Leslie, P646
"Monsieur les Deux Chapeaux," P352-355
"The Moon in the Orange Street Skating Rink," P356-358
"The Moons of Jupiter," P16, P359-368
   Radio broadcasts, P726, P727
   Read by Alice Munro, P726, P727
   Translations, P367, P368
The Moons of Jupiter: Stories, P7, P687
   Reviews, S392-461
   Sound recordings, P800-805
   Translations, P7, P805
Moore, Jean M., S1254, S1255
Moore, Lorrie, P504, P508, P581, P676; S278, S615, S1058
Moore, Michael M., P35
Moore, Tedde, P745
Moran, Maureen F., S754
Moreno, Esperanza Pérez, P7
Morgan, Ted, S148
Morgan, William, S176
Morley, Patricia, S431, S665
Morrell, Stuart, S1059
Morrison, Ray, S733

Morrissy, Mary, S279
Mort, Mary-Ellen, S432
Moschapidakis, Helen Kafatou, S71
Moss, John, S1060, S1061, S1291
Moss, Laura F., S72
Motei, Angela Cozea, S220
Moyles, R.G., S757
"Mrs. Cross and Mrs. Kidd," P369-371
    Radio broadcasts, P728
    Read by Alice Munro, P728
Muço, Betim, P26, P93, P474
Mukherjee, Bharati, S221, S433
Muller, Gilbert H., P205
Müller, Klaus Peter, P69
Munro, Alice
    Awards, S1325-1442
    Fictional works (books, stories). *See individual titles in this index*
    Interviews, P839-910
    Letters, P681, P688-690, P693, P695, P697, P704, P705
    Memoirs, P651, P652
    Nonfiction (articles, essays), P653-P706
    Poems, P650
Munro, Sheila, S765
Murch, Kem, P849
Murphy, Georgeann, S1062
"My Mother's Dream," P372, P373
    Radio broadcasts, P729
    Read by Alice Munro, P729
    Translations, P373
Myerson, Jonathan, S280

Nadkarny, Prema, S73
Naglin, Nancy, S699
Narins, Brigham, P702
Næss, Gunn Reinertsen, S74
Nemiroff, Greta Hofmann, P289
"Nettles," P374, P375
Neufeld, K. Gordon, S281
New, William Herbert, P58, P63, P97, P100, P103, P107, P118, P561; S1063, S1064, S1308, S1309
Newman, Judie, S768
Nichol, James W., P734, P743

Nicholl, Kristina, P736
Nicholson, Colin, S757
Nielsen, Richard, P748, P759
Nielsen, Rose-Marie, P4
Nischik, Reingard M., S1065
Nolan, Tom, S700
Nölle-Fischer, Karen, P3, P8
Noonan, Gerald, S701, S734, S754, S768, S770, S1066, S1067
Norris, Gloria, P336
"The Novels of William Maxwell," P691
Nowlan, Michael, P407
Nunes, Mark, S1069

Oates, Joyce Carol, P49, P541, P542, P631; S149, S150, S177, S223, S557, S702
Ober, Warren U., S1018-1021
Obexer, Regina, S75
Off, Carol, S735, S1071
"The Office," P376-384
    Translations, P384
"Oh, What Avails," P385-389
    Translations, P389
Ohl, Manfred, P7
Ohm, Viveca, S1072
"On John Metcalf: Taking Writing Seriously," P692
"On Writing 'The Office,'" P694
Ondaatje, Michael, P248, P268, P307, P338, P339, P419, P660, P664
"Open Secrets," P390, P391
Open Secrets: Stories, P8
    Reviews, S462-521
    Sound recordings, P806-813
    Translations, P8
Orange, John, S703, S1074
"Oranges and Apples," P392-394
    Radio broadcasts, P730
    Read by Alice Munro, P730
Osachoff, Margaret Gail, S76, S1075
Osborne, Linda Barrett, S435
Osler, Ida Reichardt, P790
Osmond, Rosalie, S224, S1076
Østby, Inger-Mette, S77

"The Ottawa Valley," P395-398
    Radio broadcasts, P732
    Read by Alice Munro, P732
    Television broadcasts, P731
    Translations, P397, P398
"An Ounce of Cure," P399-411, P659
    Film adaptations, P756
    Sound recordings, P814
    Television broadcasts, P733
Overduin, Hendrik, S320
Owen, Ivon, P308
O'Brien, Peter, P620
O'Connor, Mary, S1070
O'Faolain, Julia, S151, S496
O'Faolain, Nuala, S434

Pacey, Desmond, P552, P554
Packer, Miriam, S78, S1077
Paletta, Anna, S79
Palmer, Jill, S436
Palusci, Oriana, S1078
Panofsky, Ruth, S753
Pardee, Martha Harmon, P778
Park, Christine, P441
Parker, Paula, P792, P794
Passaro, Vince, S616
Passek, Lynn, S80
"Passion," P412, P413
Patterson, Troy, S283
"The Peace of Utrecht," P414-424
    Television broadcasts, P734
    Translations, P424
Peck, Edward, P380, P694
Peddie, David, P708, P734, P735, P741, P743
Peltier, Mary Damon, S321
Penner, Maxine Dawn, S81
Pérez, Esperanza, P3
Perkin-McFarland, Anne Louise, S82
Perlman, David, P256
Perrakis, Phyllis Sternberg, S1079
Persky, Stan, S372
Peter, John, S178
Peters, Joanne K., S577
Petersen, Arne Herlov, P1
Peterson, Kevin, S322
Peterson, Leslie, S1080, S1081

Petry, Florence, P9
Petry, Hildegard, P1, P5
Pfaus, B., S766
Philip, Neil, S437
Phillips, Kate, S666, S667
Philpott, Joan, S668
"The Photographer," P425, P426
Picard, Geneviève, S243
Pickering, James H., P325, P383, P562
"Pictures of the Ice," P427-430
Pilz, Joan, P105
Pitts, Charles Kristian, P724, P754, P758
Platt, Janice, P733, P750, P756
Plimpton, George, P535
Polderman, Jeanne, P7, P9, P14
Polk, James, S323
Pollard, Derek, S770
Pool, Gail, P642
Porteus, Neil, S1082
Portman, Jamie, S179, S1379, S1381
Posesorski, Sherie, S373
"Post and Beam," P431-433, P674
"Postcard," P434-439
    Radio broadcasts, P736
    Television broadcasts, P735
    Translations, P437-439
Poteet, Lewis J., S324
Potocco, Marcello, P384
Potter, John, S83
Powell, Barbara Pezalla, S84
Powell, Dorothy M., S704
"Powers," P440
Premoli, Marina, P8
Prendergast, Christopher, P29
Prendergast, Kathleen, S85
Prentice, Christine, S1084
Prince, Peter, S180
"Princess Ida," P441, P442
    Translations, P442
Pritchard, William H., S284, S705
Pritchett, V. S., S181
"Privilege," P443, P444
Probst, Robert E., P76
"The Progress of Love," P16, P445-449
    Read by Alice Munro, P820
    Sound recordings, P820

The Progress of Love: Stories, P9
    Read by Alice Munro, P818
    Reviews, S522-578
    Sound recordings, P815-819
    Translations, P9
Prokop, Mary, S225
Prose, Francine, S1085
Proulx, Annie, P2
"Providence," P450, P451
    Radio broadcasts, P737
    Sound recordings, P821
"Prue," P452-462
    Translations, P462
Pruitt, Virginia D., S1086
Putnam, Conan, S375

Quartermaine, Peter, S1087, S1310
"Queenie: A Story," P463, P464
Queenie: A Story, P10
    Reviews, S579
"A Queer Streak," P465-467
Querengesser, Neil, S756
Quigley, Ellen, S756
Quigly, Isabel, S439
Quinn, Alice, P904; S1088
Quinn, Anthony, S499

Raabe, David, S1089
Rabinowitz, Dorothy, S153
Rabkin, Eric S., P496
Radin, Victoria, S560
Rampton, David, P215, P621
Ramraj, Victor J., S1090
Rang, Zhang, P4
Rankin, Linda Marie, S86
Rasporich, Beverly, P861, P889; S183, S285, S578, S754, S757, S763, S767-769, S1091, S1092
Ravenel, Shannon, P125, P153, P318, P320, P354, P541, P625, P648, P667, P668, P673, P680
Ravitch, Michael, S286
Ready, Kathryn, S763
"A Real Life," P468-474, P675
    Translations, P474
Reaney, James, S1093

Rebar, Kelly, P724, P751, P754
"Red Dress—1946," P475-482
Redekop, Magdalene, S227, S759, S768, S1094, S1095
Redmon, Anne, S440
Reed, Nancy Gail, S154
Reese, Jennifer, S619
Regan, Stephen, S1096
Reid, Robert, S620, S671
Reid, Susan E. Bryan, S87
Reid, Verna M., S88, S1097
Reimer, Elizabeth Anne, S89
Reiser, Anna, P731
Reisman, Rosemary M. Canfield, S1098, S1311
Relke, Diana, S1099
"Remember Roger Mortimer," P696
Renwick, Meredith, S377
Renzetti, Elizabeth, S1359
Reppy, Jessie M., P73
Rerolle, Raphaelle, S461
Rexford, Alex, S441
Ricard, Jean-Pierre, P9
Ricciardi, Caterina, S1100
"Rich As Stink," P483-485
    Radio broadcasts, P738
    Translations, P484, P485
Richler, Mordecai, P595
Richter, David H., P249
Rico, Gabriele L., P75
Ricou, Laurie, S1101
Riddell, Elizabeth, S1102
Ridge, Mary Blanche, S621
Rifkind, Donna, S500
Rikman, Kristiina, P1, P4, P6, P8, P9, P11
Rimanelli, Giose, P569
Rimstead, Roxanne, S1103
Ripin, Sarah, P5
Rix, Beverley, S325, S706
Rizzardi, Biancamaria, S1104
Ro, Sigmund, P363
Roark, Margaret S., S90
Roberts, Edgar V., P204, P208, P322
Roberts, Michele, S622
Roberts, Tammy, P702
Robertson, Branka, P347

Robertson, Sarah, S378, S501, S623
Robertson, Tony, P858
Robinson, Helen, S561
Robson, H. P. Nora, S91, S1105, S1106
Rocard, Marcienne, S1107-1109
Rocca, Chiara Spallino, P9
Rochon, Lisa, S1382
Rogalus, Paul William, S92
Rogers, Jane, S1312
Rogers, Shelagh, P761
Roland, Herbert, P717
Rompf, Kraft, P458
Ronnestad, Trude, S93
Rooke, Constance, P277, P340, P498, P543, P663, P701, P702; S562, S1110, S1111
Rooke, Leon, P277, P353, P386, P393, P454, P498, P649, P702
Rosborough, Linda, S502
Rose, Anita R., S94
Rosen, Gayle, P408
Rosenberg, Donna, P149
Rosengarten, H. J., P118, P561
Ross, Catherine Sheldrick, P755, P890; S767, S769, S776, S1112-1116, S1313
Ross, Cecily, S1117
Ross, Gary Stephen, P686
Ross, Liza, P780, P783, P812
Ross, Tory, P797
Ross, Val, S503, S1118, S1350, S1435
Rothstein, Mervyn, S1119
Rouse, L. J., S563
Rowe, Percy, S736
Roy, James, P723
Roy, Michel, S95
"Royal Beatings," P486-501
　Translations, P501
Rubens, Pamela, S96
Rubenstein, Roberta, P382
Ruberto, Roberto, P569
Rubin, Merle, S672
Rubio, Jennie, S97, S1120
Rubio, Thalia, P196
Rudzik, O. H. T., S326, S707
Rule, Jane, S327
"Runaway," P502-504, P676

Runaway: Stories, P11
　Reviews, S580-637
　Sound recordings, P822-824
　Translations, P11
Rusconi, Anna, P3, P14
Russ, Margaret, S460
Ruta, Suzanne, S504
Rutledge, Margie, S1121
Rutten, Kathleen, P4
Rylski, Nika, P741

Sabin, Stefana, P622
Saggini, Francesca, S1122
Saint-Louis, Louise, S98
Sallot, Jeff, S1123
Salter, Mary Jo, S228
Samuels, Maxine, P731
Samuels, Selina, S99
Sand, Cy-Thea, P875; S442
Sandor, Suzanne, P887
Saricks, Joyce, S637
Sartorius, Hans, P7
"Save the Reaper," P505-509, P677, P678
　Translations, P509
Savoy, Eric, S752, S762
Scanlan, Larry, S443
Schiedel, Bonnie, S287
Schiefer, Nancy, S379, S444, S624, S771
Scholes, Robert, P104, P526
Schuck, Paula, S380
Schwaller-Balaÿ, Céline, P8
Schwartz, Lynne Sharon, S564
Schwartz, Narda Lacey, S1257
Scobie, Stephen, P874; S1124, S1125
Scott, Jay, S229
Scott, Sandra, P807, P813
Seaman, Donna, S288, S381, S673
Seamon, Roger, S827
Seatle, Dixie, P716
Seaton, Aileen, P713, P714, P718, P801, P804, P828
"Secrets between Friends," P510
Sedaris, David, P225
See, Carolyn, S625
Segedin, Benjamin, S505
Seidenbaum, Art, S445, S565

Selby, Pamela, S100
Selected Stories, P12
    Reviews, S638-677
    Sound recordings, P825, P826
    Translations, P12
Seligman, Lawrie, P722, P789
Sellers, Peter, P806
Sellwood, Jane, S1126
Seneca College of Applied Arts and Technology, P72
Sexton, Melanie, S101
Seyersted, Per, S1127
Shaffer-Koros, Carole M., P73
Shapiro, Anna, S446
Shaumian, Mariam, S566
Sheckels, Theodore F., S1128
Shepard, Jim, P285
Sheppard, R. Z., S382, S506
Sherman, Jason, P886
Shetterly, Caitlin, P117
Shields, Carol, S230
Shih, Elizabeth A., S1129
Shilling, Jane, S626
"The Shining Houses," P511-514
    Radio broadcasts, P739
Shoebridge, Tom, P757
Shojania, Moti Gharib, S102
Shollar, Barbara, P203
Showalter, Elaine, S627
"Silence," P515-517, P679
Simonds, Merilyn, S289
Simonson, Harold P., P572
"Simon's Luck," P15, P518-522
    Translations, P522
Simpson, Leo, S184, S447
Simpson, Mona, P895; S290, S1130-1132, S1410, S1428
Sims, Peter, S1133
Singer, Peter, P423
Singer, Renata, P423
Sinklier, Laurie Jill, S103
Skinner, David, S628
Skurnick, Lizzie, S629
Slavitt, David R., S231
Slopen, Beverley, P880; S567, S1134
Slung, Michele, S1135

Smee, Sebastian, S630
Smiley, Jane, P5, S1136
Smith, A. J. M., P136, P137
Smith, Dinita, S1137
Smith, Elaine, S737
Smith, Jennifer, S1213
Smith, Margaret, S1138
Smith, Rebecca, S1139
Smith, Roger J., P406
Smith, Ron, P901
Smith, Rowland, S1140
Smith, Stephen, P896; S328
Smythe, Karen E., S104, S770, S1141, S1142
Snyder, Rebecca Lynn, S105
Soete, Mary, S568
Solecki, Sam, S448, S738, S765
Solomon, Charles, S449
Solotaroff, Ted, S507
Somacarrera, Pilar, S1143-1145
Somerville, Christine, S106, S751, S754
"Something I've Been Meaning to Tell You," P523-530
    Translations, P528-530
Something I've Been Meaning to Tell You . . . . : Thirteen Stories, P13
    Reviews, S678-715
    Sound recordings, P827-832
    Translations, P13
Sonnenberg, B., P652
Sonnenfeld, Jean E., S329
"Soon," P531, P532
Soper-Jones, Ella, S1146
Sorestad, Glen A., P404
Soto, Cristina Sánchez, S1147
"Spaceships Have Landed," P533-535
"The Spanish Lady," P536-538
    Translations, P538
"Spelling," P539-544
Spettigue, Doug, S1148
Spotton, John, P757
Staines, David, P214, P493
Stainsby, Don, S182
Stainsby, Mari, P839
Stanley, Deborah A., P702
Stanley, Don, P381, S1149
Stapleton, Margaret, S1150

Stark, Myra, P478
Stead, Katrina M., S107
Stead, Kit, S1151
Steele, Apollonia, S1254, S1255
Steele, Clare, S108
Steele, Fraser, P755; S776
Stephens, Donald, P570
Stephenson, Craig, P582
Stern, Bezalel, S631
Stevens, John, P48, P147, P246, P406
Stevens, Peter, S739
Stevens, Susan, P784
Stewart, Ralph, S1152
Stewart, Robert, S569
Stich, Klaus P., S759, S772, S1153, S1154
Stipe, Stormy, S383
Stoffman, Judy, S771, S1155-1157, S1373, S1436, S1437
"The Stone in the Field" *see* "Chaddeleys and Flemings. 2: The Stone in the Field"
Stone, Claire L., S109
Stone, Robert, P87, P665
Stone, William B., S155, S450, S762
"Story for Sunday," P550
Story, Norah, S1314
Stott, Jon C., P160, P371
Stouck, David, S708, S1315, S1316
Stovel, Nora Foster, S1158
Straif, Barbara, S110
Stratford, Philip, S1159
Strauss, Jennifer, S1160
Strickland, Nicole, S1161
Struthers, John Russell (Tim), P269, P323, P457, P494, P659, P664, P694, P702, P862; S111, S508, S709, S740, S1044, S1162-1166, S1258, S1273, S1317
Stubbs, Andrew, S1167
Stuewe, Paul, S185, S741
Sturgess, Charlotte, S112, S1168-1170
Sturtevant, Jan, P28
Suárez Lafuente, M. S., S828, S1171
Suissa, Daniele J., P731
Sullivan, Nancy, P455
Sullivan, Rosemary, P24, P180, P420, P526
Summers, Merna, S509
Sumrall, Amber Coverdale, P28

"Sunday Afternoon," P551-555
Suppan, Christiane, S113
Sutherland, Katherine Gail, S114
Sutton, Brian, S1172
"The Sweet Second Summer of Kitty Malone," P698
Switocz, Barbara M., S115
Symons, Julian, S330
Szalay, Edina, S1173

Tallman, Warren, S182
Tamarkin, Civia, S156, S451
Tan, Amy, P507, P677
Tanaszi, Margaret, S116, S117
Taube, Eva, P481
Tausky, Thomas E., S774, S1174, S1175
Taylor, David, S452
Taylor, Michael, S742, S1176
Taylor, Stephanie, P834, P836
Teahen, Kelley, S118, S1366
"Tell Me Yes or No," P556, P557
Tench, Helen, S186
Tener, Jean F., S1177, S1254, S1255
Tessier, Vanna, S384
Thacker, Robert W., S119, S570, S751-754, S757, S759-761, S764, S767-772, S1178-1188, S1259, S1318
"Thanks for the Ride," P558-565
    Film adaptations, P757
    Radio broadcasts, P742
    Television broadcasts, P741
Thieme, John, P426; S762, S1254
Thomas, Audrey, S187, S232, S710
Thomas, Clara, S331
Thomas, Joan, S233
Thomas, Sue, S1189
Thompson, Elizabeth, P3; S754, S757, S1190
Thompson, Kent, S188, S189
Thompson, Richard J., S711
Thorburn, Jan Ellen, S120
Thoreen, David, S632
Thornton, Louise, P28
Thorpe, Michael, S234
"Through the Jade Curtain," P699
Tiffin, Audrey, S1191
Tihanyi, Eva, S771

Till, Eric, P748, P759
Tillinghast, Richard, S385
"The Time of Death," P566-572
Timson, Judith, S235, S453, S633, S1192, S1193
Tobin, Anne-Marie, S1360, S1361, S1367, S1423
Todaro, Lenora, S634
Todd, Paula, P910
Todd, Tamsin, S386
Tomalin, Claire, S236, S332, S571
Tong, Murray, S291
Tonge, Colette, P2, P7, P14, P838
Toolan, Michael, S1194
Towers, Robert, S237
Toye, William, P596
Tracy, Laura, S1195
Trant, Jennifer, S121
Trehearne, Brian, P762
Treisman, Deborah, P908
"Trespasses," P573
"Tricks," P574
Trimmer, Joseph F., P251
"A Trip to the Coast," P575-577
    Television broadcasts, P743
Truax, Alice, S292
Trudel, Danielle, S122
Trumpener, Katie, S1319
Truss, Lynne, S1196
Trussler, Michael, P79
Tucker, Eva, S157
Tudor, Kathleen, S712
Turbide, Diane, P724; S387, S510
"The Turkey Season," P578-584
    Radio broadcasts, P744
Turnbull, Deborah, P708
Turner, Gordon Philip, S123
Twigg, Alan, P857; S454, S743, S1197
Tyler, Anne, S572

Underhill, Ian, P645
Upchurch, Michael, S635
Updike, John, P328; S674
Urquhart, Jane, P15, P25, P33, P39, P92, P119, P230, P300, P330, P351, P521; S388, S636, S1198

Valleau, Al, P366
Van Herk, Aritha, P193; S389
Van Rys, John C., S1199
Van Ryzin, Jeanne Claire, S675
Van Wart, Alice, S769
"Vandals," P585-587
    Read by Alice Munro, P762
    Sound recordings, P762
Vanstone, Ellen, S1200
Varley, Jill, S124
Vasey, Paul, S1201
Velden, Maria Cecilia, S125
Veldhuizen, Dorien, P3
Ventura, Héliane, S773, S1202-1209
Vickers, Reg, S1210
Vieira, Joan, P811
"The View from Castle Rock," P588
"Visitors," P589-593
    Translations, P592, P593
Visser, Carla, S126

Wachtel, Eleanor, P893, P903, P909
Wainwright, J.A., P900; S1211, S1212
Walbert, Kate, S238
"A Walk on the Wild Side," P700
"Walker Brothers Cowboy," P594-608
    Sound recordings, P833
    Translations, P606-608
Walker, Scott, P600
"Walking on Water," P609
Wall, Kathleen, S1214
Wallace, Bronwen, S1215
Waller, Gary, P292
Walsh, Nancy, S1216
Walters, Colin, S239, S391
Wang, Yuanfei, S127
Ward, Audrey, S1217
Ward, Olivia, S1218
Ward, Sandra Lee, S128, S762
Ward-Harris, E. D., S190
Ware, Tracy, S511, S757, S1219
Warkentin, Germaine, P418, P597
Warley, Linda, P340
Warren, Rosalind A., S240
Warwick, Susan J., S762, S1220
Waterston, Elizabeth, S1221

Watmough, David, S1222
Watson, Dana Cairns, S1320
Watson, Patricia, P708
Watson, Patrick, P851, P876
Watters, Reginald E., P512
Watts, Janet, S1223
Wayne, Joyce, S241, S1224
Wear, Delese, P544
Weaver, John, S1225
Weaver, Robert, P134, P275, P309, P321, P333, P415, P417, P421, P513, P567, P575, P596, P683, P840
Weaver, Rosalie Mary, S129
Wehmeyer, Paula J., S130
Weil, Herb, S1321
Weinhouse, Linda, S1226
Weintraub, William, P751
Weiss, Allan, S1227, S1260
Weiss, Charlotte, S191
Wenger, Barry, S1228
"Wenlock Edge," P610
West, Kathleene, S573
"What Do You Want to Know For?" P701
"What Is Real?" P702
"What Is Remembered," P611-613
"What Should Cynthia Do With the Rest of Her Life?" P703
Wheeler, Anne, P758
"White Dump," P614-616
Whiteway, Doug, S744, S745, S1229
"Who Do You Think You Are?" P617-622
　　Translations, P622
Who Do You Think You Are?: Stories, P14
　　Reviews, S716-749
　　Sound recordings, P834-838
　　Translations, P14, P838
"The Widower," P623
Wiebe, Rudy, P193, P267, P306, P560, P564, P565
Wieckowska, Katarzyna, S1230
Wiedemann, Barbara, S1322
Wiedemann, Margaret Anne, S1231
Wiesenfeld, Joe, P750
Wiggins, Lee, S746
Wigod, Rebecca, S1232
"Wigtime," P624-627, P680

"Wild Swans," P628-635
　　Radio broadcasts, P745, P746
　　Translations, P635
"A Wilderness Station," P636-643
　　Film adaptations, P758
　　Translations, P643
Williams, David, S1233
Williams, John A., P205
Williams, Lynna, S293
Williamson, David, S457, S574, S747
Williford, Lex, P329
Wilner, Paul, S158
Wilson, Ethel, P655
Wilson, Lionel, P425
Wilson, Mary Louise, P814
Wilson, Patricia A., S131
Wilson, Ronald, P724, P754
Wilson, Trish, S1234
"Winter Wind," P644-646
Winter, Ernest H., P59
Wise, Kristyn, S132
Withers, Jim, S458
Wolfe, Morris, P139, P308
Wolff, Geoffrey, S333
"Wood," P647-649
Wood, James, S676
Woodcock, George, S512, S713, S756, S1236, S1237, S1323, S1324
Woods, Grahame, P741
Wordsworth, Christopher, S334, S459
"Working for a Living," P651, P652
Wray, John, S1238
Wright, Jim, P863

Yan, Qigang, S133
Yang, Yu-tsan, P528
"The Yellow Afternoon"
　　Radio broadcasts, P747
York, Lorraine M., S134, S762, S766, S767, S774, S1242-1248
Young, Elizabeth, S677

Zagratzki, Uwe, S1249
Zaleski, Jeff, S294
Zerning, Heidi, P4, P6, P11, P44, P122, P131, P280, P301, P373, P484, P485, P509
Zilm, Glennis, S749

Introduction to the Subject Index

This is a subject index to the interviews and nonfiction writings of Munro, as well as to the secondary works (books, articles and theses) that have been written about Munro and her work. The subject headings are based on notes taken at the time of verification. For the small number of items that were not available to the compiler, index entries were usually based on the information in the title and abstract, or, in the case of theses, a combination of title, table of contents, and abstract. The index is one alphabetical sequence of subjects, titles (stories and collections), names of characters, places, and names of other writers or persons discussed in the primary and secondary sources.

Subjects

Subject entries containing two concepts, for example "reality" and "truth," have been cross-posted under both terms. Concepts essentially the same, but termed differently by authors in their criticism, have been indexed under the term most commonly used, with a cross reference from the lesser used terminology.

Cross references are also made to topics that are related to each other. For example:

> Endings. *See also* Closure

The cross references to subjects found under the title of a collection or story usually refer to subjects listed under that title unless otherwise specified. For example:

> *Lives of Girls and Women*
>   Artistic development. *See* Kunstlerroman
> but
>   Protagonist. *See* Del Jordan *in main listing*

Titles

The criticism or commentary relating to a particular story or collection will be found under its title. For a subject that is common to several stories in a particular collection, such as the theme of connection in *The Moons of Jupiter*, there will be entries for that subject both under the individual stories of the collection and under the collection title itself. In the case of the novel, *Lives of Girls and Women*, and the short story cycle, *Who Do You Think You Are?* the main subject entries are found under these titles unless certain chapters are highlighted in the criticism, in which case cross-postings will also be found under the individual chapter titles.

Names

The names of people (writers, artists, psychologists, etc.) and their works are posted in the main listing and may also be cross-posted under a story or collection title if used in a comparative or elucidatory treatment of that work. In many cases, particularly in the case of theses, Munro's work is considered along with that of other authors when dealing with a topic. For these, the names of the other authors have also been listed, along with the works discussed, but no further indexing relating to these authors has been done.

Characters are listed under first names (e.g. Benny, Uncle, Austin Cobbett) or under surname if no first name is given or if the surname is used predominantly (e.g., Lougheed, Mr.) It should be noted that the inclusion of characters' names is not comprehensive; names were generally included where the character formed a significant part of the criticism. Users should also look under the titles of individual stories for information on characters, which is usually contained in the general criticism.

Entries of Note

An explanation is in order for certain headings which appear in this index. Under the heading "Munro, Alice," the subheading, "General (life, career, writing)" is followed by a long list of entry numbers. Most of these numbers lead to the numerous brief articles which have appeared in newspapers and popular magazines, many of which are based on interviews with Munro after the release of one of her books. Due to the nature and brevity of the topics covered in these pieces, it was not feasible to annotate or index them in detail. In general they contain a combination of information about Munro's personal life and career highlights, including awards, commentaries on her writing, and Munro's explanations of her writing process, writing routine, and fictional aesthetics.

Studies which discuss Munro's work as a whole are listed under "Criticism of Alice Munro—General." Under the titles of individual stories and collections, the subject heading "Critical analysis, overview, interpretation" represents the broadest treatment of the work in terms of criticism, summary, or interpretation, ranging from a simple plot summary to a book-length critical examination of the work. Entry numbers appearing directly after the title of a story represent items that did not warrant separate subject entries because they refer to only brief references to some aspect of the story.

Entry Numbers

Primary sources have numbers that are prefixed with a P (e.g., P12). Secondary sources have numbers that are prefixed with an S (e.g., S205). Bolded numbers indicate that the topic is the main focus of the work or that the subject is discussed in relative detail. Unbolded numbers indicate topics that are touched on more briefly or are secondary to the discussion. All bolded numbers associated with the subjects listed under a specific story or collection are also cross-posted in the main listing under the subject. For example:

Metaphors
    Snow, **S799**
"Winter Wind"
    Metaphors, snow, **S799**

Subject Index

*All references are to entry numbers: P = Primary Works, S = Secondary Works.
Book titles are in italics. Story titles are in quotation marks.
Bold indicates that the topic is the main focus of the work.*

"1847: The Irish" (television script), P852

Abandoned/unchosen women. *See under* Characters (types)
Abelhart, Miss ("The Dimensions of a Shadow"), S753
Abjection, **S755**, S1230
Absence
    Discourse of, S41, S757
Absurdity, **S100**, **S992**
    of Female subject, S768
    Horror of the absurd, S56
"Accident," P874: S29, S41, S52, S65, S121, S127, S757, S827
    Critical analysis, overview, interpretation, S752, S759, S762
    Reality, S962
    Woolf, Virginia, influence of, **S1000**
Acting. *See* Role-playing; Theatricality
Ada Jordan (*Lives of Girls and Women*), **P846**: S39; S63, **S88**, **S108**, S786, S926, **S1099**, S1247
Adler, Renata. *Speedboat*, S27
Adolescence, S74
    Perception in, and self-development, S989
    and Socialization, S50
    and Voice of adult narrator, S798
Adolescent literary heroine. *See under* Hero, female/heroine
Adult adolescents. *See* Characters (types)—Male
Adultery. *See* Infidelity, marital

Aesthetic distance. *See under* Narrative perspective
Aesthetic (artistic) vision, **P653**, **P702**, P840, **P843**, P852, **P858**, P863, **P865**, P867, P889, **P902**; S17, **S36**, S57, S87, **S100**, **S750**, **S786**, S904, S932, **S1024**, S1039, S1043, **S1052**, S1223
   Abdication of writer to story, P865
   Detachment of writer, P865, P894
   Distrust of art, illusions of art, **P886**; S981, **S1066**
   "Feeling," getting into a story, vs. plot, **P702**, P865, P867, P880
   Function of the writer, **P843**, **P865**, P901
   Inadequacy, limitations of art/writing, **P860**, **P862**, **P903**; S1043
   Objects, treachery to, in writing, P660, **P664**
   Purpose of writing, **P843**, P845, P857, P887, P897, **P903**, P910
   Story, P865, P886, P889, P892
   Style, P852, P889
   Texture, **P843**, P886
   Truth and writing, P847, P855, **P860**, **P891**; S790, S986, S1059
   Writer as observer, voyeur, **P881**; S36
   Writing process as a private investigation, **P653**, P865, P891, **P893**, **P897**, **P906**
"Age of Faith," S41, S757
   Critical analysis, overview, interpretation, **S751**
   Faith and consolation, S104, S770
   Religion
      and Death, **S29**
      and Small town, **S1158**
   Summary, **P846**
Agee, James
   A Death in the Family, P862; S1162
   Influence of, P841; S5, S134, S774
   Let Us Now Praise Famous Men, P862; S134, S774, S855, S1246
Aging, S753. *See also* Elderly persons; Men, middle-aged; Women, middle-aged
   and Culture, **S973**
   and Female body, S767, **S975**
   Feminist theories of, S64
   and Munro, Alice, P844, P848, P857, **P858**, P861, P872, **P892**, **P893**, **P903**, P905, P906, P910
      Effect on writing, **P873**, P882, P886, P894, **P895**, **P896**, P898, P903, P904, P909; S778, S823, S857, S882, S890, S905, S1022, S1187
   and Women, **S64**, **S767**
Ailsa Kirkham ("My Mother's Dream"), S90
"The Albanian Virgin," S29, S999
   Characters, **P897**
   Critical analysis, overview, interpretation, **S887**
   Identity formation, **S846**
   Language and women, **S129**
   Narrative strategy, S846
   Origin of story, P653, **P897**, P901, P902; S800

"The Albanian Virgin" (cont.)
    Senses, **S846**
    Writing process: **P897**
Albert ("Visitors"), S757
Alienated, fragmented characters. *See under* Characters (types)
Alienation, **S91**. *See also* Connection; Dislocation
    and Connection, **S82**, **S128**, **S1064**, **S1244**
Allegory. *See* Reading, allegories of
Allusions, **S753**, S853, **S872**
    Biblical, **S754**, S768, **S839**, **S840**
    Historical, **S754**
    Literary, **S754**, S768
Almeda Roth ("Meneseteung"), S17, S114, S753, S757, S768, S1030, S1092, S1140, S1154, S1212
Alter egos (characters). *See under* Characters (types)
Alva ("Sunday Afternoon"), S753, S767, S832
Alvin Stephens ("Open Secrets"), S835
Ambiguity **S17**, **S72**
    in Character description, S38
    of History, past, **S848**, **S965**
    and Storytelling by narrators, **S52**
American national characteristics vs Canadian, **S808**, **S1127**
American South
    and Southwestern Ontario, P843, P845
    Writers of the white American South. *See also names of individual writers*
        Influence of, P660, P841, P848, P860, **P862**, P865, P877, P889, P895; **S16**, S28, **S47**, S91, S855, **S1105**, **S1162**, S1232
        Melodrama and psychological truth, **S880**
        and Regionalism, **S16**, **S47**, **S91**
        and Religion, **S1105**, **S1199**
American values vs Canadian. *See* American national characteristics vs Canadian
Amor and Psyche myth. *See under* Myths
Analytical discourse. *See* Discourse, analytical
Anamorphosis, baroque, **S1207**
Ancestors (of Alice Munro)
    Maternal and paternal, **S765,** S769, **S771**
    Scottish, **P663**, **P899**; **S35**, **S765**, S769, **S771**, S924
Anderson, Sherwood. *Winesburg, Ohio*, P877; **S113**
Angle of vision, **S19**, **S762**, S1052
Annie, Aunt ("The Peace of Utrecht"), S767
Annie Herron ("A Wilderness Station"), S15, S17, S72, S105, S129, S831, S885, S924, S1021, S1140
Anouilh, Jean. *Eurydice*, **S833**, S1095
Antidetection. *See under* Mystery
Antoinette ("Hold Me Fast, Don't Let Me Pass"), S1013, S1019
Appearance and reality. *See* Surface appearance and reality/truth

Arbus, Diane, P862; S134, S774, S856
Archetypes, S36, **S754, S875**
    Biblical, **S754, S840**
    Bluebeard, **S1032**
    Dionysus, Medusa, **S1154**
    Female, of the 1940s, **S55**
    Joker, **S840**
    Oppositional (inclusive and exclusive), **S19, S867**
Archives, literary, **S67, S763, S771, S1027, S1177,** S1186
Arrangement. *See under* Narrative strategy
Art/fiction. *See also* Metafiction
    and Authority, **S970**
    and Autobiographical material, autobiography, P664, P702, P868; S763, S1072
    and Chaos, control over, S56, **S992**
    and Environment, **S1164**
    House as metonym for, **S1035**
    Inadequacy, limitations of, **P860, P862, P903; S901, S1066, S1175**
    and Life, **S41,** S56, **S100, S757, S992, S1066**
    and Reality/truth, S12, **S752, S1066, S1167, S1175, S1205.** *See also* Fictional reality *in main listing*
        Transforming reality into fiction, **P687, P702, P891, P897**
    and Retrospective reordering of experience, **S87**
Art Chamberlain (*Lives of Girls and Women*), S5, S28, S50, S63, S79, S91, S108, S110, S123, S753, S767, S802, S876, S979, S1038, S1122, S1173, S1212
Artist/writer figures. *See under* Characters (types)
Artistic
    Ambition, female, **S77**
    Development. *See under Lives of Girls and Women*; *Who Do You Think You Are?*; *See also* Künstlerroman
    Influences (Alice Munro), P843, P889. *See also under names of artists and photographers*
    Mind, **S77**
Artists/writers, female. *See* Writers/artists, female
Ashapurna Devi, *Pratham Pratishruti*, **S50**
Authur Comber ("Something I've Been Meaning To Tell You"), S761
Arthur Doud ("Carried Away"), S843, S998, S1086
"At the Other Place," S753, S1015
    Critical analysis, overview, interpretation, S762
    Narrative technique, development of, **S32, S119, S1182**
Atmospheric evocation, P845; **S5**
Attachment and separation. *See under* Identity formation
Attachment theory (psychology). *See under* Psychology, psychoanalysis
Atwood, Margaret, S18, **S48, S49, S82, S101, S112, S117, S810, S856,** S890, S968, S1114
    Alias Grace, **S72, S1031**
    "Bluebeard's Egg," S958
    Bodily Harm, **S102,** S961

Atwood, Margaret (cont.)
 Cat's Eye, **S61**, **S130**, S801, S806, S957
 Dancing Girls, **S59**
 The Edible Woman, **S59**, **S78**, **S102**
 "Giving Birth," **S1214**
 The Handmaid's Tale, **S51**, **S59**, **S79**, S806
 Lady Oracle, **S8**, **S9**, **S59**, **S61**, **S78**, S969, **S1245**
 "Rape Fantasies," S987
 "Significant Moments in the Life of My Mother," **S99**
 Surfacing, **S9**, **S59**, **S61**, **S78**, **S102**, S961
 "Two Stories about Emma: 'The Whirlpool Rapids' and 'Walking on Water,'" **S829**
 Wilderness Tips, **S129**
 "Wilderness Tips," **S852**
Audrey Atkinson ("Friend of My Youth"), S914
Aurality and vision, **S31**, **S1095**
Austen, Jane, P848
Austin Cobbett ("Pictures of the Ice"), S41, S757
Australia, P901; S1059, S1102
Authentic selfhood. *See under* Self
Authority, **S27**
 and Art/fiction, **S970**
 and Alice Munro, **S67**, **S763**, **S1027**
 of Narrators, **S106**, **S752**
 and Paradox, **S1126**
 and Writers, **S937**
Authors. *See* Writers
Authorship (Alice Munro)
 and Class, S67, S763
 and Gender (female), P875, P894; **S67**, **S129**, **S763**, S1011, **S1027**, S1210
 and Genre (short story), **S67**, **S129**, **S763**
 and Nationality (Canadian), P842, **P843**, P848, P877, P886, P889, P894, P903; **S67**, **S129**, **S763**, S1011, **S1027**, S1102
Autobiographical material, autobiography. *See also* Writing (Alice Munro)—Autobiographical, personal aspects
 and Art/fiction, P664, P702, P868; S763, S1072
 and Artists, female, **S75**, **S768**, **S801**, **S937**
 Confession, **S1075**
  Confessional fiction, S1222
 and Creativity, **S936**
 Female autobiography, **S45**
 Meditation, **S1075**
 Memoir, **S765**, **S1075**, **S1125**
 and Narrative perspective, first person, **S24**
 and Personal material, distinction between, **P845**, **P886**
 Place, autobiographical
  and Female writers, **S1180**

and Self-definition. **S1187**
and Voice of narrator. **S1075**
Awards. P910; **S771**, S786, S814, S825, S854, S877, S923, S949, S1059, S1216. *See also* Awards section *of this bibliography*
Governor General's Award. P886; S1115
Marian Engel Award. P887

Bacon, Francis. "Of Parents and Children." S1100
Bakhtin, Mikhail. S24, S89, S755, S1070
"Baptizing"
Body. S38
Critical analysis, overview, interpretation. **S751, S753, S759**
Protagonist, female
and Escape. **P846**
Barbara Zeigler ("Oranges and Apples"). S1004
Barber, Virginia
and Munro's authority as an author. **S67, S763, S1027**, S1029
as Munro's literary agent. **P902**; S67, S763, S771, S797, **S1027**, S1181
"Bardon Bus." S3, S29, S62, S128, S768, S900, S961, S971, S1076, S1111
Body, female. **S30**
Characters, male. **S44**
Critical analysis, overview, interpretation. **S752, S753**, S759, S762, S796
Emotional tone, climate. **P871, P874**
Grief, mourning
and Loss of love. S104, S770
Male-female relationships. **S44**, S82
Mother-daughter relationship
Ambivalence in. **S1129**
Origin of story. P861
Phallicism. **S1129**
Reader response. **S34**
Summary. **P871, P874**
Voice. **S30, S121**
Barker, Elspeth. *O Caledonia*. **S1120**
"A Basket of Strawberries"
Atmosphere. P865
Critical analysis, overview, interpretation. **S753**, S762
Bea Doud ("Vandals"). S866, S904, S914
"The Bear Came Over the Mountain." S907
Old age and loss of memory. P905
Space and identity. **S955**
Beauty rituals and fashion. *See also* Women—Appearance, personal
and Self, care of. **S102**
Becky Tyde ("Royal Beatings"). S80, S753, S757, S1038, S1211, S1230
"Before the Change." S896
The Beggar Maid. See Who Do You Think You Are?

"The Beggar Maid," P865; S806
  Critical analysis, overview, interpretation, **S753**, S762
  Gender roles, **S86**
  Revisions, **S103**
Ben Jordan (*Lives of Girls and Women*), S2, S86, S110, S122, S801
Ben Jordan ("Walker Brothers Cowboy"), S41, S86, S757, S768, S1046
Benny, Uncle (*Lives of Girls and Women*), S18, S25, S63, S73, S80, S95, S110, S112, S122, S766, S811, S867, S876, S1007, S1010, S1057, S1087, S1212
  and Parallel worlds, S13, S41, S757, S880, S901, S937, S1087
  and Storytelling, S41, S104, S106, S757, S770
  Strange and familiar, S87, S1017, S1087, S1104, S1167
Bert Matthews ("Baptizing"), S1122
Bible/biblical
  Allusions, **S754**, S768, **S840**
  Archetypes, figures, **S754**, **S840**
  Cycles/patterns, **S754**, **S840**
  Myths, **S1032**
  Story groups, **S754**, **S840**
    Egypt, **S839**, **S840**
  Typology, **S754**
Bierce, Ambrose. "An Occurrence at Owl Creek Bridge," S53
Bildungsroman, **S6**, **S9**, **S26**, S63, S101, **S123**, **S130**, S751, **S798**, **S910**, **S1079**, **S1122**, **S1139**, S1160
  and Amor and Psyche myth, **S45**
Bill, Uncle ("Princess Ida"), S41, S87, S104, S110, S122, S124, S757, S770, S926, S1084
Billy Doud ("Spaceships Have Landed"), S1018
Biography
  Feminist, **S89**
  Metabiography, fictional, **S89**
Birdsell, Sandra, P877
Black, Mr. ("The Stone in the Field"), S757, S768, S959
Blais, Marie-Claire
  Une saison dans la vie d'Emmanuel, **S1159**
Blaise, Clark, S1236
  Lunar Attractions, **S56**, S992
  A North American Education: A Book of Short Fiction, **S56**, **S111**
  Tribal Justice, **S56**
Bluebeard. *See under* Archetypes
Bobby Sherriff ("The Photographer"), S41, S80, S87, S106, S757, S767, S892, S1007, S1087
Body
  Gothicized, **S1230**
  Grotesque, **S85**
  Humiliation of, **S753**
  "The Living body," **S916**
  Metaphorical, **S752**

Teaching about the body, **S876**
    as Text, **S811**
Body, female, **S767**
    Aging female body, S767, **S975**
    and Calvinism, **S1120**
    and Change, physical and social, **S967**
    Framed representation of, **S1214**
    Idealization and fragmentation of, **S1049**
    and Language, **S55, S63, S112, S926, S979**
    Sexuality and, **S4**
    as Subject, **S30**
    Women's, men's views of, P849; **S1049**
Body/self imagery. *See under* Imagery
Bonnie Ferguson ("The Ferguson Girls Must Never Marry"), S753
Book tours. *See* Publicity and book promotion
Bourdieu, Pierre. *The Field of Cultural Production*, S763
Bowen, Elizabeth
    The Last September, **S37**
    A World of Love, **S37**
Boyce, Mr. ("Changes and Ceremonies"), S120
"Boys and Girls," **S106, S765, S969, S1048, S1215**
    Critical analysis, overview, interpretation, **S752, S753, S762, S822, S1047, S1078**
    Gender roles, **P659, P852, P889; S757**
        and Space, **S30, S928, S1202**
    Imagination in childhood, **S83**
    Voice, **S30**
Bremond, Claude, S60
Brodeur, Hélène, **S122**
Brontë, Charlotte
    Jane Eyre, **S914**, S1032
    The Professor, S914
    Villette, S914
Brontë, Emily. *Wuthering Heights*, P653, P879, P890; S83, S769
Brother-sister relationship. *See under* Family relationships
Browning, Robert, **S1247**
    "The Bishop Orders His Tomb at St. Praxed's Church," S1247
    "Andrea del Sarto," S1247
Buckler, Ernest. *The Mountain and the Valley*, **S6**, S865
Bud Salter ("The Love of a Good Woman"), S830

Callaghan, Morley, P876
Callie Kernaghan ("The Moon in the Orange Street Skating Rink"), P884; S753, S768
Calvinism. *See under* Religion
Cam ("Forgiveness in Families"), S86, S100, S761, S1203
Cameron, Elizabeth Jane [Jane Duncan, pseud.], **S1221**

Canadian
- Culture and Alice Munro, **S67**, **S763**
- Literature. *See* Literature, Canadian
- National characteristics, S1102
    - Pretension, disapproval of, **P893**; S1127
    - vs. American, **S808**, **S1127**
- National identity, S65
- Society and social class, P875
- Values and happiness, **S808**
- Writers. *See* Writers, Canadian

Care of others, **S71**, **S90**

Care of self. *See* Self, care of

Career (Alice Munro). *See also* Barber, Virginia; *The New Yorker*; Weaver, Robert
- Chronology, life and career, **S765**, **S771**, **S890**
- Early career, P852, P877, P879, P894, P903; **S765**, **S769**, **S771**, S804, S905, S908, S1042, S1111, S1137, S1148, S1149, S1161
    - Isolation from other writers, P877, P894, P903; S790, S1135
- Feminist socio-historical, cultural study of, **S67**, **S763**, **S1029**
- Promotion of in the United States, **S1045**, **S1181**
- Writing as a career/vocation, P839, **P879**; S1241

Careers, choice of, P703

Carey, Peter, S17

Caroline Halloway ("Epilogue: The Photographer"), S63, S753, S768, S880, S1173

Carr, Emily. *Klee Wyck*, **S1180**

"Carried Away," P665, P901; S757, S944, S999, S1094
- Community, S105
    - and Postwar industrialization, **S998**
- Ending, **P897**
- Gender roles
    - and Marriage, **S105**
- Grotesque, **S85**
- Hardy, Thomas, **S809**, **S836**, S843
- Letters and letter writing, **S755**
- Male-female relationships
    - and Self, **S1086**
- Multilayered and parallel lives, P896, P897
- Mystery, **S805**
- Narrative structure, **S836**
    - Instability of, **S129**
- Origin of story, P653, P897; S771
- Reading, readers, **S843**, **S998**
- Reality, alternate, P665, **P897**
- Title, **S836**
- Wilderness, frontier, images of, **S105**
- Writing of, **S998**

Carstairs
    Archetypal and mythical status, **S1018**
    as Community landscape, S105
Carver, Raymond, S974
Cather, Willa, S36, **S1178**
    "Before Breakfast," **S1179**
    A Lost Lady, **S1153**
Catherine ("Lichen"), S768
Cece Ferns ("The Love of a Good Woman"), S830
Censorship
    and Children, P693, P857
    and Chinese writers, P662, **P699**, P864
    in Huron County, P693, P854, **P856**, **P857**, **P879**, P900; S771, S994, S1068, S1071, S1102, S1123, S1197, S1239
    Writers' Union of Canada censorship handbook, P705
"Chaddeleys and Flemings," S82, S118, S827, S1224. *See also* "Connection"; "The Stone in the Field"
    Critical analysis, overview, interpretation, S759, S762
    Dislocation, S956
    Middle-aged women, S64, S1013
    Narrative strategy
        and Triggering event, **S845**
Chamney, Anne Clarke. *See* Laidlaw, Anne Clarke (Chamney)
Chamney family history, **S765**, **S771**
Chance. *See under* Fate
"Chance," P908
Change, S41, S757
    in Characters, S42
    and Connection, S1062
    in Life, and pivotal moments, **P883**
    Personal change and travel, S1064
    Physical and social change in women, S64, S967
        and Wilderness (metaphorical), **S1146**
    and Small town, S1018
"Changes and Ceremonies," S127, S768, S1167, S1243
    Critical analysis, overview, interpretation, **S751**
    Imagination in childhood, **S83**
    Male-female relationships, **P846**
    Welty, Eudora. "June Recital," **S826**
"Changing Places" (essay)
    Laidlaw family history, **P663**
Chaos/disorder and order
    Art/fiction as control over, S56, **S992**
    and Double vision of the world, S66
    and Fragmentation (narrative technique), S22, **S92**
    "The other country" and the garrison, **S767**

Char Desmond ("Something I've Been Meaning to Tell You"), S761
Characterization
    Methods/techniques of, S19, **S42**, **S86**, **S910**, **S930**, **S990**
        Projection, **S898**
Characters, **P861**, **P865**. *See also under individual works and names of characters*
    Ambiguity, contradictions in, S38
    Change in, **S42**
        and Short-story genre, **S944**
    Details and creation of, **P842**, **P843**
    in Early stories, S32, S119
    Knowing and understanding characters, P845, P865, P882, P885, P904, P907, P909
    Layering of, **S900**
    and Munro's vision of life, **P865**; **S100**
    Names of, S754
    and Narrative technique, **S813**
    and Narrators, S121
        Narrator/character/reader relationship, **S126**
    and Place, interdependence of, **S16**, **S32**, **S1183**
    Reader response to, **S25**
    Real people as, P847, P850, P855, P861, P865, P881 P886, P894, **P897**, P899, **P906**; S912, S1039
Characters (types), **S5**, **S753**, **S754**, **S839**, **S840**, **S945**, **S990**. *See also* Father(s); Hero, female/heroine; Mother(s); Protagonists, female
    Alienated, fragmented, **S42**
    Alter egos, S753
    Artist/writer figures, **S25**, **S36**, **S74**, **S75**, **S81**, S1175
    Biblical, S754
    Controlled and controlling, **S753**
    Doll figures, **S768**
    Eccentric, unconventional, P673; **S1030**
        Autobiographical aspects, P886
    Female, P865, **P892**; **S25**, **S55**, **S74**, **S81**, **S86**, **S767**, **S816**, S1059
        Child-women, S1091
        Domestic women, S767
        and Female gender roles, **S131**
        Folk women, **S767**
        Losing and lost, **S788**
        Madonna figures, **S768**
        Mock mothers/mothering clowns, **S768**
        Munro's identification with, **P854**
        and Narration, narrators, S942
        Old(er) women, S131
            Autobiographical aspects, P886
        as Personae of Munro, **S100**, **S776**, **S831**, **S1021**, S1022
        Primitives, **S767**, **S1091**
    Fools, **S768**, **S829**

Subject Index 373

    Grotesque. **S80**
    Historians, archivists, S1225
    Humiliated. **S753**
    Jokers, **S768, S840**
    Male, **S44, S86**
        Aging men, **P882**
        Marginality of, **S802**
        Writing about. P882
    Mentrix figures, mentors, **S1099**
    Music teachers and pupils. **P845**; **S826**
    Mysterious, **P884**
    Observers and observed/participants, **P659**; **S753**
    Orphan figures. **S768**
    Outsiders. **P869**; **S867**
    Prostitute figures. **S768**
    Puppet figures, **S768**
    Readers, **S768, S843, S883**
    Voyeurs, **S753**
"Characters," S753
    Critical analysis, overview, interpretation, S762, **S862**
    Sensibility. **S754**
Charlotte ("Mrs. Cross and Mrs. Kidd"), S872
Cheever, John, P848, P858; S1232
Chekhov, Anton, P877, P907
    and Munro, similarities in themes, style, **S109**
Child-women. *See under* Characters (types)—Female
Childhood, S74, **S125**
    Imagination in, **S83**
    Portrayal of, **S23, S824**
    Remembered childhood
        and Fictional topography, **S18**
            Language of. **S1101**
    and Space, natural, **S97**
    and Stories and storytelling, **S83, S106, S1101**
    Writing about, P894, **P904, P906; S1237**
Children, **P906**; **S753**
    Censorship and, P693, P857
    and Parents. P909
"The Children Stay"
    Anouilh, Jean. *Eurydice*, S1088, S1095
        Ironic intertextualization. **S833**
    Choices, P666
    Epiphanic sites and secrets. **S1204**
    Mother as watcher and keeper. S1095
    Pivot point. **S755**

"The Children Stay" (cont.)
    Senses, smell
        and Reader response, **S847**
China, Munro's trip to, **P699**, P864
Chinese writers. *See also* Ding, Ling
    and Censorship, P662, **P699**, P864
Christian readers. *See under* Readers
Christianity. *See under* Religion
Cinderella fairy tale. *See under* Fairy tales
Cinematic technique. *See under* Narrative technique
"Circle of Prayer," S29, S975, S1012
    Critical analysis, overview, interpretation, **S752**
    Origin of story, P667
Circular narrative structure. *See under* Narrative structure
City. *See* Town/city and country
Class. *See* Social class
Clayton ("The Found Boat"), S761
Cleaver, Mr. ("Characters"), S753, S862
Clifford ("Mischief"), S41, S753, S757, S1005
Close, Ann. *See* Publisher/editor relations
Closure
    Happy endings and, **S808**
    Techniques of, **S80**, **S861**
Code (Porterfield), Maud, P895; S765, S771
Code, Sarah, P895; S765, S771
Coffin, Audrey. *See* Publisher/editor relations
Cohen, Matt. *The Sweet Second Summer of Kitty Malone*, **P698**
Colin ("Monsieur les Deux Chapeaux"), S753
Collections, short story. *See* Story collections
Colours, patterns of, S754
Comedy, S767, S768, **S1020**. *See also* Humour; Irony; Satire
"Comfort"
    Religious, spiritual quest, S29
Communication
    Deception in, **S102**
    Gender differences in, P874, P894
    Inability to communicate, non-communication, **S125**, **S766**
    Not-telling, **S41**, **S755**, **S757**, **S830**, **S1172**
        and Storytelling, **S1051**
    Telling and deferral, **S41**, **S757**
    between Women, P874, P894
Community, place
    Communal identity
        and Postwar industrialization, **S998**
    and Identity, female, **S112**

Landscape of, S105
Narrative of, **S129**
Complexity. *See* Narrative complexity; Narrative structure, Complexity in
Complicity, **S41**, **S757**. *See also* Readers, complicit
Compression. *See under* Style
Confession, confessional fiction. *See under* Autobiographical material, autobiography
Confinement
    Female, S821, **S928**, **S1057**, **S1202**
    Small town and, **P845**; **S88**, **S120**
Connection, **S39**, S82, **S752**, **S1062**, **S1244**. *See also* Alienation; Human relationships; Isolation
    Collapse/absence of, **S41**, **S757**
    Family and, P899; **S82**, **S1108**
    Identity and, P899; **S2**, **S16**, S82, **S1062**
    Love, responsibility and, **S90**
    Place and, **S16**, **S1183**
    and Space, cultural and non-cultural, S97
    Theme of, and voice, S121
"Connection," S3, S17, S65, S121, S768, S959, S999, S1183, S1187
    Body, female, and language, **S979**
    Connection, S128
        and Family, **S1108**
    Critical analysis, overview, interpretation, S752, S759
    Middle-aged women, **S1013**
    Narrative strategy
        and Triggering event, **S845**
    Narrative structure, **S1108**
Connor, Ralph, **S1249**
Consolation
    Epiphany as, **S104**, **S770**, **S1141**
    and Faith, S770
    Memory as, **S104**, **S770**
Contradiction/incongruity. *See also* Narrative devices—Oxymoron
    Contradictory realities, **S72**, **S962**, **S963**
    and Opposition, **S19**, **S752**, **S762**, **S963**
Contrapuntal
    Structure. *See under* Narrative structure
    Technique. *See under* Narrative techniques
Control
    Chaos, control over
        and Art/fiction, S56, **S992**
    and Loss of control, **S753**
Controlled and controlling characters. *See under* Characters (types)
Conventional society. *See under* Garrison
Cora ("Privilege"), S41, S110, S752, S753, S757, S767, S768, S1005

"Cortes Island"
    Motifs
        and Brontë, Charlotte. *Jane Eyre*, **S914**
    Origin of story, **P903**
Country and town/city, **S767**, **S1034**, **S1106**
    as Moral opposites, **S1205**
    Rural and urban landscape, **S1106**
Craig, Uncle ("Heirs of the Living Body"), **S5**, **S6**, **S28**, **S41**, **S63**, **S83**, **S86**, **S87**, **S91**, **S99**, **S116**, S122, **S757**, S802, **S811**, **S865**, S958, **S1084**, S1167, S1175
    as Literary model, **S41**, **S132**, **S757**, **S926**, **S937**, **S1084**
    Writing (local) history, **S28**, **S41**, **S95**, **S104**, **S757**, **S770**, S1017, **S1225**
Creativity and autobiography, **S936**
Criticism of Alice Munro
    Critical reception, P852, P866, P889; S814
    Feminist, **S4**, **S64**, **S67**, **S79**, **S116**, **S763**, **S767**, **S893**, **S926**, **S1215**
        Socialist-feminist, **S57**
    General (overviews of Munro's writing), **S39**, **S752**, **S756**, S758, **S759**, S762, **S766**, **S769**, **S838**, **S855**, S862, **S879**, S907, **S911**, **S912**, **S980**, **S990**, **S999**, S1044, **S1052**, S1061, **S1088**, S1130, **S1131**, S1136, S1148, **S1174**, S1236, **S1237**, S1242
    Literary, S1234
        Deficiency in, **S1166**, **S1178**
        Evaluation of, **S1184**, **S1188**
        Place of praise in, **S1029**
Cross, Mrs. ("Mrs. Cross and Mrs. Kidd"), **S872**, S875
Cryderman, Mr. ("Jesse and Meribeth"), S753
Cryderman, Mrs. ("Jesse and Meribeth"), S753
Cultural
    Space. *See* Space, cultural
    Studies theory, feminist, **S67**, S763
    Translation, and Scottish pioneers, **S15**, **S35**, **S924**, **S1249**
Cycles, **S754**, **S839**, **S840**. *See also* Patterns; Short-story cycle

Dance of the Happy Shades
    Absent and potential meaning, **S41**, **S757**
    American South, writers of the, **S91**
    Atmospheric evocation, **S5**
    Autobiographical aspects, **P842**; S769
    Autobiographical material
        Memoir and voice, **S1075**
    Characterization, **S86**
    Characters (types), **S5**, S758, S945
        Artist figure, female, **S74**, **S81**
        Controlled and controlling, **S753**
        Female, **S55**, **S86**, **S788**, **S1091**
            and Gender roles, **S131**
        Humiliated females, **S753**

Mock mothers, S768
Childhood, S125, S824, S1237
Closure, techniques of, S80
Connection, S1062
Control and loss of control, S753
Critical analysis, overview, interpretation, S752, S756, S759, S762, S766, S767, S769, S771, S855, S1078, S1174
Critical reception, S771
Death, S1142
    and Transience of life, S881
Defense, psychological
    from Painful past, S78
Discourse, paradigmatic, S41, S757
Double vision, S66, S963, S1007
Elegiac fiction, S1142
Endings of stories, P862
Feminine world, S55
Focalization, S752
Fragmentation, S22
Garrison
    and "The Other country," S766
    and the Wilderness, S78
Gender roles, S86, S115, S131
    Socialization of girls, S11, S131
Gluck, Christoph von. *Orfeo ed Euridice* (opera), S752
Gothicism, S759
    Themes and techniques, S28
Humour, S5
Human relationships, unconsummated, S756, S863
Humiliation, sexual and social, S753
Identity, feminist self-discovery, S767
Images, imagery and themes, S13
Isolation, S756, S863
Joyce, James. *Dubliners*, S1014
Language and power, S115
Legends and reality, S752, S1113
Linking devices, S58
Loss, S1142
Magic realism, S125
Maps and mapping, S759
Memory, S785, S945
    and Narrative time, S758
Mother-daughter relationship, S74, S81
Mothers, role of, S131
Munro, Alice
    Commentary on stories, **P862**

Dance of the Happy Shades (cont.)
- Narrative perspective, P845; **S24**, S753
  - Retrospective, S81
- Narrative structure, S18, S788
  - and Iterative technique, S758
- Narrative technique, S28, S80, S886. *See also* Magic realism
  - Development of, S762, S1074
    - Dual-voiced, retrospective, S119
  - Retrospective, S81
  - and Themes, S92
  - Time as an element of, S58, S74, S758
- Narrative time, S758, S945
- Narrator, S752
  - First person, S18
- O'Connor, Flannery, influence of, S47
- Opposition, rhetorical, S963
- "The Other country"
  - and Conventional society, S66, S766, S1007
- Paradox, S963
- Patterns, S754
- Photography, S134, S774
- and *The Progress of Love*, story comparisons, S96
- Publication of, P879, P895; S771, S950, S1115, S1137, S1161
- Regionalism, S125
- Rejection, S863
- Secrecy and women, S967
- Self, authentic selfhood, S115
- Self-development, female, S25
- Space and time, S128
- Stories and storytelling, S106, S1211
- Strange and familiar, S41, S757, S1113
- Style, S981, S1067
  - and Feminine sensibility, S117
- Super-realism, S5, S1237
- Texture, S117, S125
- Themes, S28, S39
  - and Images, imagery, S13
- Time
  - Passing of, impermanence, S128, S752, S1142
- Tone, emotional, S117
- Uncontrollable elements, S753
- Unity, S58
- Voice, S788, S1075
- Writing of, P841, P861, **P862**, P895; S771, S1174

"Dance of the Happy Shades." S18, S128, S768, S862, S1007
    Absurdity, horror of, **S56**
    Angle of vision, rhetorical, **S19**
    Characters, protagonist, **P845**
    Critical analysis, overview, interpretation, S752, S759, S762, S1078
    Grotesque, horror of, **S56**
    Joyce, James. "The Dead," S1014
    Narrative devices, oxymoron, **S874**
    Origin of story, P664, P865; S765
    Voice, and reader response, S886
    Welty, Eudora. "June Recital," S759, **S826**
"The Dangerous One," S754
    Critical analysis, overview, interpretation, S762
Darbelnet, Jean, S98
Daughter-father relationship. *See* Father-daughter relationship
Daughter-mother relationship. *See* Mother-daughter relationship
David ("Lichen"), P882; S753, S767, S975, S1049
Davies, Robertson, **S88, S1158**
    Fifth Business, **S51**, S1097
"Day of the Butterfly," S40, S827, S1007. *For original version see* "Good-By, Myra"
    Angle of vision, archetypal, **S19**
    Critical analysis, overview, interpretation, S752, S762
    Elegiac fiction, elegy, S104, S770, S1142
    Estes, Eleanor. *The Hundred Dresses*, **S984**
    Exclusion, **S873**
    Narrative technique, development of, **S32, S119**
    Victimization, S873, S984
Death, **P846, P873**, P905; S38
    Control over, and detached observer, S753
    and Elegiac fiction, elegy, **S104, S770, S1142**
    and Father-daughter relationship, **P873**; S104, S770
    and Gothic themes, Gothicism, P660; S10
    and Life, transience of, **S881, S1142**
    and Quest, religious/spiritual, **S29**
    as an Uncontrollable element, S753
Deception, dissimulation, **S1100, S1206, S1208**
    Lies, S766
    and Promoting/undoing of reality, **S41, S757**
    as Technique of self-care, **S102**
Defense, psychological
    from Painful past, **S78**
    and Wilderness (metaphorical), **S78**
Deferral and telling. *See under* Storytelling by narrators
Deformity
    and Body, Gothicized, **S1230**
    and Sin, **S1105**

Del Jordan (*Lives of Girls and Women*)
    Artistic
        Ambition, **S77**, S1127
        Development. *See under Lives of Girls and Women in main listing*
        Mind, **S77**
    as Comic protagonist, **S862**
    Hero, female/heroine, **S9**, **S108**, S1114
        Tennysonian, rejection of, S1245, S1247
    Identity formation. *See under Lives of Girls and Women in main listing*
    Independence, freedom, **S77**, **S110**, S784
    Mother, relationship with. *See Lives of Girls and Women*—Mother-daughter relationship *in main listing*
    as Narrator. *See Lives of Girls and Women*—Narrator *in main listing*
    Observation, capacity for, **S77**
    as Persona of Alice Munro, **S25**, **S100**, S776
    as Reader of texts, **S811**
    Religion. *See under Lives of Girls and Women in main listing*
    Self-development. *See under Lives of Girls and Women in main listing*
    Sensitivity and understanding, **S77**
    Temperament, **S77**
Deleuze, Gilles, S965
Delusion, **S1206**
Demeter and Persephone myth. *See under* Myth(s) and mythology
Denise Vogelsang ("White Dump"), S41, S753, S757
Desire
    Female. *See also* Sexual desire, female
        Absence of, **S1195**
        and Power, female, **S971**
    Personal, and sacrifice, **S71**
Destiny. *See* Fate, destiny
Detail(s), use of, P695, P865, P886, P905; S129, **S879**, **S1008**, S1059. *See also* Surface detail(s)
    and Characters, creation of, **P842**, **P843**
    and Complexity, S1116
    Documentary, and fictional reality, **S126**
Detective fiction, **S14**, S835
Devi, Ashapurna. *See* Ashapurna Devi
Dialectics. *See* Narrative technique—Narrative dialectics: Separation and distance, dialectics of
Dialogism, **S101**
Dialogue. *See* Speech
Dick ("Thanks for the Ride"), S753
Dickens, Charles
    A Child's History of England, **P696**, P890
"Differently," P668; S62, S861, S980, S1069
    Male-female relationships and self, **S1086**

"The Dimensions of a Shadow," S753, S1113
    Critical analysis, overview, interpretation, S762
    Narrative technique, development of, **S32, S119**
Dina ("Lichen"), S1049
Ding, Ling. *Miss Sophie's Diary and Other Stories*, P864
Dionysus. *See under* Archetypes
Disarrangement. *See under* Narrative strategy
Discourse. *See also* Speech
    of Absence, **S41**, S757
    Analytical, and love, S1226
    Contradictory, of fantasy and reality, S961
    Discursive practices and self-construction, **S102**
    Double-voiced, S755
    Feminine, **S101**
        and Female body, **S55**, S979
        and Voice, **S55**
    Masculine/patriarchal, **S63, S101**. *See also* Language—Male
        Subversion of, and mother-daughter storytelling, **S70**
    Paradigmatic, **S41**, S757, **S886**
    Postcolonial, and feminine identity, S1168
Disempowerment of women. *See under* Women
Disguise
    Alice Munro
        Concealment of early writing, **P843**, P844, P854, **P893**, P903; S765, S769, S1009, S1135, S1137, S1149, S1223
        Early life, need for disguise, P906; S1039, S1119, S1223
    Female, **S993**
    Human frailty and, **S125**
Dislocation, **S82**, S956. *See also* Alienation
    and Identity, S955
Disorder. *See* Chaos/disorder and order
Disruption. *See under* Narrative strategy
Distancing. *See* Narrative techniques—Double distancing
Distortion. *See* Anamorphosis, baroque
Documentary
    Details. *See under* Detail(s)
    Evidence. *See* Historical fiction
    Photography. *See* Arbus, Diane; Evans, Walker
    Realism. *See under* Realism
Dodie, Aunt ("The Ottawa Valley"), S41, S753, S757, S761, S768
Doll figures. *See under* Characters (types)
Dolly Cross. *See* Cross, Mrs.
Domestic
    Objects, and women, **S1070**
    Women. *See under* Characters (types)
Dorrie Beck ("A Real Life"), S17, S105, S914

Dorothy ("Marrakesh"), S41, S753, S757, S761
Dotty ("Material"), S761
Double distancing. *See under* Narrative techniques
Double vision, P848, P858, P865; **S66**. *See also* Strange and familiar; Surfaces and depths; Vision of the world
    and Narrators, retrospective, **S87**, S752, **S841**, **S1060**, S1101
    Order and chaos and, **S22**, **S66**
    "The Other country" and conventional society, **S66**, **S767**, **S1007**, S1008
    and Paradox, **S963**, **S1038**
    Parallel lives, **P897**
    and Social world, **S862**
Dreams, S842, S1116
Drowning and drowned characters, **S753**
Dual-voiced, retrospective technique. *See under* Narrative techniques—Retrospective
Duality, female, **S860**, S927
    and Role-playing, **S1170**
Dudley Brown ("Hold Me Fast, Don't Let Me Pass"), S1019
"Dulse," P875; S3, S40, S106, S128, **S771**, **S971**, **S1076**, **S1187**
    Angle of vision, syntactical, **S19**
    Artist/writer, female, **S36**
    Body, female, **S30**
    Cather, Willa
        "Before Breakfast," S1178, **S1179**
        A Lost Lady, **S1153**
    Characters, P865; S1153, **S1179**
    Critical analysis, overview, interpretation, **S752**, S762
    Elegiac fiction, S104, S770
    Hero, female/heroine, **S94**
    Isolation, **S870**
    Separation and distance, dialectics of, **S870**
    Storytelling and truth, S52, **S1026**
    Voice, **S30**, S121
Duncan, Jane (pseud.), **S1221**
Duncan, Sara Jeannette, **S88**, S1114
DuPlessis, Rachel Blau, **S64**

Early stories (Alice Munro). *See under* Stories
Eccentric, unconventional characters. *See under* Characters (types)
Edgar ("Open Secrets"), S914
"The Edge of Town"
    Narrative technique, development of, **S32**, **S119**, S762, S1182
    Patterns, **S754**
    Setting, P845; S1182, S1183
Editors. *See* Publisher/editor relations

Education
    Desire for, and small town, **S120**
    Imagination in, P856; S83
    Teaching Canadian literature, P848
Egan, Kieran, **S83**
Egypt. *See under* Bible/biblical—Story groups
Eileen ("Memorial"), S753, S761
Elderly persons, **P872**, P885
    Women, **S131**
    Writing about, **P858, P872**
Elegiac fiction, elegy, **S104, S770, S1141, S1142**
    and Ethics, **S770**
    Reader response, **S104, S770**
    and Realism, **S104, S770**
Ellipsis. *See under* Narrative devices
Elsa ("Hired Girl"), S832
Elspeth, Aunt and Auntie Grace (*Lives of Girls and Women*), S28, S41, S63, S77, S91, S99, S102, S108, S122, S123, S131, S132, S757, S766, S767, S801, S839, S901, S926, S1051, S1091, S1122, S1212
    Gender roles, S2, S86, S110, S116, S802, S816
    Stories and storytelling, S77, S83, S101, S106, S1084, S1211
Emancipation
    of Consciousness, **S116**
    Female, and female duality, **S860**
Embedding. *See under* Narrative devices
Emotion(s), S753. *See also* Feeling
    Portrayal of, P841; **S117**
    and Writing, P857, P861
Emotional tone. *See under* Tone
Empowerment of women. *See under* Women
Endings, P848, P865, P889, P894, P897. *See also* Closure
    Happy endings, **S808**
    Nonconventional, **S892**
    Nonending, open-endedness, P893, P901; **S109**
    Postmodernist elements, **S983**
Engel, Marian, P657; **S48, S49**, S968
Enid ("The Love of a Good Woman"), S830, S883, S914, S1116
Entanglement. *See under* Narrative techniques
Environment
    and Art, **S1164**
    and Artistic development, **S110**, S1077
"Epilogue: The Photographer," P862; S18, S63, S765, S768, S827, S892
    Art, inadequacy of, S1175
    Critical analysis, overview, interpretation, **S751, S753**, S759
    Magic realism, S12

"Epilogue: The Photographer" (cont.)
    Photography, S12, **S1133**
        Paradox of photographic vision, **S134**, S774
        Reality/truth and perception, **S1233**
        Strange and familiar, **S1246**
    Revisions, S769, S1175
    Summary, **P846**
    Surface appearance and reality/truth, **S1087**
Epiphany, epiphanies, **S40**, **S754**, **S944**
    as Consolation, **S104**, **S770**, **S1141**
    Epiphanic sites and secrets, **S1204**
    Epiphanic techniques and closure, **S861**
    and Religion/spirituality, **S29**
    and Short-story genre, **S755**
Eric Cryderman. *See* Cryderman, Mr.
Escape
    of Female characters from expected roles, **S942**
    and Female protagonist, **P846**; **S1057**
    from Small towns, **S88**, **S120**, **S1010**, **S1128**
"Eskimo," S62, S121, S1012
    Critical analysis, overview, interpretation, **S752**, **S753**, S762
Estes, Eleanor. *The Hundred Dresses*, **S984**
Et Desmond ("Something I've Been Meaning to Tell You"), S41, S753, S757, S761, S767, S768, S1007, S1051, S1091
Ethics. *See also* Morality/moral behaviour
    and Elegiac fiction, **S770**
    Ethical narrative
        and Feminist ethics, **S90**
    of Gossip, **S51**, **S976**
    and Small town, **S120**
Eugene ("Walking on Water"), S41, S100, S753, S757, S862
Eunie Morgan ("Spaceships Have Landed"), S1018
Eurydice (Orpheus myth), S833
Eva ("Labor Day Dinner"), S753, S914
Evangeline Cryderman. *See* Cryderman, Mrs.
Evans, Walker, S134, S774, S855, S856
    Let Us Now Praise Famous Men, P862; S1162
Eve ("Save the Reaper"), S837, S1051
Ewart ("Memorial"), S753, S761
Exclusion, S19, **S873**
"Executioners, The," S18
    Critical analysis, overview, interpretation, **S761**, S762
    Homer. *The Iliad*, **S1152**
Experience
    of Life. *See under* Life
    Women's. *See under* Women

Extraordinary and ordinary. *See* Strange and familiar
Eye and ear, interplay of. *See* Narrative technique—Cinematic

Fact and fiction. *See* Reality and fiction (other-than-real)
Fairy tales
    Cinderella fairy tale, S929
    Grimm's Fairy Tales
        "Fitcher's Bird," S1032
        "The Robber Bridegroom," S1032
Faith. *See also* Religion
    and Consolation, S770
    in Love, S52
Fame, success (Alice Munro), P865, P867, P892, P896, P903; S796, S986, S1043, S1192
Familiar and strange, S41, S125, S757, S762, S1017, S1087, S1104, S1113, S1167, S1208
    See also Double vision
    and Fictional landscape, S1243
    and Photography, S1246
Family
    Death in families, S104
    Heritage, S82, S91, S954
    History (Scottish)
        and Cultural translation, S35, S924
    Lore and self-definition, S65
    Relationships, S18, S753, S759, S1015. *See also* Father-daughter relationship: Mother-child relationship: Mother-daughter relationship
        Brother-sister, S1203
        and Connection, P899; S82, S1108
        and Identity formation, S2, S61
        Parent-child, P706, P909
    Secrets, S1169
"Family Furnishings"
    Origin of story, P669
    Social class, S864
Fantasy
    Fantasizing in childhood
        and Romantic imagination, S83
    and Reality/realism, S41, S56, S127, S752, S757, S952, S961, S1019. *See also* Fiction (other-than-real) and reality/fact
        and Artistic development, S1245
        and Self-development, female, S1245
        and Silence, S62
    Romantic and Gothic fantasy, S1173
    Sexual. *See under* Sex/sexuality, female
Farce. *See* Comedy
Farris, Miss ("Changes and Ceremonies"), S6, S28, S41, S80, S83, S87, S102, S110, S757, S766, S768, S801, S826, S1084, S1167, S1175, S1211, S1212

Fashion. *See* Beauty rituals and fashion
Fate, destiny, **S124**
    and Chance, **S752**
    and Pivotal moments in life, **P883**
    and Self, **S752**
Father(s), **P855**; S40, S91, **S753, S768, S850**. *For father of Alice Munro, see* Laidlaw, Robert
Father-daughter relationship, **S18**, S33, **S81**, S759, **S768, S850**
    and Death, loss, **P873**; S104, S770
    and Secrecy, S896
"Fathers," P706
    Father-daughter relationship, **S850**, S896
Faulkner, William, S91
    "A Rose for Emily," **S880**
Fear. *See* Garrison mentality
Feeling. *See also* Emotion(s)
    and Language, **S927**
Female
    Archetypes. *See under* Archetypes
    Artist figures. *See* Characters (types)—Artist/writers figures
    Artists. *See* Writers/artists, female
    Body. *See* Body, female
    Characters. *See under* Characters (types)
    Confinement. *See under* Confinement
    Culture. *See* Folklore of female culture
    Desire. *See* Desire, female
    Disguise. *See* Disguise, female
    Duality. *See* Duality, female
    Experience. *See* Women—Women's experience
    Hero. *See* Hero, female/heroine
    Identity formation. *See under* Identity formation
    Repression. *See* Women—Repression of
    Self development. *See* Self development, female
    Sexuality. *See* Sex/sexuality, female
    Voice. *See* Voice, female
    Writers. *See* Writers/artists, female
Feminine, femininity, P857
    and Artist, female, **S1092**
    Discourse. *See* Discourse, feminine
    Feminine Gothic, self-reflexive, **S801**
    Ideal, **S55**
    Identity. *See* Identity, female/feminine
    Quest. *See* Identity—Quest for
    Sensibility, approach (Alice Munro), **S74**, S778, S890, S909, S1085, S1092, S1193
        and Style, **S117**
    Values, **S55, S118**
    World, **S55**

Feminism, P841, P846, P848, P875, P879, P889, P894, P906; **S7**, **S8**, **S30**, S790, S844, S1197, S1218
    Feminist aspects of Munro's writing, **S767**
    and Political correctness, **S1004**
    and Women in fiction, **S79**
Feminist
    Biography. *See* Biography, feminist
    Criticism. *See* Criticism, feminist
    Ethics, **S90**
    Fiction
        as Counter-hegemonic, **S79**
    Materialist-feminist theory, **S64**
    Revisionary mythopoesis, **S64**
    Themes. *See under* Themes
    Theory of language and the feminine, **S70**
"The Ferguson Girls Must Never Marry," P865
    Critical analysis, overview, interpretation, **S762**
    Neo-Gothicism, self-reflexive, **S801**
    O'Connor, Flannery, influence of, **S47**
Fern Dogherty, (*Lives of Girls and Women*), S55, S110, S766, S801
Fiction. *See* Art/fiction
    of Distance. *See* Geographic metafiction
    Self-referring. *See* Metafiction
Fiction (other-than-real) and reality/fact, **S10**, **S41**, **S752**, **S757**, **S827**, **S1167**, **S1171**
    in Mysterious characters, **P884**
Fictional
    Aesthetic. *See* Aesthetic (artistic) vision
    Elegy. *See* Elegiac fiction
    Landscape. *See* Landscape—Fictional terrain
    Realism
        Rhetorical strategies for, **S827**
    Reality, P852, P867; **S126**, S981
        and Control over chaos of life, **S992**
        and Emotional tone, **S117**
        Memory and, **P664**
        and Personal reality in writing, **P845**, **P664**
    Space/place, **S1035**
        and Real place, **S1034**
    Topography. *See* Topography, fictional
    Truth. *See* Art/fiction and reality/truth
Fictive imagination. *See under* Imagination
Findley, Timothy, **S134**, **S774**, **S856**
    The Last of the Crazy People, S989
Fiona ("The Bear Came Over the Mountain"), S955
"Fits," S3, S62, S755, S975, S999, S1012
    Anamorphosis, baroque (distortion), **S1207**

"Fits" (cont.)
    Autobiography and creativity, **S936**
    Critical analysis, overview, interpretation, S752
    Narrative perspective
        Double distancing, **S884**
    Narrative technique, indeterminacy, **S953**
    Objects, domestic
        and Women, **S1070**
    Ordinary and horrific, S1070
    Secrets/secrecy, **S997**
    Surface appearance
        and Illusion, camouflage, deception, **S1207**
"Five Points," S10, S21, S861
    Grotesque as narrative strategy, **S85**
"The Flats Road," S122, S1243
    Angle of vision, archetypal, **S19**
    Archetypes, oppositional, **S867**
    Confinement, female, **S1057**
    Critical analysis, overview, interpretation, **S751**, S759
    Escape, **S1057**
    Outsiders, **S867**
    Place, S1106
        and Identity, female, **S112**
        and Setting, feeling of, **P846**
    Space, natural
        and Childhood, **S97**
    Strange and familiar, **S1017**, **S1087**
    Translation into French, **S95**
Flaubert, Gustave. *Madame Bovary*, S763, **S922**
Flo ("Characters"), S753, S862
Flo (*Who Do You Think You Are?*), P895; S39, S41, S50, **S51**, S80, S93, S99, S106, S110, S111, S112, S753, S757, S758, S762, S767, S768, S938, S944, **S976**, S1170
"Floating Bridge," P670, P905
    Critical analysis, overview, interpretation, **S1132**
    Jokes/joking, S955, S960
    Religious, spiritual quest, **S29**
    Secrets/secrecy, **S960**
        and Epiphanic sites, **S1204**
    Space, subjective
        and Identity, **S955**
Flora Grieves ("Friend of My Youth"), S757, S812, S893, S914, S942
Focalization, S752
Folklore of female culture, S767
Food, symbolism of, **S1111**
Fools. *See under* Characters (types)

"Forgiveness in Families," P860, **P878**; S18, S86, S100
    Brother-sister relationship, **S1203**
    Critical analysis, overview, interpretation, **S761**, S762
    Narrator, narrative strategies used by, **S1203**
    Structure (linguistic, narrative, rhetorical), **S84**
    Voice, **S84**
Foucault, Michel, **S51**, **S102**
"The Found Boat," S1060
    Critical analysis, overview, interpretation, **S761**, S762
    Male/female relationships, P849
    Paradox and authority, **S1126**
Fragmentation, **S22**
    of Body, female, **S1049**
    as Narrative technique, **S22**, **S92**
    in Narrative time, **S27**
Frances Farmer ("Wild Swans"), S1124
Frances Wright ("Accident"), S41, S52, S753, S757
Franklin, Miles
    My Brilliant Career, **S1160**
    My Career Goes Bung, **S1160**
Franny McGill ("Privilege"), S41, S757, S768, S1038, S1230
Fraser, Sylvia, **S49**, S968
    Pandora, S969
Freedom of women. *See* Emancipation, female
Fremlin, Gerald, P895, P898; S765, S771, S905
French Canadian literature. *See under* Literature
French family (*Lives of Girls and Women*), S116
Freud, Sigmund, S936, S1226
    "A Child Is Being Beaten," S753
    Phallicism, **S1129**
Friedan, Betty. *The Feminine Mystique*, **S7**
Friend of My Youth
    Characters
        Female, **P892**; S55
            and Narration, narrators, S942
    Closure, techniques of, **S861**
    Connection, **S1062**
        and Dislocation, **S82**
    Critical analysis, overview, interpretation, **S759**, **S834**, **S1053**, **S1098**, **S1190**
    Critical reception, S771
    Deception, S757, S759
    Discourse, paradigmatic, S757
    Elegiac fiction, **S104**, **S770**
    Feminine world, **S55**
    Fragmentation, **S22**
    Gothicism, **S10**

Friend of My Youth (cont.)
    Identity
        Female, and male/female relationships, **S112**
        Personal and universal, **S65**
    Loss, **S948**
    Mystery, surprise, bewilderment, **S39**
    Narrative perspective, **S24**
    Narrative strategy, **S107**, **S1151**
        Contingency and piecing, **S1069**
    Narrative technique
        and Theme, **S92**
    Past, ethos of, **S1140**
    Patterns, **S754**
    Political correctness
        and Attitudes to sex, **S1004**
    Reality and fiction (other than real), **S10**
    Secrecy, **S759**
    Self, shifting subject of, **S107**, **S1151**
    Self-definition, **S65**
    Silence, **S62**, **S759**, **S948**
"Friend of My Youth," **S29**, **S62**, **S65**, **S755**, **S757**, **S768**, **S827**, **S861**, **S900**, **S1069**
    Autobiographical aspects, **P891**, **P895**; **S755**, **S769**, **S771**
    Calvinism and female body, **S1120**
    Characters, **S812**
        Female, and narration, **S942**
    Critical analysis, overview, interpretation, **S759**, **S812**
    Elegiac fiction, elegy, **S104**, **S770**, **S1141**
    Gothic realism, **S10**
    House as a metaphor, **S10**, **S1151**
    Memory and women's experience, **S1221**
    Meta-narrative, feminist, **S893**
    Metonymic meaning, **S893**
    Mother, **P891**
    Mother-daughter relationship, **P891**; **S82**, **S99**, **S107**, **S842**, **S1120**
    Motifs
        and Charlotte Brontë, *Jane Eyre*, **S914**
    Narrator, **S757**
        Perspective of, **P891**, **P899**
    Origin of story, **P653**, **P671**, **P891**, **P893**, **P895**
    Past and uncertainty, **S757**, **S965**
    Scottish
        Cultural translation, **S15**, **S35**, **S1249**
        Influence, **S1094**, **S1221**
    Self, shifting subject of, **S107**, **S1151**
    Sex/sexuality, **S812**, **S1120**
        and Political correctness, **S1004**

Stories and storytelling, S893
    Narrator's perspective, **P891**, **P899**
Writing of, P671, P893, P895
Frontier
    Small town as colonial outpost, **S88**
    and Wilderness, **S105**, **S1140**
    and Women, **S105**, **S1140**
Frontier society. *See* Pioneer/settler society
Fullerton, Mrs. ("The Shining Houses"), S767, S1211
Gabriel ("Material"), S753
Gail Massie ("The Jack Randa Hotel"), S759, S1020
Gallant, Mavis, P690; S17, S18, **S101**, **S104**, **S112**, **S770**, S931, S1110
    "Acceptance of Their Ways," **S930**
    Linnet Muir stories (*Home Truths*), **S46**
    "The Pegnitz Junction," **S1143**
Garnet French (*Lives of Girls and Women*), S38, S76, S87, S91, S116, S753, S802, S811, S899, S901, S915, S961, S1007, S1105, S1245
    and Del Jordan, S6, S25, S28, S54, S63, S79, S101, S108, S110, S116, S122, S123, S124, S130, S133, S798, S801, S1077, S1122, S1128, S1173, S1189, S1212, S1247
Garrison
    Conventional society
        and "The Other country," **S66**, **S766**, **S767**, **S1007**, S1008
    Imprisoning
        and Defense, psychological, **S78**
    Mentality, and love, **S1110**
    Small town as garrison-prison, **S88**, **S120**
Gender
    and Cultural space, **S97**
    Differences, **P858**, P861, P874, P894; **S1212**, **S1215**
        in Identity formation, **S2**
        in Social expectations of behaviour, P857; S1161
        in Storytelling about the past, P906
    Female
        and Short-story genre, **S129**, **S763**, **S767**
        and Social class, **S43**
Gender roles, P852; **S7**, **S9**, **S86**
    Female, **S55**, **S86**
        and Female characters, **S59**, **S131**
        and Identity formation, **S2**, **S11**, **S59**, **S61**
        Mothers, role of, **S61**, **S131**
        and Small-town values, **S118**
        Social expectations of, P875; **S61**, **S129**, **S767**
            and Role-playing, **S11**
        and Writers, female, P848, P861
    Freedoms and restrictions of, **P659**
    Male, P842, P843, P858

Gender roles (cont.)
    and Marriage, **S105**
    Munro's views on, **S86**, S131
    Socialization of girls, **S8**, **S11**, **S50**, **S131**, **S928**, **S1202**
    and Space (house), **S928**, **S1035**, **S1202**
    and Women in the wilderness, **S105**
Genesis story groups. *See* Bible/biblical—Story groups
Geographic metafiction, **S1034**, **S1035**
Geography (historical, physical, social), **S795**, **S956**, **S966**
George ("Labor Day Dinner"), S753
George Herron ("A Wilderness Station"), S105
George Kirkham ("My Mother's Dream"), S90
Georgia ("Differently"), S1086
Gibson, Douglas, S750, S763, **S771**, S777, S782, S797, **S919**
Gilchrist, Ellen
    In the Land of Dreamy Dreams, **S61**
    Net of Jewels, **S61**
    Rhoda: A Life in Stories, **S61**
Gilman, Charlotte Perkins. "The Yellow Wallpaper," **S821**
Girard, René, S873
Girls. *See* Gender roles—Socialization of girls
    and Boys. *See* Male-female relationships
Gladys Healey ("Day of the Butterfly"), S873
Godwin, Gail. *Violet Clay*, **S75**
"Good-By, Myra." *For revised story see* "Day of the Butterfly"
    Narrative technique, **S119**, **S1182**
    Revisions, **P845**; S763, **S1182**
"Goodness and Mercy," **S861**, S1069
    Characters, female
        and Narration, **S942**
    Elegiac fiction, S104, S770, S1141
    Mother-daughter relationship, **S853**, **S942**
    Voyage, **S853**
Gossip, **S51**, **S976**
Gothicism, Gothic, P660, P847; **S10**, S759, **S1032**
    and American South, writers of the, **S880**
    and the Body, **S1230**
    Gothic realism, **S10**, **S28**
    Gothic romance, fantasy, S56
        and Female fantasy, **S1173**
    Neo-Gothicism, self-reflexive, **S801**
    Pauline Gothic, **S883**
    and Self, feminine, **S801**
    Southern Ontario Gothic, P843, P845; S10, **S1031**
        Huron (Wawanash) County, **S28**
    Themes, **S10**, **S28**

Grace, Auntie. *See* Elspeth, Aunt and Auntie Grace
Grace, Patricia. *Potiki*, **S1084**
Greer, Germaine. *The Female Eunuch*, **S7**
Grief, mourning
    and Art/fiction as consolation, **S104**, **S770**
    and Death, **S104**, **S770**, **S1141**, **S1142**
    and Loss of love, **S104**, **S770**, **S1142**
Grimm's Fairy Tales. *See under* Fairy tales
Grotesque
    Characters. *See under* Characters (types)
    and Christian readers, Christianity, **S1199**
    and Closure, technique of, **S80**
    Horror of the, **S56**
    as Narrative strategy, **S85**
    in Photography, **S134**, **S774**
    Scottish nostalgic grotesque, **S1094**
Grove, Frederick Philip. "Snow," **S799**
Guattari, Felix, S965
Guilt of daughter. *See under* Mother-daughter relationship

Hale, Mabel. *Beautiful Girlhood*, P890
"Half a Grapefruit," **S1143**
    Angle of vision, syntactical, **S19**
    Autobiographical aspects, P856, P865
    Critical analysis, overview, interpretation, S934
    Embedding (narrative device), **S868**
    Linguistic modality, **S1144**
    Revisions, **S103**
    Speech, **S1145**
Hanratty, **S110**, **S120**, **S938**, **S1005**
    and Wingham, Ontario, P889; S931
Happiness
    and Aging (Alice Munro), P857, P861, **P892**, **P893**; S778, S1039, S1201
    and Closure, endings in stories, **S808**
    and Marriage, P858
    and Values, Canadian vs American, **S808**
"Hard-Luck Stories," P865; S18, S971, S1140, S1167
    Critical analysis, overview, interpretation, **S752**, S762
    Discourse, analytical
        and Love, **S1226**
    Storytelling by narrators, **S1025**, **S1226**
        and Truth, **S1026**
Hardy, Thomas, **S836**, S843s
    "An Imaginative Woman," **S809**

Hateship, Friendship, Courtship, Loveship, Marriage, P905, P906
    Critical reception, **S771**
    Dislocation, **S955**
    Marriage, **S813**
    Narrative technique and characters, **S813**
    Religious, spiritual quest, **S29**
    Space, subjective
        and Identity, **S955**
"Hateship, Friendship, Courtship, Loveship, Marriage," S1024
    Secrets/secrecy, **S997**
    Space, subjective
        and Identity, **S955**
Hazel Curtis ("Hold Me Fast, Don't Let Me Pass"), S1013
Hébert, Anne
    Les Chambres de Bois, **S818**
    Kamouraska, **S33**, **S46**, **S818**
    Le Temps Sauvage, **S818**
    Le Torrent, **S818**
Heidegger, Martin, S1204
Heilbrun, Carolyn, *Writing a Woman's Life*, S20
"Heirs of the Living Body," S768, S839, **S965**, S1111
    Critical analysis, overview, interpretation, **S751**, **S753**, S759
    Death, **P846**
    Grotesque as narrative strategy, **S85**
    Imagination in childhood, **S83**
    Inheritance, patriarchal, **S954**, **S958**
    Religion, spirituality
        and Eros, **S29**
    Strange and familiar, **S1017**
    Translation into French, **S95**
    Women and secrecy, **S991**
Helen ("Day of the Butterfly"), S873
Helen ("The Peace of Utrecht"), S117, S125, S753, S860
Helen Louise ("Postcard"), S30, S753
Helena ("Executioners"), S753, S1211
Hemingway, Ernest
    The Nick Adams Stories, **S2**
Henshawe, Dr. (*Who Do You Think You Are*), S1099
Herb Abbott ("The Turkey Season"), S3, S41, S121, S757, S820
Herk, Aritha Van
    Judith, S806
    No Fixed Address, S957
    The Tent Peg, S806
Hero, female/heroine, **S9**
    Adolescent literary, **S108**
    Archetypal, **S875**

    Gothic, **S1173**
    and Quest, **S94**
    Romantic, S1114
    Tennysonian, S1245, S1247
Heroic imagination
    and Questing in childhood, **S83**
"Hired Girl"
    Autobiographical aspects, S771
    "Sunday Afternoon," comparison with
    and Narrative technique, development of, **S832**
Historians, archivists. *See under* Characters (types)
Historical
    Allusions. *See under* Allusions
    Fiction
        and Historical method, S795, **S1056**
    Geography, **S795, S956, S966**
History. *See also* Pioneer/settler society
    Ambiguity of, **S848, S965**
    Industrialization, postwar, **S998**
    Public and private, **S1096**
    of Small towns, **S1225**
    and Women narratives, **S965**
Hodgins, Jack. *Spit Delaney's Island: Selected Stories*, **S69, S111**
Hogg, James, P899; S765, S1094, S1196
    The Private Memoirs and Confessions of a Justified Sinner, S831, S1120
Hogg, Margaret (Laidlaw), P899; S765, S1094
"Hold Me Fast, Don't Let Me Pass," S104, S1094, S1212, S1221
    Ending, nonending, **S109**
    Fantasy and reality, **S1019**
    Middle-aged women, **S64, S1013**
    Scottish cultural translation, **S35**
    Setting, P899
    Tam Lin (Scottish ballad), **S1019**
Home
    Autobiographical place
        and Writers, female, **S1180**
    and Identity formation, **S1005**
    Small town as symbol of, **S88**
"Home," P865, P886; S771, S983, S1075, S1175
    Autobiographical aspects, S765
    Critical analysis, overview, interpretation, S762, **S1185**
    Deformity and sin, **S1105**
    Narrative perspective, **S121**
    Neo-Gothicism, self-reflexive, **S801**
    O'Connor, Flannery. *Wise Blood*, S1105
    Patterns, **S754**

"Home" (cont.)
    Voice, **S121**
    Writers and writing, P848
Homer
    The Iliad, **S1152**
    The Odyssey, S832
Homosexuality, P875
Hood, Hugh, **S856**, S1236
    Around the Mountain: Scenes from Montreal Life, **S111**
Hopper, Edward, P843, P889, S855
    "The Barber Shop" (painting), S134, S774
Horror, **S56**, **S992**
Hospital, Janette Turner, S82
House
    and Feminine Gothic, **S801**
    and Identity, **S37**
    as Metaphor, S10, **S112**, **S818**, S1151
        for Story, **P702**; S18, S753, S953
    as a Metonym for fiction, **S1035**
    as Narrative device, **S818**
    and Social class, **S1103**
    Space of
        and Gender roles, **S928**, **S1035**, **S1202**
    in Town, and in country, S1106
"How Could I Do That?"
    Critical analysis, overview, interpretation, S762
"How I Met My Husband," S18, S76, S768, S862, S935, S1060, S1083, S1217
    Critical analysis, overview, interpretation, S752, **S761**, S762, S1227
    Narrative technique
        Development of, retrospective, **S119**
    Secrecy, not-telling, **S1172**
    Structure (linguistic, narrative, rhetorical), **S84**
    Translation into French, **S98**
    Voice, **S84**, **S1001**
    Woolf, Virginia, influence of, **S1000**, **S1001**
Huber, Sherry, S771
Hugo Johnson ("Material"), S753, S839, S1175
Human
    Attachment theory, *See under* Psychology, psychoanalysis
    Frailty and disguise, **S125**
Human relationships, P855, P885; **S752**, **S759**, **S766**. *See also* Alienation; Connection;
        Family relationships; Isolation;Male/female relationships
    Rejection, humiliation in, **S3**, **S91**, **S753**, **S863**
    in Small towns, S73
    Surface appearance and reality in, **S3**, **S1167**
    Unconsummated, S766, **S863**

Subject Index 397

Humiliated characters. *See under* Characters (types)
Humiliation, **S753**. *See also* Shame
Humour, P865; **S5**, S766. *See also* Comedy; Satire
    and Irony, S74
    in Elderly persons, P872
    of Paradox, **S1038**
Huron County (Southwestern Ontario), P843, P845, P889; S882, S894, S986, S988. *See also* Rural Ontario; Wawanash County; Wingham, Ontario
    Censorship in, **P693**, **P856**, **P857**, **P879**, P900; S771, S994, S1068, S1071, S1102, S1123, S1197, S1239
    Gothic aspects, P843, P845; S10, **S28**, **S1031**
    Munro's affinity to, **P653**, P684, P879, P895; S797, S1093, S1224, S1234
    Munro's return to, P700, P858, P865, P886, P909; S1196, S1201
    Story events and physical places in, **S859**
    Traditional conservative environment in, P893, P903; S1022, S1119, S1197, S1224

Identity, P848; S93, S752, S1109
    Character identity, technique of. *See* Characterization—Methods/techniques of
    and Connection, P899; S2, S16, S82, **S1062**
    and the Past, S759
    and Place, S16, S17, S112, S767, S1005, S1183
    Quest for, S59, S63, S130, S133, S766, S767, S1160
    and Space, S37, S955
Identity, female/feminine, S2, S129, S991
    and Desiring female body, S30
    Feminist self-discovery, S767
    and Masculine discourse, S63
    and Place, space, S112
    as Postcolonial discourse, S1168
    and Role-playing, S11, S112, S1170
    and Sexual fantasy, S127, S987
    Sexuality and, S4
    and Social class, S43
    Twin identity of mother and daughter, S860
    and Victorian female repression, S1091
Identity formation, S2, S846. *See also* Individuation; Self-development
    Alternative female identity, S11
    and Artistic development, S61, S63
    Attachment and separation and, S2
    and Family relationships, S2, S61
    Female, and mass culture, S54
    and Gender roles, female, S2, S11, S59, S61
    Gossip and, S51, S976
    and Love, S6, S1005
    and Mother-daughter relationship, S61, S82
    and Place, home, S16, S1005

"The Idyllic Summer," S754, S818
    Critical analysis, overview, interpretation, S762
    Narrative technique, development of, **S32**, **S119**, S1182
Illusion and reality. *See* Surface appearance and reality
Imagery, images S767, S768
    Body/self, S38
    Images and incidents, recurrent, **S1186**
    Patterns of, **S754**, **S839**, **S840**
    Themes and, **S13**
"Images," P865; S18, S91, S106, S755, S768, S788, S839, S1046, S1111
    Autobiographical aspects, P653, **P664**
        Personal and fictional reality, **P845**; S765
    Childhood, portrayal of, **S824**
    Critical analysis, overview, interpretation, **S752**, S762
    Death, S40, S104, S770, S1142
    Legend and reality, **S40**
    Narrative technique, iterative, **S758**, **S945**
    Objects, treachery to, in writing, **P664**
Imagination
    in Childhood, **S83**
    in Education, P856; S83
    Female, and rape fantasy, **S899**
    Fictive, **S83**, S129, S763, **S1163**
    and Legends, **S41**, **S757**
Immigrants, visible, **S852**
Impermanence. *See* Time, passing of, impermanence
Imprisonment. *See* Confinement
Inclusion, **S19**
Incongruity/contradiction and opposition. *See* Narrative techniques—Opposition and incongruity/opposition
Independence, freedom
    and Artistic ambition, female, **S77**, **S110**, S784
Indeterminacy. *See under* Narrative techniques
Individuation, **S2**, S794
Industrialization, postwar. *See under* History
Infidelity
    and Faith, love, **S52**
    Marital, P893, **P909**; S52, S922
Ingram, Forrest L., **S111**
Inheritance, **S954**
    Literary
        and Artist/writer, female, **S132**, **S958**
            Female, cross-generational, **S99**
    Maternal, **S828**
    Patriarchal, **S958**

Initiation rites, female
    Rape fantasy and, **S899**
    Sex, sexuality and, **S4**
Instability
    of Narrative, **S41, S129, S757**
    of Reality, **S41, S129, S757**
Interconnections/parallels between stories. *See under* Stories
Intertextuality, **S754, S1100**
    Ironic intertextualization, **S833**
Interviews (Alice Munro), **S771**. *See also* Interviews section *of this bibliography*
    Feelings about, P865, P880, **P898**, P910; S1080
    Paris Review, **S1131**
Inventories. *See* Lists and list-making
Inversion. *See under* Narrative devices
Iona Kirkham ("My Mother's Dream"), S90
Ireland, P686; S882
Irigaray, Luce, **S842**
Iris, Cousin ("Connection"), S3, S17, S1013
Irony, **S19, S767**
    and Absurdity, horror of life, **S992**
    and Humour, **S74, S1020**
    Munro's ironic vision, **S22**
    and Narrative perspective, retrospective, **S74**
Isabel Vogelsang ("White Dump"), P886; S3, S41, S753, S757
Isolation, S56, **S91, S128, S863, S870**. *See also* Alienation; Human relationships
    and Loneliness of men, **S974**
Iterative technique. *See under* Narrative techniques

Jack Agnew ("Carried Away"), S843, S998, S1086
Jack MacNeil ("Mrs. Cross and Mrs. Kidd"), S872
"The Jack Randa Hotel," P898; S755
    Comedy, farce, **S1020**
    Critical analysis, overview, interpretation, **S759**
    Middle-aged women, **S64, S1013**
    Narrative strategy, **S129**
    Narrative structure, circular, **S60**
"Jakarta," S29
    Review, **S1200**
Jameson, Anna, S78
    Winter Studies and Summer Rambles in Canada, S117
Janet ("Connection"), S17, S118, S753
Janet ("The Moons of Jupiter"), S41, S82, S118, S753, S757
Jarvis Poulter ("Meneseteung"), S17, S757, S1030, S1140, S1154
Jeanette Quinn. *See* Quinn, Mrs.
Jeanette ("Marrakesh"), S753, S757, S761, S767, S1091
Jeffrey Toom ("The Children Stay"), S833

Jerry Storey (*Lives of Girls and Women*), S76, S86, S87, S91, S116, S122, S123, S817, S915, S1245
    and Del Jordan, S6, S25, S28, S63, S101, S108, S110, S130, S766, S767, S1122, S1128, S1173, S1189, S1212
Jessie ("Jesse and Meribeth"), S753
"Jesse and Meribeth," S3, S18, S62
Jimmy Box ("The Love of a Good Woman"), S830
Jinny Lockyer ("Floating Bridge"), S955
Jocelyn ("Mischief"), S753
Joe Phippen ("Images"), S41, S73, S80, S753, S757, S839, S1211
Jokers/joking, P905; **S768**, S955, S960
Journey. *See* Travel
Joyce, James, S119
    "Araby," S861
    "The Dead," S1014
    Dubliners, **S113**, **S1014**
    Portrait of the Artist as a Young Man, S18, S95, S798, S916, S926, S937, S1014, S1162, **S1165**
    Stephen Hero, S1162
    Ulysses, S832, S926, S1165
Jubilee. *See Lives of Girls and Women*—Small town (Jubilee); *See also under* "The Peace of Utrecht"; Wingham, Ontario
Judges story groups. *See* Bible/biblical—Story groups
Judy Armstrong ("Hold Me Fast, Don't Let Me Pass"), S1019
Julie ("Hard-Luck Stories"), S1025, S1026, S1226
June ("Memorial"), S753, S761, S767
Jung, C. G. (Carl Gustav), **S33**, S794

Karin ("Pictures of the Ice"), S757
Kidd, Mrs. ("Mrs. Cross and Mrs. Kidd"), S872, S875
Kiil, Toivo. *See* Publisher/editor relations
Kincaid, Jamaica.
    At the Bottom of the River, **S99**
King, Thomas. *Truth and Bright Water*, **S31**
Kingdom story groups. *See* Bible/biblical—Story groups
Knister, Raymond, P689
Knowledge, knowing
    and Linguistic modality, **S1144**
    Quest for knowledge, **S752**
    and Uncertainty, modality of, **S1143**
Kristeva, Julia, S755, S1126
Künstlerroman, **S20**, **S77**, S751, S1060, **S1159**, **S1165**

"Labor Day Dinner," S3, S29, S44, S62, S65, S121, S1076, S1111
    Critical analysis, overview, interpretation, **S752**, S762

Desire, female, S971
   Absence of, **S1195**
   Family relationships, **S1015**
Lacan, Jacques, S63, S951, S1151, S1226
Ladner ("Vandals"), S866, S904
Laidlaw, Anne Clarke (Chamney), P848, P855, P865, **P891**, **P893**, P895, P909; **S765, S769**, **S771**, S882, S890, S905, S1000, S1043, S1112, **S1150**, S1241
   as Character in stories, P855, P886, P895; S755, **S765**, S767, S769, S823, S860, S890
Laidlaw family history, **P663**; S765, S769, S771, S924. *See also* Scottish ancestors
Laidlaw, James, **P663**; S771
Laidlaw, Margaret. *See* Hogg, Margaret (Laidlaw)
Laidlaw, Mary Etta, S765, S771
Laidlaw, Robert, P681, **P855**, P895, P909; **S765, S769, S771**, S985, S1112, S1241
   Boyhood Summer, 1912, S765
   The McGregors: A Novel of an Ontario Pioneer Family, P855, P879, P909; **S15**, S771
Laidlaw, Thomas, **P663**; S765, S771
Landscape, **S73**, S767. *See also* Place; Rivers; Space
   Body, female as, **S112**
   of Community, **S105**
   as Epiphanic site, **S1204**
   Fictional terrain, **S1243**
   Layering of, **S900**
   Mapping of, **S956**, **S966**
   Rural and urban landscape, **S1106**
Language, **S27**, **S40**, **S753**, **S762**, **S835**, **S849**, **S901**, S951. *See also* Discourse, masculine/patriarchal; Names
   of Childhood, remembered, **S1101**
   and Feeling, **S927**
   Keywords, **S1194**
   Male, **S115**
   and Power, control, **S101**, **S115**
   Pronouns, **S1063**
   Silence as, S835, **S1051**
   and Superrealism, **S5**, **S1104**
   as Surface, and truth beneath, **S125**
   and Women, females, **S70**, **S927**
      Female body, **S55**, **S63**, **S112**, **S926**, **S979**, **S1230**
      and Female expression, **S767**, **S926**
      in Patriarchal society, **S63**, **S115**, **S129**
      Self-development, **S61**, **S115**, **S927**
      and Sexuality, **S4**, **S63**, **S112**
   Words, P841, P851; **S1176**
Laurence, Margaret, P888, P900; S18, **S43**, **S48**, **S49**, **S88**, **S117**, S968, S994, S995, S1110, S1114, **S1127**, **S1158**, **S1180**
   A Bird in the House, **S26**, **S75**, **S108**, **S798**, S865, S933, S969, S1097, **S1101**
   Dance on the Earth: A Memoir, **S70**

Laurence, Margaret (cont.)
- *The Diviners*, **S26**, **S70**, **S78**, **S97**, **S102**, **S118**, **S820**
- *The Fire-Dwellers*, **S70**, **S78**, **S102**, S969
- *A Jest of God*, **S9**, **S78**, **S102**, **S118**, S969, S1128
- *The Stone Angel*, **S78**, **S102**, **S118**
- "Ten Years' Sentences," **S70**
- "To Set Our House in Order," **S930**

Lawrence, D. H. "The Fox," P909
Laxness, Halldór. *Independent People, An Epic*, S765
Layering. *See under* Narrative techniques
Leacock, Stephen, **S88**
- *Sunshine Sketches of a Little Town*, S1097

Lee, Sky. *Disappearing Moon Cafe*, **S852**
Lefebvre, Henri. *The Production of Space*, S955
Legend(s)
- Imagination, memory and, **S41**, **S40**, S757
- Legend-making and demythologizing, **S827**
- and Reality, **S40**, S752
- and Surface reality, S1113

Leona Parry ("The Time of Death"), S767
Lessing, Doris. "To Room Nineteen," **S821**
Letters and letter-writing, S124, **S755**, **S885**
Levine, Norman, S931
- "By a Frozen River," **S799**

"Lichen," S44, S65, S121, S768, S806, S856, S1012
- Artist/writer, female, **S36**
- Body, female, S975, **S1049**
- Critical analysis, overview, interpretation, S752, S762
- Middle-aged men, women
  - and Love, **P882**
- Photographs, photography, **S869**

Lies. *See under* Deception, dissimulation
Life. *See also* Munro, Alice—Life; Real life; Surface of life; Vision of life (Alice Munro)
- and Art/fiction, **S41**, S56, **S100**, S757, **S992**, S1066
- Choices, female sacrifice of, **S33**
- Experience of life
  - and Artistic development, **S903**, **S937**
  - and Legends, **S40**
  - Retrospective reordering of, **S87**
  - and Storytelling, **S41**, S757
- Ordinary life, and mystery, **S29**
- Pivotal moments in, P865, **P883**
- Transience of, impermanence, **S128**, S752
  - and Loss, death, **S881**, S1142

Linguistic
    Modality, and knowledge, knowing, **S1144**
    Structure, **S84**
Linked short stories. *See* Short-story cycle
Linking and linking devices
    and Open form, unity in, **S58**
    Pronouns, **S1063**
Liza ("Vandals"), S866, S904
Lispector, Clarice, "Pig Latin," S987
Lists and list-making, **S915**
Literary
    Agents. *See* Barber, Virginia
    Allusions. *See under* Allusions
    Archives. *See* Archives, literary
    Authority. *See* Authority
    Criticism. *See* Criticism (Alice Munro), literary
    Influences
        Mother as, **S132**, **S1099**
        on Munro, Alice, P686, P841, P848, P862, **P877**, P890, P894, **P906**, **P907**; **S109**, S758, S769, **S809**, **S836**, **S914**, **S922**, S984, S1000, S1001, S1014. *See also under names of individual writers*
        American, P848; **S1178**, **S1179**
        Writers of the American South, P660, P839, P841, P848, P860, **P862**, P865, P877, P889, P895; **S16**, **S28**, **S47**, **S91**, S855, **S1105**, **S1162**, S1232
    Inheritance. *See* Inheritance, literary
    Mentors. *See* Metcalf, John; Weaver, Robert
    Translation. *See* Translation
Literature
    Canadian. *See also* Short-story genre in Canada
        Cultural nationalism in, S763
        Postcolonial, **S789**
        and Scottish literature, S35
        Survey of readers, S781
        Teaching, P848
    French Canadian, **S23**, S28, S920
    Minor, **S965**
    Popular vs. literary, **S1054**
    Women, portrayal of, **S79**
        by Female writers, P657, P853; S778, S941
        by Male writers, P841, P848, P852, **P858**, **P909**
Lives of Girls and Women. See also under titles of individual chapters
    Absent and potential meaning, **S41**, S757
    Absurdity, **S56**, **S100**
    Adolescence, **S50**, S130
        and Perception, **S989**
        and Voice of adult narrator, **S798**

Lives of Girls and Women (cont.)
- American South, writers of the, S91, S1105, S1162
- Art/fiction, S87, S100, S1175
- Artist/writer, female, S25, S36, S74, S75, S77, S81, S132, S926, S1113
  - and Autobiography, S46, S75, S768, S801, S937
- Artistic ambition, female, S77, S1127
  - and Independence, freedom, S77, S110, S784
- Artistic development, P860; S36, S77, S87, S110, S755, S798, S1077, S1245. *See also* Künstlerroman
  - and Environment, S110, S1077, S1160
  - and Identity formation, S61, S63
  - and Life experience, S903, S937
  - and Masculine image, S794
  - and Mother, influence of, S77, S108, S110, S132, S1099
  - and Self-development, female, S39, S61, S75, S865, S1079
  - and Stories, Storytelling, S106, S903
- Artistic mind, S77
- Atmospheric evocation, S5
- Authority and writers, S937
- Autobiographical aspects, P851, P895; S77, S769, S771, S776
- Beauty rituals and fashion, S102
- *Bildungsroman*, S6, S9, S26, S63, S123, S130, S751, S767, S798, S1079, S1122, S1139, S1160
  - and Amor and Psyche myth, S45
- Blais, Marie-Claire. *Une Saison dans la Vie d'Emmanuel*, S1159
- Blaise, Clark. *Lunar Attractions*, S992
- Body, S61, S752, S811, S876, S916
  - Female, and language, S63, S926, S979
- Browning, Robert, S1247
- Censorship of *Lives*, P856, P857, P879; S771, S1123, S1197
- Characterization, technique of, S910
- Characters, S38, S944. *See also under names of individual characters in main listing*
- Characters (types)
  - Female, P846, P852, P865; S5, S55, S74, S86, S131, S767, S768, S816, S1091
    - as Personae of Alice Munro, S25
  - Male, S86, S802
  - Mentrix figures, S1099
- Childhood, S23, S97, S130, S1101
- Closure, techniques of, S80
- Confinement, female, S1057
- Connection, S1062, S1244
- Control, loss of control, S100, S753
- Critical analysis, overview, interpretation, S751, S752, S756, S759, S762, S766, S767, S769, S838, S889, S891, S920, S977, S1077, S1138, S1174
- Critical reception/reviews, P852; S761, S771
- Cycles/patterns, S754, S839, S840

Death, S6, S38, **S104**, S770, **S881**
Defense, psychological
    and Wilderness (metaphorical), **S78**
Detail(s), use of, **S1008**
Discourse, **S41**, **S63**, **S101**, **S102**, S757
Double vision, **S66**, **S963**, **S1060**. *See also* Narrative perspective, retrospective;
    Strange and familiar; Surfaces and depths
Elegiac fiction, **S104**, **S770**
Emancipation of consciousness, **S116**
Escape, **P846**; **S1010**, **S1057**, **S1128**
Faith. *See* Religion
Familiar and strange. *See* Strange and familiar
Family, **S2**, **S61**, **S91**, S1015
Fantasy. *See also* Rape fantasy
    Female, and Gothic fantasy, **S1173**
    and Reality, S56, S127, **S752**, **S952**, **S961**, **S1245**
Feminine. *See also* Women
    Language. *See* Body, female and language
    Self. *See* Self, feminine
    World, **S55**, S1215
Feminism, **P846**, P865; **S7**
Feminist
    Criticism, **S57**, **S79**, **S926**
Fiction (other-than-real) and reality, **S41**, **S757**, **S901**
Garrison (metaphorical), **S78**
Gender differences, **S1212**, S1215
Gender roles, **S7**, **S9**, **S86**, **S118**, **S131**
    and Identity formation, **S2**, **S59**, **S61**
Gothic, Gothicism, **S28**, **S56**, S880
    Gothic and female fantasy, **S1173**
    Self-reflexive neo-Gothicism, **S801**
Grotesque, horror of, **S56**
Heroine, **S9**, **S108**, S1114, **S1245**, S1247
Humour, **S5**, **S1038**
Identity, **S43**, **S1168**
    Quest for, **S59**, **S63**, **S130**, **S133**, **S767**, **S1160**
Identity formation, **S2**, **S6**, **S11**, **S54**, **S61**, S762
Illusion and reality. *See* Surface appearance and reality
Images, imagery, **S13**, **S839**
Imagination, **S83**, **S899**
Incongruity. *See* Opposition and incongruity
Individuation, **S2**, S794
Inheritance, **S132**, **S954**, **S958**
Initiation rites, female, **S26**, S108, **S899**
Isolation, S56, **S91**

Lives of Girls and Women (cont.)
- Joyce, James, S40
  - *Portrait of the Artist as a Young Man*, S18, S95, S798, S916, S926, S937, S1014, S1162, **S1165**
  - *Stephen Hero*, S1162
  - *Ulysses*, S926, S1165
- Jubilee. *See* Small town
- *Künstlerroman*, **S20**, **S77**, S751, S1060, **S1159**, **S1165**
- Landscape. *See* Nature—Natural landscape; Rural and urban landscape
- Language, **S61**, **S115**, S901, **S1101**, S1176
  - and Female body, **S63**, S926, S979
- Linking devices, **S58**
- Lists and list-making, **S915**
- Literary
  - Influence, mother as, **S132**, S1099
  - Models, **S132**
- Love, S6, **S52**, S75
- Magic realism, **S125**, S1104
- Male-female relationships, **P842**, **P843**, P849; S59
- Marriage, resistance to, S79
- Masculine
  - Discourse, **S63**
  - Image, **S794**
- Mother. *See also* Ada Jordan *in main listing*
  - Role of, and gender roles, **S61**, **S131**
- Mother-daughter relationship, S49, **S74**, **S75**, **S81**, **S108**, **S755**, S752, S828, S969
  - Influence of mother
    - and Artistic development, S108, **S110**, **S132**, S1099
    - and Self-development of daughter, **S61**, **S108**, S933
- Mystery. *See* Strange and familiar
- Narrative form. *See also* Short-story cycle
  - and Narrative time, **S46**, S755
  - Novel structure, P859
    - or Linked short stories, S113, S751, S762, **S1107**
  - Open form, **S58**
  - and Theme, **S124**
- Narrative perspective, retrospective, **S81**, **S87**, **S841**, **S1060**, S1101
- Narrative space, gaps, S999, **S1147**
- Narrative strategy, S57, **S920**
- Narrative structure, P841; **S18**, **S69**, **S116**, **S758**, **S801**, **S818**, **S892**, S903, **S916**, **S920**, **S999**, **S1008**
- Narrative technique, **S80**, **S81**, **S124**. *See also* Magic realism
  - Development of, **S762**, **S1074**
  - Time as an element of, **S46**, **S74**, **S758**, **S1220**

Narrator, S751, S752
    First person, S18
    as Observer and observed/participant, S753, S920
    and Retrospective double vision. *See* Narrative perspective, retrospective
Nature
    Natural landscape, space, S97
    and Technology, S76
Observer and observed/participant. *See under* Narrator
Opposition and incongruity, S762
Ordinary and extraordinary. *See* Strange and familiar
"The Other country," S867
    and Conventional society, S66, S1007, S1008
Paradox, S762, S963, S1038, S1104
Parody, S1233
Patterns/cycles, S754, S839, S840
Perception, and reality, S38, S989
Photography, S134, S751, S774, S820, S856, S1133, S1233, S1246
Place, S91
Power, and language, S115
Protagonist. *See* Del Jordan *in main listing*
Quest. *See under* Identity; Real life
Rape fantasy, S899
Readers and reading, S768, S811
Real life, S752, S1087
    Quest for, S77, S91, S751, S1105
Realism, S77, S117, S751. *See also* Magic realism; Super-realism
Reality, S38, S41, S124, S757, S766, S901, S962, S963, S1087, S1175. *See also*
    Double vision; Strange and familiar
    Fantasy and reality, S56, S127, S752, S952, S961, S1245
    and Legend, S40
Regionalism, S122
Religion, S25, S38, S47, S48, S120, S770, S1105, S1158
Revisions. *See* Writing of *Lives*
Rites of passage. *See* Initiation rites, female
Role models, female, S767
Role-playing, S11
Roy, Gabrielle. *La Route d'Altamont*, S920
Rural and urban landscape, S1106
Secrets/secrecy, S967, S1147
Self, S102
    Feminine, and Gothicism, S801
Self-development, female, P860; S6, S9, S25, S26, S45, S61, S115, S116, S123, S130,
    S756, S794, S798, S801, S910, S1077, S1220, S1245. *See also* 'Bildungsroman'
    and Artistic development, S39, S61, S75, S865, S1079
    and Mother-daughter relationship, S61, S108, S933
Self-image, S38

Lives of Girls and Women (cont.)
- Sex/sexuality, **S7**, **S8**, S15, **S753**, **S876**, S939
    - and Language, feminine, **S63**
    - Rape fantasy, **S899**
    - and Religious, spiritual quest, **S29**
    - Sexual desire, female, **S8**, **S1173**, **S1189**
- Short-story cycle, **S1**, **S69**, **S99**, S751, **S758**, S789, S980, S990, **S1041**, **S1065**, **S1147**
    - Unity and separation, **S113**
- Small town (Jubilee), S43, S73, S88, **S110**, S118, **S120**, **S122**, S938, **S1010**, **S1097**, S1127, **S1128**, **S1158**, **S1225**
- Social class, **S43**, **S864**, **S1158**
- Space
    - and Artistic development, **S97**, **S110**
    - Cultural, and noncultural, S97
- Stories and storytelling, **S52**, **S75**, **S106**, **S903**, **S1084**, S1101, S1211
- Strange and familiar, **S125**, **S1017**, **S1087**, **S1113**. *See also* Double vision; Opposition and incongruity; Paradox; Surface appearance and reality
- Style, **S40**, **S116**, **S981**, **S1067**, S1159
    - Feminine sensibility and, **S117**
- Superrealism, **S5**, **S1237**
- Surface appearance and reality, **S901**, **S1087**
- Surfaces and depths, **S125**, **S1113**, S1167
- Tennyson, Alfred Lord, S106, S926, S1245, **S1247**
- Texture, **S117**, **S125**
- Themes, **S13**, **S116**, **S124**, **S125**, S791
    - Feminist, **S7**
- Tone, **S117**
- Undset, Sigrid. *Kristin Lavransdatter*, **S25**, S926
- Unity, **S58**, **S69**, **S113**, S758
- Voice, S63, **S101**, S798
- Welty, Eudora. *The Golden Apples*, **S28**, S1162
- Wilderness (metaphorical)
    - and Defense, psychological, **S78**
- Wolf, Christa. *Kindheitsmuster*, **S841**
- Women, **S79**, **S99**, **S116**, **S131**, **S784**, **S816**, S967
- Writing of *Lives*, **P841**, **P842**, **P843**, P848, P874, **P862**, **P889**, **P895**; S57, S113, **S762**, **S765**, **S771**, S1210
- "Lives of Girls and Women," P894; S768
    - Critical analysis, overview, interpretation, **S751**
    - Women
        - Appearance, personal, P868
        - Repression of, **P846**
- Lois ("Thanks for the Ride"), S91, **S125**, **S753**, **S1091**
- Loneliness, male. *See* Isolation and loneliness of men
- Longinus. "On the Sublime," **S824**

Loss, **P893**; **S3**, **S948**
    and Elegiac fiction, elegy, **S104**, **S770**, **S1142**
Loss of control. *See* Control and loss of control
Lou, Auntie ("The Peace of Utrecht"), S767
Lougheed, Mr. ("Walking on Water"), S41, **S100**, S753, S757, S862
Louisa Doud ("Carried Away"), S105, S843, S904, S998, S1086
Love, **P882**, **P885**, P893, **P909**; **S6**, **S39**, **S52**, **S55**, **S75**, **S90**, S752, S753, S767, S1005, S1086, S1198, S1226, S1241
    Loss of, and mourning, **S104**, **S770**, **S1142**
    Writing about, S1102
The Love of a Good Woman
    Critical reception, S771
    Discussion guide, **S1003**
    Mystery, surprise, bewilderment, **S39**
"The Love of a Good Woman," S17, S29, S999, S1095
    Archetypes, Bluebeard, **S1032**
    Biblical myths, **S1032**
    Brontë, Charlotte. *Jane Eyre*, **S914**, **S1032**
    Care of others, and self interest, **S71**
    Characters, **S1116**
    Communication, not-telling, **S755**, **S830**
    Critical analysis, overview, interpretation, S759, **S848**
    Gothic elements, **S883**, **S1032**
    History/past, ambiguity of, **S848**
    Legend and reality, **S40**
    Motifs, **S914**
    Narrative complexity, **S830**, S1024
        and Detail, use of, **S1116**
    The New Yorker, publication in, S771, **S807**
    Origin of story, P672
    Pauline poetic, **S883**
    Reader response, **S807**, **S847**, S1116, S1194
    Sacrifice, female
        and Personal desire, **S71**
    Senses, smell, **S847**
    Space and identity, **S37**
    Time and place/space, **S805**
    Writing of, **P686**
Lydia ("Dulse"), S41, S52, S104, S753, S757, S770, S870, S971, S1026, S1153, S1179
"Lying under the Apple Tree"
    Autobiographical material, memoir, **S1125**

MacLennan, Hugh, **S1249**
MacLeod, Alistair. "Vision," **S31**
Maddy ("The Peace of Utrecht"), S117, S860, S1091

Madeleine ("The Flats Road"), S41, S63, S106, S110, S112, S120, S753, S757, S767, S801, S867, S876, S937, S1084, S1091

Madonna figures. *See under* Characters (types)—Female

Magic realism, P841; **S12, S125, S1061**, S1095, **S1104**

Male

    Characters. *See under* Characters (types)

    Discourse. *See* Discourse, masculine/patriarchal

    Domination. *See* Power/domination, male

    Gender roles. *See* Gender roles, male

    Image, **S794**

    Language. *See under* Language

    Loneliness. *See* Isolation and loneliness of men

    Writers. *See* Writers, male

Male-female relationships, **P842, P843,** P844, **P846,** P847, **P849,** P857, P886, **P909; S3, S44, S59, S82,** S86, **S112, S115,** S752, S817, S996, **S1086, S1173.** *See also* Infidelity, marital; Marriage

Malouf, David, S17

Mansfield, Katherine, S17

Maps and mapping, P701; **S759, S956, S966, S1243**

Margaret Dobie ("Hold Me Fast, Don't Let Me Pass"), S1019

Marian Kidd. *See* Kidd, Mrs.

Marin, Louis, S1208

Marion Sherriff ("Epilogue: The Photographer"), S28, S880, S1087

"Marrakesh," S76, S1217

    Critical analysis, overview, interpretation, **S752, S761**

Marriage, **S105, S813,** S1000, S1001. *See also* Infidelity, marital; *See also under* Munro, Alice

    and Happiness, P858; **S808**

    and Victimization, subordination of women, **S79**

Marsalles, Miss ("Dance of the Happy Shades"), **P845;** S80, S91, S767, S768, S826, S874, S1091

Marshall, Owen, S17

Martin, Claire. *In an Iron Glove,* S939

Mary Agnes Oliphant ("Heirs of the Living Body"), S80, S95, S839, S991

Mary Jo ("Eskimo"), S753

Mary McQuade ("Images"), S41, S131, S753, S757, S767, S768, S839, S914

Mass culture, **S54**

"Material," S18, S52, S82, S112, S128, S770, S783, S839, S935, S944, S1215, S1217, S1244

    Art/fiction, S100, S1175

        and Authority, **S970**

    Critical analysis, overview, interpretation, **S752, S761,** S762

    Disarrangement, **S109**

    Elegiac fiction, elegy, S104, S770, S1142

    Language, pronouns, **S1063**

    Narrative structure

        and Narrative time, **S758**

Structure (linguistic, narrative, rhetorical), **S84**
    Voice, **S84**
Maternal inheritance. *See under* Inheritance
Maureen Stephens ("Open Secrets"), S759, S835, S904
Mavis ("Wild Swans"), S102, S1124
Maxwell, William, **P691**, P895
Maynard, Fredelle Bruser. *Raisins and Almonds*, S23, S933
McCarthy, Mary. *Memories of a Catholic Girlhood*, **S45**
McCullers, Carson, P841, P848: S91
    Sojourner, **S34**
McGrath, Charles. *See* Publisher/editor relations
Meditation. *See under* Autobiographical material, autobiography
Medusa. *See under* Archetypes
Melancholy, **S104**, **S770**
Memoir. *See under* Autobiographical material, autobiography
"Memorial," S18, S29, S76, S102, S935, S967
    Angle of vision, archetypal, **S19**
    Art/fiction and authority, **S970**
    Body, female, **S30**
    Critical analysis, overview, interpretation, S752, **S761**, S762
    Elegiac fiction, S104, S770, S1142
    Narrative perspective, P862
    Narrative technique, **S871**
    Voice, **S30**
Memory, **P906**; S18, S40, S41, S753, S757, S758, S785, S945, S1062, S1064, S1221
    as Consolation, **S104**, **S770**
    and Fictional reality, P664
    Intrusions of
        and Narrative structure, **S84**
    of Mother, **S753**, S828
    as Narrative technique, **P893**; S785
    and Past, P859, P894, P906, P907; **S41**, S755, S757
    and Reality, **P886**, P907; S785
Men. *See also* Characters (types)—Male
    and Isolation, loneliness, **S974**
    Middle-aged men, and love, **P882**
    Munro's relationship with, P848, P861
    Portrayal of, P841, P849, **P882**; **S802**, S1218
Menaker, Daniel. *See* Publisher/editor relations
"Meneseteung," S15, S17, S21, S65, **S757**, S771, S827, S1069, S1212
    Archetypal mythical figures (Dionysus, Medusa), **S1154**
    Artist/writer, female, **S36**
        and Femininity, paradox of, **S1092**
    Biography, feminist, **S89**
    Body, female, S114, **S1214**
    Critical analysis, overview, interpretation, S759

"Meneseteung" (cont.)
- Grotesque and Christianity, **S1199**
- Hero, female, **S94**
- Menstruation
    - and Metonymic meaning, **S951**
    - and Voice, female, **S114**
- Narrative strategy, S1030
    - Historical method, **S795**
- Origin of story, P673
- Protagonist
    - and Escape from expected roles, **S942**
- Self, S107, S768, S1151
- Sexuality, female, **S114**
- Space and time, **S795**
- Wilderness and frontier, **S1140**
- Women
    - Narrative and history, **S965**
    - and Victorian patriarchal society, P673; **S1030**

Mentrix figures, mentors. *See under* Characters (types)
Meriel ("What Is Remembered"), S906, S955
Metabiography, fictional. *See under* Biography
Metafiction, **S52**, **S62**, S1163
- Geographic, **S1034**, **S1035**

Metanarrative, feminist, **S893**
Metaphors, P865; **S752**, **S753**, **S768**, S839
- Body as, **S752**
- House, **P702**; S10, S18, **S112**, S753, **S818**, S953, S1151
- Patterns of, **S754**
- Snow, **S799**
- Translation of, **S98**

Metcalf, John, P656, **P692**, P697; S67, S763, **S771**, S1181, S1236
- "The Teeth of My Father," **S982**

Metonymic meaning, **S893**, **S951**
Middle-aged men. *See under* Men
Middle-aged women. *See under* Women
Mildred ("Visitors"), S757
"Miles City, Montana," S18, S29, S65, S104, S1012, S1193, S1243
- Autobiographical aspects, P889; S765, S771, S1186
- Critical analysis, overview, interpretation, **S752**, S762
- Disarrangement, **S109**
- Narrative structure
    - and Narrative time, **S758**
- Origin of story, P889, P904
- Secrets/secrecy, **S997**

Millett, Kate. *Sexual Politics*, **S7**
Millicent ("A Real Life"), S17, S1020

Milton Homer ("Who Do You Think You Are?"), S80, S100, S111, S768, S926, S927, S930, S980, S1005, S1038, S1094, S1110, S1168, S1246
Mimicry, imitation, S752
    and Self-construction, S102
Mind/body
    and Care of the self, S102
Minor literature. *See* Literature, minor
"Mischief," S768
    Critical analysis, overview, interpretation, S753, S762
    Disarrangement, S1023
    Flaubert, Gustave. *Madame Bovary*, S922
    Revisions, S103
Mitchell, W. O., S88
    Who Has Seen the Wind, S865
Modality. *See* Linguistic modality; Uncertainty, modality of
Moira, Aunt ("Heirs of the Living Body"), S28, S766, S767, S784, S802, S839
"Monsieur les Deux Chapeaux," S856, S1012
    Critical analysis, overview, interpretation, S752
    Narrative structure
        and Narrative time, S758
Montgomery, L. M. (Lucy Maud)
    Anne of Green Gables, S6, S1114
    Emily of New Moon, P654, P862, P879, P890; S77, S83, S97, S769
Moodie, Susanna, S78
    Roughing It in the Bush, S117
"The Moon in the Orange Street Skating Rink," P884, P895; S29, S121, S768, S975, S1012, S1015
    Characters (types)
        Mysterious, truth and fiction in, P884
    Critical analysis, overview, interpretation, S752, S762
The Moons of Jupiter
    Art/fiction
        as Consolation, S104, S770
    Chance and fate, S752
    Chaos of life, S92
    Characters (types), S768
        Artist figures, female, S74
        Controlled and controlling, S753
        Female, P867; S55, S74, S972
    Closure, techniques of, S80
    Connection, S39, S121, S752, S1108, S1244
        Collapse/absence of, S41, S757
        and Separation, dislocation, S82, S128, S1064
    Control and loss of control, S753
    Critical analysis, overview, interpretation, S752, S759, S762, S766, S767, S769, S911, S972, S1174

The Moons of Jupiter (cont.)
- Critical reception, S771
- Desire, female
    - and Power, S971
- Discourse, paradigmatic, S41, S757
- Double vision, S66
- Elegiac fiction, elegy, S104, S770
- Father-daughter relationship, S81
- Feminine world, S55
- Human relationships, S3, S759, S766. *See also* Connection
- Humiliation, S3, S753
- Knowledge, quest for, S752
- Language, S1064
    - and Power, S115
- Love, S39
    - Humiliation in, S753
- Maps and mapping, S759
- Memory, S785, S1064
- Munro, Alice
    - Comments on, P874; S1234
- Narrative
    - Perspective, S24, S81, S96, S121, S753, S759, S959
    - Strategy, S121
    - Structure, S18, S759, S762, S959
        - and Narrative time, S758
    - Technique, S74, S80, S81, S92, S959
        - Development of, S762, S1074
    - Time, S753, S758
- Narrator, first-person, S18
- Opposition and contradiction, S752, S762
- Past, S1096
- Patterns, S754
- and *The Progress of Love*, story comparisons, S96
- Self
    - Authentic selfhood, S115
    - Self-definition, S65
- Silence, S62
- Small town, social and cultural aspects, S1225
- Stories and storytelling, S106
    - by Narrators, S1025, S1211
    - and Truth, S1025, S1026, S1064
- Style, S981
- Surprise, poetics of, S41, S757
- Time and space, disjunction in, S128
- Travel and personal change, S1064

Voice, S121
Writing of, S771
"The Moons of Jupiter," S18, S65, S106, S121, S128, S768, S771, S971, S1076, S1167
    Autobiographical aspects, S765, S771, S1187
    Critical analysis, overview, interpretation, S752, S762
    Death, **P873**
    Disarrangement, S109
    Elegiac fiction, S104, S770
    Ending, nonending, S109
    Father-daughter relationship, S82, **S768**
    Narrative structure, S759, S959
        and Narrative time, S758
    Stories and storytelling, S1026
    Understatement, S109
Moore, Brian. *The Doctor's Wife*, P852
Moore, Lorrie
Who Will Run the Frog Hospital? **S130**
Morality/moral behaviour, P865; **S90**, **S120**, S946, S981, **S1205**, **S1236**. *See also* Ethics
Morris, Wright, P841
Morrison, Toni. *The Bluest Eye*, **S910**
Mother(s), **S18**, **S49**, S753, **S768**. *For mother of Alice Munro see* Laidlaw, Anne Clarke (Chamney)
    Mock mothers/mothering clowns, S768
        Role of female artist as, S768
    Munro as mother, P910; S765, S790, S996, S1043, S1118
    Role of, and female gender roles, **S61**, **S131**
Mother-child relationship, S90, S1095
Mother-daughter relationship, **S18**, S33, **S49**, **S74**, **S75**, **S81**, **S99**, **S108**, **S132**, S752, S753, S755, S759, **S768**, **S842**, S942. *See also* Storytelling, mother-daughter
    Ambivalence in, **S49**, **S132**, S969, S1129
    and Connection, **S82**
    Daughters as narrators, **P891**, **P899**; **S99**, S842
    Death, loss of mother, S104, S770
    Demeter and Persephone myth, **S837**
    and Gossip, **S51**, S976
    Guilt of daughter, S24, S860
    and Identity formation, **S61**, S82
    Influence of mother
        and Artistic development of daughter, S108, **S110**, **S132**, **S1099**
    Irigaray, Luce, **S842**
    Maternal inheritance, **S828**
    Memories of mother, S828
        as an Uncontrollable element, S753
    Mourning of daughter, S104, **S770**, S1141
    Munro's relationship with daughters, **S765**

Mother-daughter relationship (cont.)
    and Secrets/secrecy, **S896**
    and Self-development of daughter, **S61, S108, S933**
    Twin identity of mother and daughter, **S860**
Motifs, S73, **S754, S914**
Motion and stillness. *See* Photography—Paradox of photographic vision
Mourning. *See* Grief, mourning
"Mrs. Cross and Mrs. Kidd," S106, S121
    Allusions, **S872**
    Angle of vision, stylistic and structural, **S19**
    Archetypes, S872, **S875**
    Critical analysis, overview, interpretation, S752, S762
    Elderly in nursing homes, **P872**
    Narrative structure, circular, S872, **S875**
    Narrative technique, contrapuntal
        and Characters, **S19**
    Symbolism, **S872, S875**
Munro, Alice. *See also* Aesthetic (artistic vision); Awards; Career; Publication; Vision of life; Vision of the World; Writing (Alice Munro)
    General (life, career, writing), **S775,** S778, S783, S786, S790, S793, **S797,** S804, S814, S815, S825, S844, S854, S877, S882, **S890,** S894, **S905,** S908, S909, S931, S932, S946, S947, S949, **S950,** S972, S985, S986, **S988,** S996, **S1009,** S1011, S1022, S1036, S1039, S1042, **S1043,** S1050, S1059, S1072, S1080, **S1085,** S1102, S1118, S1119, S1135, S1136, S1137, S1138, S1149, S1161, S1192, S1193, S1196, S1197, S1201, S1210, S1216, S1218, S1223, **S1224,** S1232, S1234, S1235, S1241
    Life, S750, S752, S758, **S765, S769, S771,** S890
        Early life (childhood, adolescence), P658, P684, P841, P842, **P843,** P847, P855, **P893, P906, P909,** P910; S39, **S765, S771,** S815, S882, S939, S985, S1039, **S1112,** S1161
            Disguise, need for, P906; S1039, S1119, S1223
            Imagination in, **S83**
            Outsider, feelings of being an, P660, **P869,** P887; S1119, S1174
            Reading in, **P696, P862, P869, P879, P890; S83, S769,** S1039, S1234
            in Wingham, **P695,** P857, **P909;** S905, S950, S1043, S1119, **S1150,** S1174
            Writing in, P653, P841, **P843,** P857, P877, P878, **P879,** P893, P903; S39, S765, S769, S825, S877, S882, S950, S985, S1039, S1161, **S1174,** S1201, S1223
        Employment, P893, P902
        Marriage, **P910,** P855; **S765, S769, S771,** S815, S905, S1043, S1115, S1201, S1223
        Public readings, S819, S923, S932, S946, S947, S1081, S1155
        Socioeconomic background, P865, P875; S763, S1000, S1241
Munro, Catherine, P910; S765, S771
Munro, James (Jim), P861, P895, P902, P910; **S765, S771,** S786, S905, S1072, S1137, S1149
Munro, Sheila, **S765,** S771
    Lives of Mothers and Daughters, S780, S925, S1117, S1157
Munro's Book Store, S765, S908, S985, S1235
Munrovia. *See* Huron County (Southwestern Ontario)
Murdoch, Iris. *An Unofficial Rose,* **S1054**

Subject Index 417

Muriel Snow ("A Real Life"), S17, S1020
Murray Zeigler ("Oranges and Apples"), S1004
Music teachers and pupils. *See under* Characters (types)
"My Mother's Dream," P910; S999
    Artist, female, S755
    Moral behaviour and empathy, S90
Myra Sayla ("Day of the Butterfly"), S873
Mysterious characters. *See under* Characters (types)
Mystery, **P701**; S39. *See also* Secrets/secrecy
    Antidetection, S14
    Mystery story and time, S805
    and Ordinary life, S29
    and Presence in photography, S820
    Silence and, S62, S1051
    and Truth, S14, S62
Mystification. *See under* Narrative techniques
Myth(s) and mythology. *See also* Archetypes; Legend(s)
    Amor and Psyche, S45
    Biblical, **S1032**
    Demeter and Persephone, S837
    Demythologizing and legend-making, S827
    and Imagination in childhood, S83
    Landscapes, mythical, S767
    Orpheus, S833
    Rivers, mythical qualities of, **P682**; S73, **S91**
    of Scottish nation-builder, frontier myths, S15

Names, P865; **S754**, **S849**
    Lists of, **S915**
Naomi (*Lives of Girls and Women*), S2, S50, S86, S91, S102, S110, S116, S118, S123, S130, S131, S766, S767, S801, S901, S926, S979, S1038, S1104
Naomi's father (*Lives of Girls and Women*), S25, S767
Naomi's mother (*Lives of Girls and Women*), S131
Narration, S752, S845
    and Characters, female, S942
    and Letter-writing, S885
    and Truth, S41, S52, S757
    and Voice, S84
Narrative complexity, S830, S1116. *See also* Narrative structure, complexity in
Narrative devices. *See also* Letters and letter-writing
    Ellipsis, **S109**, **S1012**
    Embedding, **S19**, **S21**, **S868**, **S1012**
    Gothic, **S10**
    House as narrative device, **S818**
    Inversion, S19
    Irony, **S19**, **S74**, **S767**, **S1020**

Narrative devices (cont.)
    Linking, S58
    Oxymoron, S19, S874
    Pronouns, S1063
Narrative form
    Connectedness of form, S92
    and Content, S17
    Linked short stories and novel form, S1107
    and Narrative time, S46
    Open form, S58
    and Theme, evolution of, S124
Narrative implication, S940
Narrative instability, S41, S129, S757
Narrative method. *See* Narrative technique
Narrative movement
        and Travel, journey (metaphorical), S1243
Narrative perspective. **P862**: S24, S31, S93, S121, S752, S753, S759, S959, S1060. *See also under individual works*
    Aesthetic distance and reader response, S53
    and Double distancing, S24, S884
    in Early stories, S32
    Female, S24, S30, S38, S64, S96, S1059
    First-person, S18, S24
        and Confessional narrative, S24, S1222
    Male, P901: S24
    Multiple, S41, S757, S996
    and Narrative technique, **P862**, P886
    Retrospective, S24, S74, S81, S87, S841, S1060, S1101, S1182
    and Subjectivity, S129
    Variable dual, S119
Narrative space, gaps, S999
    and Secrets, S1147
Narrative strategy, S57, S121, S1171. *See also under individual works*
    Arrangement, S1076
    Contingency and piecing, S1069
    Disarrangement, S17, S109, S785, S809, S1023, S1076
    Disruption, S41, S757, S935
    and Fictional realism, S827
    Grotesque as, S85
    Historical method, S795, S1056
    and Shifting subject of self, S107, S1151
    and Short-story genre, S944
    and Triggering event, S845
    Unsettlement, S1209

Narrative structure, P886, **P902**; **S17**, **S18**, **S22**, **S60**, **S69**, **S84**, **S754**, **S759**, **S762**, **S788**, **S836**, **S959**, **S999**, **S1052**,**S1108**. *See also under individual works*
    Circular, **S60**, **S754**, **S875**
    Complexity in, **P893**, P896; **S17**
    Contrapuntal, **S1016**
    House (metaphorical) and, **P702**; **S818**, S953
    and Iterative technique, **S758**
    and Narrative time, **S60**, **S755**, **S758**
    and Neo-Gothic connectedness, **S801**
    Story collections, arrangement of, **S759**, **S959**, **S1016**
    and Style, **S1067**
Narrative technique, **P843**, P886; **S129**, **S752**, **S753**, **S886**, **S980**, **S1063**, S1104. *See also under individual works*
    Characterization, character identity, S19, **S42**, **S86**, **S813**, **S898**, **S910**, **S930**, **S990**
    Cinematic, **S1095**
    Development of, **P862**, **P886**, P896; **S40**, **S92**, **S119**, **S758**, **S759**, **S762**, **S832**, **S855**, **S959**, **S1074**, **S1076**, **S1182**
        and Vision, development of, **S32**
    and Elegiac fiction, **S104**, **S770**
    Memory, use of, **P893**; **S785**
    Munro's lack of analysis of, **P862**; S761
    and Narrative perspective, **P862**, P886
    and Photography, **S134**, **S774**
    and Theme, **S81**, **S92**, **S124**
    Time, use of, **S46**, **S74**, **S758**, **S861**, **S945**, **S1220**
    and Unity, **S58**, S1109
Narrative techniques. *See also under individual works*
    Ambiguity, **S17**
    of Closure, **S80**, **S861**
    Contradiction and opposition, **S19**, **S752**, **S762**, **S963**
    Contrapuntal, in character construction, **S19**
    Double distancing, **S24**, **S884**
    Entanglement, **S1209**
    Fragmentation, **S22**, **S92**
    Indeterminacy, **S17**, **S80**, **S759**, **S953**
    Iterative technique, **S758**, **S945**
    Layering, P893, **P896**; **S900**, **S904**
        of Voice, male and female, **S121**
    Mystification, **S19**
    Narrative dialectics, **S1182**
    Nonending, **S109**
    Opposition
        and Incongruity/contradiction, **S19**, **S752**, **S762**
        Rhetorical opposition, **S963**
    Projection, **S898**

Narrative techniques (cont.)
    Retrospective, **S81**, **S1182**
        Dual-voiced, **S119**, **S1182**
    Synecdoche, **S916**
    Understatement, suggestion, **S109**
Narrative time, **S18**, **S762**. *See also* Time
    Fragmentation in, **S27**
    and Iterative technique, **S758**, **S945**
    and Narrative structure, **S60**, **S755**, **S758**
    Time shifts, **P881**; S1220
Narrator(s), **S119**, **S752**, **S757**, **S830**, **S942**. *See also* Storytelling by narrators
    Authority of, **S106**, **S752**
    Daughters as narrators
        and Mother-daughter relationship, **P891**, **P899**; **S99**, S842
    First-person, **S18**, **S752**, S1222
    Narrative strategies used by, **S1203**
    Narrator/character/reader relationship, **S126**
    as Observers and observed/participants, P659; **S119**, **S753**
    Perspective of, **P891**, **P899**; S1171
    Retrospective
        and Double vision, **S87**, **S752**, **S1060**, S1101
    Voice of, **S84**, S798, **S1001**
        and Autobiographical material, **S1075**
        and Characters, **S121**
Nature. *See also* Pastoralism; Space, Natural
    Natural environment
        and Small town, **S73**
    Natural landscape, space, **S97**
    and Postmodernism, **S810**
    and Technology, **S76**
    and Violence, **S866**
"Nettles," P905
    Senses, smell
        and Reader response, **S847**
The Newcomers [series]. *See* "1847: The Irish"
The New Yorker
    Editorial advice, P865, P895, P902
    Editors and editorial policy, P902, P905; **S771**, S890, S1088
    Publication in, P862, P897
        and Munro's career, **P904**; S771, S985, S1011, S1027, S1040, **S1045**, S1181, S1219
        and Reader response, **S807**
Newmark, Peter, S98
Neo-Gothicism, self-reflexive. *See under* Gothicism, Gothic
Nile Morrison ("Princess Ida"), S102, S122, S767
Nin, Anaïs. *The Early Diary of Anaïs Nin*, **S45**
Noncommunication. *See* Communication—Inability to communicate

Nora Cronin ("Walker Brothers Cowboy"), S753, S757, S767, S768, S769, S840, S1046
Nostalgia
 as the Grotesque, **S1094**
 and Pastoralism, S76
Not-telling. *See under* Communication
Novel form. *See* Narrative form—Linked short stories and novel form; Short-story genre—
 Short story vs. novel

O'Brien, Mary, S70
Objects, P865
 Domestic, and women, **S1070**
 Layering of, **S900**
 Treachery to, in writing, P660, **P664**
 Treatment of, and teaching, **S1089**
Observation, capacity for. *See* Artistic mind
Observers (narrators, characters)
 Detached, and control over death, S753
 and Participants/observed, **P659**; S119, S753
O'Connor, Flannery, P841, P848; **S16**, **S47**, S91, **S1105**, **S1199**
 "A Good Man Is Hard to Find," S1058
"The Office," S18, S40, S768, S862
 Artist/writer, female, **S36**
 Autobiographical aspects, **P694**; S765, S771
 Critical analysis, overview, interpretation, S752, S762, S1078
 Hero, female, **S94**
 Narrative structure, open, **S60**
 Narrative technique, **S119**, **S886**
 Space, private, and women, **S821**
Old(er) women. *See under* Characters (types)—Female. *See also* Women, middle-aged
Old age. *See* Elderly persons
Ondaatje, Michael, **S134**, **S774**, **S856**
Ontario, rural. *See* Rural Ontario
Open-endedness. *See* Endings—Nonending
Open form. *See under* Narrative form
Open Secrets, P896, **P897**, P898, P901; S771, S800, S882, S1118
 Critical analysis, overview, interpretation, S759
  Discussion guide, **S1073**
 Critical reception, **S771**
 Fate, destiny, **S124**
 Identity, female, **S129**
 Language and women, **S129**
 Layering of narrative, P896; **S904**
 Mystery, surprise, bewilderment, **S39**
 Narrative form and theme, **S124**
 Narrative structure
  and Narrative time, **S758**

Open Secrets (cont.)
    Narrative technique, **S124, S129**
    Reality, **S124**, S129
    Time, passing of, **S755**
    "Vandals" as coda to, **S904**
    Wilderness (metaphorical)
        and Change in women, **S1146**
    Women's experience, **S129**
"Open Secrets," P653; S17, S960
    Critical analysis, overview, interpretation, S759
    Language, **S835**
    Mystery, anti-detection, **S14, S805**
    Narrative
        of Community, **S129**
        Narrative implication, **S940**
    Pivot point, **S755**
    Steinbeck, John. *Of Mice and Men*, **S835**
    Truth, multiplicity of, **S14**
    Wilderness (metaphorical)
        and Change in women, **S1146**
Opposites and similarities, patterns of, **S754**
Opposition and incongruity/contradiction. *See under* Narrative techniques
Oppositional archetypes. *See under* Archetypes
"Oranges and Apples," S65, S960
    Critical analysis, overview, interpretation, **S759**
    Immigrants, visible, **S852**
    Political correctness, S852, **S1004**
    Revisions, P892
Order and chaos/disorder
    Art/fiction and control, order, S56, **S992**
    Double vision of the world, **S66**
    and Fragmentation, **S22, S92**
    Garrison (conventional society)
        and "The Other country," **S767**
Ordinary and extraordinary. *See* Familiar and strange
Origins of stories. *See under* Stories. *See also under individual stories*
Orphan figures. *See under* Characters (types)
Orpheus myth. *See under* Myths
"The Other Country." *See also* Outsiders
    Archetypes, oppositional (inclusive, exclusive), **S867**
    and Garrison (conventional society), **S66, S766, S767, S1007, S1008**
"The Ottawa Valley," S18, S856, S967, S983, S992, S1141, S1175, S1183, S1215
    Artist/writer, female, **S36**
    Autobiographical aspects, P849; **S771**, S1187
    Critical analysis, overview, interpretation, **S752**, S759, **S761**, S762
    Grotesque as narrative strategy, **S85**

Imagination in childhood, **S83**
Mother, S104, S768, S770
Mother-daughter relationship, **S99**, **S132**, **S896**, **S969**
    Twin identity of mother and daughter, **S860**
Narrative structure
    and Narrative time, **S758**
  Past, **S1096**
"An Ounce of Cure," S18, S52, S765, S992, S1060, S1104
    Critical analysis, overview, interpretation, S762
    Narrative technique, **S886**
        Development of, **S32**, **S119**
    Narrator as observer and observed/participant, **P659**
Outsiders, **P869**; **S867**, **S873**. *See also* Characters (types)—Eccentric, unconventional; "The Other country"
Owen Jordan ("Age of Faith"), S86, S130, S801
Oxymoron. *See under* Narrative devices

Paradigmatic discourse. *See under* Discourse
Paradox(es), S752, S753, **S766**, **S1104**
    and Authority, **S1126**
    and Double vision, **S963**, **S1038**
    of Femininity, and female artist, **S1092**
    Humour of, **S1038**
    and Parallels, S762
    of Photographic vision, **S134**, **S774**, **S1233**, **S1246**
    and Style, **S1067**
Parallel lives. *See under* Double vision
Parallels/interconnections between stories. *See under* Stories
Parent-child relationship. *See under* Family relationships
Parody, **S1233**
Participants/observed (narrators, characters)
    and Observers, **P659**; **S119**, **S753**
"Passion," P909
Passion story groups. *See* Bible/biblical—Story groups
Past, P909; **S128**, **S1096**. *See also* Family heritage
    and Connection, dislocation, **S82**
    Defiance of, **S1002**
    Ethos of, **S1140**
    and Identity, **S759**
    and Memory, P859, P894, P906, P907; **S41**, **S755**, **S757**
    Painful past and defence, psychological, **S78**
    and Present, **S901**, **S1096**
        and Photography as technique, **S134**, **S774**
    Public and private history, **S1096**
    and Small towns, heritage of, **S118**, **S120**
    Truth of, **S848**, **S954**

Past (cont.)
    and Uncertainty. **S965**
    Uncontrollable elements of. **S753**
Pastoralism
    and Industrialization, technology. **S76**, **S998**
Patriarchal
    Domination. *See* Power/domination, male
    Inheritance, female resistance to. **S958**
    Language. *See* Discourse, masculine/patriarchal
    Society. P673: **S63**, **S129**, **S1030**, S1212
Patricia Parry ("The Time of Death"). S753
Patrick Blatchford (*Who Do you Think You Are?*). S3, S41, S55, S100, S102, S110, S111, S120, S757
Patterns. **S754**, **S762**, **S767**, **S839**, **S840**. *See also* Cycles; Story collections—Story patterns/interconnections
    of Imagery, images. **S754**, **S839**, **S840**
    Images and incidents, recurrent. **S1186**
Pauline ("The Children Stay"). S833
Pauline poetic. **S883**
"The Peace of Utrecht." P862: S18, S40, S791, S818, S827, S862, S1015, S1164, S1215
    Autobiographical aspects. P842, P843, P886; S755, S765, **S771**, S1174, S1186, S1187
    Critical analysis, overview, interpretation. **S752**, **S753**, **S759**, **S762**, S1078
    Elegiac fiction. S104, S770, S1141
    Ending, nonending. **S109**
    Mother-daughter relationship. S49, **S99**, S755, S768, **S860**, S968
    Narrative technique, development of. **S32**, **S119**
    Past. **S1096**
    Small town (Jubilee). S37
        Autobiographical place. **S1180**
        Place and identity. **S1183**
    Space and identity. S37
    Stories and storytelling. S70, **S106**
    Surfaces and depths. **S1113**
    Understatement. **S109**
Peg Kuiper ("Fits"). S3, S41, S753, S757, S884, S1207
Perception
    Adolescent, and self-development. S989
    and Reality/truth. **S38**, **S831**, **S989**
        and Photography. **S134**, **S774**, **S820**, **S1233**
Performance. *See* Theatricality
Perry, William G., S929
Persecution. *See* Victimization
Persephone and Demeter myth. *See under* Myth(s) and mythology
Personal appearance. *See* Women—Appearance, personal
Phallicism. *See under* Psychology, psychoanalysis
The Photographer ("Epilogue: The Photographer"). S63

Photographic
> Realism, and elegiac fiction, **S104**, **S770**
> Style, and Gothic realism, **S28**
> Superrealism, **S134**, **S774**

Photography, photographs, **S12**, **S134**, **S768**, **S774**, **S820**, **S856**, **S1133**
> as Narrative technique, **S134**, **S774**
> Paradox of photographic vision, **S134**, **S774**, **S1233**, **S1246**
> and Reality/truth, **P862**; **S12**, **S134**, **S774**, **S820**, **S851**, **S869**, **S1233**
> Strange and familiar, **S1246**

"Pictures of the Ice," **S62**, **S107**, **S1151**
> Aging and culture, **S973**
> Deception, **S757**, **S1100**, **S1208**
> Discourse, double-voiced, **S755**
> Familiar and strange, **S1208**
> Intertextuality, **S973**, **S1100**
> Secrecy/secrets, **S1100**
>> and Epiphanic sites, **S1204**
> Silence, **S755**

Piecing, narrative. *See* Narrative strategy—Contingency and piecing

Pioneer/settler
> Culture, and attitudes to the past, **S1140**
> Scottish pioneers
>> and Cultural translation, **S15**, **S35**, **S924**
>> Mythology of, **S15**
> Society, **S17**, **S965**

Pivot points. *See under* Stories

Place, **P860**, **P862**, **P865**, **P869**; **S91**, **S105**, **S1034**, **S1106**. *See also* Maps and mapping; Regional settings; Regionalism
> Autobiographical place, and female writers, **S1180**
> and Characters, interdependence of, **S16**, **S32**, **S1183**
> in Early stories, importance of, **P845**; **S32**, **S119**, **S1183**
> Feeling of, **P846**, **P889**
> Geographical and historical place, **S956**
> and Identity, **S16**, **S17**, **S112**, **S767**, **S1005**, **S1183**
> and Space, **S1035**
> and Women, **S99**, **S112**

Poetry, Victorian. *See* Victorian poetry

Point-of-view. *See* Narrative perspective

Political correctness, **S852**, **S1004**
> Welty, Eudora. *The Golden Apples*, **P901**

Politics and writing. *See under* Writing (Alice Munro)

Poor, lower classes of women. *See* Women and social class

Poppy Cullender ("The Stone in the Field"), **P869**; **S1231**

"Post and Beam," **P674**; **S29**
> Secrets, family, **S991**

Possibility
    and Paradigmatic discourse, **S41**, **S757**
"Postcard"
    Body, female, **S30**
    Critical analysis, overview, interpretation, S762
    Narrative technique, **S886**
    Structure (linguistic, narrative, rhetorical), **S84**
    Voice, **S30**, **S84**
Postcolonial
    Discourse. *See under* Discourse
    Literature. *See under* Literature
Postmodernism. *See also* Metafiction; Metanarrative, feminist
    in Endings, **S983**
    and Nature, place, **S810**
Post-realism. *See under* Realism
Poverty, **S43**, **S864**, **S1103**
Power, **S27**
    Gossip and, **S51**, **S976**
    Language and, **S101**, **S115**
    Not-telling, withholding and, **S41**, **S757**
    and Powerlessness, **S753**
    and Social class, P865; **S43**, **S879**
Power, female, P865; **S753**, **S806**. *See also* Women, empowerment of
    and Desire, female, **S971**
    and Desiring female body, **S30**
    and Rape fantasy, **S899**
Power/domination, male, **S1217**. *See also* Patriarchal society
    Female struggle against, **S115**
        and Accommodation, **S57**
    and Language, male, **S115**
    and Poor, lower classes of women, **S43**
    and Sacrifice, female, **S33**
Pratt, Mary, S1092
Present and past. *See* Past and present.
Pretension, disapproval of. *See under* Canadian national characteristics
Price, Reynolds, P841
Primitives. *See under* Characters (types)—Female
"Princess Ida," S768, S1111
    Critical analysis, overview, interpretation, **S751**
    Elegiac fiction, S104, S770
    Storytelling, mother-daughter, **S70**
    Themes, feminist, **S7**
"Privilege," S768, S839, S856
    Autobiographical aspects, P854, P855, P859
    Love, and identity formation, **S1005**
    Revisions, **S103**

The Progress of Love
- Aging women, **S767**
    - and Body, female, **S975**
- Characters (types)
    - Controlled and controlling, **S753**
    - Female, **S55**
- Complicity, deception, **S41, S757**
- Connection and dislocation, **S82**
- Control and loss of control, **S753**
- Critical analysis, overview, interpretation, **S39**, S752, S759, S767, S769, **S911, S978**, S1009, **S1012**, S1036
- Critical reception, **S771**
- and *Dance of the Happy Shades*, story comparisons, **S96**
- Discourse, paradigmatic, **S41, S757**
- Elegiac fiction, **S104, S770**
- Fate, destiny, and self, **S752**
- Feminine world, **S55**
- Human relationships, **S3**
- Memory, **S41, S757, S785**
- and *The Moons of Jupiter*, story comparisons, **S96**
- Narration and truth, **S41, S752, S757**
- Narrative devices, **S1012**
    - Ellipsis, S759, **S1012**
    - Embedding, **S1012**
- Narrative form and theme, **S124**
- Narrative perspective, **S24, S96, S121, S1012**
- Narrative space, gaps in, **S999**
- Narrative strategy, **S121**
- Narrative structure, **S18**
    - and Narrative time, **S758**
- Narrative technique
    - Development of, **S762**
    - and Theme, **S92, S124**
- Narrative techniques
    - Fragmentation, **S22**
    - Indeterminacy, **S759, S953**
- Narrator, first-person, **S18**
- Paradoxes and parallels, **S762**
- Past, **S1002, S1096**
- Patterns, **S754**, S1012
- Reality, **S41, S124, S757**
- Self-definition, **S65**
- Short-story cycle, **S113**
- Silence, **S62**
- Style, **S981**
- Themes, **S92, S96, S124**

The Progress of Love (cont.)
    Title, selection of, P882
    Voice, **S121**
"The Progress of Love," P886; S18, S82, S768, S771, S999, S1076
    Critical analysis, overview, interpretation, **S752**, S759, S762
    Elegiac fiction, S104, S770, S1141
    Identity, female, S755
        and Space/place, **S112**
    Morality
        and Country and town/city, **S1205**
    Narrative structure, **S60**
        and Narrative time, **S758**
    Narrative technique, **S1169**
        Indeterminacy, **S953**
    Origin of story, P881, P886, P889
    Past, **S755**, **S1002**, **S1096**
    Reality/truth and art/fiction, **S957**, **S1205**
    Secrets
        Family secrets, **S112**, **S1169**
        and Mother-daughter relationship, **S896**
    Storytelling, mother-daughter, **S70**
Projection. *See under* Narrative techniques
Pronouns. *See under* Language
Prostitute figures. *See under* Characters (types)
Protagonists, female
    and Escape, **P846**; **S1057**
        from Expected roles, **S942**
    as Narrators, **S752**
    and Small town, S88, **S110**, **S118**, **S120**, **S938**, **S1010**, S1127, **S1128**
Protestant ethic, P852, P855, P893
Proust, Marcel, S861
"Providence," S1111
    Critical analysis, overview, interpretation, S762
    Deception and delusion, **S1206**
    Duality, female, **S860**
    Revisions, **S103**
"Prue," S3
    Critical analysis, overview, interpretation, S762
Prue ("Visitors"), S1025
Psychological
    Defense, **S78**
    Violence, **S880**
Psychology, psychoanalysis
    and Art/fiction, S71
    Attachment and separation, **S2**

Attachment theory, **S34**, **S53**
Individuation, **S2**, S794
Phallicism, **S1129**
Schizothymia in characters, **S901**
Public readings. *See under* Munro, Alice
Publication (Alice Munro), P841, P848, P891
    in Canadian journals, P903; S771
    and Short-story length, P897
Publicity and book promotion, P841, P848, P855, P863, P867, P868, P874, P886, P891; **S825**, S917, S972, S986, S1059, S1080, S1192
Publisher/editor relations, **P879**; **S67**, **S763**, **S771**, S777, S782, **S807**, S890, **S919**, S964, S1027. *See also* Gibson, Douglas; *The New Yorker*
Puppet figures. *See under* Characters (types)
Puritanism. *See also* Sexuality, female—Repression of
    and Disempowerment of women, **S15**

"A Queer Streak," **P885**; S100, S121, S900, S975, S1012
    Critical analysis, overview, interpretation, **S752**, **S753**
Quest. *See also under* Identity; Real life
    and Female characters, P865
    and Female hero, **S94**
    for Knowledge, **S752**
    Religious, spiritual, **S29**
    for Self, and other, **S752**
    Questing in childhood
        and Heroic imagination, **S83**
Quinn, Alice. *See* Publisher/editor relations
Quinn, Mrs. ("The Love of a Good Woman"), S830, S883, S1032, S1116

Ralph Gillespie ("Who Do You Think You Are?"), S41, S44, S100, S102, S111, S757, S883, S927, S930, S1005, S1212, S1246
Rape fantasy. *See under* Sex/sexuality, female
Reader(s)
    Christian, and the grotesque, **S1199**
    Complicit, **S883**
    Expectation, **S935**, **S942**
    Narrator/character/reader relationship, **S126**, S886
    Response, P848, P856, P887, P891; **S31**, **S807**, **S824**, **S929**, S932, S946, S1082, S1116
        and Aesthetic distance, **S53**
        Attachment theory and, **S34**, **S53**
        and Elegiac fiction, **S104**, **S770**
        Female characters and, **S25**
        and Smell, **S847**
    and Stories as experiences, **P892**
    Survey of readers, S781

Reader(s) (cont.)
    Survey of writers as readers, S1240
    and Textual and extratextual reality, **S126**
    Women as reader figures, S768

Reading
    Allegories of, **S843**
    Body as text, text as body, **S811**
    Eating as a metaphor for, **S768**
    as a Historically conditioned act, **S998**
    Munro, Alice, P839, P841, P846, **P856**, **P865**, **P879**, P886, P894; S759, S765, S946
        in Early life, **P696**, **P862**, **P869**, **P879**, **P890**; **S83**, **S769**, S1039, S1234
        Favourite books/stories and writers, **P862**, P865, P877, P895
        Method of reading stories, **P653**, **P698**, **P702**, P867, **P869**, P894, **P904**, **P906**; S750
    and Writing, links between, P865, P879, **P890**

Real life, S752, S1087
    Illusion of, and use of detail, S129
    Quest for, **S91**, S1105
        and Artistic mind, S77

"A Real Life," P675; S17, S1118
    Gender roles, **S129**
        and Marriage, **S105**
    Satire and irony, **S1020**
    Wilderness and women, **S105**
    Wilderness (metaphorical)
        and Change in women, **S1146**
    Women's experience, **S129**

Realism, S72, S759
    and Artistic mind, S77
    Documentary realism, S126
    and Elegiac fiction, **S104**, **S770**
    Fictional realism
        Rhetorical strategies for, **S827**
    Gothic realism, **S10**, **S28**
    Heightened realism, **S879**, S990
    Magic realism, P841; **S12**, **S125**, **S1061**, **S1104**
    Postrealism, **S101**
    Superrealism, **S5**, **S129**, **S1237**
        Photographic superrealism, **S134**, **S774**

Reality, P891; **S22**, **S38**, **S124**, **S752**, **S766**, **S962**, **S963**. *See also* Double vision; Fantasy and reality; Fictional reality; Strange and familiar; Surface appearance and reality/truth
    Alternate, contradictory realities, **P897**; S72
    Epiphanic understanding of, S104, S770, S1141
    and Fiction (other-than-real), **S10**, **S41**, S752, S757, **S827**, **S1167**, **S1171**
        in Mysterious characters, **P884**
    Instability of, S41, S129, S757

and Legend, S40, S752, S1113
and Memory, **P886**, P907; S785
and Perception, S38, S831, S989
Photography and, **P862**; S12, S134, S774, S820, S851, S869, S1233
Promoting/undoing of, S41, S757
and Truth, S754
Reality/truth and art/fiction, S12, S752, S1066, S1167, S1175, S1205
    Transforming reality into fiction, **P687, P702, P891, P897**. *See also* Writing (Alice Munro)—Autobiographical, personal aspects—Reality as basis for fiction
"Red Dress—1946," S49, S828, S969, S1069, S1212
    Autobiographical aspects, S771
    Critical analysis, overview, interpretation, S762
    Past, **S1096**
    Reader response, **S929**
Regional settings, S990. *See also* Huron County; Rural Ontario; Small town
    Characters in, S16, S32, S1183
    Importance of, in early stories, **P845**; S32, S119, S1183
Regionalism, P841, **P858**, P862, P894, P901, **P906, P907**, P909; S73, **S767, S1106, S1164**. *See also* Place
    and American South, writers of the, S16, S47, S91
    Functional relationships within region, S122
    and Identity, S16, S1183
    Spatial and historical discourse of region, S956
Rejection, S3, S91, S753, S863
Religion, S25, S38
    Calvinism, S35, S1120, S1196
    Christianity and the grotesque, **S1199**
    and Church, S48
    O'Connor, Flannery, S47, S1105, S1199
    Puritanism, Scottish fundamentalist
        and Disempowerment of women, S15
    and Small town, S25, S120, S1158
    Spirituality
        and Vision of life (Alice Munro), S29
Repression, female. *See* Sexuality, female—Repression of; Women—Repression of
Retrospective perspective. *See under* Narrative perspective
Retrospective technique. *See under* Narrative techniques
Reverend Walter McBain ("A Wilderness Station"), S15, S924
Revision, **P653**, P702, P865, **P895**, P896; S789, S1210. *See also under individual works*
    and Editors, importance of, **P879**
Rhea ("Spaceships Have Landed"), S1018
Rhetorical
    Angle of vision, S19
    Opposition, S963
    Strategies for fictional realism, S827
    Structure, **S84**

"Rich as Stink"
    Motifs
        and Brontë, Charlotte. *Jane Eyre*, **S914**
Richards, David Adam
    Blood Ties, **S120**
    Road to the Stilt House, **S120**
Rites of passage, female. *See* Initiation rites, female
Rivers, mythical qualities of, **P682**; S73, **S91**
"The Robber Bridegroom," *See under* Fairy tales—Grimm's Fairy Tales
Robert Deal ("Friend of My Youth"), S812, S914, S1004
Robert Kuiper ("Fits"), S41, S753, S757, S1207
Roberta ("Labor Day Dinner"), S3, S753, S1195
Robina ("Executioners"), S80, S753, S1091
Role-playing, **S22**, **S93**, **S752**. *See also* Theatricality
    and Identity, female/feminine, **S11**, **S112**, **S1170**
    and Self-construction, **S101**, **S102**
Romantic
    Fantasy. *See* Fantasy, romantic and Gothic
    Heroine. *See under* Hero, female/heroine
    Imagination
        and Fantasizing in childhood, **S83**
Rose ("Characters"), S753, S862
Rose (*Who Do You Think You Are?*), **P854**, **P859**; S768, S877
    Artistic development, **S39**, **S81**, **S110**, **S903**, **S1099**
    Characterization, **S42**, S102, **S930**, S1039
    Garrison mentality, S1110
    Heroine, **S9**
    Identity and identity formation. *See under Who Do You Think You Are?*
    as Persona of Alice Munro, **S100**
    Revisions to character of, **S103**
    Role-playing; Self-construction; Self-development. *See under Who Do You Think You Are?*
    Self-knowledge, P857
    Vision of the world, multi-world, **S66**
Ross ("Monsieur les Deux Chapeaux"), S753
Ross, Sinclair, **S88**
    As for Me and My House, S1097
    "One's a Heifer," S865
Roy Fowler ("Wood"), S753, S839
Roy, Gabrielle, **S122**, S931
    La Route d'Altamont, **S87**, **S920**
    Rue Deschambault, **S23**
"Royal Beatings," P653; S765, S1106, S1143, S1211
    Critical analysis, overview, interpretation, **S753**, S759, S762, **S1248**
    Disarrangement, **S1023**
    Father, **P855**; S33, S93

Linguistic modality, **S1144**
Narrative perspective, **S92**
New Yorker, editors and editorial policy, P902; S771, **S1088**
Revisions, **S103**
Role-playing, P886; S93
Speech, **S1145**
Storytelling, mother-daughter, **S70**, S93
Strange and familiar, **S1017**
Themes, **S93**
Violence and female sacrifice, **S33**
Vision and aurality, **S31**
Ruby Carruthers ("Privilege"), S768
Runaway: Stories, **P908**, **P909**; S825
"Runaway"
Names and naming, **S849**
Origin of story, P676
Rupert Quinn ("The Love of a Good Woman"), S830, S883, S1116
Rural
Life, pattern of, **P870**
Ontario
Characters' connection with, **S1183**
Gothic, grotesque aspects of, P865
Preservation of public land in, **P700**
Social and cultural history, **S1225**
and Urban. *See* Country and town/city
and Urban landscape. *See under* Landscape

Sacrifice, female, **S33**
and Desire, personal, **S71**
Sam Grazier ("The Moon in the Orange Street Skating Rink"), S753
Sapphire. *Push*, S20
Satire, S753, **S1020**
"Save the Reaper," P677; S765
Mother-daughter relationship
Demeter and Persephone myth, **S837**
O'Connor, Flannery, "A Good Man Is Hard to Find," **S1058**
Origin of story, P678
Silence, not-telling, **S1051**
Time, **S805**
"Vandals," similarities with, S837
Scott, Walter, "Marmion," S1100
Scotland, S823
Scottish
Ancestors (Alice Munro), **P663**, **P899**; **S35**, **S765**, **S769**, **S771**, S924
Influence, **S15**, **S1094**, S1221

Scottish (cont.)
    Literature, and Canadian literature
        Cross-cultural perspective, S35
    Pioneers
        and Cultural translation, S15, S35, S924, S1249
        Mythology of, S15
Seasons
    and Landscape, rural and urban, S1106
    Patterns of, S754
Secrets/secrecy, **P701**; S753, S759, S773, **S906**, **S960**, **S997**, **S1100**, **S1172**. *See also* Mystery
    and Epiphanic sites, S1204
    Family secrets, S991, S1169
    and Mothers, fathers, S896
    and Narrative space, gaps, S1147
    and Women, S967, S991
Selected Stories, P902
    Critical reception, S750, S771
    Publication of, S771
Self
    Authentic selfhood, S115
        and Male-female relationships, **S1086**
    Care of, S102
    and Fate, destiny, S752
    Feminine self, and Gothicism, S801
    and Other, S752
        Care of others, S71, S90
    Shifting subject of, S107, S1151
    Subject of self and female artist, S768
Self-construction, S102
    Gossip and, S51, S976
    Role-playing and, S101, S102
Self-definition, S65
    and Autobiography, S1187
Self-development, female, **P848**; S6, S9, S25, S26, S45, S101, S116, S123, S794, S798, S910, S989, S1077, S1245. *See also* 'Bildungsroman'
    and Artistic development, S39, S61, S75, S865, S1079
    and Gothicism, S801
    and Language, S61, S927
    and Mother-daughter relationship, S61, S108, S933
    and Storytelling, S1084, S1211
    Theme of, and narrative technique, S1220
    as a Universal experience, S130
Self-image, self-imaging, S38, S768
Self-knowledge, S877
    and Human relationships, S3

Self-referring fiction. *See* Metafiction
Senses, S846
    Smell and reader response, S847
Sensibility
    Feminine, **S74**, S778, S890, S909, S1085, S1092, S1193
        and Style, **S117**
    and Sense, **S40**, S754
Separation
    and Attachment, and identity formation, **S2**
    and Distance, dialectics of, **S19**, S870
Setting, **P846**. *See also* Regional settings; Regionalism; Small town
    in Early stories, importance of, **P845**; **S32**, **S119**, S1183
    Historical and social setting, S1096
    and Postmodernism, S810
Settler. *See* Pioneer/settler
Sex/sexuality, female, P893, P909; **S4**, **S112**, **S114**, S800, S890, **S1046**, S1137, S1241
    and Aging, P844, P848, P892
    Attitudes toward, **S812**, S1004
    Fantasy, sexual, **S127**, S987
        Rape fantasy, and female initiation rites, S899
    and Quest, religious, spiritual, **S29**
    Repression of, **S7**, **S8**, S1195
    Sexual humiliation, S753
    Teaching about sexuality, S876
    as an Uncontrollable element, S753
Sex roles. *See* Gender roles
Sexual desire, female, **S8**, S768, **S1173**, **S1189**. *See also* Desire, female; Sex/sexuality, female
Shame, **S93**. *See also* Humiliation
Sherriff family ("Epilogue: The Photographer"), S41, S87, S110, S757, S801, S1087
Sherriff, Mrs. ("Epilogue: The Photographer"), S131
"The Shining Houses," S765, S818, S839, S862, S1149, S1243
    Critical analysis, overview, interpretation, S752, S762
    Narrative technique, **S886**
        Development of, **S32**, **S119**
    Poverty, **S1103**
Short stories. *See* Stories
Short-story collections. *See* Story collections
Short-story cycle, P859; S1, S69, **S93**, **S99**, **S111**, **S113**, S980, S990, **S1005**, **S1147**
    Canadian short-story cycles, **S1006**, **S1065**
    Gaps between stories, P859
        and Secrets, S1147
    Modernist view of, **S1041**
    and Time, function of, S758
    Unity in, **S27**, **S111**, **S113**, S1109

Short-story genre
    in American literary culture. S763
    in Canada. P865; **S22.** S763. S931
    and Epiphany. **S755**
    and Gender, female. **S129.** S763. S767
    and Munro, Alice. P906. P907; S22. S844. S895. **S980.** S986. S1011. S1036. **S1136**
        Authority. **S67.** S763. **S1027**
        and Family responsibilities. **P653.** P863. P889. **P906**
        Innovation in. **S129**
        and Minor literature. **S965**
        Preference for short-story genre. P852. P862. P865. P878. P897; S790. S1055. S1119. S1197
        Short story vs. novel. P840. P841. **P842. P843.** P848. P857. P862. P863. P874. P880. P886. P892. P894. P901; S1043. S1241
        and Vision of life, the world. P853. P854. P860. P880. P908; **S1024**
    and Narrative strategy. **S944**
Siddicup. Mr. ("Open Secrets"). S835
Silence, silences. **S62. S755. S948**
    and Ellipsis. **S109**
    as Language. S835. **S1051**
    and Mystery. **S62. S1051**
"Silence." P679. P908. P909
Simon Herron ("A Wilderness Station"). S105
Simon ("Simon's Luck"). S55. S111. S133. S753. S767. S961. S1005. S1212
"Simon's Luck." S12. S806. S1066. S1076. S1095. S1111
    Critical analysis, overview, interpretation. S759. S762
    Gossip. **S976**
    Revisions. **S103**
Sister-brother relationship. *See* Family relationships—Brother-sister
Small town(s). **P695.** P854. P881. P886; **S73. S88. S118. S120. S1018. S1097.** S1232. *See also* Carstairs; Hanratty; *Lives of Girls and Women*—Small town (Jubilee); Town/city and country; Wingham, Ontario
    and Confinement. **P845; S88. S120**
    Escape from. S88. **S120. S1010. S1128**
    and Identity. **S37**
    Outsiders in, identities and roles. **P869**
    and Protagonist. S88. **S110. S118. S120. S938. S1010.** S1127. **S1128**
    Regional aspects of. **S122**
    and Religion. S25. **S120. S1158**
    Social and cultural aspects. **S1225**
    and Social class. **P909;** S43. S985. **S1158**
Smell. *See under* Senses
Snow. *See under* Metaphors
Social
    Class. **P853.** P875; S55. **S1103**
        and Small town. **P909;** S43. S985. **S1158**

Subject Index 437

  and Women. P865; **S43. S64. S864**
 Expectations
  of Behaviour, gender differences in. P857; S1161
  of Gender roles, female. P875; **S61. S129. S767**
 Humiliation. **S753**
 Transformation of women. *See* Change—Physical and social change in women
 World, and double vision. **S862**
Socialist-feminist criticism. *See under* Criticism, feminist
Socialization of girls. *See under* Gender roles
Society, conventional. *See under* Garrison
Something I've Been Meaning to Tell You
 Absence, discourse of. **S41. S757**
 American South, writers of the. **S91**
 Art/fiction and life. **S1066**
 Atmospheric evocation. **S5**
 Autobiographical material
  Confession, meditation. **S1075**
  and Voice of narrator. **S1075**
 Characterization, methods of. **S86. S898**
 Characters (types). **S768**
  Controlled and controlling. **S753**
  Female. **S74. S81. S86. S131. S767. S1091**
  Humiliated. **S753**
 Communication
  Inability to communicate. **S102. S766**
  Noncommunication. **S125**
  Telling and not-telling. **S41. S757**
 Connection. **S1062. S1244**
  and Dislocation. **S82**
 Control and loss of control. **S753**
 Critical analysis, overview, interpretation. **S39. S752. S756. S759. S761. S762. S766. S767. S769. S855. S911. S1174**
 Critical reception. **S771**
 Death. **S104. S770. S1142**
  and Transience of life. **S881**
 Deception. **S102**
 Defense, psychological
  and Wilderness (metaphorical). **S78**
 Discourse, paradigmatic. **S41. S757**
 Double vision. **S66. S963**
 Drowning. **S753**
 Elegiac fiction. **S104. S770. S1142**
 Epiphany. P860
 Gender roles. **S86. S131**
 Humiliation. **S753**
 Humour. **S5**

Something I've Been Meaning to Tell You (cont.)
- Identity, female
  - and Male/female relationships. S112
  - Quest for. S767
- Images, imagery, and themes. S13, S128
- Language
  - and Power. S101, S115
  - Pronouns. S1063
  - as Surface. S125
- Loss. S104, S770, S1142
- Love and hate/hostility, female. S767
- Memory. S785
- Mind-body. S102
- Mother-daughter relationship. S74, S81
- Munro, Alice
  - Comments on stories. P862
- Narrative form, open. S58
- Narrative perspective. S24, S81
- Narrative structure. S18, S756, S999, S1067
  - Contrapuntal structure. S1016
  - and Narrative time. S758
- Narrative technique. S74, S92, S1063
  - Development of. P862; S762, S1074
- Narrative techniques
  - of Closure. S80
  - Fragmentation. S22
  - Projection. S898
  - Retrospective. S81
- Narrator
  - Authority of. S106, S752
  - First-person. S18
- Observer and observed/participant. S753
- Order and chaos. S66
- "The Other country" and conventional society. S1007
- Paradox. S963
  - of Conflicting realities. S766
- Past. S128, S1096
- Patterns. S754
- Photography. S134, S774
- Religion, spirituality
  - and Sexuality, eros. S29
- Secrecy and women. S967
- Self
  - Authentic selfhood. S115
  - Care of. S102
  - Quest for, and other. S752

Small town, social and cultural aspects. **S1225**
Story collection
    Links between stories. **S1063**
    Story arrangement and patterns. **S762, S1016**
Storytelling. **S106, S1211**
Style. **S981, S1067**
    and Feminine sensibility. **S117**
Superrealism. **S5**
Surfaces and depths. **S125**
Suspicion. **S41, S757**
Texture. **S117**
Themes. **S13, S92, S125**
Time
    Passing of. **S881, S1142**
    and Space, displacement of. **S128**
Tone. **S117**
Translation, social and cultural aspects. **S787**
Truth
    and Fiction. **S752**
    Need to tell. **S102**
Voice. **S1075**
Wilderness (metaphorical)
    and Defense, psychological. **S78**
Writing of. **P862**; **S771**
"Something I've Been Meaning to Tell You." **S12, S18, S19, S128, S768, S1007, S1076, S1111, S1243**
    Absurdity, horror of. **S56**
    Control and loss of control. **S753**
    Critical analysis, overview, interpretation. **S752, S759, S761, S762**
    Ellipsis and silence. **S109**
    Grotesque, horror of. **S56**
    Language, pronouns. **S1063**
    Linguistic modality. **S1144**
    Narrative structure. **S84**
        and Narrative time. **S758**
    Narrative technique. **S1063**
    Place. **S1034**
    Storytelling. **S759, S1163**
        and Silence, not-telling. **S1051**
    Structure (linguistic, narrative, rhetorical). **S84**
    Uncertainty, modality of. **S1143**
    Voice. **S84**
Sophie ("Save the Reaper"). S837
Sophie Vogelsang ("White Dump"). S41, S753, S757, S767, S768

Southern
    Gothics. *See* American South—Writers of the white American South
    Ontario Gothic. *See under* Gothicism, Gothic
    Writers. *See* American South—Writers of the white American South
Southwestern Ontario. *See* Huron County
Space
    and Artistic development, female. S97, S110
    Cultural. S97
    Fictional. **S1035**
        and Real space. **S1034**
    and Gender roles. **S928**, **S1035**, **S1202**
    and Identity. S37, S955
    Narrative space. **S999**
    Natural. S97
    and Place. **S1035**
    Psychic space
        and Geographical, historical place. **S956**
    Subjective space and dislocation. S955
    and Time. **S128**, **S795**, **S805**
    and Women
        Interior, private space. **S767**, **S821**, S1070
"Spaceships Have Landed"
    Publication in *Paris Review*. P897
    Small town, archetypal. **S1018**
    Wilderness (metaphorical)
        and Change in women. **S1146**
"The Spanish Lady." S18, S29, S102, S1076, S1246
    Critical analysis, overview, interpretation. **S752**, **S761**
    Ending, nonending. **S109**
    Narrative structure
        and Narrative time. **S758**
    Translation into French. **S98**
Speech. P863, P889, P892, P902; S882, **S1145**
"Spelling." S768, S1111, S1163
    Critical analysis, overview, interpretation. S762
    Revisions. **S103**
Spirituality. *See under* Religion
Stangel, F. K., S18
Stanley, Mr. ("Dulse"). S52, S1153, S1179
Steinbeck, John. *Of Mice and Men*. **S835**
Stella ("Lichen"). P882; S753, S767, S975, S1049
Stillness and motion. *See* Photography—Paradox of photographic vision
"The Stone in the Field." S3, S15, S17, S121, S128, S768, S959
    Autobiographical aspects. P861; S1187
    Critical analysis, overview, interpretation. **S752**, **S759**
    Elegiac fiction. S104, S770

Family heritage. **S954**
Middle-aged women. **S1013**
Narrative strategy
    and Triggering event. **S845**
Outsiders. **P869**; **S1231**
Rural life, pattern of. **P870**

Stories
    Early stories (Alice Munro). P865, P886; **S762**, S765, S769, **S771**
        Characters in. **S32**, **S119**
        Imitative writing. P894; S984, S1174
        Narrative technique, development of
            Dual-voiced, retrospective technique. **S119**, **S1182**
            and Vision, development of. **S32**
        Patterns. **S754**
        Place, setting. **P845**; **S32**, **S119**, **S1183**
    House as metaphor for story. **P702**; S18, S753, S953
    Interconnections/parallels between stories. **S753**, **S754**, **S839**
    Length of story, and publication. P897
    Origins of stories (general). **P653**, P687, **P881**, P889, **P895**, **P897**, P902, P907; S823, S921. *See also under individual stories*
    Pivot points. **S755**, S1119, S1223
        and Closure, techniques of. **S80**
    as Reader experiences. **P892**

Story collections
    Links between stories. **S1063**
    Story arrangement/juxtaposition. **S754**, **S762**, **S1016**
    Story patterns/interconnections. **S754**, **S904**
    Structure of
        Centre and orbiting structure. **S759**, **S959**
        Novel vs linked stories. **S1107**
    Titles, selection of. S1196

Story
    Events, patterns in. **S754**
    Groups, biblical. **S754**, **S839**, **S840**
    as Idea and scene. P886
    Importance of. P865, P889
    Types, patterns of. **S754**
    and Voice, theory of. **S84**

"Story for Sunday." S767
    Critical analysis, overview, interpretation. S762
    Narrative technique, development of. **S32**, **S119**, S762, **S1182**

Storytelling. **S41**, **S106**, **S757**, **S1084**, **S1163**
    and Artistic development. **S106**, **S903**
    in Childhood. **S106**
        and Mythic imagination. **S83**
    Female, cross-generational. **S99**

Storytelling (cont.)
    Mother-daughter. **P891**, **P899**; S70, S828
    of the Past, gender differences in. **P906**
    and Silence, not-telling. S1051
Storytelling by narrators. S106, S1025. *See also* Communication
    Deferral and telling. S41, S757
    and Language of remembered childhood. S1101
    and Love, experiences of. S52, S1226
    and Metafiction. S52
    and Self-development. S1211
    and Truth. S52, S1025, S1026, S1064
Strange and familiar. S41, S125, S757, S762, S1017, S1087, S1104, S1113, S1167, S1208. *See also* Double vision
    and Fictional landscape. S1243
    and Photography. S1246
Style. P852, P889; S5, S767, S824, S1052. *See also* Detail(s), use of; Realism; Sensibility; Texture; Tone
    Chekhov, Anton, similarities to. S109
    Compression. S980
    Development of. S40, S981, S1067
    and Feminine sensibility. S117
    Interrogative. S965
    Photographic, and Gothic realism. S28
Subordination of women. *See under* Women
Subversion. *See under* Discourse, masculine/patriarchal
Suggestion. *See* Narrative techniques—Understatement, suggestion
"Sunday Afternoon." S76
    Autobiographical aspects. P893; S771
    Critical analysis, overview, interpretation. S762
    "Hired Girl," comparison with. S832
    Narrative technique. S832
        Development of. S32, S119
Superrealism. *See under* Realism
Surface
    Appearance
        and Reality/truth. S901, S1087
            in Human relationships. S3, S1167
            and Illusion, camouflage, and deception. S1207
    Detail(s), Munro's fascination with. P849, P865, P889. *See also* Detail(s), use of
    of Life
        and Absurdity, horror beneath. S992
        and Dark underground. S753
        Munro's excitement in. P660, **P843**
Surfaces and depths. S39, S1167
    Layered structures. S900
    in Photography. S134, S774

Surface reality and legend, **S1113**
and Themes, **S125**
Surprise, **S39**, **S41**, S757
in Endings, P865
Suspicion, **S41**, S757
Symbols, symbolism, P664, P865, P882; S767, **S872**, **S875**
Food, **S1111**
Synecdoche. *See under* Narrative techniques

Tam Lin (Scottish ballad), P899; **S1019**
Taylor, Charles, S29
Teaching
Canadian literature, P848
Writing, P860, P863, P865, P898, P907
Technology
and Pastoralism, nature, **S76**, **S998**
Ted Braddock ("The Ferguson Girls Must Never Marry"), S753
Ted Makkavala ("Accident"), S753
Television scripts. *See under* Writing (Alice Munro)
"Tell Me Yes or No," S18, S128, S768, S1212, S1215, S1243
Body, female, **S30**
Critical analysis, overview, interpretation, **S752**, **S761**
Elegiac fiction, elegy, S104, S770, S1142
Narrative technique, entanglement
and Unsettlement, **S1209**
Time, **S758**
Voice, female, **S30**
Tennyson, Alfred Lord, P890; S106, S768, S769, S811, S937, **S1247**
"Mariana," S1245, S1247
"The Passing of Arthur" (*Idylls of the King*), S1100
"The Princess," S926, S1247
Teresa Gault ("Wigtime"), S914
Text, body as. *See* Body as text
Textual reality. *See* Fictional reality
Textuality, **S41**, S757
Texture, **P843**, P886
Atmospheric evocation, P845, P865; **S5**
and Feminine sensibility, **S117**
Realism of, **S125**
"Thanks for the Ride," P886; S18, S76, S753, S771, S818, S1007, S1054, S1060, S1183
Angle of vision, rhetorical, **S19**
Critical analysis, overview, interpretation, S762
Faulkner, William, "A Rose for Emily," **S880**
Grotesque as narrative strategy, **S85**
Narrative technique, development of, **S32**, **S119**, **S1182**
Origin of story, **P845**, P895

"Thanks for the Ride" (cont.)
    Sexuality, eros
        and Religious, spiritual quest, **S29**
    Social class, **S864**
    Structure (linguistic, narrative, rhetorical), **S84**
    Violence, psychological aspects, **S880**
    Voice, **S84**, S788
Theatricality, **S102**, **S752**, **S1170**. *See also* Role-playing
Themes, **S22**, **S39**, **S93**, **S96**, **S125**, **S762**
    Chekhov, Anton, similarities to, **S109**
    Feminist, **S7**
    Gothic, **S10**, **S28**
    and Images, **S13**
    and Narrative form, evolution of, **S124**
    and Narrative technique, **S81**, **S92**, **S124**
Thomas, Audrey, S890
    "Crossing the Rubicon," S958
    "Initram," S763
    Songs My Mother Taught Me, **S8**, **S108**, S933
Time, **S752**. *See also* Narrative time; Past
    and Mystery story, **S805**
    and Narrative form, **S46**
    and Narrative structure, **S758**
    and Narrative technique, **S46**, **S74**, **S758**, **S861**, **S945**, **S1009**, **S1220**
    Passing of, impermanence, **S128**, **S752**, **S767**
        and Loss, death, S881, **S1142**
    and Short-story cycle, **S758**
    and Space, **S128**, **S795**, **S805**
"The Time of Death," P845; S771, S818, S1007
    Critical analysis, overview, interpretation, S762
    Death, **S29**, S104, S770, S1142
    Ellipsis, temporal, **S109**
    Narrative technique, development of, **S32**, **S119**
    Structure (linguistic, narrative, rhetorical), **S84**
    Voice, **S84**
Tolstoy, Leo
    Portrayal of women, P858, P909
Tone, **P843**
    Emotional tone, **P871**, **P874**; **S5**, **S117**
    and Feminine sensibility, **S117**
    Pauline Gothic, **S883**
Toolan, Michael J., S24
Topography, *See also* Maps and mapping
    Fictional, **S68**, **S1243**
        and Childhood, remembered, **S18**
Toppings, Earle, *See* Publisher/editor relations

Torrance, Mr. ("A Basket of Strawberries"), S753
Town. *See* Small town(s)
Town/city and country, S767, S1034, S1106
    as Moral opposites, S1205
    Rural and urban landscape, S1106
Traill, Catherine Parr, S78
    The Backwoods of Canada, S117
Transience of life. *See under* Life
Translation
    French, S95, S98
    Hindi
        Social and cultural aspects, S787
    and Income of Canadian writers, P866
    "Turkey Season," **P867**
Travel, **P701**
    and Change, personal, **S1064**
    Metaphorical journey
        and Narrative movement, S1243
    Voyage, S853
Treisman, Deborah. *See* Publisher/editor relations
Triggering event/experience
    and Narrative strategy, S845
    and Writing process, P702, P857, P865, P902
"A Trip to the Coast," S818, S1106
    Critical analysis, overview, interpretation, S762
    Narrative technique, development of, **S32**, S119
Truth. *See also* Reality/truth and art/fiction
    Aesthetic (artistic) vision, P847, P855, **P860**, **P891**; S790, S986, S1059
    and Fiction (other-than-real), S752
        in Mysterious characters, **P884**
    and Legend, S752
    and Mystery, S14, S62
    in Narration, S41, S752, S757
    Need to tell
        and Deception, dissimulation, S102
    of Past, S848, S954
        and Memory, S41, S757
    and Reality, **P891**; S38, **S124**, S754, S1205
    in Storytelling, S52, **S1025**, **S1026**, **S1064**
"The Turkey Season," P865; S3, S12, S18, S121, S820, S856, S917
    Critical analysis, overview, interpretation, S752, S762
    Origin of story, **P653**, P687, P867, P874
    Translation, P866, **P867**
    Understatement, S109
    Work and workers, **P867**
    Writing of, **P687**; S771

Turning points. *See* Stories—Pivot points

Uncertainty, **S41**, **S757**
    Modality of, **S1143**
    and Past, **S965**
Uncollected stories, early. *See* Stories—Early stories (Alice Munro)
Uncontrollable elements, **S753**
Understatement, suggestion. *See under* Narrative techniques
Undset, Sigrid. *Kristin Lavransdatter*, **S25**, **S926**
United Church. *See* Religion and church
Unity
    and Open form, **S58**
    and Short-story cycle, **S27**, **S111**, **S113**, **S758**, **S1109**
Unsettlement. *See under* Narrative strategy
Updike, John, **P848**, **P858**
Urban and rural. *See* Town/city and country
Urquhart, Jane. *The Underpainter*, **S31**

Val ("Forgiveness in Families"), **S761**, **S1203**
Values
    Canadian vs. American
        and Happiness, **S808**
    Feminine, **S55**, **S118**
    of Small town, **S118**
    of Society, and industrialization, **S998**
"Vandals," **S999**, **S1118**
    Abjection, **S755**
    as Coda to *Open Secrets*, **S904**
    Fictional space, **S1035**
    Nature and violence, **S866**
    "Save the Reaper," similarities with, **S837**
Vanderhaeghe, Guy, **S122**
Victimization, **S873**, **S984**
    of Women, **S79**
Victor Sawicky ("Oranges and Apples"), **S852**
Victorian
    Patriarchal society
        and Women, **P673**; **S1030**
    Poetry, **S1247**
Vinay, Jean-Paul, **S98**
Violence, **S33**, **S79**, **S85**, **S753**
    and Nature, **S866**
    Psychological aspects, **S880**
Viola ("Marrakesh"), **S761**
Violet Thoms ("A Queer Streak"), **S41**, **S753**, **S757**
Vision and aurality, **S31**, **S1095**

Vision of life (Alice Munro). P853; S3, **S17**, S117, S129, S752, **S758**, S820, S879, S881, S1118, S1186, S1223
    and Characters' lives. **P865**
    Development of, and development as a writer. **S32**, S124
    Ironic vision. **S22**
    Pivotal moments in life. P865, **P883**
    and Religion, spirituality. **S29**
    and Short-story genre. P853, P854, P860, P880, P908; **S1024**
    Surface of life. P660, **P843**
Vision of the world. **P865**; **S19**, S80, S752, **S758**
    Double vision. P848, P858, P865; S13, **S22**, **S66**, **S100**, S134, S774, **S1007**
    Multi-world. **S66**
    Objects. P865
        Treachery to, in writing. P660, **P664**
    Perception of reality. **P891**; S992
        and Short-story genre. **S1024**
"Visitors." P865; S1076
    Critical analysis, overview, interpretation. S752, S762
    Elegiac fiction. S104, S770
    Grotesque as narrative strategy. **S85**
    Stories and storytelling
        and Truth in narrative. S52, **S1025**
Voice. **S31**, **S886**, **S1046**
    and Connection. **S121**
    Female. **S30**, **S101**, **S121**, **S788**
        in Early stories. **S32**
        and Menstruation. **S114**
    Male. **S121**, S788
    and Narrative technique, retrospective. **S119**, S1182
    of Narrators. P889; **S84**
        Adult narrator and adolescent experience. **S798**
        and Autobiographical material. **S1075**
        and Characters. **S121**
        Woolf, Virginia, influence of. **S1000**, **S1001**
    Story and voice, theory of. **S84**
Voyeurism, voyeurs. S753
Waddington, Miriam. **S82**
Walker, Alice. *The Color Purple*. **S79**
"Walker Brothers Cowboy." S18, S86, S91, S768, S788, S862, S900, S999, S1054, S1174, S1212, S1243
    Critical analysis, overview, interpretation. S752, S759, S762, S1078, **S1213**
    Dislocation, subjective. **S956**
    Epiphany. **S29**
    Imagination in childhood. **S83**
    Loss. S104, S753, S770, S1142
    Narrative perspective. S753

"Walker Brothers Cowboy" (cont.)
    Narrative technique, iterative, **S758**, **S945**
    Secrets/secrecy, **S960**
    Sexuality, female, **S1046**
    Strange and familiar, **S1017**, **S1113**
    Understatement, **S109**
    Voice, **S1046**
"Walking on Water," S76, S100, S102, S128, S862, S935, S1217
    Angle of vision, stylistic and structural, **S19**
    Atwood, Margaret
        "Two Stories about Emma: 'The Whirlpool Rapids' and 'Walking on Water,'" **S829**
    Critical analysis, overview, interpretation, **S752**, **S753**, **S761**, S762
    Language, pronouns, **S1063**
Watchers. *See* Observers (narrators, characters)
Watson, Sheila, S1236
Wawanash County, **S91**. *See also* Huron County
    Gothic aspects, **S28**
    Mythical landscape of, S767
Weaver, Robert
    Role of, P656, P661, P683, P851, P852, P877, **P903**: **S67**, **S763**, S765, **S771**, S897, S912, S918, S1027, S1028, S1029, **S1045**, S1148
Weinzweig, Helen, **S107**
Welty, Eudora, P841, P848; S5, S91, **S1178**, S1180
    The Golden Apples, **P685**, P841, P862, P901; **S27**, **S28**, S134, S762, S774, S1162
    "June Recital," S759, **S826**
    "Livvie," **S94**
    "A Curtain of Green," **S94**
    "Lily Daw and the Three Ladies," **S94**
    "A Worn Path," P865
"What Do You Want to Know For?" (essay)
    Autobiographical aspects, **P701**, P898
    Dislocation, **S956**
    Maps and mapping, P701; **S956**, **S966**
    Mystery, secrets, **P701**; S759, **S960**
    Travel, **P701**
"What Is Remembered," P905; S755
    Discourse, paradigmatic relations of, **S886**
    Secrets/secrecy, **S906**
    Space, subjective
        and Identity, **S955**
"White Dump," **P886**: S3, S121, S768, S975, S999, S1012, S1066, S1111, S1212
    Critical analysis, overview, interpretation, **S752**, **S753**, S762
    Happiness and ending, **S808**
    Narrative technique, indeterminacy, **S953**
    Revisions, S753, S953

Who Do You Think You Are? (*The Beggar Maid*)
    Absence, discourse of, **S41**, S757
    Absurdity, **S56**, **S100**
    Adolescence, **S50**
    Angle of vision, archetypal, **S33**
    Art/fiction and life, control over, **S100**
    Artistic development, **S39**, **S81**, **S110**, **S903**, **S1099**
    Authority, **S27**
    Autobiographical aspects, **P853**, **P854**, **P855**, P856, P859, P889; S769
    Bildungsroman, **S9**, **S26**, S101
    Body, female
        and Change, social, **S967**
        Gothicized, **S1230**
    Characterization, S762
        of Protagonist, **S42**, S102, **S103**, **S930**
    Characters, **P854**, P859. *See also* Rose *in main listing*
        Evolution of, and time shifts, S42, S944
    Characters (types), **S768**
        Artist figure, female, **S74**, **S81**
        Controlled and controlling, **S753**
        Female, **S55**
        Grotesque, S1038, S1094
    Closure, techniques of, **S80**
    Connection, **S1062**, **S1244**
    Control and loss of control, **S753**
    Critical analysis, overview, interpretation, **S752**, **S756**, **S759**, **S762**, **S766**, **S767**, **S769**, S803, **S838**, **S888**, **S911**, S1138, **S1174**
    Critical reception, P866; **S771**, S902
    Double vision, **S66**
        and Paradox, **S963**
    Escape, **S1010**
    Family relationships, **S3**, S1015
    Fantasy and reality, **S127**, **S752**, **S952**, **S961**
    Father-daughter relationship, **P855**; S33
    Feminine world, **S55**
    Fragmentation, **S22**, **S27**, **S92**
    Garrison mentality, **S1110**
    Gender differences, **S1212**
    Gender roles, female, **S9**, **S59**, **S118**
    Gossip, **S51**, **S976**
    Gothic elements, S56, **S1230**
    Grotesque, horror of, **S56**
    Heroine, **S9**
    Home. *See* Place of origin
    Human frailty and disguise, **S125**
    Human relationships, **S3**

Who Do You Think You Are? (cont.)
- Humiliation. *See under* Love
- Humour. **S1038**
- Identity. S33, **S42**, **S93**, S752, S1109, S1124
    - Female. **S1168**
        - Quest for. **S59**, S133, S766, S767
        - and Role-playing. **S11**, **S112**, **S1170**
        - and Sexual fantasy. S127, **S987**
        - and Social class. **S43**, S93
    - Identity formation. **S51**, **S976**
        - Alternative female identity. **S11**
        - and Place of origin. **S1005**, S1127
    - Images, imagery, and themes. **S13**
    - Isolation. S56, S93
    - Language. **S27**, **S115**, **S926**, **S1176**, **S1230**
    - Love. **S52**, S55, S93, S115, S1005, S1110
        - Humiliation of. **S753**
        - and Storytelling. **S52**
    - Magic realism. **S125**
    - Male-female relationships. P855; S59, **S752**
    - Memory. **S785**
    - Mimicry and mimesis. **S102**, S752
    - Mother-daughter relationship. S33, **S74**, **S81**, **S99**, S752, S755
        - and Gossip. **S51**, **S976**
    - Narrative form and unity. **S58**
    - Narrative perspective. **S24**, **S31**, **S41**, **S757**
    - Narrative strategies
        - Disarrangement. **S1023**
        - Disruption. **S41**, S757
    - Narrative structure. P859; **S18**, **S111**, **S1067**, **S1107**. *See also* Short-story cycle
        - and Narrative time. S755, **S758**
    - Narrative technique(s). **S80**. *See also* Fragmentation
        - Closure, techniques of. **S80**
        - Development of. S40, **S762**, **S1074**
        - Retrospective. P859; **S81**
        - and Themes. **S92**
        - Time, use of. **S74**, **S1220**
        - and Unity. **S111**, **S1109**
    - Narrator. **S18**, **S31**
    - Opposition
        - and Incongruity. **S762**
        - Rhetorical. **S963**
    - Paradox. **S963**, S1104
    - Parody. **S1233**
    - Patterns. **S754**

Performance. *See* Theatricality
Photography. **S134. S774. S1246**
Place of origin. S93. **S1005.** S1127
Power. **S27. S43. S115**
    and Gossip. **S51. S976**
Poverty. **S43.** S93. **S1103**
Protagonist. *See* Rose *in main listing*
Reality. **S41. S757. S962. S963**
    and Fantasy. **S127. S752. S952. S961**
    and Legend. **S40**
Revisions (textual alterations and story arrangement). **P859. P862.** P865. **P889**; S18, **S58. S67. S103.** S762. **S763.** S769. **S771.** S797. S803. S919. **S964.** S985. S988. **S1134**
    and Publisher relations. P859. P862. P865; **S771.** S964. S1027
Role-playing. **S11. S93. S101. S102. S112.** S901. **S752. S1170.** *See also* Theatricality
Sacrifice. female. **S33**
Self. P85; **S115**
Self-construction. **S51. S101. S102. S976**
Self-development. female. **S9. S26. S39. S101.** S1168. **S1220**
Shame. **S93**
Short-story cycle. **P859**; **S1. S27. S93. S99. S111. S758.** S980. S990. **S1005. S1006. S1065**
Small town (Hanratty). **S43. S1005. S1225**
    and Protagonist. **S110. S118. S120. S938. S1010.** S1127
Social class. **P853**; **S43.** S93. **S1103**
Space
    and Artistic development. **S110**
    and Time. **S128**
Speech. S93. **S1145**
Storytelling. **S41. S52. S106. S757.** S762. **S903**
Style. **S40. S981. S1067**
Surfaces and depths. **S125**
Theatricality. **S102. S752. S1170**. *See also* Role-playing
Themes. **S93. S125**
    and Images. **S13**
Time and space. **S128**
Title. P862. P865; **S31. S1109**
Translation. P866; S902
Uncertainty. **S41. S757**
Uncontrollable elements. **S753**
Unity. **S27. S58. S111. S1109**
Violence and female sacrifice. **S33**
Vision and aurality. **S31**
Vision of the world. multi-world. **S66**
Voice. **S31**
Writing of. **P854. P862**

"Who Do You Think You Are?" S1133
    Characterization. S930
    Characters, male. S44
    Critical analysis, overview, interpretation. S759, S762
    Disarrangement. S1023
    Language. S927
    Place (of origin) and identity formation. S1005
    Revisions. S964
"The Widower." S754
    Critical analysis, overview, interpretation. S762
"Wigtime." P680, P892, P894; S21, S861
    Self. S107, S1151
"Wild Swans." P853; S29, S112, S927, S1243
    Critical analysis, overview, interpretation. S762, **S1090**
    Fantasy, sexual. S127, **S987**
    Objects, treatment of. **S1089**
    Revisions, prepublication. S41, S103, S757
    Speech. S1145
Wilderness
    and Frontier. S105, S1140
    as Metaphor for painful past. S78
    Women in. S105, S1140
        Metaphorical wilderness. S1146
"A Wilderness Station." S17, S944, S1094, S1118
    Ambiguity, contradiction. S72
    Atwood, Margaret. *Alias Grace*. S72, **S1031**
    Calvinism, S35
    Characters as Munro's alter ego. **S831**, **S1021**
    Critical analysis, overview, interpretation. S759
    Gender roles and marriage. S105
    Gothic, southern Ontario. **S1031**
    Historical fiction. **S1056**
    Identity, female. S129
    Laidlaw family history. P898, P899; **S35**, S765, S924, S1021
    Letter-writing and narration. **S885**
    Mystery, antidetection. S14
    Narrative perspective and subjectivity. **S129**
    Narrative structure, retrospective. **S60**
    Narrative technique. **S831**, **S885**
    Pioneers, Scottish
        and Cultural translation. S15, S35, S924
    Reality/truth. S72
        and Perception. **S831**
    Truth. S14, **S885**
        of Past. **S954**

Wilderness
> and Women. **S105**, **S1140**

Wilderness story groups. *See* Bible/biblical story groups

Wilfred ("Visitors"), S41, S757, S1025

Will Thornaby ("The Jack Randa Hotel"), S1020

Willens, Mr. ("The Love of a Good Woman"), S883, S1032

Wilson, Ethel, **S88**
> "Lilly's Story," P655
> "Tuesday and Wednesday," P655

Wingham, Ontario. *See also* Munro, Alice—Early life (childhood, adolescence) in Wingham; Huron County (southwestern Ontario)
> and Hanratty, P889; S931
> and Jubilee, P695; **S1180**, S1225
> Lower Town, S765, S771, S931
> Munro's relationship with as a writer, P688, P704, P865, P886, P889, P895; S771, **S779**, S950, **S1156**, **S1224**, **S1229**
> in Munro's writing, P862; S931
> Reception of Munro's writing in, P688, P862, P865, P868, P906; S763, S771, S792, S815, S878, S1033, S1037, S1191, S1224, **S1228**, **S1229**, S1232, S1234, S1238, S1241
> Story events and physical places in, S859

"Winter Wind," S18, S102, S818, S992, S1007, S1106, S1142, S1164
> Autobiographical aspects, P861; S765, **S771**
> Critical analysis, overview, interpretation, S752, **S753**, **S761**, S762
> Imagination in childhood, **S83**
> Metaphors, snow, **S799**
> Past, **S1096**
> Reader response
> > and Aesthetic distance, **S53**
> > and Attachment, **S53**

Wolf, Christa, *Kindheitsmuster*, **S841**

Wollstonecraft, Mary, S784

Women *See also* Characters (types), female; Confinement, female; Duality, female; Emancipation; Feminine, femininity; Gender differences; Gender roles; Hero, female/heroine; Language and women; Male-female relationships; Patriarchal society
> and Aging, **S64**, **S767**
> Appearance, personal, P844, P848, P868; S932, S1241. *See also* Beauty rituals and fashion
> Bonds between women, P874, P886
> and Change, physical and social, **S64**, **S967**, **S1146**
> Communication between women, P874, P894
> Cross-generational interrelationships, **S99**, **S828**
> Cultural models, **S55**
> Disempowerment of
> > and Puritanism, Scottish fundamentalist, **S15**
> Emotional dependence of, **S784**

Women (cont.)
 Empowerment of. S1210
  and Story-telling. S70
 Female expression and language. S767. S926
 in Literature. portrayal of. S79
  by Female writers. P657. P853; S778. S941
  by Male writers. P841. P848. P852. **P858. P909**
 Middle-aged. P844. P859. P882. **P886. P909**; S64. S753. S1013
 Narratives and history. S965
 and Objects. domestic. S1070
 Older. **S131**
 and Place. **S99. S112**
 Poor. *See* Social class
 as Reader figures. S768
 Repression of. **P846**; S116. **S1091**
 and Secrecy. **S967. S991**
 and Small town. **S88**. *See also* Protagonists. female and small town *in main listing*
 and Social class. P865; **S43. S64. S864**
 and Space. interior. private. S767. S821. S1070
 Subordination of. S55. S79
 and Values. S55
 Victimization of. S79
 and Wilderness. frontier. S105. S1140
  Metaphorical. **S78. S1146**
 Women's experience. **S129. S1215. S1221**
Women writers. *See* Writers/artists. female
"Wood." P865; S839
 Critical analysis. overview. interpretation. S753. S762
 Isolation and loneliness of men. S974
 Origin of story. P886
Woolf. Virginia. S784. S861. **S1000. S1001**
Words. *See under* Language
Wordsworth. William. P862
Work
 Processes of work. P865. P874
 and Workers. **P867**
"Working for a Living." **S754. S765. S771. S981**
 Detail. accuracy of. P865
Writers. *See also* American South—Writers of the white American South
 Artistic mind. S77
 and Authority. **S937**
  Munro. Alice. **S67. S763. S1027**
 Canadian. **P843**. P851. P866. P874. P877. P889. *See also* Writers' Union of Canada
  Income of. P840. P866
  as Readers. S1240

Characters as writers. *See under* Characters (types)—Artist/writer figures
Writer, character and reader. **S25**
Writers/artists, female. P841. P843. P861. P887. P889; **S36**. S909. S1072. *See also Lives of Girls and Women*—Artist/writer, female
   and Autobiography. **S75**. **S768**. **S801**. **S937**
      Autobiographical place. **S1180**
   and Duality, female. **S860**
   and Feminine sensibility. **S117**
   and Femininity, paradox of. **S1092**
   Feminist perspective of. **S926**
   and Gender roles, female. P848. P861; **S860**. S1196
   and Literary heritage/parentage. **S132**. **S958**
   and Love. **S75**
   Munro's views on. S86. S129. **S753**. **S858**. S1241. *See also* Authorship (Alice Munro)—and Gender (female)
   Role of, as mock mother. **S768**
   and Self-imaging. **S768**
   and Short-story genre. **S129**. **S763**. **S767**
   and Space. **S110**
   Writing about
      Men. P841
      Old age and death. **P858**
      Women. P657. P853; **S79**. S778. S941
Writers, male. P857. P889; S1241
   Writing about women. P841. P848. P852. **P858**. **P909**; S1232
Writer's block. *See under* Writing (Alice Munro)
Writers' Union of Canada. S771
   Censorship handbook. P705
Writing
   to Control humiliation. **S753**
   as a Historically conditioned act. **S998**
   as Space. **S110**
Writing (Alice Munro). *See also* Aesthetic (artistic vision); Career (Alice Munro)
   Aging, effect on writing. **P873**. P882. P886. P894. **P895**. **P896**. P898. P903. P904. P909; S778. S823. S857. S882. S890. S905. S1022. S1187
   Autobiographical, personal aspects. **P664**. **P687**. **P694**. **P701**. P841. **P842**. **P843**. **P845**. P849. P851. **P853**. **P854**. **P855**. P856. P857. P859. P861. P862. P889. **P891**. **P893**. **P895**. **P898**. P904. P910; **S77**. S107. S752. **S753**. **S755**. S759. S762. S765. S766. S767. **S769**. **S771**. **S776**. S980. S981. S1009. **S1125**. S1149. S1174. **S1180**. **S1186**. **S1187**. *See also under individual works*
   Characters and real people. P847. P850. P861. P865. P881. P886. P894. **P897**. P899. **P906**; S912. S1039
   and Creativity. **S936**
   Distinction between autobiography and personal. **P845**. **P886**
   Family stories. **S70**. S943
   Laidlaw family history. P898. P899; **S35**. S924. S1021

Writing (Alice Munro). Autobiographical. personal aspects (cont.)
- Mother as character in stories. P855. P886. P895: S755. S765. S767. S769. S823. S860. S890
- Reality as basis for fiction. P664. P702. P868: S786. S917. S1059. S1234. S1235
- Writing autobiography. vs fiction. P894

Compulsion to write. P898: S825. S946. S947. S1042. S1234

Confidence in. P895. **P909**: S877. S947. S1042. S1072

Criticism. critical reception. *See in main listing*

Development as a writer. P886. P901. **P904**: **S32**. **S36**. **S769**. **S771**. S797. S857. **S890**. S988. S1044. S1174. S1216. S1237. *See also* Narrative technique—Development of *in main listing*; Style—Development of *in main listing*

and Imagination. **S83**. **S1163**

Disguise. concealment (of early writing). **P843**. P844. P854. **P893**. P903: S765. S769. S1009. S1135. S1137. S1149. S1223

Early life. writing in. P653. P841. **P843**. P857. P877. P878. **P879**. P893. P903: S39. S765. S769. S771. S827. S877. S882. S950. S985. S1039. S1161. **S1174**. S1201. S1223

Early stories. *See under* Stories *in main listing*

and Emotion(s). P857. P861

Family responsibilities and writing. **P653**. P839. **P843**. P848. P852. P863. P875. P889. P895. **P903**. P904. **P906**. P910: S755. S763. **S765**. S769. **S771**. S790. S804. S815. S857. S894. S905. S932. S941. S1009. S1042. S1072. S1085. S1115. S1118. S1121. S1137. S1149. S1161. S1192. S1193. S1218. S1223. S1235. S1241

Female approach. **S74**. S778. S890. S909. S1085

Feminine sensibility. **S117**. S1085. S1092. S1193

Feminist aspects. S767

Happiness in. importance of writing. P892. P893: S947. S1192

Income as a writer. **P903**: S985. S1102

Influence on other writers. S834. **S982**. **S1031**

and Politics. **P662**. P879. P886. P894. P901

Popular writing. **S1054**

Retrospective aspect of. P862. **P903**. **P906**. P909: S790

Style. *See in main listing*

Sublime. sublimity. **S824**

Television scripts. P852

Writer's block. P910: S765. S769. S778. S797. S858. S905. S1042. S1072. S1115. S1137. S1174

Writing as a career/vocation. P839. **P879**: S1042. S1241

Writing process. **P653**. **P664**. **P687**. **P702**. P839. P840. P841. **P842**. **P843**. P865. **P878**. **P879**. P880. **P881**, P886. **P892**. **P895**. **P904**: **S750**. S752. S766. S778. S797. S823. S905. S932. S946. S949. S986. S996. S1042. **S1053**. S1201. S1235. *See also* Revision *in main listing*

About the Authors

Carol Mazur, reference librarian (retired), McMaster University Library, Hamilton, Ontario. Compiler of *Women in Canada: A Bibliography 1965-1982* (1984). Former contributor to the "Notable Documents" section of the journal *Government Publications Review* and to the Government of Canada website: *Canadian Government Information on the Internet*, <http://cgii.gc.ca/index-e.html>. Carol graduated from university with a major in English literature and has devoted much of her personal time to reading and creative writing.

Cathy Moulder, curator, Lloyd Reeds Map Collection, McMaster University Library, Hamilton, Ontario, GISP. Editor of the *Bulletin of the Association of Canadian Map Libraries and Archives*. Author of numerous articles in *ACMLA Bulletin* and other library literature, and of *Current Literature on GIS and Libraries*, <http://www.mcmaster.ca/library/maps/GIS_lib.htm>.

Z8605.55
.M39
2007

S&F
3/4/08

5487468

DISCARDED
MILLSTEIN LIBRARY

LIBRARY
UNIVERSITY OF PITTSBURGH
AT GREENSBURG